DAVID O. MCKAY LIBRARY
P9-CKX-954

CAPTIVES & COUSINS

CAPTIVES & COUSINS

SLAVERY, KINSHIP, AND COMMUNITY IN THE SOUTHWEST BORDERLANDS

JAMES F. BROOKS

Published for the

Omohundro Institute of Early American History and Culture,

Williamsburg, Virginia, by the

University of North Carolina Press,

Chapel Hill and London

The Omohundro Institute of Early American History and Culture is sponsored jointly by the College of William and Mary and the Colonial Williamsburg Foundation. On November 15, 1996, the Institute adopted the present name in honor of a bequest from Malvern H. Omohundro, Jr.

Manufactured in the United States of America
Library of Congress
Cataloging-in-Publication Data
Brooks, James, 1955–
Captives and cousins : slavery, kinship, and community in the Southwest borderlands / by James F. Brooks.
p. cm.
ISBN 0-8078-2714-2 (cloth : alk. paper)
ISBN 0-8078-5382-8 (pbk. : alk paper)
1. Southwest, New—Ethnic relations. 2. Southwest, New—Social conditions. 3. Spaniards—Southwest, New—Social conditions. 4. Indians of North America—Southwest, New—Social conditions. 5. Spaniards—Kinship—Southwest, New—History. 6. Indians of North America—Kinship—Southwest, New—History. 7. Slavery—Southwest, New—History. 8. Sex role—Southwest, New—History. 9. Southwest, New—Colonization—Social aspects. 10. Culture conflict—Southwest, New—History. I. Omohundro Institute of Early American History & Culture. II. Title.
F790.A1 B76 2002
305.8′00976—dc21 2001058528

The paper in this book meets the guidelines for permanence and durability of the Committee on Production Guidelines for Book Longevity of the Council on Library Resources.

A portion of the author's royalties from the sale of this book are paid to the Katrin H. Lamon Endowment for Native American Art and Education at the School of American Research, Santa Fe, New Mexico.

06 05 04 03 02 5 4 3 2 1

For

Frances Leon Quintana,

a woman of vision.

CONTENTS

MAPS, ILLUSTRATIONS, AND TABLES

MAPS

ILLUSTRATIONS

TABLES

You cannot build bridges between the wandering islands;
The Mind has no neighbors, and the unteachable heart
Announces its armistice time after time, but spends
Its love to draw them closer and closer apart.

—A. D. Hope (1955)

CAPTIVES & COUSINS

1

VIOLENCE, EXCHANGE, AND THE HONOR OF MEN

To Dance with Yearning

They came at dusk, as the low winter sun slipped behind the snow-capped rim of Mount Taylor. Moving softly into the adobe-muffled plaza while the villagers attended Christmas Eve Mass, *los Comanches* fanned out to pilfer *mantas* (cloaks), ropes, and tools from the various automobiles, buggies, and wagons parked around the village church. Numbering some twenty men clad in buckskin, beaded *tewas* (moccasins), and feather headdresses, they took orders from their chief, El Capitán. This man also led his young daughter, La Cautiva, by a rawhide thong tied about her wrist. Her white communion gown mirrored the small drifts of snow that had settled on the leeward side of the massive church walls.

They searched for one house among the dozens that clustered around the plaza. There they would find El Santo Niño, or the Christ child, a commercially made male doll swaddled in new cloth and lying in a wooden manger in the home of his *padrinos.* El Capitán sang softly:

A los Padrinos del	From the Godparents of the
Niño	Christ Child
le pido en primer	I ask first for
lugar	permission
si me da paso y entrada	to come within
que al Niño vengo	for I seek the Christ
a buscar.	Child.

Finally, at the seventh house the door swung open at the pressure of his hand.

Ya consiguimos	Now that we are allowed
le entrada	within

congusto y con	with pleasure and
buen cariño	affection
pasaremos los Comanches	we Comanches will enter
a ver a ese hermoso	to see that handsome
Niño.	Child.

They had found their quarry. Overcoming the defense of his protectors, the Comanches seized the sacred image and retreated into the plaza, where the villagers had begun to issue from the church in response to the padrinos' cries for assistance. A spirited fight ensued, but the raiding band made good their escape. Behind, however, they left La Cautiva, taken by the villagers in the fray.

Once beyond the village, the Comanches suddenly halted. Forming into a processional line, they turned about and reentered the firelit plaza. El Capitán led the column, carrying El Santo Niño before him. Pausing at the doors of elderly or ill villagers, he begged permission to bring the blessings of the Christ child into their homes and praised the child's healing powers. As each door opened, the Comanche chief continued to sing:

Por los enfermos	In the name of the sick
Niñito te pido	I beg of you, Christ
en primer	Child that
lugar con tus mano poderosa	with your powerful touch
Tú los tienes que sanar	you will cure them.
Tú que eres tan bondadoso	You who are so generous
y me diste mi salud	and gave to me my health
aqui me tienes presente	you now see me before you
bailando con ansiedad.	dancing with yearning.

While the Comanche visitations proceeded, the village men formed their own processional march. Leading La Cautiva by her small hands, they too called upon the homes of the infirm, proclaiming her pure and curative nature. Both processions were accompanied by the music of violin and guitar, whose players had taken seats in one of the wagons in the plaza.

At the conclusion of these visitations, ringing church bells and a staccato pounding of *tombés* (hand drums) summoned both parties to gather in the plaza before the church doors. Piñón *farolitos* (small bonfires) cast wavering shadows on surrounding walls as the two processions formed ranks facing each other.

Once silence had fallen, a *rescate* began. El Capitán, negotiating with the *majordomo* of the village, established terms of exchange for their respective captives. In return for the surrender of El Santo Niño, the Comanches were offered quarts of local wine, meals in the homes of the blessed, and hard cash in the form of quarters, dimes, and nickels. To regain his daughter, El Capitán promised that his people would again visit the village on its saint's day or when a villager wished to sponsor a *velorio* (death vigil). As darkness descended, another snow squall moved into the valley. The two leaders shook hands and exchanged their prizes. Los Comanches shed their headdresses and buckskins, becoming familiar *aldeanos* (village men) once again. Rejoined to their families, they moved from home to home for the feasts that would precede midnight Mass. La Cautiva changed into a warmer dress, then counted the pennies and sweet *bizcochitos* (cookies) given her during her captivity.[1]

Whether performed by the residents of Placitas, New Mexico, in 1938 or in Hispano villages and Indian pueblos today, the conquest romance of "Los Comanches" variously summons and silences a past rich in social possibility and burdened with malign realities. Rituals of violence, exchange, and redemption were central to the men whose societies met in the Southwest Borderlands during the colonial era. Cloaking pragmatic need for social and economic transfers between antagonistic groups, these rituals allowed men to elaborate a shared understanding of honor out of traditions both indigenous and European. Native and European men fought to protect their communities and preserve personal repute yet participated in conflicts and practices that made the objects of their honor, women and children, crucial products of violent economic exchange. This nexus of honor, gender, and kinship provided the sacred canopy under which painfully profane intersocietal trade could occur. Beneath

1. This description draws from Wesley R. Hurt, "The Spanish-American Comanche Dance," MS in New Mexico State Records Center, Santa Fe, N.Mex., in possession of the author, 1–17, esp. 6–7; Lorin W. Brown, "Los Comanches," Works Progress Administration Federal Writer's Project, Dec. 29, 1939, file 5, drawer 5, folder 45, in Museum of New Mexico Archives, Santa Fe (author's translation); field notes, interview with Francisco "El Cumanche" Gonzales, Aug. 19, 1990, in Ranchos de Taos, N.Mex. For a similar ritual in Mexico as far south as Ixcatepec, Huasteca, see Luís Reyes Garcia, *Pasión y muerte del cristo sol: Carnaval y cuaresma en Ichcatepec* (Xalpa, Mex., 1960), esp. 54–59. A different poetic drama by the same name, probably celebrating the New Mexican defeat of Comanche captain Cuerno Verde (Green Horn) in 1778, is also performed on occasion. See Gilberto Espinosa, trans., "Los Comanches," *New Mexico Quarterly*, I (1931), 133–146.

its poetic and performative architecture, a timeless transaction at once pious and erotic concealed the voices and deeds of people making history.[2]

The Comanche Dance, which villagers in northern New Mexico continue to perform during the Christmas holy days and at saint's days throughout the year, suggests the long memory of this borderland region. The ritual makes visible one rendition of the area's deep history, where exchanges of captives and culture instigated conflicts and congruities between peoples of vastly different heritage. Those who enact the communal ritual re-create fundamental elements of their past, but now, through the prism of time, in performances that neatly suture some of the wounds that once marked its initial meaning. Beneath the shroud of artifice lie details that connect to a specific history in the Southwest Borderlands.

First, "Los Comanches" points to a long and ambivalent relationship between New Mexican villagers and their nomadic and pastoral indigenous neighbors and kin, a relationship both violently competitive and simultaneously mutualistic and cooperative. Although the Comanches were confined to an Indian Territory reservation by 1875, their presence in the ritualized history of New Mexican villages during the ensuing century establishes in symbol their once-formidable role in life and death along the Río Grande.

Second, persistent ritual elements highlight the role of violence, gender, kinship, and masculine honor in long-term negotiations between colonists and Indians in the Southwest Borderlands. Mutual thievery between the groups is raised above the mundane by the capture of precious symbols: the contested icons of the Christ child and the Comanche chieftain's beloved daughter. Each is imbued with innocence, purity, and sacred healing power, qualities lent poetic immediacy by their vessel's vulnerability. But the everyday necessities behind these reciprocal captures are attested to in each group's implication in their loss: the padrinos succumb to the seduction of the Comanche's song, whereas El Capitán has brought his daughter along on a dangerous raid. In each case, these icons represent an essence of their communities, and their exchange through capture indicates the essential linkages between their communities.

2. I borrow here from Marshall Sahlins, who examines how culturally disparate English and native notions of sexuality, sacrality, gift giving, and obligation conjoined to "precipitate social forms" in eighteenth-century Hawaii; see "Introduction," in *Islands of History* (Chicago, 1985), vii–xix, especially his phrasing, "With transactions such as these, the erotic commerce ceased to repeat tradition and began to make history" ("Supplement to the Voyage of Cook; or, *Le Calcul Sauvage*," 1–31, esp. 6).

Clearly, the rescate of these cherished symbols serves as the denouement of the drama. Through ransom, the symbols return to their natal homes but now carry with them webs of understanding and commitment. As in years past, and through the cycles of generations, villagers and Indians will prey upon one another and, in doing so, lose a little bit of themselves in return for vital exchanges. The struggle will always center on community preservation, but each community's survival will depend upon a capacity to surrender and adopt, exchanging self and other. The drama will always contain within its ritual a latent tragedy and hope of catharsis.

The origins of "Los Comanches" in New Mexico remain obscure. Popular memory conflates two events, one in 1760 and the other in 1777, as its genesis. The earlier date involves a Comanche raid on the fortified home of Pablo Villalpando in Ranchos de Taos, where, after the male defenders had been slain, some fifty women and children were carried into captivity on the Great Plains. Among those captured was María Rosa Villalpando, a house servant who found herself traded to the Pawnees and then into a career that would reach its height only much later and in a distant place. Her story will emerge below and serve to illustrate one of the more satisfying experiences of a captive *Nueva Mexicana.*[3]

The other point of origin lies to the south, where the village of Tomé suffered repeated raids by Comanches in the 1770s. These proved especially damaging in 1777, when some thirty villagers died in several different attacks, and two women, Dolores Baca and María Antonia Sánchez, were kidnapped. Later ransomed from captivity in New Orleans, where they came to reside after French traders purchased them from the Comanches, these young women faced social opprobrium upon their return and died spinsters in the village. Their fate was a common one within the captive experience, suggestive of how "redemption" as well as capture might be filled with pathos for those involved.[4]

Common to both tales, however, is the popular understanding of the motive behind the raids. In each case, a Comanche chieftain had visited the villages

3. Jack B. Tykal, "From Taos to St. Louis: The Journey of María Rosa Villalpando," *New Mexico Historical Review* (hereafter cited as *NMHR),* LXV (April 1990), 161–174.

4. Stanley Noyes, *Los Comanches: The Horse People* (Albuquerque, N.Mex., 1993), 60–68; Ervin Jaskolski, "The Tomé Indian Raid," paper presented at the Annual Conference of the Historical Society of New Mexico, Taos, N.Mex., Apr. 22, 1994; Fray Angélico Chávez, *Origins of New Mexico Families: A Genealogy of the Spanish Colonial Period,* rev. ed. (1954; Santa Fe, N.Mex., 1992), 281–282.

some years before on a trading expedition and, while conducting his business, had cast eyes upon the beautiful young daughter of his host. Extracting from her father a commitment of marriage when the girl would be of age, the chieftain departed for the Plains. When the requisite number of years had passed, the Comanche returned to take his new bride, only to find her betrothed to a village youth. Filled with anger and wounded pride, the chieftain then led his men to sack the village and to seize what in honor had been promised him. The legend as enacted in the Comanche Dance remembers the conflict and praises the conciliation, with the massacre recast as resurrection of the ill or infirm.[5]

The experiential roots of the drama actually lie much deeper and darker in time, with origins in native America and the Mediterranean. Honor, gender, and kinship remain central, however. La Cautiva occupies an ambiguous position in the social drama, coded as both the daughter of the chieftain, destined for captivity by her name, and the native equivalent of Christ in the ceremony of reconciliation. Yet kinship and captive statuses blur when considered within what we know of the captive exchange traditions of the borderlands. Plains Indian groups in general, and the Comanches in particular, had multiple social locations into which captives could be incorporated, not the least of which was as adoptive sons and daughters. So too did New Mexican villagers have adoptive institutions by which captive Indian children could become "kin": either as criadas ("servants," or, literally, "those raised up," from the root *criar),* or as godchildren of adoptive padrinos. "La Cautiva" is thus the blood daughter and the adoptive captive of the Comanche chieftain, with the tragic separations safely ritualized and the sometimes-favorable cultural consequences publicly celebrated.[6]

The young girl's ambiguity reverberates even more richly when considered

5. For an early version of this tale, see Josiah Gregg, *Commerce of the Prairies,* ed. Milo Milton Quaife (1844; Lincoln, Nebr., 1966), 139–140; for its association with Tomé, see Tykal, "From Taos to St. Louis," *NMHR,* LXV (April 1990).

6. See Ernest Wallace and E. Adamson Hoebel, *The Comanches: Lords of the South Plains* (1952; Norman, Okla., 1988), 241–242, for various captive locations; see also Noyes, "The Meaning of Captivity," in *Los Comanches,* 69–73. Neither of these authors, however, places captives in a broader network of exchange relations within and between native and New Mexican society; see Frances Leon Quintana, *Los Primeros Pobladores: Hispanic Americans of the Ute Frontier* (1974; rpt., Aztec, N.M., 1991), 206–210, for New Mexican patterns of *compadrazgo.* The best treatment of the Old World origins and New World elaborations of the institution remains that of Sidney W. Mintz and Eric R. Wolf, "An Analysis of Ritual Co-Parenthood *(Compadrazgo),*" *Southwest Journal of Anthropology,* VI (1950), 341–368.

within a larger framework of village-based conquest drama. In "Los Matachines," a ritual dance performed often on Christmas Eve in both Hispano villages and the Río Grande pueblos, the sole female performer is La Malinche, a prepubescent girl clad in a white communion gown, Hernan Cortéz's slave / consort / interpreter in his 1520 conquest of Mexico. In the Matachines Dance, she is presented in an elaborate ritual of courtship to "El Monarca," presumably Moctezuma, the Aztec emperor at the time of the Spaniards' arrival. Her age, purity, and the great deference paid her by the masked male dancers both conceal and intensify the sexual nature of this conquest romance. Amid pantomimes of sword combat by the male dancers, La Malinche makes several approaches as a supplicant to El Monarca, who finally "accepts" her by his side and orchestrates a concluding dance of reconciliation.[7]

Like the Comanche Dance, "Los Matachines" borrows from "Los Moros y Cristianos" of the Iberian reconquest, where the object of contestation and redemption is usually the *Santa Cruz* (Holy Cross). But, in New Mexico, the solitary girl of virgin purity, whose exact ethnic and kin affiliations seem deliberately shrouded, is the focal point for expressions of masculine violence and sentimentality.

If El Santo Niño and La Cautiva serve as sacred symbols of intercultural contestation and accommodation in "Los Comanches," they do so within the broader field of violence, exchange, and honor that was mutually understood among the male protagonists. Without such understandings, the rescate, redemption, and negotiation of future obligations could not occur. What emerges from the drama is a sense that, despite the social distance between European and native societies, men from both groups share a need to protect the honor of their communities and construct avenues for intercultural transfers. "Trade" here is, not a matter of marketplace bargaining, but an exercise of power between "others" enacted by mutualistic and competitive bestowal of gifts. The tensions between community self-sufficiency, a matter of honor

7. Flavia Waters Champe, *The Matachines Dance of the Upper Rio Grande: History, Music, and Choreography* (Lincoln, Nebr., 1983); field notes, Picurís Pueblo, N.Mex., Dec. 24, 1989, Los Cordovas, Dec. 31, 1989. Sylvia Rodríguez, *The Matachines Dance: Ritual Symbolism and Interethnic Relations in the Upper Río Grande Valley* (Albuquerque, N.Mex., 1996), looks at "the beautiful dance of subjugation" in both Pueblo and Hispano villages from an ethnographic perspective. She finds significant differences in symbolic function between the two; Pueblo Indians "subtly subvert" the conquest narrative, whereas Hispano performers focus the dance internally as a community identity ritual vis-à-vis the majority Anglo population.

for male "providers," and the absolute fact of intercommunity dependency, a matter of shame for those same men, required that negotiations be both calculating and giving, both profane and sacred.[8]

Shame, or *vergüenza,* turns deep in the male culture of New Mexican villages, the term often synonymous with *honor.* A man lacking a sense of honor is *sin vergüenza,* or without a shameful sense of poor behavior. Facundo Valdez, a native of Mora, writes that *un hombre con mucha vergüenza* is a rancher or farmer who owns his own land and rights to common land and is therefore "neither dependent on a boss nor taking advantage of others as a merchant." Dependence on outside resources beyond one's immediate control, whether it be wage labor or commercial exchanges, is inherently dangerous to a man's vergüenza and requires a sacred framework to divest it of its dishonorable qualities. Valdez makes explicit his view of the bicultural nature of the value, stating, "One reason [vergüenza] is so developed and has survived so long in rural New Mexico, in my opinion, is the Indian part of us. It was not a case of a clash of cultures but a reinforcement. . . . People I have known were personally acquainted with '*Indios de patarado*' (loincloth), and knew *criados* and *criadas* who were Indians captured as children. The Indian usually has the role in jokes of the grave and reserved man, with wisdom and sagacity."[9]

This idealization of self-sufficiency within the individual, family, and community suppresses resentment and justifies inequalities, however. A poor man without land of his own might work for low wages as a sheepherder but explain that "whether you accept a job for fifty cents or ten dollars, you must do it well and thoroughly." Hence, the honor of a job lies in the worker's willing-

8. For the centrality of "exchanges of violence" between men as part of socioeconomic exchange between segmentary groups of the Iqar'iyen in the Moroccan Rif, see Raymond Jamous, "From the Death of Men to the Peace of God: Violence and Peacemaking in the Rif," in J. G. Peristiany and Julian Pitt-Rivers, eds., *Honor and Grace in Anthropology* (Cambridge, 1992), 167–192. Among the Iqar'iyen, endemic violence in contests of honor can be suspended only by the intercession of the *shorfa,* descendents of the Prophet, who negotiate an end to hostilities by invoking *baraka,* or "divine blessing," the only essence more powerful than honor. The comparison here is more than simply suggestive, since many Iberian notions of honor seem linked with the period of Islamic conquest. See Mintz and Wolf, "An Analysis of Ritual Co-Parenthood," *Southwest Journal of Anthropology,* VI, no. 4 (1950), 341–368.

9. Facundo Valdez, "Vergüenza," in Paul Kutsche, ed., *The Survival of Spanish American Villages,* publication no. 15 of the Research Committee of the Colorado College (Colorado Springs, Colo., 1979), 99–106, esp. 100.

ness to fulfill his duty, regardless of the honorableness of the compensation. Likewise, the vergüenza of wives and children always reflects that of the husband or father; "if a woman is *sin vergüenza,* she has destroyed the manliness of the man." Since neither *patrónes* nor wives and children can be counted on to act honorably always, the threat of dishonor imbues all social relations.[10]

The capture and ransom of sacred symbols allowed mundane, and latently shameful, economic transfers to occur as a subtext to the dominant narrative of men's contests over honor. In this sense, captive exchange fits within a larger honor-laden framework of gift exchange, where face is continuously reaffirmed yet constantly at risk. It is simultaneously egalitarian, in that only equals may contest honor, and competitive, in that honor is never secure. One gives not to receive but that others must, in order to maintain their honor, give. To borrow from a lifetime student of honor and shame, "The function of the concept of honor is precisely, despite the frailty of the logic involved, to equate [honor and shame] and establish thereby the dialectic between 'the world as it ought to be and the world as it is.'" "Los Comanches" as performed over the centuries in the villages of northern New Mexico is a condensed version of a once-was world as its male members thought it ought to be.[11]

When cultural worlds collide and coalesce, the social languages that give them voice become mixed. New words and meanings are born; others are lost to the opacity of mixture itself. Hence any historical view is limited that treats notions of honor in the borderlands as simply a type of Mediterranean cultural baggage hauled across the Atlantic and deposited on the pristine landscape of *El Nuevo Mundo.* Honor, it has been claimed, served as a distancing value through which Europeans defined themselves as superior to natives, who lacked both the quality of and capacity for honorable action. In fact, there existed a particular resonance between indigenous and European notions of honor and shame, of male violence and exchange imperatives in the region, a resonance persisting well after the United States' conquest of the region in 1846. In the Southwest Borderlands, diverse social traditions of honor and shame, of violence, kinship, and community met, merged, and regenerated in

10. The first quotation, in its original Spanish, is "si te comprometes por cuatro reales o por diez pesos a un trabajo, es necessario hacerlo bien y completo." See Valdez, "Vergüenza," Kutsche, ed., *The Survival of Spanish American Villages,* 102–103.

11. See Marcel Mauss, *The Gift: The Form and Reason for Exchange in Archaic Societies,* trans. W. D. Hall (1909; London, 1990). For a critical evaluation of Mauss, see Sahlins, "The Spirit of the Gift," in *Stone Age Economics* (Chicago, 1972), 149–183; Peristiany and Pitt-Rivers, "Introduction," in *Honor and Grace in Anthropology,* 8.

new expressions. Over time, they produced an intricate web of intercultural animosity and affection that lingers today in the mixed sounds of hand drums and violins, of battle cries and love songs.[12]

Behind the ritual of gentle memory in "Los Comanches" lie centuries of conflict, of many groups conducting violent exchanges to protect sacred honor —and to force from their neighbors the "gift" of those things deemed most valuable. To see more clearly, we look back in time, toward the center of native North America, and witness similar transactions in the realms of the sacred.

She Wears the Clothes of the Shooting Star

Pahukstatu village, in the time before time. Across their floodplain fields along the Loup River, only stubble remained after the Skiri Pawnees' harvest of corn and squash. With dawn's break, news of the man's vision traveled quickly from lodge to lodge throughout the village. Tears staining his cheeks, he had run to the lodge of the *Upirikutsu* (Morning Star) priest, crying, "He comes, he comes, father; I am seeking for you." The priest filled the pipe and smoked with the man, listening to his vision, and heard in his voice the words of the Morning Star: "I am the man who has power in the east. I am the great star. You people have forgotten about me. I am watching over your people. Go to the man who knows the ceremony and let him know. He will tell you what to do."[13]

While four days passed, and the visionary was transformed into the earthly representation of Upirikutsu, other men of the village made preparations to

12. For the contradictory, yet productive, aspects of social and linguistic hybridities, see Mikhail M. Bahktin, *The Dialogic Imagination: Four Essays,* ed. Caryl Emerson, trans. Michael Holquist (1975; Austin,Tex., 1981), esp. 358. Ramón A. Gutiérrez explores Spanish notions of honor most thoroughly in *When Jesus Came, the Corn Mothers Went away: Sexuality, Love, and Conquest in New Mexico, 1500–1846* (Stanford, Calif., 1991), 176–240, but he does not engage similar ideas among the region's indigenous men. Lyman L. Johnson and Sonya Lipsett-Rivera, *The Faces of Honor: Sex, Shame, and Violence in Colonial Latin America* (Albuquerque, N.Mex., 1998), illustrates the breadth and diversity of the honor complex but with little reference to native codes. See also Verena Martínez-Alier, *Marriage, Class, and Colour in Ninteenth-Century Cuba* (Cambridge, 1974).

13. This re-creation of the Pawnee Morning Star ceremony is drawn from an extensive scholarly literature, including James R. Murie, in Douglas R. Parks, ed., *Ceremonies of the Pawnee,* I, Smithsonian Contributions to Anthropology, no. 27 (1981), 114–136; Sakuru Ta

travel. Their wives sewed special moccasins and prepared cornballs for the journey. Some of the assistants would represent stars themselves: Fools-the-Wolf, the Black Star, Wind-Ready-to-Give, traditional allies of the Morning Star as he journeyed westward to subdue and seduce *Cupirittaka,* the Evening Star. From the union of Morning Star and Evening Star had come the Girl Child, the first human, whose warm and moist breath represented the merging of (male) fire and (female) water.[14]

The priest dressed the visionary in articles from the Morning Star bundle—an otter skin, Mother Corn, a hawk skin, a pipe, soft down feathers, and a wildcat skin whose legs were stuffed with tobacco and paints. As the Morning Star rose in the darkness to the east, the visionary and his assistants set out westward, traveling fifteen or twenty miles before they rested. Each day's journey began with the Morning Star's rising, until finally their scouts reported that an enemy village had been sighted. Gathering his men, the visionary led them in a recitation of the process of creation, the sequences by which the Morning Star had overcome the Hard Things placed in his path by Evening Star—the floods, serpents, cactus thorns, thick woods, monsters, and evil animals—ten hindrances in all, like the ten forms of human kinship.[15]

As the Morning Star rose for the final time, the men approached the sleeping village. The visionary signaled the attack by opening his robe to expose

---

(Coming Sun), "The Morning Star and the Evening Star," in *The Indian's Book: Songs and Legends of the American Indians* (1907; New York, 1968); Gene Weltfish, *The Lost Universe, with a Closing Chapter on "The Universe Regained"* (New York, 1965), 106–118; Dorothy V. Jones, "John Dougherty and the Pawnee Rite of Human Sacrifice: April 1827," *Missouri Historical Review,* LXIII (April 1969), 293–316; Melburn D. Thurman, "The Skidi Pawnee Morning Star Sacrifice of 1827," *Nebraska History,* LI (1970), 269–280; Von del Chamberlain, *When Stars Came down to Earth: Cosmology of the Skidi Pawnee Indians of North America* (College Park, Md., 1982); Philip J. Duke, "The Morning Star Ceremony of the Skiri Pawnee as Described by Alfred C. Haddon," *Plains Anthropologist,* XXXIV (August 1989), 193–203. For a dated discussion of its "diffusion" from Mesoamerica, see Clark Wissler and Herbert J. Spinden, "The Pawnee Human Sacrifice to the Morning Star," *American Museum Journal,* XVI, no. 1 (1916).

14. Murie, "Human Sacrifice to the Morning Star," in Parks, ed., *Ceremonies of the Pawnee,* I, 114–136; Chamberlain, *When Stars Came down to Earth,* 21–26.

15. Chamberlain, *When Stars Came down to Earth,* 23. Weltfish lists thirteen kin terms in all, but these include a generic "child" *(piirau)* and compounds for grandson and granddaughter; otherwise, they represent lineal terms from grandparents through sons and daughters, with the noteworthy addition of the mother's brother *(tiwatciriks)* in this matri-

his naked body, then closed his arms to symbolize taking the captive. His men attacked the dazed enemy until they found the girl for whom they searched, a girl at the dawn of puberty. Skiri scouts had already stampeded the village horse herd, retaining just enough mounts for the escape. With the girl placed behind her captor on his horse, they now retreated, knowing that a pursuit could not be undertaken. Retribution would surely come, but later, by a formal war party.

They set fire to the prairie to announce their return. As the warriors recounted coups and tallied war counts, the women of Pahukstatu village celebrated with a victory dance. The Morning Star priest took charge of the captive girl, calling to his lodge Fools-the-Wolf, the keeper of the Wolf Bundle. He would now watch over the girl and take her to the visionary's lodge for meals. The priest smudged both the Wolf Bundle keeper and the captive with the smoke of burning Sweetgrass, then took the girl's costume from the Morning Star Bundle. Rubbing her first with an ointment of red pigment and bison fat, he proceeded to dress her in a calfskin skirt, soft overblouse, warm buffalo robe, and black moccasins and finally placed a down feather in her hair. She was given a wooden bowl and buffalo horn spoon with which to eat and treated as an honored guest.

Winter passed, and the girl was taken along with the villagers on their winter buffalo hunt. The visionary warrior undertook to kill a fat buffalo cow, whose tongue and heart would be carefully dried for use in the impending ceremony. As months went by, the Morning Star priest watched the skies for the crucial sign, the rising of the Morning Star, ringed in red.

When finally the portent appeared, a five-day ritual began. The priest again clothed the visionary in the accoutrements of the Morning Star and directed that a ceremonial lodge be constructed in which holders of celestial bundles would conduct four days of prayer. The captive girl was bathed in Sweetgrass smoke and anointed with the red ointment, as ceremonies of the four semicardinal directions overcome by the Morning Star in his journey were performed. Elder men and her protector, the Wolf Bundle keeper, spoke soothing words to the girl, now transformed into the Evening Star, or White Star Woman.

During the four days of ceremony, other men erected a scaffold somewhat east of the village. Again, the semicardinal directions were represented by dif-

---

lineal society (see *Lost Universe*, 27). Chamberlain notes that Pawnee songs mirror the kin system in containing ten "steps," or stanzas (*When Stars Came down to Earth*, 23 n. 10).

ferent types of wood, elm for the northeast, box elder for the southwest, cottonwood for the northwest, and willow for the southeast. Each symbolized as well the Evening Star's animal protectors: the bear, the mountain lion, the wildcat, and the wolf. Spanning the uprights was another cottonwood pole, representing the heavens, and to it was tied an otter skin, symbolizing the renewal of life. Beneath the scaffold the men dug a shallow rectangular pit, the Garden of the Evening Star, where all life originated. It was called *Kusaru,* or the "bed."

With the scaffold complete, the girl was taken from the lodge and brought out for her final role. The right side of her body was painted red, for day, the time of the Morning Star, and her left side black, for night, the time of the Evening Star. Around her hips hung a soft skirt, and across her shoulders a painted hide robe. As night passed and the rising of the Morning Star neared, the men sang to her of celestial transformation:

> You wear the clothing of the
>   shooting-star grandfather,
> You wear the clothing of the
>   shooting-star father,
> You wear the clothing of the
>   shooting-star uncle,
> You wear the clothing of the
>   shooting-star brother.

As the star appeared on the horizon, the girl was led up to the scaffold and her wrists and ankles tied to the supporting poles by elk hide thongs, facing east. The Southeast Bundle keeper approached her with a burning firebrand and touched her sides, symbolizing the seasons of the sun. The visionary warrior, using a bow from the sacred Skull Bundle, then loosed a single arrow into her heart. With a sacred flint, the Northeast Bundle keeper took her blood to anoint the sacred tongue and heart of the buffalo cow. As her body slumped in its bonds, "it was said that her soul went straight to the zenith [of the heavens], to *Tiriwahat,*" the creator. He directed the Morning Star to clothe "her [soul] in his glowing flint" and make of her a star, "to look down upon the people for whom she had given her life."[16]

Through the Morning Star ceremony, Skiri Pawnees restored the balance of contentious but complementary male and female powers that had first brought

16. Chamberlain, *When Stars Came down to Earth,* 66.

human life to the world. Its performance was so fraught with beauty and danger that it occurred only rarely. Like "Los Comanches," its origins are shrouded in timelessness. One earthlodge and burial mound in Geary County, Kansas, may represent a Pawnee Morning Star ritual complex dating to approximately A.D. 1300. Historical references to the ritual began in 1816, when a *Ietan* (Comanche) girl was taken captive and sacrificed at Pumpkin Vine village, despite intervention by its political head, Knife Chief, whose accommodationist relation with Superintendent of Indian Affairs William Clark included a commitment to suppressing the ceremony. In 1817, Pawnees seized a ten-year-old "Spanish" boy accompanying a party of New Mexican *ciboleros* and dedicated him to the Morning Star, but Knife Chief was able this time to ransom the captive, with the assistance of the trader Manuel Lisa and his interpreter, Papin. Bloody factionalism accompanied an 1827 attempt to sacrifice a Cheyenne woman, who died in the fray. The last documented occurrence took place on April 22, 1838, when Haxti, a captive Oglala Sioux girl of fifteen, became a sacrifice to the Morning Star.[17]

Although attracting polemical coverage, both condemnatory and apologetic, this ceremony is an archetype for a wider system of sacred violence and exchange in native North America. The Pawnees were perhaps the most central of "center-people" in the great captive exchange complex that operated throughout the continent, stretching from the Southwest Borderlands northward to the Great Lakes and beyond. Before European penetration of the area, the system combined sacred and secular exchange imperatives: sacrificial subjects, kin replacements for those lost in war, and forcible seizures of women and children for marriage and adoption. After the system connected to the Euro-colonial world, "Panis" (Pawnees) came to predominate among the several thousands of Plains Indian captives transported throughout its increasingly market-driven conduits to French Canada and British America, some even to

17. Patricia J. O'Brien, "Evidence for the Antiquity of Women's Roles in Pawnee Society," *Plains Anthropologist,* memoir 26, XXXVI, no. 134 (1991), 51–64. Drawing from osteological and lithic materials scattered on a burial mound at this site, O'Brien suggests that at this early date both a captive boy and girl might have been sacrificed, one to the Morning Star and the other to the Evening Star. For the capture of the New Mexican boy, whose case hints that gender could be ritually reinscribed to meet ceremonial needs, see George E. Hyde, *Pawnee Indians* (Denver, Colo., 1951), 108–109; Jones, "John Dougherty and the Pawnee Rite of Human Sacrifice," *Missouri Historical Review,* LXIII (April 1969), 295–316; Thurman, "Skidi Pawnee Morning Star Sacrifice of 1827," *Nebraska History,* LI (1970), 269–280; Weltfish, *Lost Universe,* 115–117.

the Spanish Caribbean. At least twenty-five Pawnee captives were baptized in colonial New Mexican parishes. As both captors and captives, Pawnees occupied a central node in the network of human exchanges that predated Europeans and intensified with Spanish, French, and British imperial intrusions. Whether sacred or profane, these transfers created an increasingly heterogeneous Indian world across the heartland of North America.[18]

Underlying the Morning Star ceremony were wider implications concerning mixed descent. The intertwined displays of violence, honor, and gender facilitated the exchange system and its sacred resolution in the indigenous world. When Pawnee visionaries set forth westward to take captive a human representative of the Evening Star, they confirmed both the sophis-

18. See John B. Dunbar, "The Pawnee Indians: Their Habits and Customs," *Magazine of American History with Notes and Queries,* VIII (1882), 734–754; Chamberlain, *When Stars Came down to Earth.* The "central Plains tradition" origin of the Pawnee is undergoing radical revision; see John Ludwickson et al., "An Evaluation of Central Plains Tradition: Pawnee Ancestry," paper presented at the 49th Annual Plains Conference, Lawrence, Kans. (1991); David H. Snow, "Pots, Pipes, and Trade Partners: Aspects of the Social and Cultural Contexts of Southern Plains–Eastern Pueblo Exchange Systems," paper presented at the 49th Annual Plains Conference. Marcel Trudel counts 1,710 "Panis" (63.5 percent) among the 2,692 known American Indian slaves in French Canada. Other culturally identified Indian peoples in French colonial slavery were 126 Fox, 51 Patocas (Paduccas?), 46 Sioux, 24 Montagnais, 18 Cicachas (Comanches?), 6 Cree, 5 Sauteux (Salteurs), 2 Têtes-de-Boules, 2 Ottawa, 1 Naskapi, 1 Nipissing, and 13 Esquimaux. See *Dictionnaire des esclaves et de leurs proprietaires au Canada français* (Ville LaSalle, Quebec, 1990); W. J. Eccles, *The Canadian Frontier, 1534–1760* (1969; Albuquerque, N.Mex., 1990), 149–150; J. C. Hamilton, "The Panis: An Historical Outline of Canadian Indian Slavery in the Eighteenth Century," Royal Canadian Institute, *Proceedings,* I (Toronto, 1898), N.S. See also Brett Rushforth, "Savage Bonds: Panis Slavery in Eighteenth-Century New France," paper presented at the 8th Annual Conference of the Omohundro Institute of Early American History and Culture, Glasgow, Jul. 14, 2001. For the meaning and experience of captives in Iroquois society, where some Pawnees might have been sold, see Daniel K. Richter, *The Ordeal of the Longhouse: The Peoples of the Iroquois League in the Era of European Colonization* (Chapel Hill, N.C., 1992), 65–74. For the connections between the Plains captive network and the Caribbean in the eighteenth century, see Tanis Chapman Thorne, "People of the River: Mixed-blood Families on the Lower Missouri" (Ph.D. diss., UCLA, 1987), 73–76. For Pawnee captives in New Mexico, see "Claim Made by Lucia Ortega against Roque Novato concerning a Donation, in the Year 1769," in *Spanish Archives of New Mexico* (hereafter cited as *SANM),* I, no. 657, roll 4, frames 369–390; David M. Brugge, *Navajos in the Catholic Church Records of New Mexico, 1694–1875,* 2d ed. (Tsaile, Ariz., 1985), 22–23.

tication of their astronomical observations and their embeddedness in what anthropologist Patricia Albers calls "geographically far-ranging and ethnically mixed social formations." That the historically known captives dedicated to the Morning Star came from Comanche, Cheyenne, Sioux, and Spanish backgrounds lends credibility to this expansiveness, as does the fact that the sacred Morning Star pipe was decorated with a woven belt of "Navajo or other southwestern origin." In their renewal of the very first act of human creation, Pawnee warriors engaged in an act of sacred violence that confirmed the centrality of long-distance interethnic exchange to group genesis and survival. The action also brought honor to individuals and the lineage they represented. At the same time, the captive seizure was understood as a de facto dishonoring of the "enemy" villagers, who, although they accepted that the capture "was a kind of cosmic destiny," knew also that their honor required redemption. Within a formal pattern of warfare that pursued territorial, demographic, and strategic advantages, captive seizure was recognized by all as the offense to honor that energized future exchanges.[19]

As in most ranked, matrilineal Plains Indian societies, Pawnee brothers "were called on to preserve the reputation of the family." Accumulation of wealth in horses, wives, kinspeople, and captive slaves served to enhance family honor and solidify its economic status. Since each of the thirteen Skiri villages reckoned kinship from legendary ancestral parents, family honor contributed to village honor generally. Dishonor was expressed in terms of poverty: "The worst insult one could hurl at a man was to call him *ruti-kapakis-kawitat,* 'the one who is-poor-ragged.' " Brothers sought to preserve family and village repute by sharing wealth among siblings and acquiring horses and captives to elevate the village itself. Thus, raiding enemies for captives, especially women and children—the special responsibility of fraternal obligations—combined honor and shaming in a single action.[20]

19. Patricia C. Albers, "Symbiosis, Merger, and War: Contrasting Forms of Intertribal Relationship among Historic Plains Indians," in John Moore, ed., *The Political Economy of North American Indians* (Lincoln, Nebr., 1993), 94–132, esp. 96; Murie, "Human Sacrifice to the Morning Star," in Parks, ed., *Ceremonies of the Pawnee,* I, 121; Weltfish, *Lost Universe,* 109. For a larger view of how revenge for wife stealing encouraged intertribal warfare in South America, see Elsa M. Redmond, *Tribal and Chiefly Warfare in South America,* vol. V of Joyce Marcus, ed., *Studies in Latin American Ethnohistory and Archaeology,* Memoirs of the Museum of Anthropology, University of Michigan, no. 28 (Ann Arbor, Mich., 1994).

20. Weltfish, *Lost Universe,* 33. For a comparative discussion of gender and power in Comanche, Cheyenne, and Kiowa society, see Jane Fishburne Collier, *Marriage and In-*

Working within a guiding metaphor of sexual conquest, capture, and marriage, the Morning Star ceremony also establishes the centrality of gender and kinship to the larger exchange processes at work in native North America. Albers has made clear that mutually understood mobilizations of real or fictive kinship structured intertribal relations, whether competitive, cooperative, or symbiotic. Marriages across ethnic lines bound families in relations of reciprocal obligation, often providing the intermediate actors in economic exchanges. Likewise, membership in ritual and military sodalities involved affinal ties often expressed in adoptive terms, with no lessening in the weight of reciprocal obligation.[21]

For the Pawnees, kinship fictions made possible diplomacy and trade relations with other groups:

> People with whom one dealt as equals had to be placed in some kin category; lack of such a relation could only imply slave or enemy status. In the various trade or gift exchange ceremonials that were conducted between tribes or bands, a whole kin structure was built up so that they could communicate on a peaceful level.[22]

Although this affirms kinship's importance to trade relations, it tends to reinforce an analytically troublesome dichotomy between productive peaceful exchanges and destructive exchanges of violence. Marshall Sahlins's typology of exchange reciprocity as generalized, balanced, or negative perpetuates thinking of exchange as an alternative to war: "The gift is the primitive way of achieving peace that in civil society is secured by the state." In reality, the political economy of captive exchange was not an alternative to violence but an assimilation of violence into mutually productive exchange relations.[23]

The capture of "enemy" women and children was, therefore, one extreme expression along a continuum of exchange. As captives often assimilated to the kin nexus of their "host" society in affinal or fictive terms, they could serve

---

equality in Classless Societies (Stanford, Calif., 1988). Although Collier does a masterful job of detailing the manner in which men negotiated power through exchanges of women, her analysis fails to account for women's own status objectives in these exchanges, an issue that will prove important below, in later chapters; see Weltfish, *Lost Universe*, 34.

21. Albers, "Symbiosis, Merger, and War," in Moore, ed., *Political Economy of North American Indians*, 119–122.

22. Weltfish, *Lost Universe*, 31.

23. Sahlins, "Spirit of the Gift," in *Stone Age Economics*, 168; here I follow Raymond Jamous's work on the Iqar'iyen of the Moroccan Rif, where he argues, "Even where violence

as agents and objects of the full range of potential exchanges, from the peaceful to the violent. Albers describes the ambiguity of this process, arguing that abduction not only contained

> the grounds for conflict, but it also embodied (quite literally) the terms of reconciliation. . . . The capture of women and children was both a quintessential element of war, and a fundamental opportunity for peace. It maintained, yet rearranged, the social nexus through which tribes were able to rework their relationships.[24]

The Morning Star captive, clothed in honor while condemned to death, experienced perhaps the most permanent form of incorporation through her "marriage," reinscription, and ascension to the heavens as a new star in Pawnee cosmology. Few captives suffered this kind of "elevation" within the exchange system; many were slain in retribution for the loss of a loved one or traded throughout wide exchange networks. But the majority seem to have experienced some form of incorporation into their host society. From that position most lived out their lives in social and historical obscurity. Yet their importance was inescapable, both in their categorical role in the social sphere and in the individual cases that reveal the cultural sharing involved. Women and children were both "gift" and "offense": sometimes offered so that others must give, sometimes captured so that wounds to honor, salved by redemption or aggravated by refusals, might ensure continued cycles of "giving."[25]

Like La Cautiva and La Malinche, the Morning Star captive served as the sacred symbol through which Pawnee men engendered vital exchanges in the interests of community renewal and survival. She was not alone in her role. In the 1780s, a Shoshone medicine man used sacred powers to locate and capture Walks-at-Dusk, a Hidatsa boy whom he thought strong enough to buy Shoshone sacred rites. Walks-at-Dusk would return to his Hidatsa people, but as

---

escapes regulation, it takes on forms which are a function of the encompassing ideology." See "From the Death of Men to the Peace of God," in Peristiany and Pitt-Rivers, eds., *Honor and Grace in Anthropology,* 173.

24. Albers, "Symbiosis, Merger, and War," in Moore, ed., *Political Economy of North American Indians,* 128.

25. For another case in which captives achieve cosmological significance in native American society, in this case among the Zuñis, see the role of "enemy ancestor captives" in their quadrennial *Kan'a:kwe* ceremonies. See Will Roscoe, *The Zuni Man-Woman* (Albuquerque, N.Mex., 1991), 147–169.

a changed man and founder of a schismatic movement. In the 1820s the Cheyennes and some Sioux allies "moved against" the Crows on the Tongue River in an action that netted "over 100 young women and boys." These captives became Cheyennes through adoption, and the excuse for competitive feasts between Cheyennes and Crows in which they repeatedly tested the loyalties of the adoptees. By the nineteenth century, Comanches' and Kiowas' sun dances incorporated a sacred role for the captive women they seized from Spanish settlements, extending even further across cultures the stitching together of ritual spheres. And, throughout Plains Indian and Spanish colonial societies, more mundane exchanges "made kin" through blood brotherhood, adoption, marital ties, and the theft of women and children. Beneath sacred discourse, these transactions served the everyday exchange of material goods.[26]

This phenomenon, however, was not confined to indigenous America. Its constellation of values, attractions, and oppositions had parallels in the "Old World" that would prove meaningful when both worlds met in the Southwest Borderlands.

I Cannot Marry You

In an anonymous ballad of the fourteenth century, King John of Castile summons to his side Abenámar, son of a Moorish father and a *cristiana cautiva* (Christian captive woman). The setting is on the Granadan frontier, the mountain fastness of southwestern Spain that remained the last foothold of Islam on the Iberian Peninsula. A long period of truce holds overt conflict in abeyance, a lull in the *reconquista,* summoning memories of the centuries of *la convivencia* that characterized Christian, Muslim, and Jewish Iberia since the ninth century.[27]

26. For Walks-at-Dusk, see James F. Brooks, "Sing away the Buffalo: Faction and Fission on the Northern Plains," in Philip Duke and Michael C. Wilson, eds., *Beyond Subsistence: Plains Archaeology and the Postprocessual Critique* (Tuscaloosa, Ala., 1995), 143–168, esp. 161–164. As an indication of just how socially mixed intertribal politics were at this point, the Crows were urged to negotiate through feasting by Big Mountain, a Kiowa chief "visiting the Crows at the time." See letters of George Bent to George Hyde, Apr. 10, 1905, Feb. 7, 10, 12, 19, 1914, Western Americana MSS, 32, folders 3, 27–29, Beinecke Library, Yale University, New Haven, Conn. The captive role in Kiowa and Comanche sun dances is developed below, in Chapter 5.

27. *La convivencia,* of course, did not mean harmonious coexistence. Rather, low-scale endemic violence, with occasional eruptions of ethnically or religiously motivated riot or

King John looked across the rugged peaks to the gleaming city of Granada and asked

Que castillos son aquellos?	What are those castles?
Altos son y relucían!	How high they are and shining!

Abenámar responded, naming each in turn: the Alhambra, seat of Muhammad V; the Mosque; the Alixares; the gardens of Genaralif; and the Torres Bermejas, *castillo de gran valía* (castle of great value). The Christian king and Moorish kingdom then addressed each other, an exchange that suggests some of the ambiguities that confound any simple reading of the reconquest as a strictly religious military endeavor:

Si tú quisieses,	If you were willing,
Granada	Granada
contigo me casaría;	I would marry you;
daréte en arras	and for dowry I would
a dote	give you
a Córdoba y a Sevilla.	both Córdoba and Seville.

And Granada responded

Casada soy, rey don Juan,	I am married, King John,
casada soy,	I am married, and not a
que no vuida;	widow;
el moro que a mí	and the Moor to whom I
me tiene	belong
muy grande bien me queria.[28]	loves me very well.

Castilians were not alone in viewing the city through the poetry of romance. Beneath the landscape of ethnoreligious violence lay corresponding labyrinths of affection and desire, however paradoxical. "Abenámar" simply places in the domain of conquest contemporary imagery of Granada expressed in the court

massacre, served to maintain community cohesion and local parity in power relations. See Mark D. Meyerson and Edward D. English, eds., *Christians, Muslims, and Jews in Medieval and Early Modern Spain* (Notre Dame, Ind., 1999); David Nirenberg, *Communities of Violence: Persecution of Minorities in the Middle Ages* (Princeton, N.J., 1996); Vivian B. Mann, Thomas F. Glick, and Jerrilynn D. Dodds, eds., *Convivencia: Jews, Muslims, and Christians in Medieval Spain* (New York, 1992).

28. "Abenámar y el rey don Juan," in Rafael Mesa y Lopez, comp. and ed., *Antología de los mejores poetas castellanos* (London, 1912), 10–14.

poetry of Ibn Zamrak, Muhammad V's chief minister, who personified and sensualized the city made beautiful by his patron:

> Stay awhile here on the terrace of the Sabīka [Alhambra], and look
> about you.
> This city is a wife, whose husband is the hill:
> Girt she is by water and by flowers,
> Which glisten at her throat,
> Ringed with streams; and behold the groves of trees which are the
> wedding guests, whose thirst is being assuaged by the water-channels.
> The Sabīka hill sits like a garland on Granada's brow,
> In which the stars would be entwined,
> And the Alhambra (God preserve it)
> Is the ruby set above that garland.
> Granada is a bride whose headdress is the Sabīka, and
> Whose jewels and adornments are its flowers.[29]

In these two poems from either side of the apparently impenetrable Christian-Muslim divide, metaphors of gender, sexuality, marriage, and conquest illustrate the forces of attraction that underlay the more overt conflicts in Early Modern Spain. Other examples abound, as in the ballad *Pártese el moro Alicante* (the Muslim is leaving Alicante), where a Muslim king gives a nameless *morica doncella moça y loçana* (virginal Muslim serving girl) to his defeated and imprisoned adversary, the Christian Ganzalo Gustos. Ostensibly a gift to soothe the nobleman's loss of his seven sons in battle, the young woman's virginity, sexuality, and fecundity are in fact the avenue by which Gustos will obtain new sons and reconquer Muslim Iberia. Like the Comanche Dance and the Morning Star ceremony, men's poetry elevated and rendered sensible the strands of desire and repulsion that stretched across cultural frontiers. Romantic, erotic, and suffused with notions of military honor, such poetry responded to a specific unfolding of conflict and accommodation across the region in the Early Modern era.[30]

At the end of the fourteenth century, the peninsula contained complex societies nurtured in war but driven as well by the need to coexist, if not to tolerate.

29. Ibn Zamrak, as translated by L. P. Harvey, in *Islamic Spain, 1250–1500* (Chicago, 1990), 219.

30. See Louise Mirrer, *Women, Jews, and Muslims in the Texts of Reconquest Castile* (Ann Arbor, Mich., 1996), 17–30.

As the demographic advantage swung in favor of the Christian kingdoms of Castile and Aragon, Islamic Spain gradually gave ground to Christian frontier raiders who more often sought land and cattle than religious conquest. The ethnically mixed social formation that had characterized Spain remained secure even following Christian advances, as the military orders showed a marked preference for settling their new lands with Muslim tenants, better equipped culturally and technologically for commercial agriculture and transport.[31]

Whatever the large-scale antagonisms between Christian and Muslim empires, local relations in this multiethnic society remained relatively balanced, mirroring each other in widely shared values and expectations. One historian has explained that local Iberian

> communities survived with strongly local loyalties and culture, linking up with other regions only for trade and, if they were of the same faith, for marriage. In these communities and *pueblos*, tolerance rested on mutual respect, on repute within the local society, on good opinion or "honour." . . . [The term] never lost its basic and most important meaning of good opinion within the community comprising one's kinfolk and one's home region or *país*.[32]

As the reconquista expanded in scope during the fifteenth century, this tradition of economic mutualism and religious endogamy became strained, with frontier regions suffering endemic warfare punctuated only occasionally by truces that allowed the temporary return of economic prosperity. Each cycle of recovery would be followed by renewed hostilities. During this period, *romances fronterizos* (frontier ballads) like "Abenámar" achieved their highest elaboration. Beneath the obvious narrative of conflict, however, lay a continuing acknowledgment of shared values. L. P. Harvey argues:

> In the Castilian ballads both sides are presented as imbued with the same admirable moral qualities, both respect the same chivalric code of conduct. What marks off the one group of men from the other is a purely superficial set of differences of dress and language.[33]

31. Harvey, *Islamic Spain*, 70–71. For a treatment that includes the role of Jewish *conversos* (converts) in creating this mixed society, see Robert I. Burns, *Muslims, Christians, and Jews in the Crusader Kingdom of Valencia: Societies in Symbiosis* (Cambridge, 1984).

32. Henry Kamen, *Spain 1469–1714: A Society of Conflict* (London, 1983), xiii.

33. Harvey, *Islamic Spain*, 221–222.

A broadly held code of male honor superseded ethnic and religious differences in Early Modern Spain, providing the moral framework within which contests for honor, territory, subjects, and women took place. That men's control of women provided the focus of struggles to define honor and shame, evoked in the conquest romance of "Abenámar," appears more clearly in Spanish village dramas of "los moros y cristianos," whence "Los Comanches" in essence derives.

The earliest reference to this version of the conquest drama occurs in 1150, when companies of Moors and Christians feigned combat in honor of the marriage of Queen Petronilla of Aragon to the Catalan Count Ramón de Berenguer IV. By the fifteenth century it appeared throughout Spain, especially in frontier towns most involved with the violence of the reconquista. Commonly, the drama unfolded in a manner by now familiar: the Moors besiege a Christian village and either by guile or force of arms capture a "miraculous image" of the town. This is usually the Santa Cruz, but in some cases the cause of the attack is attributed to the failure of the town to pay an annual tribute of *cien doncellas* (one hundred maidens), and the Moors take *a fuerza de armas* what has been denied them in honor. After their initial setback, the Christian knights always prevail in subduing the *jinetes* and returning the sacred symbols, either the Holy Cross or the town maidens, to their proper place.[34]

This sanguine conclusion, like that in the Comanche Dance, was what people wished to "remember" and perhaps influenced later intercultural tactics. The practice of rescate, or ransom and redemption, mentioned earlier has its immediate origins in the Spain of the reconquista. The Redemptionist Orders of the Mercedarians and Trinitarians appeared during this period, charged with the task of raising alms for ransom and negotiating captives' repatriation. The years between 1529 and 1830 found some 9,500 Christian captives rescued from Muslim bondage in North Africa, and similar thousands must have preceded these before the conquest of Granada in 1492. In the Granadan sack of Zahara in 1410, for example, 61 women and 122 children were carried into captivity, and their redemption became a point of honor for Ferdinand I of Aragon.[35]

Not all captives were rescued, however, and many from both sides remained

34. "Fiestas of Moors and Christians," in George M. Foster, *Culture and Conquest: America's Spanish Heritage* (New York, 1960), 221–225.

35. Ellen G. Friedman, *Spanish Captives in North Africa in the Early Modern Age* (Madison, Wisc., 1983); Harvey, *Islamic Spain,* 235.

to become either *mozárabes* (Christians living under Muslim rule), *mudéjares* (Muslims living under Christian rule), *moriscos* (Muslim converts to Christianity), or *muladí* (Christian converts to Islam). Captured women and children formed only a portion of these categories, as most were composed of families and villages over which the tides of battle raged without displacing them, but captives played crucial roles as intermediaries between societies. A Christian captive scout of the Moors saved Infante Ferdinand by exaggerating the size of the enemy's rear guard, thereby persuading him to retreat from Sentil (1407). The scout was a nephew of Juana Martínez, a servant in Ferdinand's household staff. On the other hand, the Kingdom of Navarre maintained a core of artillery specialists who were Muslim and who proved their loyalty over several generations. Likewise, Ridwan Bannigash (Vanegas), born of Christian parents and taken captive when still a child, became chief minister under Muhammad VIII (1428–1430) but maintained contacts with his Christian relatives during his tenure.[36]

Religious endogamy seems the rule in Early Modern Spain, but captives who converted (whether moriscos or muladí) could, and did, marry into the "host" society. In time, however, the loyalty both of "New Christians" and muladí like Ridwan Bannigash became suspect; this seems primarily a sixteenth-century development, when *limpieza de sangre* (purity of blood) became increasingly important to membership in noble families, military confraternities, or religious orders. Earlier, during the centuries of the reconquista, marriage was largely a matter of fostering social stability; interethnic marriages were condoned and even encouraged. In Alfonso X's (1252–1284) legal code *Las Siete Partidas,* marriage was defined as a state necessary "to avoid quarrels, homicides, insolence, violence, and many other wrongful acts that would take place on account of women if marriage did not exist." Accordingly, crown and church authorities promoted *unidad doméstica* as part of their frontier policy, offering significant property and citizenship rights to married or marriageable women who would migrate to frontier towns. In their charters, many of these same towns decriminalized the kidnapping and forcible abduction of Moorish women if the captive could be converted and married to her abductor.[37]

36. Harvey, *Islamic Spain,* 1–5, 138–150, 233–234, 246–247.

37. Bartolomé Bannassar, *The Spanish Character: Attitudes and Mentalities from the Sixteenth to the Nineteenth Century,* trans. Benjamin Keen (1975; Berkeley, Calif., 1979), 82–83; Samuel Parsons Scott, trans. and ed., *Las Siete Partidas* (Chicago, 1931), 886; Antonia Castañeda, "Gender, 'Race,' and Representation: The Politics of Colonialism in Alta California,"

Although preoccupations with purity of blood had become profound by the time of Spanish colonialism in the Americas, the pragmatics of creating a stable colonial society required that this issue be subordinated on the new frontiers. La Malinche, the central symbol in the New Mexican conquest drama of "Los Matachines," serves well as a starting point for questions about sexual violence, colonialism, and *mestizaje* in the New World. Enslaved when sold to the Huastec Maya by her Aztec family to simplify an inheritance, she became at age fourteen Cortéz's concubine and interpreter during his *entrada* into Mexico. Her children by Cortéz were hardly the first from such conquest unions but hold a special place in the ideology of *la raza cósmica*. Less often recognized is the fact that her oldest child, Martín Vallejo, died fighting Muslim corsairs in the Mediterranean. At least one child of New World interethnic relations found himself embroiled in similar patterns of the Old.[38]

Spanish crown policy in the early years of conquest reflected the Spaniards' experiences in Iberia. In 1500, Queen Isabella appointed as governor of the Indies Fray Nicolás de Ovando, *comendador major* of the military order of Alcántara, who had experience in the governance of the conquered provinces of Granada. Acknowledging that capture and concubinage had become the rule in the Indies (with native women fetching as much as one hundred *castellanos),* Ovando recommended formalization of these unions under Spanish law. Accordingly, Isabella instructed that Spanish men be induced to marry Indian women, and Indian men marry Spanish women (although the latter was hardly likely), in order more rapidly to attain full Christian conversion.[39]

After Isabella's death, Ferdinand continued her policies, prohibiting in 1514 any discrimination against Spanish men who took Indian wives. In practice, few marriages were confirmed (in 1514 in Española, only 63 of the 672 *encomiendas* granted to Spanish men included formalized unions of grantees with Indian women), and concubinage continued as common practice. But the policies themselves reflect an administrative willingness to continue customary conquest marriages even in the more foreign setting of the Americas. Policy

---

paper presented at the "New Directions in American Indian History" conference, Kalamazoo, Mich., Mar. 17–19, 1994; see also Mary Elizabeth Perry, *Gender and Disorder in Early Modern Seville* (Princeton, N.J., 1990), 53–74.

38. Sandra Messinger Cypess, *La Malinche in Mexican Literature: From History to Myth* (Austin, Tex., 1991).

39. Leslie Byrd Simpson, *The Encomienda in New Spain* (Berkeley, Calif., 1966), 10–12.

failures had more to do with differential power relationships in the Indies than changes in Spanish values.[40]

In the sixteenth century, indigenous and European traditions of violence, exchange, honor, and shame began to meet in the Southwest Borderlands. Although confusion, revulsion, and massacre characterized much of this encounter, such conflicts' roots in shared customs and values of honor would also promote long-term patterns of coexistence and cultural exchange.

He Left a Child among the Heathen

The indigenous and Iberian societies that met in the borderlands shared several broadly sketched notions about the nature and negotiation of intergroup relationships. First among these was the idea that men's repute rested largely in their ability to preserve, protect, and dominate the well-being and social relations of their families and communities. Concurrent with this idea existed the acknowledged (and disquieting) reality that in-group survival depended to some degree on social and economic interactions with out-groups, a continual challenge to men's sense of honor. Second, men undertook exchange relations within an honor-and-shame nexus that would allow interdependency without lessening their normative control over women and children, the mutually understood focus of contestation, negotiation, and exchange.

Finally, long-term interdependency produced unresolved tensions in the maintenance of stable cultural identities. The exchange of culture-group members fostered accommodation, eroded linguistic and cultural boundaries, and concomitantly placed stress on the production and preservation of in-group identity. So painful were these pressures that they found expression in terms of the sacred, where beauty and danger, death and healing, tragedy and romance reflected in the spiritual realm the violence of everyday life. Resolutions to violence also lay in the realm of the sacred, whether in the rescate at Placitas, the sacrifice on the Morning Star scaffold, or the metaphoric marriage of Castile and Granada (or Spain and Mexico). Although the capacity to maintain shared levels of violence between societies lay as much with military and economic parity as it did with any divine intervention, the fact that such reso-

40. Ibid., 35, 177 n. 3. For a recent treatment of miscegenation and acculturation in New Spain that includes the African aspect, see Claudio Esteva-Fabregat, *Mestizaje in Ibero-America,* trans. John Wheat (Tucson, Ariz., 1994).

lutions took place in sacred discourse confirmed the primacy of these mutual values for both sets of social protagonists.[41]

Where sacred or secular parity did not exist, intergroup exchanges took on a real and tangible aura of tragedy. Consider the following passage from the *relación* of Alvar Núñez Cabeza de Vaca. Some years into his journey across the Southwest (probably 1532), he and his companion Andrés Dorantes spent eighteen months with the "Mareames" of the Gulf Coast, a hunting and gathering group perhaps later known historically as the Muruam. The castaways reported that, among these Indians,

> when daughters are born to them they let the dogs eat them and throw them away. The reason they do this, according to them, is that all the Indians in that land are their enemies and they carry on continual warfare with them; and if by any chance their enemies should marry their daughters, these enemies would increase so much that they would conquer them and take them as slaves; and for this reason they preferred to kill their daughters rather than let a possible enemy be born to them.[42]

When he asked why they did not marry these girls themselves, Dorantes received further details that reveal how prescriptive exogamy could become distorted by unequal power relations:

> They said that to marry women to their kinfolk was a bad thing, and that it was much better to kill them than to give them to their own kin or to their enemies; and both they and their neighbors called the Yguazes have this custom, but only they, for none of the other tribes in the land practice it. And when these Indians [Mareames and Yguazes] want to marry they buy wives from their enemies, and the price each man gives for his wife is

41. René Girard maintains: "The sacred consists of all those forces whose dominance over man increases or seems to increase in proportion to man's effort to master them. Tempests, forest fires, and plagues, among other phenomena, may be classified as sacred. Far outranking these, however, though in a far less obvious manner, stands human violence—violence seen as something exterior to man and henceforth as a part of all the other outside forces that threaten mankind. Violence is the heart and secret soul of the sacred." See *Violence and the Sacred,* trans. Patrick Gregory (Baltimore, 1977), 31.

42. Enrique Pupo-Walker, ed., *Castaways: The Narrative of Alvar Núñez Cabeza de Vaca,* trans. Frances M. López-Morillas (Berkeley, Calif., 1993), 59–60; Nancy P. Hickerson, "How Cabeza de Vaca Lived with, Worked among, and Finally Left the Indians of Texas," *Journal of Anthropological Research,* LIV (Summer 1998), 199–218.

> a bow, the best that can be procured, with two arrows, and if perchance he does not own a bow, a fishing net two cubits wide and one long; they kill their own children and trade in those of others.[43]

Even if we discount its sensational aspects, this remains a description of exogamous bands practicing bride-price exchange amid a larger atmosphere of violent conflict and captive seizure. It seems from Nuñez's account that these Coahuiltecans were trapped between the Gulf Coast and more numerous and more powerful endogamous bison-hunting Jumanos to the north. In this shrinking niche Coahuiltecans resorted to female infanticide to preserve their group identity, while taking wives from their neighbors. Here we see a most desperate expression of women's sacrifice in the name of group survival, and one destined to fail, for Coahuiltecans disappeared by the end of the eighteenth century.[44]

More often than not, however, the exogamous exchange of women seems to have bolstered group vitality, albeit at the expense of women's security. A variation operated in the borderlands through the "gift" of a woman-as-wife to an out-group man toward establishing diplomatic, trade, and kinship connections: the woman remains with her natal group and the man cohabits with her only seasonally. It may well have organized Plains Indian–Pueblo relations during the protohistoric period in New Mexico. Turning the conventional notion of hypergamy (Pueblo Indian women's marrying into more prestigious Plains Indian bands) around, one wonders whether underprivileged Pueblo men, deprived of wives by their male seniors, married out into matrilocal Plains Apache or Jumano bands, given what seems intense competition for women within Pueblo Indian society.[45]

These marriages might have been only seasonal, after autumn harvest had ended and as autumn antelope or bison hunts commenced on the Plains. A Pueblo man would travel onto the Plains and take a wife, thereby gaining kinship rights to products of the hunt. He then brought his family back to winter "under the eaves" of the pueblo, carrying along meat products to exchange for less perishable corn. As the spring "season of want" approached on the Plains, his family migrated eastward, carrying the agricultural products to their kinspeople. Among the historically Plains-dwelling Jicarilla Apaches, at

43. Pupo-Walker, ed., *Castaways,* trans. López-Morillas, 60.

44. Ibid., app. B, 136–137.

45. For evidence of this competition, but not out-marriage, see Gutiérrez, *When Jesus Came,* 8–16.

least, corn-growing knowledge was attributed to the efforts of men, suggesting a possible link to migrating Pueblo males.[46]

With the advent of Spanish colonialism in New Mexico the practice stretched to admit new players. In the early autumn of 1660, Diego Romero, *alcalde ordinario* of Santa Fe, and five companions, including one Pecos Indian and the villa's *mestizo* blacksmith Juan de Moraga, set out for the eastern Plains under orders from Governor Bernardo López de Mendizábal to "barter for skins of buffaloes and antelopes." Arriving among the *rancherías* of the "Apaches of the Plains," Romero announced that—like his father Gaspar Pérez before him—he had come to trade and to leave a son "among those heathens." After his hosts debated his proposal,

> at about four in the afternoon they brought a tent of new leather and set it up in the field; they then brought two bundles, one of antelope skins, and the other of buffalo skins, which they placed near the tent. Then they brought another large new buffalo skin which they stretched on the ground and put Diego Romero upon it, lying on his back. They then began to dance the *catzina,* making turns, singing, and raising up and laying Diego Romero down again on the skin in accordance with the movements of the dance of the catzina. When the dance was ended about nightfall, they put him again upon the skin, and taking it by the corners, drew him into the tent, into which they brought him a maiden, whom they left with him the entire night. On the next day in the morning the captains of the rancherías came to see whether Diego Romero had known the Indian woman carnally; seeing that he had known her, they anointed [his] breast with the blood. They then put a feather on his head, in his hair, and proclaimed him as their captain, giving him the two bundles of skins and the tent.[47]

Aside from the anomalous reference to the catzina dance, which seventeenth-century Spanish observers seem to associate with any ceremonial activity of sensual content, we have here a description of a marriage and adop-

46. Snow, "Pots, Pipes, and Trade Partners."

47. The case of Diego Romero is contained in Inquisition depositions, "Letter of Fray García de San Francisco, Senecú . . . ," Oct. 13, 1660, "Testimony of Fray Nicolás de Freitas, Mexico," Jan. 24, 1661, both in Charles Wilson Hackett, trans. and ed., *Historical Documents Relating to New Mexico, Nueva Vizcaya, and Approaches Thereto, to 1773,* III (Washington, D.C., 1937), 156–163; for Diego Romero's ultimate conviction for bigamy and sentence to galley slavery, see John Kessell, *Kiva, Cross, and Crown: The Pecos Indians and New Mexico, 1540–1840* (Albuquerque, N.Mex., 1987), 193–197.

tion ritual that probably vastly predated Spanish presence in the borderlands. Like his father before him (whose expedition had occurred in 1634 and who escaped Inquisitorial punishment), Romero established commercial connections with the "Apaches Vaqueros" (bison-hunting Apaches) by participating in the gift exchange of an Apache maiden. By "leaving sons" among the rancherías, these Spanish men established kinship linkages that would be recognized, at least on the Apache side, across generations. In years to come, some socially marginal Pueblo and Spanish men would desert the colony altogether in pursuit of Indian kinship, assuming new identities as culturally indeterminate plainsmen, or *llaneros,* and generate real concern among their colonial administrators.

During the decades leading up to the Great Southwestern Revolt of 1680, other Athapaskan (Apache and Navajo) groups expanded their attacks on the southern Piros and western Pueblos. But the Apaches Vaqueros remained relatively peaceful, attending seasonal rescates at Pecos Pueblo, the main Spanish connection to the Plains. Although they arrived laden with hides and dried meat to trade for corn and knives, they also brought with them captives from Quivira (probably Wichitas), whom they sold to Pueblos and Spanish alike. Honoring connections to Pueblo and Spanish kin, they also became suppliers in a burgeoning colonial slave trade.[48]

Native American and Spanish colonial men found that the survival of their communities depended, in part, on their ability to exchange both human and material resources across cultural boundaries. Often undertaken in acts of violence, these exchanges also produced unexpected, often fortuitous results because the women and children who crossed cultures proved remarkably adept at making something of their unfortunate circumstances. The combined product of these structural imperatives and the creative potential of human action emerged as a system of slavery unique to the Southwest Borderlands but with strong similarities to other regions where colonial and indigenous people met in relative parity. Old and New World traditions of honor, violence, and captivity that had emerged from very different circumstances were to mesh in a far-flung tapestry of conflict and exchange across their borderland meeting ground. Over several centuries, borderland peoples would be drawn, in the words of the poet, "closer and closer apart."[49]

48. Jack D. Forbes, *Apache, Navaho, and Spaniard,* 2d ed. (1960; Norman, Okla., 1994), 156–176; Kessell, *Kiva, Cross, and Crown,* 222.

49. For South American cases that bear resemblance, see Susan Migden Socolow, "Spanish Captives in Indian Societies: Culture Contact along the Argentine Frontier, 1600–1835,"

This, then, is a story about how peoples of markedly different cultural heritage found solutions to the crises of the colonial encounter. In the Southwest Borderlands, two powerful social impulses, inclusion and exclusion, met on the historical terrain of colonialism and resolved themselves in forms of slavery that were at once particular and mutual. Diverse traditions of capture, servitude, and kinship met and meshed to accommodate both the community-forming impulse of assimilation and the community-preserving impulse of alienation. These were the most visible aspects of borderland political and cultural economies that bound indigenous and Spanish colonial peoples in long-term relations of violence, exchange, interdependence, and interdevelopment. Within their system, native and colonizing peoples crafted a locally negotiated distribution of wealth and power that led not simply to distinctions between captives and cousins or to hierarchies of masters and victims but to the interpenetration of cultures.

The reciprocal seizure, sale, and exploitation of people by American Indians and Euramericans offers a challenge to integrated analysis. Motivations seem disparate, cultural institutions mutually inscrutable, and moralities widely at odds. Yet in the Southwest Borderlands indigenous and colonial practices joined to form a "slave system" in which victims symbolized social wealth, performed services for their masters, and produced material goods under the threat of violence. Although captives often assimilated through institutions of kinship, they seldom shed completely their alien stigma, and even then their numbers were regularly renewed through capture or purchase, thereby reinvigorating the servile classes. Grounded in conflict, the pattern developed through interaction into a unifying web of intellectual, material, and emotional exchange within which native and Euramerican men fought and traded to exploit and bind to themselves women and children of other peoples. As these captives became cousins through native American and Spanish New Mexican kinship structures, they too became agents of conflict, conciliation, and cultural redefinition.[50]

Hispanic American Historical Review, LXXII (February 1992), 73–99; for similar cases along the Araucanian frontier of Chile, see Sergio Villalobos et al., *Relaciones fronterizas en la Araucania* (Santiago, 1982); Villalobos, *Araucania: Temas de historia fronteriza* (Temuco, 1989); A. D. Hope, "The Wandering Islands," in Ruth Morse, ed., *A. D. Hope: Selected Poems* (Manchester, 1986), 20–21.

50. An exceptional effort at integrated analysis is Theda Perdue, *Slavery and the Evolution of Cherokee Society* (Knoxville, Tenn., 1979), in which she details the Cherokees' ability

Essential to this story was the borderlands' relatively long freedom from control by western centers of power—Spain, Mexico, or the United States. Other scholars have stressed the importance of this "distance" for understanding the region. One historian has pointed out how weak Spanish and Mexican economic and political control in the area from 1780 through 1847 allowed New Mexican colonists and native Americans to maintain "all kinds of local arrangements . . . , some of which were based on mutual economic needs." Ethnohistorical work with New Mexican villagers and their Ute Indian neighbors led one anthropologist to define the region as a "non-dominant frontier community," one persisting well after the American conquest of 1847. "Because of the weakness of the government," she argued, "rank-and-file settlers in outlying communities had to learn to coexist with Indian neighbors without being able to keep them subordinate" in ways "contrary to the prescribed model . . . that . . . never gained official recognition."[51]

Middle distance from the Atlantic World's market economy was also crucial. Physical and political isolation underlay the New Mexicans' "relations with Indians in day-to-day living" and the elaborate webs of ethnic tension, friendship, conflict, and kinship that complicate regional history even to the present. This study emphasizes the relative distance from the burgeoning international economy as well. It tells a story of how local societies distributed

---

to transform their precontact institution of *atsi nahsa'i* (war captive incorporation) first into a slave-raiding and -catching complex that protected them from wholesale enslavement themselves and finally into their own chattel enslavement of Africans. For brief overviews of indigenous captivity and slavery in North America, see John R. Swanton, "Captives," Henry W. Henshaw, "Slavery," both in Frederick Webb Hodge, ed., *Handbook of American Indians North of Mexico,* 2 vols., Bureau of American Ethnology Bulletin, no. 30 (New York, 1971), I, 203–206, II, 597–600. Scholarly studies of servitude in New Mexico have concentrated on Spanish enslavement of native Americans, with only glancing reference to the reciprocal side of the dynamic. See L. R. Bailey, *Indian Slave Trade in the Southwest* (Los Angeles, 1966); Frank McNitt, *Navajo Wars: Military Campaigns, Slave Raids, and Reprisals* (Albuquerque, N.Mex., 1972); Gutiérrez, *When Jesus Came.* I borrow here from Claude Meillassoux's definition of slavery as a "social system based on the *exploitation* of a class of producers or persons performing services, renewed mainly through *acquisition.*" See *The Anthropology of Slavery: The Womb of Iron and Gold* (Chicago, 1991), 343.

51. Daniel Tyler, "Mexican Indian Policy in New Mexico," *NMHR,* LV (April 1980), 101–120, esp. 115; Frances Leon Swadesh, "Structure of Hispanic-Indian Relations in New Mexico," in Paul M. Kutsche, ed., *The Survival of Spanish American Villages* (Colorado Springs, Colo., 1979), 53–61, esp. 55, 60.

power, organized production, and exchanged resources with little disruption by centralizing forces. Thus it becomes a case study of how noncapitalist societies engaged with the growing power of the Atlantic economy and avoided incorporation for more than a century before becoming both agents and victims of its successful expansion.[52]

Comanche, Kiowa, Apache, and Navajo raid-and-trade networks extended as far south as Sonora and Durango, Mexico, as far west as the Colorado River, as far north as the Yellowstone, and eastward nearly to the Mississippi. As they connected with other market circuits, commodities like horses and captives could end up in New England, Louisiana, Cuba, Mexico City, or California. Likewise, despite their distance from these power nodes of mercantile capitalism, Spanish colonists in New Mexico traveled and traded extensively, confounding characterizations of the region as "isolated and tradition-bound." Yet, because the Atlantic economy penetrated these borderlands only haphazardly, local actors were able to control their own exchanges and to meet that larger economy for centuries largely on their own terms.[53]

To explore this region's slave economy is to complicate and enrich our understanding of North American slavery. Indigenous peoples like Apaches, Comanches, Utes, Navajos, Pawnees, and Pueblos (to name but a few) had practiced the capture, adoption, intermarriage, and occasional sacrifice of outsiders since well before European entry into the region. Similarly, the Spanish colonists who came to northern New Spain (later Mexico) in the sixteenth century also carried with them customs of capture, enslavement, adoption, and exploitation of non-Christian peoples, dating from the Iberian reconquista, when the Muslim-Christian borderlands formed a field of violence and intercultural negotiation within which a volatile coexistence prevailed across several centuries. Where Spanish conquest by arms and disease of New World

52. This broad perspective with emphasis on changing social relations of production in political-economic context owes much to the work of Howard Lamar, especially his seminal essay "From Bondage to Contract: Ethnic Labor in the American West, 1680–1890," in Steven Hahn and Jonathan Prude, eds., *The Countryside in the Age of Capitalist Transformation: Essays in the Social History of Rural America* (Chapel Hill, N.C., 1985), 293–324.

53. Gutiérrez, *When Jesus Came,* 336. Gutiérrez's statement strangely echoes Hubert Howe Bancroft's assertion that, after 1770, "New Mexico settled down into that monotonously uneventful career of inert and nonprogressive existence, which sooner or later is to be noted in the history of every Hispano-American province." See *History of Arizona and New Mexico, 1530–1888* (1889; Albuquerque, 1962), 225.

peoples was overwhelming, such traditions faded, but convivencia persisted in the daily life of the Southwest Borderlands. Here, beneath the profound cultural differences and steady conflicts punctuating Indian and Spanish colonial relations, native and Spanish men shared similar notions of honor, shame, and gender, with the control of women and children as a central proof of status. Both branches of borderland slavery could interact because they grew from shared patriarchal structures of power and patrimony that contrast sharply with the racial divisiveness and labor exploitation around which the more familiar forms of Euramerican enslavement of Africans functioned.

These common cultural motifs allowed the Indian and Spanish systems to become interwoven in the region. Unlike chattel slavery elsewhere in North America, borderland slavery found affinity with kin-based systems motivated less by a demand for units of labor than their desire for prestigious social units. The kin-embedded structures of borderland slavery created immensely different gender and class realities from those contained in labor-oriented American slaveries. Because the captive women and children in this system often found themselves integrated within the host community through kinship systems—adoption and marriage in the indigenous cases or *compadrazgo* and concubinage in the Spanish colonial cases—they participated in the gradual transformation of the host society. Most such slaves became members of the capturing society, often in marginal categories but in ways that allowed them to bring useful cultural repertoires and mediation to their new kinspeople. The ties between gender and power in the Southwest take more fertile meaning from the fact that the hapless women and children who became slaves also became the main negotiators of cultural, economic, and political exchange between groups. Yet over the years the slave system of the area displayed growing tensions between the social needs of participant societies and the economic value of bound labor, a dynamic that casts new light on just how "societies with slaves" might have in time become "slave societies."[54]

54. The borderland slave system bears comparison to the kin-based slave societies of Africa. The author recognizes ongoing disagreement regarding the significance of kinship in systems of captivity and slavery in African societies, especially those between the Miers and Kopytoff school of African slavery as a continuum of kinship and Meillassoux's assertion that true slavery can only exist as the "antithesis of kinship." While the distinction is certainly more than semantic, this study sees both qualities as historically present and mutually constitutive, in the sense that, without the earlier form of kin incorporation of captives, the later denial of kin status to captives would not be socially or analytically tren-

While the powerful steadily exploited the weak in all systems of slavery, the volatility of Southwest Borderland slavery and the thinness of formal, state-level support for the institution made those who had the most social wealth in slaves and livestock natural targets of attack by those who had the least. Hence there existed a redistributive transfer of wealth from the higher orders (caste, rank, age) in Indian and Euramerican societies to men of lower status. Of course, these lower-status entrepreneurs often reproduced the social inequalities that had initiated their own actions, triggering new cycles of brigandage. Southwest Borderland slavery, with its peculiar kin and class realities, constituted only the most dramatic aspect of larger borderland political economies operating between colonial and indigenous peoples roughly equal in power. Despite cultural differences in the region, native and colonizing peoples came to share some understanding of the production and distribution of wealth and status as conditioned by social relations of power. In this case, these mutual understandings involved a convergence in patriarchal notions about the socially productive value and exchangeability of women and children as well as sheep, cattle, and horses. This borderland violence was not solely destructive but produced enduring networks of economic and social relations. Described by contemporary observers and later historians as a chaotic and unceasing predatory war, it was a system that allowed virtually all of the protagonists in the borderlands to experience demographic or economic growth during much of the period. Stressing simply the corrosive effects of the "slave

---

chant. For overviews and debates, see Suzanne Miers and Igor Kopytoff, eds., *Slavery in Africa: Historical and Anthropological Perspectives* (Madison, Wisc., 1977); Meillassoux, *Anthropology of Slavery;* Paul E. Lovejoy, *Transformations in Slavery: A History of Slavery in Africa* (Cambridge, 1983); Suzanne Miers and Richard Roberts, eds., *The End of Slavery in Africa* (Madison, Wisc., 1988). These debates aside, the borderland "slave system" has many parallels to the African experience: wars of capture, the mediating role of kinship, the predominance of women and children as slaves, the relative absence of plantation or industrial organization, the muted role of racial as opposed to ethnic differentiations, and, finally, the agency of a "conquest" state in suppressing traditional practices. For modern syntheses of chattel slavery in the South that stress evolution in the institution in relation to changing socioeconomic factors, see Robert William Fogel, *Without Consent or Contract: The Rise and Fall of American Slavery* (New York, 1989); Peter Kolchin, *American Slavery, 1619–1877* (New York, 1993). I borrow the distinction between "societies with slaves" and "slave societies" from Ira Berlin's discussion in *Many Thousands Gone: The First Two Centuries of Slavery in North America* (Cambridge, Mass., 1998), 8–13, as separating societies where slaves were not essential to the economy from societies in which enslaved productivity was its basis.

trade" on Indian and colonial societies diffuses its major contributions to intercultural trade, alliances, and communities among groups often antagonistic to Spanish, Mexican, and American modernizing strategies.[55]

The story is not only that of a developing web across local cultures but also of its unraveling. Between 1500 and 1880, Southwest Borderland societies went through five major periods: the early Spanish colonial (1540–1680), the reconquest and Bourbon reform era (1680–1810), Mexican nationalism (1810–1846), the U.S. conquest (1847–1866), and territorial incorporation (1867–1880), at which point any "distance" from the Atlantic world's capitalism ended. In the latest of those periods, Americans fulfilled their regional war against slavery. Hence, this study gestures to broad American transitions toward wage-labor capitalism, with attendant changes in kinship systems, family structure, and ethnic identities. Whereas, in the sixteenth century, kinship served as the primary means of group and collective identity, by the nineteenth century, citi-

55. The concept of "Spanish Borderlands" has become increasingly variegated since Herbert Eugene Bolton proposed the term in *The Spanish Borderlands: A Chronicle of Old Florida and the Southwest* (New Haven, Conn., 1921). Where "borderlands" to Bolton evoked the heroic and romantic contributions of Spanish conquistadores to North American history, to later students the concept has come to mean zones of diffuse and complex exchanges between cultures, from the precolonial era to contemporary border dynamics between the United States and Mexico. For the definitive synthesis, including an overview of changing historiographical approaches to the Spanish Borderlands, see David J. Weber, *The Spanish Frontier in North America* (New Haven, Conn., 1992), esp. "The Spanish Legacy and the Historical Imagination," 335–360. For a provocative new formulation that places women and gender at the forefront, see Gloria Anzaldua, *Borderlands / La Frontera: The New Mestiza* (San Francisco, 1987). For viewpoints on the negative consequences of slavery, see Forbes, *Apache, Navaho, and Spaniard;* Bailey, *Indian Slave Trade in the Southwest;* Gutiérrez, *When Jesus Came,* 149–156, 180–190. Students of slavery in African societies have better recognized the paradoxical nature of captive exchange, especially Meillassoux; an important model for my approach to interethnic exchange has been Daniel H. Usner, Jr., *Indians, Settlers, and Slaves in a Frontier Exchange Economy: The Lower Mississippi Valley before 1783* (Chapel Hill, N.C., 1992). Usner uses the concept "frontier exchange economy" to "examine how Indians, settlers, and slaves produced and distributed goods at a regional level." In Usner's case, this economy "evolved from a network of interaction to a strategy for survival" with the emergence of a commercial plantation economy between 1763 and 1783 (5–9). In contrast, the borderland political economy of the Southwest actually expanded with increasing commercial contacts, until its ideological and military power presented strategic problems for Anglo-American expansion and development.

zenship, both national and tribal, competed as a new level of identification. Where once patrimony lay beneath most social relations, property became by the middle years of the nineteenth century a powerfully organizing concept among Euramericans and Indians alike. Concurrently, capitalist development and state order brought a measure of security to the region's women and children but foreclosed some arenas of their communal influence and participation—and severed the human heart of the intercultural network.[56]

When this study ends, each regional community had lost much of its economic vitality and cultural flexibility. Navajos, Comanches, Kiowas, Utes, Apaches, and New Mexicans found themselves negotiating new, exclusive identities among themselves and with the American state. In some cases, this involved their recruitment as scouts, fighters, or laborers for American armies and enterprises; in others, it meant their defeat or dispossession or death. Yet vestiges of the earlier formations remained, primarily in quietly acknowledged kin connections, cultural celebrations, and a modern propensity to reclaim various mixed-descent identities.

This pattern of cultural sharing through systems of violence and kinship deepens our understanding of how "mixed" groups became peoples in the Southwest and how ethnic communities themselves were historically and culturally sorted and produced. Identities like Comanche, Kiowa, Apache, Navajo, Ute, Pueblo, Spanish-American, and Hispano seem timeless and unquestioned in much historical literature. The intergroup economic, cultural, and biological exchanges across the centuries show that ethnicities in the Southwest were often a matter of biological interchange, strategic reconstruction, and political invention, as sexual enslavement, market penetration, and state pacification policies closed some avenues of identity while fostering others. Current Indian reservations and closed, corporate Spanish-American

56. Stephanie Coontz, *The Social Origins of Private Life: A History of American Families, 1600–1900* (New York, 1988), best synthesizes this discussion. Nonetheless, she overstates her case when, in chap. 2, "The Native American Tradition," she surveys major shifts in descent patterns and the sexual division of labor with European expansion and concludes that this resulted in the "destruction of Native American kinship systems" (68). The study at hand notes remarkable adaptation and persistence in customary kinship relations. For distinctions between patrimony as a "set of goods [including captives], in principle inalienable, in the possession of an organized collectivity, transferred unilaterally within it (by gift or inheritance) independently of exchange" and property "in the Roman sense of *usus, fructus, abusus,*" see Meillassoux, *Anthropology of Slavery,* 341–342.

villages are less romantic enclaves of premodern cultures than homelands and townships devoted to labor regulation and the commodification of culture for tourist markets.[57]

Any long-term historical study of borderland dynamics requires a blending of social theory with empirical research and sources. Along with the insights of a legion of Spanish Borderland and American Indian specialists, this work is especially indebted to several important analytical frames: it emphasizes cycles of conquest by Spanish, Mexican, and American colonizers, focuses on land-tenure systems as sites of conquest and resistance struggles, and takes cognizance of world-systems theory to describe the engulfment of local societies by Euramerican capitalism. Earlier scholars cue this work about broad patterns, periodization, and development.[58]

The many archaeologists, historians, folklorists, and ethnographers who have made New Mexico and the region's indigenous people their subject of

57. Gary Clayton Anderson, *The Indian Southwest, 1580–1830: Ethnogenesis and Reinvention* (Norman, Okla., 1999), provides a crucial rethinking of the cultural creativity shown by Jumanos, Apaches, and Comanches in Coahuila and Texas. Among the many works that, despite gifted analysis in other areas, refrain from considering the "mixed" nature of Southwest identities, see Morris W. Foster, *Being Comanche: A Social History of an American Indian Community* (Tucson, Ariz., 1991); Wallace and Hoebel, *The Comanches;* Richard L. Nostrand, *The Hispano Homeland* (Norman, Okla., 1992). Noteworthy exceptions to this tendency include Forbes, *Apache, Navaho, and Spaniard;* John H. Moore, *The Cheyenne Nation: A Social and Demographic History* (Lincoln, Nebr., 1987); Quintana, *Los Primeros Pobladores;* Anderson, *Indian Southwest.* Works in other regions have also served as models for variegated paths to collective identity, principally Karen Blu, *The Lumbee Problem: The Making of an American Indian People* (Cambridge, 1980); Richard White, *The Middle Ground: Indians, Empires, and Republics in the Great Lakes Region, 1650–1815* (Cambridge, 1991); and the brilliant work of Gerald M. Sider, *Lumbee Indian Histories: Race, Ethnicity, and Indian Identity in the Southern United States* (Cambridge, 1993). For comparative cases in state-sponsored ethnic identities, see Terence O. Ranger and Eric J. Hobsbawm, eds., *The Invention of Tradition* (Cambridge, 1983); Leroy Vail, ed., *The Creation of Tribalism in South Africa* (Berkeley, Calif., 1991). For a deeper look at the internal production and meaning of an ethnic identity formed from economic and state pressures, see Bill Bravman, *Making Ethnic Ways: Communities and Their Transformations in Taita, Kenya, 1800–1950* (Portsmouth, N.H., 1998).

58. Edward S. Spicer, *Cycles of Conquest: The Impact of Spain, Mexico, and the United States on the Indians of the Southwest* (Tucson, Ariz., 1962); Roxanne Dunbar Ortiz, *Roots of Resistance: Land Tenure in New Mexico, 1680–1980* (Los Angeles, Calif., 1980); Thomas D. Hall, *Social Change in the Southwest, 1350–1880* (Lawrence, Kans., 1989).

study—too numerous to list here but whose work is levied throughout—have done the exhaustive work in archives, in mountain *placitas,* and on Indian reservations that bring the "messiness" of history-as-lived into this analysis, in ways that meet one of the region's most revered anthropologist's standards for ethnohistory: "A basic yardstick of acceptability would be that the people portrayed be able to recognize themselves in the portrait."[59] The detailed work of these scholars on life, settlement patterns, marriage choices, feuds, friendships, and community politics grounds this study in the rich contortions of historical experience, while social theory speaks to broader patterns that ultimately extend meaning and clarify paradoxes. Finally, this exploration of intercultural relations brought together in a system of slavery maintains depth of field by placing anthropological and historical scholarship in productive dialogue with a wealth of underused primary materials and my own ethnohistorical fieldwork in the region.

These sources are surprisingly rich because the system of slavery excited moral and military anxiety among church and state administrators, whether Spanish, Mexican, or American. Captive seizure and exchange data appear repeatedly in traditional archival sources like baptismal and burial registers, *diligencias matrimoniales,* and military reports. Likewise, since captive exchange combines elements of romance and danger, the custom inspired an extensive body of written and oral folk literature in both Indian and New Mexican communities, heretofore untapped partly because of interpretive difficulties and partly because of the value charge attached to "slavery."

Between 1540 and 1880, several thousands of Indian and Euramerican women and children in the Southwest Borderlands crossed cultures through the workings of a captive exchange system that knit diverse communities into vital, and violent, webs of interdependence. These women and children, whether captives of Euramerican origin or native Americans ransomed at rescates, proved crucial to borderland political and cultural economies that used human beings in far-reaching social and economic exchange. Whatever the large-scale antagonisms between European colonists and native Americans, at the local level, problems of day-to-day survival required cross-cultural negotiation. Prolonged, intensive interaction between Spanish colonial *pobladores* and nomadic and pastoral Indian societies required some mutually intelligible symbols through which cultural values, interests, and needs could be

59. Swadesh, "Structure of Hispanic-Indian Relations in New Mexico," in Kutsche, ed., *Survival of Spanish American Villages,* 53.

defined. Horses, sheep, guns, and buffalo hides spring immediately to mind as customary exchange items, but women and children proved even more valuable (and valorized) as agents (and objects) of cultural negotiation. In the Southwest Borderlands, as elsewhere in North America, the exchange of women through systems of captivity, adoption, and marriage provided European and native men with widely understood symbols of power with which to penetrate cultural barriers. Their tales must be fretted from more familiar narratives where they have long lain hidden beneath epics of exploration and conquest. Yet, while in their vulnerability they knit diverse peoples in webs of painful kinship, their captures and exchanges violated the masculine cultures of honor and social integrity of the victimized group and inspired the raids and reprisals that would punctuate everyday life in the Southwest Borderlands for three centuries.

The slave system of the borderlands grew from the exercise of power between the native American and Euramerican inhabitants of the Southwest. Struggling to preserve and protect the integrity of their power within families and communities, men from both sides of the Atlantic negotiated interdependency and maintained honor by acknowledging the exchangeability of their women and children. Disguising necessity in sacred artifice, they produced a mutually recognizable world of violence and retribution, of loss and redemption that drew the protagonists together while forcing them apart. Eventually the power, economy, and moralism of the broader modernizing world ended this local system, though its remnants are what give special qualities to the region even today where these local political and cultural borderlands once flourished.

MAP 1. *Southwest Borderlands, c. 1780.* Drawn by Carol Cooperrider

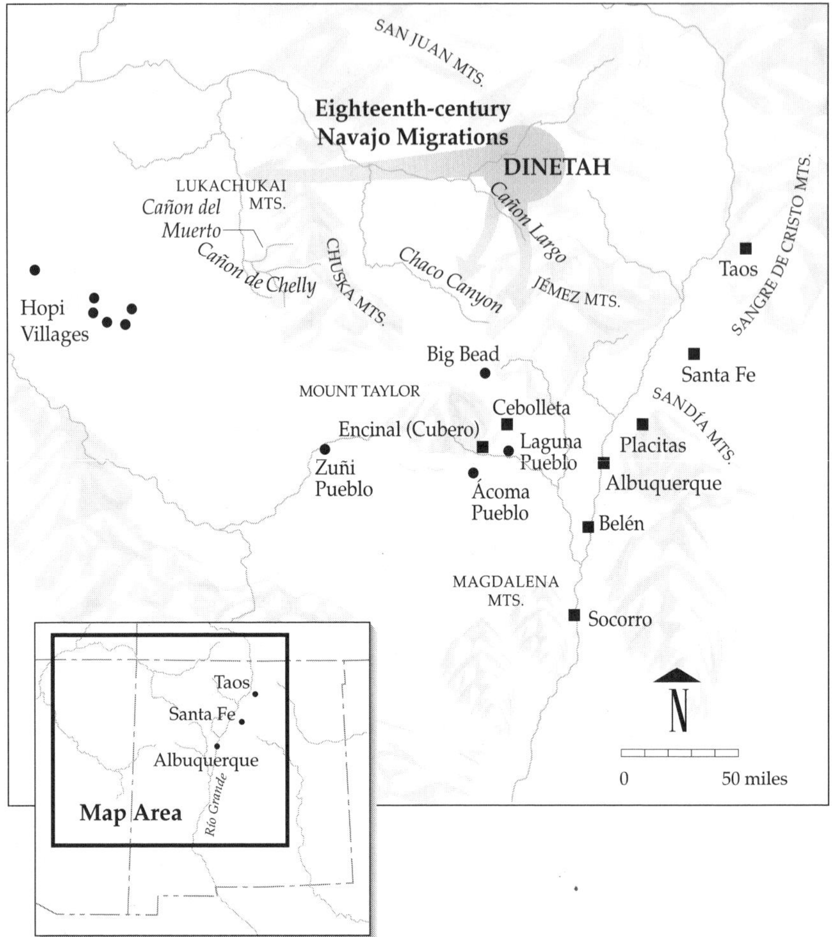

MAP 2. *Pastoral and Mountain Borderlands, c. 1800.* Drawn by Carol Cooperrider

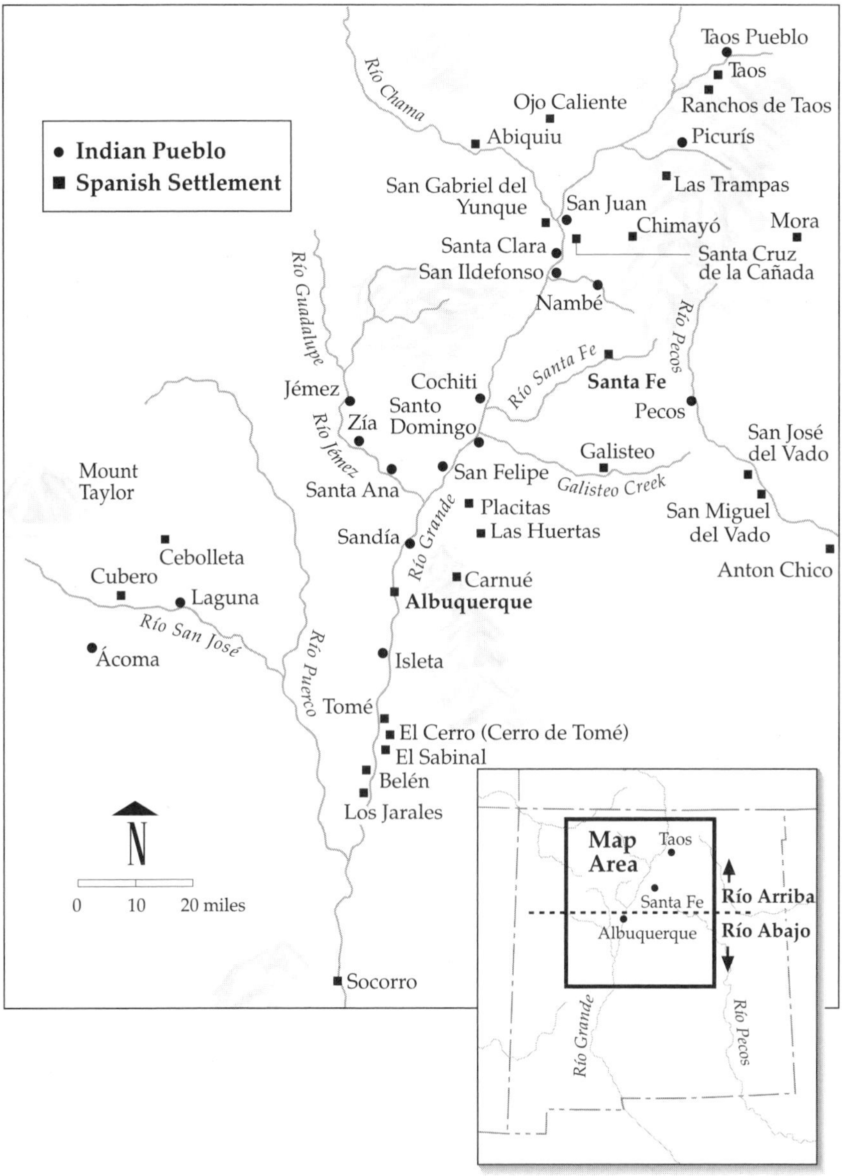

MAP 3. *New Mexico, c. 1800.* Drawn by Carol Cooperrider

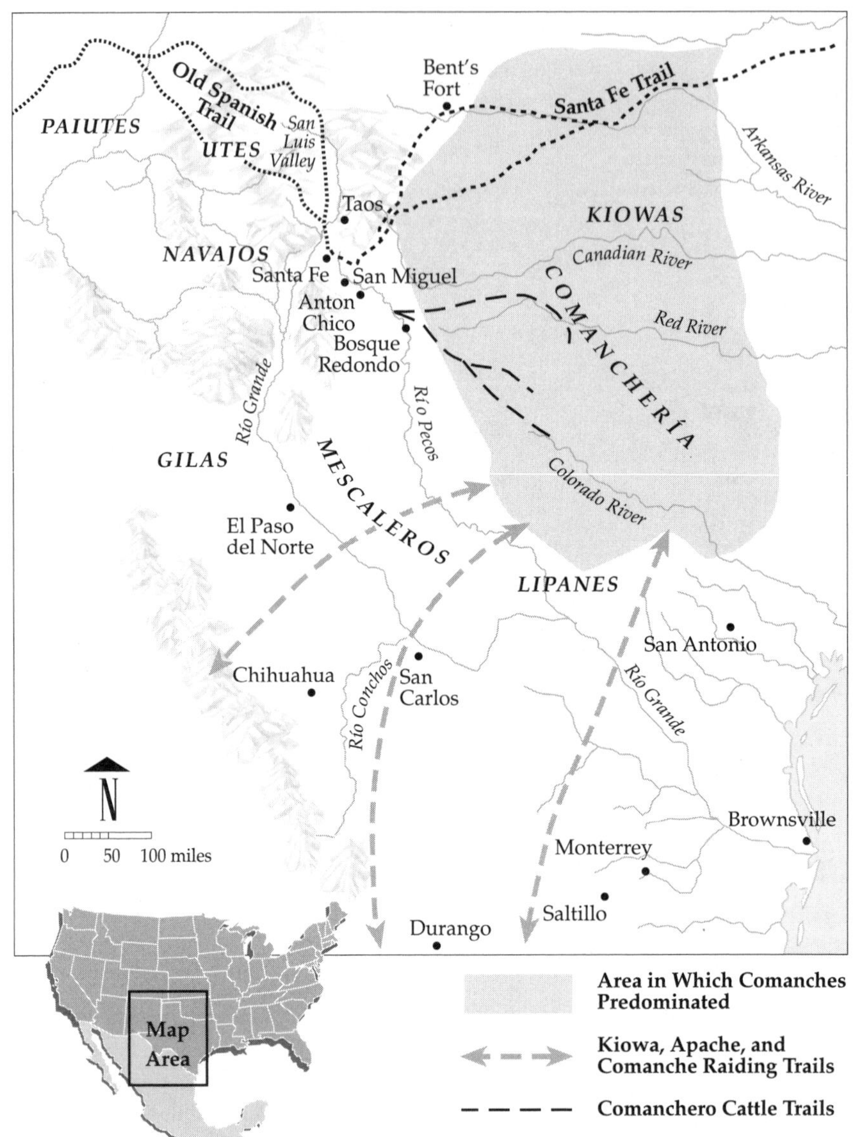

MAP 4. *Southwest Borderlands, c. 1840.* Drawn by Carol Cooperrider

2

LOS LLANEROS

CREATING A PLAINS BORDERLAND

Nothing but Bison and Sky

Fatigued with disappointment and bitter fighting throughout a hard winter among the Tiguex pueblos of the Río Grande, Francisco Vásquez de Coronado arrived at the Towa pueblo of Cicúye (Pecos) in the spring of 1541 with renewed hope. Situated on a high mountain pass that bridged the Río Grande valley with the Great Plains, the fortified town was perhaps the most powerful ally the enterprising conquistador might make among the peoples of the region. The Zuñi town of Hawikuh had failed to fulfill the riches promised by Cabeza de Vaca and Fray Marcos de Niza, tales that had inspired Coronado's entrada in the first place. Moving on to the pueblos of the Tiguex along the Río Grande, the Spanish found a reluctant and belligerent people who had only been subdued after sieges, executions, and enslavement. Indian peoples to the east seemed to promise more.

Capable of fielding five hundred warriors, Cicúye was "feared throughout the land," according to chronicler Pedro de Castañeda. Among the gifts laid before Captain Hernando de Alvarado at Cicúye during his reconnaissance the previous autumn were piles of thick bison robes, indicative of the pueblo's situation on the edge of the Plains grasslands. These probably derived from two sources—seasonal bison hunting by Cicúye sojourners and a vigorous trade network in specialized commodities between the pueblo and nomadic hunter-gatherers residing on the Plains. Pueblo trade goods like obsidian, turquoise and shell jewelry, ceramics, and pipes appear abundantly in presumably Athapaskan camps dating from the sixteenth century. The trade went beyond luxury items, however: one of Coronado's men later reported that the Querechos (Athapaskans) and Teyas (Jumanos) of the Plains exchanged "*cueros de Cíbola* [bison hides] and deer skins that they do not need, and the meat dried in the sun [pemmican] . . . for maize and blankets to the natives at the [Río Grande]."[1]

But more intriguing than these commodities was the presence of Plains peoples living as *esclavos* (slaves) at Cicúye. Alvarado had brought two of these, Ysopete and El Turco, along with two Towas, Bigotes and Cacique, back to the Tiguex winter quarters for Coronado's interrogation. Ysopete drew attention because his body featured a "painting" of a bison (notice of adventures yet to come), but El Turco proved more immediately provocative. His name, usually attributed to a "Turkish" appearance (perhaps he was tall with a prominent nose), also makes an implicit cultural connection back to Mediterranean captives familiar to Spaniards, and to his role, that of coerced cross-culture negotiator. This no doubt had been his function among the Towas of Cicúye, and, now, "by signs and in the Mexican tongue [Nahuatl] of which he knew a little," he enticed Coronado with stories of his natal peoples, the "Harahey" (Pawnees). Distant on the Plains lay Quivira, ruled by a great lord who traversed lakes in boats with golden oarlocks; beyond, in Harahey, lived King Tatarrax, "bearded, grey-haired, and rich," his kingdom perhaps "the richest prize in the Indies." Although Ysopete, a Quiviran (Wichita), hinted his doubts to the Spanish from the very beginning, El Turco's imagination fueled Coronado's resolve.[2]

So, the following April or May of 1541, Coronado set out for Quivira with his reportedly fifteen-hundred-strong force of Europeans (Castilians, Portuguese, Italians, French, German, even a Scot), Africans (perhaps thirty), some eight hundred Mexican Indians (Tarascans, Mexicas, Tlatelolcans, Tlaxcalans),

1. Pedro de Castañeda, "Relación de la jornada de Cíbola," in George Peter Hammond and Agapito Rey, trans. and eds., *Narratives of the Coronado Expedition, 1540–1542* (Albuquerque, N.Mex., 1940), 191–283; Herbert E. Bolton, *Coronado: Knight of Pueblos and Plains* (Albuquerque, N.Mex., 1949); John L. Kessell, *Kiva, Cross, and Crown: The Pecos Indians and New Mexico, 1540–1840* (Albuquerque, N.Mex., 1987), 20–21. For Pueblo trade goods in Plains-Indian archaeological sites, see Christopher Lintz, "Texas Panhandle–Pueblo Interactions from the Thirteenth through the Sixteenth Century"; Timothy G. Baugh, "Ecology and Exchange: The Dynamics of Plains-Pueblo Interaction," in Katherine A. Spielmann, ed., *Farmers, Hunters, and Colonists: Interaction between the Southwest and the Southern Plains* (Tucson, Ariz., 1991), 89–106, 107–127; for trade in meat and corn, see Castañeda, "Relacion del Suceso," in Hammond and Rey, trans. and eds., *Narratives,* 293.

2. Bolton, *Coronado,* 189, 232–233. On cultural affiliations of El Turco, Ysopete, and other Plains groups, see Carroll L. Riley, *Rio del Norte: People of the Upper Rio Grande from Earliest Times to the Pueblo Revolt* (Salt Lake City, Utah, 1995), 169, 196.

and scores of new Tiguex slaves acquired in fighting over the winter. Guiding them were El Turco, Ysopete, and Xabe, an additional Quiviran slave supplied by his captors at Cicúye. This polyglot group would encounter an equally complex cultural array of nomadic bison-hunting Querechos and Teyas and sedentary riverine farmers like the Quivirans. Even the Quivirans, it was reported, spoke seven different tongues in their well-spaced villages along the Arkansas River.

But the entrada was a dismal failure: Quivira held no riches. The expedition nearly exhausted itself on the immensity of the Plains before straggling back to the Río Grande. Small satisfaction came when Coronado, finally heeding Ysopete's accusations, ordered El Turco executed with a garrote. The young Quiviran was rewarded with gifts and released to remain with his kinspeople. Xabe returned to Tiguex with the Spanish, urging yet another expedition beyond Quivira the following year. Perhaps he wished to be himself repatriated, but it appears that he traveled with Coronado back to Mexico.[3]

Male slaves like El Turco, Ysopete, and Xabe attain some prominence in the Coronado narrative. At the very least they provide strong evidence for a precontact Plainswide trade in slaves and the role of Pueblo Indians as their captors or purchasers. But deeper in the story lies another case that may well be emblematic of a more widespread pattern, the capture and enslavement of women. While Coronado and his chosen thirty (including El Turco and Ysopete) had separated from the main force for their dash to Quivira at the *barrancas* (canyons) of the llano estacado escarpment, the main force encamped and hunted bison, killing at least five hundred to feed their large contingent. It was there that Castañeda reported that "a painted Indian woman ran away from Juan de Zaldívar. She fled down the barrancas when she recognized the land, for she was a slave at Tiguex where [the Spanish] had obtained her." A tattooed Indian woman from the llano, almost certainly a Teya, had been a captive among the Tiguex before the Spanish had subdued and enslaved many of those Pueblo people. Zaldívar had in turn taken her as a consort, a layering of violence and domination that presages much of what was to come. That the Spanish found little to remark about her presence among the defeated

3. For modern scholarship on Coronado's trek to Quivira and back, see pertinent essays in Richard Flint and Shirley Cushing Flint, eds., *The Coronado Expedition to Tierra Nueva: The 1540–1542 Route across the Southwest* (Niwot, Colo., 1997). Cultural affiliation of the Teyas as Jumano is discussed therein by Carroll L. Riley, "The Teya Indians of the Southwestern Plains," 320–343; see also Bolton, *Coronado,* 300–306, 311–312.

Tiguex suggests her presence was not unusual; indeed, perhaps many more Plains Indian women suffered her condition than the few men usually featured in this narrative. In a vast region crisscrossed by trade in meat, hides, maize, jewelry, obsidian, and pottery, women might have been the most mobile, and negotiable, item of exchange. Unlike other "goods," they sometimes had the capacity to affect in some small way the outcome of their experience, as would many of those who followed in the centuries ahead.[4]

Yet that ability was subject to fates and powers beyond their control as well. Just "nine days distant" to the southeast, near the headwaters of the Red River of Texas, the Teya woman ran into a small force of Spanish men led by Luis de Moscoso. Moscoso had taken command of Hernando de Soto's Florida expedition (1539–1543) after the death of the latter in May and had been attempting to link up with Coronado to the west. The lost and increasingly desperate Spanish force seized the woman and marched back to the Mississippi River. After building seven boats, the three hundred men, two Coosa Indian women, and one nameless "painted" Teya slave woman set sail for Mexico, arriving on the gulf coast at the Panuco River in September 1543. From there we lose her to the illegible past, like most of her enslaved kindred.[5]

As If They Were Calves and Colts

In 1598, Juan de Oñate would establish the first Spanish settlement in New Mexico at San Gabriel del Yunque, across the Río Grande from San Juan Pueblo. By 1610, tensions with those Indian neighbors would force his successor, Pedro de Peralta, to move the Spanish capital to Santa Fe. In Oñate's wake came dozens of Franciscan priests bent on harvesting the ripe field of Pueblo Indians so conveniently congregated along the Río Grande and its tributaries. Spanish military men like Oñate and his successors would spend much of the next seventy years locked in church-state combat with the Franciscan fathers over the rewards that Indian lands, labor, and tribute enabled them to accu-

4. Castañeda, "Relación de la jornada de Cíbola," in Hammond and Rey, trans. and eds., *Narratives*, 241–243.

5. Ibid. For Soto and Moscoso, see David J. Weber, *The Spanish Frontier in North America* (New Haven, Conn., 1992), 49–55. Weber suggests that the Teya woman connected with Soto in Arkansas in the fall of 1541. This would seem to depend on whether "nine days distant" implies time or distance. I read it as meaning the latter.

mulate. Most of these struggles took place within the Río Grande valley, but the Great Plains held enticements and trouble as well.[6]

Driven as they were by the desire for wealth and conversion of heathen souls in the ledger books of state and church, Spanish men both secular and religious saw the numerous peoples of the Plains as yet another field for dual endeavor. Cicúye, now referred to in Spanish documents as Pecos, would play a key role in both respects. Utilizing thousands of hours of Pecos's labor, by 1625 Fray Andrés Júarez had completed construction of the most imposing mission-*convento* complex in New Mexico. With walls forty feet high containing some 300,000 adobe bricks, the church dominated the mountainous horizon and the lives of Pecos's peoples. It also stood watch over the autumn trade fairs that took place in the grassy meadows immediately to the east, where Querechos, more commonly referred to now as "Apaches Vaqueros," arrived with hides, meat, and Quiviran slaves to exchange for Pueblo maize, pottery, and blankets. At these fairs in the 1630s, according to his ecclesiastical enemy Fray Estevan de Perea, Governor Francisco de la Mora y Ceballos issued *vales* (permits) authorizing the seizure of Indian boys and girls "as if they were calves and colts" to be placed in "perpetual slavery." The Franciscans were similarly eager purchasers but cloaked their commerce in the notion that Christian charity required the redemption of young captives from the heathen.[7]

The long-standing indigenous trade in captives did not prove equal to Spanish demand, however. Pueblo peoples could be encumbered by the tributary demands of the encomienda and labor drafts of the *repartimiento,* but the relatively strong legal protections for converted Indians made their exploitation somewhat costly, at least in the political implications for those who found themselves recalled to Mexico City to account for their actions. As early as 1620, therefore, Governor Juan de Eulate attacked a peaceful Apache trading encampment to obtain captive laborers, some of whom he was accused of selling to the silver mines of Nueva Vizcaya. He also extended permission to his soldiers to seize orphans from within the Christian pueblos and put them to

6. For the first Spanish colony, and tensions between secular and religious leadership, see France V. Scholes, *Church and State in New Mexico, 1610–1650* (Albuquerque, N.Mex., 1937), vol. VII of Historical Society of New Mexico, *Publications in History;* Scholes, *Troublous Times in New Mexico, 1659–1670* (Albuquerque, N.Mex., 1942); Ramón A. Gutiérrez, *When Jesus Came, the Corn Mothers Went away: Sexuality, Love, and Conquest in New Mexico, 1500–1846* (Stanford, Calif., 1991), 39–140.

7. Kessell, *Kiva, Cross, and Crown,* 124–127, 155; Scholes, *Church and State,* 94 n. 21.

domestic service, ostensibly a paternalistic gesture aimed at their education. Subsequent governors would extend this artifice even further, as when Felipe de Sotelo Osorio sent a detachment of Pueblo Indian auxiliaries onto the Plains to an Apache Vaquero encampment. Although the Apaches vowed to become Christians, their chief was put to death and his kinspeople were brought back to the colony in bonds. Governor Luís de Rosas (1637–1641) included Utacas (Utes) among his quarry in similar raids, at one time carrying at least eighty women and children back to work in his *obraje* in Santa Fe, where they were to produce mantas for the Plains trade. Governor Diego de Peñalosa (1660–1664) held so many Apache slaves that he declared he had once given away more than one hundred, presumably to political allies who supported him during the church-state civil war under his administration.[8]

By the late seventeenth century in Spanish colonial New Mexico, non-Pueblo slaves numbered some five hundred Quivirans, Apaches, and Utes, or 21 percent of the colony's 2,347 subjects. At least 60 percent of these were concentrated in twelve wealthy households like that of Captain Alonso García, who held twenty-two, but another thirty-four households held at least one or two slaves. Other households held from three to nine. Well more than half of the approximately two hundred Spanish heads of family held at least one Indian captive. Once situated in those households, Indian slaves faced a variety of experiences dependent largely upon the character of their masters. If brutal and lacking in Christian principle, masters might treat Indian slaves no better than the *galeotes* (galley slaves) of the Iberian wars and literally work them to death or force young women into concubinage like a morica. Many others, probably numbering in the hundreds, were shipped south for sale as laborers or as gifts to patrons in Mexico. Gentler masters made use of the alternative Iberian custom of compadrazgo and extended the embrace of fictive kinship to their still subordinate criados or criadas. In most cases, slaves' lives probably reflected some middle range between these two extremes.[9]

8. See Charles R. Cutter, *The Protector de Indios in Colonial New Mexico, 1659–1821* (Albuquerque, N.Mex., 1986), for the ongoing struggle to protect Christian Indians from exploitation by soldiers and friars alike; see also Scholes, *Church and State,* 73, 118; Kessell, *Kiva, Cross, and Crown,* 138; Jack D. Forbes, *Apache, Navaho, and Spaniard,* 2d ed. (1960; Norman, Okla., 1994), 156. For a recent overview of encomienda in the colony, see H. Allen Anderson, "The Encomienda in New Mexico, 1598–1680," *NMHR,* LX (October 1985), 353–377.

9. Although impossible now to determine in the dearth of pre-1680 documentary materials, cautious estimates are useful. Forbes estimates "700 Indian servants and captives" among the Spanish during the siege of Santa Fe and suggests some might have escaped to

Although Spanish enslavement displayed considerable variation in sources and treatment of Indians, and never (exempting the "just war" doctrine) received royal or church sanction, in seventeenth-century New Mexico the practice was a keystone in the colony's economic and social architecture. Indian slaves wove blankets, served as domestics, weeded fields, herded livestock, and suffered humiliation as their masters used slave subjugation to affirm their fragile sense of superiority. Yet the violence and domination visited upon Indian women and children included several intrinsic elements that would constantly erode its stability as well. The insinuation of kinship linkages between Spanish masters and Indian slaves—whether fictive in form through the kinship implicit in *crianza,* explicit in church-sanctioned compadrazgo relations, or literal (though illegal) in children born of rape and concubinage—constantly undermined the fixity of slavery as an institution. Likewise, the Indian impulse toward kinship creation with the Spanish newcomers brought some Spanish men, women, and children into the indigenous kin nexus. That impulse could take either cordial and diplomatic form, as we saw earlier in Diego Romero's "marriage" to the Apache woman, or violent symmetry with Spanish slave raids, as Indians took Spanish women and children captive into their own camps.

Who Kills a Spaniard Shall Get an Indian Woman for a Wife

The capacity of Pueblo and nomadic Indians alike to exercise violence on Spanish society became obvious in August of 1680, when a carefully planned rebellion delivered 422 Spanish subjects to death or captivity. The surviving

---

join the rebels in the confusion *(Apache, Navaho, and Spaniard),* 179. Muster rolls taken after the 1680 revolt show 426 Indian *servientes* among 125 surviving households that gathered in El Paso del Norte. These are distinguished from *agregados* (relatives, orphans, or poor people), who had attached themselves to the patronage of a head of family. See "Muster, September 29, 1680," in Charles Wilson Hackett, *Revolt of the Pueblo Indians of New Mexico and Otermín's Attempted Reconquest, 1680–1682,* I (Albuquerque, N.Mex., 1942), 134–153. I follow Gutiérrez's extrapolation of population figures in *When Jesus Came,* 107, 171–172; see also Salomé Hernández, "*Nueva Mexicanas* as Refugees and Reconquest Settlers, 1680–1696," in Joan M. Jensen and Darlis A. Miller, eds., *New Mexico Women: Intercultural Perspectives* (Albuquerque, N.Mex., 1986), 18–41, esp. 44–46. For Indian slaves sent south to Mexico, see David M. Brugge, "Captives and Slaves on the Camino Real," in Gabrielle G. Palmer and Stephen L. Fosberg, comps., *El Camino Real de Tierra Adentro* (Santa Fe, N.Mex., 1999), 103–110.

1,946 colonists, allies, dependents, and slaves were expelled from the northern colony. Triggered in large part by local enforcement of the Spanish Inquisition, which sought to erase covert native spiritual practices among nominally Christianized Pueblo Indians, the Great Southwestern Revolt also sprang from economic hardships that played havoc with customary trade between those Pueblos and their nomadic neighbors. Droughts and famines beset the region between 1666 and 1671, seriously diminishing Pueblo agricultural production. Coupled with constant demands for tithes and tribute from the Franciscan fathers and Spanish *encomenderos* alike, Pueblo peoples along the borders found themselves without the necessary grains and textiles to entice and entertain their long-term trading partners. Alienated Plains Apaches and Navajos quickly shifted their trading economy to one based in raiding and during the 1670s forced the abandonment of several pueblos east of the Manzano Mountains. Seizing crops from fields and granaries and taking captives—sometimes as many as thirty in a single attack—these onetime allies of the southeastern Pueblos now turned into eager enemies of the reeling colony. When Governor Juan Francisco Treviño added to their misery in 1675 by launching an internal war against Pueblo idolaters and sorcerers, hanging several Indian spiritual practitioners and flogging forty-seven more, the seeds of insurgency were sown.[10]

But Spanish slavery also fueled the rebellion, whence fractures more complex than the simple Pueblo-Spanish split became manifest. When an army of diverse Pueblo groups laid siege to Santa Fe on August 13, 1680, their first demand was for the head of Maese de Campo (secretary of government and war) Francisco Javier, who was "the reason we have risen." Javier had only days before been at Pecos, where, after extending his guarantee of safe conduct to a visiting band of Plains Apaches, he had disarmed and distributed them among his friends as captives, retaining some to sell south in Parral. This offense to Pecos's economic and diplomatic relations with Apaches certainly mobilized that pueblo to revolt. But Javier's treachery was not the sole reference to slavery

10. Despite modern treatments of the Pueblo revolt, Forbes's *Apache, Navaho, and Spaniard* continues to be the only scholarly discussion to take seriously the breadth of its origins and the close connections between Pueblo rebels and surrounding Athapaskan groups; see 156ff. For Treviño's campaign against Pueblo spiritual practitioners, see Henry Warden Bowden, "Spanish Missions, Cultural Conflict, and the Pueblo Revolt of 1680," in *Church History*, XLIV (June 1975), 217–228; Gutiérrez, *When Jesus Came*, 130–140; Kessell, *Kiva, Cross, and Crown*, 226–227.

lying at the root of rebellion. Three days into the siege of Santa Fe, the allied Indians elected as their captain a renegade "Christian" Tano Indian named Juan who had recently slipped away from the Spanish camp and who came forth to parlay with Governor Antonio Otermín. Mounted on horseback and armed with a harquebus, he bore two banners, white and red, by which he asked the Spanish to chose either peace (and departure) or war (and extermination). The "apostate" made clear what the choice of peace entailed.

> His people asked that all classes of Indians who were in our power be given up to them, both those in the service of the Spaniards and those of the Mexican nation [Nahuatl-speaking Tlaxcalans] of that suburb of Analco. He demanded also that his wife and children be given up to him, and likewise that all the Apache men and women whom the Spaniards had captured in war be turned over to them, inasmuch as some Apaches who were among them were asking for them. If these things were not done, they would declare war immediately.[11]

Speaking beyond personal interest in recovering his wife and children, Juan made clear the extent to which slavery figured prominently in the grievances of Indian peoples throughout the region. His declaration also indicates that enslavement inspired some "Apaches of the Achos nation" to join with the Pueblo insurgents in hopes of rescuing their own kinspeople. Finally, his reference to slaves held by peoples of the "Mexican nation" residing in the Barrio de Analco (just across the Río Santa Fe from the presidio) hints at a phenomenon that would mark developments in the next century—the central role of Indian military auxiliaries in perpetuating and expanding slavery beyond the marches of the colony. But, as in the case of *genízaro* military auxiliaries in the eighteenth century, enslavement formed the foundation of their condition as well. Indian slave-soldiers who seized Indian slaves would become yet another layer of growing complexity in slavery in the Southwest Borderlands.

11. Kessell, *Kiva, Cross, and Crown,* 231–236; account by don Antonio Otermín, in Hackett, *Revolt of the Pueblo Indians,* 94–105, esp. 99. Tlaxcalan fighters and their families were used extensively in the Spanish northward expansion throughout the seventeenth and eighteenth centuries, usually settled as military colonies and relieved of taxation for their service. See David Bergen Adams, "The Tlaxcalan Colonies of Spanish Coahuila and Nuevo Leon: An Aspect of the Settlement of Northern Mexico" (Ph.D. diss., University of Texas at Austin, 1971). For Tlaxcalans as residents of Analco, see Marc Simmons, "Tlascalans in the Spanish Borderlands," *New Mexico Historical Review* (hereafter cited as *NMHR),* XXXIX (January 1964), 101–110.

The rebels' demand in 1680 centered on the return of enslaved women and children, and in that challenge, at one level, we can feel the anguish of families torn asunder. But under contest as well during the insurgency was the multivalent issue of men's control over their own (and others') women and children. Pedro García, a Christian Tano Indian "in the service of" *estanciero* Captain Joseph Nieto, reported to Governor Otermín the inducements proffered by the rebels. An Indian from the pueblo of Galisteo approached García and warned that the rebellion had commenced. Its leaders had declared a scale of rewards for those Indians who joined them:

> The Indian who shall kill a Spaniard will get an Indian woman for a wife, and he who kills four will get four women, and he who kills ten or more will have a like number of women; and they have said that they are going to kill all the servants of the Spaniards and those who know how to speak Castilian, and they have also ordered that rosaries be taken away from every one and burned.[12]

If the uprising was inspired in part by a desire to redeem Indian women and children from Spanish bondage, it also served to make available to the successful rebels new (and multiple) wives. These might have been meant to come from within the pueblos themselves, but it also seems likely that they would be drawn from the Spanish population. Implicit here is an indigenous pattern: Spanish men and their subordinated male Indian *servientes* would die, while their spouses and children were assimilated through marriage and adoption into victorious Indian families. Indeed, in García's case, this might have proved true—as he ran toward Isleta Pueblo, where Otermín and the survivors had taken shelter after abandoning Santa Fe, rebels from Santo Domingo Pueblo came out on horseback and took away his "wife and an orphan girl" who fled with him. He himself was rescued by the Spanish rearguard.[13]

Twelve years would pass before Spanish soldiers, friars, and families reoccupied the northern reaches of the Río Grande. Few Indian sources exist by which we may understand their long decade of autonomy, but the alliance seems to have quickly unraveled as interpueblo friction grew and assaults by freshly mounted Apaches and Navajos haunted their days. Popé, the San Juan spiritual practitioner whose nativistic millennialism had organized the

12. "Declaration of Pedro García," Aug. 25, 1680, in Hackett, *Revolt of the Pueblo Indians*, 24.

13. Ibid., 24–25; Kessell, *Kiva, Cross, and Crown*, 233–236.

various pueblos to revolt, now acted the tyrant himself. Ordering every vestige of Catholic religion destroyed, every marriage sealed by the church abandoned, every article of Spanish agriculture destroyed, he instituted a reign of terror by which even use of the Castilian tongue could lead to execution. Concurrently he made heavy demands for women, grain, and livestock. In 1681, he was deposed, and factional leaders from contending pueblos stepped forward. Drought again visited the land, and hunger followed. Alone among the pueblos, Pecos seemed to prosper, for it had resumed its economic and military alliance with Plains Apaches, whom Spaniards now called "Los Faraones" for their resemblance to the swift cavalries of the biblical pharaohs—and, perhaps metaphorically, to the depth of their involvement in the slave system of the borderlands.[14]

Made Captives and Held Slaves

Huddled in their quarters at El Paso del Norte, the Spanish refugees from the Great Southwestern Revolt reported with certainty the deaths of the 422 priests, soldiers, and settlers who failed to make the retreat. But the reconquest undertaken by don Diego de Vargas between 1692 and 1696 offers us a somewhat different insight as to what became of at least some of the seventeenth-century colonists. During his initial entrada between August and December 1692, Vargas and his small force of sixty Spanish soldiers and one hundred Indian auxiliaries redeemed some sixty-three Spanish and Indian captives from their Pueblo captors. How many more were held among Apaches and Navajos is unknown, although at least one Navajo case survives, whose story follows in the next chapter. But those enumerated in the census of October 29 and sent back to El Paso under the protection of Sargento Mayor Cristóbal de Tapia tell a story fraught with ambiguity but meaningful nonetheless.

Vargas's muster roll reveals a picture of heterogeneous ethnic kin connections. Racial designations indicate that twenty of the redeemed captives were nominally Spanish, probably mestizo, sixteen of whom were female and four male. Thirty-six were *indio,* some described as of Pueblo origin (Tewa, Isleta, Piro), of whom twenty-two were female and fourteen male. Those not designated as Pueblo might have been of Jumano, Apache, Ute, or other cultural

14. Forbes, *Apache, Navaho, and Spaniard,* 185–186; Kessell, *Kiva, Cross, and Crown,* 238–243; Gutiérrez, *When Jesus Came,* 135–140.

background. Four mulattas and one mulatto comprised the remaining captives. Forty-two of the rescued were female, eighteen of whom were adults. Nineteen were male, eight of them adults. Two additional *hijos* (children, probably male) made the list, but of their sex we cannot be certain. Almost all, mestiza and Indian alike, were addressed as sisters, aunts, kinswomen, or relatives by their redeemers. In three cases, unmarried women with children were claimed by men who intended to marry them upon their safe return to El Paso.

Twelve years had passed since they fell into captivity, and doubtless each would have a singular story to tell. Of these we have little evidence. But the matter-of-fact language of the muster does suggest a pattern that was familiar: captivity and resulting kinship ties blurred and insinuated themselves into the social relations of captive women. Vargas's secretary took care to differentiate between a "grown" daughter or son *(hijo grande)* and children not yet at the age of maturity. We may surmise that at least thirty-three of the children had been born after 1680 to the twelve mothers enumerated, whether by rape or consensual union. Only one of the redeemed women connected with a redeemed man who declared his intentions to be her husband once they were again in the embrace of the church. The reuniting of Spanish colonial families rent by captivity meant sundering families created in captivity, an ironic twist on notions of freedom. And, although we must be cautious about imputing too much generosity of heart to their Spanish liberators, children born in captivity seemed to be implicitly accepted as attached dependents, if not affinal kinspeople, in their mothers' transition from captivity to freedom. Thus, even in the severance of one set of kin relations, an undercurrent of affinity between former captors and redeemed women and children tugged against the segregation of societies. Such underlying connections would perhaps resurface in years to come.[15]

For now the reconquest remained incomplete. In 1696, after six months of bitter skirmishes, devastation, executions, and reprisals, don Diego de Vargas succeeded in suppressing a second Pueblo revolt. This latest rebellion had divided the pueblos of Río Grande from without and within. The northern pueblos of Taos, Picurís, San Ildefonso, San Juan, and Jémez were among the rebels, whereas the southern Keres pueblos had joined the Spanish as auxil-

15. Don Diego de Vargas, "List of the People Found in the Pueblos of New Mexico . . . in This Present Year 1692," and facsimile of original, both in John L. Kessell and Rick Hendricks, eds., *By Force of Arms: The Journals of Don Diego de Vargas, New Mexico, 1691–93* (Albuquerque, N.Mex., 1992), 525–531.

iaries. Although it contributed warriors to the Spanish, Pecos Pueblo suffered factional disputes that would not be resolved until the anti-Spanish contingent fled in 1700 to find sanctuary with the Jicarilla Apaches.[16]

During the revolt of 1696, several hundred people from Taos and Picurís Pueblos also fled in fear of Spanish reprisals to join their longtime trading partners, the Apaches of El Cuartelejo ("fortified buildings"). These Athapaskans lived north of the Arkansas River, in rancherías that featured a strong Pueblo architectural influence, as their Spanish name suggests. By 1706, many of the refugees had returned to Picurís, for Fray Juan Alvarez noted of that pueblo that "there are about three hundred Christian persons, and others keep coming in who have been among the Apaches." But those who returned claimed other Picurís remained involuntarily among the Cuartelejos.[17]

In October of that year, Governor Cuervo y Valdez sent a report to the Spanish crown concerning the remaining Picurís people at El Cuartelejo:

> There they had sought refuge in the asylum of barbarity, but they found, instead of the relief which they sought, labor twice as great as that which they had endured. For, many of them being able-bodied men, they were made captives and held as slaves and obliged to do all kinds of work. In this they have suffered such great hardship that in an effort to escape from their oppressors, [they have requested us] to send several squadrons of soldiers to take them away and restore them to their old pueblo.[18]

Whether this report of exploitation was a Spanish fiction to justify the resettlement of Picurís Pueblo or a legitimate statement of conditions remains

16. Kessell, *Kiva, Cross, and Crown*, 295–297. For a thorough treatment of the second revolt, see J. Manuel Espinosa, trans. and ed., *The Pueblo Indian Revolt of 1696 . . .* (Norman, Okla., 1988).

17. Archaeological investigations of the Athapaskan rancherías north of the Arkansas have revealed several settlements composed of rectangular adobe room-blocks containing Río Grande Pueblo material culture. See James H. Gunnerson, *The Archaeology of the High Plains* (Washington, D.C., 1987), 106. For a 1778 reference to a group of Taos Indians who fled to the Plains in the 1640s and "fortified themselves at a place which afterwards was called El Cuartelejo," see Fray Sylvestre Velez de Escalante to Fray Juan Augustin de Morfí, Apr. 2, 1778, in Ralph Emerson Twitchell, *The Spanish Archives of New Mexico*, 2 vols. (Cedar Rapids, Iowa, 1914), II, no. 779, 279–280; see also "Declaration of Fray Juan Álvarez," Jan. 12, 1706, in Hackett, trans. and ed., *Historical Documents Relating to New Mexico, Nueva Vizcaya, and Approaches Thereto, to 1771* (Washington, D.C., 1937), III, 374.

18. "Cuervo y Valdez to His Majesty," Oct. 18, 1706, in *Historical Documents*, III, 383.

unclear. If true, it appears to be a very early case of male captives' suffering enslavement for their labor value. In Apache society, women served as the primary agriculturalists; thus, these male captives would have the double humiliation of bondage and consignment to "women's work." Given the ease of their repatriation, the Picurís might have offered their (male) agricultural skills to the Cuartelejos in return for shelter during the reconquest. Once return home appeared safe, they perhaps sought the security of a Spanish escort to make their passage across increasingly dangerous territory.

Captain Juan de Ulibarrí led the recovery expedition, composed of forty Spanish soldiers and settlers and one hundred Pueblo Indians under the leadership of José Naranjo, a Spanish / Pueblo mixed-blood from Santa Clara Pueblo. With several Picurís as guides, Ulibarrí crossed the Sangre de Cristo range east of Taos and descended into the homeland of the Jicarillas, the valley of the Cimarron (from the Spanish *cimarrones,* "fugitives") River. Continuing to the northeast, he met or heard of numerous bands of Apaches in the area, some of whom approached his party with gestures of peace, including crudely constructed crosses. The Jicarillas "occupied themselves with their maize and corn fields which they harvest, because they are busy with the sowing of corn, frijoles, and pumpkins." These people, too, lived at least seasonally in adobe dwellings, as one dating from 1700 has been excavated on the Ocaté River. The mixed economy and semisedentary settlement pattern of these Apache groups indicates a strong Pueblo cultural linkage and hints at a long tradition of exchange, probably involving exogamous marriages along the lines discussed earlier.[19]

Upon his arrival at El Cuartelejo, Ulibarrí began negotiations for the return of the Picurís people. His diplomacy worked, for "having treated the heathen nations with much affection, flattery, and cordiality, he succeeded in getting them to turn over readily and voluntarily seventy-four persons." Some women, however, who had married Apaches probably stayed behind voluntarily, for the Cuartelejos much later claimed kin connections to Picurís. Ulibarrí's success might have been due to his ability to flatter and persuade, but, before the

19. "The Diary of Juan de Ulibarri . . . ," in Alfred Barnaby Thomas, trans. and ed., *After Coronado: Spanish Exploration Northeast of New Mexico, 1696–1727* (Norman, Okla., 1935), 63–64; James H. Gunnerson, "Apache Archaeology in Northeastern New Mexico," *American Antiquity,* XXXIV (January 1969), 23–39. This site is on the western margins of the Dismal River Aspect (Apachean) culture area, 1640–1725, typified by village-based horticultural / hunting societies. Unlike Dismal River "earthlodge" dwellings, however, this site features Pueblo-style *jacal* structures.

expedition left New Mexico, the people at Picurís Pueblo had loaded it down with "cotton and woolen blankets and as many horses as they could collect." While these might have served primarily as diplomatic gifts, the goods probably indemnified the Cuartelejos for the loss of labor incurred by surrendering the Picurís, indicating exchange values at issue as well.[20]

Besides repatriating the Picurís captives, the Ulibarrí expedition gathered information that suggests an expansion in the scope of traditional captive exchange. Containing the earliest-known reference to the presence of Comanches on the borders of New Mexico, a report from the people of Taos Pueblo warned of an impending attack by a combined force of Utes and their Comanche cousins. Although this attack failed to materialize, on his return through Jicarilla country, Ulibarrí learned that crop and captive raids by Utes and Comanches on several Apache bands had taken place while he visited El Cuartelejo. A new people had moved out onto the Plains.[21]

A Great Multitude of Both Sexes

Early in the eighteenth century, Shoshonean-speakers whom their Ute cousins termed *komántcia,* or "enemy," completed their centuries-long migrations out of the Great Basin and onto the buffalo plains. Taking advantage of the presence of feral horse herds and abundant buffalo, in less than a century the *Nemenu* ("People") would develop an equestrian military culture that swept the semisedentary Plains Apaches from the foothills-plains ecotone of the Rocky Mountains. By the end of the century, Comanches had imposed their control over an exchange network that reached from the upper Missouri to northern Mexico.[22]

20. "Don Francisco Cuervo y Valdez to His Majesty," Oct. 18, 1706, in Hackett, *Historical Documents,* III, 384. Ulibarrí reported a total of sixty-two returned Picurís, including "Don Lorenzo and Don Juan Tupatú . . . two of the most noteworthy Indians of the entire kingdom and provinces." ("Diary of Ulibarri," in Thomas, trans. and ed., *After Coronado,* 74); see also Dolores A. Gunnerson, *The Jicarilla Apaches: A Study in Survival* (DeKalb, Ill., 1974), 172.

21. "Diary of Ulibarri," in Thomas, trans. and ed., *After Coronado,* 61, 76.

22. See D. Bernard Shimkin, "Shoshoni-Comanche Origins and Migrations," Sixth Pacific Science Congress of the Pacific Science Association, *Proceedings,* IV (1940), 17–25; Marvin K. Opler, "The Origins of Comanche and Ute," *American Anthropologist,* XLV (1943), 155–158. Pekka Hämäläinen argues that Comanches established a seasonal trading

During those hundred years, Comanches maintained a social organization in which the basic unit was a band-level "household" *(numunahkahni)* of three to five bilaterally extended families, sometimes more, and usually referred to by the Spanish as a ranchería. These immediate kin groupings also understood themselves as members of larger "divisions," numbering up to several hundred people, often named in reference to important aspects of their livelihood, like the Yamparicas (Yap Eaters), Penetakas (Honey Eaters), or Kotsekas (Buffalo Eaters). These basic units were linked by a variety of sodalities arranged around politics, medicine, and military cohorts, but flexibility of membership was always central at all levels of Comanche society. Marriage occurred outside the kin group but within the division, and marital residence was predominantly patrilocal. Bride service, through gifts of horses and lifelong hunting offerings to the bride's family, provided the mechanism through which young men could claim wives. Since marriage, by supplying a man the labor to assure his independence, proclaimed his adulthood, a man's capacity to claim women stood at the very center of Comanche power relations. This system promoted the individual pursuit of wealth by young men, since only through personal gain could a man assert his right to a woman or women free of obligations to other men—to "borrow" marriage gifts from senior men would call into question a husband's prestige and power.[23]

With men's honor linked to their ability to give gifts in return for wives, and little intragroup reciprocity beyond the obligations of bride service, eighteenth-century Comanche society seems acquisitive and egalitarian to an extreme. Lacking any coercive capacity, leaders exercised authority by example and persuasion. Thus, prestige, acquired through feats of arms and hunting excellence, as well as the capture of horses and human beings, represented the "cultural capital" for which all Comanche men strove. As Euramerican traders

---

center on the upper Arkansas River equal in import to the better-known Mandan-Hidatsa center on the upper Missouri, which lost its centrality only after the Bent brothers and other Americans established trading posts in the 1830s. See "The Western Comanche Trade Center: Rethinking the Plains Indian Trade System," *Western Historical Quarterly*, XXIX (Winter 1998), 485–513.

23. Ernest Wallace and E. Adamson Hoebel, *The Comanches: Lords of the South Plains* (Norman, Okla., 1952), 22–24; Morris Foster, *Being Comanche: A Social History of an American Indian Community* (Tucson, Ariz., 1991), 31–38; Thomas W. Kavanagh, *Comanche Political History: An Ethnohistorical Perspective* (Lincoln, Nebr., 1996), 41–56. On Comanche gender and kinship systems, see Jane Fishburne Collier, *Marriage and Inequality in Classless Societies* (Stanford, Calif., 1988), 15–70.

brought additional prestige items onto the Plains, new commodities and new commodification of local products, including captives, would enter into the calculation of power.

Ulibarrí also obtained news of French participation in the Plains exchange economy. Questioning the Cuartelejos about neighboring tribes, he discovered that these and other Plains Apaches fought with the Pawnees, who were themselves allied with the French and the Jumanos. Slavery was clearly at the root of the conflict.

> The Pawnee Indians sell to the [French] the Apache women and children whom they take prisoners as they themselves sold to us those of the Pawnees they captured. . . . In the forays which they have made on them, they have taken from these Pawnees some fowling pieces, clothes, small short swords, French iron axes . . . and two French guns.[24]

Settling at Cahokia and Kaskaskia in 1700, French missionaries, traders, and farmers introduced an additional layer of complexity to the exchange network of human beings. Ulibarrí's report indicates that the French had extended their trading ties as far as the Platte and Loup Rivers. Soon Pawnees would find themselves even more deeply involved in the captive system. "Panis" captives became an important exchange item for the French in the eighteenth century, who purchased them from Ottawa and Cree middlemen to barter for the freedom of Anglo-American captives taken by French Mission Indians. Early articulation of the Plains system with the Atlantic economy also occurred about this time. French fur-traders in Saint Louis (established 1730) purchased captive Plains Indian women from the neighboring Omaha and Ponca tribes for use as hide processors. After French expulsion in 1763, the Spanish governor of Louisiana suggested that captive Plains women be exchanged for "Florida Indian girls" raised by the Catholic orders in Cuba, thereby providing a supply of marriageable women in the Louisiana colony without loss of labor at the convents. These anonymous Plains Indian women presumably spent their lives in Cuba, presaging the deportation of Apaches to that island in the later eighteenth and nineteenth centuries.[25]

24. "Diary of Ulibarri," "Declaration of Garduño," both in Thomas, trans. and ed., *After Coronado*, 70–74, 173, esp. 74.

25. W. J. Eccles, *The Canadian Frontier, 1534–1760* (1969; Albuquerque, N.Mex., 1983), 149–150; Tanis Chapman Thorne, "People of the River: Mixed-Blood Families on the Lower Missouri" (Ph.D. diss., UCLA, 1987), 72–74. The best treatment of the French trade is in

Although the direct export of captives from New Mexico to Mexico declined after the reconquista, the regional demand for Indian captives continued to grow. Even as they were being pressed upon by southward-moving Comanche bands, Apache groups in customary trade relationships with Pecos Pueblo sought to maintain their own market niche. In 1711, Governor Peñuela reported of the Pecoseños that

> they are and have always been involved in trade, and that they enjoy very great advantage from the Apache Indians, Faraones, Chipaynes, and Jacindes, who are accustomed to come to their pueblo most years. The Pecos buy from [the Apaches] buffalo meat, lard, grease, buckskins, buffalo hides, buffalo or elkskins, and some Apache children slaves [and other Plains Indians] whom they capture from the enemies with whom they wage war. These the Pecos buy from said Apaches for a horse or two at most and sell them to the Spaniards for four or five horses, from which they realize very great profits.[26]

But in less than a decade the tables would begin to turn for these once-dominant Plains Apaches, who would soon become victims rather than masters in an expanding slave trade.

In 1719, Comanche and Ute attacks on the Jicarillas yielded sixty-four women and children captives who would later be brought to Pecos for resale. Throughout the eighteenth century, Spanish church and secular authorities vied to gain control of this trade, variously blaming each other or the local alcaldes for "the saddest" of this commerce. In 1761, Fray Pedro Serrano chided the Spanish governors, who when "the fleet was in" scrambled to gather as many horses, axes, hoes, wedges, picks, bridles, and knives in order to "gorge themselves" on the "great multitude of both sexes" offered for sale. Fifteen years later, Fray Atanasio Domínguez reported that the Comanches brought

---

Juliana Barr, "The Seductions of Texas: The Political Language of Gender in the Conquests of Texas, 1690–1810" (Ph.D. diss., University of Wisconsin, 1999). For Apache deportations, see Christon I. Archer, "The Deportation of Barbarous Indians from the Internal Provinces of New Spain," *Americas,* XXIX (1973), 376–385; Max L. Moorhead, "Spanish Deportation of Hostile Apaches: The Policy and the Practice," *Arizona and the West,* XVII (1975), 205–220. Cuba also became the point of deportation for army deserters and other social marginals in the late eighteenth century. See Archer, *The Army in Bourbon Mexico, 1760–1810* (Albuquerque, N.Mex., 1977), 269–284.

26. Peñuela to the viceroy, Oct. 20, 1711, quoted in Kessell, *Kiva, Cross, and Crown,* 364.

to Taos for sale "pagan Indians, of both sexes, whom they capture from other nations." The going rate of exchange, which seems to have held quite steady until the mid-nineteenth century, was "two good horses and some trifles" for an "Indian girl twelve to twenty years old"; for a male captive, "a she-mule" or one horse and a "poor bridle . . . garnished with red rags" was the going price. Girls were clearly more highly valued than boys. The general atmosphere, according to Domínguez, resembled "a second-hand market in Mexico, the way people mill about."[27]

This regional market for captives competed against their internal labor value in the expanding equestrian economy of the Plains. Beyond ecological constraints like quality of forage and availability of water, labor was the single greatest factor determining the vigor of these expanding pastoral societies. Livestock herds required constant management, especially when subject to theft by competing nomads and pastoralists like Utes, Arapahos, and Cheyennes. Ethnographic surveys reveal that 73 percent of pastoral societies include some form of slavery in their social organization, as compared to 43 percent of agricultural societies and 17 percent of horticulturists. The southern Plains seems no less a region in which emerging pastoral economies were associated with forms of human bondage. By midcentury, Comanche horse herds probably outnumbered those in colonial New Mexico, and the need for pastoral labor increased accordingly. In addition to "Indian slaves, men and women, small and large, a great multitude of both sexes," the Comanches now brought horses, "deer and buffalo hides," and, at times, French firearms. They accepted payment in maize, beans, and iron goods—awls, pails, hoes, axes, bridles, and knives of all sizes. These extending networks of interdependency increasingly reworked the character of servitude on the Plains and in the New Mexican colony.[28]

27. See "Diary of Antonio Valverde," in Thomas, trans. and ed., *After Coronado,* 112–115; "Report of the Reverend Father Provincial, Fray Pedro Serrano, to the Most Excellent Señor Viceroy, the Marquis of Cruillas," 1761, in Hackett, trans. and ed., *Historical Documents,* III, 486–487; Fray Francisco Atanasio Domínguez, *The Missions of New Mexico, 1776,* trans. and ed. Eleanor B. Adams and Fray Angélico Chávez (Albuquerque, N.Mex., 1956), 252. See also Amando Represa, "Las ferias hispano-indias del Nuevo México," in *La España ilustrada en el lejano oeste: viajes y exploraciones por las provincias y territorios hispánicos de Norteamérica en el siglo XVIII* ([Valladolid], 1990), 119–125.

28. Pierre Bonte, "Ecological and Economic Factors in the Determination of Pastoral Societies," in John G. Galaty and Philip Carl Salzman, eds., *Change and Development in Nomadic and Pastoral Societies* (Leiden, 1981), 33–49; Gerald Betty, "'Skillful in the Man-

The need to meet both internal labor demands and external market demands shifted Comanche captive raiding to New Mexican targets as well as to Apaches, Utes, and Pawnees. In August 1747, Comanches and a few Muache Ute allies swept down upon Spanish settlements in the Río Chama valley. At Santa Rosa de Lima de Abiquiu, established in 1737, the raiders carried off twenty-three women and children, forcing abandonment of the village until 1754. Seven years later, Spanish authorities redeemed one woman, but the rest disappeared into the captive system. Ojo Caliente, north of Abiquiu, also suffered captive raids and temporary abandonment. In 1760, the Taos Valley rancho of Pablo Francisco Villalpando suffered a concentrated attack that yielded approximately sixty women and children for the Comanches, including María Rosa Villalpando, whose story below illustrates the geographic breadth of the captive network and its consequences for one New Mexican woman. Less spectacular raids throughout the eighteenth century yielded captives by the handful. Redemption negotiations repatriated perhaps a dozen of these; the remainder seem to have been either integrated into Comanche society or traded throughout the Plains network.[29]

---

agement of the Horse': Comanches as Southern Plains Pastoralists," *Heritage of the Great Plains,* XXX, no. 1 (1997), 5–31; George Peter Murdock, "Ethnographic Atlas: A Summary," *Ethnology,* VI (April 1967), 109–236; "Report of Fray Serrano," in Hackett, *Historical Documents,* III, 487; on trade in French guns, see Governor Codallos y Rabal's report of 1748, in which thirty-three Frenchmen resided with Comanches north of Taos, "sold them plenty of muskets in exchange for mules," and planned to enter Taos to continue this trade (Twitchell, *Spanish Archives of New Mexico,* I, no. 499, 148–151, esp. 148); Amando Represa, "Las ferias hispano-indias del Nuevo México," in *La España ilustrada en el lejano oeste,* 119–125; Bishop Pedro Tamarón y Romeral, "Bishop Tamarón's Visitation of New Mexico, 1760," in Eleanor B. Adams, ed., Historical Society of New Mexico, *Publications in History,* XV (1954), 57–58; "Report of Fray Serrano," in Hackett, ed., *Historical Documents,* III, 486–487.

29. "An Account of Lamentable Happenings in New Mexico . . . Written by Reverend Father Fray Juan Sanz de Lezaún," 1760, in Hackett, ed., *Historical Documents,* III, 477; "Petition of Inhabitants of Abiquiu, Ojo Caliente, and Pueblo Quemado to Remove, Presented to Governor Codallos y Rabal, 1748," in *Spanish Archives of New Mexico* (hereafter cited as *SANM),* I, no. 28, roll 1, frames 263–266. Tamarón, "Bishop Tamarón's Visitation," in Adams, trans. and ed., Historical Society of New Mexico, *Publications in History,* XV (1954), 58, gives the number of captives as fifty-six; the text included in don Bernardo de Miera y Pacheco's map of 1779 puts the number at sixty-four. See Pacheco, "Plano de la Provincia Interna de el Nuebo Mexico . . . 1779," in Domínguez, *Missions of New Mexico,* trans. and ed. Adams and Chávez, 2–5. Small-scale raids netted individuals like Alejandro Martín in 1775

The complex intermediation of kinship and commodity pressures was already evident in the case of the women and children captured at Abiquiu in 1747 and Taos in 1760. Some five years after the first event, Governor Tomás Vélez Cachupín surrounded and defeated a Comanche band on the Plains. The survivors begged for liberty, which Vélez Cachupín promised if they would find and return the women and children taken at Abiquiu. Assured that at least three of the women and two boys were living within another ranchería to the north of the Arkansas River, the governor took four hostages toward their safe return and went back to Santa Fe to await the repatriates. Meanwhile, he satisfied a request by his superior in Mexico City, the marqués de Altimira, that he make use of the four Comanche hostages to learn more about their people and thereby "establish good relations" between them and the colony. He could do so only through a circuitous process of translation, by which his lieutenant Juan José Lobato utilized the services of a Kiowa woman, captured by Comanches, in turn captured by Utes in battle, and subsequently sold to the Spanish settler Antonio Martín. She, however, could not speak Spanish, so Lobato also employed "an Indian woman servant of Sebastian Martín" whose "sincerity" he trusted. With this tenuous chain of communication established, Lobato learned from the hostages that the Spanish captives were held in the ranchería of a captain named El Oso (the Bear), and that his brother, Nimiricante (Man Eater?), had attempted to ransom one woman by offering El Oso an Apache woman captive in return. El Oso refused, and the brothers parted in anger. Despite this failure, Vélez Cachupín remained so encouraged by the Comanche effort to return a captive to the Spanish that he released his four hostages without further ado; one, the son of Captain Guanacante, refused to leave the governor's household, which the Comanches took as "proof that he was pleased" with Vélez's Cachupín's hospitality. One Spanish woman would finally be returned in 1754. The others, it seems, simply "became Comanche" through cultural assimilation.

Likewise, although the Comanche raiders of 1760 did return two years later and offer to ransom "three women and four boys" seized in that attack, the negotiations with interim governor Manuel Portillo Urrisola collapsed when one of the boys refused to leave the Comanche camp. A battle ensued, involving the Spanish, some Muache Utes who were also attending the rescate,

---

and Dolores Baca and María Antonia Sánchez at Tomé in 1777. For the latter instance, see Angélico Chávez, *The Origins of New Mexico Families: A Genealogy of the Spanish Colonial Period* (1954; Santa Fe, N.Mex., 1992), 281–282.

and the Comanches. It ended with hundreds of Comanches dead or captured. When Vélez Cachupín used some of these Comanche captive women as emissaries to find the 1760 captives, he was told that "some of the prisoners might have died or have been traded to the French and Jumanos." The capture of Spanish women and children, therefore, slipped almost seamlessly into well-established indigenous patterns of abduction and exchange, wherein the kin-building impulse of assimilation was always in tension with the captives' value within both the indigenous and wider colonial world. And, in turn, on at least some occasions, Indian captives among the Spanish, like the son of Guanacante, would assert a kinship with their captors, extending the fictive and affinal enmeshment of the two societies.[30]

Dynamic filaments of kinship reached even beyond the immediate protagonists in the 1760 case. Among the scores of women and children seized in that raid was twenty-one-year-old María Rosa Villalpando, Pablo's second daughter, carried with the others into captivity on the Great Plains. María's young husband, Juan José Xacques, was slain in the assault, but her infant son José Juliano Xacques somehow escaped both death and captivity. The Comanches apparently traded María shortly thereafter to the Pawnees, not as a sacrificial object (her maturity and motherhood would prohibit that role), but as a woman. By 1767 she lived in a Pawnee village on the Platte River and had borne another son, who would come to be known as Antoine Xavier. In that year, the French trader and cofounder of Saint Louis, Jean Salé dit Leroie, visited the Pawnees and began cohabiting with María. About one year later, she bore Salé a son, whom they named Lambert. This arrangement apparently suited Salé's trading goals, for not until 1770 did he end María's Indian captivity and bring her to Saint Louis, where they married. Although Salé agreed to extend his name to Antoine, the marriage contract between María Rosa and Jean Salé

30. "General Campaign, 1752: Report of Governor Vélez Cachupín to Conde de Revillagigedo, November 27, 1751," Marqués de Altamira to Vélez, Apr. 26, 1752, Juan Jose Lobato to Vélez, Aug. 28, 1752, "Report of Vélez to Marqués de Cruillas, 1762," in Thomas, trans. and ed., *The Plains Indians and New Mexico, 1751–1778* (Albuquerque, N.Mex., 1940), 73, 79, 114–117, 150–153, esp. 151. See also "Information Communicated by Juan Candelaria, Resident of the Villa de San Francisco Xavier de Albuquerque, Born 1692," *NMHR*, IV (December 1929), 274–297; E. A. H. John, *Storms Brewed in Other Men's Worlds: The Confrontation of Indians, Spanish, and French in the Southwest, 1540–1795* (College Station, Tex., 1975), 323–335. Gary Clayton Anderson claims an additional eleven captives were returned before the battle in *The Indian Southwest, 1580–1830: Ethnogenesis and Reinvention* (Norman, Okla., 1999), 209.

made clear that Lambert would "be legitimate heir of his parents in every respect." Thus the indigenous system of adoptive kinship met the Euramerican incentive toward formalized descent.[31]

Jean and María (now Marie Rose Salé) had three more children, but in 1792 their father returned to France, where he remained the rest of his life. María stayed in Saint Louis to become one progenitor of the Leroux and Provost families, later prominent in the Plains fur and hide trade. Her New Mexican son, José Juliano, would visit her there in 1803, with unexpected results. She paid him two hundred pesos "hard money" and sent him packing, requiring that he relinquish any interest in her estate. María died at the home of her daughter Helène in 1830, at well over ninety years of age. For María Rosa, a captivity begun in bloody violence and the terror of deracination had culminated in a circuitous and ultimately successful passage across cultures into security and longevity. At each phase of her journey, kinship, whether coercive or voluntary, shaped and defined her experience. This might have been the case among her fellow captives as well, but the Comanche comment that some might have been sold indicates commodity pressures were also at work, a transformation that would place them in much more vulnerable conditions.[32]

In addition, kinship often organized the fate of young male captives. Strong as affinal ties might have been, however, they did not prevent captives from being exchanged in the interests of intercultural communication and diplomacy. In 1770, Comanches seized eight-year-old Francisco Xavier Chaves while he herded his family's sheep near Tomé. He grew to adulthood among his captors, but, when his Comanche mother died, depriving him of the protections of kinship, he was sold to the Taovayas, village farmers along the Red River who were often allies of the Comanches. In 1784, at the age of twenty-two, he slipped away from the Taovayas and presented himself to Governor Domingo Cabello at San Antonio de Béxar. Eyelids tattooed in the Taovayas fashion, he began a long career as cultural emissary in the service of Spain.

31. "Marriage Contract between Jean Salle and Marie Rose Videlpane," Jul. 30, 1770, instrument no. 2023, Old St. Louis Archives, Missouri Historical Society, St. Louis, Mo., quoted in Jack B. Tykal, "From Taos to St. Louis: The Journey of María Rosa Villalpando," *NMHR*, LXV (April 1990), 170.

32. "Marriage Contract between Jean Salle and Marie Rose Videlpane," in Tykal, "From Taos to St. Louis," *NMHR*, LXV (April 1990), 161–174. José Juliano took his money and ran, but not home to his wife and family, for in 1809 he resided in San Antonio de Béxar, where Comandante Salcedo ordered his return to Santa Fe. See *SANM*, II, no. 2239, roll 16, frames 920–922.

With the Frenchman-turned-Indian Pedro Vial, he participated in the earliest Euramerican trailblazing expeditions between Tejas (Texas) and New Mexico in the 1780s and 1790s. Chaves managed also to reclaim kin and cultural ties with the Comanches, for as late as 1792 Vial encountered him on the Plains east of Pecos traveling with seven Comanches and their wives. He had spent the last three years among these Comanche kinspeople, and now Chaves told Vial that they were heading for New Mexico in order to see his parents. Chaves found ways to connect the flexible kinship relations of his adoptive people with those blood relatives he had left behind more than twenty years before. Throughout his life, he inhabited, or coexisted in, multiple social worlds, fluidly crossing back and forth between them.[33]

They Take up the Barbarous Life of Those Who Consider Them Slaves

Ecological and epidemiological forces also played a role in driving the expansion of a Plains capture-and-slavery complex. A prolonged drought gripped the Southwest from 1777 to 1779, reducing agricultural production in the Río Grande valley and affecting the western provinces of the Hopis and Navajos even more severely. A devastating series of smallpox epidemics, beginning in the 1770s and extending until 1781, accompanied this famine in a plague extending from the Gulf of Mexico northward into the headwaters of the Missouri River. Whereas several hundred Spanish settlers died, more than five thousand Pueblo Indians succumbed to the disease. Plains Indian losses might have run even higher. It appears that the smallpox entered New Mexico from the southern Plains with nomadic trading parties, including the Comanches. No reliable death figures are available for the Plains tribes, but epidemiologists believe that all people not immune to the disease will contract it upon exposure, with attendant fatality rates ranging between 10 and 50 percent. One division of the Comanches was reported to have lost two-thirds of its member-

33. Chaves's first mission is recorded in "El viaje de una embajada de paz a la nación Comanche," in Represa, ed., *La España ilustrada en el lejano oeste,* 11–28, 17, 26. Elizabeth A. H. John and Adán Benavides, Jr., have edited and translated this diary as "Inside the Comanchería, 1785: The Diary of Pedro Vial and Francisco Xavier Chaves," *Southwestern Historical Quarterly,* XCVIII (1994–1995), 25–56. John discusses his many diplomatic achievements in *Storms Brewed,* 649–652. For Vial's life, see Noel M. Loomis and Abraham P. Nasatir, *Pedro Vial and the Roads to Santa Fe* (Norman, Okla., 1967), 357, 360, 373.

ship by 1785. Compounding the crisis, in the late 1780s drought withered Plains grasslands, depleting bison herds and visiting famine on the Comanches.[34]

Comanches responded with an increase in captive and livestock plundering along all the northern borderlands, suggesting a strategic shift in their raiding economies. When Comanche populations flourished, as they did before the 1770s, the seizure and resale of captives seems the predominant pattern, given their value in the regional exchange economy. But, with severe population losses and widespread hunger, captures for assimilation and livestock thefts for food became the favored pattern. In the six years between 1771 and 1776 alone, Nueva Vizcaya suffered 1,674 persons killed and 154 captured, 116 haciendas abandoned, and 68,256 head of livestock stolen.[35]

No definitive figures for Spanish losses exist to substantiate an increase in Plains captive raiding, but in 1780 an *expediente* issued by Teodoro de Croix from Arizpe suggested that the *Provincias Internas* "establish an alms gathering . . . all proceeds of which go to the ransom of captives" from the various Indian *naciones del norte.* In that "the parents or relatives may be so poor that they have no property or funds with which to pay," such a plan would "be beneficial to humanity, to the state, and to the Faith." In response, Inspector General Antonio Bonilla betrayed the anxiety felt by Spanish elites at the presence of an alternative worldview on their borders. His comments characterized well the complexity of a system of bondage in which violence, attraction, deracination, subjugation, fictive kinship, sexual desire, and affinal ties were interwoven. By the late eighteenth century, the borderlands had become a place of cultural exchange:

> These prisoners adopt and take up the debauched, barbarous life of those who consider them slaves. This evil extends even to adults, especially those

34. Marc Simmons, "New Mexico's Smallpox Epidemic of 1780–1781," *NMHR,* XLI (October 1966), 319–326; John, *Storms Brewed,* 593. For a 1785 firsthand report in which Comanche losses are reported at two-thirds of their population, reducing their numbers to two thousand men-at-arms, or six to eight thousand total, see "El viaje de una embajada de paz a la nación Comanche," in Represa, ed., *La España ilustrada en el lejano oeste,* 1–28, 17, 26. In response to the Comanche starvation, Governor Fernando de la Concha sent 200 *fanegas* from the presidial warehouses, and the people of Santa Fe contributed another 160 fanegas. See "Ugarte y Loyola to Concha, 7 December, 1789," in *SANM,* II, no. 1067, roll 12, frames 221–226.

35. Croix to Bucareli, Sept. 27, 1777, cited in Bernard E. Bobb, *The Viceregency of Antonio María Bucareli in New Spain, 1771–1779* (Austin, Tex., 1962), 151–152.

of the feminine sex . . . on the account of the lascivious vice of sensuality at which [Spanish captives] are at the greatest liberty to indulge themselves. Contributing to the release and liberty of the unfortunate persons who grieve under the most unmerciful bondage is a most pious and charitable act.[36]

By 1784, don Phelipe de Neve had instituted the almsgiving plan, but "scarcely were enough funds produced to pay for the first expedition." At least "one hundred and fifty-two captives, of both sexes" were known to be held in captivity, but collections had "been insufficient to defray the costs entailed." Citizens of provincial Texas had donated only 479 pesos, and New Mexicans contributed none at all. Redemption costs in the form of trade goods could rise as high as 200 pesos per captive, and, although twenty repatriations were effected, by 1791 the *limosna* fund quietly expired. Plains Indians drove a hard bargain in order to retain their captives. Beyond their immediate value as new kinspeople, children born of captive Spanish women probably carried greater resistance to European microbes, a quality that the epidemics of the 1770s and 1780s might well have made obvious. Those who remained among their captors in "unmerciful bondage" probably spent their lives there, herding horses, tanning hides, making robes, and perhaps strengthening Indian populations through indulgences in sensuality.[37]

Poverty in the Spanish provinces might also have prevented redemption of lost kinsfolk, since most, but not all, captives came from poor families. Wealthy families who underwrote the gathering of alms might simply have sought their own private rescue strategies. But, also, poor borderland settlers possibly made some hard choices concerning the loss of their relatives and its potential social and economic rewards. Given the likelihood that their captive relatives had become members of Plains Indian societies, and that this membership extended social and economic privileges along kin lines, lower-order settlers might have seen the almsgiving and redemption plan as commendable but expensive and potentially harmful, meddling with what was becoming a workable system.

36. "*Expediente* of El Caballero de Croix to Domingo Cabello, Señor Governador de Texas, June 6, 1780," "Bonilla's Certification of June 15, 1780," 4 fols., Bexar Archives, Barker Texas History Collection, University of Texas, Austin (hereafter cited as Bexar Archives), 42.

37. "*Bando* of Don Phelipe de Neve, Governor and Commandant General of the Interior Provinces of New Spain, Dated May 8, 1784," Bexar Archives; Russell Mario Magnaghi, "The Indian Slave Trader: The Comanche, a Case Study" (Ph.D. diss., St. Louis University, 1970), 144–147.

Had Plains Indian societies been entirely self-sufficient, servitude might have remained strictly within the arena of kinship and its several beneficial results. But consistent need for agricultural products and European trade goods pulled against ties of kinship when captives simultaneously embodied real value in the exchange economy. The captive exchange system predated European contact, forming a core element in a Plainswide exchange complex, but, by the late eighteenth century, it began to intersect with the expanding Atlantic economy. Although the indigenous system functioned independently for some time, intensive interaction among the Spanish, Apaches, Pawnees, French, and Comanches would rapidly expand the geographic scale and cultural meaning of human exchange. This transformation would overlay exchanges in the realm of kinship with new incentives toward commodification, although the kinship element would persist and shape the experience of its victims.

As the regional webs of the captive network expanded, the system also became more internally complicated. In Indian societies, the prestige attendant on the conspicuous display of dependents enlarged the servile population and fueled more captive raiding. The cultural consequences of captive absorption in New Mexican colonial society created a people who would ultimately knit these webs into a more unified whole through intermarriage and cultural exchanges yet simultaneously pose internal challenges to the stability of colonial society. These people were the genízaros, whose story will unfold below. But, first, we need to examine the internal political consequences for Comanche peoples of their increasing interdependence with the Spanish colony in New Mexico.

A Barbarian Has Raised Himself up among That Nation

In their initial expansion out of the Great Basin and onto the Plains, the Comanches' highly localized and personalistic social and political organization had worked to put them in a position of power on the southern borderlands. By the 1780s, however, broader processes placed new pressures on this adaptation. The Comanche economy had become more complicated, with horse pastoralism developing alongside subsistence bison hunting. Comanche horses became a commodity sought by other Indian groups, New Mexicans, Texans, and Anglo-American traders on the Mississippi. Likewise, bison products — dried meat, tallow, and hides — acquired increased market values in New Mexico and Texas. Growing market involvement required additional laborers, especially herders and hide processors, customarily boys and women, respectively. A Comanche man's ability to benefit from market participation correlated with the number of such laborers in his household. Accordingly, polygamous marriage increased during the period, as did competition between men for wives. But natural increase could not meet this need, and captive seizure and adoption provided a perilous but effective way of increasing the dependent labor pool.[38]

Paradoxically, as the Comanches grew in economic strength, they also experienced a growing sense of vulnerability. Participation in larger market circuits fostered an increasing dependency on forces beyond their control. The drought in the Southwest during the late 1770s produced famine in New Mexico and depleted grazing resources on the southern Plains, reducing Comanche ability to trade for New Mexican agricultural products, to find bison, and to maintain their horse herds. Their first experience with smallpox in the same period probably shook the psychological foundations of Comanche society. These latent and tangible crises pushed Comanches to pursue cultural and political innovation.

For all the attention that scholars have given to geopolitical conflicts in stimulating the Spanish-Comanche Peace of 1786, trade imperatives, drought, and disease played equally significant roles. The stunning defeat of Comanche captain Cuerno Verde (Green Horn) in 1779, while humbling to Comanches generally and boosting morale among New Mexican militiamen, highlighted little more than the futility of military solutions. In the years following this battle, Plains Indians and New Mexicans alike needed new regional accommodations that would permit mutual survival.

The case of the Cuerno Verdes, for the name applies to two men, demonstrates some of the difficult adjustments facing Comanche society in the late eighteenth century. Whether these men rose to leadership among the Jupes or Yamparikas remains unclear, but they probably claimed adherents in young men from both groups, whose territorial core included the drainages of the Arkansas River. The first documentary mention of Cuerno Verde occurs shortly before a 1768 attack on the genízaro outpost of Ojo Caliente north of Abiquiu.

38. Dan Flores, "Bison Ecology and Bison Diplomacy: The Southern Plains from 1800 to 1850," *Journal of American History,* LXXVIII (1991–1992), 472. For Comanche trade in horses and bison products with New Mexico and Texas, see John, "Nurturing the Peace: Spanish and Comanche Cooperation in the Early Nineteenth Century," *NMHR,* LIX (October 1984), 345–369.

Questioning a Comanche captive held by Taos Indians in 1767, Governor Pedro Mendinueta learned that

> a barbarian has raised himself up among that nation with the appearance and accoutrements of those of a little king. He has near his person a guard of armed men, pages who serve him when he mounts and dismounts from his horse, holding a canopy or shade of buffalo skins for him in which he takes his seat. All obey him.[39]

The subsequent attack at Ojo Caliente was led by a captain "whose leather headdress bore a green horn." This man was slain in the raid, but another, who might well have been his son, quickly donned his headdress, name, and claim to leadership.[40]

The younger Cuerno Verde engaged in a ten-year war against New Mexicans and the eastern pueblos of Galisteo and Pecos. His motivation might have lain with blood revenge, but Governor Mendinueta's decision to shift alliance-building efforts from the Comanches to the Natagé and Sierra Blanca Apaches at this moment could have figured just as prominently. Having heard from a recently repatriated Taos Indian held captive by Comanches that the Comanches had lately traded horses to the Jumanos for "seventeen loads of [English] guns and munitions," the governor panicked and sought an Apache alliance. This switch in the beneficiaries of New Spain's dwindling diplomatic gifts probably provoked Comanche anger as much as did the loss of the senior Cuerno Verde.[41]

The targets of Cuerno Verde's raids bear out this suggestion. Although some Comanche bands "did not find it inconvenient to present themselves peacefully at Taos to trade," Cuerno Verde's warriors dealt brutally with the Galisteo and Pecos Pueblos, where the Natagés and Sierra Blancas came to collect their gifts. By the late 1770s, Galisteo was abandoned, Pecos decimated to a

39. Mendinueta to viceroy, June 18, 1767, in Thomas, trans. and ed., *Plains Indians*, 167.

40. John, *Storms Brewed*, 468–469; she draws upon Anza's diary, in which he claims Cuerno Verde's father "held the same command and power" and "met death at our hands." See also Thomas, trans. and ed., *Forgotten Frontiers: A Study of the Spanish Indian Policy of Don Juan Bautista de Anza, Governor of New Mexico, 1777–1787 . . .* (Norman, Okla., 1932), 135–136; Kavanagh, *Comanche Political History*, 92–93.

41. Mendinueta to viceroy, June 18, 1767, in Thomas, trans. and ed., *Plains Indians*, 162. Jumanos and their relations with Comanches and colonial New Mexicans: Nancy Parrott Hickerson, *The Jumanos: Hunters and Traders of the South Plains* (Austin, Tex., 1994).

population of 269 people, and Pecos's stock reduced to "eight old cows and a dozen sorry horses." With Apache access points destroyed, the Apache alliance quickly unraveled, and the Natagés and Sierra Blancas moved south to join their Lipan cousins in developing a raiding economy in the borderlands of Nueva Vizcaya.[42]

Such was the situation that Juan Bautista de Anza inherited when he became governor of New Mexico in 1778. Understanding that a Comanche peace could be built only upon stable trading relations, and that Cuerno Verde, whatever his motives, must be punished to restore provincial morale, Anza embarked on the single most successful military expedition in New Mexican history. His campaign's success derived from innovative tactics, fortunate timing, and probable internal dissension among the Comanches.

The governor refused to follow traditional routes from the Río Grande valley to the Plains, traveling instead northward through the San Luis Valley of Colorado and over Ponca Pass into the South Park area before turning eastward into the *comanchería.* His approach, therefore, was not detected until he engaged Cuerno Verde's encampment on present-day Fountain Creek, Colorado. In a stroke of good fortune for Anza, Cuerno Verde was gone—engaged in an unsuccessful attack on Taos Pueblo with a force of 250 warriors at the same time Anza moved against his ranchería. By the time Anza's force, moving southward with their booty of thirty-four captive women and children and five hundred horses, engaged Cuerno Verde, he had with him only "fifty men of his daily and personal guard, to attack six hundred men in good formation." The other two hundred men seem to have melted away in the aftermath of the Taos failure, perhaps anticipating a momentous change in Comanche leadership. Some Comanche bands, and some of his own people, appear to have grown tired of his relentless raiding and self-aggrandizement.[43]

42. "Governor Mendinueta's Proposals for the Defense of New Mexico, 1772–1778," *NMHR,* VI (January 1931), 26–36, esp. 34; John, *Storms Brewed,* 483. For a detailed firsthand report of Spanish-Apache relations in eighteenth-century Nueva Vizcaya that shows a remarkable sensitivity to the historical problems of Apache groups, see José Cortés, *Views from the Apache Frontier: Report on the Northern Provinces of New Spain,* ed. Elizabeth A. H. John, trans. John Wheat (Norman, Okla., 1989). For the Apache "raiding and poaching economy," see Anderson, *Indian Southwest,* 128–143; for the nineteenth century, see William B. Griffen, *Utmost Good Faith: Patterns of Apache-Mexican Hostilities in Northern Chihuahua Border Warfare, 1821–1848* (Albuquerque, N.Mex., 1988).

43. "Diary of Anza's Campaign against the Comanche, 1779," in Thomas, trans. and ed., *Forgotten Frontiers,* 136.

Cuerno Verde's defeat in 1779 did not bring the Comanches to their knees, however. The limited evidence suggests that after 1770 various factions had competed for political sway. More conservative band leaders like Cuerno Verde and Captain Toroblanco of the Yamparicas had conducted freelance raids against the border pueblos, whereas innovators like Paruanarimuca of the Jupes and Cuetaninabeni and Ecueracapa of the Cuchanticas sought stabilized relations. The issue was largely resolved in 1785, when Ecueracapa's agents killed Toroblanco as he attempted to flee his ranchería on horseback.[44]

While Cuerno Verde's death marked a singular achievement of Spanish arms, it also signaled a new era in Comanche political organization. Henceforth, Comanche band leaders like Cuerno Verde, who sought power and prestige at the expense of trade relations with New Mexico, would find themselves abandoned or, in the case of Toroblanco, assassinated. Probably aware of an emergent Sioux-Cheyenne alliance in the north-central Plains, which drew its military hardware from American traders, Comanches realized the need for stable relations with a European ally. By 1786, the Comanches had created a new political structure aimed specifically at seeking "a new adjustment and establishment of their commerce in New Mexico."[45]

Fittingly, initial steps toward treaty making involved Spanish colonists and Comanches in a chance meeting on the Plains, where the former were venturing to emulate the latter in a bison hunt. Fraught with danger, the encounter owed its success to the presence of a captive acting as an intercultural emissary. On December 10, 1785, some two months before the Spanish and Comanches would solidify their agreement in Santa Fe, Anza's lieutenant Pedro Garrido y Duran reported,

> It happened that a party of Spaniards were buffalo hunting [when] an Indian called José Chiquito, having become separated from [the Spanish] was made prisoner by spies of Ecueracapa, who took him for a pagan whose costume he was wearing. They wished to let him go immediately on noticing the mistake, but because of his having resisted and entreated them in the Comanche language, which he spoke fairly well, they took him to the *ranchería*. Being conducted into the presence of the above-mentioned captain, he was

44. Pedro Garrido y Duran, "An Account of the Events concerning the Comanche Peace, 1785–1786," in Thomas, trans. and ed., *Forgotten Frontiers*, 298–299.

45. John H. Moore, *The Cheyenne Nation: A Social and Demographic History* (Lincoln, Nebr., 1987), esp. 77, 133–139; Garrido, "An Account of the Events concerning the Comanche Peace," in Thomas, trans. and ed., *Forgotten Frontiers*, 295.

> fed, clothed and treated with the greatest generosity and humanity. Ecueracapa thus took advantage of this happy accident to initiate his commission.[46]

Testimony to the ease with which a potentially violent moment could be transformed through a captive's agency and Comanche diplomatic customs of generosity, the report also provides a glimpse at the cultural indeterminacy some captives showed even after years in the power of another people. José Chiquito still offered the appearance of a "pagan" Indian and was initially mistaken for a member of an enemy people. He still spoke Comanche "fairly well" and seems to have understood the honor Ecueracapa bestowed on him in offering hospitality. Ecueracapa seized the opportunity to initiate peace negotiations through José Chiquito rather than have peace proposed from without by Anza.[47]

Ecueracapa's initiative had its origins in a significant change in Comanche political organization. Some months earlier, probably following the autumn buffalo hunt, more than six hundred "camps or rancherias" had gathered at "La Casa de Palo" on the Arkansas River. The gathering, sponsored by the Kotseka (Buffalo Eaters) division, included two additional divisions of the Comanches, the Jupes and the Yamparicas. As such, it constituted a temporary assemblage of three northern divisions who ranged from the Rocky Mountains to the crosstimbers country of Texas and probably numbered some four thousand people.[48]

At this meeting, the Comanches "resolved to elect and designate one among them in order" to negotiate a peace and establish stable commerce with New Mexico. They chose Ecueracapa, or Cota de Malla, known in Comanche as "Contatanacapara," "one without equal in military achievements." Ecueracapa accepted the commission with the assurance that he "would be abandoned

46. Garrido, "An Account of the Events concerning the Comanche Peace," in Thomas, trans. and ed., *Forgotten Frontiers*, 294–321, esp. 296.

47. In a debate around the "band" or "tribal" nature of Comanche social organization, both Melburn D. Thurman and Daniel J. Gelo deny the Comanches' initiative in seeking the treaty of 1786. See Thurman, "A New Interpretation of Comanche Social Organization," *Current Anthropology*, XXIII (October 1982), 578–579; Gelo, "On a New Interpretation of Comanche Social Organization," ibid., 551–555; the evidence clearly supports the alternative viewpoint of Kavanagh, *Comanche Political History*, 110–121.

48. Garrido, "An Account of the Events concerning the Comanche Peace," in Thomas, trans. and ed., *Forgotten Frontiers*, 294–295.

neither by [the other captains] nor by their subjects" and that, if betrayed, he "would attach himself to the Spanish party." Having reached this general understanding, when the chance arose months later with José Chiquito, Ecueracapa dispatched him to Santa Fe.[49]

Following in the path of his emissary, Ecueracapa arrived in Santa Fe on February 25, 1786, riding in triumph through formal ranks of soldiers and citizens, to which were added "spontaneous festive demonstrations of the somewhat large crowd." The Comanche leader offered his terms: a general and binding cessation of hostilities in return for the right to "settle and subsist a short distance from the settlements"; free passage through the Pecos corridor "for greater cultivation of the reciprocal friendship and commerce of both parties"; a combined campaign against the Apaches; and, finally, suitable tokens or credentials from Anza to confirm the peace among the "scattered rancherías" of his people.[50]

Ecueracapa's election and subsequent negotiations illuminate the Comanches' strategic needs at the end of the eighteenth century. The Casa de Palo gathering was probably the first such congress in Comanche history, a recognition that stable commercial relations with New Mexico stood to deliver better results than the earlier pattern of freelance raiding and trading. Such a negotiation required at least a nominal leader with whom New Mexicans would treat, and Ecueracapa filled that role well. A highly respected man among Comanches and Spanish alike, he understood that his authority depended upon the good opinion of his fellow captains, and he consistently sought their council. In this and later meetings with Spanish authorities, he included a wide array of colleagues, thus honoring the diffused nature of Comanche local authority while responding to the situational need for concentrated leadership in diplomatic negotiations.

Ecueracapa's treaty terms also indicate that trade relations were the primary goal to which the other terms were linked. Often attributed to the "traditional enmity" between the Comanches and Apaches, the anti-Apache alliance of 1786 was clearly grounded in material realities. The right to dwell safely near New Mexican villages and to trade at Pecos and Santa Fe required the elimination of the Apaches, since Pecos had historically served as the Apache trading point, as had Taos for the Comanches. Ecueracapa showed remarkable fore-

49. Ibid., 295–296.

50. Ibid., 300–301.

sight in pursuing the Pecos gateway, since the route up the Pecos River would soon become a major commercial artery for Euramericans as well, while the Taos trade remained more local in character.

Anza acceded to all the Comanches' requests, and the conflicts of preceding years were ritually buried in the soil. A new relationship was forming that would hold well into the next century, and the Comanches took seriously their role in that peace. One of the captains who accompanied Ecueracapa, Tosapoy of the Jupes, offered a stirring confessional in which he promised a new commitment to "equity and justice in the particular matter of commerce." He admitted that the fault for "violence and deceit" that sometimes had occurred at trade fairs lay with him, especially in the matter of a quarrel between himself and "an individual Spaniard who was present." As an act of repentance, and a deft tactical move, he "delivered (on his knees) a native of Santa Fe whom they had there. This good fortune fell upon Alezandro Martín who was a prisoner among them for eleven years." From his base at San Miguel del Vado, Martín would become a key actor in cultural exchanges between Comanches and New Mexicans through the early decades of the nineteenth century.[51]

This symbolic transaction smoothed the way for more mundane exchanges, and the following day a full-fledged *feria* commenced. In return for New Mexican iron knives, *serapes,* and hard bread, the Comanches traded more than "six hundred hides, many loads of meat, animal fat, fifteen mounts and three guns." Well satisfied, they concurred with Anza that another fair be held at Pecos in July, and, with "extravagant farewells," the Comanches returned to the Plains.[52]

Several months later, as spring brought the first combined Spanish-Comanche campaign against the Apaches, Ecueracapa sealed his agreement with Anza in a distinctively Comanche manner. On May 28, he sent his twenty-year-old third son, Tahuchimpia, to Santa Fe with the charge that Anza "instruct his son in the language and customs of the Spanish as if he were his own child." Familiar with the forms of Comanche institutionalized friendship and adoptive ritual, Anza accepted the young man and apparently arranged for his education in Mexico City. Tahuchimpia and his elder brothers, Oxamaquea and Tomanaguene, would accompany Anza in his combined Spanish-Comanche-Navajo campaign against the Gila Apaches in July 1786. Later that fall, Tahuchimpia and Tomanaguene joined the annual *cordón* to Chihuahua

51. Ibid., 303–304; Kessell, *Kiva, Cross, and Crown,* 405–407, 430, 551 n. 20.

52. Thomas, *Forgotten Frontiers,* 76–77.

with ten other Comanches to formalize the treaty with Comandante General Jacobo Ugarte y Loyola. When Ecueracapa died at the hands of the Pawnees in 1793, the Cuchanticas requested that the now-literate Tahuchimpia return to lead them. He was doing so as late as 1812, according to at least one Spanish source.[53]

By 1786, customs of captivity and servitude in Plains Indian and New Mexican society alike had facilitated economic and cultural exchanges that contributed directly to the establishment of formal diplomatic relations. With these developments, certain indigenous and colonizing peoples on the Plains would begin to utilize their distinct interpretations of commerce, kinship, and coercion to craft various "borderland communities of interest" that often stood in marked opposition to the social boundaries their political superiors sought to maintain. Similar processes west of the Río Grande involving Navajos and New Mexicans yielded another type of borderland, organized around a common sheep-raising culture and drawing again upon the reciprocal captive trade. The very success of their pastoral adaptation would, in the nineteenth century, make them the first focus of American pacification and emancipation programs.

53. This is the first occasion of Comanches' acting as a border cavalry in the service of Spain. Few, if any, Spanish accompanied this foray, but its progress was carefully recorded in a *Tarja* (Tally sheet) that Anza had prepared and sent with Ecueracapa. Five hundred ninety-three Comanches from the Cuchantica, Yamparica, and Jupes divisions participated and killed six Apaches, taking two captive as well as seizing eighty horses and mules. It seems that the Comanches retained the latter, as rewards for their services. This document is treated in Thomas, "An Eighteenth Century Comanche Document," *American Anthropologist,* N.S., XXXI (1929), 289–298; with additional details, it is discussed in Kavanagh, *Comanche Political History,* 116–117; Thomas, *Forgotten Frontiers,* 313–314; John, *Storms Brewed,* 714; don Pedro Baptista Pino, *The Exposition on the Province of New Mexico, 1812,* trans. and ed. Adrian Bustamante and Marc Simmons (Albuquerque, N.Mex., 1995), n. 130.

3

LOS PASTORES

CREATING A PASTORAL BORDERLAND

Less than one month after Comanche captain Ecueracapa and don Juan Bautista de Anza affirmed their historic treaty in Santa Fe, some eighty Navajos gathered at a crossing of the Río Puerco to negotiate treaty terms themselves with the governor. Like the Apaches, Comanches, and Kiowas of the Plains borderlands, Navajos and the Pueblo and Spanish residents of the Río Grande valley were enmeshed in enduring patterns of contention and accommodation. Building upon and intensifying a mixed economy of trading and raiding for foodstuffs and captives that had characterized precontact Athapaskan / Pueblo relations, Navajos and New Mexican colonists developed a new focus of contentious exchange in a colonial import: sheep. Whereas on the Plains bison and horses underlay much of the emergent political economy, during the century following the Great Southwestern Revolt, sheep pastoralism would emerge as the primary subsistence practice among many Navajos. New Mexican pobladores also began to place greater weight on sheepherding, since a burgeoning colonial population increasingly depleted irrigable farming lands in the Río Grande valley. But with these stepwise adjustments in subsistence practices came tensions within and without both societies. Pastoral wealth in sheep, and the dependent labor to manage those flocks, proved unequally distributed among Navajos and New Mexicans alike. The eighteenth century would see class tensions emerge within both groups and play themselves out across cultural boundaries. As the indigenous and colonial *pastores* sought to maintain cultural integrity while elaborating a common sheep culture, systemic patterns of coexistence and conflict were driven by relative access to three resources: people, livestock, and land. This borderland, too, had its making much earlier, in relations between the indigenous peoples of the Río Grande valley and those of the plateaus to the west.

They Carry on Trade with Those in the Settlements

> At last two couriers were sent to the north. When these got back to their kindred they said they had found a race of strange men, who cut their hair straight in front, who lived in houses in the ground and cultivated fields. These people, who were engaged in gathering their harvest, the couriers said, treated them very kindly and gave them food to eat. . . . The newly discovered race—Kisáni (Pueblos) they were called—entered the camp of exiles and guided the latter to a stream of water. . . . The Kisáni gave the wanderers corn and pumpkins to eat, and the latter lived for some time on the food given to them daily by their new friends.[1]

Yet Navajo-Pueblo comity in the fourth world would prove fragile in this, the fifth. Hungry, cold, and frightened on the island that survived the great flood of the fourth world, and unable to find game, some young Navajo men looked at the camp of the Kisáni who had accompanied them to the fifth world and saw that they "had brought with them from the lower world an ear of corn for seed." They demanded corn of the Kisáni. And, although the Kisáni broke their ear of corn to share with the Navajo, the damage had been done. "The Pueblos had become alarmed at the threats and angry language of their neighbors and moved away from them, and this is why the Navajoes and Pueblos now live apart from one another."[2]

Food as substance and symbol, then, lay at the very center of amity and dissension in the passage between the worlds of the Navajos' origin narrative. But so too did women and children serve as objects of contestation. In fact, harmony in the fourth world had been riven by conflict between men and women, when each in their pride had claimed the ability to survive without the other. They split for a time, separated by a deep river. Although the women came to accept that their horticultural domain could prosper only with men's assistance, and men to understand that without women "surely [their] race would perish," in their attempt to reunite across the river two girls were lost to Tiéholtsodi, the water monster, who dragged them beneath the swift current. Accompanied by Coyote, a man and woman braved the river and rescued

1. Washington Matthews, comp. and trans., *Navaho Legends* (1897; Salt Lake City, Utah, 1994), 68.

2. Ibid., 78.

the girls—but did not see that Coyote had stolen two of Tiéholtsodi's children in return, concealing them beneath his robe. In retaliation for this offense, Tiéholtsodi flooded the fourth world, in turn ushering men and women, both Navajos and Pueblos, into the perils of the fifth.[3]

The quality of intercultural relations between Pueblos and Athapaskans on the eve of Spanish colonialism has long proved a ground of scholarly debate. Until archaeological dating methods proved it impossible, many assumed that predatory Athapaskans were to blame for the collapse of ancestral Pueblo civilization in the Southwest. Documentary evidence from seventeenth-century New Mexico, showing warfare between Pueblos and Athapaskans, was "upstreamed" to the fifteenth century to show long-term conflict. Jack D. Forbes challenged this view, asserting instead, "The essential relationship existing between the Athapascans and the Pueblo Indians prior to Spanish interference was one of peace and commerce." Forbes offered strong evidence for Athapaskan-Pueblo comity while acknowledging that warfare occasionally marred this condition. Modern scholars have applied ecological cooperation and competition models to the Southwest and found widespread economic interdependency between Pueblos and their semisedentary neighbors. But competition and conflict also seem common, and not always in association with periods of ecological stress. Cultural factors seem to lie at the heart of this violence, frustratingly concealed by time. Human exchanges must have been part of material relations such as trade, in ways that entailed both accommodation and conflict.[4]

3. Ibid., 71–74. For an account that places the transition from hunting to agriculture and sexual infidelity among Navajos as the crux of gendered conflict in this origin narrative, see Berard Haile, "Women versus Men: A Conflict of Navajo Emergence," in Karl W. Luckert, ed., *American Tribal Religions*, VI (Lincoln, Nebr., 1981); the standard modern exegesis of the Navajo origin narrative, using Matthews's text as starting point, is Paul G. Zolbrod, *Diné Bahané: The Navaho Creation Story* (Albuquerque, N.Mex., 1984).

4. Drawing on his fieldwork for the Bureau of American Ethnology, Adolph F. Bandelier popularized the notion of predatory Athapaskans in his novel, *The Delight Makers* ([1890]; New York, 1971); see also his *Final Report of Investigations among the Indians of the Southwestern United States*, I (Cambridge, 1890). For recent chronology and current theories involving resource depletion, internal social strife, and gradual, sequential abandonment, see Linda S. Cordell, *Prehistory of the Southwest* (Orlando, Fla., 1984), 303–326. Herbert Eugene Bolton, in his efforts to criticize the Black Legend of treasure-hunting Spaniards brutalizing all the Indians they encountered, portrayed the Pueblos as eager to embrace the Spanish alliance. See "The Mission as a Frontier Institution in the Spanish American Colonies," in John

The Athapaskan-speakers who came to be known historically as the Navajos probably entered New Mexico in the fifteenth century. Although scholars differ whether these people were a branch of bison-hunting Plains Athapaskans or Great Basin–Frémont migrant hunter-horticulturists, most agree that a distinctive linguistic and cultural group appears in the archaeological record by 1600, in the northern drainages of the modern San Juan River. Here, in the region known as *Dinetah,* or the Navajo homeland, kin clusters of three to five nuclear family groups lived in forked-stick hogans near the canyon bottoms, practicing a mixed economy of men's hunting and women's horticulture. The matrilineal organization of Navajo society seems to draw upon this deeply rooted horticultural practice, in contrast to "pure pastoralists," who are almost exclusively patrilineal. This matrilineal orientation was embedded in Navajo cosmology and reinforced over time by the absorption of refugees and captives from the matrilineal Pueblo peoples of New Mexico.[5]

Francis Bannon, ed., *Bolton and the Spanish Borderlands* (Norman, Okla., 1964); Jack D. Forbes, *Apache, Navaho, and Spaniard* (1960; Norman, Okla., 1994), 282. For ecological conflict and accommodation, see Katherine A. Spielmann, "Coercion or Cooperation? Plains-Pueblo Interaction in the Protohistoric Period," in Spielmann, ed., *Farmers, Hunters, and Colonists: Interaction between the Southwest and the Southern Plains* (Tucson, Ariz., 1991); for an argument that sees interpueblo warfare (often over the theft of women) as the dominant force in Southwestern prehistoric settlement types and patterns into which Athapaskans and Spaniards might have introduced some interpueblo stability, see Steven A. LeBlanc, *Prehistoric Warfare in the American Southwest* (Salt Lake City, Utah, 1999), esp. 197–276.

5. The earliest dendrochronological date to which Navajo traits have been ascribed is A.D. 1421-plus on Mariana Mesa, north of Quemado, New Mexico. For the next two centuries, we have thirty-five dates that cluster heavily on Mariano Mesa (twenty-three) and another, smaller cluster farther north in the Chacra Mesa / Gobernador region (seven). See Vivian R. Gwinn, "The Navajo Archaeology of the Chacra Mesa, New Mexico" (master's thesis, University of New Mexico, 1960), 156 and table A; Joseph C. Winter and Patrick Hogan, "The Dinetah Phase of Northwestern New Mexico: Settlement and Subsistence," in Bradley J. Vierra, ed., *Current Research on the Late Prehistory and Early History of New Mexico* (Albuquerque, N.Mex., 1992); J. Loring Haskell, *Southern Athapaskan Migration, A.D. 200–1750* (Tsaile, Ariz., 1987), esp. 92; for modern scholarship that generally supports the sixteenth-century arrivals, see Ronald H. Towner, ed., *The Archaeology of Navajo Origins* (Salt Lake City, Utah, 1996). For a discussion of pastoral social organization, see Paula G. Rubel, "Herd Composition and Social Structure: On Building Models of Nomadic Pastoral Societies," *Man,* N.S., IV (June 1969), 268–273; Stephen Pastner, "Camels, Sheep, and Nomad Social Organisation: A Comment on Rubel's Model," *Man,* N.S., VI (June 1971),

Although sixteenth-century Spanish explorers recorded these peoples under the generalized term *Querechos* (from the Jémez [Towa] *Kearai+tsa'a),* the farming tradition is reflected in the name by which they later appear in Spanish colonial documents, as "Indios Apaches del Navaju." Combining the Zuñi word *apachú* ("enemies") with the Tewa compound noun *navahuu* meaning a "large arroyo [stream course] with cultivated fields," Padre Gerónimo Zarate Salmerón in 1626 invented an identity for a people who termed themselves *Diné.* Zarate's invention, however, conveys descriptive and analytical significance, for it points to a historically ambiguous relationship between the Navajos and their Puebloan neighbors—peoples sharing some elements of subsistence practice and social organization, yet often in conflict with each other.[6]

On the one hand, archaeological investigations reveal Pueblo ceramics in Navajo sites as early as the late fifteenth century, suggesting that finer Pueblo wares might have been prestige items in economic exchanges. Although cache-pits and granaries at Navajo settlements are an indication for some surplus maize and squash production, hunting appears the dominant subsistence strategy. The greater mobility of Navajo camps (as compared to Pueblo villages) increased their ability to kill and process game into exchangeable com-

---

285–288. Of course, horticultural and agricultural societies contain matrilineal, patrilineal, and cognatic descent systems. For Navajo kinship and social organization, see Gary Witherspoon, *Navajo Kinship and Marriage* (Chicago, 1975), 15–22. Haskell's thesis that Navajos descended from Great Basin–Frémont hunter-horticulturalists, rather than bison-hunting Plains Athapaskans, lends credence to this view that sees matrilineality preceding the influence of Puebloan adoptees *(Southern Athapaskan Migrations,* 92–97). For strong evidence of horticultural practice during the Dinetah Phase (1550–1700), see Michael P. Marshall and Patrick Hogan, *Rethinking Navajo Pueblitos* (Albuquerque, N.Mex., 1991), 299–312.

6. For a reference to Querechos in Coronado's 1540 expedition, see George Peter Hammond and Agapito Rey, trans. and eds., *Narratives of the Coronado Expedition, 1540–1542* (Albuquerque, N.Mex., 1940), 185; for the Towa derivation of the name, see John P. Harrington, "Southern Peripheral Athapaskawan Origins, Divisions, and Migrations," *Smithsonian Miscellaneous Collections,* C (1940), 503–532. Usually suffixed to a clan name (such as *Cinzakadiné,* "Cedar Standing by Themselves People," or *Cahiskidni,* "Sagebrush Hill People"), this term should not be understood as constituting a "national" identity. See also Forbes, *Apache, Navaho, and Spaniard,* 114–115; L. R. Bailey, *If You Take My Sheep: The Evolution and Conflicts of Navajo Pastoralism, 1630–1868* (Pasadena, Calif., 1980), 37; Donald E. Worcester, "The Navajo during the Spanish Regime in New Mexico," *New Mexico Historical Review* (hereafter cited as *NMHR),* XXVI (April 1951), 101–118.

modities. In the historic period, Spanish sources contain some evidence of amicable trade relations between Athapaskans and Pueblos. In 1583, in an exploratory entrada seeking gold and silver, Antonio de Espejo reported that "Curechos" visited the pueblo of Ácoma to

> carry on trade with those in the settlements, taking them salt, game such as deer, rabbit, and hares, tanned deer skins and other things to trade for cotton *mantas*.[7]

Under optimal ecological conditions, Navajo and Pueblo subsistence strategies seemed to encourage small-scale economic exchanges. Peaceful trading during years of plenty proved mutually beneficial—Navajos taking advantage of their mobility to exchange surplus game and skins for the maize, beans, and squash surplus of the Pueblos.

During lean years, however, when game was short and Navajo plantings insufficient for survival, the greater efficiency of Pueblo irrigation agriculture produced an imbalance in negotiating power. Incentives for Pueblos to barter might be so few as to preclude trading altogether. Navajos could gain access to Pueblo surpluses only through higher-risk strategies: giving women in marriage to create ties of reciprocity, stealing food in raids on Pueblo fields, or attacking the Pueblos themselves to provide motivation for the Pueblos to accept less costly trading exchanges.[8]

Some human exchanges indeed occurred, lending support to the first scenario. During Espejo's 1583 expedition, he acquired "Curecho" women for his men from the Hopi villages and subsequently skirmished with Querecho war-

7. Winter and Hogan, "Dinetah Phase of Northwestern New Mexico," in Vierra, ed., *Current Research*, 299–312, discuss a "dual residence pattern" of seasonal alternation between canyon-bottom summer camps and upland winter hogan clusters that allowed for vertical integration of agricultural and hunting resources. For a discussion of Pueblo influences during the Gobernador Phase (1700–1770), see Marshall and Hogan, *Rethinking Navajo Pueblitos*. The authors question the evidence for large-scale migrations of Pueblo refugees after 1680 but do find evidence for trade relations between these groups. Espejo is quoted in Bolton, *Spanish Exploration in the Southwest, 1542–1706* (New York, 1952), 183; Haskell, *Southern Athapaskan Migrations*, 76, 81.

8. These scenarios build upon models offered by Spielmann in her discussion of protohistoric Plains-Pueblo exchange patterns, where "outcome- and situation-specific" interactions range from "competitive to parasitic to mutualistic," depending upon ecological factors like availability of game, crop yields, and population pressures. See her "Coercion or Cooperation?" in Spielmann, ed., *Farmers, Hunters, and Colonists*, 36–50.

riors who hoped to liberate these captives. Just why these Querecho women lived among the Hopis is unexplained, but ethnographic analogy suggests a possible pattern of hunter, horticultural, and agricultural hypergyny, where Navajo women were offered to junior Hopi men unable to find wives within their home village. Echoes of this fragile symbiosis may be heard from Navajo oral historians, who claimed that, when "the Navajo were hungry, they went to the Hopi country. The Hopi would treat them well and feed them. When the Navajo had been fed the Hopi would throw them off the mesa. In revenge the Navajo would organize a war party." By claiming shared cultural notions of kin reciprocity, during lean times Navajos could feed off their Hopi neighbors, but only insofar as Hopis were willing to share their own scarce resources. Navajo women later appear frequently in the baptismal records of Río Grande pueblos (especially Jémez and Zía) in the early historic period. In all, cross-cultural extensions of kinship could promote mutually beneficial economic exchanges, but at a risk to the exchanged women. Marginal in Hopi society as incompletely assimilated outsiders, Navajo women might have been more vulnerable than native Hopi women to becoming "gifts" to Espejo's soldiers.[9]

Such exchanges did not flow simply from Navajo to Pueblo, however. Frederick W. Hodge reported that, in the 1850s, five of the nineteen Navajo clans claimed descent from Pueblo clan mothers, and evidence of Pueblo material culture in Dinetah Phase (1550–1700) Navajo sites suggests that cultural exchange might have included Pueblo women. Navajo origin narratives given by Torlino and Náltsos Nigéhani to Washington Matthews in the 1890s recount a long accretion through which small bands were accepted as new clans by the original Tsedzinkini clan. Most of these were fellow Athapaskans, but at least eight derive "from women of alien races." In 1598, after Oñate's destruction of rebellious Ácoma Pueblos, disabled and elderly Ácomas were "freed and entrusted to the Indians of the Province of the Querechos" with the understanding that they would be cared for and not allowed to leave the Querecho

9. [Diego Pérez de Luxán], *Expedition into New Mexico Made by Antonio de Espejo, 1582–1583 . . .*, trans. and ed. Hammond and Rey (Los Angeles, 1929), 111–114. See John D. Speth's discussion of the literature on hypergyny in "Some Unexplored Aspects of Mutualistic Plains-Pueblo Food Exchange," in Spielmann, ed., *Farmers, Hunters, and Colonists*, 18–35; W. W. Hill, "Navaho Warfare," in *Yale University Publications in Anthropology*, no. 5 (1936), 3–26, based on 1933 interviews with Curley of Chinlé, Roan Horse of Crystal, and Son of the Late Smith, all of Fort Defiance, quote 3. See also David M. Brugge, *Navajos in the Catholic Church Records of New Mexico, 1694–1875*, 2d ed. (Tsaile, Ariz., 1985), 33–39.

rancherías. This evidence implies some long-term human exchange between Navajos and Pueblos, although whether exploitative or benign remains unsettled.[10]

Hints of violence in these transfers are also evident. Marriages of Navajo women to Pueblo men probably triggered reprisal raids by unmarried Navajo men; an absence of Navajo brides would have tangibly expressed an affront to their honor. Navajo oral history seems to support this proposition and points to competition between Navajo bands themselves for wives. Traditional Navajo historians recount a past steeped in contention over women:

> Long before [we were taken to] Fort Sumner, the people [Diné] on both sides of the Lukachukai Mountains were very prosperous, while those in del Muerto and de Chelly were poor. However, the people of the Canyons were noted for their beautiful women. The men who had horses would sneak into the Canyons and steal one or two wives from these people. The reason for this stealing was that the people of del Muerto and de Chelly were originally of Pueblo stock while those in the mountains were of the Old Navajo stock and the Canyon girls were much prettier than those of the mountains. For revenge, the Canyon people would raid. First they raided the Pueblos, then the Ute.[11]

10. Frederick Webb Hodge, "The Early Navajo and Apache," *American Anthropologist,* O.S., VIII (1895), 223–240. Among these clans were the Nanashte'zi (Zuñi), Ma'ideshgizni (Jémez), Dibélishini (San Felipe), Xogi (Zía), and one unidentified Pueblo group. Note that these all represent Pueblos on the margins of Navajo territories, hence most likely to be involved in trading and raiding exchanges. For detailed discussion of Navajo clan relations, see Malcolm Carr, Katherine Spencer, and Doriane Woolley, "Navajo Clans and Marriage at Pueblo Alto," *American Anthropologist,* N.S., XLI (1939), 245–257; Matthews, comp. and trans., *Navaho Legends,* 29–32; Hammond and Rey, *Juan de Oñate and the Founding of New Mexico,* I (Sante Fe, N.Mex., 1927), 116–123. Brugge argues that as many as twenty-four, or one-third, of modern Navajo clans "claim Pueblo origins." See "Navajo Archaeology: A Promising Past," in Towner, ed., *Archaeology of Navajo Origins,* 255–271, esp. 262. More than five hundred Ácoma women and children were taken and distributed among the Spanish colonists after this defeat as well. For evidence of violence and captive seizure within Pueblo society, see Chris G. Turner II and N. T. Morris, "A Massacre at Hopi," *American Antiquity,* XXXV (1970), 320–331, on the Hopi devastation of their kinspeople at Awatovi in 1700, when male captives were mutilated and killed and women and children absorbed into the western Hopi villages.

11. Hill, "Navaho Warfare," in *Yale University Publications in Anthropology,* no. 5 (1936), 3.

This oral narrative suggests that clans (principally the *Ma'ideshgizni* ["Coyote Pass"], also known as the Jémez Clan) residing in the Cañons del Muerto and de Chelly formed before European contact. After contact, they became susceptible to wife-stealing raids by their newly mounted cousins, and they in turn raided the Pueblos and Utes for women. A network of forcible exogamy may explain the 1583 Espejo expedition's seemingly contradictory declaration that, while at times engaged in barter with Athapaskans, the Ácoma Pueblos lived on their fortified mesatop "because of the war this Pueblo has with the Querechos Indians."[12]

Depending upon ecological and cultural conditions, these exchanges of women probably included both peaceful marriage diplomacy between sedentary Pueblos and semisedentary Navajos as well as the theft of women between rivals. Since the marginal environment of the Greater Southwest seldom guaranteed subsistence needs for the region's large population, cultural strategies of marriage, raiding, and warfare were often employed to redistribute resources. Evidence of contention and accommodation between Navajos and Pueblos in the protohistoric period should not be seen as inexplicably contradictory—rather, it suggests that exchange strategies ranged along a continuum, from peaceful bartering to systematic violence.

The Spirit of the Sheep Has Always Been with Us

Spanish colonialism in New Mexico intensified existing tensions and introduced radically new historical forces. Population loss, cultural crises, and tributary burdens expanded concentrically from the Pueblo villages into the borderlands. First, Spanish military actions and European pathogens reduced the Pueblo population by some 80 percent, from eighty thousand in 1598 to seventeen thousand in 1679. Concurrently, Spanish administrators and missionaries vied for control of this dwindling pool of Pueblo laborers, seriously disrupting the Pueblo subsistence economy. Attempting to find alternative sources of wealth and labor, Spanish soldiers and missionaries entered into the captive trade at a new level of commodification, for captives now had cash value as slaves in the mines of northern New Spain. Seeking to preserve and augment their own populations, Pueblos joined this effort and campaigned autonomously (or as Spanish auxiliaries) to take Navajo and Ute captives. Not

12. [Luxán], *Expedition into New Mexico,* trans. and ed. Hammond and Rey, 112–114.

surprisingly, Navajos retaliated and seized Pueblo and Spanish captives themselves.[13]

Yet, as important as these developments would prove to be, the creation of a pastoral borderland rested on a new variable. The Spanish introduction of livestock husbandry into the region allowed Navajos to adopt and refine sheep pastoralism, a subsistence strategy often associated with territorial expansion, social stratification, and military aggressiveness. Lest these qualities be subsumed under some belligerent pastoral ethos, scholars caution that they represent functional components of pastoral reallocation systems, wherein expansion redistributes both people and animals across new landscapes, conflict shifts wealth between richer and poorer regions, bands, and families, and stratification reorganizes production between regions and sectors of pastoral communities. Although this does not encompass the emotional and destructive aspects of resentment and retribution, redistributive elements appear common in the Navajo case.[14]

In 1598, Juan de Oñate's soldiers, families, and servants set forth from Zacatecas for the Río Grande valley with some 1,000 cattle, 150 mares and colts, and 3,600 sheep and goats. Although thinned by the journey, these herds and flocks were reported to be flourishing by 1601, to the point that cattle alone provided the colony's need for meat and the sheep could be reserved for their fleece. Within a few decades, local wool production developed to the point of being a major source of revenue for colonial governors like Juan de Eulate (1618–1625) and Luís de Rosas (1637–1641) in the production of serapes and *frazadas* woven by "Christian Indians" and Apache, Navajo, or Ute "war-captives" in their Santa Fe obrajes.[15]

Navajos spared little time in taking advantage of the new resources on their

13. Ramón A. Gutiérrez, *When Jesus Came, the Corn Mothers Went away: Sexuality, Love, and Conquest in New Mexico, 1500–1846* (Stanford, Calif., 1991), table 2.1, 92–93; France V. Scholes, *Church and State in New Mexico, 1610–1650* (Albuquerque, N.Mex., 1937), 73 and n. 20, 118–119 and n. 11; for a modern treatment that stresses population erosion by intimidation and control throughout the seventeenth century, see Andrew L. Knaut, *The Pueblo Revolt of 1680: Conquest and Resistance in Seventeenth-Century New Mexico* (Norman, Okla., 1995); Oakah L. Jones, Jr., *Pueblo Warriors and Spanish Conquest* (Norman, Okla., 1966), 175.

14. Pierre Bonte and John G. Galaty, "Introduction," in *Herders, Warriors, and Traders: Pastoralism in Africa* (Boulder, Colo., 1991), 3–30.

15. Hammond and Rey, *Juan de Oñate*, I, 44; John O. Baxter, *Las Carneradas: Sheep Trade in New Mexico, 1700–1860* (Albuquerque, N.Mex., 1987), 5–6; Scholes, *Church and State*, 118–119.

borders. Pedro de Peralta abandoned Oñate's first settlement at San Gabriel (near San Juan Pueblo) in 1610, in part because of persistent Navajo sheep and horse raids, and he moved the villa to more defensible ground at Santa Fe. Navajos continued to press against the Spanish colony, striking the Jémez mission in 1657, taking stock, killing nineteen men, and carrying thirty-five women and children into captivity. In 1669, Navajos attacked the mission *estancias* at Ácoma, seizing eight hundred sheep, nine horses, and "several captives." Three years later, Fray Juan de Ayeta declared that the province "was totally sacked and robbed by their attacks and outrages, especially of all the cattle and sheep, of which it had previously been very productive." When fifteen hundred Spanish survivors of the Great Southwestern Revolt of 1680 fled south to El Paso del Norte, they took some five thousand *ganado mayor y menor* (horses, cattle, sheep, and goats) with them but left behind other thousands, many of which, it seems, ended up in Navajo rancherías.[16]

The acquisition of sheep provided a renewable resource that stabilized Navajo subsistence while destabilizing both settlement patterns and social organization. Navajo population expanded rapidly during the period, if site frequencies from the Dinetah to Gobernador Phases are representative of general population increases. This expansion, coupled with the grazing needs of sheep flocks, soon exceeded the capacity of Dinetah to provide sustenance. One historian estimates that forage in Dinetah canyon bottoms was depleted by the 1720s (when Navajo flocks might have exceeded eleven thousand animals), and, indeed, both archaeological and documentary materials point to a two-pronged migration west and southeast out of Dinetah by the middle of

16. Worcester, "The Navajo during the Spanish Regime in New Mexico," *NMHR*, XXVI (April 1951), 101–118; for the archaeology of Oñate's settlement, see *When Cultures Meet: Remembering San Gabriel del Yunqe Oweenge: Papers from the October 20, 1984, Conference Held at San Juan Pueblo, New Mexico* (Santa Fe, N.Mex., 1987); Scholes, *Troublous Times in New Mexico, 1659–1670* (Albuquerque, N.Mex., 1942), XXII, 150–151. The Spanish retaliation for this raid freed the 35 captives, among whom was a Spanish woman, and netted 211 Navajo captives who were distributed among the expedition members; see Hammond, *The Spanish Period, 1540–1821,* MS for the Navajo Land Claim (1955), 13, in New Mexico State Records Center, Santa Fe, N.Mex.; Petition of Fray Francisco de Ayeta, Mexico, May 10, 1679, in Charles Wilson Hackett, trans. and ed., *Historical Documents Relating to New Mexico, Nueva Vizcaya, and Approaches Thereto, to 1771,* 3 vols. (Washington, D.C., 1937), III, 302; Hackett, *Revolt of the Pueblo Indians of New Mexico and Otermín's Attempted Reconquest, 1680–1682* (Albuquerque, N.Mex., 1942), I, 21–65.

the eighteenth century. Hostilities with their northern neighbors, the "Yutas," probably hastened this emigration.[17]

Changes in social organization, stratification, and exchange strategies accompanied Navajo migrations. Sheep ownership might have begun within the domain of personal property, but shifts in subsistence strategies—where women more often tended fields, crops, and flocks while men raided and defended their families from raiders—probably promoted its sedimentation within matrilines. Depending upon the quality of an outfit's grazing lands and relative vulnerability to raiders, sheep ownership gradually became unevenly distributed throughout Navajo society. A patronage complex formed with successful raiders increasing the size of their extended kin groups through marriage diplomacy and the acquisition of "pawned" dependents. Since sheep pastoralism required shepherds, and sheep provided the bridewealth necessary to gain more labor through marriage, entrepreneurial headmen established "outfits" that linked as many as a dozen families in unequal webs of reciprocal obligation. Through clan and affinal ties families and outfits maintained obligations of mutual aid and hospitality across wide reaches of their semi-desert landscape. The existence among the Navajos of dispersed, exogamous matriclans protected those who were beginning to build livestock wealth while wrapping poorer families in the ambivalence of dependency.[18]

Navajo historians quoted earlier recalled both the migratory movements and the development of nascent "classes" in Navajo society. Their reference to

17. While certainly not definitive, site frequencies give a general impression of rapid population growth in the eighteenth century: A.D. 1400–1500, 13 recorded sites; 1500–1600, 22 sites; 1600–1700, 38 sites; 1700–1800, 475 sites. See J. Lee Correll, *Through White Men's Eyes: A Contribution to Navajo History: A Chronological Record of the Navajo People from Earliest Times to the Treaty of June 1, 1868* (Window Rock, Ariz., 1979), I, 22–23, 27–28, 44–46; Brugge, "The Navajo Exodus," Archaeological Society of New Mexico Supplement no. 5 (Albuquerque, N.Mex., 1972), 1–15; Bailey, *If You Take My Sheep*, 75–87.

18. See Clyde Kluckhohn and Dorothea Leighton, *The Navajo* (Cambridge, 1946), 109–111; the authors explain that "the size of an 'outfit' tends to depend on the wealth of its leader or, more exactly, of the leader and / or his wife or wives. Wealthy Navajos who control thousands of sheep are often the focal points of 'outfits' which include a hundred or more individuals in a ramified system of dependence" (110). Outfits should not be confused with clans: in the Dennehotso Valley in the 1930s, 669 people were organized into 9 outfits but represented 21 different clans. This reflects both the needs of labor organization and the Navajo clan exogamy requirement.

the prosperous Diné on either side of the Lukachukai Mountains indicates two groups of expanding pastoralists. One group moved westward beyond the Lukachukai range into the open grazing lands of northern Arizona, where by the late eighteenth century they would displace the Havasupais, driving them into their sanctuary in the Grand Canyon. The other group, moving southward out of Dinetah across Chacra Mesa, would fan out around Mount Taylor (Mount San Mateo) in the middle of the eighteenth century. The historical experiences of these two groups diverged at this point. The western group would develop in relative isolation, husbanding immense flocks and herds while protected by distance from market forces and conflict with Europeans until the American conquest of the 1860s. The eastern group would also prosper for a time, but under more volatile conditions, for their history was inextricably bound up in market and cultural exchanges with Europeans in the Río Grande valley.[19]

Intermediate to these major migrating groups were the "poor" Navajos of the Cañons del Muerto and de Chelly. Descended from early assimilations of Pueblo women, these groups were perhaps more devoted to settlement and farming than their rich cousins and perhaps culturally distinct. In time, their vulnerability would force adaptation upon them, and from this group would emerge some of the most aggressive *ladrones* in the pastoral borderlands. Nor were these *rico/pobre* divisions solely segmented by region. Even in the rancherías of western ricos, dependents existed who had little claim to the outfit's wealth and hence no opportunity for advancement through marriage unless by the grace of a headman's loan. These pobres lived only three to five days' travel from the Spanish flocks along the Río Grande, an irresistible temptation toward freebooting. If sponsored by a shaman who knew the ritual "ways" for raiding (Blessingway, Bear Way, Big Snake Way, Turtle Way, and Frog Way), small groups, usually afoot, would approach at night and make their seizure at dawn. Successful raiders distributed captured livestock first to the sponsor, then to "parents, friends, and relatives." Customary redistribution procedures limited the amount of wealth an individual could acquire but allowed for the gradual enrichment of both the outfit and the raider's immediate kin. Captives would have an even greater potential to yield individual rewards.[20]

19. Bandelier claims this territorial conflict began by 1686 (*Final Report,* II [1892], 382–383). Tree-ring dates of confirmed Navajo sites in the area begin at 1709. See M. A. Stokes and T. L. Smiley, *Tree-Ring Dates from the Navajo Land Claim,* II, *The Western Section* (Tucson, Ariz., 1964).

20. Hill, "Navajo Warfare," in *Yale University Publications in Anthropology,* no. 5 (1936), 5, 6. The overlap between commercial exchanges and raiding is evident in the fact that the

The relationship between the eastern bands who would come to be known as the *Diné Ana'aii,* the pobres of the canyons, and the peoples of the Río Grande valley (both Pueblo and Spanish colonial) would soon revolve around exchanges of livestock and captives. The existence of economic stratification within Navajo society has long been noted, as have similar dynamics among the colonial population of eighteenth-century New Mexico. The historical interconnections between these phenomena and the long-term cultural ramifications that were their legacy have yet to be demonstrated.

In what appears their initial probe southward, "two large bands" of Navajos raided livestock from the pueblos of San Juan, Santa Clara, and San Ildefonso in the spring of 1705. In July 1705, Captain Roque de Madrid led a punitive expedition that included some one hundred Pueblo genízaros (detribalized, nomadic Plains Indians) into the Dinetah, probably punishing the wrong people—his victims were dispersed families in the throes of hunger, and he counted only thirty-two sheep on his two-week campaign. After killing at least thirty-nine Navajos and laying waste to several cornfields, he returned to Zía Pueblo with an uncounted number of captive women and children, whom he gave "as presents" to his men. A second campaign followed this action, and, by 1706, a Navajo headman named Perlaja sought out a truce. After an exchange of captives, Governor Francisco Cuervo y Valdez noted that "their good faith is attested by the confidence with which they continue to barter and trade on our said frontiers and in our pueblos." By 1709, Navajos carefully avoided taking stock from Spanish settlements but continued to build their flocks by raiding the nearby Pueblos.[21]

Blessingway was also the primary chant for trading journeys. See Hill, "Navajo Trading and Trading Ritual: A Study of Cultural Dynamics," *Southwestern Journal of Anthropology,* IV (1948), 371–396, esp. 384. Hill's work also hints at evidence of competition between shamans, wherein some sponsored raiding bands in hopes of gaining wealth and others served ricos in order to defend wealth. The prevalence of witchcraft accusations among the Navajos, especially after 1864, also points to class friction expressed in supernatural terms.

21. Statement of Captain Alphonso Rael de Aguilar, Santa Fe, January 10, 1706, *Provincias Internas,* XXXVI, no. 5, fol. 473, v, quoted in Frank D. Reeve, "Navajo-Spanish Wars, 1680–1720," *NMHR,* XXXIII (January 1958), 205–231, esp. 216; see John P. Wilson's translation of "Autos de guerra hechas en el tiempo del Sr. Gouverndour y Capn. Gnl. Don Francisco Cubro y Baldes . . . ," in Frank McNitt Papers, New Mexico State Records Center, also published as Rick Hendricks and John P. Wilson, trans. and eds., *The Navajos in 1705: Roque Madrid's Campaign Journal* (Albuquerque, N.Mex., 1996). See also Governor Cuervo y Valdez to His Majesty, Aug. 18, 1706, in Hackett, trans. and ed., *Historical Documents,* III, 381–

The southern-migrating group of Navajos established a major settlement community on the northern flanks of Mount Taylor, on what they called *yotso,* or "Big Bead" Mesa. The earliest occupational date at this settlement occurred in 1745, which, when considered with the end dates of Gobernador settlements in the north (1736–1745), reinforces the migration thesis. Although not noted in the site report, some evidence for stratification appears at Big Bead—the community seems divided in clusters of exclusively one of two styles, either forked-stick hogans (eighteen) or a newer form of circular masonry hogans (thirty-five). The forked-stick clusters are more scattered and associated with grazing areas, whereas the masonry clusters are concentrated within defensive walls on the mesa's *peñoles* (outcroppings). The clear demarcation of settlement cluster and dwelling type may represent summer-winter habitations but could point to developing social divisions between the extended family gathered around a Navajo headman and scattered dependent families among his larger outfit.[22]

The Big Bead community seems the focal settlement of one migratory Navajo group that became associated with Franciscan missionaries' efforts to congregate Navajos at Encinal and Cebolleta between 1744 and 1750. Their endeavors provide significant information on Navajo cultural adaptations in the mid-eighteenth century. During this period, New Mexican Franciscans grew nervous about the successes achieved by their Jesuit competitors in northern Sonora and Arizona, especially when news of Jesuit plans for missionary work among the Hopis reached Santa Fe. The Franciscans responded with preemptive missions among the Hopis and Navajos, which yielded few lasting converts. One strategy involved several quick missionizing forays into the Navajo homeland and met with some success. A second strategy was one of reduction and concentration, a pattern applied elsewhere in New Spain, and it aimed at settling the Navajos in the Río Puerco region below Big Bead Mesa. This experiment failed in less than a year. Both efforts, however, reveal the complex cultural negotiations underway in Navajo society.

Fray Carlos Delgado undertook the first Navajo assignment with spring journeys in 1745 and 1746, traveling northward from Jémez into Dinetah. In 1745, he visited a Navajo band at a "Pueblo de los Collotes," where several lead-

---

383; McNitt, *Navajo Wars: Military Campaigns, Slave Raids, and Reprisals* (Albuquerque, N.Mex., 1972), 23.

22. Dorothy Louise Kuer, "Big Bead Mesa: An Archaeological Study of Navajo Acculturation," Society for American Archaeology, *Memoirs,* I (Menasha, Wisc., 1941).

ing men requested baptism for themselves and their families. The name of this ranchería seems suggestive, since *collote* (coyote) served as a racial category indicating mixed Indian-Spanish descent. The next year's visit is even more revealing: at the "Pueblo Españoles," Delgado baptized eight children. His military escort, don Bernardo Antonio de Bustamante y Tagle, reported that the name derived from doña Augustina de Peralta and doña Juana Almassan, two Spanish women taken captive during the Pueblo revolt of 1680, probably from estancias near Santo Domingo Pueblo.[23]

We cannot be sure if the two pueblos mentioned by Delgado were different rancherías or the same, with "españoles" simply adding ancestry detail to the "collotes" of the previous year. It is clear, however, that Delgado's account accords with Navajo origin narratives. Matthews's informants recalled that the *Nakaídiné* (Mexican) clan derived from either one or two captive Spanish women taken by the *Notádiné* (Ute) clan in a raid "somewhere near Socorro" in the early colonial period. These captives initially served the Notádiné as "slaves," but their "descendants became free among the Navajoes" and formed a clan prohibited from intermarriage with their former captors.[24]

Archaeological data provide even more detail to this remarkable evidence for the role of captivity, adoption, and marriage in the creation of a mixed society that would be reduced in historical references to a homogeneous "Navajo." In the tributaries of the San Juan River that flow from the heartland of Dinetah, there exist dozens of major archaeological sites that represent settlements dating from the early eighteenth century to the mid-1750s. Most feature multiroomed masonry structures, defensive walls, and both forked-stick and circular hogans. At least two of these, Hooded Fireplace and Frances Canyon, contain fireplaces in the room-blocks built in the Spanish style—corner rather than central hearths, hooded with cedar laths that retain traces of

23. Reeve, "The Navajo-Spanish Peace: 1720s–1770s," *NMHR*, XXXIV (January 1959), 15–17; for detail, see "Testimony Taken at Isleta in July, 1746, from Bustamente, et al.," part 1, doc. 32, New Mexico Originals, Coronado Room, Zimmerman Library, University of New Mexico, Albuquerque; for the likelihood that these women came from the Santo Domingo Parish, see notations under Peralta and Anaya Almazán in Fray Angélico Chávez, *The Origins of New Mexico Families: A Genealogy of the Spanish Colonial Period* (Santa Fe, N.Mex., 1992), 4, 86.

24. Matthews, comp. and trans., *Navajo Legends*, 146. The Notádiné were Utes who joined the people at Dinetah shortly before these events. They were remembered as bringing with them "good arms of all kinds," and, although they were "at first unruly and impertinent," in time they merged with the Navajo and became a distinct clan.

FIGURE 1. *Frances Canyon Ruin.* 1996. View toward west showing fortified tower. Photograph by Ronald H. Towner

adobe plaster. Another, called Old Fort, is so heavily fortified and carefully planned that it has been called "a walled Spanish town" by some archaeologists. Frances Canyon is the earliest of these settlements, dating from 1710, followed by Hooded Fireplace at 1723 and Old Fort at 1740. All had been abandoned by the 1750s. Perhaps most significant for our story is the fact that at Hooded Fireplace investigators found no sweat lodges, so prevalent in other sites and still profoundly important in customary Navajo spiritual practice. Either Frances Canyon or Hooded Fireplace might have been Pueblo Españoles, home to the Peralta and Almassan women, where in their captivity they constructed a reminder of their earlier lives in the hearths over which they worked daily. They might even have introduced some of their mixed-descent children to some elements of Catholicism—at Pueblo Españoles, Fray Delgado received a reception so warm he was "overcome with emotion" and unable to chant the *Te Deum Laudamus.* Perhaps these children, or other Spanish fugitives and captives invisible in the historical record, drew upon family and cultural memory to build the walled Spanish town on the escarpment overlooking San Rafael Canyon.[25]

25. Hooded Fireplace was first reported in Roy L. Carlson, *Eighteenth-Century Navajo*

FIGURE 2. Spanish-style corner fireplace at Frances Canyon Ruin. 1999. Photograph by James F. Brooks

The people of Pueblo Españoles might also have provided the seed for the Franciscan's reduction efforts at Cebolleta and Encinal. Between 1746 and 1748, drought made travel to Dinetah difficult because streams and springs were dry, and Delgado was unable to follow up his early success. In the summer of 1748, however, a Navajo headman named "Fernando de Orcazitas" visited Fray Juan Miguel Menchero at Isleta and requested a missionary. Menchero suggested his group move to the southern slopes of Mount Taylor (the sacred moun-

---

Fortresses of the Gobernador District (Boulder, Colo., 1965), 36–42, and reconsidered by Marshall, with assistance from Paul S. Grigg, in "The Pueblito as a Site Complex: Archaeological Investigations in the Dinetah District," *1989–1990 BLM Pueblito Survey,* New Mexico Buerau of Land Management Cultural Resources Survey No. 8 (1991), 33–51. In their effort to question the "pueblo refugee" origin thesis for these pueblitos, the authors do not consider captive seizure as the source for "intrusive" elements in the Gobernador Phase. For Frances Canyon, see 141–182; for Old Fort, see Ronald H. Towner and Byron P. Johnson, *The San Rafael Canyon Survey: Reconstructing Eighteenth-Century Navajo Population Dynamics in the Dinétah Using Archaeological and Dendrochronological Data* (Tucson, Ariz., 1998), 19–34; "walled Spanish town" quote from Towner, personal communication with the author, Feb. 26, 2001. For Delgado's report, see Reeve, "Navajo-Spanish Peace," *NMHR,* XXXIV (January 1959), 16.

tain of the south to the Diné), where a mission could be established. That autumn, the headman don Fernando and his followers accompanied Menchero and don Pedro Romero in a survey that located the proposed mission church in Cebolleta Canyon. Since the bilingual don Fernando served as interpreter in these negotiations and his band seemed particularly amenable to conversion, this event likely records the migration of some Nakaídiné to the Mount Taylor area.[26]

Within a year, another Navajo band requested a padre, claiming pointedly that although residents of the area they had not previously been preached to by Fray Delgado. They might have been the Big Bead community, now attempting to take advantage of an alliance with the Spanish. The Franciscans scrambled to establish another mission at Encinal, southwest of Cebolleta, and by autumn had done so, bringing Indian laborers from Laguna Pueblo to begin building a church. Unfortunately for their efforts, however, supplies of trade goods, farming implements, and livestock had run short, and the Navajos quickly lost interest in the reduction. By April of 1750, Governor Vélez Cachupín heard that the Navajos had revolted against the padres and run them out of the missions. The apostates claimed they "could not become Christians or stay in one place because they had been raised like deer." But, although the padres departed, some Navajos continued to occupy the area, and the governor himself was accused of carrying on trade in skins and baskets with the rebels.[27]

The Navajos of the Mount Taylor region had, by midcentury, successfully gained access to the resources they desired without surrendering autonomy to the Spanish. They did so by absorbing migrants and captives from other Indian groups and Spanish colonial society, a strategy that increased their technological and cultural repertoires of action. Concurrently, more distant Navajos adopted a seminomadic lifestyle that vastly enhanced their emergent pastoralism. They embraced a sacred ritual complex, the Blessingway, that prescribed dispersed pastoral settlements and norms of reciprocity between the strong and weak and solidified an emergent identity as a unified people. But, for those bands around Mount Taylor and the Río Puerco valley, successful adaptation to

26. Reeve, "Navajo-Spanish Peace," *NMHR,* XXXIV (January 1959), 19–23. Fernando de Orcazitas was probably named after don Juan Francisco de Guemmes y Horcacitas, viceroy 1746–1755.

27. Ibid., 23–28, esp. 27; Fray Manuel Bermejo and Fray Juan Sanz de Lezuan, *Relato,* Oct. 29, 1750, part 3, doc. 67, New Mexico Originals, Coronado Room, Zimmerman Library, University of New Mexico, Albuquerque.

Spanish pastoralism would be culturally troubling, and finding a stable identity would prove elusive. The drought of 1746–1748 probably acted as a catalyst, but their geographic and cultural migration toward the Spanish colony started around their hearths and in their minds much earlier.[28]

They Had Kept Her for So Long

Not all Spanish captives spent their lives among the Navajos. Even when Spanish captives experienced redemption, however, the sexual, cultural, and kinship connections they had forged in captivity sometimes allowed Navajos greater access to and leverage over Spanish wealth and power. In the lives of two half sisters, daughters of the encomendero Andrés Hurtado, we have relatively complete stories that span the period during which captivity and sheep pastoralism helped to shape relations between Navajos and residents of the Río Grande valley. Their tales lend some texture and detail to the constellation of exchange, kinship, and exploitation sketched above and hints at some of the varieties of experience in which captive women found themselves enmeshed.

Early in the summer of 1680, shortly before the conflagrations of the Great Southwestern Revolt, a band of *Apaches del Nabajo* swept down upon the Jémez River rancho of Captain Andrés Hurtado. They took captive his daughter Juana Hurtado de Salas, her two-year-old daughter María Naranjo, and her seven-year-old illegitimate sister also named Juana but subsequently described as "la coyota," indicating mixed Indian-Spanish descent. For the next twelve years, their lives in captivity are a blank in the historical record that can be reconstructed only by inference and imagination. But those years of captivity seem to hold the key to understanding much of their subsequent lives, which, although they went in seemingly different directions, illustrate

28. Brugge argues that the Blessingway emerged in the 1750s as a boundary-marking and identity-building ritual complex with strong incentives toward reciprocity between wealthy and poor in the form of gift giving and social deference, respectively; see *Navajo Pottery and Ethnohistory* (Window Rock, Ariz., 1963), 22–23. The most complete critical treatment of the Blessingway is Leland C. Wyman, *Blessingway: With Three Versions of the Myth Recorded and Translated from the Navajo by Father Berard Haile, O.F.M.* (Tucson, Ariz., 1970). Wyman notes elements in the "Leaving for the Wide Country" segment, which features clan accretions, "an early tendency of the clans to increase their numbers through captures. Slavery may have been an accepted institution even at that early date" (452 n. 339).

the myriad forms in which captivity and kinship could intermesh families and societies in the region.[29]

Juana Hurtado de Salas and the two-year-old María Naranjo might not have remained long with their Navajo captors, for they would later be redeemed by Juana's brother Martín at the Zuñi pueblo of Halona in 1692, as part of Vargas's initial reconquest effort. But in the intervening twelve years Juana had borne a young son and a daughter "about three years old," presumably by either her Navajo or Zuñi captors. María and these two mixed-descent children would follow their mother back into Spanish colonial society, probably to join the household she created in 1694 with Cristóbal de Cuellar in Bernalillo near Albuquerque. Cuellar died in 1700, leaving Juana with yet another daughter, María de Cuellar. Five years later Juana (now some forty years old) married twenty-year-old Tomás García de Noriega of Albuquerque and bore two more daughters and one son over the next six years. Over the course of her life, Juana gave birth to seven children from at least four different fathers of at least two different racial backgrounds, apparently suffering little social stigma in the process. Both of her postcaptivity marriages were to men of good repute in the Spanish community. Her first daughter, María Naranjo, would have an illegitimate daughter herself, Bartola Hurtado, who would in 1742 marry Spanish-born José de Bustamante y Tagle, cousin to Governor don Juan Domingo de Bustamante (1722–1731).[30]

Juana's half sister, Juana la Coyota, experienced her captivity and subsequent redemption as a more marginal figure to the Spanish community, but her history suggests remarkable personal creativity and autonomy. When she died in 1753 at some eighty years of age, Juana owned two ranchos with three houses, 330 head of goats, ewes, and rams, 42 cows with calves, 6 oxen, 3 bulls, 38 heifers and steers, 31 mares and stallions, a jenny and a jack mule, and a

29. See Chávez, *Origins of New Mexico Families,* 49–50, for reference to Hurtado's encomienda rights at Santa Ana and neighboring pueblos.

30. J. Manuel Espinosa, trans. and ed., *First Expedition of Vargas into New Mexico, 1692* (Albuquerque, N.Mex., 1940), 237; Chávez, *Origins of New Mexico Families,* 80, 150, 182. Juana Hurtado de Salas and her half sister Juana Hurtado de Galván (or Juana la Coyota) might have enjoyed the company of an abjurant Spanish priest, Father Juan de Bal, or "Father Greyrobe," at Halona. For a critical and compelling reconstruction of his story through Zuñi oral histories, see Andrew Wiget, "Father Juan Greyrobe: Reconstructing Tradition Histories, and the Reliability and Validity of Uncorroborated Oral Tradition," *Ethnohistory,* XLIII (1996), 459–482.

respectable amount of personal property. Her illegitimate son Juan Galván served as the *teniente* of the Zía district. Nativity had given Juana linkages to both Spanish and Zía Pueblo society, and in her captivity she developed linguistic and kinship ties with the Navajos. Throughout her life, her experience as a captive woman would afford her special negotiating skills with which she pursued security for her lineage.[31]

Juana's mother had come from the pueblo of Zía. She was sister to pueblo governor Juan Checaye, for he would later claim Juana as his niece. Her mother might have worked as a domestic servant in the household of the encomendero Hurtado, but we know little more about her life. No doubt sexually used by the Spaniard, she bore a daughter in 1673 who was just one among hundreds of such coyotas resulting from the Spanish colonization of New Mexico. The mother's connection with Zía Pueblo, however, remained central to her daughter's story. Four years after Juana's ransom from Navajo captivity, the young woman petitioned for and received a private land grant at the northwest corner of the Zía Pueblo lands, near the village later known as San Ysidro. Her rancho proved a key locus of trade between Navajos, Pueblos, and Spanish pobladores for the next half-century—and the source of Juana's wealth and influence.[32]

Although restored to her natal society, Juana never severed connections with her onetime captors. Frequent visits by Navajos to her rancho suggest that she had experienced adoption into a Navajo band. She might even have married in captivity; she never formalized any future conjugal relationship. Kin-

31. "Inventory and Settlement of the Estate of Juana Galvana, *Genízara* of Zia Pueblo, 1753," in *Spanish Archives of New Mexico* (hereafter cited as *SANM),* I, no. 193, roll 1, frames 1365–1372. See *Archdiocesan Archives of Santa Fe* (hereafter cited as *AASF), Burials,* roll 43, frame 371, for an inventory of the estate of Juana's daughter Luisa, who preceded her in death in 1735, as well as *SANM,* II, no. 406, roll 7, frames 458–475. Although not as wealthy as her mother, Luisa had ten cows with six calves, two horses, and ten sheep, as well as personal objects. I thank Frances Leon Quintana for pointing to Juana Hurtado as a case study in captivity and for sharing her notes with me. Her essay, "They Settled by the Little Bubbling Springs," *El Palacio,* LXXXIV, no. 3 (Fall 1978), 19–49, treats the history of the Santísima Trinidad grant at "Los Ojitos Hervidores."

32. "Proceedings against Raman Garcia Jurado, Alcalde Mayor of Bernalillo, for Coerced Labor and Other Extortions against Pueblo Indians of Zia, Jemez, and Santa Ana," in *SANM,* II, nos. 367, 370, 378a, 380, reel 6, frames 1010–1126, esp. frame 1084, for reference to Juan Checaye as Juana's uncle. For Juana's landholdings, the rancho at San Ysidro, and a smaller rancho at the border of the Zía Pueblo grant, see *AASF, Burials,* reel 43, frame 420.

ship aside, her trilingual skills and cultural intermediacy facilitated economic exchanges between potential enemies. Her wealth certainly derived from her role as trader and interpreter, while her affinity with the Navajos remained so close that Fray Miguel de Menchero commended her usefulness in assisting proselytization efforts. "They had kept her for so long," he wrote in 1744, "[that] the Indians of said Nation make friendly visits to her, and in this way the father of the said mission has been able to instruct some of them."[33]

Juana's conduct, however, also attracted criticism from church authorities. Throughout her life, she persisted in maintaining a long-term liaison with a married man of Zía Pueblo, presumably named Galván. By 1727, this relationship had resulted in four children and charges of scandalous behavior leveled against her by the padres. Her son Juan also maintained an unmarried relationship with a Zía woman named Magdalena, and, although *Alcalde Mayor* Ramón García Jurado banished him to Santa Fe in punishment, Juan obtained a writ from the governor allowing his return, upon which he again took up the affair. When the alcalde placed Juan in the stocks for punishment, his mother—asking whether García took her son for an Apache to be treated so—promptly freed him. García then ordered Juana placed in the stocks, but the people of Zía "threatened that the whole pueblo would move to the mesa tops, rather than have her mistreated." Like the Navajos, the people of Zía saw benefits in the presence of this kinswoman on their borders. In hearings subsequent to the dustup, one witness claimed that Juana often acted "saucy" with Spanish authorities because she was "favored by certain people." It seems so. Juana could claim kin connections with a prominent Spanish encomendero (she consistently used the Hurtado name), to the governor of Zía Pueblo, to her Zía consort, Galván, and probably some affinal or adoptive kinship to a Navajo band. Working within this expansive notion of kinship, Juana, her children, and her various kinspeople all found tangible rewards in having a human bridge across three cultures. Drawing upon her qualities and talents as a negotiator, Juana "la Galvána" had utilized her experience as a captive to carve out an intermediate niche in the complex power relations of colonial New Mexico.[34]

33. "Declaration of Fray Miguel de Menchero, Santa Bárbara," May 10, 1744, in Hackett, trans. and ed., *Historical Documents,* III, 404–405.

34. Abandonment of the pueblo for defensible mesatop positions often preceded Pueblo-Spanish conflict; see Fray Francisco Atanasio Domínguez, *The Missions of New Mexico, 1776,* trans. and ed. Eleanor B. Adams and Fray Angélico Chávez (Albuquerque, N.Mex.,

When viewed together, the lives of the two Juanas cast light on just how thoroughly enmeshed Indians and Spanish colonial peoples could become through the captive system. By the time Juana la Coyota died, three generations of people, at least twenty-two in number and from five or six (Zía, Navajo, mestizo, Spanish, and perhaps Zuñi) ethnic/racial backgrounds, were relatives to one another, even though the relationships might not always be acknowledged. Juana Hurtado would move relatively effortlessly from captivity back into the mainstream of Spanish colonial society, whereas her half sister lingered on the margins of several cultures. But in so doing Juana la Coyota apparently acquired social influence and personal wealth in greater measure than her sibling. The bloodlines and affinal ties consequent to slavery in the borderlands knitted diverse peoples in a social fabric at once intimate and distant, depending on one's ability to embrace the complex politics and social networks of which it was composed.

Without Sufficient Land to . . . Maintain My Herds and Horses

About the same time that Juana la Coyota received her grant at San Ysidro and the southern Navajos were establishing themselves at Big Bead Mesa, Cebolleta, and Encinal, New Mexican pobladores undertook a migration of their own westward into the Río Puerco valley. In the relative quiet after 1710, the Spanish colonial sheep industry began to expand, but in a manner that concentrated ownership in either church *cofradías* or a few elite families. Pueblo flocks also grew per capita in the Río Grande valley, as the Pueblo population stabilized and then expanded in the latter half of the eighteenth century. The earliest comparative population and stockholding data available are based on Governor Francisco Marín de Valle's inspection tour of 1757, as reported in the margins of don Bernardo de Miera y Pacheco's 1758 map of the province.[35]

But many colonial New Mexicans suffered during this period. In the 1750s,

---

1956), 332. For "la vida escandolosa" of Juana and Galván and the Zía Pueblo incident, see *SANM*, II, no. 345, reel 5, frames 524–541. For a broader historical context, see Frances Leon Swadesh, "Structure of Hispanic-Indian Relations in New Mexico," in Paul M. Kutsche, ed., *The Survival of Spanish American Villages* (Colorado Springs, Colo., 1979), 53–61.

35. John O. Baxter, *Las Carneradas: Sheep Trade in New Mexico, 1700–1860* (Albuquerque, N.Mex., 1987), 29–31, reproduced in John L. Kessell, *Kiva, Cross, and Crown: The Pecos Indians and New Mexico, 1540–1840* (Albuquerque, N.Mex., 1987), 508–512.

TABLE 1. Census of the Province of New Mexico, 1757–1758

Spanish and Non-Indian Citizens	
Total Population	5,170
Households	1,032
Men Capable of Bearing Arms	1,360
Horses	2,543
Cattle	7,832
Sheep and Goats	47,621

Genízaro Indians	
Total Population	225
Households	58
Men Capable of Bearing Arms	63
Horses	0
Cattle	48
Sheep and Goats	89

Pueblo Indians	
Total Population	8,694
Households	2,346
Men Capable of Bearing Arms	2,800
Horses	4,813
Cattle	8,325
Sheep and Goats	64,561

Conducted by don Bernardo de Miera y Pacheco. Note the relative equality in livestock wealth between Spanish and Pueblo peoples and the poverty of the genízaro caste. Although few in number, adult genízaro men available for military campaigns were an equivalent percentage of population to their Spanish and Pueblo neighbors and highly valued for their knowledge. See Kessell, *Kiva, Cross, and Crown*, 512. The El Paso del Norte district is excluded in this table.

José Montaño of the village of Atrisco complained that his sons were obliged to labor for the Pueblos near Albuquerque, weeding fields and gathering firewood, for which they received only "a few ears of corn." Accordingly, his sons undertook a migration to the Puerco and petitioned with ten other families for lands upon which to winter their stock. Antonio Baca pleaded that he found himself without "sufficient 'land to enable me to raise, pasture, and maintain my herds and horses.' " Likewise, Baltazar Baca of Belén declared himself "very badly provided for the maintenance of the small means which I have, consisting of herds of livestock."[36]

A look at migrants' settlement strategies reveals some similarities to the Navajo cases. The Montaño boys linked up with a patrón of their own, Antonio Gurulé, whose household included his wife Antonia Quintana, five children, and some thirteen criadas, probably Indian house slaves and their offspring. The other eleven families totaled sixty persons, only four of whom were servants. Gurulé probably played a role similar to the entrepreneurial Navajos, lending stock under *partido* to his neighbors. The communal land grant that Governor Vélez Cachupín confirmed on March 29, 1754, instructed the grantees to form a defensive plaza, ready to interdict any Navajo raiders moving toward the Río Grande valley. But the actual settlement pattern tended more toward the scattered *poblaciónes* typical of the area, with dwellings strung along the course of the Río Puerco. The settlers were warned in 1759 that they must adhere to the original instructions before receiving reconfirmation of the grant, but no evidence exists on the ground to confirm this, suggesting that they followed the time-honored colonial tradition of *obedezco pero no cumplo* (I obey but do not comply).[37]

These poblaciónes were the product of small-scale sheepherding, which works against large consolidated villages. The reproductive vitality of small

36. Reeve, "Navajo-Spanish Peace," *NMHR,* XXXIV (January 1959), 9–40, esp. 31; "Particíon de las tierras, Nuestra Señora de la Luz San Fernando y San Blas, 1772," in *SANM,* I, no. 277, roll 2, frames 479–482; *Antonio Baca v Inhabitants of the Rio Puerco,* Jul. 20, 1762, in *SANM,* I, no. 105. See also *Report of the Surveyor General, New Mexico,* roll 23, frames 191–221, roll 31, frames 453–462, New Mexico State Records Center; Baltazar Baca Grant, 1769, in *SANM,* I, no. 114.

37. "Particíon de las tierras," in *SANM,* I, no. 277, roll 2, frames 479–482; U.S. Bureau of Land Management, *Report of the Surveyor General,* New Mexico Land Grants, Records of Private Land Claims Adjudicated by the U.S. Surveyor General, 1855–1890, case 49, file 93, reel 18, New Mexico State Records Center; field survey by David H. Snow, personal communication, Jul. 23, 1992.

flocks can be destroyed by the loss of a few ewes or a single ram. Early New Mexican settlers on the Puerco employed a bedding-and-grazing strategy similar to their Navajo neighbors', by which flocks were bedded in brush enclosures at night and driven to grazing ranges during the day. But this intensive grazing practice had a centrifugal effect on settlement, since sheep quickly exhausted forage near the bedding corrals. Navajos and New Mexicans evolved a common settlement strategy wherein satellite *jacales* and *torreónes* were scattered across grazing grants from which pastores could continue bedding-and-grazing practices. Although this pattern perturbed Spanish administrators as it created a patchwork of mixed Navajo–New Mexican settlement, the mode gave settlers a way to manage small flocks with limited family labor. It also offered a dispersed defense should hostilities commence. Both Navajos and New Mexicans utilized this technique effectively, spreading out livestock and taking to their heels when raided. Although some livestock would be lost, and occasionally a shepherd killed or captured, the tactic avoided devastating losses. Frances Leon Swadesh (Quintana) points out, however, that wealthy stockowners whose flocks and herds suffered attrition under this system "never failed to comment on the cowardice of their herders in the face of an attack."[38]

The settlers who followed the Gurulés and Montaños also struggled to meet the needs of their animals, directives coming out of Santa Fe, and local settlement exigencies. Antonio Baca, the alcalde of the Zía–Santa Anna–Jémez district, headed another settlement on the Río Puerco, receiving a grant in 1759

38. Swadesh, "Jémez, Zía, and the Babbling Springs: A New Mexico Ethnohistory," MS in Laboratory of Anthropology, Santa Fe, N.Mex., 1–21, esp. 14. For Navajo grazing practices, see Bailey, *If You Take My Sheep,* 115–126. On Hispanic settlement patterns and land-use strategies along the Río Puerco, see Jerold Gwayne Widdison, "Historical Geography of the Middle Rio Puerco Valley, New Mexico," *NMHR,* XXXIV (October 1959), 248–284. For the various environmental, economic, and cultural factors behind ranchos, estancias, poblaciones, and plazas, see Snow, "Rural Hispanic Community Organization in Northern New Mexico: An Historical Perspective," in Paul Kutsche, ed., *The Survival of Spanish American Villages* (Colorado Springs, Colo., 1979), 45–52; Swadesh, "Archaeology, Ethnohistory, and the First Plaza of Carnuel," *Ethnohistory,* XXIII (Winter 1976), 31–44; for the tendency toward scattered poblaciones, see Marc Simmons, "Settlement Patterns and Village Plans in Colonial New Mexico," *Journal of the West,* VIII (January 1969), 7–21; for a discussion of dispersal and mobility as an effective defensive strategy, see M. J. Rowlands, "Defence: A Factor in the Organization of Settlements," in Ruth Tringham, ed., *Territoriality and Proxemics: Archaeological and Ethnographic Evidence for the Use and Organization of Space* (Andover, Mass., 1973), 447–462.

north of San Fernando. Its western boundary was "the high mountain, where the Navajo Apaches cultivate," or Big Bead Mesa. His actual control over the grant seems tenuous—three years later Baca had to eject fourteen squatters on the grant, who claimed "that they were grazing upon said tract about ten thousand head of sheep and cattle."[39]

Over the next six years, provincial governors confirmed ten more grants, ranging from Ojo de San Miguel due north of Mount Taylor to San José del Encinal due south. Each was devoted to livestock grazing, with petitioners reporting flocks (usually under partido) of some 700–1,000 sheep, several dozen cattle, and horse herds up to 800 *yeguas* (mares). A census taken in 1765 counted 39 families with 154 *gente de razón* at San Fernando and 14 families of 83 *vecinos* at San José del Encinal (de la Laguna), the Bacas' settlement. Each of these grants cautioned the petitioners not to intrude their settlements upon the "peaceful Navajo Indians" nor to allow their flocks to trample the planting or pastoral lands belonging to the Navajos. On Santiago Duran y Chaves's grant at the Ojo de San Mateo, "seven ranchos of Apache Navajo" did not object to his settlement, because "they were friends" and Duran would assist them if their enemies the Utes attacked. Reciprocal needs in defense and pastoral exchange created a condition for fragile coexistence.[40]

By 1770, the extensive nature of their pastoral economies scattered Navajo rancherías and New Mexican poblaciones across several hundred square miles around Mount Taylor. Spanish administrators and settlers took some pains to avoid infringing on Navajo crop and range land, and some degree of mutualism existed between the two societies. Navajos experimented with and quickly rejected the Franciscans' effort at reduction and congregation; pobladores felt comfortable enough with their own adaptations to ignore orders from Santa Fe to do the same.

A Congregation of Dissident, Discordant, Scattered People

Navajo–New Mexican relations on the Río Puerco during this period formed a mixed ethnic community that balanced between the cultural strategies and economic needs of Indian and European settlers. But the Navajo–New Mexi-

39. *Baca v Inhabitants,* Jul. 20, 1762, in *SANM,* I, no. 105; *Report of the Surveyor General,* roll 31, frames 453–462, esp. 460.

40. Reeve, "Navajo-Spanish Peace," *NMHR,* XXXIV (January 1959), 31–34; Donald C. Cutter, trans. and ed., "An Anonymous Statistical Report on New Mexico in 1765," *NMHR,* L

can pastoral borderland contained latent local tensions and a vulnerability to external market forces that made such stability fractious and contested. Likewise, treating the suspension of Navajo raids on Spanish settlements as evidence for half a century of "peace and goodwill" neglects continuities in tensions that would spark open hostilities again in the 1770s. Competition over people, livestock, and land became exacerbated with the pastoral borderlands' increasing involvement in the market-oriented economy of Bourbon New Mexico.[41]

During the eighteenth century, Navajos became full-fledged suppliers to the Spanish in the captive trade. Traces of this role appear as early as 1694, when Padre Juan Amando Niel reported that, in addition to "yutta" captives, Navajo raiders ventured as far east as the rancherías of the "*pananas y jumanes*" (Pawnees and Jumanos) to seize "*multitud de muchachos y muchachas*" for ransom to the Spanish at annual July ferias. In 1699, Navajo raiders returned with even more remarkable captives: *dos hijuelas de franceses.* Fray Gerónimo de Zarate quickly baptized the two French girls "María" and "Antonia," after which they disappear from history. By the middle of the eighteenth century, Navajos increased their captive raiding and had begun incorporating some as *b'yisná,* probably children who worked as herders. When Ventura, an "*yndio genízaro y christiano de la nación Caigua*" (Kiowa) returned in 1748 from a year's residence among the Navajo, he reported to Francisco Guerrero, alcalde of Taos Pueblo, that, although they were suffering drought and crop loss, they had recently killed twenty-eight "Yutas" and captured two boys and two women, at least one of whom they traded to Spanish purchasers at Abiquiu. The two children and one woman presumably remained with their captors. Ventura also noted that the Navajos held many sheep and traded often at Jémez Pueblo.[42]

(October 1975), 347–352, at 350; *Baca v Inhabitants,* Jul. 20, 1762, *Miguel and Santiago Montoya v Juan Pablo Martín,* 1766, in *SANM,* I, nos. 105, 571, roll 8, frames 1178–1217; Reeve, "Navajo-Spanish Peace," *NMHR,* XXXIV (January 1959), 35.

41. Richard White, *The Middle Ground: Indians, Empires, and Republics in the Great Lakes Region, 1650–1815* (Cambridge, 1991); Reeve, "Navajo-Spanish Diplomacy, 1770–1790," *NMHR,* XXXV (July 1960), 200. Reeve admits confusion as to the sources of the renewed hostilities after 1770, rejecting simple economic resource competition as the driving cause yet concluding only that "there must have been some other specific factor." See "Navajo-Spanish Peace," *NMHR,* XXXIV (January 1959), 40.

42. Padre Juan Amando Niel, "Apuntamientos que las memorias del Padre Gerónimo de Zarate hizo, no tan solo sestando practico del terreno que se cita, si no es llevada en la

Navajo participation in captive trading did not prevent them from becoming victims themselves. Although the majority of the 229 Navajo baptisms between 1720 and 1770 seem to represent voluntary conversions associated with mission efforts out of Encinal and Cebolleta, at least 33 of these are clearly designated as cautivos. Governor Cruzat y Góngora's 1732 *bando* prohibiting the sale of captives to Pueblo Indians suggests that Spanish raiders accounted for much of this traffic. Since both Navajos and New Mexicans utilized their children or family dependents as herders, scattered with their flocks across a broad landscape, the temptation to snatch these *piezas* proved irresistible.[43]

Continuities in the regional captive trade are the most overt reminder that, despite generally peaceful relations between Navajos and New Mexicans, tensions existed between the haves and have-nots of both societies, which ultimately produced more open conflict in the 1770s. The type of mixed society taking shape in the Mount Taylor–Río Puerco region was innovative, expansionistic, and little restrained by convention. As Navajo outfits grew in size, so too did the numbers of poor dependents attached to them. These pobres saw the flocks of the Río Grande and Río Puerco as tempting avenues to wealth and by the late 1760s had commenced a petty thievery in the area. Wealthy Navajo headmen like Antonio el Pinto protested that they had little control over these dependents but did attempt to repay stock losses in an effort to prevent general reprisals. In 1776, Fray Francisco Atanasio Domínguez saw this stealing at the root of a *"casi guerra civil"* around Cebolleta and Encinal, where "said Navajos live almost in the midst of our people."[44]

New Mexican pobladores also saw the looser society as an opportunity for aggrandizement. Although some settlers, like Antonio Gurulé, seem to have

---

mano las memorias para cortejaras con el," in *Documentos para la historia de México,* 3d Ser., part 2 (Mexico City, 1856), 108–110, in the Bancroft Library, University of California, Berkeley; "Statement relative to the Condition of the Navajó Country and Its Inhabitants, July 20, 1748," in *SANM,* II, no. 494, roll 8, frames 827–834.

43. For the general pattern, see Brugge, *Navajos in the Catholic Church Records,* 22–23; for captive entries, see May 30, Jul. 1, 1731, Nambé Burials, B-16; Mar. 22, 1733, San Ildefonso Baptisms, B-24; Apr. 1, 1737, Dec. 8, 1749, Jan. 6, 1753, Dec. 22, 1759, Feb. 18, 1760, Jémez Baptisms, B-17; Jan. 2, 1738, Jan. 1, 1739, Cochiti Baptisms, B-14; Aug. 10, 1755, San Juan Baptisms, B-27; Feb. 23, 1762, June 30, 1770, Laguna Baptisms, B-17a; Dec. 2, 1764, Santa Clara Baptisms, B-31, New Mexico State Records Center. See also Cruzate's bando of Dec. 6, 1732, in *SANM,* II, no. 378, roll 6, frames 1243.

44. See Domínguez's report in Domínguez, *Missions of New Mexico,* trans. and ed. Adams and Chávez, 253–254.

been men of standing, most were of markedly less substance. While serving as alcalde mayor of the district, Antonio Baca ran sheep under partido from Nicolas Ortiz, Bentura Romero, and Antonio Armijo, each of whom had to sue Baca to collect payments from him. Baca's eldest son, Juan Antonio, dabbled in the captive trade and was brought before Governor Vélez Cachupín in 1762 for illegally selling an Indian woman. Baltazar Baca, settler of the 1768 Encinal grazing grant, was of similarly questionable character. In his early twenties, he and Gregorio Benevides were fined "35 pesos and costs" for the theft of six melons from the fields of Asencio, an Indian from Nambé Pueblo. Ten years later, Baltazar and his father Bernabe, then serving as alcalde mayor of Ácoma and Zuñi Pueblos, suffered reprimands and fines for exploiting Indians under their charge as sheepherders.[45]

Baltazar's petition for lands near Encinal in 1768 would have long-term consequences for the borderlands of the Puerco. On December 16, 1768, Governor Mendinueta confirmed to Baltazar and his married sons José Francisco and Laureano a grazing grant of one Castilian league, or five thousand *varas*, running due west of the old Navajo mission at Encinal. In addition to cautions regarding noninterference with Laguna and Ácoma Pueblo plantings in the area, the grantees were specifically ordered to "endeavor to attract . . . by Christian and faithful treatment" the "Apaches del Navajo" who dwelt nearby. The Bacas interpreted this injunction loosely, for sometime between 1768 and 1772 one of them impregnated a local Navajo woman, whose coyote son bore the name "Francisco Baca." This mixed-descent man would, by the 1820s, become headman of the Diné Ana'aii.[46]

Although this schismatic band would not appear in Spanish records as "ene-

45. *Nicolas Ortiz contra Juan Gutiérrez y Antonio Baca,* Jul. 9–24, 1766, in *SANM,* II, no. 600, roll 8, frames 974–981; *Antonio Armijo contra Antonio Baca,* Sept. 3, 1767, *Ventura Romero contra Antonio Baca,* Aug. 22–Sept. 4, 1767, in *SANM,* II, no. 623, roll 10, frames 188–230; "Pleito contra Juan Antonio Baca, 10 deciembre, 1762," in *SANM,* II, no. 564; "Pleito contra Baltazar Baca y Gregorio Benvides, 11–24 septiembre, 1742," in *SANM,* II, no. 447, roll 8, frames 146–172; "Autos criminales contra Baltazar y Bernabe Baca, agosto 2–septiembre 7, 1752," in *SANM,* II, no. 523, roll 8, frames 1070–1105. See also Myra Ellen Jenkins, "The Baltazar Baca 'Grant': History of an Encroachment," *El Palacio,* LXVIII (Spring 1961), 47–64.

46. Confirmation by Governor Pedro Fermín de Mendinueta, Dec. 16, 1768, in *SANM,* I, no. 114, *Report of the Surveyor General,* roll 23, frames 191–221; Jenkins, "The Baltazar Baca 'Grant,'" *El Palacio,* LXVIII (Spring 1961). McNitt, *Navajo Wars,* 29, contains a transposition of "1786" for what should be "1768" in his discussion of Baca's grant. This has unfortunately obscured the connections between the Spanish and Navajo Bacas.

mies of their own people" until 1818, when a headman named Joaquín brought his outfit into alliance with the Spanish, their difficult history began in the 1770s. That Francisco Baca replaced Joaquín as headman by the 1820s suggests this band derived from those Navajos located at Encinal in the 1770s. Baca himself was semiliterate, able to sign his own name in communications with the Spanish governor and capable of participating in legal wrangles over land and crop ownership in the 1830s. In these disputes, Baca claimed a right to plantings at Cubero, the major irrigated lands of the Encinal mission. These links indicate a direct connection between the eighteenth-century mixed settlement at Encinal and the later Diné Ana'aii.[47]

Joaquín's statement to Jémez alcalde Ignacio Vergara in 1818 claims that his band opposed the thievery practiced by "rebel" Navajos and had made attempts to interdict raiders with their booty in order to prevent Spanish reprisals. Invariably, only a few animals would be returned—countless others were absorbed into Joaquín's band's flocks and herds. Francisco Baca would go one step further. In 1823 he began delivering Navajos as captives to Spanish militias operating against ladrones. By this time, captive women and children brought some 100 pesos each in Santa Fe. Between 1820 and 1830, 259 Navajos would be baptized as *indios de rescate* in local parishes. While Spanish campaigns netted most of these, at least twenty-four were delivered into bondage by their breakaway kinsmen. For half a century, the Diné Ana'aii would enrich themselves in the sheep and captive trade. Their ultimate fate in the nineteenth century, however, would be imprisonment and ostracism.[48]

Francisco Baca and his successor in leadership with the Diné Ana'aii, "Cebolla" (Antonio) Sandoval, would become the best-known mixed Navajo–New Mexican bordermen in the region. But mestizaje was part of the culturally flexible pastoral society generally taking shape there, a phenomenon both born of and deeply implicated in the captive trade. The Baltazar Baca family, Spanish progenitors of the Diné Ana'aii, were themselves products of an earlier mixed cultural community, the Río Grande settlements around Belén, south of Albuquerque.

47. McNitt, *Navajo Wars,* 56, 70–73; Francisco Baca to Narbona, Jan. 15, 1826, *Governor's Papers,* Letters Received from within New Mexico, Mexican Archives, New Mexico State Records Center.

48. Sánchez Vergara, "Re. Loyal Navajos in Current Outbreak," Jémez, Jul. 21, 1818, in *SANM,* II, no. 2736, roll 19, frames 172–176; McNitt, *Navajo Wars,* 59, 68; Brugge, *Navajos in the Catholic Church Records,* 22–23.

Governor Domingo de Mendoza had established the *paraje de Belén* in 1740 as a congregation of genízaro warriors and their families to defend the southern door to the colony against Apache raiders. By 1744, Fray Miguel de Menchero reported some forty families in residence and noted the "great bravery and zeal" with which they fulfilled their obligations as military auxiliaries. The Bacas were not genízaros but seem to have dwelt in the adjoining Plaza de Jarales, a heterogeneous community of poor Spanish, mestizo, and genízaro members. These people also took pride in their contributions to the defense of the province—as Baltazar would later claim, "Our persons are devoted to the Royal service whenever we are called upon."[49]

Although evidence does support both Menchero and Baca in that claim, the people of Belén also proved adept at illicit borderland trading and larceny. Two prominent leaders of the Belén genízaros, Luís Quintana and Antonio Casados (both Kiowa Apaches), had fled from their master in the northern outpost of Ojo Caliente in 1742, taking two criadas with them. After Quintana received two hundred lashes and served two years in the Chihuahua mines, he and Casados resettled in Belén, where in 1746 they led a minor revolt against land encroachments by don Diego de Torres discussed below. The following year two other residents of the outpost stood accused of stealing livestock and goods from the rancho of don Juan Miguel Alvares del Castillo in nearby San Clemente. The settlement also served as a dumping ground for undesirables—in 1747, Antonio Santistevan of Abiquiu was banished to Belén after allowing the escape of a Ute captive taken during the Ute campaign of that year. Twenty years later, the coyote Miguel Tafoya, originally of Belén and now a resident of the Río Puerco, was sentenced to five years hard labor in the wool mills of Encinillas (near Ciudad Chihuahua) after stealing livestock from the Río Abajo, taking refuge among (and probably marrying into) local Navajos, and "inciting them to rebellion."[50]

49. "Declaration of Menchero," in Hackett, *Historical Documents,* III, 400–401. For the mixed character of Jarales, see "Spanish Colonial Census of 1790," in Virginia Langham Olmsted, comp., *Spanish and Mexican Censuses of New Mexico, 1750–1830* (Albuquerque, N.Mex., 1981), 78–80; see also Baltazar Baca petition, in *SANM,* I, no. 114.

50. "Proceedings against Luis Quintana and Two Other Indians, July 18, 1741 to July 31, 1742," in *SANM,* II, no. 441, roll 8, frames 67–95; Steven M. Horvath, "The Social and Political Organization of the *Genízaros* of Plaza de Nuestra Señora de Los Dolores de Belen, New Mexico, 1740–1812" (Ph.D. diss., Brown University, 1979), 180–184; "Proceedings . . . against Two *Genízaro* Indians," in *SANM,* II, no. 480, roll 8, frames 736–747. No record exists whether they were actually convicted of the crime. See also "Proceedings against Antonio

Given the cultural mélange from which settlers like the Bacas, Montaños, and others derived, it is little wonder that the mixed society in the Río Puerco region seldom drew praise from Spanish administrators. Writing in 1776, Antonio de Bonilla described the Spanish settlers as "a congregation of dissident, discordant, scattered people, without subordination, without horses, arms, knowledge of their handling, and governed only by caprice." Bonilla argued that enlistment of borderlanders in a formal militia held the only hope for their betterment and the creation of stability in the province. Accordingly, he recommended sufficient powder be sent from New Spain to "drill them in the use of firearms" and requested at least fifteen hundred horses be sent northward as well, to allow the formation of *compañías volantes* (light cavalries).[51]

But Bonilla's proposals were too little, too late. Military discipline and organization of borderlanders would not occur for nearly another century. By 1774, the volatile communities on the Río Puerco erupted into violence. The dependents of Navajo headmen apparently expanded their local pilfering of livestock to small raids on Indian pueblos and Spanish settlements in the Río Puerco valley. Perhaps more important, Comanches and Gila Apaches also repeatedly struck the region in considerable force, especially at Albuquerque and Belén in the Río Grande valley itself, tying up the small force of *presidiales* available in the Río Abajo. During the summer of 1775, Navajo ladrones raided stock from Jémez, Zía, San Ildefonso, the Río Chama valley, and outlying ranchos near Albuquerque. Spanish and Pueblo reprisals recaptured most of the animals and took some women and children captive but failed to subdue the pillaging. By the end of 1775, the Navajos had expelled Spanish settlers from the Mount Taylor region. Navajo bands established themselves at the sites of their former neighbors and henceforth became known by the names of these initial settlements—San Mateo in the west, Guadalupe and Cabezon in the north, Cebolleta and Encinal in the east.[52]

Santistevan," in *SANM*, II, no. 482, roll 8, frames 769–772; "Criminal Proceedings against Miguel Tafoya, *Coyote*, June 21, October 6, 1768," in *SANM*, II, no. 638, roll 10, frames 446–474; see also Brugge, "Eighteenth-Century Fugitives from New Mexico among the Navajos," in June-el Piper, ed., *Papers from the Third, Fourth, and Sixth Navajo Studies Conferences* (Window Rock, Ariz., 1993), 279–283.

51. Alfred B. Thomas, "Antonio de Bonilla and Spanish Plans for the Defense of New Mexico, 1772–1778," in Hackett, ed., *New Spain and the Anglo-American West* (Los Angeles, 1932), 183–209, esp. 203.

52. On October 5, 1774, Navajos attacked ranches near Laguna Pueblo, probably the Baltazar Baca settlement of San José del Encinal, where they killed four men and took two

During the next decade struggles ensued between older Navajo headmen controlling wealth in livestock and dependents, like Antonio el Pinto (known to his people as Hashke Lik'ishi, or Spotted Warrior) or his competitor don Carlos, and younger men seeking their own power and prestige. After Spanish administrators elevated don Carlos to a chieftainship with gifts of staffs, medallions, and annuities, Antonio formed a brief alliance with Gila Apache raiders, probably an attempt to retain the support of the younger Navajos. Concurrently, Navajos from the area struck westward and "by warlike acts and by other deeds of violence . . . possessed themselves of many of the Moqui [Hopi]," a major expansion of the captive network, seizing so many that Governor Anza feared that they "might aspire to be our declared enemies again, when they realize their strength." Anza's military expeditions accomplished little in pacifying the border, so he turned to a more successful strategy. In the spring of 1785, he forbade New Mexican settlers from "all trade, exchange, and communication" with Navajos.[53]

The fact that this injunction brought the Navajos to treat with Anza says much about the nature of these borderland societies. Antonio el Pinto broke with his Gila allies, and fourteen other headmen agreed to assist the Spanish in subduing the southern border. In return for the service of Navajo auxiliary warriors in his campaigns against the Gilas, Anza offered a resumption of trade relations and a bounty of one hundred pesos for every Apache captive delivered to Santa Fe.

In March 1786, eighty Navajos led by Antonio el Pinto and don Carlos agreed reluctantly to a military alliance that included a short-lived nonaggression pact with the Comanches, who had negotiated a treaty with Anza some

---

captives; in November they killed one shepherd and captured another near Zía at Ojo del Espiritu Santu and in December struck Laguna Pueblo, capturing a boy and taking thirteen sheep. See Reeve, "Navajo-Spanish Diplomacy," *NMHR*, XXXV (July 1960), 207. According to Governor Mendinueta, during the nine months between October 1774 and July 1775, there had been five invasions by Comanches and ten by the Gilas in the Río Abajo district; see Mendinueta to Bucareli, Mar. 30, 1775, *Provincias Internas*, LXV, file 10, fol. 36, v, cited ibid., n. 21; Mendinueta to Bucareli, Aug. 18, 1775, ibid., 209. See also "An Account of the Events concerning the Dissolution of the Gila-Navajo Alliance, 1785–1786," in A. B. Thomas, *Forgotten Frontiers: A Study of the Spanish Indian Policy of Don Juan Bautista de Anza, Governor of New Mexico, 1777–1787 . . .* (Norman, Okla., 1932), 350.

53. Anza to Croix, Jan. 17, 1781, Rengel to the conde de Galvez, Aug. 17, 1785, in Thomas, *Forgotten Frontiers*, 241–242, 259–260.

months earlier. Later that summer, twenty-six Navajo warriors joined twenty-two Comanches, a few Pueblo auxiliaries, and a handful of Spanish under Salvador Rivera for an expedition into the Apachería. The campaign accomplished little other than to net fourteen Apache captives and seal the fate of el Pinto, who seven years later would receive mortal wounds in a Gila revenge raid. Although the Navajo-Spanish Peace of 1786 would never prove as resilient as the Comanche-Spanish accord, it did point to an enduring, if volatile, economic interdependence.

Within two years, Navajos in the Mount Taylor region associated with Antonio el Pinto drew praise from Vicente Troncoso, Governor Fernando Chacón's special envoy and trading partner to those Indians. "They resemble us" Troncoso noted,

> in having some ideas of religion, having previously and at present some Christians, although apostates, among them. The women grind corn and wheat in the same way as the Spanish women. The activities of the men are their plantings, raising of livestock (more sheep and goats than cattle), having of the former a considerable proportion. Their women . . . make the best and finest serapes that are known, blankets, wraps, cotton cloth, coarse cloth, sashes, and other [things] are for sale [and] esteemed . . . even in Mexico City [by] persons who order them from me.

Río Puerco Navajos had moved closer to their Spanish allies, and, although Troncoso would protest that his interests were only that "they proceed well" with their "imitation of the customs, food, clothing, and undertakings of the Spanish," he clearly was deeply involved in the Indian trade as a middleman for the governor. In this respect, at least, Navajos conformed more closely to Chacón's ideal than did many Spanish villagers. Who could blame the common citizenry if they wished to join in the rewards of little-regulated interethnic trade? In time, that impulse would lead to Spanish resettlement of the Mount Taylor area, but their love of liberty would put them at odds with their colonial administrators.[54]

The pastoral economy of the Río Puerco Navajo bands had supplanted, for a time, the area's Spanish settlers and their pastoralism. Navajo basketry and wool blankets became valuable commodities in the colony, bringing Navajo women into direct market production and increasing the need for dependent

54. "Troncoso to Chacón, re: Antonio El Pinto, 12 April, 1788," TS trans. Brugge, Dec. 17, 1969, McNitt Papers, New Mexico State Records Center.

shepherds. Navajos now sold a few Hopi, Havasupai, Ute, and Gila captives to the Spanish but seem to have retained many more for their own labor and demographic needs. Better than their recent New Mexican neighbors, Navajos had adapted to local economic and military realities and established themselves in former Spanish settlements. But internal struggles would again make them vulnerable, and New Mexicans would again push to gain a foothold in the borderland commerce.[55]

In the meantime, to the north, within the network of mountains, canyons, and arroyos that had cradled the Navajo genesis in Dinetah, another set of relations had begun to form between the Utes and New Mexicans who sought to make homes amid the region's sheltering pine forests and snow-fed rivers. This mountain borderland would stand in marked contrast to those frontiers created by the llaneros and pastores.

55. Revilla Gigedo to Governor Concha, Dec. 14, 1791, discusses his satisfaction with the growing trade in baskets, blankets, and peltries by the Navajos *(SANM,* II, no. 1176, roll 12, frames 794–798); see also Brugge, *Navajos in the Catholic Church Records,* 50–53. On July 12, 1791, Governor Concha reported to Revilla Gigedo that Navajos had taken seventy-one Gila slaves in the last few months *(SANM,* II, no. 1132, roll 12, frames 559–563).

4

LOS MONTAÑESES

TRAVERSING BORDERLANDS

Thrusting south between the plains and plateau landscapes across which were emerging the borderland societies of los llaneros and los pastores was a chain of mountain ranges that descended from the alpine massifs of Colorado into New Mexico for some two hundred miles. Breaching timberline for much of their length, the source for many of the creeks and intermittent streams that provided life to agricultural peoples along their courses, the Sierras de Sangre de Cristo, Jémez, Sandía, and Magdalena seemed a substantial geologic barrier between the histories unfolding to their east and west. But these thickly timbered, well-watered, and relatively temperate heights may better be seen as linking landscapes and societies than separating them. Even before the advent of Spanish colonialism, mountain-nestled pueblos like Taos, Picurís, Pecos (Cicúye), and Jémez had served as centers for trade and exchange between the Río Grande valley and the plains and plateaus. And, while the core of the Spanish colony would form in the valley itself at San Gabriel del Yunque, Santa Cruz de la Cañada, Santa Fe, and Albuquerque, after 1700 much of the colonial population would migrate up tributaries and across hills to found new villages in the mountains. Crucial to our story, however, is that these settlements on the outer fringes of the colony would often be formed by peoples that were themselves on the margins of that social core. Poor or landless pobladores, genízaros, fugitives, and cultural renegades composed a substantial proportion of these villagers. These marginal types along with their Pueblo, Jicarilla, and Ute Indian neighbors would create a mixed society that simultaneously stood apart from the colonial center and played prominent roles in stitching together the plains and pastoral borderlands, producing a wide network of intercultural relations in the Greater Southwest.

No Commerce with the Infidels

On June 28, 1700, in the villa of Santa Fe, Governor Pedro Rodríguez Cubero ordered the execution of Miguel Gutiérrez, a condemned criminal who had escaped from Spanish authorities and been recaptured. Cubero instructed that the dead man's head be impaled upon a pole in the plaza of Taos Pueblo in order that "the Apaches de la Xicarilla and other nations know that they must not shelter fugitive Spaniards." Gutiérrez's crime remains unclear, as do the details of his recapture, but the incident suggests that within a few years of don Diego de Vargas's reconquista there existed an occasional, if illicit, intercourse between Spanish colonists, Pueblo Indians, and the Indian inhabitants of the mountains and plains northeast of the colony.[1]

In these early years of New Mexico's resettlement, Apache groups like the Jicarillas, Nataxes, and Faraones troubled its mountainous borders. Vargas began his second term as governor and captain general of the Province of New Mexico with a campaign against the Faraon Apaches, who had "committed . . . various thefts of cattle and flocks from farms . . . at Cieneguilla . . . and Bernalillo." Leading a combined force of 47 Spaniards and at least 120 Pueblo Indian auxiliaries, on March 31, 1704, the aging warrior began to scour the canyons of the Sandía Mountains in search of the "rabble," which left many dead sheep in its wake. Just three days into the campaign, however, Vargas took seriously ill and died at Bernalillo on April 8. Although the expedition was a failure, it forecast a line of historical interpretation that posed a dichotomy between a Spanish-Pueblo alliance on the one hand and belligerent *indios bárbaros* on the other.[2]

Were the "frontiers" of colonial New Mexico so clearly delineated? The case

1. "Order for the Execution of Miguel Gutiérrez, according to the Sentence of Death, 28 June, 1700," in *Spanish Archives of New Mexico* (hereafter cited as *SANM*), II, no. 77, roll 3, frame 686; for similar cases, see Dolores A. Gunnerson, *The Jicarilla Apaches: A Study in Survival* (DeKalb, Ill., 1974), 167–168.

2. "Report of the Marqués de la Nava Brazinas, 27 March–2 April 1704," in *SANM*, II, no. 99, roll 3, frames 889–899. Oakah L. Jones, Jr., argues that the Vargas campaign "was a most significant forecast of the nature of Indian warfare, which was to be almost characteristic of the entire eighteenth century. The Apache would continue to be the dominant menace until the Comanche arrived on the northern and eastern frontiers. As a result, the conflict hereafter would center around Spanish-Pueblo unity on the one hand and the indios

of the fugitive Miguel Gutiérrez implies that at least one element of Spanish society looked upon the indios bárbaros as potential allies rather than feared enemies. Other evidence further clouds the conventional dualism between the Río Grande valley and the "heathen frontier." On August 5, 1705, Vargas's successor Governor Cuervo y Valdez responded to complaints that "Spanish settlers had been entering the country of the 'Apaches de la Xicarilla' to trade . . . two or three horses for one boy or girl." He issued a bando prohibiting "the citizens of the Pueblos of Pecos, Taos, Picuries, and others on this frontier" from "entering into commerce with the indios infieles." Those who gambled or traded with these Indians were threatened with confiscation of property or loss of life.[3]

The common citizenry of New Mexico was not alone in taking advantage of the opportunities offered by trade with nomadic societies. In 1730, Bishop Benito Créspo visited the province and in his report to Viceroy Juan Vázquez de Acuña bemoaned the disjuncture between the timid missionary efforts of the resident padres and their lively interest in commerce:

> There are many who have been in residence eighteen or twenty years, not one has dedicated himself [to conversion]. . . . For this reason not many of the pagans on the borders are converted. They are bartering and trading with them every day, as I have seen.[4]

Secular authorities seem to have been similarly enticed by the allure of commerce. Despite repeated governmental edicts regulating or prohibiting traffic with *los indios infieles,* local settlers seldom resisted the temptation to enter the trade when the opportunity arose. In 1726, seven Spanish colonists suffered prosecution when their hard bargaining created disorders among Apaches visiting Pecos Pueblo to trade captives and hides. In 1735, the teniente of Santa Cruz de la Cañada, Diego de Torres, was accused of having "opened a trade

---

bárbaros, whether they were Comanches, Apaches, Utes, or Navajos, on the other" *(Pueblo Warriors and Spanish Conquest* [Norman, Okla., 1966], 65–68).

3. Cuervo, in Gunnerson, *Jicarilla Apaches,* 168; "Petition to the Governor and Captain-General by the Cabildo of Santa Fe, November 26, 1703," in *SANM,* II, no. 91, roll 3, frames 823–828; "Report of Governor Cuervo y Valdez, *Bando* regarding Barter in Towns, August 5, 1705," in *SANM,* II, no. 118, roll 3, frames 1062–1065.

4. "Documents concerning Bishop Crespo's Visitation, 1730," in Eleanor B. Adams, trans. and ed., "Bishop Tamarón's Visitation of New Mexico, 1760," *New Mexico Historical Review* (hereafter cited as *NHMR),* XXVIII (July 1953), 222–233, esp. 230.

with a group of Comanches at Ojo Caliente before arrival of the responsible authorities." A witness testified that Torres had "sent a servant to negotiate for buffalo robes in exchange for *belduques* [hunting knives]." In his own defense, Torres pleaded the urgency of the situation, arguing that the Comanches had threatened to "burn their goods unless trading started because they were nervous about Utes camped in the vicinity." His pleading failed to mollify the court, and Torres was punished by confiscation of the illegally obtained robes.[5]

New governors arriving in the province recognized the peril and promise of the Indian commerce and sought either to control it by strict licensing of approved traders or to establish regular exchange rates that would prevent bad blood between settlers and Indians. Yet neither measure could arrest the alternating flow of goods and insults across cultural boundaries. Whether loci of warfare or trade, the Pueblo Indian villages of Taos, Picurís, Jémez, and Pecos served as the main points of intercultural exchange throughout the eighteenth century. But, as informal trade centers, mountain-based Spanish colonial settlements like Ranchos de Taos, Talpa, Llano Quemado, Ojo Caliente, Abiquiu, Las Trampas, Las Truchas, Chimayo, Cundiyo, Las Huertas, Chilili, and Carnué conducted an almost constant, usually illicit, traffic in furs, hides, livestock, and captives with los indios bárbaros. In the nineteenth century, Spanish settlements like San Miguel del Vado, Mora, Anton Chico, La Cuesta, Las Huertas, Manzano, Cubero, Cebolleta, and Nacimiento would extend these exchanges out into the plains and pastoral borderlands themselves. However, in both centuries, these villages represent geographical, temporal, and cultural elaborations of the earlier Plains-Pueblo trade in that each grew from nuclei of genízaros purchased at rescates. Providing domestic labor, commercial go-betweens, and military auxiliaries for the Spanish colony, genízaros would prove central in the formative years of the exchange economies of the borderlands.[6]

5. See "Miguel Enriquez de Cabrera, Alcalde Major de Taos y Picurís, Bando relative to Trade with Apaches, 17 Sept., 1725," in *SANM,* II, no. 339, roll 6, frame 356; "Governor Bustamante, Bando Prohibiting Alcaldes Majores from Trading with Un-Christianized Indians, 17 Sept., 1725," in *SANM,* II, no. 340, roll 6, frames 357–360; "Criminal Proceedings against Spaniards for Creating Disorders with Un-Christianized Indians at the Pueblo of Pecos, 3 Aug.–7 Sept., 1726," in *SANM,* II, no. 340a, roll 6, frames 383–401; "Proceedings in the Complaint against Diego Torres, Teniente de Alacalde Mayor de Chama, 13 April–16 May, 1735," in *SANM,* II, no. 402, roll 7, frames 364–397; see also Frances Leon Quintana, *Pobladores: Hispanic Americans of the Ute Frontier* (1974; Aztec, N.Mex., 1991), 41.

6. Governor Henrique de Olvide y Michelana, "Bando Forbidding Trade with Los Indios

Servants among Our People

Sometime in the 1750s, Father Phillipe von Segesser, a Jesuit missionary working in the northern province of Sonora, sent to his family in Lucerne, Switzerland, a "box" and "three colored skins, which can be considered curios and of little value." Two of those colored skins (painted bison hides) survive, depicting in a vernacular mission style certain events in Spanish-Indian relations in northern New Spain. The more famous of the two almost certainly depicts the violent end of an expedition sent by New Mexican governor Antonio Valverde y Cosío under his *teniente general* don Pedro de Villasur onto the Great Plains in 1720 to search for signs of French among the river-dwelling Pawnees. Attacked by some five hundred Pawnees (and perhaps some French as well) along the South Platte River, only fourteen of forty-two Spanish and forty-eight of sixty Pueblo auxiliaries returned to New Mexico to report on the "Villasur Massacre." While an important work of visual evidence toward understanding the extensive nature of indigenous and colonial politics on the Plains, this hide painting, known as "Segesser II," is of lesser value than its more obscure cousin when it comes to representing the complexity of intercultural exchanges in the Southwest Borderlands.[7]

"Segesser I" depicts a raid by mounted horsemen on a mountain tipi encampment whose defenders are afoot and armed only with bows and arrows. Watching the conflict unfold are the women of the ranchería, gathered behind a defensive palisade. The men who confront the attackers are clearly of a single cultural group—their hairstyles, weaponry, and shields are nearly identical—and probably represent an Apache band. The nine aggressors (probably

---

Gentiles, 7 January, 1737," in *SANM*, II, no. 414, roll 7, frames 552–552. In the 1750s, Governor Vélez Cachupín established prices for exchangeable goods, predominantly domestic manufactures and foodstuffs, while prohibiting the sale of arms, ammunition, powder, horses, mules, and oxen. See A. B. Thomas, *The Plains Indians and New Mexico, 1751–1778* (Albuquerque, N.Mex., 1940), 129–143.

7. Both hide paintings are in the Museum of New Mexico, Palace of the Governors, Santa Fe; for an extensive, if speculative, treatment, see Gottfried Hotz, *The Segesser Hide Paintings: Masterpieces Depicting Spanish Colonial New Mexico* (1970; Santa Fe, N.Mex., 1991); for a primary account pertaining to the Villasur Expedition, see "Declaration of Martínez, Mexico, Nov. 13, 1720," in Thomas, *After Coronado: Spanish Exploration Northeast of New Mexico, 1696–1727* (Norman, Okla., 1935), 170–173.

FIGURE 3. *Segesser I (detail).* c. 1720–1729. Probably an eighteenth-century Spanish-genízaro slaving expedition against Apaches. Courtesy Museum of New Mexico

more, for a section of the hide is missing), on the other hand, are signified as from diverse indigenous cultures and seem to have been outfitted by Spanish patrons. Their horses are equipped with Spanish bits, bridles, and rawhide *cueros* (leather armor), they wield Spanish *espadas anchas* (cavalry sabres) and steel-tipped lances, and they attack in a formation that puts the lancers in the vanguard. But eight are also unmistakably Indian; they exhibit distinctive and different headdresses and hairstyles and carry round leather shields. One of their number may be a Spanish soldier, for he wears what seems to be a steel helmet.[8]

That the Villasur Massacre would be a worthy subject for artistic commemoration seems obvious, for the defeat shocked Spanish authorities from Santa Fe to Madrid. Yet why was equal attention given to what appears a rather everyday battle between Spanish-allied Indian militias and an encampment of

8. For detailed examination of the figures and material culture, see Hotz, *Segesser Hide Paintings,* 15–78; his treatment is unfortunately constrained by an insistence on seeing this scene as a "Mexican Indian militia" operating in "the Sierra Madre mountains of northern

los infieles? The answer probably lies with the artist and whatever priest or captain commissioned the work, but it is a historical jewel nonetheless, for it provides a visual opening into one of the most distinctive and complicated phenomena that the Southwest Borderlands would produce—the creation of "slave militaries" in the region that in time came to express a sense of community, if not ethnic, identity.

Neither "Spanish" nor "Indian," los genízaros have attracted significant attention in modern studies. Much of the debate centers on whether these peoples constituted a racialized and degraded social category imposed from without by Spanish authorities or whether, in time, they developed an internally generated positive ethnic identity. We will see that the answer lies somewhere within this dualism, but we must first look at how the category and the people came to exist in the first place.

The Recopilación of 1681 reiterated the ban on buying and selling Indian slaves first set forth in 1542 and prohibited even their ransom through the artifice of rescate. Just war doctrines of enslavement remained in place, however, which allowed Spanish field commanders and troops enormous latitude in determining appropriate victims during pursuits and engagements. Military exigencies could cover a wide range of war captive possession. As early as 1694, Padre Juan Amando Niel claimed that Carlos II himself condoned the use of royal funds to ransom Pawnee and Jumano boys and girls held captive by Navajo raiders, to prevent their "atrocious treatment"—in this case, Navajos were said to behead those children not purchased. If the king felt justified in setting aside his own law, who were local Spaniards to obey the strictures, especially when engaged in acts of Christian charity? Army officers more often invoked military strategy to justify the ransom of captives but also took note of the humanitarian aspects. In 1786, Comandante General of the Internal Provinces Jacobo Ugarte y Loyola endorsed the ransom of Apache captives "less than fourteen years old" from Comanches on two grounds: to "stimulate" Comanches to make war on the Apaches and to "conserve life"—at least of those young enough to assimilate easily into servile life among the Spaniards. Throughout the eighteenth century, Spanish colonists redeemed indigenous captives from their captors, baptized them into the Catholic faith, and set out to acculturate them as new detribalized royal and Christian subjects. Cus-

Sonora" and misses the more specific genízaro or *nixora* connections. For the latter's role as mixed-descent military auxiliaries in northern Sonora, see Henry Dobyns et al., "What Were Nixoras?" *Southwestern Journal of Anthropology*, XVI (Summer 1960), 230–258.

tom required that these indios de rescate, "saved" from slavery among their "heathen" captors, owed their Spanish redeemers loyalty and personal service in return for their ransom. Defeated enemies and redeemed captives came to carry the appellation "genízaro" in New Mexico, although the term encompassed other statuses as well.[9]

These and other servile peoples fell under the Spanish laws governing slavery that had originated in Las Siete Partidas in A.D. 1265, doctrines noteworthy for their "liberal" position that "all the laws of the world should lead towards freedom." Under these regulations, slaves were conferred rights in marriage and against cruel treatment. They were also allowed to hold property and testify as plaintiffs or defendants and to pursue manumission. Any one of these rights, virtually unknown in the English colonies of North America, might occasionally find exercise among genízaros in New Mexico. Far more often, genízaros—especially if young, female, or isolated in Spanish households—experienced their bondage in forms as brutal as that of their African counterparts throughout the Americas. Since application of protective principles lay in the realm of a local magistrate or protector de indios, the enlightened elements of Spanish slave law fell far short of the ideal, for Indian and African alike.[10]

Enslavement of Indians under the just war doctrine was rampant during the seventeenth century but tapered off after the reconquista of New Mexico between 1692 and 1696 as the Spanish sought alternative, diplomatic routes to pacification of the "wild" Indians. Redemption of captives from Kiowas, Comanches, and Navajos, however, increased in scale during the eighteenth century. These occurred in roughly two forms, either through formal ransoming at ferias or rescates or through small-scale *cambalaches* in local villages or

9. For provisions of the Recopilación that prohibited the purchase, sale, barter, exchange, and ransom of Indians, see Silvio Zavala, *Los esclavos indios en Nueva España* (Mexico City, 1967), 95 n. 146; Padre Juan Amando Niel, "Relaciones de Nuevo Mexico," in *Documentos para la historia de Méjico*, 3d Ser., part 2 (Mexico, 1856), 108; Ugarte to Anza, Oct. 5, 1786, in Thomas, trans. and ed., *Forgotten Frontiers: A Study of the Spanish Indian Policy of Don Juan Bautista de Anza, Governor of New Mexico, 1777–1787*... (Norman, Okla., 1932), 335–336, 386 n. 130.

10. For Las Siete Partidas and the African slave experience in colonial New Mexico, see Colin A. Palmer, *Slaves of the White God: Blacks in Mexico, 1570–1650* (Cambridge, Mass., 1976), esp. 84–118. For Indian slaves in New Mexico, see David J. Weber, *The Spanish Frontier in North America* (New Haven, Conn., 1992), 126–129.

at trading places on the Great Plains. Extrapolating from extant New Mexican parochial registers, between 1700 and 1880, reveals that some five thousand members of plains or pastoral Indian groups entered New Mexican society as indios de rescate, indios genízaros, criados, or *huérfanos,* primarily through the artifice of "ransom" by colonial purchasers. Ostensibly, the debt of ransom would be retired by ten to twenty years of service to the redeemers, after which time these individuals would become vecinos. In practice, these people appear to have experienced their bondage on a continuum that ranged from near slavery to familial incorporation, but few shed the stigma of servility.[11]

Evidence from the eighteenth-century genízaro community of Abiquiu on the Río Chama and Hispano settlements northward in the San Juan river system suggests that most genízaros achieved familial assimilation in the households of their masters through the Spanish institution of compadrazgo. Through the means of this fictive kinship system, genízaros gradually influenced and became a part of a larger Hispano identity group in northern New Mexico. Alternative explanations have asserted a more narrowly circumscribed ethnic genízaro identity, based on the existence of several relatively homogeneous and endogamous genízaro settlements in the Río Grande valley, or have emphasized exploitation, enslavement, and social alienation. One historian, for example, argues that the genízaros were "slaves and criados . . . who had no genealogical ties to the Hispano community, who were dishonored by their status as thralls, and who were deemed socially dead amid men and women of honor." Numerous cases of complaints brought by genízaros against their Spanish masters, charging labor exploitation, cruel discipline, and sexual misuse, buttress evidence of their subordinate position. Characterizations drawn from two contemporary observers, Fray Atanasio Domínguez and Fray Juan Agustin de Morfí, also show contempt for the caste. Domínguez, writing in 1776, claimed that the genízaros were "servants among our people," unable to speak Spanish "without twisting it somewhat," whose "weak" characters turned them into "gamblers, liars, cheats, and petty thieves." Reporting on the state of the province in 1778, Morfí (who never actually visited New

11. Since only some 75 percent of baptismal registers still exist, extrapolating outward would bring the total to 5,116. This would not include captives who were resold so quickly that they never received baptism (David M. Brugge, *Navajos in the Catholic Church Records of New Mexico, 1694–1875,* 2d ed. [Tsaile, Ariz., 1985]). For breakdown by tribal derivation and date, see 22–23.

Mexico and drew his information from interviews) characterized the genízaros as landless "on account of their poverty, which leaves them afoot and without arms . . . they bewail their neglect and they live like animals."[12]

A deeper look into the genízaro experience reveals even more complexity and variation than heretofore proposed, with power distributions operating at all levels of society in colonial New Mexico. The view that, beneath the level of Spanish elites, ethnic boundaries between Spanish and Indian societies eroded under the pressure of kinship and interdependency suffices only so long as we recognize that they did so within a context of unequal and often contested power. The "ethnic identity" position finds some support but requires refinements that include those villages where genízaros and vecinos shared residence, often under the same roof. Although such cases imply easy social mixing, evidence also points to asymmetrical power relations even at the household level. Likewise, the dichotomy between honorable españoles and dishonored genízaros might have been the ideal of elite Spanish ecclesiastics like Domínguez and Morfí but probably reflects prescriptive anxieties about the existence of a mestizo caste neither Spanish nor Indian that was all too important to the colony's survival. Troubled by evidence of social and cultural mixing in distant villages, administrators and churchmen proved eager to find ideological devices by which genízaros could be subsumed within the fragile Spanish social hierarchy. Questions remain, therefore, around the origins of the category in colonial New Mexico, the quality of day-to-day relationships between genízaros and lower-order New Mexican vecinos, and historical

12. For the debate on the genízaros, see Frances Leon Swadesh, *Los Prímeros Pobladores: Hispanic Americans of the Ute Frontier* (Notre Dame, Ind., 1974); Gilberto Espinosa and Tibo Chavez, *El Río Abajo,* chap. X, "The *Genizaro*" (Albuquerque, N.Mex., n.d.); Fray Angélico Chávez, *"Genizaros,"* in Alfonso Ortiz, ed., *The Handbook of North American Indians* (Washington, D.C., 1988), 198–200; Robert Archibald, "Acculturation and Assimilation in Colonial New Mexico," *NMHR* (July 1978), 205–217; Steven M. Horvath, "The *Genizaro* of Eighteenth-Century New Mexico: A Re-examination," *Discovery* (Santa Fe, N.Mex., 1977), 25–40; Russell M. Magnaghi, "The Plains Indians and New Mexico: The *Genizaro* Experience," *Great Plains Quarterly,* X (Spring 1990), 86–95; Ramón A. Gutiérrez, *When Jesus Came, the Corn Mothers Went away: Sexuality, Love, and Conquest in New Mexico, 1500–1846* (Stanford, Calif., 1991), 188; Fray Francisco Atanasio Domínguez, *The Missions of New Mexico, 1776,* trans. and ed. Eleanor B. Adams and Fray Angélico Chávez (Albuquerque, N.Mex., 1956), 42, 126, 208, 259, quoted in Gutiérrez, *When Jesus Came,* 189; for Morfí, see Marc Simmons, trans. and ed., *Father Juan Agustín Morfí's Account of Disorders in New Mexico, 1778* (Isleta Pueblo, N.Mex., 1977), 34–35, quoted in Gutiérrez, 189.

transformations in the nature of their servile status as the borderland economies and societies matured.

The genízaros' origins lay within a larger framework of borderland conflict and accommodation unfolding across the Early Modern Spanish world. Between 1529 and 1830, Spain (and much of Christian Europe) suffered almost continuous harassment from the Ottoman corsairs of North Africa's Barbary Coast. In addition to plunder, these raiders seized Christian captives by the score, either as prisoners of war or in attacks on coastal settlements. Held as slaves and hostages by the Moors, these captives were pawns in a great rivalry between Islam and Christianity. Their ransom was achieved through the efforts of two orders of religious Redemptionists, the Mercedarians and Trinitarians, who undertook the raising of limosnas for ransom and negotiated for captive repatriation. Thus, while Spanish colonists in New Mexico were obtaining thousands of Indian captives at the Taos and Pecos rescates, their counterparts in Spain were rescuing thousands of Christians from the presumed horrors of captivity among the infidels. And, just as the riches obtained through ransom proved crucial to the economies of North Africa, so too did the purchase of captives fuel extension of the market economy into native North America.[13]

Many of these indios de rescate came to be known as "genízaros" in New Mexico, but just why they did so is unclear. The internal politics of the Barbary States yields clues to this puzzle, however. Although within the Ottoman Empire, real power lay locally with the Janissary Corps, the slave armies raised by the Ottomans through the tributary demands of the *devshirme,* or "levy of the boys," imposed upon Balkan subjects. Although the Balkan States had few natural resources to offer, they did contain large populations from which mercenary armies could be raised. Supplementing these levies were renegade Christians from the northern Mediterranean, who found adventure and prestige in the renowned military prowess of the Janissaries. These Janissaries (from *yeñi çeri,* "new troops"), known as "los genízaros" in Spanish, had been created in the fifteenth century, as Ottoman rulers found native Turkish troops often owed allegiance to local chiefs and royal competitors rather than to the expanding Muslim state. Thus the twin meanings ascribed to the term "genízaro" in Spanish are, first, a subject people descending from parents of alien

13. For the Redemptorist orders in the medieval period, see James William Brodman, *Ransoming Captives in Crusader Spain: The Order of Merced on the Christian-Islamic Frontier* (Philadelphia, 1986); for the later era, see Ellen G. Friedman, *Spanish Captives in North Africa in the Early Modern Age* (Madison, Wisc., 1983).

nations or races and, second, prestigious military units that owed a particular loyalty to the crown and that ostensibly stood above the petty intrigues of court politics.[14]

These double attributes attached to the genízaros of New Mexico as well. Both slaves and soldiers, individual genízaros certainly occupied a low status in the colony yet collectively proved crucial in colonial defense and ultimately acted as slave raiders themselves. Colonial New Mexico—rent from within by conflicts between secular and religious authorities, as well as between españoles and mestizos, and threatened from without by the inscrutable politics of contending *indios gentiles*—was fertile ground for the development of a "slave soldiery."[15]

14. For the origins of the Ottoman Janissaries and their relation to slavery and servility in Middle Eastern and Muslim thought, see Cemal Kafadar, *Between Two Worlds: The Construction of the Ottoman State* (Berkeley, Calif., 1995), 17–18, 112; Bernard Lewis, *Race and Slavery in the Middle East: An Historical Enquiry* (Oxford, 1990), 11–14, 62–71; for their role in the Barbary States, see Andrew C. Hess, *The Forgotten Frontier: A History of the Sixteenth-Century Ibero-African Frontier* (Chicago, 1978); John B. Wolf, *The Barbary Coast: Algiers under the Turks, 1500–1830* (New York, 1979); Chávez, *"Genízaros,"* in Ortiz, ed., *Handbook of North American Indians*, 198–199.

15. When viewed in comparative perspective, this ambiguity is less exceptional than it first seems. The enslavement of women and the military mobilization of captive men and male children often went hand in hand not only in the Ottoman Empire but in Africa and Asia as well. For comparative cases, see Wendy James's treatment of Ethiopia, "Perceptions from an African Slaving Frontier"; for the Sudan, see Douglas H. Johnson, "Sudanese Military Slavery from the Eighteenth to the Twentieth Century," both in Léonie J. Archer, ed., *Slavery and Other Forms of Unfree Labour* (London, 1988), 130–156; for Asia and Africa compared, see Jack Goody, "Slavery in Time and Space," in James L. Watson, ed., *Asian and African Systems of Slavery* (Berkeley, Calif., 1980), 16–42. Slave soldiers filled a need where complex cultural and political subdivisions threatened centralization of power, and rulers required both concubines and soldiers who were free of kin and factional obligations. Claude Meillassoux terms these "symplectic [societies] . . . whose *heterogeneous social components* are not amalgamated but are held together by various compulsive *alliances* which can carry out some functions of a centralizing power." "By replacing free men with slaves, the masters could protect themselves from ambitious relatives or rebellious subjects; and at the same time they could protect themselves from these henchmen, by granting them differentiated privileges which divided them among themselves and further attached them to their master" *(The Anthropology of Slavery: The Womb of Iron and Gold* [Chicago, 1991], 64, 140, 344). See also France V. Scholes, *Church and State in New Mexico, 1610–1650* (Albuquerque, N.Mex., 1937), vol. VII of Historical Society of New Mexico, *Publications in History.*

Only one reference to this mysterious status exists in records that predate the Pueblo revolt of 1680, and even that is opaque. Under investigation for abuses during his governorship (1661–1664), Diego Peñalosa stood accused of removing "a genízara, daughter of an Apache-Quivira mother and a Pueblo Indian" from the home of a political enemy. The girl was crippled, and allegedly she was suffering abuse in her position as family servant. The term might have denoted her mixed Indian descent (indeed, from three cultural roots), her servile status, or both. References after the revolt are more numerous but only make the picture more complex. Carlos de Sigüenza y Góngora reported that Diego de Vargas employed a genízaro guide during the reconquista of 1692. Vargas also liberated seventy-four "mestizos, y genízaros" in his progress northward, who then enjoyed "the freedom to return to their brothers, relatives, and spouses." Here the category could indicate a role in military service, mixed-Indian descent (distinguished from the Spanish-Indian mixture of mestizos), and presumably a low social status associated with origins in the regional slave trade. Vargas himself once complained in private correspondence that he "felt no better than a genízaro," so beset with humiliations and isolated from his family in Spain was his position in New Mexico. Only a decade later, yet another use of the term pertained to the Jémez Pueblo warriors who accompained Captain Roque de Madrid in his Navajo campaign of 1705. In this and subsequent cases, when applied to Pueblo Indians, "genízaros" described their military role rather than an enslaved status.[16]

But the term more often applied to members of non-Pueblo Indian cultures who were incorporated into the colony through war or rescates. In 1733, genízaros representing "over one hundred families" petitioned for the right to resettle the abandoned pueblo of Sandía. Extant records of their request indicate that the male heads of households derived from Jumano, Pawnee, Apache, Kiowa, Crow, and Ute heritage; only one was a Pueblo. Seventeen of

16. Scholes, *Troublous Times in New Mexico, 1659–1670* (Albuquerque, N.Mex., 1942), 219, vol. II of Historical Society of New Mexico, *Publications in History;* John L. Kessell, personal communication, Oct. 20, 1995; don Carlos de Sigüenza y Góngora, *Mercurio volante (The Flying Mercury): An Account of the Recovery of the Provinces of New Mexico,* trans. and ed. Irving Albert Leonard (Los Angeles, 1932), 88; "Campaign Journal of Don Diego de Vargas Zapata Luján Ponce de León, 8 January 1692," in J. Manuel Espinosa, trans. and ed., *First Expedition of Vargas into New Mexico, 1692* (Albuquerque, N.Mex., 1940), 128, 263. In his 1705 campaign into Navajo country, Captain Roque de Madrid referred to his Jémez Pueblo auxiliaries as "genízaros." See Rick Hendricks and John P. Wilson, trans. and eds., *The Navajos in 1705: Roque Madrid's Campaign Journal* (Albuquerque, N.Mex., 1996), 19, 44.

the twenty-five men were married, but the tally ignored the cultural derivation of their wives. Judging from later censuses, the thirty-five children born of these marriages probably carried the status of genízaro into adulthood, making them into a hereditary caste. The petitioners took pains to distinguish themselves from those servants residing as "children" in Spanish homes and bound to service by the costs of their redemption. They cast their request as an opportunity to overcome the destitution and separation of their condition while serving the kingdom as guardians and scouts along the Apache frontier. Governor Gervasio Cruzat y Góngora denied their plea, instructing instead that they settle only in established towns and villages. By 1750, the majority were concentrated in the Plaza de los Jarales in Belén and the Barrio de Analco in Santa Fe, but seventeen genízaro families resided alongside vecino neighbors in Ranchos de Taos and San Juan de los Caballeros.[17]

These census data suggest a reconsideration of the presumed landlessness of the caste. After the initial appeal for lands near Sandía Pueblo was refused in 1733, census reports confirm that groups of genízaros received land grants for settlement near Belén in 1740, at Ranchos de Taos in 1750, at Las Trampas in 1751, at Abiquiu and Ojo Caliente in 1754, at San Miguel de Carnué in 1763 and San José de las Huertas in 1765, at Socorro near El Paso del Norte in 1773, at San Miguel del Vado in 1794, and at Anton Chico in 1822. Spanish colonial authorities had a strategic objective in these settlements, namely, to establish buffers on the frontier between nomads and villages in the Río Grande valley. Far from being landless, genízaros occupied key posts in the colonial defense perimeter.[18]

17. "Petición para los genízaros de diversos tribus a poblar el pueblo antiguo de Sandía, 21 avril, 1733," in *SANM,* I, no. 1208, roll 6, frames 687–696; census of July 12, 1750, in Virginia Langham Olmsted, comp., *Spanish and Mexican Censuses of New Mexico, 1750–1830* (Albuquerque, N.Mex., 1981), 47–48; see also Horvath, "The *Genízaro* of Eighteenth-Century New Mexico," *Discovery,* 34.

18. For these dates, see "Declaration of Fray Miguel de Menchero, Santa Bárbara," May 10, 1744, in Charles Wilson Hackett, trans. and ed., *Historical Documents Relating to New Mexico, Nueva Vizcaya, and Approaches Thereto, to 1771,* 3 vols. (Washington, D.C., 1937), III, 401; Spanish colonial censuses of 1750, 1760, and 1790, in Olmsted, *Spanish and Mexican Censuses of New Mexico;* "Las Trampas Grant," in *SANM,* I, no. 975, *Records of the Surveyor General of New Mexico,* no. 27, New Mexico State Records Center, Santa Fe, N.Mex.; Swadesh, *Los Prímeros Pobladores,* 38; Andrew T. Smith, "The People of the San Antonio de Las Huertas Grant," MS in the New Mexico State Records Center; "Description

Other settlements featured a mix of caste residents, which would seem to have bearing on the relative legal and social autonomy of genízaros. The village of San José de las Huertas, in the Sierras de Sandía east of Bernalillo, offers such an example. The land grant petition of 1765 contains the names of eight families, both español and genízaro. By 1767, the village had increased to twenty-one families of mixed-caste status. In its early years, "there was much intermarriage with Indians of San Felipe, Santa Ana, and Sandia [Pueblos]," and villagers who died were buried in the *campo santo* at San Felipe. This alliance with nearby Pueblo people suggests that ethnic alliances were often negotiated at the local level, however much Spanish elites might have wished to maintain ethnic differences and political distinctions between their subject peoples.[19]

The Spanish colonial census of 1750 taken in Ranchos de Taos displays another blending of caste groups. Of the village families, 37 percent were considered Spanish, 26 percent coyotes, and 35 percent genízaros. The census taker reported nine Spanish households of fifty-seven persons, six coyote households of fifty-five persons, and eight genízaro households of twenty-five persons. Even the Spanish households showed a blurring of caste relations; the house of Antonio Atiensa included his coyota wife María Romero, their son Domingo Romero *(castizo),* and the widow Juana with her daughter Manuela, no doubt criadas. Likewise, the household of Juan Rosalio Villalpando, an important español, included his wife María Valdes and their six children, all of whom are termed "coyote," indicating that María was an india, though whether she entered the household as an india de rescate or from nearby Taos Pueblo is unknown. Pablo Francisco Villalpando's household contained three female and two male servientes, two of whom carried the family name. María Rosa Villalpando, whom Comanche raiders would seize ten years later, either was his daughter through marriage to Francisca Lujan or she was the "servant" María Villalpando, a daughter born out of wedlock to a woman from the Martín family. In either case, the Villalpando household illustrates the man-

---

of the Most Notable Characteristics of the Settlement at El Paso del Río del Norte," Sept. 1, 1773, in Hackett, trans. and ed., *Historical Documents,* III, 508; E. Boyd, "The Plaza of San Miguel del Vado," *El Palacio,* LXXVII, no. 4 (1971), 17–27; Magnaghi, "Plains Indians and New Mexico," *Great Plains Quarterly,* X (Spring 1990), 88. Gutiérrez also makes note of this military role *(When Jesus Came,* 305–306).

19. Smith, "The People of the San Antonio de las Huertas Grant, 1767–1900," MS in New Mexico State Records Center, 37.

ner in which Spanish kinship systems, fictive, affinal, and biological, mixed peoples across class and caste lines in a single village family.[20]

The fact that the census arranged households by caste categories reveals a conscious concern about caste status on the part of Spanish administrators, but the data also demonstrate how informally these categories might be arranged at the village level. Census findings from a cluster of plazas at Belén show yet another pattern. In 1790, the third plaza, "Nuestra Señora de los Dolores de los Genízaros," contained thirty-three households, all designated as genízaro, strong evidence that in some cases homogeneous communities developed among some indios de rescate. But the adjacent second "Plaza de Jarales" held thirty Spanish, twelve mestizo, four coyote, and two genízaro households. The marriage patterns from these communities reveal little caste-anxious endogamy; of the twenty-eight unions, only one is español-española. Six marriages involved genízaro-genízara and five mestizo-mestiza. The remaining sixteen show a crossing of caste lines. In most of these, hypogamy seems the rule, with women marrying men of "lower" status. Children of these unions, for example genízaro-coyota, seem to follow the father's status and are later enumerated as genízaros. Thus some genízaros formed genealogical ties to the vecino community. Within households, intercultural mixing became even more complex, as servientes (many the illegitimate children of the patrón) designated coyotas or *de color quebrado* (of broken color) cast the purity of the family line into doubt.[21]

Whatever their residence pattern, as military slaves genízaros played crucial roles in the defense of the province. From 1744 forward, when Fray Miguel del Menchero commended the genízaros of "Cerro de Tomé" (Belén) for the "great bravery and zeal" with which they patrolled the "country in pursuit of the enemy," these auxiliary soldiers utilized their knowledge of the geographic and cultural landscape of the borderlands to preserve the colony. In campaigns against Gila Apaches in 1747, Comanches in 1751 and 1774, and Sierra Blanca Apaches in 1777, in the defeat of Cuerno Verde in 1779, and doubtless in many more local engagements, genízaros played important roles as scouts and

20. See "Ranchos de Taos," in Olmsted, comp., *Spanish and Mexican Censuses of New Mexico,* 47–48; Jack B. Tykal, "From Taos to St. Louis: The Journey of María Rosa Villalpando," *NMHR,* LXV (April 1990), 166.

21. Analysis drawn from Horvath, "The *Genízaro* of Eighteenth-Century New Mexico," *Discovery,* 25–40; for examples, see households in Ranchos de Taos, Spanish colonial census of 1750, in Olmsted, comp., *Spanish and Mexican Censuses of New Mexico,* 47–48.

auxiliary units in forays that also yielded hundreds of captive Indian women and children. We see their centrality and ambiguity vividly portrayed by the anonymous artist of "Segesser I" in the "slave militia" bearing down upon the Apache ranchería, whose defenders know full well the main object of the raid—they stand forward to defend the women and children who watch above from the mesatop palisade. As the century progressed, genízaro military indispensability would provide them some leverage within the social and legal constraints that governed their condition, but often at the cost of violence against their own kinspeople.[22]

Genízaros did more than defend the frontiers against surrounding indios bárbaros. They also mobilized to protest encroachments on their communal lands by colonial estancieros. In October 1745, two genízaros of Belén brought a complaint before Viceroy don Pedro Cebrian y Agustín in Mexico City. They claimed that intrusions on the lands of their pueblo by Diego de Torres, Fulano Barreras, and Antonio Salazar had forced many members of their community to abandon that place, thereby leaving the southern marches of the colony undefended. Furthermore, a grant issued in 1740 to Torres and thirty-one others (among whom was don Nícolas de Chaves, alcalde of Albuquerque) "was illegal and should be null and voided . . . since the land in question included Indian [p]ueblos." Assisted in preparing their complaint by the lawyer Francisco Cordova in Mexico City, the plaintiffs Antonio Casados (Kiowa Apache) and Luís Quintana (Apache) claimed membership in the pueblo of Our Lady of Belén. Casados stated that, "as a young Apache, he was sold into the household of Francisco Casados" before settling in the Belén area in the household of Captain Torres, where he had "paid off his ransom" and joined the genízaro community. There he "became a war captain of the genízaros." Quintana had

22. See "The Declaration of Fray Miguel de Menchero, May 10, 1744," in Hackett, trans. and ed., *Historical Documents,* III, 401–402; "Codallos y Rabál, Santa Fe, Report of Campaign of Alonzo Rubín de Celis against Gila Apaches," in *SANM,* II, no. 483, roll 8, frames 773–339; "Report of the General Campaign, 1751," in Thomas, *Plains Indians and New Mexico,* 64–74, 114–116, 120–121; "Vélez Cachupin, Certified Copy of His Account of Campaign against Comanches in the Fall of 1751," in *SANM,* II, no. 518, roll 8, frames 1049–1054; Pedro Fermín de Mendinueta to Viceroy Antonio María Bucareli y Ursua, Sept. 30, Oct. 20, 1774, in Thomas, *Plains Indians and New Mexico,* 169–176. For the campaign against the Sierra Blanca Apaches by fifty-five genízaros in 1777 that yielded a score of captives, see Cavallero de Croix to Governor Mendinueta, Jul. 2, 1777, in *SANM,* II, no. 701, roll 10, frame 701.

apparently been expelled from the colony some years before, but, having met his countryman in Mexico City, now sought "to return to his land."[23]

With the assistance of Cordova, Casados and Quintana deftly finessed legal details by situating their claim within the tradition of royal protections granted Indian pueblos, thereby sidestepping the question of their social or juridical status as genízaros. The strategy worked, at least for a time. The viceroy ordered Governor Joaquín Codallos y Rabal to hold hearings in Santa Fe to clarify the question of ownership—or suffer a thousand-peso fine. When the day of the hearing arrived, Casados marched to the villa with "seventy Indians from all the different Pueblos" in his entourage. But Codallos seized this opportunity to accuse Casados of "inciting all of the friendly Pueblos against the Spaniards." Given that the genízaro had gone outside the province "to file his charges before the Viceroy without license or permission from proper authorities," he ordered Casados held in the military guardhouse. Here we see the dual nature of genízaros in close focus: sufficiently bold and knowledgeable to journey to Mexico City and appeal to the viceroy's sympathies under the principles of Indian law, in New Mexico Casados remained a "public and notorious fugitive" subject to arrest and confinement when detached from the collective military role of his community.[24]

Governor Codallos called a series of Spanish witnesses who impugned the validity of Casados's complaint, suggesting that "since he has acquired a certain degree of high intelligence" he had become a troublemaker in the community. Don Nícolas de Chaves came forward to claim that on his authority as alcalde he had given "possession to the Spaniards" in 1740 and that the "twenty or so Indians" resident thereon were only so "with the consent of . . . Diego de

23. "Order of Viceroy, Count of Fuenclara, 20 Oct. 1745," "Declaration of Antonio Quintana, 12 Feb. 1746," both in "Antonio Casados and Luís Quintana, *Genízaros,* Proceedings against Fulano Barreras, Diego de Torres and Antonio Salazar over Lands at Puesto de Belén," in *SANM,* I, no. 183, roll 1, frames 1302–1327. For a discussion, see Steven M. Horvath, "The Social and Political Organization of the *Genízaros* of Plaza de Nuestra Señora de Los Dolores de Belen, New Mexico, 1740–1812" (Ph.D. diss., Brown University, 1979), 180–181; Malcolm Ebright, "Advocates for the Oppressed: Indians, Genízaros, and Their Spanish Advocates in New Mexico, 1700–1786," *NMHR,* LXXI (October 1996), 305–339, esp. 317–320; Casados's statement that he had "paid off his ransom" suggests that, at least in some cases, unfree labor in New Mexico more closely resembled indentured servitude than chattel slavery. No documentary evidence has yet come to light describing formal indenture contracts between captives and their Spanish ransomers like that hinted at by Casados.

24. "Obedience and Writ of Codallos y Rabal, 11 Feb. 1746," in *SANM,* I, no. 183.

Torres." Casados, probably brought before the court in chains, was allowed to testify only through a court-appointed interpreter, despite his fluency in Castilian. Even then, the governor cut off his statement and proceeded to cross-examine with sole emphasis on Quintana's flight from the colony, asking no questions regarding the Indian (or genízaro) rights to the arable lands at Belén. He did proceed to collect considerable testimony in favor of the Torres claim from members of the Spanish community, who also spoke unanimously to the seditious nature of Casados's complaint. With the Spanish claim thus bolstered and the genízaro complaint apparently discredited, the governor forwarded his findings to the viceroy. Unfortunately, the viceroy's decision on this case does not survive. But in 1749 the genízaros of Belén again brought a complaint, this time against don Nícolas de Chaves, for "allowing his livestock to foul their acequias." Petitioning in this instance through ecclesiastical channels, rather than secular courts, they won a ruling whereby Chaves was instructed to "build bridges and protect the springs from his cattle." This case suggests that, whatever the resolution to the Casados / Quintana claim three years before, the ability of genízaros to mobilize as a community and assert their rights as wards of the crown or church allowed them some measure of power in the face of local opposition.[25]

Female genízaras also were perilously suspended between the exploitative designs of their masters and the legally mandated guardianship of the secular and religious representatives. In 1763, two genízaras, María Paula and Manuela, servants in the household of Tomás Chávez of Albuquerque, filed a complaint with the alcalde mayor of that villa. Purchased as children, they were now young women. Both claimed that the requisite religious instruction had been denied them by their mistress, Ysabel Chávez, that their master had forced them to herd sheep rather than learn domestic arts—and, in the case of Manuela, that Tomás Chávez had forced himself upon and impregnated her while she worked in the pastures. When Governor Vélez Cachupín reviewed their petition, he found the Chávezes in "neglect of Christian charity" and placed the women in new homes where they would be instructed in Christian doctrine and put to services appropriate to their sex and status as wards of the state. Their slim victory, born of their ability to invoke Christian mores, presumably saved the women from the worst abuses of the master-slave rela-

25. "Declaration of Don Nícolas Chaves, 19 Feb., 1746," ibid.; "Peticíon de los genízaros de Belén, 28 marzo, 1749," *Archdiocesan Archives of Santa Fe,* reel 52, frames 68–72, in New Mexico State Records Center.

tion but did not move them toward freedom. That condition probably awaited Manuela's illegitimate child, who would carry the surname of her adoptive padrinos.[26]

A similar fate, in which sheer good fortune played a hand, awaited ten genízaros swept up in a witchcraft frenzy that erupted in the village of Abiquiu that same year. Its roots lay in 1756, when the Franciscan padre Felix Ordóñez y Machado, founder of the mission to the genízaro settlement, died unexpectedly of suspicious causes. Others in the community, including the new missionary Juan José Toledo, experienced strange illnesses over the next seven years, and when a genízara "on her death bed" accused Joaquín Trujillo, a Kiowa genízaro, of *maleficio* (sorcery), all of the settlements along the Río Chama exploded in accusations and counteraccusations. Joaquín and his brother, Juan Largo, defended themselves as simple healers and seers suffering the resentment of their neighbors and pointed instead to the genízaros Miguel Ontiveros (Pawnee), Agustín Tagle (Kiowa), and Vicente Trujillo (perhaps from San Juan Pueblo) as among some fifteen genízaros (eleven men, three women, and a twelve-year-old girl) who had adopted "the idolotrous and sexually promiscuous Turtle Dance" from their Río Grande Pueblo neighbors. Although none of the accused men confessed to sorcery, María Candelaria Tagle, Vicente Trujillo's wife and perhaps a sister or daughter of Agustín, broke after being lashed to a gun carriage for eight hours. She offered that she had mixed *sangre de drago* ("dragon's blood," a medicinal tea) into some tamales she had made for Father Toledo.

Despite its harmlessness, María's confession coincided with an outbreak of *energúmenas* (violent spirit possession) among dozens of women and girls from Spanish settlements along the Chama. Padre Toledo's masses were continually interrupted by the possessed women falling to the earthen floor of the church, writhing and shrieking obscenities. Even after exorcism the spirits continued to speak, but now in clear voices that demanded the destruction of any and all heathen shrines and sacred petroglyphs in the area. Spanish settlers,

26. "Proceedings in the Complaint of Two Genízara Indian Women of the Jurisdiction of Albuquerque against Their Masters, 12–15 Oct. 1763," in *SANM*, II, no. 547, roll 9, frames 524–526; I thank Dedra S. McDonald for bringing this case to my attention. See her Ph.D. dissertation, "Women Domestic Servants in the Spanish Colonial and Mexican Borderlands, 1700–1860" (University of New Mexico, 1999), for a sweeping examination of labor relations and strategies of survival employed by Indian and Spanish women in the context of bound labor.

probably resentful of the attention the church showered upon its Pueblo and genízaro wards (only the major Spanish towns of Santa Cruz de la Cañada, Santa Fe, and Albuquerque had resident priests), seemed to have found a way to strike out at their Indian neighbors. But not at all of them. The spirits praised Joaquín Trujillo, the original suspect, for his "great work" in exposing the evils of Indian paganism. After four months of incarceration in Sante Fe, five of the imprisoned men had died, probably from the acute infectious hepatitis that seems to have underlain the hysteria. The remaining prisoners were found guilty of sorcery but granted conditional amnesty in honor of a royal wedding in Spain. Rather than hang or burn at the stake, the survivors—six men, three women, and the girl—suffered consignment to service and instruction in Spanish settlers' homes, where they would spend the rest of their lives.[27]

By the mid-eighteenth century, dependent service seems most often the punishment settled on genízaros who stepped beyond the support of a cohesive community or failed to recruit the sympathy of their crown-appointed guardians. Some ten miles south of San José de las Huertas, in Tijeras Canyon, the village of San Miguel de Carnué del Laredo featured mixed social composition. In 1763, seventeen families received an agricultural grant from Governor Vélez Cachupín; among them were ten españoles, three coyotes, and the families of the genízaros Gregorio Montoya, Francisco García, and Bartolo Anzures. Five years later, Montoya and García stood accused of stealing eight cattle from Zía Pueblo. The facts of the case made clear that the Spanish teniente de alcalde Cristóbal Jaramillo had put them up to the crime, since livestock was in short supply in the village. Although they had acted in the interests of the community, their vecino neighbors failed to come to their defense. The genízaros were put to low-paid labor until the owners were compensated, but Jaramillo went unpunished. The larcenous spirit of these socially mixed villages might have been evenly distributed, but egalitarianism did not apply when courts chose to enforce the law. Household or village coresidence and mutual economic needs fostered daily interaction across caste lines, while

27. See copies of "Autos seguidos contra unos indios jenízaros del pueblo de Abiquiú, 1760–1766," in Pinart Collection, Bancroft Library, University of California, Berkeley; see also *Records of the Surveyor General of New Mexico,* report no. 140, Town of Abiquiu Grant, in New Mexico State Records Center; Gilberto Benito Córdova, "Missionization and Hispanicization of Santo Thomás Apóstol de Abiquiu, 1750–1770" (Ph.D. diss., University of New Mexico, 1979). See also Quintana, *Pobladores,* 23–29; Quintana attributes these symptoms to acute infectious hepatitis, culminating in cirrhosis of the liver (25).

racial resentments and social inequalities promoted divisions and relegated genízaros to subservient positions.[28]

Those Indians captured in war and los indios rescate came to constitute a caste of genízaros over the course of the eighteenth century. Their position within colonial society ranged from near-slave status initially to autonomous conditions within their own communities by midcentury. Their standing, however, was always precarious and could slip quickly back into permanent dependent servitude. Yet expansion of the borderland economies broadened the role of social marginals like genízaros in mediating between los indios bárbaros and the Spanish colony, which would open new negotiating spaces for those peoples so disparaged by the colonial elite.

Lest We Go in Search of Relief to Our Lands and Our Nation

An unusual audience occurred in the Sonoran town of Arizpe, seat of the comandante general of the Interior Provinces of New Spain, early in the summer of 1780. Bentura Bustamante, "Lieutenant of the Genízaro Indians of the Villa of Santa Fe in the Kingdom of New Mexico," laid a bold challenge before Spain's highest-ranking representative in the provinces, the newly appointed comandante general Teodoro de Croix. Speaking in the name of thirty-three petitioners, four of whom accompanied him, Bustamante swore that, unless Croix addressed their community's grievance, they faced little choice but to "go in search of relief to our lands and our Nation." As is too often the case in Spanish colonial legal proceedings, neither the exact nature of Bustamante's complaint nor precisely what remedy he and his traveling companions had in mind was ever explicitly mentioned. But Bustamante asserted without hesitation his community's right to make a claim. As "yndios genízaros," he argued, his people had been delivered from infidelity into the mysteries of the Holy Catholic Faith by their Spanish "parents and masters." After that, they had purchased lands, built houses, and "remained obedient to the Royal Service for campaigns and war activities," even when to do so meant they had "betrayed their own Nation." For "loyal Christian Indians" to confront their superiors in such a manner seems unusual. But it becomes startling when we consider that

28. "Diligencias criminales contra los jenízaros de Carnué," in *SANM*, II, no. 636, roll 10, frame 400; see discussion in Swadesh, "Archaeology, Ethnohistory, and the First Plaza of Carnue," in *Ethnohistory*, XXIII (Winter 1976), 31–44.

the threat to desert the colony and find succor with their "own Nation" issued from people whom custom treated as servants and slaves.[29]

A careful look at the wider context of Bustamante's protest illustrates how his people were in the vanguard of the colony's growing interdependence with and interpenetration of the plains and pastoral economies. In 1776, Carlos III finally approved a massive reorganization of New Spain's northern frontier into the Provincias Internas and appointed Teodoro de Croix as comandante general. Aimed at promoting immigration and expanding the economy in the northern provinces, the creation of new or relocation of existing presidial defenses composed one aspect of Croix's strategy. Croix selected Juan Bautista de Anza, fresh from success in establishing the presidio at San Francisco in Alta California, as governor of New Mexico. As part of his military reorganization of the province, Anza considered several options. He proposed that the scattered poblaciones associated with the settlements like Santa Cruz de la Cañada and San Buenaventura de Chimayo be consolidated into fortified plazas capable of defense against Indian attacks. There, church and state might better monitor the unruly settlers' behavior. He also considered relocating the capital and presidio to a new site on the Río Grande between Santo Domingo and Cochiti Pueblos. Barring that, he proposed a less dramatic move of the Santa Fe presidio from the north bank of the Río Santa Fe (where it remains today in the form of the governor's palace) to higher ground on the south side, where the Barrio de Analco clustered around the Church of San Miguel. This barrio had long embraced the lands and homes of Santa Fe's genízaro population, which in 1780 numbered some 142 individuals in 42 families, or 12 percent of the town's population. Anza's plans would have included resettlement of many "lower order" vecino residents in the new capital and relocation of the Analceño genízaros to frontier settlements, which Bustamante had termed "gateway of the enemy Comanche."[30]

29. "Petición de Bentura Bustamante, 20 junio, 1780," in *SANM,* I, no. 1138, roll 6, frames 323–325. I thank David H. Snow for bringing this case to my attention.

30. For reorganization of the Interior Provinces, see Weber, *Spanish Frontier,* chap. 8; for Anza's proposals, see *SANM,* I, no. 1118, roll 6, frames 149–160; for genízaro occupation of Analco, see Domínguez, *Missions of New Mexico,* trans. and ed. Adams and Chávez, 42; "Geographical Description of New Mexico Written by . . . Fray Juan Agustín de Morfi . . . 1782," in Thomas, trans. and ed., *Forgotten Frontiers: A Study of the Spanish Indian Policy of Don Juan Bautista de Anza, Governor of New Mexico, 1777–1787 . . .* (Norman, Okla., 1932), 92; see also Anza to Croix, May 26, 1780, in Thomas, *Forgotten Frontiers,* 177; "Petición de Bentura Bustamante, 20 junio, 1780," in *SANM,* I, no. 1138, roll 6, frames 323–325.

Although Anza's relocation plans were never explicitly stated, other evidence makes clear that they lay at the root of Bustamante's complaint. The genízaro petition was part of a larger protest against consolidation and reorganization in which the interests of settler society and those of their despised castes converged for a brief time to transcend barriers of race and caste. Bustamante and his companions probably arrived in Arizpe with a larger party of twenty-four petitioners led by Manuel de Armijo and José Miguel de la Peña, who had fled Santa Fe in May after offending Governor Anza by their own refusals to relocate. Also among that party traveled Cristóbal Vigil and Salvador Maestas, representing La Cañada and Chimayo respectively. Thus Anza's reorganization schemes sufficiently distressed four different communities to send emissaries across some five hundred miles of uncharted territory to plead for their repeal.[31]

Each community expressed different grievances. The citizens of Santa Fe, according to Armijo and Peña, had labored too long and hard to build irrigation dams and acequias, maintain the chapel, and till their fields to abandon them now. They complained too that Anza's prohibition against the sale or purchase of Indian servants, whom Anza claimed they treated like "infidel slaves," deprived them of the additional profits and labor with which to make good the relocation. The outlying villages of La Cañada and Chimayo, on the other hand, found Anza's orders to congregate vexing, for to do so would distance them unnecessarily from their fields and orchards. Anza later told the comandante general that this concern was trivial; rather, their resistance emerged from a general disposition toward "separation and solitude" that came from the "old custom of living dispersed . . . in order to enjoy greater liberty" and participate in illicit Indian trading.[32]

Bustamante's genízaros argued somewhat differently. Although his people did not wish to abandon their communal lands or their centrality in military affairs, foremost among their fears over relocation stood the danger of "losing their women and children" to capture by Comanche raiders, a peril

31. "Manuel de Armijo y José Miguel de la Peña, 2 junio 1780," Document Five, Sender Collection, roll 1, frames 27–38, New Mexico State Records Center; for Vigil and Maestas, see Anza to Croix, Jan. 12, 1781, in *SANM*, I, no. 1118, roll 6, frames 149–160; for Croix's reception of the petitioners, see Croix to Anza, Jul. 29, 1780, in *SANM*, I, no. 1260, roll 6, frames 949–959.

32. Document Five, Sender Collection, roll 1, frames 27–38, New Mexico State Records Center; Anza to Croix, Jan. 12, 1781, in *SANM*, I, no. 1118, roll 6, frames 149–160.

that had plagued frontier settlements since the colony's inception. The genízaros of Analco knew the pattern of reciprocal slave raiding all too well, for they were one consequence of the trade and often took cautivos themselves during their campaigns against los indios bárbaros. Years of military service and coresidence with colonial New Mexicans had made them devout Catholics and loyal subjects, yet Anza's expulsion and relocation plan left Bustamante's people only two alternatives—to "endure their burdens and travails" or to depart the colony altogether.

The latter option raises intriguing questions about just how the Analceños conceived of themselves as a community. Bustamante thrice employed the term "nación" in his appeal, once declaring his genízaro *compañeros* an "Indian Nation, all united in due conformity," again when he threatened that they might seek refuge in their "lands and Nation," and finally when he claimed that in military service for the Spaniards they "betrayed our own Nation." That Bustamante described Comanches as enemies and that by 1780 Anza had implemented a strategy of taking war to the Sierra Blanca and Lipan Apaches suggest that the betrayal his genízaros felt might have derived from a common descent with Apaches. Indeed, Apaches comprised some 65 percent (675 of 1,045) of the Plains Indians baptized in New Mexican parishes between 1730 and 1780, and perhaps the Analceños represented a concentration of these in a single barrio. Yet possibly the unified community of which Bustamante spoke grew among peoples of diverse cultural backgrounds sharing similar historical experiences and united by Catholicism, military service, coresidence, and an ascribed servile status. Thus their "Indian Nation" might have loomed larger within and without their minds, meaning any who were simply not Spaniards. Whether Bustamante's threat meant literal desertion and apostasy or merely temporary flight to the Plains while Anza reconsidered his decision remains unclear. It does hint that these genízaros had not entirely severed their familial and cultural connections to their native kinspeople, who presumably remained willing to take them in to their rancherías.[33]

Bustamante's people did not need to risk fugitive status, however, for Anza reported to Croix in 1781 that Analco was not sufficiently expansive or well

33. "Petición de Bentura Bustamante, 20 junio, 1780," in *SANM,* I, no. 1138, roll 6, frames 323–325. The phrases at issue are, in sequence, "compañeros que semos de dicha Nación Yndios todos unidos en devida conformidad"; "o nos iremos a buscar alivio a nuestra tierras y Nación"; and "quando hemos salido a Campaña hemos entregado a nuestra propia Nación." For Apache baptisms, see Brugge, *Navajos in the Catholic Church Records,* 22–23.

watered to support a new presidio. His preferred plan, relocation of the capital, hung in abeyance for lack of funds—and, by 1787, when a more modest construction of barracks adjacent to the presidio did occur, was largely unnecessary. He still fumed that his intended expedition to open a route between New Mexico and Sonora had to be abandoned due to the "malicious and needless flight of the settlers of this Villa" but appeared heedless to the irony that the path had been trailblazed by the mixed group of vecinos and genízaros the previous year. For a few months, at least, the Spanish citizenry of New Mexico and the genízaros of Analco found common cause. The latter seemed willing to take extraordinary risks in their search for an autonomous social space, however circumscribed, and to protect the interests of their families and growing sense of community.[34]

The troubles of 1780 do point to an emerging array of shared interests between genízaros and lower-order vecinos that occurred in conjunction with expansion on the borderland economies. Consequent to the unauthorized departure of citizens and slaves to Arizpe, Anza had reported to Croix his inability to persuade the citizens of the province to form a cordón to Chihuahua that would then have cooperated with his Sonoran expedition. He attributed this reluctance to the lack that season of "the formal trading for hides with the pagans," which took place only every two years. He explained that such a fair "stimulates and makes up the largest part of the trade of this province," without whose effects the settlers thought a cordón to be fruitless. As a drought and famine that began in the late 1770s persisted in the province, and with a smallpox epidemic just beginning, local economic conditions would become dire. Under these circumstances, genízaros and vecinos alike found neither relocation nor a major trade and military expedition appealing. In December 1780, many of the lower social order pursued an alternative strategy. Probably guided by genízaro scouts like Bentura Bustamante, more than two hundred men, women, and children from the colony took to the eastern Plains on a buffalo hunt, returning to their homes with 450 loads of meat.[35]

34. For construction of the *cuartel* between 1787–1791, see Ross H. Frank, "From Settler to Citizen: Economic Development and Cultural Change in Late Colonial New Mexico, 1750–1820" (Ph.D. diss., University of California, Berkeley, 1992), 139–142; Anza to Croix, May 26, 1780, "Geographical Description by Morfi," both in Thomas, *Forgotten Frontiers,* 92, 177, 374 n. 28, 379–380 n. 59; see also Thomas, trans. and ed., *Teodoro de Croix and the Northern Frontier of New Spain, 1776–1783: From the Original Document in the Archives of the Indies, Seville* (Norman, Okla., 1941), 107–108.

35. Anza to Croix, May 26, 1780, in Thomas, *Forgotten Frontiers,* 177; see also Kessell,

Few of Good, or Even Moderately Good, Blood

Alliances born of mutual interests between genízaros and their Spanish colonial neighbors, like those expressed in the 1780 Arizpe protests and winter bison-hunting sojourn, suggest an increasing permeability of racial or caste boundaries in the colony across the eighteenth century. Spanish ecclesiastics and administrative elites took pains to distinguish themselves from those below them, whether Indian, *casta,* or lower-class españoles. Yet the biological and social consequences of everyday intimate interaction among those lower orders, whether coercive or voluntary, mixed the colony's population in ways that elites tried but failed to control through caste distinctions.

Census data from colonial New Mexico are notoriously inconsistent, but some informed speculations as to the relative "free" and "unfree" composition of the society over time are possible. Although one Franciscan census of 1749 reported 1,350 "indios servientes" among a total non-Pueblo colonial population of 4,170 (32 percent), the next year's census counted a total Spanish and caste population of 3,809 individuals. Of these, 154 (4 percent) were genízaros and 693 (18 percent) servientes or criados. The lower orders were more heavily represented in peripheral villages (447 of 1,052 inhabitants, or 42 percent) than in the villas of Santa Fe and Albuquerque (400 of 2,757 inhabitants, or 15 percent), although Albuquerque did hold the highest representation of families who included mulattoes of African descent (18 of 191 households) among their members. Consistent with their role as scouts and military auxiliaries and probable precursors to Bentura Bustamante's people, 112 genízaros resided near the Santa Fe presidio in the Barrio de Analco, with an additional 24 in the frontier outpost of Ranchos de Taos.[36]

An anonymous report of 1765 listed a combined español, gente de razón, casta, and genízaro population of 5,168 in the Río Arriba and Río Abajo re-

---

Miera y Pacheco Map of New Mexico, 1776–1789, n. 11, facs. reproduction from don Bernardo de Miera y Pacheco, "Plano de la Provincia Interna de el Nuebo Mexico . . . 1779," map in Domínguez, *Missions of New Mexico,* trans. and ed. Adams and Chávez.

36. Henry W. Kelly, *The Franciscan Missions of New Mexico, 1740–1760* (Albuquerque, N.Mex., 1941), 19; Olmsted, comp., Spanish colonial census of 1750, *Spanish and Mexican Censuses of New Mexico,* 1–97; for the African presence in colonial New Mexican society, see Dedra S. McDonald, "Intimacy and Empire: Indian-African Interaction in Spanish Colonial New Mexico, 1500–1800," *American Indian Quarterly,* XXII (1998), 134–156.

gions but failed to distinguish each category other than a genízaro total of 288. In the El Paso del Norte region, 389 genízaros (including 36 "with the status of citizens," an upward movement not noted in the northern colony) represented 12 percent of the combined Spanish and caste population of 3,142 individuals. Eleven years later, Fray Atanasio Domínguez counted 650 genízaros in a combined Spanish and caste population of 9,742 in the Río Arriba and Río Abajo, or 7 percent of the total. But, of the racial composition in some mountain villages, wherein genízaros and vecinos intermixed in residence and intimate relations, Domínguez commented, "There are few of good, or even moderately good, blood."[37]

Despite their obvious preoccupation with purities of blood, neither the 1765 nor 1776 enumerators took care to give precise figures of casta individuals other than those for genízaros. Given the moral anxiety that local customs of rescate provoked in church and secular authorities, who served as census takers, Spanish householders seem likely to have hidden many servants as minor dependents or fictive sisters and brothers. The census of 1790 counts only 248 sirvientes or criados, or 1.5 percent of a total Spanish and caste population of 16,081. At first glance, this suggests that servitude had virtually disappeared in a society that was expanding at the extraordinary rate of 8 percent per annum. If we look, however, at the percentage of casta individuals in the Spanish colonial population and compare this figure to those of "composite" families, which include dependents attached to the biological family, and to those of "incomplete" (female-headed) families, we see a very different picture.[38]

The census of 1790 counted a high proportion of mestizos, coyotes, and people de color quebrado within the Spanish and caste population in the major regions of Spanish settlement: 26 percent at Santa Cruz de la Cañada, 26 percent at Santa Fe, and 38 percent in the Albuquerque region, totaling 3,522 of 11,485 people in all three regions, or 31 percent. Composite families in the principal Spanish settlements of Santa Cruz de la Cañada (16 percent), Santa Fe (21 percent), and the Albuquerque region (27 percent) represented 22 percent (442 of 1,997) of all families, reflecting "the ample group of domestic servants

37. Donald C. Cutter, trans. and ed., "An Anonymous Statistical Report on New Mexico, 1765," *NMHR*, L (October 1975), 347–352; Gutiérrez, *When Jesus Came*, 171; Domínguez, *Missions of New Mexico*, trans. and ed. Adams and Chávez, 98–99.

38. Gutiérrez, *When Jesus Came*, 172. Since only sixty-eight individuals in the 1790 census had been born outside of New Mexico, this growth was the combined product of natural increase (probably not more than 3 percent annually), the "slippage" of acculturated Pueblos into New Mexican society, and the importation of Indian captives.

and the peons" living within or around the house or rancho. The 132 families who did report holding servientes or criados averaged 1.87 such persons per household. If we apply the same number to the 309 composite families "hiding" their servants as quasi kin, we find another 577 servile people in the population.[39]

Furthermore, a high proportion of "incomplete" families occurred in these same districts: 22 percent in Santa Cruz de la Cañada, 25 percent in Santa Fe, and 28 percent in Albuquerque. Averaging some two children per family, the members of 515 incomplete families totaled 1,541 individuals. About one-third of these families were headed by "widows," but many of these, as well as the nonwidowed, female-headed households, seem a thinly concealed concubinage of unwed mothers attached to Spanish households. Even if we reduce the total by one-third to reflect the widowed population, we still find 1,026 women and children living in a dependent status in these districts. The smaller frontier and mountain villages are not so carefully detailed in this census, but, given the much larger representation of racially mixed and socially marginal people in earlier enumerations of those locales, we may conservatively extend the patterns above to the colony as a whole.[40]

The servile population of 1790s New Mexico might have totaled some 1,851 individuals, or 12 percent of the Spanish and caste population. Many of these people derived from the slave trade, either as indios de rescate or descendants of the same. Between 1700 and 1800, 1,646 non-Pueblo Indians received baptism in local parishes and hence were the source for many of these servile people (Table 2). Although no precise correlation exists between the casta population and members of composite and incomplete families, mixed-descent people of full or quasi-servile status in 1790s New Mexico likely represented some one-half of the total casta population (1,851 of 3,522, or 53 percent). That one-half of these people were perhaps not slaves or servants points to the fluid quality of human bondage in New Mexico, where children of slaves could be, though were not always, born free.[41]

39. Alicia V. Tjarks, "Demographic, Ethnic, and Occupational Structure of New Mexico, 1790," *Americas,* XXXV (July 1978), 45–88, esp. 83, table 14; see also 74, 77, table 12. For average slaves per household, see Gutiérrez, *When Jesus Came,* 171, table 4.5.

40. Tjarks, "Demographic, Ethnic, and Occupational Structure," *Americas,* XXXV (July 1978), 67, 77, table 12.

41. Brugge, *Navajos in the Catholic Church Records,* 22–23. Gutiérrez, *When Jesus Came,* 171, cites Albert H. Schroeder's estimation of genízaros' numbering about one-third of New Mexico's population in the late eighteenth century to postulate 9,680 genízaros in a 1793

TABLE 2. Baptisms of Selected Non-Pueblo Indians, 1700–1800

Tribe	1700s	1710s	1720s	1730s	1740s	1750s	1760s	1770s	1780s	1790s	Total
Apaches	47	26	97	143	320	170	23	24	14	36	900
Jumanos	3	2		8	1			1			15
Pawnees	3	4	9	1	2	1				1	21
Aàs (Crows)					8	17	4	2	18	24	73
Kiowas				12	5	2	3	2	7	4	35
Comanches			3	4	7	11	33	48	57	30	193
Utes		5		1	5	8	9	9	23	14	74
Navajos	19	3		11	178	32	8	77	7		335
Overall	72	40	109	180	526	241	80	163	126	109	1,646

The non-Pueblo Indians who entered the colony further increased its ethnic complexity. Apache captives predominated in baptisms throughout the eighteenth century, testimony to their growing vulnerability in the face of Comanche expansion. These Apaches doubtless formed the early core of the colony's genízaro population and those of the Barrio de Analco community. The large number (178) of Navajo baptisms in the 1740s was the result of voluntary conversions at the Cebolleta and Encinal missions, but the hundred or so that followed thereafter were not. This would continue to be the case for the nineteenth century, when they would far outnumber any other Indian group. The 193 Comanches baptized in the latter decades of the century reflect the era of warfare that concluded in the 1780s; fewer than 30 more Comanches would be taken in this manner across the nineteenth century. Overall, these baptisms make clear the close relationship between cycles of warfare and enslavements of women and children in the Spanish colony.

The censuses of 1750 and 1790 provide two fairly reliable data points to consider another element of racial and servile complexity in the colony—the growth of the free, yet socially marginal, mixed-blood population through the childbearing of servile women. A random sample of baptismal entries indicates that the female-to-male ratio of indios de rescate was approximately two to one; some two-thirds of all captives were women and girls. Judging from marital and baptismal registers and anecdotal materials, we may presume that most of these ended up in conjugal relationships with New Mexican men, either as concubines to Spaniards or wives of male castas. Analysis of births to Navajo captives in New Mexican households shows that 84 percent (135 of 160) were designated illegitimate, suggesting either concubinage or unsanctified unions. Of the 25 legitimate births, 21 listed a captive Navajo man as father and a mestiza as mother; hence Navajo women bore legitimate children in fewer than 3 percent of these cases. It should be noted, however, that, in 113 cases, the children did have baptismal padrinos, indicating a limited integration into New Mexican forms of fictive kinship.[42]

---

population of 29,041. See Schroeder, "Río Grande Ethnohistory," in Alfonso Ortiz, ed., *New Perspectives on the Pueblos* (Albuquerque, N.Mex., 1979), 62.

42. Brugge, *Navajos in the Catholic Church Records,* 116, estimates a sixty to forty female-male ratio for the Navajo captives he has studied between 1694 and 1875. Working again with the Spanish colonial census of 1750, where individuals are designated either by proper name or by a gendered noun (criada / criado, genízara / genízaro, india / indio), I find that women total 153 of 282 individuals, or 54 percent. Since some bondwomen, for example, are

Given that the 1790 census reported only 66 of the 16,081 Spanish and caste individuals as Mexican immigrants and 2 from Spain, the remarkable growth rate between 1750 and 1790 of 8.2 percent must have resulted from the combined influx of captives and acculturated Pueblos, their mixed offspring, and the natural increase of the Spanish population. Even with renewed migration from Mexico after 1790, the mixed population grew with each generation. Beginning in the eighteenth century and proceeding well into the nineteenth, the mountain borderlands would bring new strains of Indian blood into New Mexico, as would the colony send those of the "pure Castilian" into Indian societies. The path for both lay to the north.

To the Kingdom and Provinces of Teguayo

The darkly timbered and perennially snowcapped mountain country rising in the northern reaches of the colony had long held a fascination for New Mexicans. Neither teeming with herds of buffalo nor well suited to sheep, the massifs of the San Juan Mountains did conceal abundant game like deer and elk. But to many New Mexicans the region seemed to hold deeper mysteries—people who had huge ears *(los orejones),* people who ate their own children for sustenance, dangerous "strawheads" *(cabezas pajizos)* who were "enemies of all the other nations," even people who were made of stone *(las piedrases).* To the north might also be found the nation of the Yuta and, beyond that, the mythic region of Teguayo, in the center of which spread the Great Lake of Copala and the caves from which the Aztecs were said to have originated. Most intriguing of all, however, were the persistent stories of abundant silver,

designated simply *"cinco indias criadas y ocho coyotitos"* ("Francisco Romero, Alias Talache Coyote, Settlement of Estate," *SANM,* I, no. 780, roll 4, frame 1175), we cannot determine a precise gender breakdown. Nineteenth-century figures show persistence in these proportions: Lafayette Head's 1865 census of Indian captives held in Costilla and Conejos Counties, Colorado Territory, shows females numbering 99 of 148 captives (67 percent), with children under age fifteen accounting for 96 of the 148 (National Archives, New Mexico Superintendency, microcopy 234, roll 553); baptismal entries for the *parrochia* of Sapello, east of the Sangre de Cristos, between 1861 and 1871 show a total of 49 captives, of whom 34 are female, of which 13 are above age fifteen. Only one of the boys is above age fifteen. See *Archdiocesan Archives of Santa Fe,* Sapello Baptisms, Our Lady of Guadalupe, Jan. 20, 1861, to Mar. 5, 1871, microfilm in New Mexico State Records Center; Brugge, *Navajos in the Catholic Church Records,* 116.

in some cases so abundant that streams flowed with silver ingots. And it is no surprise to find that the colony's earliest native informant on the region was "a captive two years in the province," a Jémez Pueblo man, don Juanillo.[43]

On a more mundane level, the deer, elk, and timber of the San Juan Mountains offered sustenance and security that attracted Ute migration in the seventeenth century and would entice New Mexicans northward in the century following the reconquista. These plentiful subsistence resources—and the absence of intensive production of easily marketable commodities like bison hides or sheep fleeces—would influence the style of settlement and cultural interaction in the north well into the nineteenth century.

While Ute bands, their Jicarilla Apache neighbors, and New Mexican pobladores would jointly create a borderland in the north, they did not develop the social relations of production in conjunction with external markets in the same manner as their pastoral or plains cousins did. Consequently, neither did they elaborate internal social inequality to the same degree as did those other groups. But the absence of internal relations of servitude did not prevent these mountain groups from participating in the slave system of the Greater Southwest Borderlands. Utes and Jicarillas began as victims of the commerce but in time learned to protect themselves as suppliers of Navajo captives. Likewise, New Mexican *montañeses*—often themselves descended from the genízaro products of the trade—soon became slave traders themselves.

As such, Indian and New Mexican mountain people created a permeable borderland wherein captives and commodities like deerskins and peltries moved through their respective societies without working major internal transformations. Throughout the eighteenth century, this meant that los montañeses were insulated to some degree from the internal tensions developing with commercial integration in the plains and pastoral economies. But, also, by the early years of the nineteenth century, they would be without the wealth in horses, weaponry, and labor that would allow them to compete for the fruits of the Greater Borderlands' political economy. To understand the long-term meaning of their contradictory relationship to the larger economy, we need to

43. "Diarios de Juan María Antonio Rivera, 1765," in Cutter, "Prelude to a Pageant in the Wilderness," *Western Historical Quarterly*, VIII (January 1977), 5–14; Joseph P. Sánchez, *Explorers, Traders, and Slavers: Forging the Old Spanish Trail, 1678–1850* (Salt Lake City, Utah, 1997), 7–11; Alonso de Posada, *Alonso de Posada Report, 1686: A Description of the Area of the Present Southern United States in the Late Seventeenth Century*, trans. and ed. Alfred Barnaby Thomas (Pensacola, Fla., 1982).

look at the means by which los montañeses created their distinctive borderland in the mountains and valleys of the north.

As we saw earlier, southward migrations by Shoshonean-speaking "Yutas" and associated warfare contributed to Navajo abandonment of Dinetah in the eighteenth century, a movement largely complete by the late 1770s. But all was not enmity, for according to Navajo accounts a band of Utes "with good arms of all kinds" camped as neighbors in the San Juan area, and, although at first they were "unruly and impertinent," over time they merged with Navajos to form the Notádiné ("Ute People") clan. At the same time, Utes' proximity to the Spanish colony led to enslavement by New Mexicans. On some occasions in the seventeenth century, Yuta captives were brought into the governor's obrajes in Santa Fe or sold south to work in the silver mines of Zacatecas. Across the eighteenth century, baptismal records show seventy-four Utes brought into New Mexico as indios de rescate, more often the result of local snatches than the major expeditions for military slaves suffered by their Apache neighbors.[44]

For the first half of the eighteenth century, the Utes maintained generally good relations with their Comanche cousins. These included combined horse and captive raids and efforts to supplant the Plains Apaches as New Mexico's principal trading partners. Testifying in 1719, Captain Miguel de Coca stated that "the Ute nation and that of the Comanche commonly go about together for the purpose of interfering with the little barter that this kingdom had with the nations that come in to ransom." The Jicarilla Apaches were the early victims of this alliance; in his autumn campaign of 1719, Governor Antonio de Valverde visited a Jicarilla ranchería that had lost sixty-four women and children to Ute and Comanche raiders the previous year. The fact that 62 percent of Apache baptisms as indios de rescate in New Mexican parishes occurred between 1700 and 1750 suggests that the Ute-Comanche alliance rapidly gained ascendancy in the Plains captive trade and contributed to Jicarilla withdrawal from the Plains. By 1733, the church had established a mission for the Jicarillas five leagues north of Taos, perhaps in the Cieneguilla Valley, but found those Apaches little interested in a *reducción.* Although they would often serve as auxiliary scouts and fighters for the Spanish, the Jicarillas were the first group to look for security in the northern mountains.[45]

44. Washington Matthews, trans. and comp., *Navajo Legends* (1897; Salt Lake City, Utah, 1994), 146; Scholes, *Church and State in New Mexico,* 301; Brugge, *Navajos in the Catholic Church Records,* 22–23.

45. "Opinion of Captain Miguel de Coca, August 19, 1719," "Diary of the Campaign of Governor Antonio de Valverde against the Ute and Comanche Indians, 1719," both in

By the late 1740s, however, the Comanches began to operate independently of the Utes and by 1750 had secured peaceful (although probably coercive) trading arrangements with the Jumanos, Pawnees, and French traders working out of the Great Lakes region. The year 1747 featured the last combined Ute-Comanche actions, when some Muache Utes joined Comanches in the captive raid against the genízaro settlement of Abiquiu and succeeded in carrying off twenty-three women and children. After that time, references to Comanches indicate a shift to new allies. In 1748, a Comanche trading encampment northeast of Taos included thirty-three Frenchmen, and one year later Comanches brought ten Frenchmen along on an expedition "to sell slaves to the Spaniards" in New Mexico. With these autonomous movements by the Comanches, the Utes found themselves foreclosed from trade opportunities on the Plains and often at odds with their former allies. By 1750, relations between them deteriorated into overt hostilities.[46]

The Utes began a gradual withdrawal into the mountains about this time, although the eastern band, the Muaches, continued to risk substantial time on the Plains hunting buffalo along the Arkansas, Purgatoire, and Canadian Rivers. The Capote and Weeminuche bands occupied the San Luis Valley and the drainages of the San Juan River, relying principally on the deer and elk herds of the area for sustenance and trade items, especially the *antas blancas* (white elkskins) coveted by New Mexicans and other Indian groups alike.

By the middle years of the eighteenth century, both Jicarilla Apaches and southern Ute bands pursued peaceful relations with the New Mexicans. Gov-

---

Thomas, *After Coronado*, 105, 110–133, esp. 115 (see also table 1); Brugge, *Navajos in the Catholic Church Records*, 22–23; Joseph Antonio Villa-Señor, *Teatro Americano*, part 2 (Mexico, 1748), cited in Thomas, *After Coronado*, 46; for a view that stresses the mountain orientation of Jicarilla culture, tempered by Plains and Pueblo influences, see M. E. Opler, "A Summary of Jicarilla Apache Culture," *American Anthropologist*, N.S., XXXVIII (1936), 202–223.

46. Henri Folmer, "Contraband Trade between Louisiana and New Mexico in the Eighteenth Century," *NMHR*, XVI (July 1941), 249–274; "An Account . . . by Fray Juan Sanz de Lezaún, 1760," in Hackett, trans. and ed., *Historical Documents*, III, 477; Herbert Eugene Bolton, "French Intrusions into New Mexico, 1749-1752," in John Frances Bannon, ed., *Bolton and the Spanish Borderlands* (Norman, Okla., 1964), 150–171; Fray Antonio Duran de Armijo to Governor Joaquín Codallos y Rabal, Feb. 27, 1748, Codallos to viceroy, Mar. 4, 1748, both in Ralph Emerson Twitchell, *The Spanish Archives of New Mexico* (Cedar Rapids, Iowa, 1914), I, no. 499, 148–149; for the 1749 visit, see Bolton, "French Intrusions," in Bannon, ed., *Bolton and the Spanish Borderlands*, 162; Opler, "The Origins of Comanche and Ute," *American Anthropologist*, N.S., XLV (1943), 155–158.

ernor Vélez Cachupín negotiated a treaty of friendship between Utes and New Mexicans in 1750 that allowed for resettlement of those villages terrorized by the Comanche-Ute raids of 1747. The following decades saw Utes developing particularly close commercial ties with the genízaro villages of Abiquiu and Ojo Caliente immediately to the south of their territory. Writing in 1776, Fray Francisco Atanasio Domínguez reported that "many heathens of the Ute nation" came to Abiquiu each autumn "very laden with good deerskins" solely for the purpose of bartering for horses. The going rate was "fifteen to twenty good deerskins" per horse; if horses were not available, the Utes might trade two deerskins for one high-quality belduque. A little deer or buffalo meat might be traded as well, for maize or corn flour.[47]

Although these good relations might have been assisted by the presence of some Utes in the villages, most of the genízaros in the north seem to have been either Kiowas, Kiowa Apaches, Pawnees, or, at Abiquiu, descendants of seventeen Hopi-Tewa criados brought to the village in 1743 by Miguel de Montoya. Antonio Casados and Luís Quintana, both Kiowa Apache genízaros, had served originally in the household of Francisco Casados at Ojo Caliente. Pawnee genízaro Miguel Ontíveros was accused of sorcery at Abiquiu along with several Kiowas and an expatriate San Juan Pueblo Tewa. These northern outposts seem the most ethnically heterogeneous communities in New Mexico, and, although the witchcraft outbreak points to unmistakable tensions between Spanish and genízaro coresidents of the area, that social mixture would work toward increasing mutualism throughout the next century.[48]

47. For the abandonment and resettlement of Abiquiu and Ojo Caliente, see "Petition of Inhabitants to Remove, 1748," in *SANM,* I, no. 28, roll 1, frames 267–271; "Town of Abiquiu, Order for Resettlement, 1750, by Order of Governor Velez Cachupín," in *SANM,* I, no. 1100, roll 5, frames 1561–1564; "Town of Ojo Caliente, Resettlement, 1753," *SANM,* I, no. 650, roll 4, frames 265–274. For an archaeological report and site plan for the first village of Santa Rosa de Lima de Abiquiu, see Charles A. Hoffman and Charles M. Carrillo, "Archaeological Investigations at River Banks in the Vicinity of Santa Rosa de Lima de Abiquiu," report prepared for the U.S. Army Corps of Engineers (September 1980), in New Mexico State Records Center; for Ojo Caliente's settlement history, see Boyd, "Troubles at Ojo Caliente, a Frontier Outpost," *El Palacio,* LXIV (November–December, 1957), 347–363; Domínguez, *The Missions of New Mexico,* trans. and ed. Adams and Chávez, 252–253.

48. That Kiowa, Kiowa Apache, and at least one Pawnee captive turn up in Abiquiu and Ojo Caliente records in the eighteenth century suggest that the Ute-Comanche alliance had preyed upon these groups for slaves between 1700–1750; the Hopi genízaros at Abiquiu seem unique, perhaps a remnant of those Tewas who had fled to the Hopi mesas

With the peace of 1750, the captive trade continued but in a subdued form compared with other regions. Fray Domínguez drew a distinction between the heavy trade in captives he had earlier observed at Comanche trade fairs in Taos and at Abiquiu, noting that the Utes only "sometimes" brought "little captive heathen Indians (male or female)" for sale there each October. Barred from the products of the Plains, the Utes concentrated on small-scale hide-for-horse trading and shifted their own captive raiding to neighboring Paiute peoples of the Great Basin.[49]

Generally isolated in the mountains and valleys of the north, the Ute bands did not participate in the social adjustments that occurred within Indian groups on the Plains or among the pastoral Navajos. Without the opportunity to undertake major collective bison hunts, they had no need for the hunt police formed by groups like the Sioux, Cheyennes, and Arapahos. Likewise, warfare remained more in the vein of small raiding ventures; hence, the Utes did not feature soldier societies. With subsistence largely a matter of small game hunting and wild plant gathering, supplemented by a minor trade in peltries, the Utes had little need for dependent labor like the Navajo *naalté,* and so neither did the Utes develop institutionalized categories for marginal social members. Although in their equestrianism they came to look more like Plains groups than did their hunting-and-collecting Paiute cousins in the Great Basin, their culture retained the extended bilateral family, matrilocal residence, and diffused gender division of labor associated with the Great Basin region.[50]

Relations between the southern Utes and their Paiute cousins are difficult

---

after 1693 and later returned as servants to Montoya. The upper plaza at Abiquiu is still referred to as *Moquino,* the Spanish colonial term for Hopi sites, by locals. See Quintana, *Pobladores,* 22–29; author's interviews at Abiquiu, Aug. 23, 1991; Horvath, Social and Political Organization of *Genízaros,*" 181–183; "Autos seguidos contra unos indios jenízaros del pueblo de Abiquiú, 1760–1766," in Pinart Collection, Bancroft Library, University of California, Berkeley. Gilberto Benito Córdova includes a transcription of these documents in his "Missionization and Hispanicization of Santo Thomás Apóstol de Abiquiu, 1750–1770" (Ph.D. diss., University of New Mexico, 1979), app. 1.

49. Domínguez, *Missions of New Mexico,* 253.

50. On Ute culture history, see Opler, "The Southern Ute of Colorado," in Ralph Linton, ed., *Acculturation in Seven American Indian Tribes* (New York, 1940), 119–206; on Ute-Paiute relations, see Opler, "The Ute and Paiute Indians of the Great Basin Southern Rim," in Eleanor Burke Leacock and Nancy Oestreich Lurie, eds., *North American Indians in Historical Perspective* (New York, 1971), 260–276; for taxonomy of "True Plains" cultural traits, see Symmes C. Oliver, "Ecology and Cultural Continuity as Contributing Factors in the Social

to discern from eighteenth-century sources, but some hints exist of human exchanges both benign and hostile. When Joaquín María Antonio Rivera departed on an exploratory venture in 1765—spurred by the recent arrival in Abiquiu of an "ancient Ute" with an ingot of silver—he hired Juachinillo, a Ute genízaro, as his guide. This man led Rivera's small party on two expeditions through Ute country into what is today southeastern Utah, home to the "Payuchis." On the first, they met with a band of Capote Utes along the Río de las Animas, hoping to find Cuero de Lobo (Wolfskin), the man who had brought the silver to Abiquiu. To their dismay they heard he had left to visit his mother-in-law in the lands of the Payuchis, proof that marriage exchanges did occur between Utes and Paiutes. On the other hand, their Ute informants also regaled the Spanish party with tales of the depraved and dangerous nature of their western neighbors, those child-eating, straw-haired monsters with huge ears or bodies of stone. Since the well-horsed and -armed Utes clearly had little to fear from these groups militarily, their vilification of the Paiutes might have served to justify raids, captures, and enslavements.[51]

The next several decades saw continual seasonal and illegal *viajes* by New Mexican settlers into the province of Teguayo to trade with various Ute bands, and nearly as often visits by Utes to Abiquiu and Ojo Caliente to conduct exchanges of dried meat, peltries, skins, and Paiute or Navajo captives. Local authorities were so complicit in this covert trade that Teodoro de Croix felt compelled to issue his own edict in 1778, assuring settlers, genízaros, and Indians alike that transgressions would be punished by incarceration, fines, and, in the case of the latter two groups of people, floggings of one hundred lashes. The citizens of Santa Fe who traveled to Arizpe in 1780 included the prohibition among their complaints, all the while continuing the trade as evidenced by the numerous prosecutions undertaken by authorities through the remainder of the century. We can only wonder how many *traficantes* slipped through the scant legal net governors were able to cast across the northern frontier.[52]

Organization of the Plains Indians," in University of California, *Publications in American Archaeology and Ethnology,* XLVIII, no. 1 (1962), 1–90.

51. Cutter, "Prelude to a Pageant in the Wilderness," *Western Historical Quarterly,* VIII (January 1977), esp. 6, 8–9; for Rivera's diaries, see Sánchez, *Explorers, Traders, and Slavers,* apps. A, B, 135–157.

52. "Bando of Cavallero de Croix, Prohibiting Trade with the Utes, 17 Sept. 1778," in *SANM,* II, no. 740, roll 10, frames 1055–1066; for prosecutions, see "Proceedings against the Settlers of Abiquiu for Having Traded with the Utes without Permission, Feb., 1783," in

On occasion, local clerics interposed in the trade, for better or worse. When the custodian of Abiquiu, Fray José Vela Prada, discovered in 1805 a young Navajo woman held captive among a band of visiting Utes, he ransomed her for two horses at a cost to the church of 1,001 *pesos fuertes.* She had been badly injured, apparently in her capture, for she "had wounds all over her body from the stabs of their arrows." It "broke his heart" to see "the tears she poured upon being set free." Yet we must wonder why, although the Navajos wished her back, she "chose" now to remain in Abiquiu as the newly baptized María Candelaria. The gentle padre's motives might not have been entirely altruistic.[53]

By 1805, Governor Joaquín de Real Alencaster could speak of "the customary commerce in furs, horses, and Paiute captives" carried on for nearly fifty years by longtime Ute interpreter and trader Manuel Mestas, genízaro of Abiquiu. In 1809, two English trappers, James Workman and Samuel Spencer, encountered some New Mexicans near present-day Moab, Utah, on a slave-trading venture to the Utes. In 1813, Mauricio Arze and Largos Gracia nearly suffered execution, or so they claimed, by a group of Utes who insisted the New Mexicans purchase twelve "Indian slaves" before any other trading could take place. With the advent of the "Old Spanish Trail" linking New Mexico to California in the 1830s, the principal commerce in sheep and horses was augmented by Paiute children, "with boys fetching on an average $100, girls from $150 to $200," according to Daniel W. Jones, who worked the trade in the nineteenth century.[54]

SANM, II, no. 855, roll 11, frames 520–524; "Case against Vicente Serna and Others for Trading Illegally with the Utes, 31 Mar.–29 April, 1785," in *SANM,* II, no. 920, roll 11, frames 837–844; "Case against Marcelino Manzanares and Others for Illegally Trading with the Utes, 10–29 April, 1785," in *SANM,* II, no. 912, roll 11, frames 845–852; "Case against Salvador Salazar and Others for Trading Illegally with the Utes, 22 April–9 May, 1785," in *SANM,* II, no. 913, roll 11, frames 853–863; "Proceedings against Cristóval Lovato et al., Río Arriba, 2 Aug.–2 Sept., 1979," in *SANM,* II, no. 1393, roll 14, frames 112–127. For a fine detailing of these cases, see Sánchez, *Explorers, Traders, and Slavers,* 91–98.

53. Father José Vela Prada, Custos, to Governor Real Alencaster, Abiquiu, Aug. 18, 1805, *SANM,* II, no. 1876, roll 15, frame 780; Sanchez, *Explorers, Traders, and Slavers,* 99.

54. See Real Alencaster to Comandante Salcedo, Sept. 1, 1805, item no. 7, in *SANM,* II, no. 1881, roll 15, frames 810–836. Alencaster also praises the interpretive services to *"los pananas"* (Pawnee) rendered by Joseph Chalvet, an expatriate Frenchman. For Mestas's Ute-genízaro background and service as interpreter, see *SANM,* II, no. 1886, roll 15, frames 849–851; Leland Hargrave Creer, "Spanish-American Slave Trade in the Great Basin, 1800–1853," *NMHR,* XXIV (September 1949), 171–183; Daniel W. Jones, *Forty Years among the Indians:*

Like captives from the pastoral and plains borderlands, the majority of Paiute captives seemed to end up in the villas of Santa Cruz de la Cañada, Santa Fe, and Albuquerque, especially between 1776 and 1825, when a commercial weaving industry developed in response to Bourbon reform programs and market connections to Mexico and the United States. Commercial development clearly played a role in maintaining demand for indios de rescate, alongside the parallel demand for domestics and concubines in rico households. This economic growth did not, however, prove sufficiently strong to bring the vecino population of New Mexico into the labor force in any great numbers. Most vecino families still sought the security and autonomy of life in small villages, where potential rewards of trade relations with Indian groups counterbalanced vulnerability to raids by those same Indians.[55]

As had been the case with Abiquiu and Ojo Caliente along the Río Chama and its tributaries, after 1750 lower-status pobladores built a constellation of small mountain villages in the Sangre de Cristos east of La Cañada, running all the way to Arroyo Hondo, just north of Taos. Beginning with poblaciones strung along small tributaries like the Río Santa Cruz, Río Quemado, Río de las Trampas, and Río de las Truchas, these had coalesced by the later years of the eighteenth century into plazas in rough compliance with the regulations associated with the creation of the Provincias Internas. Fray Domínguez noted in 1776 the existence of Cundiyo (9 families of 36 persons), Chimayó (71 families of 367 persons), Quemado (52 families of 220 persons), Truchas (26 families of 122 persons), Trampas (63 families of 278 persons), and Las Trampas (Ranchos) de Taos (67 families of 306 persons). Few of these pobladores drew his praise—the vecinos of Cundiyo and Chimayó "pass[ed] for Spaniards" and spoke a "simple Spanish"; the peoples of Trampas were for the most part "a ragged lot . . . as festive as they [were] poor, and very merry." Most were of "low class." Those few servants who did reside in village families also spoke a simple Spanish, but were generally "light colored." At Las Trampas de Taos, the "local Spanish" tongue mingled with that of Taos Pueblo, and most resi-

---

A True yet Thrilling Narrative of the Author's Experiences among the Natives (Salt Lake City, Utah, 1890), 49–50.

55. Brugge, *Navajos in the Catholic Church Records,* chap. 3, "Geographic Distributions," notes a gradual shift southward from the Río Arriba to the Río Abajo for baptismal entries of all Indian groups between 1750 and 1850, corresponding to the increased demand for labor in sheep grazing and wool processing. For the emergence of the textile industry, see Frank, "From Settler to Citizen," 232–264.

dents also spoke "to a considerable extent the Comanche, Ute, and Apache languages."[56]

Growing from families of lower-status, often mixed-descent settlers who were set apart from the core of the Spanish colony in the Río Grande valley, the mountain villagers shared with their Ute and Jicarilla neighbors exposure to raids by Navajos, Comanches, and Kiowas alike. Utes and Jicarillas used mobility and retreat to avoid complete defeat but by the 1770s were in desperate straits. New Mexican villagers suffered even more, and outposts like Ojo Caliente, Truchas, and Chimayo were occasionally abandoned, then resettled when Spanish administrators threatened forfeiture of land rights. The years of Cuerno Verde's depredations (1768–1779) proved the most devastating. Hence, when Governor Anza issued his call for an expedition against the Comanches, he found Utes, Jicarillas, Pueblos, and mountain villagers eager to join forces.[57]

We have already seen the military details of Anza's campaign, but a closer look at the composition of his force points to the local alliances that had formed in the Río Grande valley and mountain borderlands. Joining the 103 presidial veterans under Anza were 176 members of the local militia, 103 of whom came from La Cañada and the mountain villages. The Río Grande Pueblo Indians and genízaro communities contributed an additional 259 warriors. On the fifth day of their northward march, "two hundred men of the Ute and Apache nation" joined Anza's force as they crossed the Río de los Conejos in the San Luis Valley. The governor accepted their services with the understanding that, "with the exception of personal captures, they would have to agree to divide [spoils] equally with all [his] men." The Utes and Jicarillas guided Anza's secretive flanking maneuver through the Colorado mountains, joined in the attack on Cuerno Verde's encampment, then retired with their booty of horses and captives just before the fight that killed the Comanche leader.[58]

Satisfied that their enemies had suffered enough, the Utes retreated into the mountains and watched Spanish-Comanche affairs with a keen eye. When Ecueracapa's overtures brought peace negotiations with Anza in 1785, the Utes

56. Domínguez, *Missions of New Mexico,* trans. and ed. Adams and Chávez, 59–60, 83–84, 98–99, 112–113.

57. Marc Simmons, "Settlement Patterns and Village Plans in Colonial New Mexico," *Journal of the West,* VIII (January 1969), 7–21, 15.

58. "Diary of Anza's Campaign against the Comanche," in Thomas, trans. and ed., *Forgotten Frontiers,* 122–132, esp. 125.

responded angrily. Ute headmen Moara and Pinto met with the governor in Santa Fe on January 7, 1786, protesting the impending treaty so vigorously that, during the four hours of argument, "they did not wish to smoke or accept any other present." Anza treated their concerns seriously, and, when Ecueracapa arrived in Santa Fe on the twenty-fifth, he was exhorted by the governor to include Moara and Pinto in his negotiations. After "various charges and satisfactions on both sides," the parties reached a "reciprocal and perpetual reconciliation," which the Comanches and Utes sealed symbolically by "exchanging clothes in the presence of the Governor."[59]

Their reconciliation might have involved customary indigenous diplomacy as well. Comanches told later ethnographers that a historic Ute-Comanche accord had been the work of a Ute woman, long captive among the Comanches, whose mixed-descent Ute-Comanche son had become an important Comanche war captain. She negotiated a truce between two warring bands, using her influence with her Ute brother, himself a band leader. For her efforts, the Utes "made her a special honor; they took her back to the main camp where her father and mother were still living. They gave her a tipi with an antelope skin tied to the top of a pole for a special sign." The symbolic exchange of clothing before the governor might have reenacted a more profound and meaningful exchange earlier between the two camps.[60]

The "perpetual" peace also brought calls from both Utes and Comanches for free trade within their respective borderlands, requests that Anza and his successors struggled to avoid. Although semiannual trade fairs were sanctioned and rough price guidelines approved, surreptitious trade with villagers continued to create intercultural links beyond the reach of Spanish authorities. Spanish governors reached out to their Comanche allies, but they failed to meet similar Ute requests. Although they attempted to forbid the clandestine trade in the north, their generally hands-off policies allowed Utes and New Mexican mountain villagers to develop long-term social and economic ties around subsistence exchanges, the fur trade, and a steady commerce in Paiute captives.[61]

59. Pedro Garrido y Duran, "An Account of the Events Concerning the Comanche Peace, 1785–1786," ibid., 294–321, esp. 297, 301.

60. See E. Adamson Hoebel, "The Political Organization and Law Ways of the Comanche Indians," American Anthropological Association, *Memoirs,* LIV (Menasha, Wisc., 1940), 36.

61. Cheryl Foote, "Spanish-Indian Trade along New Mexico's Northern Frontier in the Eighteenth Century," *Journal of the West,* XXIV (1985), 22–33, esp. 30. For the nineteenth

During the eighteenth century, Utes, Jicarilla Apaches, and New Mexicans created a permeable borderland that paralleled in some respects those crafted among the pastoralists of the west and the plains peoples to the east. Reciprocal thievery, mutualistic bartering, and captive seizure and assimilation figured prominently in all three regions. But the borderland of los montañeses held fewer opportunities for economic intensification than did the others. Although the Paiute captive trade connected with economic development in the colony itself, much of borderland slavery's transformative potential simply passed through the participant societies. Both Indian and New Mexican montañeses brought some captives into their encampments and placitas, but not primarily as labor sources—rather, these people were incorporated as subordinate family members whose cultural repertoires would prove useful in borderland negotiations. Customs of slavery and kinship interacted with both economic intensification and isolation to foster distinctively different "borderland communities of interest" in the coming century.

century, see Leland Hargrave Creer, "Spanish-American Slave Trade in the Great Basin, 1800–1853," *NMHR*, XXIV (July 1949), 171–183.

5

ELABORATING THE PLAINS BORDERLANDS

San Carlos de los Jupes: January 1787

The thin notes of a mourning song drifted in the winter air over the half-built village. Smoke rose from untended cooking fires in several of the adobe jacales that clustered around the frozen confluence of the Rito San Carlos and the Arkansas River (Río Napestle). In brush *corrales* at the edge of the village, sheep and oxen fed on remnants of dry forage gathered from the floodplain the previous autumn. In the strange calm of that morning, the *maestro de los obreros,* Manuel Segura, walked the deserted streets of the stillborn settlement and contemplated his report to New Mexico's governor, don Fernando de la Concha.

It had started so well. Recently chosen as teniente general of the Comanche bands generally known as "los Jupes," Captain Paruanarimuca (Bear Harness) had appeared in Santa Fe the previous July, seeking an audience with then-governor Juan Bautista de Anza. Filled with urgency, he proposed that the governor assist his people in founding an *establecimiento fijado* (fixed settlement) on the banks of the Arkansas River beneath the Sierra Almagre, or the front range of the Colorado Rockies. By August, Anza had gathered thirty workers under the direction of Manuel Segura at Taos Pueblo and had contracted with *arrieros* Felipe Moya, Antonio Domínguez, and Luis Rivera for the delivery of seed, flour, sheep, and oxen to the settlement. Paruanarimuca himself arrived in Taos to receive the laborers and supplies and guide the expedition back to his chosen site on the Rito San Carlos.[1]

1. Juan Bautista de Anza to Jacobo Ugarte y Loyola, Oct. 20, 1787, in *Expediente sobre la poblacion de San Carlos de los Jupes en el Nuevo Mexico,* 1788, legajo 7.1, Qno 10, 11, Provincias Internas, tomo 65, archivo general, Mexico, trans. and ed. A. B. Thomas, in "San Carlos, a Comanche Pueblo on the Arkansas River, 1787: A Study in Comanche History

By October 1786, nineteen jacales were occupied by the Comanches, with a greater number still under construction. Some concern existed that the Jupes might not respect the effort and expense of this experiment, and Comandante General Ugarte cautioned new governor Concha that, unless they engaged in labor themselves, they might not "develop an affection for their possession." Work continued, with an expanse of irrigated fields planned for the spring. Reassured that the Comanches were themselves participating in construction, Ugarte informed his superiors that the Jupes "were numerous" and would surely "constitute a considerable settlement."[2]

But, now, except for the few laborers who had remained with Segura, the village lay deserted. On the snow-swept prairie to the east, a dark column of Comanche horses and travois followed the sorrowing Paruanarimuca, who led his people on a return to the buffalo plains. They carried with them the flexed and bundled body of his favored wife, who had died unexpectedly a few days before. Her prized possessions—horses, clothing, beadwork, awls, hide scrapers, cooking utensils—would be buried with her, once a suitable niche in riverbank or rock formation was found. Paruanarimuca himself had shaved the left side of his head in mourning, while his junior wives sliced flesh from their forearms and sang honor songs throughout the night. Segura could only wonder at the superstitions that moved these indios bárbaros to desert the safety of the village in the dead of winter and at how the governor in Santa Fe would react to a failure that had cost the province some 691 pesos, 11.5 percent of his annual budget for Indian affairs.[3]

Although Ugarte considered briefly the idea of settling the abandoned village with New Mexican pobladores, San Carlos de los Jupes disappeared from the historical record even more quickly than its adobes melted back into the earth somewhere along this tributary of the Arkansas River. But the six-month

---

and Spanish Indian Policy," *Colorado Magazine*, VI (1929), 79–91; Thomas W. Kavanagh, *Comanche Political History: An Ethnohistorical Perspective, 1706–1875* (Lincoln, Nebr., 1996), 120, 137–138.

2. Ugarte to Concha, Jan. 22, 1788, Ugarte to don Manuel Antonio Flores, March 1788, in *Expediente sobre la poblacion de San Carlos de los Jupes*, trans. and ed. Thomas, in "San Carlos," *Colorado Magazine*, VI (1929), 88–90.

3. Concha to Ugarte, June 26, 1788, ibid. For Comanche mortuary practices, see Ernest Wallace and E. Adamson Hoebel, *The Comanches: Lords of the South Plains* (1952; Norman, Okla., 1986), 149–154; account by José Maldonado, included in Concha to Ugarte, ibid., in Thomas, "San Carlos," *Colorado Magazine*, VI (1929), 91. New Mexico received six thousand pesos annually for extraordinary expenses for maintaining peace with los indios gentiles.

experiment points to a period of significant change in relations between Plains Indians and New Mexicans. San Carlos de los Jupes suggests that, although by 1787 the Comanches had emerged as the principal equestrian power on the southern Plains, they were simultaneously drawing closer to ever more intimate cultural and economic exchanges with the peoples of colonial New Mexico.[4]

The Spanish-Comanche-Ute peace was barely a year old when Paruanarimuca first proposed the settlement. In fact, as soon as Muache and Capote Ute leaders got wind of the San Carlos experiment, several headmen hurried to Santa Fe for an audience with Anza. They too requested the creation of a farming settlement and suggested a site below Abiquiu on the Chama River as an agreeable location. Anza moved more slowly on this request, probably in recognition that these Utes constituted a lesser economic partner and had less military power at their disposal. Likewise, friendly Navajo leaders like Antonio el Pinto also took advantage of the movement toward accord, participating again in the sheep trade after Anza lifted the embargo that had brought peace to the Río Puerco valley the previous year.[5]

Usually seen as evidence of Anza's diplomatic brilliance in bringing the Comanche cavalry into border service on the margins of the Provincias Internas, this complex of treaties also marked major innovations in Navajo, Ute, and Comanche borderland strategies, of which the San Carlos settlement represents only one intriguing example. The strategic goals of Comanche thinkers like Paruanarimuca involved three interrelated aspects. Eager to maintain their military superiority on the Plains, Comanches sought continued access to guns, powder, and lead. Recognizing the limits of complete dependency on bison for subsistence—a matter of unpredictable availability and simply of taste—they needed reliable access to the agricultural products of New Mexico and river-farming Indians like the Wichitas and Taovayas. Requiring addi-

4. For Ugarte's repopulation plan, see his letter to Concha of Jan. 28, 1789, in *Spanish Archives of New Mexico* (hereafter cited as *SANM),* II, no. 1039, roll 12, frames 138–139. The Rito San Carlos, now the St. Charles River, flows into the Arkansas west of the Huerfano-Arkansas confluence; for a map drawn by Jules De Mun in 1817 that shows the Rito San Carlos, see George S. Ulibarri, "The Chouteau-Demun Expedition to New Mexico, 1815–1817," *New Mexico Historical Review* (hereafter cited as *NMHR),* XXXVI (October 1961), 231–273, esp. 262.

5. Anza to Ugarte, Santa Fe, Jul. 14, 1787, no. 523 in *Expediente sobre la poblacion de San Carlos de los Jupes* in Thomas, "San Carlos," *Colorado Magazine,* VI (1929), 83.

tional labor to meet market demands and to purchase Euramerican products, they increased captive raiding, which also countered population decline. These strategies would create a political structure capable of international diplomacy, rework cultural notions of gender and social inequality, stabilize economic relations with certain Spanish colonial villages in New Mexico, and expand the Comanches' participation in the slave system of the borderlands.

Given their situation, the Comanches' initial interest in a settlement at San Carlos de los Jupes makes sense. Pastoral societies often pursued economic diversification by building trade or tribute relationships with sedentary agricultural neighbors or by establishing dependent villages of their own to provide support during times of hardship. Paruanarimuca's plan seems to reflect such a goal. As much as Spanish authorities might have thought they were fostering a "reduction" of nomadic barbarians, the Jupes' leader might have been soliciting the creation of an accessible, dependable farming village on the fringes of his territory. Such a settlement would have provided the Jupes with a hedge against famine and the New Mexicans with extraordinary access to meat, hides, and horses. The untimely death of the favored wife prevented this scenario from playing out. What Segura saw as superstition was probably no more than sensible action on the part of people recently devastated by epidemic disease: to flee the site of a painful loss and potentially deadly infection.[6]

6. The Tuareg of North Africa serve as a classic example of a pastoral society seeking economic diversification along the same lines as the Comanches; in order to guard against famine cycles they cultivated economic alliances with Hausa farmers in the Sahel or, barring that, planted their own slaves in satellite farming communities that could be called upon in times of famine. See Stephen Baier and Paul E. Lovejoy, "The Tuareg of the Central Sudan: Gradations in Servility at the Desert Edge (Niger and Nigeria)," in Suzanne B. Miers and Igor Kopytoff, eds., *Slavery in Africa: Historical and Anthropological Perspectives* (Madison, Wisc., 1977), 391–411; for a broader treatment of this phenomenon across the length of the Sahel, see James L. A. Webb, Jr., *Desert Frontier: Ecological and Economic Change along the Western Sahel, 1600–1850* (Madison, Wisc., 1995), esp. 68–96. Thomas interpreted San Carlos as "nothing less than a Comanche attempt, with Spanish assistance, to reduce themselves from rovers of the plains to growers of wheat and builders of houses" ("San Carlos," *Colorado Magazine*, VI [1929], 82); Elizabeth A. H. John, in *Storms Brewed in Other Men's Worlds: The Confrontation of Indians, Spanish, and French in the Southwest, 1540–1795* (College Station, Tex., 1975), attributes the experiment to "Paruanarimuco's enthusiasm for the Spanish way," interrupted by the need "to ease [a] chief's grief by leaving the painful reminders at the scene of death" (732–734). Neither view adequately addresses the strategic motivations beneath his actions.

The San Carlos settlement furnishes only one of many cases in which Indian groups and New Mexican vecinos, especially those of intermediate or low economic or caste status, sought to better their lives by creating together a political economy of the borderlands. From the time of their first tentative entradas beyond the immediate bounds of the colony, Spanish New Mexicans encountered Plains groups like Apaches and Comanches, plateau groups like Apaches and Navajos, and mountain-dwelling Ute bands. In all three ecological zones—the buffalo plains, the canyons and mesas west of the Río Grande, and the mountain ranges that linked them—the borderlands came to share some general similarities. Each featured indigenous and colonial societies capable of assimilating outsiders through affinal, fictive, or subordinative institutions of kinship and servitude, and these societies utilized such assimilations to enrich their own cultural repertoires. But each borderland contained salient differences as well, especially regarding the subsistence practices, settlement patterns, and styles of interaction with larger market forces that their resident societies displayed as the nineteenth century unfolded.

With the Spanish-Comanche alliance of 1786 and the accord among Navajos, Utes, and Governor Juan Bautista de Anza later that year, space for borderland intercultural negotiations expanded dramatically. Over the next several decades, Comanches, Kiowas, Apaches, and Navajos engaged in social and political innovations that allowed them to address changing needs and economic situations in their plains and plateau landscapes. Concurrently, genízaros and land-poor vecinos from the Spanish colony recast their seasonal trading and buffalo-hunting sojourns into permanent settlements along the eastern foothills of the Sangre de Cristo Mountains, as would sheepherding pastoralists extend their ranges and villages west of the Río Grande. These developments were intimately connected. Cultural transfers of the captive system contributed to the transformation of each society, which in turn facilitated the integration of these groups into larger market circuits in North America. In the space of one generation, borderland peoples, Indian and Euramerican, began to form communities of interest that redefined and expanded their way of life.

They Agree among Themselves Perfectly

The constellation of treaties and agreements among Spanish, Comanches, Navajos, and Utes in 1785 and 1786 marked the beginning of a new collaboration in the Southwest Borderlands. Its immediate effect took the shape of previously unimaginable joint military expeditions against various Apache groups who now found themselves outside the compass of the borderland economies. Where earlier in the century Faraones, Natagés, Mimbres, Gilas, and Sierra Blancas figured as central players in trade relations along the frontier, they now occupied secondary and decidedly vulnerable positions. In the spring of 1786, some 350 Comanche fighters from the three principal divisions (Jupe, Yamparica, and Cuchantica) on the llano entered the Sierras Sandía south of Santa Fe and attacked several Apache rancherías. Their rewards were relatively few; eighty-five horses seized, six Apaches killed and two taken captive at the cost of one Comanche dead and six wounded, including, apparently, Ecueracapa. That same summer an allied force of twenty-two Comanches, twenty-six Navajos, some Pueblo auxiliaries, and a handful of Spanish troops campaigned farther south against the Gilas and Mimbres and took better spoils; fourteen Apache women and children returned to Santa Fe with their captors. Two years later, another joint expedition took place. Eight Comanches, eight Jicarilla Apaches, seventy-four Spanish soldiers, and twenty Navajos under Antonio el Pinto entered Gila country, guided by an Ácoma Pueblo Indian named Casimiro, who had been a captive among the Mimbres for many years. Eighteen Apache men were killed and five women were captured in this foray. By 1790, these depredations brought some Gila and Sierra Blanca Apaches into the colony itself, when Anza's successor, Fernando de la Concha, settled several bands in a farming experiment not unlike San Carlos de los Jupes on the west bank of the Río Grande at El Sabinal, some forty miles south of Albuquerque. It would last nearly a decade before its residents abandoned it under Comanche pressure.[7]

Although these joint ventures shared common goals of local security, each participating party harbored its own objectives as well. The Spanish certainly wished to end Apache predations on their scattered settlements and perhaps sought to bind Comanches, Navajos, and even Jicarilla Apaches to their interests by fostering a common enemy. But Navajos like Antonio el Pinto, whose rancherías occupied the area of Big Bead Mesa and whose sheep grazed the

7. Thomas, trans. and ed., "Tarja," "Fourth Enclosure," both in "An Eighteenth Century Comanche Document," *American Anthropologist,* N.S., XXXI (1929), 294–295, 297–298; Adlai Feather, trans. and ed., "Colonel Don Fernando de la Concha, Diary, 1788," *NMHR,* XXXIV (October 1959), 285–304; Kavanagh, *Comanche Political History,* 115–117; for El Sabinal, see Concha to Viceroy Conde de Revilla Gigedo, Jul. 12, 1791, in *SANM,* II, no. 1132, roll 12, frames 559–563; John, *Storms Brewed,* 751–752.

lower Río Puerco, worked also to protect those flocks and to curtail competition from Gilas and Mimbres in trade with neighboring Spanish villages. Comanche leaders like Ecueracapa of the Cuchanticas and Tosapoy of the Jupes campaigned to garner the social prestige that accrued to successful warriors, to enlarge their horse herds, and to maintain free access to their valuable trading partners at Pecos Pueblo. The Gilas and Sierra Blancas at El Sabinal tried desperately to retain some hold on Spanish affections in the face of interloping Navajos and Comanches but found themselves more often the victims of widespread, multiethnic slave-raiding parties.

Thus, the communities of interest that began to take shape at the turn of the century would wear two faces: one of allies pursuing mutual ends and one of particular groups working toward specific cultural goals that intermeshed with those of other groups for a time. Intercultural agreements expressed themselves in shifting and labile affiliations that could adhere or dissolve with remarkable speed. Indeed, joint Comanche-Navajo actions faded quickly as Utes and Navajos aligned themselves to raid Comanche horse herds and take captives in the 1790s. Comanches, increasingly pressured from the east by well-armed Pawnees, drew even closer to the Spanish in New Mexico and in the summer of 1790 successfully requested firearms and a presidial escort for their summer bison hunt north of the Arkansas. Yet within five years Pawnees and Comanches would themselves reach an accord through the services of Pedro Vial, the French borderman turned Spanish emissary. During that same period, a Pawnee, Wichita, and Taovaya delegation approached the Spanish governor of Texas at San Antonio de Béxar with the enticement that thirty-three Indian naciónes were willing to join Spain to prevent further American encroachments west of the Mississippi—if trade and military assistance against expansionistic Sioux and Cheyennes were forthcoming. A closer look at local dynamics illustrates how communities of interest between societies often emerged as a consequence of alignments and tensions within Indian and Spanish communities themselves.[8]

8. For Ute-Navajo raids on Comanches and Concha's unsuccessful attempt to make peace by returning Comanche captives among the Navajos, see Concha to Viceroy Conde de Revilla Gigedo, May 6, 1793, in *SANM*, II, no. 1234, roll 13, frames 234–235; for the Comanche-Spanish summer hunt, see "Juan de Dios Peña, Diary of Campaign with Comanches against the Pawnees, 12 June–8 August, 1799," in *SANM*, II, no. 1089, roll 12, frames 262–265; Rudolph C. Troike, "A Pawnee Visit to San Antonio in 1795," *Ethnohistory*, XI (1964), 380–393; John, *Storms Brewed*, 750–766.

Anza's defeat of Cuerno Verde in 1779 and the assassination of Toroblanco in 1785 cleared the way for the ascension of a new generation of Comanche leadership devoted to closer social and economic ties with the New Mexican colony. Ecueracapa, Paruanarimuca, and Tosapoy were among the dozen or so captains who would henceforth consider themselves friends of the Spanish. But their ability to deliver perfect compliance was limited by the political culture of Comanche bands and divisions. Each *paraibo (capitancillo* in Spanish) maintained closest control over his own numunahkahni through ties of blood, affinity, and persuasion, but this authority was granted by followers rather than imposed from above. Sacred power *(puha),* hunting and military skill, and the ability to arrange or dispense prestigious marriage partners, horses, and captives lay at the heart of leadership qualities. If one were elected to divisional leadership, like Ecueracapa in 1785, similar criteria for continuing authority held true, with perhaps highest value placed on the ability to negotiate with Euramerican officials to Comanche advantage. Despite Spanish claims, little evidence exists that *jefes principales* were ever appointed from outside Comanche society; rather, their election was recognized and given greater prestige by the bestowal of gifts and titles by respected Spanish governors like Tomás Vélez Cachupín and Juan Bautista de Anza. If leaders at the band or division level failed to deliver, Comanches felt little compunction to follow them.[9]

Tenuous by Euramerican standards, the structure of Comanche political leadership mirrored the flexibility and creativity of everyday Comanche society. No Plains Indian peoples seemed to show less regard for formal rules of social organization as understood by Spanish, Mexican, or American observers. Yet, despite the fluidity and idiosyncrasy expressed in their society, Comanches operated within a system of laterally extended families and larger regional residence bands linked by affinal ties. When expanded groups focused on seasonal activities, a broader Comanche community was realized. The whole cultural association was loosely tied by movement of peoples between groups, a process stimulated by Euramerican threats and opportunities. Converging and dispersing as seasonal, strategic, and sacred exigencies re-

9. Kavanagh best describes the attributes of leadership at the local band level: "Through a combination of *puha,* hunting skill and military bravery, political skill and charisma, and control of trade and other economic activities, he attracted judicious marriages for members of his own family and *numunahkahni* and maintained peripheral families and individuals in personal support relations; conversely, if he was unable to maintain his supporters, they would look elsewhere" *(Comanche Political History,* 43, 53–55).

quired, local bands, divisions, and even larger groups bedeviled all attempts by Euramerican authorities to fix Comanches in diplomatic or administrative units. The larger, often multidivisional, gatherings represent the clearest evidence for sociopolitical innovation in the face of Euramerican intrusion: huge associations at Casa de Palo to create a diplomatic corps in 1786 and to elect new Cuchantica chiefs in 1793 and 1797 (Encanaguané and Canaguaipe, respectively); war councils in 1791, 1809, and 1825; and occasional sun dances in the later nineteenth century. All of these focused activities allowed grave and respectful debate of political issues aimed at either diplomacy, defense, or the replenishment of sacred power. While such gatherings fostered a larger collective consciousness, the more commonplace dispersed pattern of band or division organization met the grazing, hunting, and raiding needs of a militarized pastoral society. Even within these smaller units, membership remained fluid, allowing easy communication and preventing concentrations of individual power.[10]

Two decades after the treaty of 1786, Governor Concha would say of the Comanches,

> They agree among themselves perfectly, and the internal quarrels never exceed the limits of the petty disputes that arise between individuals. All of the four divisions [Cuchanticas, Jupes, Yamparicas, and Orientales] live in a close union, and it frequently happens that those of one go to live among

10. Kavanagh, *Comanche Political History,* 52; Morris W. Foster, *Being Comanche: A Social History of an American Indian Community* (Tucson, Ariz., 1991), 66–67; Wallace and Hoebel, *The Comanches,* 214. Gerald Betty discusses the ecological benefits of dispersed grazing bands in " 'Skillful in the Management of the Horse': Comanches as Southern Plains Pastoralists," *Heritage of the Great Plains,* XXX, no. 1 (1997), 5–31. The precise nature of Comanche social and political organization remains a hotly contested topic. See Hoebel, "The Political Organization and Law Ways of the Comanche Indians," American Anthropological Association, *Memoirs,* no. 54 (Washington, D.C., 1940), 6; Symmes C. Oliver, "The Problem of the Comanche," app. in "Ecology and Cultural Continuity as Contributing Factors in the Social Organization of the Plains Indians," in Walter R. Goldschmidt, ed., *University of California Publications in American Archaeology and Ethnology,* XLVIII (1962), 1–90, esp. 71; Melburn D. Thurman, "A New Interpretation of Comanche Social Organization," *Current Anthropology,* XXIII (October 1982), 578–579; Daniel J. Gelo, "On a New Interpretation of Comanche Social Organization," *Current Anthropology,* XXVIII (August–October 1987), 551–552; Kavanagh, *Comanche Political History;* Kavanagh, "The Comanche: Paradigmatic Anomaly or Ethnographic Fiction?" *Haliksa'i,* IV (1985), 109–128.

the others, so that their interests are common and they share a common destiny.[11]

Comanches themselves confirmed the persistence of these ideals to later ethnographers. Band membership expanded and contracted at will, for "the linkage of the person to the band was on the basis of free association. . . . There was nothing to prevent change of residence to another band . . . mere whim being sufficient cause." Fluidity of membership and flexibility of organizational level, rather than rigid adherence to the band or wholesale adoption of tribal organization, were the two key components of Comanche society, innovations that proved successful well into the nineteenth century. Shared values of freedom of association and rejection of social control mechanisms constituted a unifying worldview. "Comanches," argues a modern student of the question, "used their distinctive means of social organization to out-compete a succession of Euro-American regimes on the southern Plains for the better part of two centuries."[12]

Kiowas present a rather different picture of sociopolitical adjustment to that we see in the Comanche case. Far smaller in numbers, perhaps never exceeding two thousand people, or 10 percent of the Comanche estimate of twenty thousand members, the Kiowas are also enigmatic in Plains Indian ethnohistory. Unlike those of their Comanche allies or Dakota enemies, Kiowa origins have proved difficult to trace along archaeological or linguistic paths. Their language derives from the Tanoan family and bears close affinity to the Tiwa subfamily spoken by the peoples of Taos, Sandía, and Isleta Pueblos of New Mexico. Kiowa origin narratives recall a migration across the Saskatchewan plains and more specifically campsites and hunting areas in the Yellowstone River region, where they made acquaintance with their longtime friends, the Crows. According to early Euramerican documents and the prominence of the Black Hills in their own historical traditions, Kiowas lived in the northern Plains in the seventeenth century. Modern work in historical linguistics, however, indicates longer duration in their presence on the southern grasslands and links them to the protohistoric Jumanos of eastern New Mexico and western Texas.[13]

11. Donald E. Worcester, trans., "Advice on Governing New Mexico, 1794, by Don Fernando de la Concha," in *NMHR,* XXIV (July 1949), 236–254, esp. 238.

12. Hoebel, "Political Organization and Law Ways of the Comanche Indians," American Anthropological Association, *Memoirs,* no. 54, 12; Foster, *Being Comanche,* 74.

13. James Mooney suggests the name derives from *Ga-i-gwu,* or "people having two

Kiowas first entered the Spanish colony in New Mexico as victims of the eighteenth-century captive trade. Church records reveal the presence of Kiowas in the colony as early as 1727, when "María Chaves," an older Kiowa woman, received last sacraments and was buried at Isleta Pueblo. Between 1730 and 1800, thirty-five Kiowas were baptized in northern parishes, among whom were Antonio Casados and Luís Quintana, leaders of the 1746 Belén protests, and Agustín and María Candelaria Tagle, implicated in the 1763 witchcraft eruption in Abiquiu. At least three children were born of Kiowa women and baptized as well. But the direction of violent captives reversed at the turn of the century. In the autumn of 1800, a large raiding band of Kiowas, Apaches, Pawnees, and Skiri Pawnees fell upon Spanish settlements around Abiquiu, seizing livestock and several women and children. Comanches, furious that the party was led by a former Skiri captive who had escaped to his kinsmen after betraying six Comanches in an ambush, offered to retaliate on behalf of their Spanish allies. Yet, in the early months of 1806, Kiowas and Comanches negotiated a peace that would last out the nineteenth century. At the San Miguel del Vado rancho of a New Mexican borderman friendly with both sides, and assisted by a Comanche captive long resident among the Kiowas, three potential antagonists realized a mutual need for peace and commerce. The parties celebrated the accord in a three-day feast and exchange of gifts. The Comanches gave "a great many horses" to their new friends, who reciprocated with "hair switches" for the Comanches' custom of "making their hair very long." Finally, the parties sealed the treaty with the marriage of Guik'áte, known to

---

halves or parts of the body or face painted in different colors," from a customary hairstyle in which Kiowa warriors cut the right side of their hair above the ear to display ear pendants and let the left side grow long, braided and wrapped in otter skin. The name may have even earlier roots in a distinctive tattooing, if indeed the Kiowas descended from the Jumanos, who were known for their facial tattoos. See "Calendar History of the Kiowa Indians," *Seventeenth Annual Report of the Bureau of American Ethnology,* part 2 (Washington, D.C., 1979), 150; for Kiowa origin and migration narratives, see Maurice Boyd, *Kiowa Voices: Myths, Legends, and Folktales,* II (Fort Worth, Tex., 1983), 1–12; for connections between Jumanos and Kiowas, see Nancy P. Hickerson: "Ethnogenesis in the Great Plains: Jumano to Kiowa?" paper read at the annual meeting of the American Assocation for the Advancement of Science, Chicago, 1991; "Kiowa: The Resurgence of Tanoan on the Southern Plains," paper presented at the annual meeting of the American Anthropological Association, San Francisco, 1992; "The Linguistic Position of the Jumano," *Journal of Anthropological Research,* XLIV (1988), 311–326; *The Jumanos: Hunters and Traders of the South Plains* (Austin, Tex., 1994), 207–208.

the Spanish as El Ronco (the Hoarse One), to a daughter of the Yamparica Comanche captain Somiquaso, with the Kiowa man taking up new residence among his Comanche affines.[14]

The most striking quality of Kiowa culture was the serious attention given to social rank, or graded categories of distinction tied to military honor, wealth in horses, and social dependents, which stands in marked contrast to the more broadly egalitarian Comanches. Kiowas described their nineteenth-century social organization to ethnographers as composed of four gradations of prestige (from highest to lowest): *óngop, óndeigúp'a, kóon,* and *dapóm.* The first rank may be understood as a noble class, attained not by blood but by a family's capacity to give generously of its wealth in horses, to mount noteworthy military efforts in pursuit of horses, honor, and revenge, and to maintain a handsome and dignified demeanor in daily affairs. Óndeigúp'a were also respectable families but without the wealth to present themselves in the noble manner of the superior rank. Estimated at 40 to 50 percent, they comprised the center of Kiowa society. Dependent families, attached to higher ranks by the loan of horses for warfare or bride-price, comprised the kóon: "They are also human. They will always be here," said one Kiowa. At the very bottom of Kiowa society lay the dapóm, considered "shiftless and lazy" and whose "own relatives had practically disowned them . . . they were virtual outcasts." These latter were recalled as constituting some 10 percent of Kiowas. As we will see, captives might also be considered among the dapóm but in practice had more opportunity for advancement than Kiowa members of that rank.[15]

The key to residence in each rank, and the potential for mobility between ranks, lay with kinship. While not strictly hereditary, óngop status tended

14. For Kiowa baptisms and burials, see David M. Brugge, "Some Plains Indians in the Church Records of New Mexico," *Plains Anthropologist,* X, no. 29 (1965), 181–189; for raids by the "Naciones del Norte," see "Chacón, Four Letters on Military and Indian Affairs, 24 Nov., 1800," in *SANM,* II, no. 1517, roll 14, frames 644–674; "Chacón, Summary of Events in the Province of New Mexico, 1 Oct. to 25 Nov., 1800," in *SANM,* II, no. 1518, roll 14, frames 652–653; John, "An Earlier Chapter of Kiowa History," *NMHR,* LX (October 1985), 379–397; for Kiowa-Comanche peace, see Mooney, "Calendar History of the Kiowa Indians," *Seventeenth Annual Report of the Bureau of American Ethnology,* part 2, 162–163; for feast and gift exchanges, see Tébodal's 1892 account of "How the Kiowa Made Peace with the Comanche," in Papers of Hugh Lenox Scott, folder 3, box 74, Manuscript Division, Library of Congress; Kavanagh, *Comanche Political History,* 146–148.

15. Bernard Mishkin, *Rank and Warfare among the Plains Indians* (1940; Lincoln, Nebr., 1992), 35–37.

FIGURE 4. *Six Kiowa Men.* Note that "2 and 3 were attendants of Little-Mountain," probably dapóm. 1845. Watercolor by Lt. James W. Abert. Courtesy Yale Collection of Western Americana, Beinecke Rare Book and Manuscript Library

to pass through family lineages, since their wealth in horses and dependents allowed young óngop men the mounts and freedom to engage in military ventures that would affirm their high standing. Similar constraints and opportunities prevailed for those of the óndeigúp'a, who could aspire to gain óngop status only through extraordinary martial achievements for men or noteworthy beauty, expertise in the arts of beadwork, tanning, and tipimaking for women. But, since these performances were often linked to the military equipage or free time associated with family wealth, such upward mobility proved difficult. The principal web between the two upper ranks of Kiowa society extended through marriage: men of lower rank would strive to acquire enough horses, usually twenty or thirty, to offer as bride-price to the óngop uncles who controlled the marriageability of their nieces. Once connected through affinal ties, a young man might ask his higher-status relatives to give him the "build-up" necessary for movement into the higher rank, but they were under no obligation to do so. With socially sanctioned mobility so difficult, not surprisingly Kiowas reported elopement as "the most common method of contracting a marriage." Even then, the bridegroom's family was subject to retaliation and loss of property by the male relatives of the bride. Eloping couples often took advantage of the ease in moving between *topotógas* (local residence bands) to put as much distance as possible between themselves and aggrieved relatives on both sides.[16]

Like Comanches, Kiowas spent the autumn months dispersed across the Plains in bands, hunting bison, tanning hides, and preparing dried meat for the winter. Early fall was also when small raiding parties of six to ten men sortied out to capture horses and military honors from other Indian groups or drive south into Mexico for livestock and captives. Some of the latter parties might be in the field throughout the winter, while their relatives took shelter in river bottoms among the cottonwood and willow windbreaks. Spring often brought lean times, and bands broke camp to hunt for subsistence.

In midsummer, Kiowas gathered for the sun dance and large-scale revenge parties. These congregations were also occasion for interband marriages and the exercise of a communal identity. There young men could speak of their recent achievements in hope of gaining the community affirmation that would allow them to move up in rank. In keeping with their extraordinary attention to social prestige and ceremonial practice by which status was negotiated,

16. Jane Fishburne Collier, *Marriage and Inequality in Classless Societies* (Stanford, Calif., 1988), 142–196, esp. 145.

Kiowas might have conferred unifying political power in jefes principales, as the Comanches did. Band-level captains, termed *topotók'i,* felt free to conduct informal diplomacy with other Indian groups and Euramericans but deferred to more prominent leaders in formal affairs. Although the Kiowa-Comanche peace of 1805–1806 was initiated by Guik'áte, he claimed that only Bulé, their principal chief, could confirm it.[17]

Comanches and Kiowas moved into the nineteenth century with some markedly different social responses to the challenge of incorporating rapid new wealth and vastly expanding territories. Comanches maintained the political egalitarianism and personal autonomy that had long been the legacy of their Great Basin roots yet proceeded to create new, multidivisional political gatherings and concentrated leadership to deal with Euramerican threats and opportunities. Kiowas refined notions of social rank that might reflect their earlier origins in a horticultural hearth or might have developed as a consequence of their newfound wealth in horses. Both groups seem to affirm Concha's remark that "they agree among themselves perfectly" and that they moved easily between band affiliations. At least in diplomatic affairs, this mobility included changes of residence across cultures themselves. Yet conflict and contention also permeated these societies in less visible ways, and in these tensions resided some of the forces that would form multiethnic communities of interest.[18]

Some Loved Their Horses More Than Their Wives

For all the ease of lateral movement among Comanches and the careful regulation of status among Kiowas, social competition, often erupting into conflict, haunted their days and nights. Where men's honor was the crucial correlate

17. Mishkin, *Rank and Warfare,* 24–34; John, "An Earlier Chapter," *NMHR,* LX (October 1985), 386–387.

18. Ethnologists generally agree that those equestrian Plains cultures exhibiting the greatest degree of attention to rank and status, with fully developed warrior and hunt police societies or elaborate age-grading, derived from an earlier horticultural tradition. Arapahos, Crows, Dakotas, Lakotas, and Cheyennes are the classic examples. It is therefore intriguing that Kiowas, conventionally understood as Plains pedestrian nomads, would likewise show such features. Hickerson's Jumano connection is at least one solution to the paradox (see "Ethnogenesis in the Great Plains"). For an overview that has stood the test of time, see

of social well-being and was expressed in the conspicuous display of horses, women, and social dependents, no amount of mobility or ceremonial control could prevent interpersonal or group schism. Horses, very simply, were the substance and symbol through which flowed success in hunting, raiding, honor, and marriage. Stealing horses under dangerous conditions brought acclaim, gifts of horses brought propitious marriages and the goodwill of spiritual specialists, and damages in the form of horses could resolve crises ranging from personal insults to wife theft to murder.

"Some men," said Post Oak Jim to an anthropologist in 1933, "loved their horses more than they loved their wives." Other Comanches added, "Or child, or any other any human being." This was no exotic hierarchy of affection but rather a condensed and powerful description of how economy, kinship, and society interwove during the florescence of Plains Indian equestrianism. If the horse afforded both the means and display of a man's prowess as horseman, hunter, and fighter, its power to do so was shaped by its social capacity to deliver to its owner the fundamental requisites for masculine respect. Horses provided the social currency of bride-price, by which a Comanche man secured a wife who would feed, clothe, entertain, and produce the hospitality by which he could enter into relationships of generosity with other men. Without horses to exchange in marriage, a Comanche man was bound by reciprocity to hunt and herd for his wife's family, thereby slowing his route to military prestige. Horses were also the currency of bridewealth, through which a Kiowa man acquired dependent lower-status relatives indebted to him by marriage to a daughter or niece. Bound by masculine codes of honor, these affines could not refuse the request of a wife-giver and were thereby engaged in the support of his career. Finally, horses provided the means through which a young Comanche man or lower-status Kiowa man could raid for livestock and seize captives, the symbolic capital, supplemental labor, and social currency through which they augmented careers or entered the marriage market as dispensers of young women.[19]

Robert Harry Lowie, *Indians of the Plains* (New York, 1954); for a recent essay that suggests horse-wealth as an inhibiting variable to age-grade development, see Jeffrey R. Hanson, "Age-set Theory and Plains Indian Age-grading," *American Ethnologist,* XV, no. 2 (1988), 349–364.

19. Post Oak Jim quoted in Wallace and Hoebel, *The Comanches,* 36. I condense substantially here Collier's discussion of Comanche and Kiowa marriage and social inequality relationships in *Marriage and Inequality,* esp. 197.

FIGURE 5. *Wild Horses on the Southern Plains.* 1834. Field sketch by George Catlin. Reproduced from George Catlin, *Letters and Notes on the Manners, Customs, and Condition of the North American Indians . . .* (New York, 1844), II, 59

Yet Comanches and Kiowas did not have equal ownership of horses. The former had even more disparity in their distribution than the latter, despite their egalitarian social profile. Some few Comanche men maintained herds of fifteen hundred to three thousand animals, but the vast majority ran strings of about twelve horses, over which number was considered a surplus and available for exchange purposes. Some indigent men had only one or two and had to borrow from relatives for war parties or, more rarely, marriage gifts. Women, too, strove for horse ownership, either by marriage to a wealthy man, through institutions like the Comanche Shakedown Dance (in which they attempted to shame successful raiders into parting with some of their spoils), or in rare cases by accompanying a raiding party and claiming their own rewards. Kiowas considered ownership of twenty to fifty horses evidence of a well-to-do óndeigúp'a family, but wealthy óngop men had many more, often in the hundreds, their generosity with which garnered them social prestige. Families of the kóon rank might have six to ten horses, and more than a few of the dapóm had no horses at all. Yet the concentration of horse-wealth was also unstable in the sense that, as social currency in societies based on asymmetrical reciprocity, wealth only had power when it moved between men and their families in the form of gifts. To hoard horse-wealth brought disparaging and dishonoring comments from those of all ranks and statuses.[20]

Comanche men might have loved their horses more than their wives, but they did so because horses, paradoxically, gave men the capacity to obtain wives and all the good things that came with them. Kiowa men loved their horses, too, but again for their ability to inaugurate the marriage transaction by which a bride's brother or uncle became wealthier in horses and, supported by kin, beholden to him for life. In both societies, men obtained full social enfranchisement through marriages, which in turn were made possible by horses. Young unmarried men, while the very core of Comanche and Kiowa military strength, also hovered as a threat to social stability and were usually made to reside on the outskirts of a ranchería or behind their parents' tipis. Since men's status in both societies was so inextricably tied to rights in horses and rights in women, struggles to obtain both lay at the heart of social conflict. "In the old days," said the Comanche Yellowfish, "lots of trouble began over women." Of the 107 prereservation Comanche customary law cases recorded by ethnographers, horse theft or woundings triggered 17 percent, often in association with the 42 percent that involved disputes between men about women; 23 cases were of adultery and 22 born of women absconding with higher-status men. Horse and women disputes figured even more prominently among the Kiowas. Horse stealing or retributive woundings composed 10 percent of their "petty disputes between individuals," usually in association with the 60 percent of actions in Kiowa law that began in "quarrels involving husband, wife, and co-respondent" (over women either absconding or committing adultery). If we include conflict between husband and wife's kin or insults to rights in women held by husband's kin (the levirate), this balloons to more than 70 per-

20. On Comanche horse ownership, see Wallace and Hoebel, *The Comanches*, 39–40, 72; Hoebel, "Political Organization and Law Ways of the Comanche Indians," American Anthropological Association, *Memoirs*, no. 54, 14–15. For the inheritance case involving three thousand horses, see "Inheritance," box 1, Comanche Field Notes, 1933, Ser. 5, Research Notes, E. Adamson Hoebel Papers, American Philosophical Society, Philadelphia, Pa. (hereafter cited as Hoebel Papers); for Kiowas, see Mishkin, *Rank and Warfare*, 19–20; Jane Richardson, *Law and Status among the Kiowa Indians*, American Ethnological Society, *Monographs*, I (New York, 1940), 14.

cent. Yet, despite the passions at work, fewer than a dozen incidents ended in overt violence between men; rather, the vast majority found resolution in kin-negotiated restitution of damages, again signified in horses.[21]

Unequal access to women was central to endemic social tension. By the beginning of the nineteenth century, women probably outnumbered men in both Comanche and Kiowa society, given the extent of casualties among men in raids and warfare. But, where social prestige expressed in horse-wealth provided men the ability to gain wives, men who either by military excellence or social rank were preferred husbands could almost always outcompete their juniors by age or rank. Comanches described this in simple terms: while women often married by age sixteen, men seldom did so until they were twenty-five or thirty, after they were able to acquire horses and repute in warfare. Even then, girls were often married to middle-aged men wealthy in horses and were placed into increasingly polygamous households. Quanah Parker, the last chief of the Comanches, had nine wives in all, including five at one time. Mrs. Asenap told ethnographers that her father Padaponi had "three or four"; she couldn't remember precisely. Kiowas also saw men of the senior óngop rank acquire wives to the detriment of young men from the lower ranks. Óngop men seem consistently to have maintained households of two to six wives, with two or three being most common. At least some cases of polygamy in Comanche and Kiowa society may be the result of a decline in the numbers of men consequent to casualties in war, but the ample evidence of contestation over women suggests that unequal access to women organized much of social conflict within these Plains Indian societies.[22]

Men constrained by youth, family poverty, or low rank faced two choices: either accept a subordinate role and hope that in time a patron would assist them in mounting a military career, or strike out on their own with others

21. See Wallace and Hoebel, *The Comanches,* 217; Hoebel, "Political Organization and Law Ways of the Comanche Indians," American Anthropological Association, *Memoirs,* no. 54; for the Kiowas, see Richardson, *Law and Status among the Kiowa Indians,* American Ethnological Society, *Monographs,* I.

22. Wallace and Hoebel, *The Comanches,* 132–133; "Polygamy," box 1, Comanche Field Notes, 1933, Ser. 5, Research Notes, Hoebel Papers; for Kiowas, see Collier, *Marriage and Inequality,* 150–157; Richardson, *Law and Status among the Kiowa Indians,* American Ethnological Society, *Monographs,* I. In the twelve cases involving ónde men, eight had more than one wife; Mishkin, *Rank and Warfare,* reports that sixteen of the twenty-five "most famous men in the tribe" had more than one wife, and five had more than two (55).

FIGURE 6. *Cassulan, His Wife, and Tiah-na-zi—Kioway Indians; Making Their Toilet.* 1845. Watercolor by Lt. James W. Abert. Courtesy Yale Collection of Western Americana, Beinecke Rare Book and Manuscript Library

of their cohort and seize the booty that could elevate them to full manhood through marriage. This was the internal force behind the expansion of the Plains raiding economy in the nineteenth century. No matter what their jefes principales might promise in diplomacy with the Spanish, Mexicans, or Americans, junior men's quest for full cultural enfranchisement required violent economic action. By 1800, Plains Indians already outclassed New Mexicans in the quality and quantity of their herds, but Texas and Mexico beckoned with vastly more animals. Whatever horses could not be absorbed by the internal economy of Comanche and Kiowa society found ready buyers among American traders on the eastern fringes of the Great Plains. And, when junior Comanche and Kiowa men returned to their rancherías, running their portable wealth before them, they did so increasingly with captives as a parallel form of social currency. Captive girls and women had value as laborers in the expanding hide trade but also as fresh, usually subordinate, participants in the marriage economy. Comanches reported that captive women might become secondary "chore wives" to the "chief wife" of a prominent Comanche. Others might be competed for between junior men. Captive boys had immediate value as horse herders for their captors but were also sold to senior men who wished to enlarge their own labor pool and social recognition as heads of large, laterally extended families. If they showed themselves culturally adept, captive boys grew to become warriors and raiders themselves. They too would desire wives but seldom competed with full-blood men for marriage into esteemed families. In the unstable and creative world of southern Plains Indians, the naturalization of these alienable dependents proved one of their most remarkable innovations.[23]

We Made Slaves of the Older Boys

As Comanches and Kiowas redirected their raiding territories southward into Texas and northern Mexico, they also set about making cultural sense of the fact that their numbers would henceforth be considerably augmented by alien peoples. It was a situation at once familiar and original. The assimilation of outsider women and children had long been a part of intercultural exchanges in the Southwest, for which adoptive practices both sacred and mundane were in place. But in the nineteenth century demographic crises and economic exigencies lent real impetus to the practice and began to transform its cultural meaning.

Pawnees, Wichitas, Apaches, Kiowas, and Comanches all engaged in captive raiding and trading across the Plains but none so vigorously as the latter two groups, who made the institution a core cultural element. Both conceived multiple locations into which captives could be assimilated—as kinsmen (if formally adopted), as blood bondsmen (exchangeable, but only within the group as patrimony), or, among the Comanches, as chattels (alienable property). Comanches made a clear distinction between peoples "born of Comanche" *(numu ruboraru)* and those "raised as Comanche" *(numu'aitu)* as well as between "captives assimilated through adoption" *(kwuhúpu)* and those "slaves"

23. For Comanche expansion southeast and connections with American traders from Nacogdoches, Natchitoches, and St. Louis after 1800, see Kavanagh, *Comanche Political History,* 177–181; for captives as chore wives, see Wallace and Hoebel, *The Comanches,* 141 (for captive men as potential, though less than ideal, husbands, see 138). The idea that captives could be both alienable, like chattels, and dependent, in the form of fictive kin, runs counter to the conventional analytical categories of patrimony and property used by students of slavery. See Claude Meillassoux, *The Anthropology of Slavery: The Womb of Iron and Gold* (Chicago, 1991), 341–342. For an argument that places gender in the form of unequal "sex divisions of valued status positions" at the center of intertribal Indian warfare, see Clifton B. Kroeber and Bernard L. Fontana, *Massacre on the Gila: An Account of the Last Major Battle between American Indians, with Reflections on the Origins of War* (Tucson, Ariz., 1986), 173.

(tai'vo) who "must do work for another" *(tiri'aiwapi)*. Several forces converged to give social impulse to these distinctions. Internal status competition was one, but the need to rebuild populations ravaged by warfare and epidemic disease also figured heavily. Finally, as market connections with American traders matured, captives became increasingly valuable as commodities in the Plains economy, given their usefulness as laborers in the bison hide and horse trade and in an emerging contraband cattle commerce.[24]

Comanches had been stunned by the smallpox epidemic of 1779–1781. Another fierce outbreak swept the southern Plains in the winter of 1815–1816, taking some four thousand people, according to the Comanche leader Chihuahua. Losses might have been more, assuming he spoke only of the devastation among his people, the "middle" tribe of the Yamparicas. Kiowas recalled that this was the first smallpox "within the memory of their tribe," and they probably suffered proportionally to their Comanche allies. The disease struck at the wisdom and hope of these Plains peoples, taking mostly the old and young. The Texas divisions lost at least four of their paramount leaders, and clear political power did not again refocus for a generation. The full shock of their loss escapes our comprehension, but at least one strategy for recovery was clear.[25]

Determining real numbers of the women and children drawn into Plains Indian captivity is even more difficult than counting their counterparts in Spanish and Mexican society. One historian estimates that from 1540 to 1820 some five to ten thousand "people of all ages, sexes, and castes" were cap-

24. Stanley Noyes, *Los Comanches: The Horse People* (Albuquerque, N.Mex., 1993), 69–73; Dan Flores, "Bison Ecology and Bison Diplomacy: The Southern Plains from 1800 to 1850," *Journal of American History* (hereafter cited as *JAH)*, LXXVIII (1991–1992), 465–485. For captive status in Kiowa society, see Mishkin, *Rank and Warfare,* 42–45. Mishkin claims the Kiowas never resold their captives, given Kiowa anxiety about their small population. For the Comanches, see Wallace and Hoebel, *The Comanches,* 241–242; Mishkin, *Rank and Warfare,* 44; Thomas Gladwin, "Comanche Kin Behavior," *American Anthropologist,* L (1948), 73–94, esp. 82. For Comanche kin terms, see Lila Wistrand Robinson, *Comanche Dictionary and Grammar* (Norman, Okla., 1990); for a nineteenth-century Comanche dictionary and grammatical source, see Manuel García Rejón, comp., *Comanche Vocabulary,* trilingual ed., trans. Daniel J. Gelo (Austin, Tex., 1995).

25. Chihuahua's estimates were reported by John Jameson, newly appointed American agent at Natchitoches, in 1817. See Kavanagh, *Comanche Political History,* 172–173; for the Kiowas, see Mooney, "Calendar History of the Kiowa Indians," *Seventeenth Annual Report of the Bureau of American Ethnology,* part 2, 168.

tured by nomadic Indian groups across the whole expanse of the northern borderlands from Sonora to Texas. Given that the population of the Provincias Internas totaled only some 34,000 vecinos in 1800, captive and livestock raiding by southern Plains Indian groups siphoned away much of the province's demographic and economic growth. But to see this borderland violence only in terms of its debilitating effect on northern New Spain overlooks the fact that one people's loss was another people's gain. Wealth in the form of human and animal resources flowed into the southern Plains as it flowed out of the northern frontier. Perhaps real numbers are inadequate in any event, when we have at hand diverse and compelling stories of human beings swept into the whirlwind of bondage set loose by the colonial encounter and expansion of market economies. And of longer-term meaning were the intersocietal consequences these exchanges would portend.[26]

The ability of Comanches, Kiowas, and Apaches to plunder northern Mexico was substantially enhanced by the crisis of the Mexican Wars for Independence that commenced when Padre Miguel Hidalgo issued his "Grito de Dolores" (a call for social and political enfranchisement for Mexico's underclasses) near Guanajuato in September 1810. Although Hidalgo's ragtag army of poor peasants was defeated the following spring and the revolutionary priest executed, the forces of rebellion set loose in his uprising spread throughout Mexico and ultimately all of Spanish America. In northern Mexico, militias once assigned to frontier defense were drawn into the camps of rebels or royalists, and the funds used to craft gift alliances between New Spain and Indian groups evaporated. Texas experienced two quickly suppressed pro-

26. Peter Alan Stern, "Social Marginality and Acculturation on the Northern Frontier of New Spain" (Ph.D. diss., University of California, Berkeley, 1984), 322. Flores has recently argued that by the early nineteenth century the Comanches had abandoned traditional Shoshonean population control such as infanticide and polyandry and turned to population augmentation through captive adoption. Flores attributes this to the efficiency of the buffalo-hunting economy, which eliminated the need for population limitations and stimulated the demand for pastoral laborers. Downplaying epidemics and cultural exchange as alternative factors, however, obscures the creativity shown by Comanches in responding to crisis and opportunity. See "Bison Ecology and Bison Diplomacy," *JAH*, LXXVIII (1991–1992), 465–485, esp. 471; his source on infanticide practices is Abram Kardiner et al., *The Psychological Frontiers of Society* (New York, 1945), 83. See also Carl Coke Rister, *Border Captives: The Traffic in Prisoners by Southern Plains Indians, 1835–1875* (Norman, Okla., 1940); Russell Mario Magnaghi, "The Indian Slave Trader: The Comanche, a Case Study" (Ph.D. diss., St. Louis University, 1970), 152.

independence revolts between 1811 and 1813, but the royalists could no longer contain the eastern Comanches, who grew so bold as to raid San Antonio itself in 1814. Coahuila lay open to Comanche and Kiowa incursions, while to the west Lipan and Mescalero Apaches penetrated Chihuahua. New Mexico, by contrast, experienced little immediate upheaval after 1810 and worked hard to maintain commercial relations with the western Comanche divisions.[27]

In August 1813, José Francisco Ruíz, a thirty-year-old *ranchero* living along the Nueces River south of San Antonio, Texas, fled for asylum among the eastern Comanches. He had joined in Bernardo Gutiérrez de Lara's liberal rebellion against Spanish authority in Texas, a rising sympathetic to the Hidalgo independence movement then underway in Mexico. Defeated by royalist forces at the Battle of the Medina River on August 18, 1813, Ruíz escaped execution and spent the next eight years living, traveling (and probably raiding) with Comanches "friendly to the revolutionary cause" and closely involved with those Americans engaged in the Plains trade along the eastern frontier. In the autumn of 1821, with Mexico's independence from Spain, the new commandant general of the eastern Interior Provinces granted Ruíz a full pardon for taking on the role of commissioner to the Comanches and Lipan Apaches as a representative of the new government. At a meeting with the "ancient Pitsinampa [Pisinampe]" in March 1822, Ruíz extended an invitation for a Comanche delegation to visit Mexico City and negotiate a treaty between the two "nations." The old chief appointed a younger man, Guonique, to lead the Comanche delegation of nine men and four women, which met with Emperor Iturbide's representative Francisco de Azcárate in the capital in December 1822. The treaty affirmed on the thirteenth of that month contained fourteen articles, including detailed provisions for mutual military support, commerce, diplomatic representation, education of young Comanche men at the imperial court, and a "mutual restitution of prisoners (unless they, of their own free will, should desire to remain in the nation where they [were] located)." In clarification of the last article, the official report on the treaty claimed that "more than two thousand, five hundred of all classes, sexes, and ages were held as captives

27. David J. Weber, *The Mexican Frontier, 1821–1846: The American Southwest under Mexico* (Albuquerque, N.Mex., 1982), 9–10; Matthew McLaurine Babcock, "Trans-national Trade Routes and Diplomacy: Comanche Expansion, 1760–1846" (master's thesis, University of New Mexico, 2001), 65–67. For the broader context of independence movements in Spanish America, see Christon L. Archer, ed., *The Wars of Independence in Spanish America* (Wilmington, Del., 2000).

in [Comanche] power," not counting the "large number" who, like Ruíz, had fled to Comanches for asylum during the wars of independence.[28]

Striking numbers, if they are to be believed, for they suggest that captive Mexicans in the 1820s comprised some 10 to 20 percent of a total Comanche population variously estimated at some twelve to twenty thousand individuals. But Guonique threw other vast figures around during his visit, offering once to mobilize eight thousand men-at-arms to defend the internal provinces against enemies "from the interior or abroad" and again in conversation with Iturbide himself to "raise a body of twenty-seven thousand men" within six months if the emperor found himself in need. Perhaps these would come from the "nine nations" the Comanches held in "subordination," but Guonique likely wished to present his people as a substantial ally and formidable foe depending on the future of relations between the respective nations.[29]

Whether the numbers were exaggerated, captives chose to remain with the Comanches, or major repatriations occurred after treaty ratification, Ruíz himself offered a lower estimate six years later. Writing in 1828, as one of many observations about his Comanche friends, he reported,

> The Comanches have always been fierce defenders of their freedom. They fought a war in New Mexico, and to this date some of the prisoners taken then are still living with the Comanches. . . . Comanches have taken hundreds of prisoners of both sexes. It is estimated that they have over 900 prisoners with them, not counting the many who have managed to escape after suffering great hardships. The lot of the women is most pitiful.[30]

Despite their disparities, if the combined "Nations of the North" held but 150 Spanish captives in the 1780s, the 1822 and 1828 estimates indicate a ferocious expansion in the scale of Indian slave raiding. And there remained some consistencies. Speaking of the eastern Comanches alone, Ruíz declared their

28. The treaty of 1822 was published with editorial commentary as "Delegación del Nación Cumanche á el congreso Méxicano," in *Gaceta del gobierno imperial de México*, Jan. 30, 1823, reprinted by Carlos J. Sierra in *Boletín bibliográfico de la secretaría de hacienda y crédito público* (Mexico, 1968), 14–15. It appears in translation in Malcolm D. McLean, comp., trans., and ed., *Papers concerning Robertson's Colony in Texas*, IV (Arlington, Tex., 1977), 426–433, esp. 428–429; Kavanagh, *Comanche Political History*, 195–198.

29. McLean, comp., trans., and ed., *Papers concerning Robertson's Colony*, IV, 431–432.

30. José Francisco Ruíz, *Report on the Indian Tribes of Texas in 1828*, ed. John C. Ewers and trans. Georgette Dorn (New Haven, Conn., 1972), 9.

total population to number some one thousand to fifteen hundred families, perhaps five to ten thousand individuals. The captive component in 1828, therefore, held somewhere between 10 or 20 percent of the total population. Most of these were probably seized in the cluster of raids across the Río Grande that followed the general collapse of Spanish military authority in the aftermath of the Gutiérrez de Lara rebellion. In 1815, for example, the authorities interrogated a redeemed Spanish woman and found that "fugitive" members of that revolution had accompanied a Comanche and Wichita campaign into Coahuila that netted dozens of sheepherders, cowherders, women, and children, along with hundreds of head of livestock. Since royalists reported that nearly one thousand revolutionaries had fled to safe haven among friendly Indian tribes, Ruíz might have seen the action firsthand.[31]

Also in 1828, Ruíz, now a colonel in the Mexican army, accompanied an expedition through Texas to establish boundaries and garner intelligence on its Indian inhabitants. Among his colleagues was Jean Luis Berlandier, a French scientist who produced a long manuscript on "Indigenes nomades" they encountered during their year in the field, borrowing heavily from Ruíz's knowledge. He too commented on a burgeoning captive population and distinguished between those of Euramerican descent and those from other Indian groups:

> The indigenous nations generally make a distinction between two sorts of prisoners, who get totally different treatment. The first are Creoles, whom they call *white men,* although some are every bit as dark as themselves. The others are other natives, whom they call *red men.*

Although he claimed it "hard to estimate the number of frontier settlers" in Indian captivity, he ventured that Comanches alone held some "five or six hundred" creole prisoners, predominantly women and small children. The women found torment at the hands of Comanche women, but the "male children, on the contrary, [were] raised with great care. . . . These prisoners do not return to their homes because the nomadic life and the marriages they have contracted afford them an independence they prize." Older boys, "taken as slaves at too advanced an age to grow to like the native life may try to escape, but if they

31. Gary Clayton Anderson, *The Indian Southwest, 1580–1830: Ethnogenesis and Reinvention* (Norman, Okla., 1999), 254–255; McLean, comp., trans., and ed., *Papers concerning Robertson's Colony,* IV, 428. For Comanche participation in the Gutiérrez de Lara rebellion, see Anderson, *Indian Southwest,* 253–254.

are unlucky enough to be recaptured they may be killed or simply sent back to slavery." Other creole captives, he said, were "often led into the [Mexican] villages and sold" for "a mule or a gun, or whatever other object the owner thinks worth the trifling value of a Christian prisoner among the savages."[32]

Of captives taken from enemy Indians, Berlandier claimed that "some are killed or tortured to death, while others are destined to replace the members of the victorious tribe killed in the war, and they are spared only if the family of the dead man agree to it. At that moment they change their names and are treated with tenderness, as if they actually were the man who died in combat." Other Indian groups who took captives, however, like the Lipan Apaches, Wacos, and various Wichita bands, he described as "ferocious and inhuman," practitioners of torture and cannibalism, and completely dedicated to enslavement of those they did not kill. "Carried in bonds to the villages, the women and children are used as slaves, not like the Creoles, to become part of the people, but as real slaves who are forced to perform all the work." Since Comanches often warred against these latter groups, Berlandier's observations in this case probably reiterated the Comanches' own biases.[33]

Although Ruíz and Berlandier's information must be filtered through the lens of prejudices on either side, both men displayed real attention to the finer points of Indian societies and the landscapes in which they lived. Ruíz, in fact, was considered by Comanches their most understanding and sympathetic Euramerican contact and served throughout the 1820s and 1830s as their principal intermediary with both Mexican and American Texan administrators. Their reports on Indian slavery carry some weight, especially when read in dialogue with statements from Comanches and Kiowas themselves.

Comanches seem to have segregated their captives by race, age, and gender, which in turn conditioned their experience of enslavement. In combination with later oral histories, the accounts of Ruíz and Berlandier suggest that Comanches held five or six hundred captives from Spanish settlements and perhaps an additional three or four hundred from "enemy" Indian nations.

32. Jean Luis Berlandier, *The Indians of Texas in 1830*, ed. John C. Ewers and trans. Patricia Reading Leclercq (Washington, D.C., 1969), 75, 76, 83. Berlandier and Ruíz accompanied a Comanche band of sixty to eighty members led by "the chiefs Reyuna and El Ronco" on a six-day bear and bison hunt northwest of San Antonio. The latter might well have been the Kiowa "El Ronco" (the Hoarse One) who married the Yamparica Somiquaso's daughter (12).

33. Ibid., 76–77.

The former carried the higher cultural value, probably because of the prestige implicit in their subjugation—a conquering people held in bondage by their putative subjects. They also embodied latent exchange value for redemption in Spanish villages. Indian captives more readily suffered torture in the context of ritual sacrifice but could also be saved if Comanche families wished to adopt them in the place of a lost loved one.

Children capable of easy assimilation fit into the traditional pattern of adoption and acculturation, and boys were especially esteemed. But age was a tangible factor. The Comanche Tasura told ethnographers that, although they "adopted the young ones into the family, we made slaves of the older boys." Herman Asenap's father was a young Mexican boy seized "while gathering beans" but then adopted and fully assimilated into Comanche life. As an adult, he returned to Mexico with some Comanches and, despite the opportunity to repatriate, "refused to leave the tribe." He later conducted raids into his former homeland. Older boys, however, depending upon the skills they carried into captivity, might be "forced to keep guns in condition" or put to "women's work" like tanning hides. The Comanche warrior Padaponi "captured a Mexican boy" to herd his horses but finally "gave him away" because it was "too much trouble teaching him the language." Hekiyan'i, a captive Mexican girl who married and remained for the rest of her life with her Comanches affines, recounted a darker story. She said that, if a Comanche man tired of his male slave, he might bind the young man astride a horse and haze it into a herd where "eventually they get killed." Such cruelty was reported by Comanches and Euramerican observers alike to be the special province of certain assimilated captives. Nayia claimed that one man "would throw captured babies in the air and catch them on [his] spear" and would castrate or crucify older boys. If true, little wonder that Berlandier wrote, "Small [captive] boys . . . grow up with such good tutors that they become so active and so evil the garrison people fear the prisoners more than the natives."[34]

Captured women, especially creoles, also found avenues to cultural assimilation open among the Comanches. In a statement rich with the paradoxes of human bondage in the borderlands, Herman Asenap declared that women were "not enslaved" but "often belonged to the men who captured them." "Enslavement" seems here to mean exclusion from opportunities inherent in the

34. "Captives," box 1, Comanche Field Notes, 1933, Ser. 5, Research Notes, Hoebel Papers; Berlandier, *Indians of Texas in 1830,* ed. Ewers and trans. Leclercq, 83.

kin relation, and "belonging" seems to refer to the patrimonial rights by which a male captor could decide his captive's fate within Comanche kin relations. In the case of Hekiyan'i, taken as a girl from her village in northern Mexico, this right in persons seems to have endured with her captor, Toyop, even after he had exchanged her with Wahawma, who told her, "When you grow up, you'll be my wife." Although Toyop was himself of Mexican captive origin, and perhaps lower in social status than Wahawma, he was able to reclaim her two years later to care for his aged (and adoptive) father, Terservakwitsi. In this case, the captor's claim was seen by the community as superior to that of the anticipatory husband, despite their different social status.[35]

Yet captive women sometimes found themselves under the protection of Comanche women. Sarah Ann Horn, taken captive in 1837, reported that she was taken in "by an old widow woman . . . a merciful exception to the general character of these merciless beings." She was "set to work to dress buffalo skins, to make them into garments and moccasins; to cut up and dry the buffalo meat, and then pound it for use, and do all the cooking for the family." Her sons Joseph and John, ages four and five, had very different experiences. John died of exposure after being "set to hold a horse throughout the night." Joseph had the better fortune of adoption into a Comanche household "whose mistress was a Spanish woman, who, with her brother had been captured by these Indians in childhood . . . she was of amiable disposition, and much interested in the care of [her] dear child." Similarly, Rosita Rodrigues, seized from northern Chihuahua in 1845 with her son Incarnación, reported she "remained a prisoner among the Comanche Indians about one year, during which time I was obliged to work very hard, but was not otherwise badly treated as I became the property of an old squaw who became much attached to me." Her son, however, remained "a prisoner among the Comanche" and herded livestock with other captive boys. Yet Incarnación's imprisoned status seems dubious, since Rosita reported to her father that she had "heard from [her son] a short time ago—he was well and hearty, but pure Indian now." Neither Horn nor Rodrigues claimed to have suffered sexual abuse. At least some captive women

35. "Hekiyani-Life," in "Captives," box 1, Comanche Field Notes, 1933, Ser. 5, Research Notes, Hoebel Papers. An abridged version is in Wallace and Hoebel, *The Comanches,* 260–263. This case lends credence to Collier's position that the fundamental kinship coercion in stateless societies lies with the power over women's fictive or biological kin to determine their marital choices and the capacity to withdraw them from those agreements. See *Marriage and Inequality,* 226–230.

FIGURE 7. *The Spanish Girl; (a Prisoner).* 1845. She had been captured four years earlier by Little Mountain and given to his father as a gift wife (see James William Abert, *Through the Country of the Comanche Indians in the Fall of the Year 1845 . . .*, ed. John R. Galvan [1846; San Francisco, Calif., 1970], 47). Watercolor by Lt. James W. Abert. Courtesy Yale Collection of Western Americana, Beinecke Rare Book and Manuscript Library

were informally adopted by older women, by which action they received the protection of the Comanche incest taboo.[36]

Horn and Rodrigues returned to tell their stories. Most captive women did not, bound either by literal coercion or the bonds of kinship. The latter was implicitly recognized by Tasura when he noted that the Comanches "captured many women—we have only a few full-bloods left." Josiah Gregg noted the presence of Mexican women among the Comanches when he began traveling the Santa Fe Trail in the 1830s. He remarked with surprise that some of these "preferred remaining with [their captors], rather than encounter the horrible ordeal of ill-natured remarks on being restored to civilized life." One woman seized in 1785, reputedly the daughter of the governor of Chihuahua, refused repatriation in 1805, even after the offer of one thousand pesos for her ransom. She sent word that the Comanches "had disfigured her by tattooing; that she was married, and perhaps *encinta* [pregnant], and she would be more unhappy returning . . . under these circumstances than remaining where she was."[37]

Kiowas also prized young boys and captive women as potential kinspeople. Although they told ethnographers that they "chose to employ the [male] captives as workers, not as warrior recruits," this seems only to have applied to those captives who did not experience assimilation through adoption, since

36. Rosita Rodrigues to don Miguel Rodrigues, Jan. 13, 1846, in Bexar Archives, Barker Texas History Collection, University of Texas, Austin (hereafter cited as Bexar Archives); *A Narrative of the Captivity of Mrs. Horn and Her Two Children* (St. Louis, Mo., 1839), reprinted in C. C. Rister, *Comanche Bondage* (Lincoln, Nebr., 1989), 157–158, 164, 183; on the incest taboo, see Hoebel, "Political Organization and Law Ways of the Comanche Indians," American Anthropological Association, *Memoirs*, no. 54, 108. I am indebted to Tressa L. Berman for suggesting the association between captive women's low incidence of sexual abuse and the adoptive incest taboo. For similar examples among other Indian groups, see James Axtell, "The White Indians of Colonial America," in Stanley N. Katz and John M. Murrin, eds., *Colonial America: Essays in Politics and Social Development* (New York, 1983), 16–47, esp. 27.

37. See Tasura's statement in "Captives," box 1, Comanche Field Notes, 1933, Ser. 5, Research Notes, Hoebel Papers. Cynthia Ann Parker, the mother of Quanah Parker, the last Comanche war chief, is the most famous example of a woman who chose to remain with her captors and found family fulfillment there. See James De Shields, *Cynthia Ann Parker: The Story of Her Capture* (St. Louis, Mo., 1886). Parker lived twenty-four years among the Comanches and died of heartbreak shortly after her rescue; see Rodrigues letter, Bexar Archives; Josiah Gregg, *The Commerce of the Prairies*, ed. Milo Milton Quaife (1744; Lincoln, Nebr., 1966), 208.

our best firsthand account of Kiowa captivity indicates that Andrés Martínez did work his way through Kiowa warrior societies in livestock raids. If captives, like Martínez, experienced a fortuitous adoption, they were given "good names" and could inherit property from their parents; if not, they received "ludicrous names" that highlighted their alien origins and were put to work at camp chores or herding horses. Captive women, if not adopted or married, "looked after the household work as helpers of their mistresses. They performed the menial work, cared for the children, [and] helped in tanning and food preserving." If brought into a polygamous household as a chore wife, they might suffer abuse and scorn from Kiowa first-wives, who were said to overwork them.[38]

Despite Kiowa concerns with the preservation of rank and status, with favorable adoptions or extraordinary bravery captives could move upward in rank, perhaps even more readily than Kiowas of the dishonored dapóm rank. The two categories meshed and separated around individual cases, but Kiowas estimated that captives composed 5 to 7 percent of their population, while dapóm hovered around 10 percent. Although nominally dapóm at the moment of capture, in that they had no kin affiliations upon which to call for protection or support, higher-rank adoptions did provide those benefits for some captives. Neither, apparently, did they necessarily carry the stigma of uselessness and criminality associated with the bottom rank. Thus Andrés Martínez, purchased by Tseitáinte (Many Bears) from his Mescalero Apache captors for one mule, two bison robes, and a red blanket, and given to Tseitáinte's daughter Etonbo as a surrogate son, found real opportunity as the adoptive grandson of an óngop topotók'i. With such prestigious sponsorship, he was soon riding in livestock raids led by another esteemed captive, Mokín, a "Black Mexican" adopted by the keeper of the sacred *taimé* (sun dance) medicine bundle. Augmenting his household through captive seizure and adoption seems to have been a custom for Tseitáinte, who had given his wife Honzipfa (Tanner of Hides) a three-year-old Mexican captive boy nearly twenty years earlier and whom Andrés knew as the Kiowa warrior Guolate. Yet, without advantageous

38. Mishkin, *Rank and Warfare,* 37, 42–45, esp. 43, 44. Donald Collier reports captive numbers at 6–7 percent, or some 140 people (most of whom were women), in "Kiowa Social Integration" (master's thesis, University of Chicago, 1938); for Martínez, see J. J. Methvin, *Andele, the Mexican-Kiowa Captive: A Story of Real Life among the Indians* (Albuquerque, N.Mex., 1996).

FIGURE 8. *Lager der Kiowäy Indianer (Kiowa Ranchería).* c. 1851. Note the Mexican apparel of the women on the left. By Heinrich Balduin Möllhausen. Courtesy Yale Collection of Western Americana, Beinecke Rare Book and Manuscript Library

kin ties, captives endured social opprobrium and constant reminders that they were not real Kiowas.[39]

Seized to labor as herders or hide processors, adopted as sons or daughters, or desired (and resented) as wives, captives found themselves in roles as various and fluid as the societies in which they were held. And yet another capacity awaited some as well, in the spiritual realm. Kiowas and Comanches reported the use of captives in their sun dances as cutters of the sacred "tree," or center pole around which their men danced to renew medicine powers. Accompanied by men from the *Koi'tseñko,* or Sacred Horse warrior society, this prestigious and spiritually perilous role was undertaken among the Kiowas by a "captive Mexican woman." She wielded the ax, alternating each blow with a song from the Koi'tseñko soldiers, then conducted the felled tree back to its place in the dance ground. Somewhat differently among the Comanches, the role went to a "virtuous Comanche woman, . . . a virtuous captive woman, [or] a captive man who had a number of war deeds to his credit." While elevation of captives to this position might have been reward for "the captive woman

39. Mishkin, *Rank and Warfare,* 42–44, 54; Methvin, *Andele,* 57; Boyd, *Kiowa Voices,* II, 155–158.

who was faithful to her master or the captive man who had won war honors," as Comanches told ethnographers, perhaps more was at risk. The social liminality of captives made them more dispensable than fully enfranchised Kiowas or Comanches should something go awry during the period when potent spiritual power roamed the encampments and dance grounds. As one respected Kiowa ethnographer noted of the center pole cutter, "She had to be a captive, because what she was going to do was dangerous, and you could not risk one of your own women to do it; she had to be dressed beautifully because what she was to do was a great honor, even if she died doing it." If simultaneous marginality and centrality were daily a part of captives' lives, the sun dance role, like that experienced by the Pawnee Morning Star ceremony's honored victim, compressed the paradox into a single, intensely conflicted moment.[40]

Some Gave Themselves Up

The violent exchange of culture-group members established an atmosphere heavy with pain and demands for retribution, which in turn spurred further conflict. But, at less obvious levels, implicit in the very notion of retribution and explicit in the cultural meanings of kinship, certain forms of reciprocity—however unequal—were being enacted as well. If Comanches and Kiowas knitted their societies together by mutual recognition of the obligations between kinspeople, however much those obligations might at times be resented and the source of social friction, so too were other Indian groups and Spanish settlers coming to participate in a shared universe of reciprocal obligations.

One expression of these phenomena was recited by the Comanche Post Oak Jim. Other Indians, he told ethnographers, "frequently snuck into [Comanche] camps to give themselves up—they came from poor tribes where there was not enough food." In effect a form of self-exchange by which destitute and vulnerable members of other Indian groups solicited the protective embrace of kinship dependency in return for their labor, the practice seems to have spread beyond individual acts of desperation into a form of pawnship. As the institution was expressed elsewhere, this involved pawning dependent women

40. Methvin, *Andele,* 52–60, esp. 58; Ralph Linton, "The Comanche Sun Dance," *American Anthropologist,* N.S., XXXVII (1935), 420–428, esp. 421; Alice Marriott, *The Ten Grandmothers* (Norman, Okla., 1945), 53–56, esp. 54.

and children either to wealthy families within the group or across ethnic lines to wealthier lineages. In return, the family or group would receive livestock, grains, or money. The pawned dependent remained "totally at the disposal of the recipient lineage" and could be repatriated only upon repayment of the loan. Redemption was rare, however, and most pawns found themselves married into the host society, where their children became full members. It seems that impoverished Shoshones sometimes sold children to their prosperous Comanche cousins in this fashion, although in such strictly economic terms seems unlikely. In at least one instance a Comanche war party was composed of "Half-Shoshoni men" who traveled with a captive Mexican cook, suggesting a considerable Shoshone representation among the Comanches, either through self-sale or pawnship. The pattern appears to have crossed the Indian–New Mexican divide as well. In the 1860s, an American administrator in New Mexico, reporting on Indian slaves held by citizens in the territory, claimed that "destitute orphans are sometimes sold by their remote relations; poor parents also make traffic of their children."[41]

Destitute Indian individuals and families used self-exchange or pawnship to survive and gather the resources of kinship, and by the middle years of the nineteenth century poverty-stricken and indentured Mexican *peones* made similar choices. But, in the early years of the century, Comanches, Kiowas, and Spanish colonists worked from somewhat more powerful and advantageous positions to recruit the benefits of linkage with their neighbors. Lean and difficult times visited all sides in various ways, and, if Comanches could call upon Spanish governors for shipments of corn during famine or to build them farming outposts on the Plains—which Quegüe of the Kotsotekas requested in 1805—so too could Spanish governors call upon Comanche warriors to pun-

41. "The Testimony of Chief Justice Kirby Benedict before the Doolittle Committee, July 4, 1865," in "Condition of the Indian Tribes," in *Report of the Commissioner of Indian Affairs, 1865* (Washington, D.C., 1866), 325–327, esp. 326. See Post Oak Jim, in "Captives," box 1, Comanche Field Notes, 1933, Ser. 5, Research Notes, Hoebel Papers; for pawnship as compared to slavery, see Suzanne Miers and Igor Kopytoff, "Introduction: African Slavery as an Institution of Marginality," in Miers and Kopytoff, eds., *Slavery in Africa: Historical and Anthropological Perspectives* (Madison, Wisc., 1977), esp. 10; for a treatment of pawnship across Africa, see Toyin Falola and Paul E. Lovejoy, eds., *Pawnship in Africa: Debt Bondage in Historical Perspective* (Boulder, Colo., 1994); Wallace and Hoebel, *The Comanches*, 241–242. Wallace and Hoebel say pawning occured "often," but they do not refer to specific cases; for half Shoshones, see "Captives," box 1, Comanche Field Notes, 1933, Ser. 5, Research Notes, Hoebel papers.

ish Apache depredations. However, beneath these overtly diplomatic bargains lay more subtle forms of negotiation performed at the local level. Forcible exchange between Indians and Spanish or Mexican settlers created a shadow kinship that reached across social barriers, seldom openly acknowledged but covertly recognized in the realm of significant silences. Whether unspoken because of the severe moral judgment that Spaniards and Mexicans might have levied against Indian-European unions or because of the very everydayness of the practice at the local level, these expressions of informal involuntary kinship were useful to all the protagonists in the borderlands.[42]

This creative, if undeniably harsh, quality is a noteworthy and discrete characteristic of borderland slavery, setting it apart from other North American slave systems, where increasingly rigid social and racial barriers allowed little conscious recognition of the asymmetrical symbiosis between masters and slaves. The multiethnic slave system of the Southwest conformed more closely to indigenous captivity and servitude elsewhere in the world, especially that in Africa. Many African systems of servitude contained aspects of risk and resource diversification deployed through coercive kinship. In their mildest forms, these aspects included the exogamous marriage of women in horticultural societies, as with the Kikuyu to male pastoralists of the Masai, fostering familial reciprocity. In a more severe expression, war captives taken by nomadic groups like the Tuareg became pastoral laborers or, if drought threatened, farmed seasonally in savanna encampments, rejoining their masters later in the transhumance cycle. Other dependents, generally Hausa subdued through warfare, formed *imrad* (client) farming villages along the Sahel, to be called upon in times of drought and famine.[43]

Although Comanches do not seem to have consciously settled their depen-

42. Quegüe requested of Governor Joaquín Alencaster that "houses of wood forming a plaza" be built for them, probably to the southeast along the Río Colorado. Alencaster offered to do so if they returned in the spring, but nothing seems to have come from the agreement. See Alencaster to Nemesio Salcedo, Nov. 20, 1805, letter no. 30, in *SANM,* II, no. 1925, roll 15, frames 993–1034, esp. 1030; Kavanagh, *Comanche Political History,* 145; Pierre Bourdieu, *Outline of a Theory of Practice* (Cambridge, 1977), notes that inegalitarian social relations are perpetuated by significant silences, or "what cannot be said for lack of an available discourse" (170).

43. Of course, in practice at the local level and especially before the nineteenth century, chattel slavery in the South often involved complications of multiple actors, economic interdependency, and mixed-race kinship, though these were little acknowledged in public discourse. For two examples, see Peter H. Wood's *Black Majority: Negroes in Colonial*

dents in client villages—their immediate labor value in the pastoral economy probably precluded this—they do seem to have cultivated a similar type of relationship with socially marginal Spanish and Mexican villagers after 1786. Perhaps San Carlos de los Jupes was an attempt to seed the Plains with this type of village. The patron-client relationship probably included the practice of Comanche men, whether born to or raised among these peoples, marrying genízaras and poor vecinas in these villages. In January 1816, the Comanche Miguel Martín married María Concepcion Ortega at San Miguel del Vado, as did the Comanche José Vigil marry María Josefa Fernandez in September 1817. By the 1820s, a man called Manuel el Comanche married into the village, where he "learned to speak Spanish quite intelligibly" and became an important cultural intermediary. Given the vulnerability of San Miguel to Comanche and Kiowa goodwill for its trade economy and survival, such marriages might well have constituted the diplomatic keys to its success. Undeniably relations of unequal dependency, the African and Southwest Borderlands systems were constantly mediated by kinship formation across social and cultural boundaries.[44]

By the early decades of the nineteenth century the peoples of the Plains borderlands were crafting an unspoken understanding that exchanges of women and children through capture and the creation of kinship in marriage and child adoption might lay the groundwork for multiethnic enterprises toward subsistence, military, and even ceremonial collaborations. But since these exchanges were seldom voluntary, affronts to honor and group pride were part of the Plainswide understanding. Added to this emotional volatility was the simple fact of finite resources, Euramerican manipulations, and expansive designs by some of the protagonists.[45]

South Carolina from 1670 through the Stono Rebellion (New York, 1974); Daniel H. Usner, Jr., *Indians, Settlers, and Slaves in a Frontier Exchange Economy: The Lower Mississippi Valley before 1783*. See also Thomas Spear, "Introduction," Richard Waller, "Acceptees and Aliens: Kikuyu Settlement in Maasailand," both in Spear and Waller, eds., *Being Maasai: Ethnicity and Identity in East Africa* (London, 1993), 1–18, esp. 8–13, 226–257; Baier and Lovejoy, "The Tuareg of the Central Sudan," in Miers and Kopytoff, eds., *Slavery in Africa*, 391–411.

44. For the Martín and Vigil marriages, see Frances Levine, *Our Prayers Are in This Place: Pecos Pueblo over the Centuries* (Albuquerque, N.Mex., 1999), table 12, "Other Indigenous Groups Identified in the Pecos Pueblo Marriage Records, 1694–1826," 80; for Manuel el Comanche, see Gregg, *Commerce of the Prairies*, ed. Quaife, 305n.

45. Patricia C. Albers, "Symbiosis, Merger, and War: Contrasting Forms of Intertribal Relationship among Historic Plains Indians," in John H. Moore, ed., *The Political Economy of North American Indians* (Lincoln, Nebr., 1993), 119–128.

The political economy of captive exchange knitted Plains Indian groups in a unified system that expressed itself in both low-scale endemic violence and constant intersocietal exchange. As New Mexican villagers became ever more deeply involved in the system, local and familial loyalties similarly cut across ethnic boundaries but sometimes put groups at odds with each other. In general, however, the participants in the political economy of the llano more often found themselves threatened from without, either by Spanish, Mexican, and American administrators or by the insinuation of a larger capitalist economy into their regional system. The migration of New Mexican genízaros and land-poor vecinos onto the Plains in the late eighteenth and early nineteenth centuries occurred in tandem with these transformations among their indigenous neighbors. They too carried with them internal social tensions and the potential for cultural redefinition that would continue the elaboration of borderland communities.

A Desire to Live in Imitation of the Wild Tribes

"The inhabitants are indolent," wrote Governor Concha of New Mexican villagers to his successor in 1794. "They love distance which makes them independent; and if they recognize the advantages of union, they pretend not to understand them, in order to adapt the liberty and slovenliness which they see . . . in their neighbors the wild Indians." As we saw earlier, efforts by Governor Juan Bautista de Anza to congregate the scattered villagers of Río Arriba and to relocate the genízaros residing in the Barrio de Analco in Santa Fe met stiff resistance in 1780, when Bentura Bustamante threatened that his genízaros might desert the colony altogether. With the peace of 1786, lower-status residents of the Río Grande valley—already seasoned llaneros either by birth, military service, or autumn buffalo-hunting forays—initiated their own migrations eastward. In a broad sense, their resettlement accorded with the objectives of Spanish administrators in that they constituted a skilled military presence on the traditional entradas to the colony. Yet their commitment to congregation in fortified plazas and farming settlements proved elusive. Instead, New Mexican llaneros presented a constant irritant to their superiors. While maintaining a village-based cultural profile, they began to move freely across the Plains, traveling seasonally to hunt buffalo as ciboleros or trade with Indians as *comancheros.* In doing so they came to wear their cultural affiliation lightly, living as Spanish or Mexican *labradores* during periods of planting and harvesting, only to slip comfortably into a nomadic lifestyle when fat buffalo or barter beckoned in the autumn.[46]

Although their "liberty and slovenliness" dismayed Spanish elites, the knowledge of borderland developments gained by backcountry sojourners proved so valuable that the authorities had to grant allowances for both travel and settlement beyond the pale of colonial control. During this period we see the establishment of key villages east of the Sangre de Cristos: San Miguel del Vado in 1794, San José del Vado in 1803, Mora in 1818, and Anton Chico in 1822. Not coincidentally, each petition for a village grant included names of men designated as genízaros, for these people had long served in the vanguard of intercultural negotiation. Like their Comanche neighbors, New Mexican llaneros drew upon customary practices and developed new strategies to exploit opportunities on the Plains. Looser, more flexible village organization and cultural hybridity were among these innovations.[47]

The fifty-two residents of the villa of Santa Fe who petitioned Governor Fernando Chacón for a grant of vacant land on the Pecos River on September 1, 1794, illustrate the blending of tradition and innovation. Though nominally Spanish New Mexicans, the settlers were a culturally mixed age group, combining families, and individuals, from both Indian and Spanish origins. Led by Lorenzo Márquez and Domingo Padilla, both vecinos, the petitioners included thirteen genízaro heads of families, all of whom claimed that, although they had "some small pieces of land" in the Santa Fe, water shortages and overcrowding made it "impossible for all of us to enjoy its use." They had already reconnoitered (and probably farmed seasonally, given the use requirements in

46. Worcester, trans., "Advice on the Governing of New Mexico," *NMHR,* XXIV (July 1949), 236–254, esp. 250. For the emergence of border peoples of ambivalent loyalties throughout the Spanish Borderlands during the period, see Weber, *The Spanish Frontier in North America* (New Haven, Conn., 1992), chap. 11.

47. For these dates, see E. Boyd, "The Plaza of San Miguel del Vado," *El Palacio,* LXXVIII, no. 4 (1971), 17–26; Miguel Montoya, "The Preservation of a Trail-Era Community in the Mora Valley Today," paper presented at the New Mexicans and the Santa Fe Trade Conference, Las Vegas, N.Mex., Aug. 12, 1990. Although the official grant for the village of Mora was not issued until 1835, in 1818 three hundred residents petitioned Santa Fe for a resident priest; for Anton Chico, see Michael J. Rock, "Anton Chico and Its Patent," *Journal of the West* (July 1980), 86–91. Since by 1822 caste designations like "genízaro" were no longer used in official record keeping, for Anton Chico it is necessary to trace the genízaro lines by following the village's first settlers from San Miguel and San José in "family chain" migrations down the Pecos River.

Spanish land law) a fertile valley twenty miles down river from Pecos Pueblo, where there lay enough land not only for themselves but also for "as many in the province who are destitute."[48]

Chacón confirmed the grant at San Miguel del Vado with the understanding that, at the end of two years, all able-bodied men must possess firearms. Only twenty-five of the petitioners did so at the time—the others, following a long tradition of using Indian weaponry instead, had bows and arrows. Chacón required that the militia muster regularly and the settlers build the requisite fortified plaza. The settlers, however, felt less urgency. The first baptismal entry for a vecino of El Vado dates from 1798, when the Pecos Indian Juan de Días Fernández married María Armijo, daughter of grantee Juan Armijo. Grantees Márquez and Padilla, however, had appeared as padrinos in the Pecos baptismal books in the early 1780s, suggesting that the Analceños had probably sojourned on the Plains and farmed the Pecos River bottom for some time before making their petition. They had apparently experienced few problems with the nomadic Indians. Since the effort and expense of building a fortified adobe plaza and equipping themselves with firearms was probably beyond the means of these families, the risk of possible attack seemed reasonable given the potential rewards of inserting themselves as middlemen in the Plains trade.[49]

Outgoing governor don Fernando de la Concha had already warned Chacón to beware of the emergence of easy relations between villagers and "wild Indians." Concha had grudgingly allowed the intercourse to grow, he explained, "with the idea of acquiring a complete knowledge of the waterholes and lands in which [the Comanches] are situated." Moreover, the presidial troops needed remounts, and "the only way to acquire horses of good quality cheaply is to . . . barter with the Comanches . . . the cost of each [being] eight pesos, more or less." By the beginning of the nineteenth century, Comanches had become the principal horse traders on the southern Plains, and New Mexicans were virtually without mounts. In 1805, the presidial herd presented such a poor spectacle that the governor declared himself unable to mount military campaigns unless he relied entirely on genízaros and Pueblo auxiliaries for

48. San Miguel del Vado grant, *Records of the Surveyor General of New Mexico,* no. 119, roll 24, frames 595–740, New Mexico State Records Center, Santa Fe, N.Mex. For the deathblow this outpost dealt to Pecos Pueblo's role in intercultural trade, see John L. Kessell, *Kiva, Cross, and Crown: The Pecos Indians and New Mexico, 1540–1840* (Albuquerque, N.Mex., 1987), 415.

49. San Miguel del Vado grant, roll 23, frame 599; Kessell, *Kiva, Cross, and Crown,* 418.

his force. These groups presumably maintained better numbers and quality of riding stock through informal trade with Comanches. This dependency on social marginals evoked increasing anxiety in colonial administrators.[50]

Concha offered cautions about the general character of these villagers as well. "Under a simulated appearance of ignorance or rusticity they conceal the most refined malice. He is a rare one in whom the vices of lying and robbing do not occur together." These character traits he attributed to "the dispersion of their settlements [and] the bad upbringing resulting from this, the proximity and trade of the barbarous tribes." The governor noted that the civilian militias upon which the province depended for defense functioned virtually free from military authority. These were forever "disturbing the Province whenever it suited them in the purpose of gaining their own ends," a chaos that derived from a "lack of obedience, willfulness, and desire to live without subjection and in complete liberty, in imitation of the wild tribes which they see nearby." With no little exasperation, he suggested that "the removal of more than two thousand labradores to another area" would be "very useful to the society and the state." Social stability could only be attained by "a new system of regulations and . . . a complete change in the actual system of control," especially the creation of a stable commercial agriculture and imposition of military discipline within the militias.[51]

His successor fared no better in effecting order on the borderlands. By 1803, Governor Chacón reported failure in promoting commercial agriculture in the province: "The majority of its inhabitants are little dedicated to farming, . . . [contenting] themselves with sowing and cultivating only what is necessary for their sustenance." In contrast, he praised "the Pueblo Indians who compose a third of the population, [who] develop large fields that are cultivated in common, so that they can take care of widows, orphans, the sick, [and] the unemployed." Noting that the Pueblos alone produced a surplus and thus "never feel the effects of hunger," he affirmed by implication their readiness for formal market participation should a more reliable trade be established between the province and the Chihuahua market centers. The governor's interest in developing an export economy was not simply a bureaucrat's endorsement of the

50. Worcester, trans., "Advice on the Governing of New Mexico," *NMHR,* XXIV (July 1949), 251; "Joaquín Real Alencaster to Nemesio Salcedo, regarding Proposed Campaign against Unfriendly Indians, 1 Sept. 1805," in *SANM,* II, no. 1881, roll 15, frame 835.

51. Worcester, trans., "Advice on the Governing of New Mexico," *NMHR,* XXIV (July 1949), 243–244.

Bourbon reforms; Chacón wished to harness the multifarious opportunities of the borderland economy to his own ends. Since he had held the tithe rental contract for the province from 1796 to 1801, his personal income had probably suffered from the vecino population's predilection for informal commerce, an issue that would come to a head just a few years later.[52]

Chacón also complained of the "natural decadence and backwardness" of the provincial economy, where "internal commerce is in the hands of twelve or fourteen merchants . . . neither properly licensed nor well versed in business matters." Even worse than this commercial core were "the rest of the citizenry [who] are so many petty merchants . . . continuously dealing and bartering with whatever products they have at hand."[53] "Formality prevail[s]" only "in the trading carried on with the nomad Indians *(Naciones gentiles),* that being a give-and-take business conducted in sign language." In exchange for New Mexican manufactures like saddlebags, bridles, bits, iron goods, textiles, and agricultural products both raw and processed, the "nomads give Indian captives of both sexes, mules, moccasins, colts, mustangs, all kinds of hides and buffalo meat." New Mexican villagers indeed produced a local agricultural surplus and practiced weaving, leatherworking, and blacksmithing but were more inclined to use that surplus in exchange with Plains peoples than to accept the low prices resulting from risky overland shippage and the uncertain markets of Chihuahua. Their assertive stance in this regard would soon be read as subversive by their colonial administrators.[54]

To Trade with the Heathens in the Customary Manner

Once officials recognized that much local production went into the Indian trade rather than south along the Camino Real, which was the web of overland routes that connected Santa Fe with central Mexico, efforts were made in both Mexico City and Santa Fe to stem the leakage. Early in 1805, the viceroy decreed that all goods bartered by New Mexicans at the annual trade fair in the San Bartolome Valley would be free from payment of the 6 percent *alca-*

52. The Bourbon reforms of 1765–1821 liberalized provincial society and economy by relaxing travel constraints, exempting the province from taxation and increasing specie circulation.

53. Marc Simmons, "The Chacón Economic Report of 1803," *NMHR,* LX (January 1985), 81–88, esp. 83.

54. Ibid., 87.

bala (tax) required of other provinces. In June, Chacón's successor, Joaquín del Real Alencaster, convened a junta in Santa Fe to discuss methods of improving manufactures and mining and to redirect existing production toward the Mexican trade. Although a lack of capital limited any significant invigoration of the textile or nascent mining industries, Alencaster attempted, first, to build up local sheep flocks by prohibiting their sale to Navajos and, second, to gain at least indirect revenue from the broader Indian trade through a taxation and licensing system. Both directives produced consequences that would confirm the worst suspicions of his predecessors.[55]

Late in the autumn of 1805, the vecinos of San Miguel and San José del Vado gathered near their new church, ostensibly to discuss raising limosnas for the upcoming Fiesta de la Señora de Guadalupe. But *Teniente de Justicia* Juan Antonio Alarí suspected otherwise and managed to eavesdrop on the meeting. Don Felipe Sandoval, *hermano mayor* of the Virgin's cofradía, led the discussion. Listening intently, Alarí discovered that "all of their conversation" involved the governor's recent interference with the Comanche trade and that Sandoval intended to incite the settlers to reject the order and "go to trade with the heathens in the customary manner." Should they fear to act alone, Sandoval reassured his listeners that the citizens of La Cañada and Río Arriba would support their challenge. Sure that an insurrection was at hand, Alarí broke up the meeting and took Sandoval, José García de la Mora of La Cañada, and Victor Vigil of Río Arriba into custody.

True to Sandoval's claim, when news of the men's arrest circulated throughout the province, enraged bands of citizens from outlying villages converged upon the capital. The governor, hoping to prevent outright revolt, quickly convened an investigation of the grievances beneath the scandal. Numerous respondents confirmed general dissatisfaction with the governor's restrictions. Limitations on the Comanche trade, though, constituted only one complaint. Sandoval's agents had circulated a letter throughout the province urging a general disobedience. García de la Mora himself complained of the Chihuahua cordón's uncertain timing, the governor's "lamentable decision" to prohibit the sale of sheep to the Navajos, and the forced collection of "hundreds of fanegas" of grain to feed the presidial soldiers in the capital. As "many men on foot and horseback" churned restively outside the seat of government, Alencaster released the insurgents from jail and forwarded his *diligencias* to Commander

55. Junta report on economic development, incomplete, June 17, 1805, in *SANM*, II, no. 1844, roll 15, frames 656–657.

General Nemesio Salcedo for review. He proffered a charge of sedition against Sandoval, but Salcedo failed to act upon his recommendation. By 1810, in fact, Sandoval found himself appointed *Protector de Indios* of the Pueblo Indians of the province.[56]

Unlike Sandoval, whose social status probably protected him until a change of governors brought more open trade policies, other men from San Miguel suffered severely as a consequence of the subversive activity. Even while the investigations of the vecinos were under way in Santa Fe, Lieutenant Alarí took four more men into custody. Francisco el Comanche, Francisco Xavier *de Nación Aà* (Pawnee), José María Gurulé *de Nación Caigua* (Kiowa), and the genízaro Antonio María were charged with seditious activities among los gentiles, especially the Comanches. Alarí claimed that the men, in disregard of the governor's licensing directives, had visited the camps of Comanche General Somicuiaio (Somiquaso), speaking "very badly of the Spanish, and the Governor." Spreading rumors and "a thousand lies," which included an accusation that customary gifts for the Indians might not be forthcoming, the men also acquired "hides, meat, and other goods" from the Indians. Alexandro Martín, the captive returned by Tosapoy in 1786 and now "interpreter to the Comanches," corroborated Alarí's testimony, claiming the men's activities resulted in "great harm to the peace." More than a little frustrated as to what measures he could take to castigate these "baptized and Christian Indians," Alencaster sent them by military escort to the assessor general of the Provincias Internas in Guadalajara, warning of the risk they "might flee and go to live among said Indians, and disrupt the peace." The resolution of their cases remains unclear, but in 1807 the genízaro Antonio María was arrested for vagrancy in Chihuahua, then sent north to be held in the guardhouse in Santa Fe, suggesting that he and whatever movement he represented remained a source of concern to Spanish authorities. Whatever became of Francisco el Comanche, his wife Juana Mes, a genízara, was buried in December 1809 at Pecos Pueblo, the church at which the settlers at San Miguel contined to serve. Francisco's

56. For the short-lived insurrection, see "Sumaria informacion indagatoria sobre combocatoria . . . ," in *SANM,* II, no. 1930, roll 15, frames 1043–1098; Kessell, *Kiva, Cross, and Crown,* 434–435; for Sandoval's appointment, see Charles R. Cutter, *The Protector de Indios in Colonial New Mexico, 1659–1821* (Albuquerque, N.Mex., 1986), 82–86. José García de la Mora would later serve as secretary of the provincial government from 1810–1812. See don Pedro Baptista Pino, *The Exposition on the Province of New Mexico, 1812,* trans. and ed. Adrian Bustamante and Marc Simmons (Albuquerque, N.Mex., 1995), 20 n. 10.

connections with the Spanish settlement still held the respect of the religious, if not the secular, authorities.[57]

The disturbances that erupted in 1805 point to the extent to which New Mexicans of several classes or castes depended upon open trade with los indios gentiles for their economic well-being and the astonishing cultural complexity of borderland villages. The "seditious" activities at San Miguel del Vado involved respectable vecinos like Felipe Sandoval, his compadres from the northern villages of the Río Arriba, genízaros like Antonio María, and mysterious social marginals like the Comanche Francisco, the Pawnee Francisco Xavier, and the Kiowa José María Gurulé. The four men sent to Guadalajara might simply have been contraband traders caught in the act, yet they and their more respectable co-conspirators might have been central to more widespread communities of interest then in formation. Although no explicit connections yet exist between the commotions at San Miguel and the Kiowa-Comanche peace agreement that same fall and winter, Kiowa recollection that the negotiations began in the house of a New Mexican Indian trader friendly with both parties seems beyond coincidence. Somiquaso, whose daughter married the Kiowa El Ronco in affirmation of the alliance, also hosted the four contrabandistas from San Miguel. Finally, if we consider that a Comanche captive had played a key role in bringing the two sides to parlay and that the Comanche captain Huarnicoruco had in 1804 claimed the Kiowa José María Gurulé to be his son—though Governor Chacón insisted that Gurulé was a Skiri Pawnee captive adopted by Huarnicoruco—we have circumstantial evidence that at least some of the San Miguel "insurgents" had also worked to foster the inter-Indian alliance.[58]

57. Although Dolores Gunnerson argues that the Aàs were Crows in *Ethnohistory of the High Plains* (Washington, D.C., 1988), 49–50, in this case it is probable that Elizabeth A. H. John's identification of the "Aàs" as the "Aguages," or Panismahas (Pawnee), is more accurate. See *Storms Brewed,* 592; "Diligencias criminales contra Francisco el Comanche, Francisco Xavier, José María Gurule, y Antonio María . . . 2 diciembre 1805–28 marzo 1806," in *SANM,* II, no. 1931, roll 15, frames 1099–1117; for Juana Mes burial, see Levine, *Our Prayers Are in This Place,* table 13, "Other Indigenous Groups Identified in the Pecos Pueblo Burial Records, 1694–1826," 81.

58. Gurulé's Kiowa identity is certainly in question, since Governor Chacón reported in 1804 that the Yamparica Comanche captain Huarnicoruco claimed him as his son. Chacón countered that Gurulé was, in fact, a Skiri Pawnee genízaro, once Huarnicoruco's captive but settled by Chacón at San Miguel del Vado in 1794 as an agent for the Comanche. Gurulé's "unruly conduct, cheating, and horse thieving" had led to his replacement by Alexandro

Provincial grievances clearly went beyond Alencaster's attempt to regulate the Plains trade and included his prohibitions against the sale of sheep with the Navajos, the burden on the local populace of maintaining an ineffective presidial troop, and petty taxation to support smallpox vaccinations and the salaries of several *aguaciles mayores.* By 1808, resentment spread from borderland villages to include Spanish military officers in the capital, who probably found some profit in contraband themselves. New threats of rebellion erupted. Lieutenant Colonel José Manrique found himself jailed by Alencaster when the former began to raise a militia company in Santa Fe, ostensibly for local defense. Commander General of the Interior Provinces Salcedo finally intervened to remove Alencaster from office, abolish taxation, and appoint don Alberto Maynez as interim governor. Maynez wisely relaxed his predecessor's trade restrictions and allowed local commercial initiatives to flourish. Although many details remain obscure, the general condition of the province at the beginning of the century seems one of barely restrained entrepreneurial frenzy of a decidedly heterogeneous type.[59]

Maynez took a different tack toward controlling traffic on the Plains, with the added incentive that Zebulon Pike's recent arrest in the San Luis Valley had given notice of growing American designs on the colony. Rather than grant such interlopers free access to the region, the governor sought to extend Spanish presence to the east. One tactic lay in organizing a mounted *tropa de genízaros* to ride reconnaissance on the Plains, an attempt to exert administrative authority over their customary sojourns and to enjoy their intelligence-gathering abilities. In the autumn of 1808, he dispatched eight members of the troop on a journey from the confluence of the Rito San Carlos and the Arkansas River—probably passing by the deserted Comanche farming settlement—well south to the Red River. Their report shed light on just how dynamic regional affairs had become. The troop quickly encountered a mixed group of Kiowas and Comanches, who declared that they were moving jointly to engage in "fearsome war" on the Utes and Jicarilla Apaches, all the while reassuring the genízaros how much they valued the Spanish trade. The scouts learned as well that among the enemy "pueblos de los panana" (Pawnees) to the east "were

---

Martín, the former captive of Tosapoy. See Kessell, *Kiva, Cross, and Crown,* 429–430; "Isidro Rey a Real Alencaster, 1 April, 1807," in *SANM,* II, no. 2043, roll 16, frame 315.

59. Salcedo to Maynez, Chihuahua, Aug. 10, 1808, in *SANM,* II, no. 2144, roll 16, frames 592–593; Salcedo to Maynez, Chihuahua, Aug. 11, 1808, in *SANM,* II, no. 2145, roll 16, frames 594–595.

several Anglo Americans who intended to enter the Province," which news surely added anxiety to Nemesio Salcedo's days. As the troop moved down the Arkansas to where the Río Huerfano joined its flow, they discovered an abandoned stockade that they attributed to Pike's expedition. They then moved south to purchase horses and dispense gifts among another band of Kiowas on the Colorado River. In all, the reconnaissance found that the Plains were alive with commerce and conflict that connected the Indian world to both the Spanish and American economies.[60]

The presence of American adventurers and explorers on the Plains borderlands after 1800 would ultimately undercut attempts by Spanish governors to rein in the informal initiatives of their own frontier villagers. The boundary between the expansionistic United States and northern New Spain remained undetermined from the time of the Louisiana Purchase in 1803 until the Adams-Onís Treaty of 1819 fixed it along the Arkansas River. Accordingly, Americans, whether official agents or freelance entrepreneurs, worked to garner the commercial potential of the horse-and-bison Plains by pursuing diplomatic and commercial alliances with Indian groups like the Pawnees, Otos, Wichitas, and Osages. In itinerant American traders Comanches and Kiowas discovered lucrative new markets for the horses and a more reliable supply of guns and ammunition. New Mexicans scrambled to retain the affections of their long-term neighbors and affines, but to do so they would have to concede increasing power to the Indians in any negotiations.[61]

Maynez and José Manrique, who would follow him as governor in 1810, also allowed their colonists to mount substantial trading expeditions onto the Plains, an effort to counter American influences. As many as two hundred colonists ventured out in the autumn of 1810 to barter with Kiowas and Comanches along the Arkansas River. In 1818, the alcalde of Taos, Juan de

60. For creation of the genízaro troop, see Salcedo to Maynez, Chihuahua, Aug. 12, 1808, in *SANM*, II, no. 2146, roll 16, frame 596; Maynez and Manrique to Salcedo, June 20, 1809, in *SANM*, II, no. 2234, roll 16, frames 907–909; for Pike's expedition and arrest, see Weber, *Spanish Frontier*, 294–295; for the report on reconnaissance of 1808, see "José Manrique, Draft of Report to Nemesio Salcedo y Salcedo," Nov. 26, 1808, in Pinart Collection, Bancroft Library, University of California, Berkeley.

61. For a synthesis of the reconfigurations in power in North American borderlands during the transition from imperial to republican rule in the United States and Mexico, see Jeremy Adelman and Stephen Aron, "From Borderlands to Borders: Empires, Nation-states, and the Peoples in between in North American History," *American Historical Review*, CIV (June 1999), 814–841.

Dios Peña, confessed that he could not meet a recent militia levy "because so many men had left to trade with the Indians." In an ironic twist that revealed how Plains commerce could simultaneously threaten local and family security, several women from the villages along the Rito Colorado north of Abiquiu petitioned their alcalde, Juan Lobato, that they be allowed to abandon their homes for a time. "The men were away trading, and the settlements undefended" against possible Ute or Jicarilla raiders. Fortunately for those women, their men returned shortly after the governor denied the request. This delicate trade-off between economic opportunities attendant to Plains sojourns and the vulnerability of those left behind would characterize life in New Mexico for decades to come.[62]

62. Governor Manrique also reported increasing incursions by Anglo-American beaver trappers into the area. See José Manrique to Comandante General Nemesio Salcedo, Mar. 27, 1810, in *SANM,* II, no. 2308, roll 17, frames 61–63; Juan de Dios Peña to interim governor Melgares, Nov. 4, 1818, in *SANM,* II, no. 2768, roll 19, frames 433–434; Juan Lobato to Melgares, Sept. 22, 1818, in *SANM,* II, no. 2750, roll 19, frames 302–304.

6

COMMERCE, KINSHIP, AND COERCION

Commerce, Stock Raising, and Planting Fields

Like their counterparts east of the Sangre de Cristos, in the relative calm after 1787 Navajos and New Mexicans gradually established a new mixed society in the lower Río Puerco region. Although the nineteenth-century mixed society would draw upon strategies of the preceding century, it differed in significant ways from the eighteenth-century pattern. New Mexican resettlement was much more condensed, concentrating in two major villages, Cebolleta and Cubero. New Mexican pastores employed a new grazing technique, blanket grazing, that put huge numbers of sheep, often in the tens of thousands, on the grasslands for whole seasons. Constantly under the care of young shepherd boys, these flocks remained vulnerable to raids, yet their sheer size improved the probability that a viable flock would survive most losses. Such vast flocks were owned by sheep ricos of the Río Abajo, whose economic fortunes blossomed with new fiscal and market policies introduced in the Bourbon reforms and expanded with commercial opportunities attendant upon open trade with the United States after 1821. But the pastoral borderlands held enticing possibilities for lower-order New Mexicans as well, especially as they found novel ways to gain sheep-wealth in concert with their counterparts among the Navajos.[1]

Navajos too increasingly committed to sheep pastoralism. In 1796, Lieutenant Colonel don Antonio Cordero noted that they were "not nomadic like other Apaches." They dwelt instead in ten congregations of rancherías dis-

1. For an overview of the cultural ecology and environmental history of the Río Puerco valley, see Jerold Gwayne Widdison, "Historical Geography of the Middle Rio Puerco Valley, New Mexico," *New Mexico Historical Review* (hereafter cited as *NMHR*), XXXIV (October 1959), 248–284.

persed widely across their plateau-and-canyon landscape from the Río Puerco in the east to Cañon de Chelly and the Carrizo Mountains in the west. In these they sowed "corn and other vegetables" and raised sheep in enough quantity to manufacture "coarse cloth, blankets and other textiles of wool which they trade in New Mexico. In past times they were enemies of the Spaniards: at present they are their faithful friends and are governed by a general who is appointed by the governor." Since Antonio el Pinto had died defending his ranchería against a Gila Apache attack in 1793, the general to whom Cordero referred was probably Pinto's successor, Segundo. His authority as general, however, was presumably limited to members of his outfit and even then constrained by respect for individual autonomy in Navajo culture and by generational tensions emerging between *na'taani* and young men who wished to attain the same status.[2]

At the dawn of the nineteenth century, Navajo headmanship and social organization more generally stood on the threshold of momentous change. Headmanship, a political position largely maintained by popular support from kinsmen, moved toward alignment with class status derived from pastoral wealth. If leadership once derived from skills in conflict arbitration, subsistence hunting, and defensive warfare, with pastoral wealth was added the ability to recruit followers through largess, followers who would provide labor in return for a headman's reciprocity. Sheep-grazing on the arid plateau and in canyon country always pushed the limits of security, as forage could fail with drought, and wolves, coyotes, and mountain lions were everyday threats. At least one shepherd was required for every 250 animals, and, with the flocks of a Navajo rico sometimes numbering in the several thousands, a headman might need as many as a dozen pastoral laborers. In the early years of the nineteenth

2. Daniel S. Matson and Albert H. Schroeder, eds., "Cordero's Description of the Apache, 1796," *NMHR*, XXXII (October 1957), 356. It is unlikely that the whole Navajo population lived in the ten communities named by Cordero, since even a large outfit or coresidential kin group probably featured only forty to fifty hogans with an average residence of five household members, or 200–250 people. Navajo population in 1800 is almost entirely conjectural, but if in 1864 it was twelve thousand to thirteen thousand, as most contemporary and modern observers agree, an estimate of seven to eight thousand seems reasonable for the turn of the century. Thus most Navajos were still dispersed throughout the hundreds of valleys and washes in the region, engaged primarily in subsistence farming and hunting. But Cordero's locations coincide with known concentrations of multiclan clusters, and this almost certainly points to communities more intensively involved in sheep raising and its labor demands.

century the extended kin and cross-clan affines of a headman like Segundo and the occasional seizure of a Paiute, Ute, or Spanish New Mexican *yisná'* met this labor demand. Yet within a few decades huge increases in flock size and mounting inequality within Navajo society would foster demand for additional dependent laborers and a new servile category—that of *naalté,* or slave.[3]

New Mexicans also sought fresh opportunities in the Río Puerco valley after 1786. Among the thirty residents who petitioned Governor Fernando Chacón for a settlement grant at Cebolleta on March 15, 1800, were descendants of the eighteenth-century settlers the Bacas, the Chavezes, and the Gallegos. Although they had officially taken shelter during the troublous 1780s and 1790s in Río Grande villages like Belén and Carnué, the fact that a lively commercial intercourse persisted during the period suggests that they sojourned as traders (often on behalf of Governor Chacón) while awaiting resettlement. Furthermore, Spanish land tenure custom required that petitioners hold "productive possession" of lands for three to five years before making a claim, so the Cebolletaños had probably returned some years earlier, in part to maintain their rights to the earlier grant. On the condition that the settlers "form a regular settlement and . . . not abandon it under any pretext," each head of household received eighty-three varas of farming land in the canyon and fifty-five varas for stock raising on the grassy uplands.[4]

The Río Puerco Navajos immediately protested the new settlement, claiming that the New Mexicans' flocks infringed upon their own grazing lands. These Navajos seemed willing to accept New Mexican farmers and traders in their territory, but competition from other sheep grazers was another matter entirely. When Governor Chacón rejected their complaint, they turned to violence, striking the high-walled plaza in a series of raids through the spring and summer of 1804. By August, Navajo raiders had seized all the livestock of the village, killed twelve shepherds and taken several captives, and finally forced the village men to hide their dependents in a deep cave one league north of

3. For a reconstruction of Navajo society and economy in the nineteenth century, drawing largely on upstreamed ethnography and land-use modeling, see Klara B. Kelley, "Navajo Political Economy before Fort Sumner," in Linda S. Cordell and Stephen Beckerman, eds., *The Versatility of Kinship* (New York, 1980), 307–332. For captive and slave terminology, see the Franciscan Fathers, *An Ethnologic Dictionary of the Navaho Language* (St. Michaels, Ariz., 1910), 437–438.

4. Town of Cebolleta grant, *Surveyor General's Reports,* New Mexico Land Grants, claim no. 46, roll 17, frames 935–1011, New Mexico State Records Center, Santa Fe, N.Mex.

the plaza. In December, the New Mexicans briefly abandoned their village "on account of the terror they experienced from the Navajo Indians" but then resettled upon the governor's orders with his promise that a small garrison of thirty presidiales would be forthcoming.[5]

Lieutenant Colonel Antonio Narbona's legendary January 1805 campaign into the Cañon de Chelly resulted in 115 Navajos killed and 33 taken captive along with 350 sheep and goats. In a suggestion of just how unreliable Spanish administrators thought their local militias, Narbona's troops were largely composed of regular soldiers from Sonora as well as a company of Opatá scouts from the village of Bacuachi. Eleven Navajo captives were distributed as rewards and the remainder brought to Santa Fe. By March, Navajo headmen Cristóbal and Vicente approached Governor Alencaster, offering two New Mexican captives in return for the Navajo prisoners. Alencaster repatriated sixteen captives, including the headman Segundo and his family, and promised that the Navajos would now be permitted "commerce, stock-raising, and planting of fields and other enterprises." But Cebolleta would remain. By October, more than forty Navajo families had established themselves near the village, and, although they were occasionally accused of pilfering in the settlers' fields, a tenuous stability again ensued.[6]

In the wake of this accord, informal commerce between Navajos and Cebolletaños became so brisk that by late 1805 it threatened to reduce formal exports in the annual cordón to Chihuahua. Accordingly, Governor Alencaster placed penalties on the unlicensed sale of sheep to Navajos, just one of his actions that sparked near-revolt in the province. Trade resumed after the governor quickly rescinded his orders, especially with those Navajo outfits settling around Cebolleta. Navajo interdependence with New Mexicans increased

5. *Spanish Archives of New Mexico* (hereafter cited as *SANM)*, II, no. 1810, roll 15, frames 439–440.

6. Narbona's campaign is commonly attributed to the origin of the place-names "Massacre Cave" and "Cañon de los Muertos" (now Cañon del Muerte). The archaeologist Earl H. Morris learned from Navajo informants in the 1920s that in 1805 the Navajos had hidden their elderly and women and children in a high cave on the canyon wall, from where a Navajo woman once held captive by the Spanish taunted Narbona's men as those "who walked without eyes." In a fusillade that expended some ten thousand rounds, the cave ceiling rained ricocheted bullets down upon the victims, whose bones were still evident to Morris during his visit. See Frank McNitt, *Navajo Wars: Military Campaigns, Slave Raids, and Reprisals* (Albuquerque, N.Mex., 1972), 37–46. Alencaster's agreement with Cristóbal and Vicente is contained in *SANM,* II, no. 1828, roll 15, frames 591–593.

thereafter, as the export market for Navajo serapes initiated under Chacón's administration developed in northern Mexico. In 1812, don Pedro Bautista Pino reported optimistically of the Cebolleta Navajos,

> This nation . . . has given itself to farming and manufacturing. . . . Many speak Spanish and entire families come and reside among us, embracing the Catholic religion. Their settlements are well policed and regulated and their woolen weavings are the most valuable in our province and in Sonora and Chihuahua.[7]

In 1818, some bands would cast their lot even more firmly with their Spanish neighbors, a move that signaled growing divisions between wealthier Navajos who were linked in commerce with the colony and those more distant who were turning to theft to accumulate similar wealth. That year, the Río Puerco headman Joaquín threw his people's lot in with the Spanish by betraying plans for livestock raids by other Navajo groups farther to the west. Although Abiquiu, Cebolleta, Taos, and Mora lost some 2,000 sheep and 100 horses and mules in the subsequent raids, with Joaquín's assistance in December of that year New Mexican volunteers recaptured 2,300 sheep and 73 horses, killing 7 of the ladrones and taking 2 women captive. In a treaty negotiated the following year, Governor Facundo Melgares rewarded Joaquín by appointing him general of the entire Navajo Nation, a move guaranteed to complete the rupture between his Río Puerco outfit and its more distant Navajo bands. Joaquín's status depended upon his ability to assure Spanish shepherds safe passage to grazing country as far west as Cañon Largo, a stipulation that could only be fulfilled by provoking the hostility of his countrymen. Nothing is known of his subsequent fate, but Joaquín's decision marked the seminal moment in the appearance of the Navajo band that other Navajos would call the Diné Ana'aii.

In 1826, now-governor Narbona recognized mixed-blood headman Francisco Baca (born about 1786 from the union of the settler Baca and a Navajo woman) as Joaquín's successor, as would later governors treat with the mixed-blood Antonio Sandoval. Ranging from their Río Puerco base as far east as the Sierras de Sandía and as far west as Zuñi Pueblo territory, the Diné Ana'aii maintained close relations, both economically and culturally, with the region's

7. Don Pedro Baptista Pino, *The Exposition on the Province of New Mexico, 1812,* trans. and ed. Adrian Bustamante and Marc Simmons (Albuquerque, N.Mex., 1995), 48–49. This language, however, is my translation of the pertinent passage in the facsimile reprinted therein.

New Mexican settlers. Serving as guides for New Mexican military expeditions and often acting as autonomous raiders themselves, the Diné Ana'aii functioned as pivots in the pastoral borderlands economy.[8]

Cebolleta would remain the major New Mexican settlement in the Río Puerco region until 1833, when Juan Chávez and sixty-one neighbors from the Río Abajo established a new village at Cubero, the spring just west of the old Encinal mission of the 1740s. This grant differed from its predecessors in one important way—the lands were purchased the previous year by Pedro Molina from Francisco Baca, headman of the Diné Ana'aii, then resold to the petitioners. The mixed-descent Navajo accepted five hundred ewes, four horses, one fat cow, twelve varas of muslin, and two varas of Bayeta cloth in return for his rights to those lands. Baca's entrance into the land business signals just how thoroughly he and his followers had integrated into a commercialized pastoral economy. The grant itself would become the object of a century of litigation, for its lands were also claimed by Laguna Pueblo. Endemic interpersonal conflict mirrored the legal wranglings, but in forms that simultaneously fastened economic exchanges. The region encompassing Cebolleta, Cubero, and the Río Puerco soon became the western counterpart to the violent and volatile borderland east of the Sangre de Cristos, a pivotal trading and raiding point for the expansion of an aggressive sheep pastoralism based in no small part on human bondage. One historian has characterized nineteenth-century Cebolleta as "a hell-raising military post brothel, a haven for army deserters, murderers, renegades, slavers, and thieves."[9]

Exchanges of local violence, occasional formal campaigns, and short-lived peace treaties came to characterize Navajo–New Mexican relations. Spanish, Mexican, and later American administrators would sign more than a dozen

8. See McNitt, *Navajo Wars,* app. B, 434–435; for Ygnacio María Sánchez Vergara's report to don Pedro Maria de Allande concerning Joaquín's defection, see report of Jul. 21, 1818, in *SANM,* II, no. 2736, roll 19, frames 172–175; see also Appendices A and B, below; McNitt, *Navajo Wars,* 50.

9. "Carta de Pedro Molina à jefe político sobre la venta de las tierras en Encinal y Cuvero para Francisco Baca, 16 deciembre 1832," in *SANM,* I, no. 1304, roll 6, frames 1176–1178; "Carta de Jose Francisco Chavez y Baca à jefe político, adjuntando uno petición de los indios de Laguna . . . , 26 mayo 1835," in *SANM,* I, no. 1310, frames 1190–1193; *Rafael Sena de Albuquerque v Francisco Baca, Nabajo, y el pueblo de Laguna, sobre tierras, Rancho de la Punta,* Aug. 27, 1835, in *SANM,* I, no. 910, roll 5, frames 1835–1838; McNitt, *Navajo Wars,* 72. The case was finally resolved in the 1930s. See Myra Ellen Jenkins, "The Baltazar Baca 'Grant': History of an Encroachment," *El Palacio,* LXVIII, nos. 1–2 (Spring 1961).

treaties with various Navajo headmen. The treaties were usually broken within a few months; their failure was attributed to "warlike dispositions" and lack of formal political control on the part of both Navajo and New Mexican leaders. But left unanswered was the question of why so many of the local peoples seemed entirely uninterested in vesting sufficient political power in their leaders that peaceful stability might be maintained. The solution lies in understanding the apparently random violence of the borderlands as a system for redistributing wealth and power across and within Indian and Eurocolonial societies. Mutual economic needs necessitated an array of local arrangements that kept peoples and resources flowing across cultural barriers, even when wealthy and powerful Indian or New Mexican leaders wished to arrest those transfers.[10]

The florescence of the borderland economy forces examination of how a slave and livestock trade, apparently corrosive and debilitating, actually promoted economic growth. Historians have long recognized the existence of this trade in the Southwest. But we have hesitated to examine the mutually advantageous aspects that clarify why this traffic persisted as long as it did, especially those involving reciprocal emotional retribution and economic redistribution. Without this perspective, we remain unable to explain why, if the first half of the nineteenth century was one of unremitting warfare, many Indian and New Mexican communities expanded demographically, geographically, or economically throughout the period. Long stagnant, New Mexico's vecino population increased dramatically after 1800, growing from 15,000 to 26,000 by 1821 and to 61,525 by 1850. In 1850, Valencia County on the Navajo border had the largest population of any territorial county (14,180). This coincides with a rapid expansion of settlement up the Río Puerco, first at Cebolleta (1800), then Cubero (1833).[11]

10. The nineteenth-century attitudes persisted in much subsequent historiography, beginning with Frank D. Reeve's work in the 1950s through McNitt's 1972 monograph and Thomas D. Hall, *Social Change in the Southwest, 1350–1880* (Lawrence, Kans., 1989), 161. Daniel Tyler pointed us in new directions when he posited the "local arrangements" between village-level New Mexicans and their Indian neighbors as the distinctive characteristic of the region between 1786 and 1847. But the "mutual economic needs" of which Tyler spoke featured more complexity and deeper internal tensions than heretofore recognized ("Mexican Indian Policy in New Mexico," *NMHR*, LV [April 1980], 101–120, esp. 115–116).

11. Reeve broke ground in the historical study of Navajo-Spanish relations, identifying cycles of peace and conflict; see "Navaho-Spanish Wars, 1680–1720," *NMHR*, XXXIII (Janu-

Several dynamics worked in concert to promote this borderland expansion. First, the province experienced increased integration with the formal sectors of the Bourbon-era Mexican economy, especially as a source of exports to northern Mexico as that region suffered through the upheavals of the wars for independence. After 1821, with the opening of the St. Louis to Chihuahua Trail, this economic growth expanded dramatically. The arrival of American-allied traders (whatever their national origin) introduced new social challenges and tensions within both Indian rancherías and New Mexican communities, where capitalist relations of exchange penetrated and placed stress on traditional customs of kinship. A nascent merchant class matured in New Mexico, as did the fortunes of the great sheepherding families of the Río Abajo. This expansion in sheep pastoralism was mirrored among certain Navajo outfits. Navajos and New Mexicans alike found that increases in market demand required wealthy sheep owners to expand their dependent labor pool, thereby lending new incentives to the regional slave trade. Illicit commerce in captives

---

ary 1958), 205–231; "The Navaho-Spanish Peace, 1720s–1770s," *NMHR,* XXXIV (January 1959), 9–40; "Navaho-Spanish Diplomacy, 1770–1790," *NMHR,* XXXV (July 1960), 200–235; "Navajo Foreign Affairs, 1795–1846," *NMHR,* XLVI, 2 parts (April–July 1971). L. R. Bailey followed with an important, but poorly referenced and conceptualized, study of Spanish and Mexican slaving *(Indian Slave Trade in the Southwest* [Los Angeles, 1966]). McNitt explored the nexus of raid and reprisal in *Navajo Wars* but paid little attention to Navajo seizure of Mexican captives, thus missing the reciprocal and redistributive aspects of the trade. David M. Brugge examined baptismal records for Navajo captives in New Mexico, as well as other tribes, and includes a chapter on Navajo slavery; see *Navajos in the Catholic Church Records of New Mexico, 1694–1875* (Tsaile, Ariz., 1985). For an in-depth treatment of New Mexican economic expansion to 1820, see Ross Harold Frank, "From Settler to Citizen: Economic Development and Cultural Change in Late Colonial New Mexico, 1750–1820" (Ph.D. diss., University of California, Berkeley, 1992). Martín González de la Vara notes a period of economic growth between 1821 and 1836 but finds the province struggling to maintain fiscal and political connections with a central government in turmoil ("La política del federalismo en Nuevo México, 1821–1836," *Historia Mexicana,* XXXVI [1986], 81–112). For a glowing (and probably exaggerated) report of New Mexico's economy in the period following independence, see "The *Ojeada* of Lic. Antonio Barreiro of 1832," in Pedro Bautista Pino, *Three New Mexico Chronicles: The* Exposición *of Don Pedro Bautista Pino 1812; the* Ojeada *of Lic. Antonio Barreiro 1832; and the Additions of Don José Agustín de Escudero 1849,* trans. and ed. H. Bailey Carroll and J. Villasana Haggard (Albuquerque, N.Mex., 1942), 109. On the increase of Navajo sheep flocks between 1800 and 1850, see Bailey, *If You Take My Sheep: The Evolution and Conflicts of Navajo Pastoralism, 1630–1868* (Pasadena, Calif., 1980), 76–77.

was part of a wider informal exchange system that moved tanned elkskins and bison hides, sheep fleeces and woolen textiles, iron implements and agricultural goods across cultures and beneath the control of customs officers and Indian headmen alike.

And, as their economies diversified, so too did these borderland societies become increasingly complex, dynamic, and unstable. In the pastoral borderlands west of the Río Grande, relations remained tense, yet low-grade military conflict between New Mexican and Navajo raiding bands began to redistribute resources, principally sheep but also women and children, from the wealthy to the poorer orders of both societies. Thus competition for control of the informal Indian trade would lie at the heart of the conflict that would come to characterize the nineteenth century.

A Brisk Commerce with Neighboring States

New Mexico's formal economy experienced systematic and sustained growth between 1790 and 1846. In the decades after 1790, Bourbon reform policies increased specie circulating in the Provincias Internas, heightened crown expenditures on presidial supplies, eased New Mexico's tax burdens, and promoted the province's market connections to Texas, Chihuahua, Sonora, and California. The province enjoyed relative immunity from the social and economic catastrophes of the wars for Mexican independence, and after 1821 American merchandise and capital further invigorated the fortunes of those mercantile families able to participate in the new transnational commerce. But the region's vitality also depended on surges in the informal trade among common New Mexicans and their Indian neighbors, a parallel economy that spanned customary and capitalist systems of exchange.

The Spanish-Comanche Peace of 1786 relieved many settlers of militia obligations and allowed them to concentrate on developing an export sheep and textile industry. Due largely to differing fertility rates and differing vulnerability to epidemics, a steadily growing colonial population (from 16,358 in 1790 to 28,436 in 1820) outstripped and replaced the Pueblo Indians (8,640 in 1790 and 9,923 in 1820) as the primary producers and laborers in the province. Whereas the colonial population grew at an annual rate of 2.1 percent between 1785 and 1820, per capita economic productivity seems to have grown at more than double that rate, or 5.6 percent. Relatively insulated from the upheavals of 1810 to 1821 that destroyed the textile industries of the Bajío, "the New Mexican economy functioned as a giant *obraje* [where] *vecinos* gathered local products and processed them for the internal market and for export to other regions," one historian argues. New Mexico's self-sufficiency, he believes, contributed to the region's ability to adapt to the opening of trade with the United States in 1821.[12]

In addition to confirming the growth of New Mexico's formal economic sector, tithe rental analyses suggest why tensions might exist between colonial administrators and their subjects and between the formal and informal sectors of the economy. Beginning in 1732, the Catholic Church levied an annual tithe of 10 percent of the annual increase of all New Mexican agricultural products and livestock. Rather than collect these tithes themselves, the church auctioned the right to collect tithes for a period of two to five years for a flat, annual rental fee. Any difference between the rental payment and actual collections went to the holder of the contract, who usually took tithes in kind (sheep, maize, and wheat), then shipped these products to markets in the south, where they were converted to specie. In many cases, the holder of the tithe rental contract was the provincial governor. Between 1806 and 1809, Governor Alencaster held the contract for New Mexico at an annual fee of four thousand pesos. The governor clearly benefited from local production passing through his control; he could then regulate its sale in Chihuahua. The restrictions against unlicensed trading he imposed upon taking office in 1805 were an attempt to maximize these profits. The commotions that resulted ultimately cost him his job in 1808.[13]

Policies more friendly to the informal sector, instituted by Governor Maynez in 1809, might have channeled some informal products into the Chihuahua trade, for tithe rental holder José Márquez was willing to pay half again more (6,153 pesos annually between 1810 and 1813) for the contract than had Alencaster. This may also reflect the rising importance of New Mexican commerce and, again, its relative insulation from the devastation of the wars for independence then raging to the south. Between 1814 and 1818, the tithe rental holder paid 8,215 pesos and between 1819 and 1822 10,000 pesos, clearly signaling the economy's growing health. Mexican independence and constitutional reforms eliminated the practice after that time, but commerce with Americans injected new goods and demands into a region eager for growth. Since the tithe rental contracts suggested only the renter's anticipation of what local economic pro-

12. Frank, "From Settler to Citizen," 190–203, esp. 407.

13. Ibid., 167–190, table 6, at 447.

duction he would be able to collect in kind—domestic livestock, maize, and wheat production as well as products of the informal Indian trade—we cannot know from that source each sector's relative share. Other evidence exists to show the growing power of the informal commercial sector, whether Navajo sheep and textiles or the Plains trade in hides, meat, horses, and captives.[14]

The Analceños' buffalo hunt of 1780 and José Chiquito's capture by Ecueracapa's spies in 1785 indicate that New Mexicans had become accustomed to making viajes onto the Plains in search of buffalo meat. After the Spanish-Comanche Peace and extension of settlements onto the Plains, these expeditions became more regular and produced lasting cultural types romanticized in the traditions of the cibolero and *comanchero.* Although these terms served initially to describe hunting and trading activities, they also came to represent real cultural adjustments in the lives of llaneros.

Like their Plains Indian counterparts, New Mexicans often involved whole communities in their bison hunts. Ciboleros treasured quick and agile *caballos ligeros* (swift, nimble horses) from which they wielded eight-foot lances tipped with twelve-inch blades, since their muskets proved of "*poco provecho*" (little advantage) against the beasts' thick hides. Hunting expeditions occurred after village fields had been planted in June, when bulls were taken for meat, and in late autumn for the "very woolly and valuable" hides of cows. In the autumn and early winter, after harvest, caravans of *carretas* (heavy, two-wheeled carts) headed for the Plains, often with much of the village population in the carts or following on horseback. Each carreta could hold the *tasajo* (dried meat) of three buffalo, which means that the 1780 hunt, netting 450 *cargas* of meat, might have resulted in as many as 1,350 dead buffalo and 45 tons of meat. In 1808, while surveying a trail between San Antonio and Santa Fe, Francisco Amangual encountered a party of 120 New Mexican ciboleros near the Canadian River. In the early nineteenth century, don Pedro Bautista Pino, a careful observer of New Mexico's economy, estimated that ciboleros took at minimum 10,000 to 12,000 animals per year.[15]

14. Ibid. Frank argues, "Despite the inflationary pressures felt within the province during the end of the colonial period, the value of the tithe contract outpaced the rise in the price of the major tithe goods" (190, 191 fig. 11).

15. This depends upon whether the 1780 use of carga meant a six-hundred-pound carreta load or a two-hundred-pound burro load. Even if carga meant the lower amount, the hunt netted some 450 buffalo, since the dressed and dried meat averaged about two hundred pounds per animal. The best contemporary description of ciboleros is found in don Antonio

The American trader Josiah Gregg offered extended observations on the cultural innovations and borrowings that New Mexican ciboleros displayed in their bison hunts when he encountered them on the Plains in the 1820s and 1830s. "Every year," he said,

> large parties of New Mexicans, some provided with mules and asses, others with *carretas* or truckle-carts and oxen, drive out into these prairies to procure a supply of buffalo beef for their families. They hunt like the wild Indians, chiefly on horseback and with bow and arrow, or lance, with which they soon load their carts and mules. They find no difficulty in curing their meat, even in mid-summer, by slicing it thin and spreading or suspending it in the sun; or, if in haste, it is slightly barbecued. During the curing operation they often follow the Indian practice of beating or kneading slices with their feet, which they contend contributes to its preservation.[16]

Although the number of bison ciboleros took seems striking, as does the cultural hybridity of their enterprises, their undertakings correspond closely in both substance and form to the buffalo harvests of another group of mixed-culture farmers and hunters on the Plains, the Red River Métis of central Canada. This mixed-descent community of some 5,000 people took between 500 and 650 tons of buffalo meat during their summer hunts in the middle years of the nineteenth century, with autumn hunts garnering another 200 tons, or about 6,000 to 9,000 animals annually. The Hudson's Bay Company made annual purchases of pemmican, dried meat, and hides from these Métis; the meat products alone probably totaled over 50 tons in 1850. These self-provisioning seasonal migrations of up to 1,000 sojourners—traveling by horseback and drawing their distinctive Red River carts behind teams of oxen—also relieved pressures on local agricultural stores. Métis buffalo hunt-

---

Barreiro's *Ojeada sobre Nuevo México* . . . (Puebla, N.Mex., 1832), which also draws upon Pedro Bautista Pino's report of 1812. Pino would have known cibolero culture well, for he made the original allotments of farming lands at San Miguel in 1803. See Pino, *Three New Mexico Chronicles,* trans. and ed. Carroll and Haggard, 100–102, 280–282; John L. Kessell, *Kiva, Cross, and Crown: The Pecos Indians and New Mexico, 1540–1840* (Albuquerque, N.Mex., 1987), 418–419; Francisco Amangual, "Diary of the Incidents and Operations Which Took Place in the Expedition from the Province of Texas to the Province of New Mexico," 1808, TS, trans. Haggard, Bexar Archives, Barker Texas History Collection, University of Texas.

16. Josiah Gregg, *The Commerce of the Prairies,* ed. Milo Martin Quaife (Lincoln, Nebr., 1966), 86.

ing proved a highly complementary adaptation to their marginal environment.[17]

Compared to the 6.5:1 bison / person ratio estimated as the annual subsistence kill rate for buffalo-hunting Plains Indians in the nineteenth century, the Red River Métis ratio is much lower at 1.2 to 1.8:1 and reflects their mixed farming, hunting, and market economy. The New Mexican ciboleros fall closer to the Métis example. In 1827, the population of San Miguel and nearby Pecos Pueblo stood at 2,893, and, when supplemented by other Río Grande consumers, the cibolero hunts could have served some 5,000 people, or a bison / person ratio of approximately 2:1.[18]

In addition to their bison harvest, the Indian trade held rewards for many New Mexicans. Whereas throughout the eighteenth century the prevailing pattern was one of Comanches and other Plains groups visiting Taos, Pecos, and even Santa Fe for ferias, by the nineteenth century this began to change, with New Mexicans more often heading onto the Plains in search of trade. Plains groups became reluctant to visit colonial settlements as their suffering from epidemic disease increased, but the San Miguel cases of 1805, in which the villagers risked imprisonment by venturing out onto the Plains to find trading partners, suggest that cambalaches to the Plains also allowed New Mexican villagers to engage in commerce far from the regulating authority of Spanish administrators like Governor Alencaster. In order to reach their trading partners and find new irrigable lands to till, New Mexicans extended small settlements eastward. Salvador Tapía and seventeen companions petitioned for the Anton Chico grant southeast of San Miguel del Vado in 1822, then abandoned it due to Indian hostilities in 1827 or 1828. Juan Martín and thirteen companions resettled its village in 1834. Seasonal stock-grazing outposts provided other op-

17. G. Herman Sprenger, "The Métis Nation: Buffalo Hunting vs. Agriculture in the Red River Settlement (circa 1810–1870)," in *Western Canadian Journal of Anthropology,* III, no. 1 (1972), 158–178; see 169–173 for hunting estimates. For a comprehensive look at the Métis phenomenon, see Jacqueline Peterson and Jennifer S. H. Brown, eds., *The New Peoples: Being and Becoming Métis in North America* (Manitoba, 1985). For the Métis's incorporation as proto-industrial producers for the hide trade between 1840 and 1870, see Gerhard J. Ens, *Homeland to Hinterland: The Changing Worlds of the Red River Metis in the Nineteenth Century* (Toronto, 1996).

18. Dan Flores, "Bison Ecology and Bison Diplomacy: The Southern Plains from 1800 to 1850," *Journal of American History* (hereafter cited as *JAH),* LXXVIII (1991–1992), 479. Narbona's census of 1827 may be found in Pino, *Three New Mexico Chronicles,* trans. and ed. Carroll and Haggard, 88.

portunities. Pablo Montoya, alcalde and a prominent citizen of La Cienega, southwest of Santa Fe, petitioned for this type of grant in 1824 along the "Colorado" (Canadian) River some one hundred miles east of Santa Fe. He claimed his desire for lands at such an extraordinary "distance from the settlements" was to gain lands upon which to raise his "cattle, sheep, and horses," but others alleged his fifteen-year occupation of the rancho was equally devoted to the Indian trade.[19]

In June 1813, Manuel Baca of San Miguel del Vado reported to acting governor Manrique that a band of comancheros had just returned from a trading visit with "los Comanches." The nature of this trade was revealed in a trial in the summer of 1814, in which José Manuel Gonzales and Juan Domingo Cordero stood accused of thieving horses from the ranchería of the Comanche captain Vicente. The two men defended themselves by claiming that they had traded Vicente 46 serapes, 121 *manojos* of *punche* (local tobacco), 5.5 fanegas of *bastimentos* (provisions), and a hide sack of *tabaco desmenusado* (rolled tobacco) for two mules, one horse, nine mares, three colts, and two cargas of meat. Later, they traded for more mules and horses with the "Monteños" Comanches, returning to New Mexico after an absence of five months.[20]

Josiah Gregg also encountered New Mexican comancheros in his travels across the Plains. These, he said, "are usually composed of the indigent and rude classes of the frontier villages, who collect together several times a year and launch upon the plains," carrying "trinkets and trumperies" that they "barter away to the savages for horses and mules." The "entire stock" of an individual trader seldom exceeded twenty dollars in value, for which was ex-

19. For Anton Chico, see Michael J. Rock, "Anton Chico and Its Patent," *Journal of the West* (July 1980), 86–91; for the Pablo Montoya grant, which, when finally surveyed in the 1870s, was found to contain 655,468 acres, see Pablo Montoya, resident of Cienega, petition for lands on the "Rio Colorado den Rincon dela Sinta a la Trinchera," Nov. 30, 1824, in *SANM*, I, roll 3, frames 1608–1610; "Manuel Armijo to Alcalde Pedro José Perea re Disposition of the Goods of the Deceased, Pablo Montoya, 14 April 1842," in *SANM*, I, roll 6, frames 1261–1262; case no. 1319, *Report of the Surveyor General, New Mexico*, New Mexico State Records Center.

20. "Manuel Baca, alcalde de San Miguel del Bado à gobernador interino Manrique, 1 junio 1813," in *SANM*, II, no. 2492, roll 17, frames 731–733; Frances Levine, "Economic Perspectives on the Comanchero Trade," in Katherine A. Spielmann, ed., *Farmers, Hunters, and Colonists: Interactions between the Southwest and the Southern Plains* (Tucson, Ariz., 1991), 158–159; see also case against Cordero and Gonzáles, in *SANM*, II, no. 2542, roll 17, frames 992–1034.

pected "a mule or two" in exchange. In an extraordinary allusion to a trait that today serves as an inside joke in describing Plains Indians, Gregg noted of comancheros, "Instead of pointing with their hands and fingers they generally employ the mouth, which is done by thrusting out the lips in the direction of the spot or object which the inquirer wishes to find out." He attributed this trait to the ubiquitous serape, which inhibited arm and hand movements.[21]

The relative allocation between subsistence and market aspects of the cibolero and comanchero bison and Indian trade economy may be impossible to determine, but there do exist some suggestive hints. Antonio Narbona claimed in 1827 that most agricultural production of the province was locally consumed, "since they cannot be exported to other provinces because of the lack of beasts of burden." But some efectos del país, principally woolen textiles and bison robes, were exported to Chihuahua and Sonora where they were "sold at ridiculously low prices." Even with those poor exchange values, he added,

> a large number of the settlers are engaged in hunting buffalo, in trading with the friendly Indians, and in raising sheep and goats. These sources of income are quite profitable in times when things are not in a turmoil because of an invasion of the wild Indians.[22]

Bison hides, textiles produced by New Mexican and Navajo weavers, and sheep comprised the principal local products exported south along the Camino Real. Between 1826 and 1845, nearly 400,000 sheep valued at 200,000 pesos were driven south, accounting for 47 percent of the total measurable exports for the period (422,907 pesos). Sixty percent of those animals were owned by the Chávez, Otero, and Sandoval families. Manuel Armijo, governor at the time of the American conquest, shipped an additional 34,916 sheep between 1835 and 1845. These same families, with the Pereas and Yrrissarris, also dominated transshipment of foreign (American) goods—predominantly cotton textiles, Chinese silks, and small manufactures like cutlery—obtained from the St. Louis trade, valued at 181,492 pesos. Fully 90 percent of the known value of exports to Mexico during the period was held by a handful of families with close ties to the mercantile elite of Nueva Vizcaya.[23]

21. Gregg, *Commerce of the Prairies,* ed. Quaife, 219, 223.

22. Narbona, in Pino, *Three New Mexico Chronicles,* trans. and ed. Carroll and Haggard, 89–90.

23. For the export economy of New Mexico between 1826 and 1845, based on assessed valuations contained in extant *guías* issued to *comerciantes* departing from Santa Fe, see

Despite the dominance of the sheep and merchant families, common New Mexicans eagerly engaged in the export trade whenever they could collect sufficient local products to hope for some profit in so arduous an undertaking. The remaining 10 percent (41,415 pesos) of the Mexico trade was distributed among the lower orders of the province and yet composed more than 50 percent of the total departures. The cargo-laden mules of these petty traders indicate the diversity of the economy in which they operated and stand in stark contrast to the dual sheep and import staples of their wealthy counterparts. Luis María Cabeza de Baca departed for Chihuahua and Sonora in the summer of 1837 with 300 blankets, 200 varas of rough cloth, and 11 serapes, probably of Navajo origin. Felipe Romero set out for Chihuahua and Durango in September of 1838 with 71 bison hides, 163 blankets, 114 pairs of socks, 4 elk hides, 6 serapes, 1 bed blanket, 13 bedspreads, 7 deerskins, and 2 bearskins, assessed at a total value of a mere 161 pesos. A similar range of local and Indian goods was displayed in the six loads Juan de Jesús Abeita took to Chihuahua, Durango, and Zacatecas in 1843: 39 bison hides, 10 bedspreads, 36 serapes, 25 deerskins, 28 woolen blankets, and 2 beaver traps were enumerated in his cargo valued at 144 pesos. Virtually all the loads carried by small traders featured combinations of bison hides, rough New Mexican blankets or knit stockings, a few fine Navajo serapes, and elk or deerskins probably bartered from Utes and Apaches in the north. Indeed, fully half of the 420 individual loads carried by New Mexicans into Mexico by 1845 were valued at less than 234 pesos. Pitiful as these cargoes may seem in comparison with the many bolts of cotton, linen, and silk scarves of the great merchant families, Cabeza de Baca, Romero, and their like stood to garner real profits if their bundles could be converted to specie. Steel from which lance blades, arrow points, and knives were crafted for the Indian trade sold for one peso per *quintal* in Guaymas and Hermosillo. These traders, though small in scale, straddled the spaces between the bison economy, the Navajo trade, and the Mexican export sector while integrating the domestic production of weavers and knitters from their own households.[24]

Negotiating exchanges within these spaces was perilous. A single cambalache could include both successful bartering and intercultural violence, as

---

Susan Calafate Boyle, *Los Capitalistas: Hispano Merchants and the Santa Fe Trade* (Albuquerque, N.Mex., 1997), 28–44, esp. tables 3, 4.

24. Boyle, *Los Capitalistas,* 38; see also Cabeza de Baca guía, in *Mexican Archives of New Mexico,* New Mexico State Records Center (hereafter cited as *MANM),* roll 24, frame 799; Romero guía, in *MANM,* roll 25, frame 1445; Abeita guía, in *MANM,* roll 34, frame 1246.

apparently occurred early in the autumn of 1831 along the Río Pecos at the small village of Cuesta. There, a mixed group of Comanches, Kiowas, Pawnees, and two Mexican captives arrived with eight horses to trade for gunpowder, blankets, and serapes. They found an avid, if meager, welcome. Among the villagers who dealt for the horses (two of which were branded and almost certainly stolen) were the widow Rafaela Tapía and her son, who purchased a horse and a yearling colt with a gun, one blanket, two hands of punche, and three charges of powder. The branded horses also were traded for two serapes, a fringed shawl, and six charges of powder. All might have ended well at that point, except that, as the Indians proceeded down the Pecos towards the Plains, they were said to have encountered an additional party of eight comancheros from settlements in the Río Arriba and Río Chama and from La Cañada. At the spring Agua del Toro, the New Mexicans suffered an ambush that left four of their group dead and two grievously wounded, with their horses and trade goods in the hands of the attackers. Whether or not the assaulting Indians were the same as those who traded at Cuesta (later Comanche visitors to San Miguel del Vado protested they might have been Arapahos or Shoshones), the two events show how easily intimate face-to-face exchanges that went so far as to include New Mexican women bartering with Comanche warriors could combine with violence between the cultures. Still, the suspicion that the nine charges of gunpowder obtained at Cuesta might have been expended in the murder of the comancheros probably fed into Governor José Antonio Chávez's decision the next month to prohibit both trading and bison hunting by New Mexicans.[25]

Despite the perils, villagers of the llano, comancheros, Navajo traders, and ciboleros all found the risk worth taking. From an average of ten to twelve thousand each year in the 1810s, the cibolero bison harvest grew to and peaked at some 25,000 animals per year in the middle years of the nineteenth century. In 1832, Antonio Barreiro noted the energy, diversity, and class asymmetries of New Mexico's economy when he reported,

> New Mexicans also carry on a brisk commerce with neighboring states. Annually they carry out large numbers of sheep, hides, piñones, coarse woolen cloth, tobacco, and other articles which they sell at good prices. There are

25. See José María Ronquillo and Donaciano Vigil, "Report on Depredations near Tierra Blanca," Sept. 17, 1831, *MANM*, roll 13, frames 559–579; José Antonio Chávez to José Antonio Vizcarra, Oct. 23, 1831, *MANM*, reel 13, frame 488; Thomas W. Kavanagh, *Comanche Political History: An Ethnohistorical Perspective, 1706–1875* (Lincoln, Nebr., 1996), 205–206.

> some men who have contracts in Durango to deliver annually fifteen thousand sheep which, delivered, bring nine reales or more each. Sheep trading is monopolized by a small number of men. Consequently, it must not be considered as beneficial as commerce in hides, coarse woolen cloth, etc. The latter type of commerce is distributed among all classes of society in New Mexico, especially among the middle and lowest classes.

Barreiro took pains to make the trade in hides and textiles distinct from "the commerce they have with the heathens," which yielded *esquisitas pieles* (luxury furs) obtained from Utes. His reference to hides and textiles probably meant the cibolero contribution to New Mexico's economy, vecino weavings, and the barter-for-export element of Navajo women's woven serapes and frazadas. Despite its small representation among measurable exports to Mexico, the bison economy and Indian trade were indispensable adjuncts to the subsistence farming of New Mexican villagers. Disruption of that component, whether by Mexican licensing and taxation, American competition, or decline in the bison herds themselves, could threaten their material well-being and sense of autonomy.[26]

Each of these threats emerged in time, but the latter would shape the broad course of New Mexican and Indian economic relations. Beginning in the 1830s and peaking in the 1850s, contemporary accounts suggest that the Comanches traded as many as 30,000 hides annually to American buyers, taking perhaps another 130,000 for subsistence if their population was 20,000 people. Kiowas traded even more heavily in bison hides than Comanches, given their much smaller population of 2,000; Indian Agent John W. Whitefield reported Kiowa sales at 20,000 hides in 1856 alone and 6,500 buffalo killed for food, shelter, and clothing. In the previous year William Bent reported that 3,150 Cheyennes delivered 40,000 bison hides to his outpost, and, if the foregoing use estimates are accurate, Cheyennes took an additional 20,410 for their subsistence needs. In these cases, per capita buffalo kills increased with market involvement from 6.5 bison per person to a range of 8:1 (for the Comanches) to 13:1 (for Kiowas), to 19:1 (for the Cheyennes). Participation in the hide trade also vastly overstressed traditional scraping-and-tanning labor conducted by Indian women. At an estimated use need of 12–14 bison per year per lodge, one woman could

26. See "*Ojeada* of Lic. Antonio Barreiro of 1832," in Pino, *Three New Mexico Chronicles*, trans. and ed. Carroll and Haggard, 109–110, 288. His reference to valuable furs indicates most explicitly the fur trade conducted by Utes at Taos, since neither Navajos nor Plains groups were much involved in trapping at this point.

keep abreast of a household's needs. But, since Plains Indian hunters were taking thousands more bison than needed for tipis, clothing, and subsistence each year, those market-bound hides, even if minimally processed, would require the recruitment of supplemental labor in the form of additional Mexican captives in the years after 1830.[27]

The bison population of the southern Plains held at approximately 6 million during the first half of the nineteenth century, able to reproduce itself at the 6.5:1 subsistence ratio if nonhuman mortality (predators, disease, and starvation) took some 600,000 annually. The southern Plains bison herds could have supported a subsistence population of 60,000 people taking 390,000 animals annually, somewhat under the "critical mortality for breeding cows" of 420,000. The Comanche, Kiowa, and Cheyenne figures suggest that, when we add an additional 5,000 New Mexicans seasonally dependent on bison for subsistence and market commerce to the Southern Plains Indian population of 30,000, market hunting put annual harvests into a range of 270,000 to 420,000 breeding cows. Market hunting alone might have proved sufficient to engender a crisis. Grazing competition from horses both domestic (250,000 to 500,000) and wild (perhaps some 2 million), intrusive bovine diseases, and prolonged drought significantly eroded the vitality of bison herds. Increased market hunting, with selection toward two-to-five-year-old cows for their easily processed, luxuriant hides, began to tip the balance in the direction of an ecological disaster.[28]

The bison economy was crucial to the lives of Plains Indians and New Mexican llaneros alike. So too was the competitive and mutualistic pastoral sheep-

27. The cibolero hunt figures I use here are based on Flores, "Bison Ecology and Bison Diplomacy," *JAH,* LXXVIII (1991–1992), 482, with corrective insights drawn from Kavanagh, "Playing a Numbers Game: Counting the Comanches in History and Anthropology, an Historiographic and Ethnographic Review" (1998), paper in possession of the author; see also Levine, "Economic Perspectives on the Comanchero Trade," in Spielmann, ed., *Farmers, Hunters, and Colonists,* 164–165. Bent quoted in Flores, "Bison Ecology and Bison Diplomacy," *JAH,* LXXVIII (1991–1992), 483.

28. Flores, "Bison Ecology and Bison Diplomacy," *JAH,* LXXVIII (1991–1992), 480–483. Kavanagh, however, points out possible errors in Flores's calculations that reduce his estimation of the annual calf crop from 1.4 million to between 252,630 and 650,000 calves, placing herd viability well below the equilibrium threshold that Flores claims. See also Andrew C. Isenberg, *The Destruction of the Bison: An Environmental History, 1750-1920* (Cambridge, 2000).

FIGURE 9. *Comanche Ranchería.* 1834. Note the women dressing bison hides. Field sketch by George Catlin. Reproduced from Catlin, *Letters and Notes,* II, 65

and-weaving economy developing among New Mexican and Navajo pastores. Peripheral in terms of the formal economy, these mixed cultural enterprises were central to those on its margins. The poverty and neglect bewailed by certain New Mexican aspiring *capitalistas* stemmed more from inequalities in access to credit and markets than any fundamental weakness in regional production. Indeed, their apparent stranglehold on the region's mercantile and sheep economies was fragile, for from the east had arrived American competitors, and to the west of the Río Grande New Mexican and Navajo pastores were creating their own solution to differential access to livestock wealth. When José Rafael Alarid felt obliged to warn in 1824 that there existed "wicked dissidents" among provincial merchants who looked favorably on associations with the encroaching United States, he highlighted these twin dangers: the overwhelming attraction of American commerce and the disorderly and subversive nature of relations between common New Mexicans and their Indian neighbors. Alarid made an explicit appeal for Mexican regular troops to maintain the stability of the province and delivered a thinly veiled warning about wavering loyalties. A complex social world was becoming even more variegated as local peoples worked new solutions to the arrival of American markets and their representatives. The danger came as much from within as without.[29]

A Babble-tongued Multitude

The advent of the St. Louis–Santa Fe–Chihuahua trade in the 1820s also introduced a new set of mixed-culture actors into the borderlands, especially those French, Canadian, Scottish, English, and American fur trade entrepreneurs who served as agents of capitalist expansion as well as cultural affines of the borderland communities. Following a commercial strategy that had proved effective east of the Mississippi, men like John Gantt, the Bent brothers, Antoine Robidoux, Ceran St. Vrain, Charles Beaubien, Charles Autobees, and Alexander Barclay sought marriage alliances with local families. They joined with longtime New Mexican bordermen like Marcelino Baca to create what Barclay termed a "babble-tongued multitude" on the upper Arkansas River.[30]

These men began their careers by making full use of the kinship incorporation offered them by the Indian groups with which they traded. Marcelino Baca of Taos married a Pawnee woman who had "rescued him from captivity among her people" and whom contemporaries described as a "woman of matronly grace and dignity." Baca insisted that their union and children be recognized by the Catholic Church and brought his family to Taos for baptism in 1843. William Bent married into the Cheyennes in 1837 and, when his first wife died, took her sister in marriage in accordance with the Cheyenne sororate. Charles Autobees, who began his career distilling whiskey at Turley's Mill north of Taos, married both a Nueva Mexicana from Taos and an Arapaho woman, "Sycamore," who lived as an "out-of-door wife in a tent," although still part of the extended household. Writing from the Arkansas River settlements of Pueblo and Hardscrabble in 1847, Thomas Fitzpatrick claimed that nearly all of the sixty male residents had Indian wives, among whom were repre-

29. For the problem of Chihuahua monopoly, see Max L. Moorhead, *New Mexico's Royal Road: Trade and Travel on the Chihuahua Trail* (Norman, Okla., 1958), 50–54; for economic hardships of the Mexican Period, see David J. Weber, *The Mexican Frontier, 1821–1846: The American Southwest under Mexico* (Albuquerque, N.M., 1982). Alarid quoted in Boyle, *Los Capitalistas,* 14.

30. Alexander Barclay to George Barclay, May 1, 1840, Barclay Papers, Bancroft Library, University of California, Berkeley.

sented Blackfoot, Assiniboine, Arikara, Sioux, Arapaho, Cheyenne, Pawnee, Shoshone, Sanpete, and Chinook women. The presence of Sanpete and Chinook women from as far north as the Columbia Plateau and coastal Oregon indicates just how extensive kin-based exchange networks in the West had become by the early nineteenth century and hints that the slave system of greater New Mexico had links to regional slave complexes in the Northwest.[31]

Expanding on these connections with Indian groups, the mixed communities on the Arkansas also maintained a web of kin relations with New Mexican settlements to the south. The thriving village of Taos served as their main point of commerce, and patterns of intermarriage illustrate the centrality of kin connections to a larger commerce in deerskins, buffalo hides, arms and ammunition, and sweetened whiskey. Between 1819 and 1846, 152 *extranjeros* married in the Catholic Church at Taos, 91 of whom married New Mexican women. Charles Beaubien married María Paula Lovato in 1829 and operated a store in Taos through the 1840s. Charles Bent formalized his union with Ignacia Jaramillo, as did Christopher "Kit" Carson with Ignacia's sister, Josefa. Others, like Antoine and Abraham LeDoux, known through diligencias matrimoniales to have married Pawnee women, lived in concubinage with the Taoseñas Polonia Lucero and Guadalupe Trujillo. Pedro Vial, the *llanero extraordinario* with close ties to both Taovayas and Comanches, never married María Manuel Martín but did name her as his heir in 1814. María Martín's sister, Paula

31. Janet Lecompte, *Pueblo, Hardscrabble, Greenhorn: Society on the High Plains, 1832–1856* (Norman, Okla., 1978), 17, 63–73; Lecompte, "A Babel-Tongued Multitude on the Upper Arkansas, 1832–1856," in Paul Kutsche, ed., *Survival of Spanish-American Villages,* The Colorado College Studies, no. 15 (Spring 1979), 63–77; Tanis Chapman Thorne, "Marriage Alliance and the Fur Trade: Bent, St. Vrain, and Co., 1831–1849" (master's thesis, University of California, Los Angeles, 1979). Thorne notes a shift on the part of Bent's Fort traders from "extensive" marriages with Indian women to "intensive" marriages with New Mexican women around 1841 (8). For an excellent analysis of the indigenous use of French Catholic marriage and godparenthood structures in promoting family economies in the Great Lakes region, see Susan Sleeper-Smith, "Women, Kin, and Catholicism: New Perspectives on the Fur Trade," *Ethnohistory,* XLVII (Spring 2000), 423–452. The Pacific Northwest featured an extensive slave system with marked similarities to that discussed in these pages, well deserving of comparative study. For a documentary history, see Robert H. Ruby and John A. Brown, *Indian Slavery in the Pacific Northwest* (Spokane, Wash., 1993); for broader synthesis concentrating on coastal slavery, see Leland Donald, *Aboriginal Slavery on the Northwest Coast of North America* (Berkeley, Calif., 1997). See also María Rosa Villalpando's story in Chapter 2, above.

Martín, was wed to José Juliano Xacques, the son whom María Rosa Villalpando left behind when she was seized by Comanches in 1760. José Juliano probably heard through Vial that his mother still lived in St. Louis.[32]

The web of kinship extended beyond simple marital ties in that marital unions also required the spiritual sponsorship of compadrazgo. Aspiring traders sought the spiritual endorsement of locals like Rafael Luna, alcalde of Taos, or extranjeros who had already established kin ties in the community. Baptiste Lalanda, who had come to New Mexico before 1804, became *compadre* (protector) to Luna, then sponsored several subsequent French traders. Charles Beaubien acted as padrino in baptisms (of converting foreigners) or marriages more than thirty times between 1829 and 1846.[33]

Compadrazgo and marriage strategies went through a rapid evolution in the first half of the nineteenth century. In the initial period of establishing cultural ties that would enhance commercial relations, these institutions seem little guided by class distinctions. Baptiste Lalanda might seek out ties with Rafael Luna, but Luna, a trapper who died in 1832, was no rico. His status as alcalde did, however, lend local legitimacy to extranjeros seeking access. Most of the commercial wealth in New Mexican society was held by ricos of Santa Fe and the Río Abajo, families whose social aspirations led them to seek marriages with prominent families in Chihuahua rather than with itinerant fur trappers and traders who often appeared distinctly Indian in dress and customs. By the late 1830s, however, choosing padrinos and marriage partners had become much more class endogamous, as families who prospered sought to guard that wealth from possible dilution through social or marriage bonds with the pobres. The Lopez, Vigil, Suaso, and Jaramillo families brought twelve different extranjeros into the fold in the 1830s and 1840s through marital matches with their daughters. These families continued to prosper and allied themselves first with the Armijo counterrevolution to the lower-class Río Arriba uprising of 1837 and later with the Americans. Governor Armijo rewarded their loyalty

32. Sandra Jaramillo Macias, "Bound by Family: Cross-Cultural Marriages in the Mexican and Territorial Periods," paper presented at the Annual Meetings of the Carson Society, Taos, N.Mex., July 30, 1994. The definitive portrait of Taos and its centrality to a wider commerce during the fur trade era remains David J. Weber, *The Taos Trappers: The Fur Trade in the Far Southwest, 1540–1846* (Norman, Okla., 1971). For the relationship between María and Paula Martín, see Vial's *testamento* of 1814, *SANM,* I, no. 1063, roll 5, frames 1343–1362.

33. Taos Baptisms, 1819–1846, *Archdiocesan Archives of Santa Fe,* rolls 19–21, New Mexico State Records Center.

with several massive (and illegal) land grants between 1841 and 1843, totaling some 9.7 million acres. In casting their lot so firmly behind land-based accumulation of wealth, some of these families would bear the brunt of the violence that erupted after the American conquest in 1847.[34]

The late 1830s also saw the mixed communities stretching from Taos to the Arkansas River start to bifurcate along lines of legal and social legitimacy. Among the scores of small-scale or seasonal settlements along the Arkansas, only William Bent's massively fortified trading depot (constructed between 1832 and 1834) at the junction of the Arkansas and Purgatoire Rivers could claim legal sanction. The lands north of the Arkansas had been United States territory since the Adams-Onís Treaty of 1819 established the northern boundary between the Louisiana Purchase and New Spain. This Indian territory had been set aside in 1834 as the exclusive domain of tribes, and only officially licensed traders like the Bent brothers were permitted. No white persons were allowed to farm or keep livestock on those lands, wear Indian clothing, use Indian tools (or, by implication, marry Indians or "go Indian" in any manner), hunt game, or hold title to land or improvements. Lands south of the Arkansas came under similar restrictions by Mexican law—as we have seen in cases in the plains and pastoral borderlands, official land grants restricted use to grazing alone, with the farming and hunting rights clearly retained by the indigenous inhabitants. Likewise, officially licensed traders might make seasonal sojourns to the Arkansas, or recipients of individual *empresario* grants

34. Deena J. Gonzáles, *Refusing the Favor: The Spanish-Mexican Women of Santa Fe, 1820–1880* (New York, 1999); for treatments that presuppose an immediate rico-extranjero alliance strategy, and thus overlook the dynamic changes wrought in class relations by the fur trade, see Rebecca Craver McDowell, *The Impact of Intimacy: Mexican Anglo Intermarriage in New Mexico, 1821–1846* (El Paso, Tex., 1982); Lecompte, "The Independent Women of Hispanic New Mexico, 1821–1846," *Western Historical Quarterly,* XII (January 1981), 17–35. None of the grants awarded by Armijo between 1832 and 1843 accorded with the Mexican Colonization Law of 1824, which limited individual grants to eleven square leagues (48,000 acres). Although the law was amended in 1828 to permit foreigners to receive land grants, the size restrictions were not lifted. The six grants in question averaged 1.6 million acres each. See Malcom Ebright, "New Mexican Land Grants: The Legal Background," in Charles L. Briggs and John R. Van Ness, eds., *Land, Water, and Culture: New Perspectives on Hispanic Land Grants* (Albuquerque, N.Mex., 1987), 15–64; Marianne L. Stoller, "Grants of Desperation, Lands of Speculation: Mexican Period Land Grants in Colorado," in John R. Van Ness and Christine Van Ness, eds., *Spanish and Mexican Land Grants in New Mexico and Colorado* (Santa Fe, N.Mex., 1980), 22–39.

like Carlos Beaubien and Guadelupe Miranda might be encouraged to place settlers on their lands, but the freelance settlements that did occur never received official sanction.[35]

Yet the mixed-culture entrepreneurs of the borderlands paid little heed to these restrictions, and neither American nor Mexican authorities were in a position to enforce them. Trading and farming outposts dotted the Arkansas's tributaries west of Bent's Fort. In 1839, a mixed group of Americans and New Mexicans established Fort Leche (its inhabitants drank goats' milk, perhaps to chase the sweet whiskey that contributed to its failure) five miles upriver from the Bent establishment. The following year, Maurice LeDuc and some fellow Frenchmen settled a post for trading with Utes near Hardscrabble Creek, ninety miles west of Bent's Fort. El Pueblo, at the mouth of Fountain Creek and the Arkansas, was founded in 1842 by four independent American traders who had, in the 1830s and early 1840s, established themselves as naturalized Mexicans and married into Taos families. In fact, Mathias Kinkaid and Francisco Conn had been among the grant petitioners for the Santa Gertrudis de Mora grant in 1835. Kinkaid and his common-law wife Terasita Sandoval experimented in 1841 with nursing captured buffalo calves on milk cows for later sale to eastern zoos or European hunting estates. In 1842, it seems he sold forty-

35. "An Act to Regulate Trade and Intercourse with the Indian Tribes, and to Preserve Peace on the Frontier," *U.S. Statutes at Large,* IV, 682–683, quoted in Lecompte, "A Babel-Tongued Multitude," in Kutsche, ed., *Survival of Spanish-American Villages,* 71. The scholarship on Mexican land law and actual land tenure in New Mexico is sparse, since most analysis has aimed at uncovering the legal chicanery that went into the dispossession of New Mexicans following the American conquest. The legality of New Mexican settlement of Indian lands has only been considered in the case of Pueblo land grants, and Pueblos, as village Indians, received better protection than did their nomadic counterparts. For the Pueblos, see G. Emlen Hall, "The Pueblo Grant Labyrinth," in Briggs and Van Ness, eds., *Land, Water and Culture,* 67–138. For provisions for the settlement of empresario grants, see section 1 of the regulations issued November 21, 1828, pursuant to the Mexican Colonization Law of 1824. The most authoritative historical source on these questions is Mariano Galván Rivera, *Ordenanzas de tierras y aguas, ó sea formulario geométrico-judicial para la designación, establecimiento, mensura, amojonamiento y deslinde de las poblaciones . . .* (1842), supplement to Joaquín Escriche y Martin, *Diccionario razonado de legislación y jurisprudenica . . .* (Paris, 1863); for an argument that sees Bent's Fort as the central element in the capitalist transformation of the Plains Tribes and New Mexico, see Douglas C. Comer, *Ritual Ground: Bent's Old Fort, World Formation, and the Annexation of the Southwest* (Berkeley, Calif., 1996).

four yearling calves for one hundred dollars apiece and gained the capital to underwrite the Pueblo post.[36]

Other outposts followed, including San Buenaventura de los Tres Arrollos (Hardscrabble) in 1844, Greenhorn in 1845, and Alexander Barclay's rancho in 1846. All lay on the Mexican side of the Arkansas and were occasionally condemned as "outlaw settlements." Their occupants often fit the description as well, for by the mid-1840s serious competition had erupted between wealthy legitimate traders and aspiring traders who lacked American or Mexican government approval.[37]

On the eastern Plains, such competition involved efforts by New Mexican comancheros to reach Comanches and Kiowas with trade goods before they made their seasonal journeys to Bent's Fort, and at times this led to conflict between comancheros and Bent's agents. On the Arkansas, however, entrepreneurial New Mexican and American traders attempted to interpose themselves between mountain-dwelling Utes and the fort some ninety miles to the east. Lacking much in the way of capital goods, they purchased Turley's whiskey on credit, undertook small-scale stock raising, and planted the bottomlands with wheat and corn. They then utilized these products in exchange for furs and deerskins, especially after 1840, when the Utes found themselves almost completely foreclosed from the buffalo plains.[38]

Juan Chiquito of Taos exemplified this outlaw type, a poor but ambitious man more than willing to blend customary patterns of violence and exchange with the more formalized system represented by William Bent's enterprise. Juan had, in the 1840s, murdered Juan Polvaderas in order to abscond with his wife, Anastasia, who apparently assisted in the crime. In 1851, Juan attached himself as a cook to a mixed group of traders at the mouth of the Huerfano, but soon cut out on his own with Anastasia and his son (from an earlier marriage) José Leon, and they took up quarters in the abandoned homestead of Marcelino Baca at El Pueblo. There they traded with local Utes and preyed upon the formal commerce, attracting some forty or fifty "bad men," including "murderers" from Mexico who had brought with them "wives whom they stole from New Mexico." These men worked as peons in Chiquito's large adobe rancho. In 1862 Chiquito's outfit grew bold and raided Charles Autobees's settlement

36. Lecompte, *Pueblo, Hardscrabble, Greenhorn,* 35–53.

37. Francisco García Conde to the governor of New Mexico, Sept. 20, 1845, *MANM,* no. 1128, roll 38, frames 600–602.

38. Lecompte, *Pueblo, Hardscrabble, Greenhorn,* 98–106.

at the mouth of the Huerfano River, taking livestock, wagons, and the wives of Carmel Medina and Choteau Sandoval. José took the Sandoval woman as his second wife and gave Louisa Medina to his compadre Jesus Romero.[39]

Chiquito's raid was of little real consequence other than for the retribution it brought from the Autobees outfit, which killed José and his companion Francisco Frederico in June 1862. Yet it illustrates the extent to which customary violence between men continued to express itself in competition over women among these mixed communities, themselves the vanguard of commercial penetration. Charles Autobees himself operated on the margins of respectability, entering the Arkansas valley in 1836 as a traveling whiskey salesman for Simeon Turley's distillery. His fortunes grew along with the multiethnic connections nourished by his polygynous household of a New Mexican woman and Sycamore, his Arapaho wife. By 1845 he had established a farm at the crossing of the St. Charles, perhaps on the same site as the San Carlos de los Jupes experiment of 1787. Supplying agricultural products to Bent's Fort, Autobees moved in 1853 to a better location at the mouth of the Huerfano. There he helped establish a village that its founders hoped to make a link on the recently proposed transcontinental railroad. Commercial boosterism, Indian trading, polygamy, stock and captive raids, and retributions all combined in the babble-tongued multitude on the Arkansas and along the Río Grande, heralding in its dynamic mix the more systematic commercial integration of the region that lay on the distant horizon.[40]

Loved as if of Our Own Blood

Extranjeros, of course, were not the only "strangers" to enter New Mexican society in the early decades of the nineteenth century. Many hundreds of Indian slaves, the vast majority of them Navajos and Utes, streamed into regional households where they occupied positions of continuing ambiguity. On the one hand, the Spanish Council of Regency in Cádiz had abolished the personal servitude of Indians in 1812, the decree of which reached New Mexico in November of that year. Explicit in its abolition of slavery, the ban implicitly undercut the long-term fiction of rescate, by which Indians ransomed from

39. Francis W. Cragin, interviews with Tom Autobees, November 1907, notebook II, 4–8, Cragin Collection, New Mexico State Records Center.

40. Lecompte, *Pueblo, Hardscrabble, Greenhorn*, 227–236.

TABLE 3. Baptisms of Selected Non-Pueblo Indians, 1800–1880

Tribe	1800s	1810s	1820s	1830s	1840s	1850s	1860s	1870s	Total
Apaches	41	19	12	13	5	24	11	3	128
Pawnees	1	2				1			4
Aàs	10	7	3						20
Kiowas	12	11	3	5	1				32
Comanches	15	9	6	2	1	1			34
Utes	162	112	49	71	157	43	26	1	621
Navajos	10	4	259	43	106	29	790	47	1,288
Hopis	7	3	15	1	2		6	3	37
Yumans	9	1	7	4	1				22
Flatheads			1	4	1	1	1		8
Shoshones			1	4	6	5			16
Overall	267	168	356	147	280	104	834	54	2,210

Adapted from David M. Brugge, *Navajos in the Catholic Church Records of New Mexico, 1694–1875* (Tsaile, Ariz., 1985), 22–23.

captivity among the "heathens" were morally bound to repay the cost of their ransom to their rescuers with personal service. But New Mexico was far from Spain, whose experiments with liberalism were tentative and incomplete. Custom continued to frame the institution of Indian slavery in the province, and even then local custom equivocated between the poles of fictive kinship and outright slavery.[41]

Notations offered by parish priests in the baptismal entries for Navajo captives entering New Mexican society are a case in point. Between the time of the 1812 abolition and the American conquest of 1847, priests baptized some 330 Navajos, perhaps two of which were voluntary conversions. The rest were

41. See Gonzales Carvajal, decree of council of 1812, in *SANM*, II, Orders and Decrees, roll 22, frames 531–533.

slaves. But none, of course, found their status so blatantly designated. Ten percent had been ransomed under the traditional artifice, whereas 17 percent were said to have been adopted according to continuing customs of ceremonial kinship. But priests did record 19 percent as "purchased," a clear indication of market status, and an additional 10 percent received designations indicating some superordinate power and patrimonial interest (for example, *bajo del dominio de,* "under the power of") on the part of the padrinos who presented them for baptism. Twenty-three percent of the captives presented for baptism lacked any designation of social status, other than their Navajo cultural derivation. In all cases, however, the simple fact of baptism provided New Mexicans moral cover for resisting mutual repatriation of captives in treaty negotiations with Navajos. The second article of an 1824 treaty declared that New Mexicans would return Navajo captives "provided they wish to go, since to send back those who had received baptism or intended to was un-Christian."[42]

Whatever their ascribed social or confessional status, captive Navajo women and children receiving baptism came at least nominally under the protection of Catholic compadrazgo practices that established some set of culturally sanctioned obligations and responsibilities between fictive kin, especially with regard to religious instruction and moral treatment. A padrino, at least in theory, would never treat violently or pursue sexual relations with a godchild. But kinship and ownership could overlap without contradiction in the New Mexican institution. Of the 272 cases for which data are available, 68 percent show some correlation between servile status and ceremonial kinship, either in direct relation through owners and godparents representing the same people or less obvious connections to godparents who derived from the laterally extended family of the owners. The 32 percent who had godparents with surnames different from their owners' families may indicate even greater vulnerability, in that their owners sought to avoid the moral burdens of godparenthood, or, conversely, a favorable status, in that the owners invited community members beyond the family to assume those obligations and to monitor the treatment of their godchildren. Thus the twin valences in the lived meaning of *criadismo*—subordinate peoples raised up by and in the power of their "parents" and masters—found semantic expression in the baptismal registers of New Mexican village churches. And, although New Mexicans would claim that many such

42. Baptismal analysis drawn from Brugge, *Navajos in the Catholic Church Records,* table 8, 112–113; for treaty of 1824, see Reeve, "Navajo Foreign Affairs," *NMHR,* XLVI, part 2 (July 1971), 244–245.

criadas and criados grew to adulthood, married Spanish men or women, and bore children who were "loved as if [they] were of our own blood," available evidence presents a less sanguine picture.[43]

Of the 160 known births of children to Navajo slaves in New Mexico between 1694 and 1875, 135 came from unconsecrated unions in which the father was seldom named. These fathers might have been Navajo or other Indian slaves, the younger sons of slaveowners, or the masters themselves. Since custom held that both male and female slaves achieved freedom with marriage to New Mexicans, and legitimate children were therefore born free as well, slaveowners had little incentive to support formal unions, since the illegitimate children fell under the dependent embrace of compadrazgo and would remain bound to the owners in some fashion. Of the twenty-five legitimate offspring, Navajo men who had married New Mexican women fathered twenty-one; only four came from marriages of Navajo women to New Mexican men. Yet, given Navajo systems of matrilineal descent, the dishonor of illegitimacy inscribed in Spanish baptismal registers possibly redounded more significantly in the cultural world of the master class than with the slave women themselves, who considered their children fully enfranchised members of the maternal clan, if only in aspiration. As elsewhere in North America, slave women carried the double burden of servile status and subordinate sex throughout their lives, with little hope for social assimilation. In New Mexico, however, the proximity of natal families, rancherías, and clans always held the possibility that repatriation would allow the recovery of cultural dignity.[44]

Just as the local Catholic Church shrouded Indian slavery in conventions of redemption, Christian uplift, and familial assimilation, so too did the law

43. The moral and economic webs established through compadrazgo relations in New Mexico remain underexamined. The best local study to date is Frances Leon Quintana, *Pobladores: Hispanic Americans of the Ute Frontier* (Aztec, N.Mex., 1991). Quintana notes a carryover of the Old World endogamous functions of the institution among New Mexican elites but also sees a New World system that "helped to stabilize relations between native Indian populations and Spanish and mestizo groups" (206–210, esp. 207). Sandra Jaramillo Macias has traced nineteenth-century compadrazgo webs in the Taos area; see "Bound by Family: Women and Cultural Change in Territorial Taos," paper presented at the Carson Foundation, Taos, N.Mex., July 30, 1994; baptismal data from Brugge, *Navajos in the Catholic Church Records,* table 9, 114–115; Sarah Garcia, "The Navajos," interview with Lester Raines, Aug. 31, 1936, in Works Progress Administration Federal Writer's Project Files (hereafter cited as WPA), file 5, drawer 5, folio 50, no. 26, Museum of New Mexico, Santa Fe.

44. Brugge, *Navajos in the Catholic Church Records,* 116–117.

in New Mexico function in contradictory ways. In some of the few cases that survive, Indian captives appear as alienable or inheritable property, as dowry wealth given at marriage, or as marital property contested in acrimonious divorces. In 1739, for instance, Manuel Saenz de Garvisu purchased a house and eleven varas of land in Santa Fe from the master tailor José García, adding "an Indian woman" to the fifty pesos in specie he paid. Nearly fifty years later, José Francisco Montoya would do the same with a Navajo woman, as did María Rufina Salazar offer a Navajo servant to Santiago Salazar in 1842. In 1844, María Antonia Espinosa took José Antonio Manzanares to court over contested ownership of some farming land near Los Ojtos and his claim to ownership of a Navajo servant woman. The estate of Francisco Romero of Taos, settled January 10, 1765, unabashedly included five Indian servant women and their eight mixed-blood children. Other wills, however, reveal occasions when both freedom and alienable property were settled upon criadas in the events of marriage or the deaths of their owners. In 1750, María de la Candelaria Gonzales emancipated her Indian servant woman on the condition that she "watch over and assist my daughter as if she were her mother." A modest emancipation, perhaps, but one that might well have been comprehensible to all parties who understood the obligatory nexus of kinship. The same woman would revise her will in 1757 to stipulate also that her daughter Marcela Antonia receive a "young Indian called Acensio Antonio" to be raised as her criado, which suggests a complex intergenerational, matrilineal system of guardianship and caretaking. The mother re-created for her daughter a servant to serve her and to care for her own daughter. Thus the obligations of kinship and the bonds of dependency found conflicted resolution in one family. Suspended somewhere between the status of patrimony and property, Indian slaves in New Mexico were simultaneously exploited and cherished, even within the same household.[45]

45. Testamento of Maria de la Candelaria Gonzales, dated 1750, *SANM,* I, no. 344, roll 2, frames 765–769, 890–893. For Indians as property, see the will of Miguel Archiveque, Aug. 14, 1727, in *SANM,* I, no. 17, roll 1, frames 183–189; conveyance of house and land from José García to Manuel Saenz de Garvisu, Sept. 26, 1739, in *SANM,* I, no. 330, roll 2, frames 736–738; inventory and settlement of estate of Antonio Durán y Armijo, in *SANM,* I, no. 240, roll 8, frame 618; likewise for the estate of Francisco Romero of Taos settled Jan. 10, 1765, *SANM,* I, no. 781, roll 4, frame 1175; conveyance of land from Cristobal Archuleta and Juan José Beita to Jose Francisco Montoya, Oct. 15, 1784, in "Land Conveyances," Borrego-Ortega Family Papers, New Mexico State Records Center. For the Mexican Period, see letter of con-

As their numbers soared after 1820, enslaved Navajos contributed to subtle cultural hybridization in New Mexican households and villages. Using distinctively Navajo upright looms (rather than colonial horizontal harness looms), captive Navajo women weavers produced "slave blankets" that utilized Mexican dyes and incorporated Mexican diamond motifs into their traditional techniques. Contemporaries admired and valued the watertight weft of Navajo serapes, and the slave blankets were doubtless of similar quality. In some cases, Navajo slave weavers might have disguised the sacred weaving convention of the spirit line—an intentional flaw introduced so as not to offend Spider-woman, who gave the arts of weaving to the Navajos—by including "lazy lines" that created a diagonal line of interruptions between the new design motifs. Although baptized and instructed in the Holy Faith, some Indian slaves appeared to sustain spiritual traditions from their natal societies.[46]

A window into other roles for Indian slaves in the households of the New Mexican mercantile families may be heard in the memories of Guadalupe Martínez, an orphan adopted into the Santa Fe kindred of José Chávez, one of the most prominent exporters in the region. She recounted the anticipation and hard labor that attended the departure of a cordón to Mexico:

> For weeks before the trip, the household was all action and bustle. Bales of goods arrived from various parts of the province and were piled high in the storerooms to await the day when they would be loaded on mule or burro for the long and dangerous journey across the Journada del Muerto. . . .

---

veyance dated June 19, 1844, in Silvanio Salazar Papers, New Mexico State Records Center, in which land was transferred for one Indian woman valued at one hundred pesos; *María Antonia Espinosa v José Antonia Manzanares,* Feb. 22, 1844, in Maria Duran collection, New Mexico State Records Center. For the American Period, see *Juan Pablo Apodaca v Manuela Chaves,* District Court Records, Valencia County, Civil Cases, no. 329 (1861); *Mariano Yrrisarri v Francisco Montoya et uxor,* District Court Records, Bernalillo County, Civil Cases, no. 259, 262 (1861, 1862); *Manuel Yrrisarri v Vicenta Arranda,* District Court Cases, Bernalillo County, Civil Cases, no. 302 (1864). For another example of property settled on a criada, see the testamento of don Santiago Roibal, 1762, granting his criada title to a parcel of land for "service without salary" (fragment in the New Mexico State Records Center, Land Grant Records); and José Riano's contestation of Gregoria Gongora's will in 1739, in which he exempted "a piece of land for the *india* who raised my youngest and other children," in *SANM,* II, no. 427, roll 7, frames 1023–1025.

46. H. P. Mera, *The "Slave Blanket"* (Santa Fe, N.Mex., 1938); Kathy Whitaker, personal communication, Nov. 18, 2000.

> A large number of servants was necessary to the smooth management of so large a household; many of these were Indian slaves bought outright by Don José or acquired through barter. They engaged in domestic duties under the watchful eyes of the mistress. Some of the servants worked in the fields, some tended stock, those working out of doors being supervised by a trusted *majordomo* who managed the estate while the master was away.[47]

Weavers, domestics, shepherds, and agricultural laborers, Indian slaves fulfilled the wide range of occupational categories necessary for an economy moving into the capitalist world. But large, multislave households such as Chávez's were rare in nineteenth-century New Mexico. By far the largest proportion of slaveholding families (75 percent) held only one Indian slave, and fully 89 percent held no more than two. And, although now virtually impossible to recover from census returns, after 1821 no "slaves" were so designated in Mexican enumerations, for the Mexican Constitution of 1824 abolished slavery and a general emancipation was declared in 1829. But law and custom did not coincide in New Mexico. If the eighteenth-century pattern persisted, most of these households were dispersed in the smaller villages on the outskirts of the settled territory. There, it seems, they continued in the role of coerced cultural mediators, much as had their genízaro counterparts in the earlier era.[48]

As had been the case with Juana Hurtado Galván in the eighteenth century, residence of Navajo kinspeople in outlying New Mexican and Pueblo villages provided linguistic and cultural facilitators for trading visits that satisfied the needs of economic exchange while remaining fraught with danger, given the tensions that underlay such fragile symbiosis. On trading days Navajos bartered woolen blankets and sashes, buckskins, and baskets in return for iron hoes, knives, brass tack fittings, and bread. But these direct exchanges took place in a larger atmosphere of competitive sociability, especially between young men who sponsored horse races upon which both real goods and personal honor were wagered. These events substantiated the intimacy of every-

47. "Tia Lupe," WPA Oral History Files, Unpublished Manuscripts no. 20, New Mexico State Records Center.

48. For these data, see Brugge, *Navajos in the Catholic Church Records,* tables 13, 14, 15 at 122, discussion at 121–124. Since his figures collapse all of the nineteenth century into a synchronic snapshot, they do not reflect what might have been changes in household composition over time. But since only ten households at any point in the nineteenth century held more than six Indian slaves, it seems reasonable to extend his figures as a general pattern. See app. A, "Households with Six or More Captives," 167–169.

day cross-cultural contacts. Fine horses, expert horsemanship, and risk taking were mutually appreciated as well as threatening. In 1818, for example, an unpaid gambling debt between local Navajos and village residents provoked violence at Cebolleta, an event unusual only in its ending in bloodshed. In its aftermath one Cebolletaño lay dead and three wounded, and two sons of the Navajo headman Vicente had fled to the backcountry to avoid revenge.[49]

Violent exchanges were more enduring when they took the form of mutual captures and enslavements, yet even then they could promote commerce and competition. Navajo boys held captive in New Mexican villages sometimes served as guides for both trading and raiding expeditions into Navajo country. Cebolletaños had an especially favored captive, raised from boyhood and named Kico, who guided their sojourns and forays into those hinterlands, where his knowledge of landscape proved even more valuable than his language skills. By the nineteenth century, Navajo had become something of a lingua franca in the borderlands, used by New Mexicans and Pueblos alike. New Mexicans would become even more deeply bound to their Navajo neighbors in the coming decades, whether by the imperatives of commerce or the coercion of borderland kinship.[50]

One Does Not Force the Horse to Run

Navajos also took captives from New Mexican and Pueblo villages and neighboring Indian groups, and in so doing they enmeshed themselves in larger exchanges of commerce, culture, and violence. Whereas New Mexicans seized more than one thousand Navajos over the course of the nineteenth century, however, Navajos reciprocated in much smaller numbers, probably fewer than

49. See earlier the case of Juana Hurtado Galván, taken captive by Navajos in 1680 and redeemed in 1696, above; see also *SANM,* II, no. 367, roll 6, frames 1010–1023. Her case, and others illustrating close trade links through kinship, are discussed in Frances Swadesh, "The Structure of Hispanic-Indian Relations in New Mexico," in Kutsche, ed., *Survival of Spanish-American Villages,* 53–61. For Navajo trading, see W. W. Hill, "Navaho Trading and Trading Ritual: A Study of Cultural Dynamics," *Southwestern Journal of Anthropology,* IV (1948), 371–396; Allande to Governor Vergara, June 25, 1818, in *SANM,* II, no. 2727, roll 19, frames 145–148.

50. See C. C. Marino, "The Seboyetanos and the Navahos," *NMHR,* XXIX (January 1954), 8–27. Ruth Underhill claims that Navajo was used both at Zuñi and the Hopi pueblos as the language of diplomacy *(The Navajos* [Norman, Okla., 1956], 65).

one hundred. But other Indian groups, especially Apaches to the south and Utes and Paiutes to the north, seem to have lost many more to Navajo raiders. By the late nineteenth century, the Navajo term for Paiute *(báyodžīn)* had become synonymous with "slave." Navajos also purchased slaves from other Indian groups like Chiricahua Apaches, Yaquis, and Mayos, whose victims included Mexicans from Sonora. Yet, as was the case in New Mexico, slavery within Navajo society took many forms, ranging from the full kinship assimilation of yisná' through customs of adoption to a harsher form, developing across the first half of the nineteenth century, that might have set slaves apart from Navajo society almost completely.[51]

As they had for the eighteenth century, in the 1930s, Navajo oral historians recalled the expanding spheres of retribution in which their predecessors were engaged as the nineteenth century commenced. After describing how the poorer Navajo outfits in Cañon de Chelly lost their "pretty" women, and thereby privilege within the marriage economy, to better-mounted and -armed kinsmen whose livestock grazed the plateaus, these Navajos added,

> For revenge, the Canyon people would raid. First they raided the Pueblos, then the Ute, and finally the Mexicans. This drew attention to the Navajo, and raids in retaliation were sent into the Navajo country. As the Canyon people were safe in their protected location, the Navajo on the outside were forced to suffer under these attacks.[52]

Documentary evidence supports the sequence of expansion recalled in Navajo memory. Of fifty-three Navajo livestock and captive raids evident in Spanish and Mexican sources between 1800 and 1847, seventeen targeted Pueblo Indian villages like Jémez, Zía, Laguna, San Juan, and Santa Ana, and fifteen of those occurred before 1836. Of the thirty-four raids on Spanish New Mexican settlements and ranchos over the period, fourteen took place in the last decade, when livestock losses exceeded twenty thousand sheep, cattle, mules, and horses. The growing wealth of New Mexican sheep ricos was a strong attraction for Navajo ladrones. When captives were mentioned, fifteen

51. The fullest treatment to date of Navajo slavery may be found in Brugge, *Navajos in the Catholic Church Records,* chap. 4, 127–144; for synonymy between báyodžīn, Paiute, and slave, see Franciscan Fathers, *Ethnologic Dictionary,* 438.

52. Hill, "Navaho Warfare," *Yale University Publications in Anthropology,* no. 5 (1936), 3–26, esp. 3; based on interviews with Curley of Chinlé, Roan Horse of Crystal, and Son of the Late Smith, of Fort Defiance (1933).

were taken from New Mexicans, two from Pueblos, and ten from Apaches. Given later estimates of *binaalté* among the Navajos, many captive raids, especially against Utes and Paiutes, never found mention in Euramerican sources.[53]

Doubtless unwilling to provoke cycles of revenge with their more powerful kinsmen, raiding bands looked beyond wealthy Navajo outfits for retribution and expanded their raids to strike distant Indian groups for captives and New Mexican villages for sheep, horses, mules, and captive women and children. Since Utes and Mexicans often failed to recognize the particular derivation and limited goals of these raiding groups, they in turn targeted Navajos in general for revenge. By extending their raiding economy to Pueblos, Apaches, Utes, and Mexicans, the poor men of the canyons and indigent dependents of ricos took a circuitous route into marriage and adulthood, their situational response to a Navajo society in which wealthy men were gradually acquiring control over access to most marriageable women.[54]

One means that men from the livestock-poor outfits of the canyons or younger sons of ricos eager for advancement employed to acquire the wealth that would buy them brides came through the acquisition of horses, mules, sheep, and captives. Horses were the ultimate masculine prestige item and the favored currency of bride-price. This could range from a minimum of one or two animals to a maximum of fifteen, although to exceed twelve was thought to court bad luck, probably in the form of witchcraft accusations against either the bride's family or that of the groom for engaging in ostentatious displays of wealth. Bride-price correlated with the wealth of the bride's family, since the groom would gain the subsidiary benefit of his wife's sheep flocks once he joined her in matrilocal residence. A family or clan rich in marriageable young women, therefore, could elevate its cultural value by increasing the size of its sheep flocks. Stolen sheep were integrated into the matrilineally managed flocks of the clan, available for wedding feasts and marriage gifts when opportunity arose. Young upwardly aspiring men might also capture Apache, Ute, Paiute, or Spanish New Mexican girls and adopt them into their maternal Navajo clans, thereby increasing the pool of potential brides. The young male captives they seized could be sold to ricos as dependent herders. When the American adventurer Albert Pike rode on campaign with Governor José Antonio Vizcarra in 1823, he noted that Navajo "great men have a number of

53. See Appendix A, below.

54. See Gary Witherspoon, *Navajo Kinship and Marriage* (Chicago, 1975), 23–28, for customary bridewealth exogamy.

servants under them" that they used to herd "vast flocks of sheep and large herds of horses." These great men could pay for their binaalté with horses or other livestock, thereby awarding young captors the cultural currency with which to enter the marriage market.[55]

Slavery in nineteenth-century Navajo society seems no less complicated than the institution in New Mexico. As was the case in Spanish households and villages, few firm lines delineated the semiservile or dependent categories of kinship and quasi kinship from the harsher condition of the slave, nor did time or circumstance prohibit mobility between statuses. Navajos themselves could disagree over just what range in status the term "naalté" could embrace. Some felt it included both poor Navajo dependents who labored for "a rich man" in return for a share of the flocks or herds and "war prisoners captured by the People . . . and used as slaves." Others claimed a distinction between naalté as "a person captured in war and brought home to work" without compensation and *na'nil,* or servants who received some payments in kind. The latter term might have applied to Paiute children whom their parents sold to Navajo ricos in exchanges reminiscent of the pawnship relation between Comanches and Shoshones noted earlier. Neither term seemed to apply to an additional semiservile category, that of kinspeople who helped "their kinsmen herd sheep and other work," for they were "members of the family." Still, agreement held in the matter that "when Navajos had slaves, the slaves changed hands just like the Negroes did in the South. They were bought and sold by the bosses of the slaves."[56]

55. Alternatively, Navajos later claimed that "the price of a slave was a set of beads, a mountain lion skin, and 'a few other things.'" This may reflect a transaction between men, outside the marriage economy, in the context of warfare. See Hill, "Navaho Warfare," *Yale University Publications in Anthropology,* no. 5 (1936), 14–16, esp. 16. For the Navajo bride-price system and marriage economy, see David F. Aberle, "Navaho," in David Schneider and Kathleen Gough, eds., *Matrilineal Kinship* (Berkeley, Calif., 1961), 96–201, esp. 123–128. Aberle notes that what few cases of adoption ethnographically exist involved "non-Navajo slaves or the children of non-Navajo female slaves"; such unions provided these slaves "with a clan affiliation," the primary benefit of which was to sanction their marriageability in Navajo society (110); see also Albert Pike, *Prose Sketches and Poems, Written in the Western Country* (Boston, 1834), 145.

56. This philological debate took place sometime in 1963, between the renowned Blessingway singer Frank Mitchell (b. 1881) and his classificatory "brother," Albert G. (Chic) Sandoval, Sr., while Sandoval was assisting Wesleyan University graduate student Charlotte I. Johnson in the translation of Mitchell's twelve-hour unmediated life story. Speaking apparently from within his own lifetime experience, Mitchell mentioned the experience of Hastiin

Despite accord among older Navajos around the existence of slavery, historical linguists argue that Navajo semantics suggest a fairly recent development of the category. The Navajo language barely acknowledges the possibility of coercion between agents and animate objects, reflected most obviously in the depth of respect for autonomy in Navajo culture. Nineteenth-century Navajo treaty makers were adamant that they could not force their kinspeople or other clans to abide by a treaty's provisions. As one linguist has explained, a Navajo "does not *make* the horse run, trot, or gallop, because the horse has a will of its own. He may trot *against his will,* at the direction of a person . . . but he still had the freedom of choice to decline or refuse to trot." Linguistic evidence suggests that the concept of "force," extended to slavery, emerged late in Navajo society and even then a slave's compliance might have lain with the security, respect, distance from safety, and affective ties she or he felt for a captor.[57]

Language does seem to have been potent in determining the fate of war captives. Even if seized in a raid and carrying the initial designation of yisná', captives could move among various conditions of servitude. If a warrior addressed his captive by the proper kinship term, thereby effecting an in-the-field adoption, the 1930s Navajo informants said that the

> prisoner was recognized as one of the tribe and no distinctions were made between him and other Navajo. However, if the adoption did not take place immediately, the status of the captive was that of a slave. Some slaves, because of their accomplishments, were more highly thought of than others. If the captor was well-to-do he kept his prisoners; otherwise he sold them to some rich man.[58]

Ch'o, who "was a slave of a man over here. Another man went and bought him, and then he was his slave. When that second boss passed away, why that slave was free. Nobody else claimed him, so he went on his own then." See Charlotte J. Frisbie and David P. McAllester, eds., *Navajo Blessingway Singer: The Autobiography of Frank Mitchell, 1881–1967* (Tucson, Ariz., 1978), 160 n. 12; for Paiute pawning, see transcripts of interviews held in the Doris Duke Oral History Collections, Special Collections, University of Utah, esp. nos. 672, 682, 684, 686, cited in Robert S. McPherson, *The Northern Navajo Frontier, 1860–1900: Expansion through Adversity* (Albuquerque, N.Mex., 1988), 11, 99 n. 26.

57. Discussion in Brugge, *Navajos in the Catholic Church Records,* 129–132, citing Robert W. Young and William Morgan, *The Navajo Language* (Salt Lake City, Utah, 1962), 507–510.

58. Hill, "Navaho Warfare," *Yale University Publications in Anthropology,* no. 5 (1936), 16.

For those slaves lacking in accomplishment, life could be harsh indeed. The Franciscan fathers who proselytized among the Navajos and produced the first ethnological dictionary of the Navajo language claimed that owners forced slaves to work at agricultural labor, to herd livestock, and to do "everything arduous." Hoeing, weeding, irrigating, and harvesting were especially shunned by prominent men and therefore "assigned to captive slaves" so that their owners could engage in "some noble raid or in complete inactivity," the Franciscans asserted. Slaves purportedly could be sold at the owner's will, put to death in blood compensation, or sacrificed upon an owner's death. Although only one case of blood compensation is known through documentary sources, on some occasions slaves were considered dispensable when sent as couriers into dangerous negotiations with enemy groups.[59]

Unlike Spanish New Mexicans, who had long made use of captive women as weavers in their obrajes, Navajo custom prohibited teaching non-Navajo captive women to weave. Rather, most captive women served in the fields as laborers, on nearby ranges as sheepherders, or in households as chore wives, activities that in turn freed Navajo women to weave for social prestige or the market. Such exclusive customary taboos, however, might actually have originated only as a consequence of market forces emerging in the late eighteenth and early nineteenth centuries. Retention of sacred knowledge allowed Navajo women to control one important aspect of production and to continue the concentration of wealth within matrilineal outfits. Likewise, excluding captives from sacred knowledge placed restrictions upon their assimilation—although adopted as clan members, and married, they could not achieve complete incorporation. By the nineteenth century, some female binaalté in Navajo society might have begun to serve as social boundary markers, especially those adopted or born into ancillary captive or slave clans, where institutional marginalization solidified in-group identities while retaining for the slave some as-

59. Franciscan Fathers, *Ethnologic Dictionary*, 259, 423–424. It seems likely that slave owners devoted themselves more to defending their families, flocks, and herds from pillagers than to engaging in "noble raids" and that their "inactivity" reflected instead a strong devotion to practicing the sacred ritual cycles of Navajo life, which assured spiritual safety and cultural presitge. The Franciscan Fathers, of course, had strong motivation to portray Navajos as needing social and spiritual uplift, but they remain highly respected authorities on Navajo culture and history. For the 1858 killing of the "Mexican captive who [had] frequently visited the garrison," in reciprocation for the killing of an officer's black slave, see McNitt, *Navajo Wars*, 335–336, and Chapter 8, below.

similative benefits of kinship. The Enemyway ceremonial complex maintained boundaries and built cohesion by driving ghosts of *ana'i* (non-Navajos, or "enemies") from their victims. The centrality of alienness to this ritual suggests that the everyday existence of outsiders within Navajo society could actually cement social solidarity.[60]

On the other hand, as commercial integration increased the size of sheep flocks, the vast desert ranges over which they foraged, and the need for male shepherds—especially New Mexican or Mexican boys already trained to the task—the naalté experience diverged. Male captives could hold personal property like livestock and marry, although whether with Navajo women or other slave women is not always clear. José Ignacio Anañe, seized as a boy from his home village of Tucklatoe (Tecolote?) in 1832, had become "the fortunate possessor of two wives and three children" by the time Americans offered him his

60. According to the Franciscan Fathers, weaving remained the "sacred trust of Navaho women" *(Ethnologic Dictionary,* 423–424). For existence of captive or slave clans, see 424–432, esp. 431–432, where the twentieth-century existence of exogamous taboos between captor and captive clans is discussed. Aberle also notes the presence of " 'slave' clans" descended from captives ("Navaho," in Schneider and Gough, eds., *Matrilineal Kinship,* 110–111). For ways in which the Enemyway (which he prefers to call the Alienway) worked to foster "combinations of kinship and nonkinship solidarity," see Witherspoon, *Navajo Kinship and Marriage,* 56–64, esp. 58. While underpinning Navajo identity, the concentration of weaving knowledge and power in women's hands probably helped to maintain the relatively egalitarian nature of Navajo gender relations, as compared to areas like the Southeast, where the deerskin trade among the Creek and Choctaw seems to have undercut the gender division of labor, and the Great Plains, where the hide trade produced similar erosion. See Kathryn E. Holland Braund, *Deerskins and Duffels: The Creek Indian Trade with Anglo-America, 1685–1815* (Norman, Okla., 1993); Richard White, *The Roots of Dependency: Subsistence, Environment, and Social Change among the Choctaws, Pawnees, and Navajos* (Lincoln, Nebr., 1983), 96–146; Alan M. Klein, "The Political Economy of Gender: A Nineteenth Century Plains Indian Case Study," in Patricia Albers and Beatrice Medicine, eds., *The Hidden Half: Studies of Plains Indian Women* (Boston, Mass., 1983), 143–174. An example of domestic slavery as a boundary-marking institution may be seen in James H. Vaughan's treatment of *mafakur* slavery among the Margi of northeastern Nigeria. Of this, Vaughan contends that "the outstanding general characteristic of mafakur is that all mafa, without regard to political position, private influence, or wealth, hold in common a status that in structural terms is fundamentally and irrevocably intermediate with regard to membership in Margi society" (emphasis removed). See "Mafakur: A Limbic Institution of the Margi," in Suzanne Miers and Igor Kopytoff, eds., *Slavery in Africa: Historical and Anthropological Perspectives* (Madison, Wisc., 1977), 85–102, esp. 100.

freedom in 1849. But he also "belonged to" the headman Waro (Guerro?), who had originally purchased him from his captors. Anañe preferred "most decidedly to remain with the Navajos, notwithstanding his peonage." Jesus Arviso, a Mexican captive from Sonora and property of the headman Tl'a (Lefthand), married one unnamed Navajo woman and later her sister Yohazbaa' under the Navajo levirate. Other slave men could acquire sacred knowledge, as in the case of Nakai Na'dis Saal, who became a Nightway Singer. Some gained political influence, like Juan Annagri (Anañe), a slave of the wealthy headman Herrera but "a shrewd, intelligent man" who "exercised more influence over the principal chiefs . . . than any other person in the country." Juan's captive brother Terribio was said also to have profound sway over Herrera. Yet other male captives encountered harsher fates, like Manuel Lucira (Lucero?), who was taken from Del Mansina (Manzano?) in 1847 at age twelve and was "sold several times and badly treated, by flogging." Although evidence is thin, as commercial interests and cultural power came to predominate in livestock management among some wealthier Navajos, the institution of Navajo slavery shaded toward more severe treatment and social differentiation, especially in regard to a slave's gender, age, and willingness to assimilate to the social positions that remained available.[61]

Numerical estimates of slaves held in Navajo society prove no easier to arrive at than full comprehension of the institution itself. In 1882, twenty years after the deaths, destruction, and dispersals of the Long Walk era, Navajo agent Dennis Riordan claimed that even then there existed "300 slaves in the hands of the tribe," who derived from Utes, Comanches, Apaches, Hopis, Pueblos, and (New) Mexicans. An additional twenty he had recently set free. One might suppose that the terrible war years of 1860 to 1868 might have reduced substantially the number of slaves held by Navajos, but strong evidence exists that most of the wealthy headmen managed to escape much of the violence and remain with their outfits far to the west in Monument Valley and northward across the San Juan River. Afterward, in 1868, they returned to regain their social prominence and prosperity. When one of these, the wealthy headman Hashkeneinii, died in 1909, he still held thirty-two Ute binaalté whom Navajos felt then belonged to the person who divided his estate, Louisa Wetherill,

61. For the cases of Anañe, Lucero, and others, see Calhoun to Brown, Oct. 1, 1849, in Annie Heloise Abel, ed., *The Official Correspondence of James S. Calhoun, while Indian Agent in Santa Fé and Superintendent of Indian Affairs in New Mexico* . . . (Washington, D.C., 1915), 29–30; for Nakai Na'dis Saal and Arviso, see Brugge, *Navajos in the Catholic Church*, 134–139.

widow of the American trader Richard Wetherill and adoptive daughter of Hashkeneinii.[62]

Slaveholding was much less dispersed among Navajos than among New Mexicans. Only wealthy headmen, able to purchase binaalté and support them as dependents, held slaves in any numbers or at all. Since outfits with such wealth numbered ten at the beginning of the century (drawing upon Cordero's ten rancherías of 1796) and at least thirteen by midcentury, one may propose that these constituted the slaveholding class among that nation. Various Americans observed at that time that these ricos held "peons or slaves, just as they have in the South, except that they are Indians" and that a headman could hold forty to fifty dependent peons in his ranchería. Overall, one ethnohistorian estimates that midcentury Navajo ricos held flocks and herds capable of supporting—and necessitating the labor of—three to five dependent households of five members each (whether indigent Navajos or slaves), or a maximum of twenty-five dependents. A total slave population among nineteenth-century Navajos likely existed in a range of three hundred to five hundred individuals, or a maximum of 5 percent of a total population of ten thousand people. But, within wealthy outfits numbering some twenty households and one hundred people, slaves might compose as much as 38 percent of the residents of a given ranchería.[63]

62. Riordan quoted in Brugge, *Navajos in the Catholic Church Records,* 142; for the success of fugitive ricos in escaping internment at Bosque Redondo, see McPherson, *Northern Navajo Frontier,* 9–10; for Hashkeneinii and Wetherill, see McPherson, 137, 140, and further discussion in Chapter 8, below.

63. In 1860, at the outbreak of the Navajo war that culminated in the Long Walk, there were thirteen wealthy headmen known to favor peace with the Americans but unable to control young or poor raiders (McNitt, *Navajo Wars,* 411). For quote, see "Samuel Yost to Editor of the *Santa Fe Weekly Gazette,* Oct. 2 1858," reprinted in J. Lee Correll, comp. and ed., *Through White Men's Eyes: A Contribution to Navajo History: A Chronological Record of the Navajo People from Earliest Times to the Treaty of June 1, 1868* (Window Rock, Ariz., 1979), II, 152. For peon numbers, see "The Arrival of Captain Dodge," *Santa Fe Weekly Gazette,* Dec. 31, 1853, microfilm in New Mexico State Records Center. For estimates of class composition of Navajo rancherías in 1850, see Kelley, "Navajo Political Economy," in Cordell and Beckerman, eds., *Versatility of Kinship,* esp. 321–327. For emergence of the "lavish giveaways" of the Blessingway Ceremony as an element of ricos' hegemonic practice to maintain social influence (and control over rangelands), see Brugge, *Navajo Pottery and Ethnohistory* (Window Rock, Ariz., 1963), esp. 22; Brugge, "Navajo Land Usage: A Study in Progressive Diversification," in Clark S. Knowlton, ed., *Indian and Spanish-American Adjustments to*

Despite the narrow distribution of slaveholding within Navajo society, rico headmen exerted extensive cultural influence as purchasers of captives and stolen livestock and as distributors of gifts and dispensers of women in the marriage economy. In order to gain access to that economy, many more Navajos had an implicit interest in the captive and livestock raiding economy than might ever aspire to be wealthy slaveholders and sheepmen themselves. This cultural investment in the Navajo institution passed back and forth across cultural barriers to stitch Navajos and New Mexicans into a wider weave of violence and social inequality.

Their Capture Bore Rich Fruit

However many pastoral slaves Navajo great men accrued within the Navajo captive exchange economy, New Mexicans reciprocated by seizing even more in their own slave raids. Vizcarra's campaigns of 1823 to 1825 yielded the greatest number of involuntary baptisms of any years on record: at least 199 Navajo women and children entered New Mexican systems of bondage during those two years alone. The 1820s would inaugurate a ferocious expansion in the New Mexican slave trade that would last until the defeat of the Navajos in 1864, but it was an expansion that would be nearly matched by the avidity with which poor and upwardly aspiring Navajo raiders took to raiding New Mexico for livestock and captives themselves. Speaking of these ladrones, whose actions they explicitly distinguished from tribal warfare, Navajos made clear the economic intent. Navajo livestock and captive raiders "never burned the villages, and always left enough sheep behind that the flocks would be good again the next year." Even the sacred ritual preparations for raids, the Blessingway, Bear Way, Big Snake Way, and Frog Way, were the same as those Navajos employed in preparing to trade with Pueblos, Mexicans, and other Indian groups. The intercultural violence of the pastoral borderlands was, until the 1860s, a matter of seizing and redistributing pastoral resources and hence must be viewed from within that larger political economy.[64]

Arid and Semi-arid Environments (Lubbock, Tex., 1964), 16–25. For a survey of changing American perceptions of Navajos, which swung from admiration of their wealth to criticism of their plundering ways by 1860, see William H. Lyon, "The Navajos in the Anglo-American Historical Imagination, 1807–1870," *Ethnohistory,* XLIII, no. 3 (Summer 1996), 483–509.

64. Brugge, "Vizcarra's Navajo Campaign of 1823," *Arizona and the West,* VI (Autumn 1964), 223–244; Brugge notes that only two of those baptisms hold any hints of voluntary

As the nineteenth century progressed, there arose several groups whose actions knitted Navajos and New Mexicans in ever tighter relations of conflict and exchange, groups whose genesis derived from pressures inherent in intra-societal social and generational inequality. The first, the ladrones, combined rico dependents and poor Navajos in raiding bands that struck Pueblo and New Mexican villages for sheep, horses, mules, and captives. Another were the Diné Ana'aii, who increasingly came to prey upon their own kinspeople. Finally, poor New Mexicans, landless and with little chance for upward mobility, found sustenance in raiding livestock and maintaining a slave-exchange economy that could flourish only in close association with that of the Navajo pillagers.

The "Enemy Navajo" under mixed-blood headmen Francisco Baca and Cebolla Sandoval (from his Navajo name Haastin Tlth'ohchin, or "Onion") maintained outfits in the Río Puerco region and formed close relations, both economically and culturally, with the valley's New Mexican settlers. Serving as guides for New Mexican military expeditions, and often acting as autonomous raiders themselves, the Diné Ana'aii functioned as pivots in the borderland economy. Their allegiance to New Mexico increased across the 1830s, as an export market for Navajo serapes developed in northern Mexico. Antonio Barreiro reiterated don Pedro Pino's optimistic 1812 assessment of friendly Navajos' commercial inclinations in 1832, and few cargas left Santa Fe for Chihuahua and points south in the decades of the 1830s and 1840s that did not contain some dozens of *serapes navajoses* that sold for fifty to sixty pesos in Mexican markets. These textiles, reported Gregg, who plied the St. Louis to Chihuahua routes after 1824, were "of so close and dense a texture that [they] will frequently hold water . . . [and are] therefore highly prized for protection against the rains."[65]

Still, reciprocal retribution in captive raiding fed the pervasive insecurity and anger in the borderlands. One would think, as did many Spanish, Mexican, American, and "peaceful" Navajo leaders, that truces that included captive re-

---

conversion. See also Hill, "Navaho Warfare," *Yale University Publications in Anthropology*, no. 5 (1936), esp. 6, 16; for trading Ways, see Hill, "Navaho Trading and Trading Ritual," *Southwestern Journal of Anthropology*, IV, no. 4 (Winter 1948), 371–396, esp. 382–387; Underhill, *Navajos*, 68–72, esp. 71.

65. For Cebolla Sandoval, see McNitt, *Navajo Wars*, 72 n. 10, and Diné Ana'aii in app. B, 434–435; "The *Ojeada* of Lic. Antonio Barreiro in 1832," in Pino, *Three New Mexico Chronicles*, trans. and ed. Carroll and Haggard, 133; Gregg, *Commerce of the Prairies*, ed. Quaife, 199.

patriation would resolve this anxiety. But social and economic inequalities in both Navajo and New Mexican society made this difficult. Military conflict proved the quickest means for social marginals to compete for and acquire wealth. Frequent skirmishes in the region, which, at first glance, seem mutually destructive, actually fostered socioeconomic expansion among certain marginal groups. One facet of this dynamic derived from the role of New Mexican villagers in the defense of the province.

Because New Mexico seldom had more than one hundred professional troops assigned to the presidio in Santa Fe, day-to-day defense largely depended on *milicias activas.* But the financial troubles besetting Bourbon New Spain and, later, independent Mexico never allowed for the payment of these local militias, which were required to furnish their own mounts, arms, and ammunition for standard forty-five-day campaigns. This requirement provoked much pain and resentment among militia men and their families. In 1812, don Pedro Pino reported that the "liberty of the children is sacrificed in order to fulfill the obligations of citizenship" when men sold their children into peonage to obtain horses and weaponry or when, in the field, they left their families at the mercy of Indian captive raiders. Militia men's only means of compensation lay in receiving spoils of war—livestock and captives. Before 1821, local custom allowed for the equal distribution of captured livestock within the war band, with women and children going to the individual captors. Although Mexican reforms sought to regularize this practice by making booty the responsibility of commanders, militia commanders generally continued customary divisions of spoils, after retaining the best prizes for themselves. Still, the poor bore the burden of frontier defense. In 1834, village civil militias totaled nine hundred men, "badly armed, poorly equipped, and without instructions in handling arms." Governor Francisco Sarracino berated wealthy New Mexicans that year for leaving provincial military affairs "in the hands of the impoverished class," from which he thought no good could come. Implicit in his warning was the fact that volunteers stood a good chance of adding to personal wealth in a victorious campaign. For example, an 1839 autumn campaign by combined militias from Cebolleta and Abiquiu netted 9,253 sheep, 222 horses and mules, 7 Navajo captives, and the redemption of 1 Mexican captive. The eighty-four volunteers received the livestock in equal parts, while their four captains shared the "prisoneros." When field commanders were less scrupulous, they and their men might engage in on-the-spot bartering over stolen livestock with Apaches and Navajos they encountered in their campaigns. Since the sheep, horses, and mules were the property of wealthy Navajos or New Mexican ricos, poor Indians and New Mexicans occasionally cut their own deals for blankets, leather goods, steel tools, and captives when out of their superiors' sight.[66]

Armed with old *escopetas* (muskets), lances, bows and arrows, and small shields termed *chimales,* the border militias entered Navajo country under the skilled guidance of captive Navajo boys like Kico. Oral tradition supports the centrality of captive raiding in these ventures, "one of the greatest rewards of a campaign." "If the captives were of average age, or young and could be domesticated and taught, then their capture bore rich fruit," either by getting resold to ricos in the valley or by adding to the prestige to their owners as house servants.[67]

Folk memory from Cubero and Cebolleta recalled significant differences in identity between the *nacajalleses* (as Navajos termed New Mexican raiders, Hispanicizing the Navajo ethnonym *Nakai)* of the border villages and those they termed the *gente del río,* or river men, who proved timid and unskilled in border raids. Primarily pastoralists, rather than farmers, nacajalleses mirrored more closely their Indian neighbors than the sedentary farmers of the Río Grande. Eschewing the social hierarchies of class and deference so prominent among the river men, they instead conferred authority in raids on famous warriors like Redondo Gallegos, "feared by the Navajos on account of his extraordinary strength."[68]

66. For a description of the milicias in the late colonial period, see Pino, *Exposicion sucinta y sencilla de la provincia del Nuevo Mexico . . .* (1812), rpt. in Pino, *Three New Mexico Chronicles,* trans. and ed. Carroll and Haggard, 67. In Spanish, Pino's full statement was, "Llega, para decirlo de una vez, á tal extremo este mal que hasta la libertad de los hijos es sacrificada para cumplir con aquella obligacion como vecino" (16 of the Cádiz edition). See also Quintana, *Pobladores,* 55–56. Militia numbers and quality from Santiago Abreú to Ministero de Guerra y Marina, Mar. 14, 1834, *MANM,* roll 14, frame 690; Sarracino quoted in Weber, *Mexican Frontier,* 117. For the 1839 campaign, see "Noticia al público, por disposición del exelentísmo sr. gobernador y comandante general deste departmento de Nuevo Mexico, diciembre 16, 1839," Huntington Library, San Marino, Calif. For a circular condemning the "grave evil" suffered by the province because of the traffic in stolen stock that New Mexicans maintained with Apache and Navajo ladrones in the Socorro, Cebolleta, and Jémez regions, see "José María Oritz, Juez de Paz de San Ildefonso á Manuel Armijo, febrero 22, 1843," Sender Collection, no. 282, roll 2, frames 533–535, New Mexico State Records Center.

67. Marino, "Seboyetanos and the Navahos," *NMHR,* XXIX (January 1954), 8–27, esp. 11, 13.

68. Ibid., 10.

Although these militia units ostensibly stood under the authority of Spanish, Mexican, or American governors, in practice they were often self-organized war bands pursuing local goals: settlement expansion, sheep herds, and captives. Since wealthy families like the Armijos, Pereas, and Chavezes had consolidated their hold on the sheep industry in the Río Grande valley by the 1820s, settlers looked beyond the Río Puerco valley for all of those objectives. Allied with members of the Diné Ana'aii, whose kin connections and strategic needs made conditions favorable for New Mexican forays, the nacajalleses pushed their control of grazing lands in a great arc to the west, as far as the borders of Zuñi, Hopi, and Dinetah.[69]

But acquiring sheep to graze on these lands was a problem for New Mexicans short on capital. There were only two options. On the one hand, New Mexican pastores could again try to build flocks through the partido system, by which *partidarios* took responsibility for a flock in return for annual payments of some 20 percent of the lamb and wool crop, with the long-term obligation to return the original number of ewes within three to five years. Since sheep flocks' rate of increase ranges between 10 and 30 percent annually, the partido placed nearly all the speculative burden on the debtor. If all went well, the partidario could create a working flock of his own during this period; but, if disease, bad weather, or Indian raids intervened, he could find himself deeply in debt to his patrón.[70]

The second avenue was quicker but more dangerous. This involved stealing sheep indirectly from ricos by "rescuing" them from neighboring Navajo pastoralists. Because Navajo ladrones built their own flocks through raids, we can see the reciprocal and redistributive nature of the borderland economy taking shape. By the middle decades of the nineteenth century, Navajo flocks probably exceeded 500,000 sheep and goats and several thousand horses, but their ownership was concentrated among the dozen or so rico headmen that dominated the grazing economy and, by extension, access to social recognition. Poor Navajo families and young men aspiring to social prestige through marriage and livestock wealth faced only two choices: attach themselves as dependents to a wealthy headman's outfit or raid the vast flocks of New Mexican ricos.[71]

69. John O. Baxter, *Las Carneradas: Sheep Trade in New Mexico, 1700–1860* (Albuquerque, N.Mex., 1987), 61–110.

70. Ibid, 28–30.

71. For livestock estimates, see Kelley, "Navajo Political Economy," in Cordell and Beckerman, eds., *Versatility of Kinship*, 320–321, n. 6.

New Mexicans might have held as many as three million sheep in the 1830s and 1840s. Of these multitudes, the majority were owned by the cartel of intermarried rico families in the Río Abajo. Although exports, both on the hoof and of woven goods, to Chihuahua and points south constituted much of their market, after 1830 a thriving trade with California developed as well. Returning traders brought some luxury goods like Chinese silks, but the major commerce was in horses and mules—many of which had been illegally acquired from missions and ranchos by Yokuts raiders from the San Joaquín Valley, then sold to New Mexican middlemen. These were poor to middling entrepreneurs who worked on speculation for the ricos of Río Abajo and who often made their homes in Cebolleta, Cubero, and Abiquiu, the departure point for the Old Spanish Trail that linked New Mexico and southern California after 1829. Henceforth, these bordermen became active in expanding the commercial circuits of the local pastoral economy. Operating in the gray area between legal trade and larcenous freebooting, they were viewed as economically crucial yet potentially dangerous by both Mexican and later American authorities.[72]

Navajo raiders took full advantage of these expanding resources and proliferating networks. The number of sheep New Mexicans claimed stolen by Navajo ladrones during the period is truly staggering: nearly 7,000 between 1800 and 1821, some 50,000 between 1821 and 1846, perhaps 200,000 by the end of 1859, and an additional 103,000 by 1864. In parties of four to ten men, Navajo ladrones swept down upon these flocks and ran them back toward the security of their deep canyons. The Navajo term for stealing *(ansh'í)* carries no moral opprobrium in that it is understood more specifically as "appropriating loose property," with its own ritual framework. As economic forays rather

72. New Mexican estimates are found in William M. Denevan, "Livestock Numbers in Nineteenth-Century New Mexico, and the Problem of Gullying in the Southwest," *Annals of the Association of American Geographers* (December 1967), 691–703, esp. 697–699. In the 1830s and 1840s, the six major sheep ricos exported some 200,000 sheep each year to Mexico; some families might have owned as many as 500,000 sheep themselves (Baxter, *Las Carneradas,* 89–110). For the New Mexico–California trade, see Joseph J. Hill, "Spanish and Mexican Exploration and Trade Northwest from New Mexico into the Great Basin, 1765–1853," *Utah Historical Quarterly,* III (1930), 3–23; Hill, "The Old Spanish Trail," *Hispanic American Historical Review,* IV (1921), 444–473; Baxter, *Las Carneradas,* 89. For the Yokuts horse-raiding network, see George Harwood Phillips, *Indians and Intruders in Central California, 1769–1849* (Norman, Okla., 1993). For the lower-order and speculative composition of the caravans, see John Adams Hussey, "The New Mexico–California Caravan of 1847–1848," *NMHR,* XVIII (January 1943), 1–16.

than military expeditions, raids by ladrones were extraordinarily successful in gaining property while avoiding loss of life on both sides: of thirty-nine such actions identifiable in documentary materials, only six involved casualties among the Navajo raiders and perhaps ten among their New Mexican and Pueblo victims.[73]

The activities of Navajo ladrones played perfectly into the needs of border militiamen in Cubero and Cebolleta. Since sheep assimilate easily into new flocks, village men, upon hearing of a Navajo raid in the Río Grande valley, could muster and ride in hot pursuit, ostensibly as a loyal civil militia. If successful in their chase, they might recapture the stolen herd. However, under customary division of spoils, the sheep would not be returned to ricos in the valley but would be divided among the militia members as compensation for their risk. During the twenty-five years of Mexican rule after 1821, New Mexican military expeditions and militia raids claimed to have recaptured 51,688 sheep, 696 cattle and oxen, and 2,034 horses and mules from Navajo ladrones. Although some had certainly been stolen, others probably derived from legitimate Navajo flocks and herds. The 243 Navajo captives taken in these same recaptures hardly fell within the range of liberated property but certainly "bore rich fruit" for their captors. Even if New Mexican militias found no Navajo flocks to raid or recapture, they might strike flocks owned by a New Mexican rico and claim to have taken them from Navajos. Rafael López nearly pulled off such a stunt in 1836 but was caught in his subterfuge by authorities and relieved of the 3,500 sheep and goats he had plucked from José de Madriaga's shepherds on the Río Salado. Now endowed with flocks of their own, and trafficking in captive Navajo women and children—desirable commodities in rico households as domestic servants or textile weavers—New Mexican bordermen were able to create their own niche in linking the pastoral to the export economies.[74]

Interacting with those economies and their agents, however, required continuous struggle and dispute over just who would establish the terms of exchange and benefit most from their exercise. Navajos, Utes, Apaches, Coman-

73. See detailed losses (including cattle, horses, mules, and captives) attributed to Navajo raiders in Appendix A, below; see also Franciscan Fathers, *Ethnologic Dictionary,* 503–504; Kelley, "Navajo Political Economy," in Cordell and Beckerman, eds., *Versatility of Kinship,* 328 n. 15.

74. For New Mexican raids and recaptures, see Appendix B, below; for López's failed adventure, see José de Madriaga to Governor Pérez, June 26, 1836, *MANM,* roll 21, frames 612–614.

ches, Kiowas, American traders, and New Mexican pobladores all understood that their economic well-being depended on a lively trade with their neighbors and used local systems of kinship to forge the relationships of reciprocity and obligation that would promote mutually rewarding exchange. Yet the vigor of the regional commerce also depended on distant markets that made new demands on the productive capacity of local peoples, whether they were weavers, fur traders, hide processors, sheepherders, or livestock thieves. Intensified forms of coercive labor emerged among Indians and Euramericans in ways that met market requirements yet strained the cultural fabric of Indian and Euramerican societies. When much of the economic activity in the borderlands occurred in the shadowy realms somewhere between informally organized free trade and outright theft, these dynamics could easily end in bloodshed, especially if Mexico or the United States attempted to subsume them within state-regulated markets and political authority.

7

PEAKS AND VALLEYS

THE BORDERLANDS SPEAK

The Old Way Gave to Many a Pleasurable Excitement

Three years after the 1846 American conquest of New Mexico, United States Indian Agent James S. Calhoun received a visitor in his Santa Fe headquarters. This man, a vecino from the western border village of Cebolleta, complained of a recent Navajo raid in which he lost four horses, one mule, sixteen oxen, and an uncounted number of sheep. Only one month before, Navajos had struck a neighboring village, killing two men, wounding one, and "carrying off, as a captive" one New Mexican woman. When told that Calhoun could offer neither military nor financial remedies for such wrongs, the man became agitated and, according to Calhoun, proceeded to contrast "the present with the former government of the territory":

> The preceding [Mexican] government permitted reprisals, which is not tolerated now; and like the Pueblo Indians, neither the Spaniards or Mexicans can see the propriety of this government interdiction unless it is the purpose of said government to make an appropriate restitution from its own treasury. The eternal state of war and reciprocal robbery under [the] former government, gave to many a pleasurable excitement, and afforded to all an opportunity of satisfying their own demands, whether founded in justice or in a mere desire to possess other peoples' property.[1]

The settler's complaint indicates one man's frustration with a conquering state that sought to suppress a vital and violent borderland economy but lacked

1. James S. Calhoun to Commissioner of Indian Affairs Orlando Brown, Nov. 15, 1849, in Annie Heloise Abel, ed., *The Official Correspondence of James S. Calhoun, while Indian Agent in Santa Fe and Superintendent of Indian Affairs in New Mexico* (Washington, D.C., 1915), 50, 76–77.

the power to replace it. He was not alone in his vexation, for many of his compadres would express similar regrets in the years to come. His anomalous characterization of an "eternal state of war and reciprocal robbery" that allowed both the satisfaction of justice and the redistribution of property suggests the complexity of motivations among protagonists in the region. And, although the settler claimed that the preceding Mexican government had coped well with the endemic conflict, we will see that he spoke from a position of some nostalgia.

But this was not the only event troubling Calhoun's mind. Just two weeks earlier, the transplanted Virginian heard from a party of New Mexican ciboleros that a band of Jicarilla Apaches had attacked travelers on the Santa Fe Trail, killing several men and taking captive a Mrs. White, her young daughter, and their "colored serving woman." Five days later, word came of a Lipan Apache raid on a caravan of German immigrants just north of El Paso, in which thirteen captives were taken and offered to Mexicans in exchange for Apache prisoners held in Chihuahua. Finally, he reported in his correspondence of June 7 certain rumors that Plains groups like the Arapahos, Cheyennes, and Comanches had united to "act in concert against the Territory."[2]

The heated conversation in Calhoun's office serves as a reference point from which to examine continuing patterns of slavery, kinship, and community formation in the Greater New Mexico Borderlands after 1821. The particular style of retributive and redistributive justice hinted at by the angry Cebolletaño reflects the quintessential local understanding of a borderland political economy that had been in formation over the past century. The capture of the three women on the Santa Fe Trail and the German immigrants illustrates how the captive exchange system expanded to include new victims: Americans, European immigrants, and African-descended slaves moving westward in the wake of the Mexican-American War. The rumors of a grand alliance—which in time grew to include reports of New Mexican insurgents joining with Plains Indians, supported by Mexican resources, to reconquer the Southwest—would persist well into the 1850s. Although never achieved in fact, the extensive and enduring evidence for intercultural interest-group activity would attest to its possibility and keep Calhoun's successors in a continual state of alarm. Mexican and American attempts to impose state order in the borderlands actually intensified the formation of communities of interest among certain families, factions, classes, and clans of Indians and New Mexicans.

2. Calhoun to Brown, Nov. 2, 1849, Nov. 7, 1849, ibid., 68–72.

After 1836, Plains Indian nations like the Comanches, Kiowas, and Cheyennes would work toward an alliance of their own, aimed at preventing encroachments on their bison economy by "immigrant tribes" and white settlers alike. But they did so with the assistance and support of their new affinal allies, American traders like the Bent brothers. Responding in some part to the new order of things emerging on the Plains and to political developments south of the Río Grande, in 1837 New Mexican villagers and various Pueblo Indians of the Río Arriba rose in rebellion and briefly overthrew the Mexican government of Albino Pérez, executing Pérez in the process. Ten years later, some of the same insurgents, in wider collaboration with Plains Indians, participated in a major uprising against the recently established American government of occupation. Again, the externally imposed governor would die. In each case, the rebels strove to protect their regional multiethnic communities and economies against what they perceived as dangerous outside intrusion.

Of course, neither Mexican nor American liberal modernizers were willing to accept that these economies contained their own implicit logic, based as they were in a regional network of raids and retributions that more easily provoked comparison to a Hobbesian "war of all against all" than to Adam Smith's fluid systems of exchange of wealth between nations. Most external authorities would have agreed with Calhoun's military colleague Colonel E. V. Sumner, who explained in 1851,

> This predatory warfare has been carried on for over 200 years, between the Mexicans and the Indians, quite enough time to prove that unless some change is made the war will be interminable. They steal women and children, and cattle, from each other, and in fact carry on the war in all respects like two Indian nations.[3]

The borderland economies and their practitioners flourished despite the major administrative changes historians generally use to mark the period: the transition to Mexican rule in 1821 and the American conquest of 1846. Although these events had long-term consequences, the fact that neither the Mexican nor the early American state exerted real military or economic control in the region allowed local groups to continue their own accommodations. Retribution through exchanges of violence and redistribution through exchanges of people and livestock lay at the heart of these local arrangements.

But the full expression of borderland economies and their communities

3. Sumner to General John G. Jones, Nov. 20, 1851, ibid., 445.

hinged in good part on the maturation of the larger regional economy and its dovetailing with American markets and associated actors throughout the Southwest after the opening of the St. Louis–Santa Fe–Chihuahua trade in 1821. These stages of modernization were, ironically, predicated in part on local and indigenous exchange networks and maintained through the region's customs of kinship and coercion. Modernizing trends evinced a shared desire to harness the wealth and power of American capitalism to local ends.

Peace. Friendship. Profit. Plunder.

The proliferation of borderland communities after 1830 had much to do with a series of diplomatic and commercial agreements worked out among Indian groups and Euramericans during that decade. A growing point of contention were the millions of bison then grazing the central and southern Plains, their traditional role in local subsistence and exchange systems, and their increasing commercial value in the American economy. Groups like the Cherokees, Creeks, Kickapoos, Sauk-Foxes, Potawatomi, Shawnees, and Delawares had begun moving westward as early as the late eighteenth century, well before the forced removals of the 1830s that culminated in the Trail of Tears. These charter generations of émigrés sought to preserve a hunting and farming way of life in the West but by the 1820s had become some of the earliest commercial bison hunters. With these migrations, the buffalo plains, especially the huge herds of the central Plains "neutral ground," became contested territory. Successful efforts to open the Plains to emigrant tribes would also open the Plains to commercial exploitation by American interests but would draw a concerted collective response from those Indian peoples who considered those grasslands their rightful hunting ranges.[4]

4. For an overview of migrations and removals of the emigrant tribes from east of the Mississippi and their relations with autochthonous Indians, see David La Vere, *Contrary Neighbors: Southern Plains and Removed Indians in Indian Territory* (Norman, Okla., 2000); Francis Paul Prucha, *The Great Father: The United States Government and the American Indians* (Lincoln, Nebr., 1984), 64–93. For the creation and maintenance, until 1840, of the central Plains neutral ground, see Elliott West, *The Way to the West: Essays on the Central Plains* (Albuquerque, N.M., 1995), esp. 60–63. The emigrant tribes were not passive in attempting to create a space for themselves on the new borderlands. One noteworthy case of alliance building can be found in the efforts by John Dunn Hunter, an adopted Quapaw captive, to create a "Red and White Republic of Fredonia," including the emigrant tribes, in Mexi-

In 1834, thirty Osages, Cherokees, Delawares, and Senecas set out westward from Fort Gibson, Indian Territory, with a company of two hundred U.S. dragoons under Colonel Henry Dodge. They brought with them two Wichita children and Gunpa'ñdama, a young Kiowa woman captured by the Osages the previous year. Meeting first with a large encampment of Comanches orientales, who received them warmly, they continued with Comanche guides to the Wichita village of Kitskukatuk on the Red River. George Catlin, the Philadelphia portrait artist who accompanied the expedition, reported, "To our very great surprise we have found these people cultivating quite extensive fields of corn maize, pumpkins, melons, beans, and squashes; so with these aids and an abundant supply of buffalo meat, they may be said to be living quite well." The Wichitas expressed their delight at the return of their captive girls and surrendered a "white boy" they themselves held prisoner.[5]

As word spread, hundreds of Kiowas and Wacos also arrived at the Wichita village, and Gunpa'ñdama returned to her people. A year later, representatives from the Comanches and Wichitas met at Fort Gibson to sign a treaty of peace and friendship between themselves, the United States, and the immigrant tribes. By 1837, the Kiowas, Kiowa Apaches, and Towakonis also agreed to a multilateral understanding that allowed the passage of seasonal hunters from the Creeks, Cherokees, and other eastern tribes. In return, licensed American traders would bring goods annually to the Red River country.[6]

The east-west accords of 1837 were followed by north-south negotiations between powerful Indian groups that concluded in the summer of 1840. Meeting along the Arkansas River some miles below Bent's Fort, the Cheyennes and Arapahos made peace with the Comanches, Kiowas, and "prairie" Apaches in order to solidify reliable access to American goods, something the expansionary Sioux in the north had already accomplished by taking control of the Missouri River trade from the Arikiras, Mandans, and Hidatsas. The Cheyennes played host to the treaty celebration and, with the Bents' contribution of provisions from the fort, offered their visitors a massive feast of rice, corn-

can Texas in 1827. See Richard Drinnon, *White Savage: The Case of John Dunn Hunter* (New York, 1972).

5. George Catlin, *Letters and Notes on the Manners, Customs, and Condition of the North American Indians* . . . , 2 vols. (New York, 1844), II, 36–86; James Mooney, "Calendar History of the Kiowa Indians," *Seventeenth Annual Report of the Bureau of American Ethnology*, part 2 (Washington, D.C., 1979), 261–269.

6. Mooney, "Calendar History," *Seventeenth Annual Report*, part 2, 169–174.

bread, and molasses. They laid dozens of guns, blankets, bolts of cloth, and brass kettles before their guests. Not to be outdone, Comanche and captive Mexican boys herded hundreds of green broke horses into the Cheyenne encampment as gifts, so many that the Cheyennes lacked sufficient ropes to lead them away.

Intercultural captivity, redemption, and marriage also figured in sealing the alliance. The Comanche captain Old Wolf held as captives (one as affinal kinsman) the former Bent employees James Hobbs and Jean Baptiste, seized some four years before. Hobbs had married one of Old Wolf's daughters and had fathered a son, now three years old, yet he allowed William Bent to effect Hobbs's ransom for six yards of red flannel, a pound of tobacco, and an ounce of trade beads. Baptiste came cheaper at the cost of one old mule. Two of Old Wolf's sons, however, would not part with their wives, two white sisters named Brown, aged eighteen and twenty-one, captured near San Antonio several years earlier. Alien men might be replaced with new captures, but women, especially white women, were a rare and valued commodity. Exchanges between the Indian participants went better. Jennie, George Bent's Cheyenne cousin, married Kiowa Dutch, a German immigrant captive turned Kiowa warrior, in a ritual expression of intertribal friendship. This accord resolved one of William Bent's biggest anxieties, for the hostilities between these peoples had made his economic venture and military survival highly doubtful. By 1842, Bent sent two employees, John Hatcher and Robert Fisher, to the South Canadian River with orders to establish a secondary trading post for the southern tribes, a settlement that would later become known as Adobe Walls.[7]

The central-southern Plains accords of 1840 were also an indigenous at-

7. For the context of the 1840 alliance, see George Bird Grinnell, *The Fighting Cheyennes* (Norman, Okla., 1956), chaps. 5–6; the Kiowas probably acted as intermediaries in these north-south negotiations, given their earlier residence in the Black Hills region and evidence for Kiowa-Cheyenne trading as early as 1815. See Mooney, "Calendar History," *Seventeenth Annual Report,* part 2, 168. On Sioux expansionism, see Richard White, "The Winning of the West: The Expansion of the Western Sioux in the Eighteenth and Nineteenth Centuries," *Journal of American History,* XLV (1978), 319–343; Letters of George Bent to George Hyde, June 4, 1909, Dec. 13, 1913, Western Americana MS, 32, Beinecke Library, Yale University, New Haven, Conn. James Hobbs, *Wild Life in the Far West: Personal Adventures of a Border Mountain Man* (Glorieta, N.Mex., 1969), claims that the sisters were sold to William Bent three months after the council, that one then lived out her life in San Antonio, and that the younger sister, Matilda, returned to the Comanches within a few days in order to be with her mixed-descent children (45–50); see also David Lavender, *Bent's Fort* (Garden City,

tempt, underwritten by mixed-culture trading interests, to establish political control over the Great Plains in general. The losers in this regard were river-based Indians like the Pawnees, Omahas, and Wichitas, who lost their primacy in agricultural trade in the early decades of the nineteenth century and now faced new pressures from the immigrant tribes of the Southeast. The riverine Indians needed continued access to the buffalo plains, but so did the migrating tribes.

The Pawnees never managed to insert themselves in peace negotiations. Once the fulcrum of the central Plains indigenous economy and arguably the keystone in the region's spiritual architecture, they would soon find themselves outside the embrace of casual yet enduring alliances that cast nets across the Plains after 1840. The Pawnees suffered perhaps more than any other river people for being in the wrong place at the wrong time. Driven by a burgeoning population and continued demand for buffalo hides, the Sioux pushed southward into the hunting territories of the Platte, long Pawnee country. A series of devastating Pawnee defeats followed the Sioux expansion. By the mid-1840s, the Pawnees' mixed economy was in shambles, and they grew increasingly dependent upon American annuities for bare survival. Their only recourse seemed to be alliance with the Americans, who soon began making use of Pawnee scouts in their Plains campaigns.[8]

The other "nations" with whom some Plains Indians waged long-term warfare after 1830 were Mexican settlements in Texas and south of the Río Grande. Whereas the Texan Republican rebels who sought independence from Mexico in 1835 used the services of skilled diplomats like José Francisco Ruíz and Sam Houston to avoid direct conflict with their Indian neighbors, outlying settlements remained vulnerable, especially those around San Antonio, which some Indians still considered a Mexican outpost. In 1836, various European immigrant colonies in the hill country west of that town found themselves under attack, and women like Sarah Ann Horn, Rachel Plummer, Cynthia Ann Parker,

---

N.Y., 1972), 199–203. On the first Adobe Walls, see Janet Lecompte, *Pueblo, Hardscrabble, Greenhorn: Society on the High Plains, 1832–1856* (Norman, Okla., 1978), 17.

8. White, "Winning of the West," *JAH*, XLV (1978), 319–343. For the Pawnee decline in Plains power relations, see White, *The Roots of Dependency: Subsistence, Environment, and Social Change among the Choctaws, Pawnees, and Navajos* (Lincoln, Nebr., 1983), 147–211; for Pawnee assistance to the U.S. Army, see Thomas W. Dunlay, *Wolves for the Blue Soldiers: Indian Scouts and Auxiliaries with the United States Army, 1860–90* (Lincoln, Nebr., 1982). Delawares, Shawnees, Potawatomies, and Kickapoos were also in high demand both as regular scouts and informal hunters for furs and scalps.

and the Brown sisters were captured. But, for every one white woman garnered in Comanche raids, dozens more Mexican mestizas and their children suffered capture and enslavement. Now-independent Texans recognized the difference: the republic's standing committee on Indian affairs asserted in 1837 that no substantial barriers stood in the way of treaties of friendship between Texas and the Comanches but that Comanches "are the natural enemies of the Mexican whom they contemptuously discriminate their 'stock-keepers' and out of which nation they procure slaves."[9]

Kiowas, Apaches, and Comanches suffered deep population losses as smallpox spread southward from the Missouri River down the Plains between 1837 and 1840. Real numbers are again elusive, but the disease struck the Kiowas with such force that they recorded the winter of 1839 to 1840 as "Smallpox Winter" in their pictorial calendar histories. The demographic and psychological shock of the epidemic surely provided strong incentive for working out the Plains alliance the coming summer. But peace alone would not allow their recovery. A more aggressive response was in order. The Lone Star Republic and northern Mexico both sheltered large numbers of horses, cattle, and women and children in small settlements vulnerable to captive and livestock raiding. Periodic forays in the preceding decade had continued the traditional pattern: lightning-quick descents by small bands of ten to twenty warriors on moonless nights to strike isolated haciendas and ranchos and relieve them of their livestock and peons. In the summer of 1835, for example, Rancho de las Animas near Parral, Chihuahua, suffered a Comanche attack in which nine buildings were set aflame, six men died, and thirty-nine captives aged five to twenty-five were carried into captivity. Twenty-two of those lost were female. James Hobbs himself had accompanied a Comanche foray west of Monclova about the same time that netted 1,400 horses and mules and 9 Mexican women and children.[10]

9. For treaty relations between the Republic of Texas and Comanches from 1838 to 1845, aimed in particular at giving eastern Comanches reliable market outlets for livestock and hides, see Thomas W. Kavanagh, *Comanche Political History: An Ethnohistorical Perspective, 1706–1875* (Lincoln, Nebr., 1996), 258–278; "Report of the Standing Committee on Indian Affairs, Texas Congress, Oct. 17, 1837," in Dorman H. Winfrey and James M. Day, eds., *Indian Papers of Texas and the Southwest,* I (Austin, Tex., 1995), 24. The Republic of Texas would become part of the United States in 1845.

10. For Smallpox Winter among Kiowas and extensions to Apaches and Comanches, see Mooney, "Calendar History," *Seventeenth Annual Report,* part 2, 274–275; for a survey of Indian conflicts with Chihuahua, see Víctor Orozco, *Las guerras indias en la historia de Chi-*

The next decades would bring dramatic expansion in the range and style of the raiding economy. Beginning in October of 1840 and continuing into January of 1841, Comanches and allied raiders undertook three incursions deep into Mexican territory for the plunder that would allow them to reassert themselves as powers on the Plains. Encountering thin and disorganized resistance from state militias in Tamaulipas, Nuevo Leon, and Coahuila, large Indian cavalries penetrated as far south as the northern boundaries of Zacatecas and San Luis Potosi states, more than 350 miles below the crossings of the Río Grande. The last invasion proved the most rewarding. Some two hundred to three hundred Comanches swept through defenseless haciendas, ranchos, and pasturelands near Saltillo, rounded up eighteen thousand head of horses, mules, and cattle, snatched more than one hundred captives, and left behind three hundred casualties. Mexican militias pursued and rescued forty of the captives and several thousand head of stock, but the rest were run northward. On January 21, the grazing outpost of Pozo was literally swept clean of inhabitants: one adult man died, and nineteen women and twenty-two children were carried away. In what may be indicative of shifting needs in Comanche labor demand, eighteen of the captured children were male. An incursion in the autumn of 1844 suggests a similar pattern. Mexican militia surprised a Comanche column running captives and livestock out of southeast Chihuahua and retook 32 stolen children and 2,500 horses and mules. Although many more head of livestock and several adult women captives could not be saved, the majority (twenty-two) rescued were boys. A Durango militia ambush the following year yielded the same distribution when fifty boys and twenty girls aged four to twenty were recaptured from a combined Kiowa and Comanche incursion. Since boys as young as five years old could be put to the task of watching livestock, and postpubescent women quickly assimilated into the marriage economy of their captors, Plains raiders addressed the paired crises of labor and population in their targets.[11]

---

huahua: Antología, compilación, ensayo preliminar, y notes (Ciudad Juárez, 1992). For the attack on Rancho de las Animas, see *El noticioso de Chihuahua* (hereafter cited as *ENCH),* June 12, 1835, rpt. in Orozco, *Las guerras indias,* 89; for Hobbs's experience, see Hobbs, *Wild Life in the Far West,* 32.

11. Details of the 1840–1841 invasions may be found in Isidoro Vizcaya Canales, *La invasión de los indios bárbaros al noreste de México en los años de 1840 y 1841* (Monterrey, 1968). For the Saltillo attacks, see Vizcaya Canales, "Noticia en *El voto de Coahuila,* 12 enero, 1841," 181–185; for an inventory of the Pozo captives, happily rescued three days later, see 200–201.

FIGURE 10. *The Little Spaniard.* 1834. His-oo-san-ches (Jesús Sánchez) was a Spanish-Comanche "half-breed, for whom they generally have the most contemptuous feelings"; yet, for his daring, he "commanded the highest admiration and respect of the tribe." Field sketch by George Catlin. Reproduced from Catlin, *Letters and Notes,* II, 68–69

At least some of the captives whom pursuers failed to rescue seem to have found life among their captors not entirely objectionable. When General Pedro García Conde interrogated Roque de Jésus Flores, "rescued" in 1835 after fifteen years in Comanche captivity, the general found it "disgraceful" that the twenty-two-year-old "from one of the principal families of Santa Rosa [Chihuahua]" had been "made a captive at such a young age that by his facial features alone could he be distinguished from the Comanches." The young man told García Conde, "There exist among [the Comanches] many captives, although it is not possible to say a firm number, and none of the former have fled their captivity voluntarily, because of the good treatment they receive." But others were more ambivalent. When the U.S. Whipple Survey expedition encountered several Mexican captives in a Kiowa ranchería near the Canadian River in 1853, surveyor John Pitts Sherburne reported that one, Andrés Nuñares, "had no desire to leave since he was well treated" and had acquired in his five years of bondage "considerable property in mules and horses." The Mexican proved culturally fluent enough to give the expedition the first Kiowa vocabulary of some two hundred terms for the natural and spiritual world. An eighteen-year-old woman, however, married to an "old chief" with whom she had produced a child during her seven-year captivity, "wished to return" despite Sherburne's observation that she "appeared quite happy and quite probable [sic] was as contented as she would have been in Mexico." So too did the third man, who apparently had not fared as well as Nuñares. But when the Americans proposed to buy the "prisoners" the Kiowas became indignant and said that "it was not the part of friends to try and take their Captives." The American party left them all behind, lest their forcible seizure "raise the Kioway and Comanche tribes against us." The Kiowas watched their departure, "secure in the fleetness of their horses, with their captives guarded."[12]

For the 1844 raid and rescue, see Ralph A. Smith, "Indians in American-Mexican Relations before the War of 1846," *Hispanic American Historical Review,* XLIII, no. 1 (February 1963), 34–64, esp. 54; for 1845, see Smith, "The Comanches' Foreign War: Fighting Head Hunters in the Tropics," *Great Plains Journal,* XXIV–XXV, no. 5 (1984–1985), 21–44, esp. 27. For historiography, see Cuauhtémoc Velasco Ávila, "Historiografía de una frontera amenazada: Los ataques Comanches y Apaches en el siglo XIX," in Antonio Escobar Ohmstede, ed., *Indio, nación y comunidad el en México del siglo XIX* (Mexico, 1993), 315–327.

12. Roque de Jesús Flores, interrogation, in *ENCH,* Jul. 17, 1835, republished in Orozco, *Las guerras indias,* esp. 90; [John Pitts Sherburne], *Through Indian Country to California: John P. Sherburne's Diary of the Whipple Expedition, 1853–1854,* ed. Mary McDougall Gordon (Stanford, Calif., 1988), 84–85 n. 16, 88.

FIGURE 11. *Comanches Meeting U.S. Dragoons.* 1834. The man featured at the center is His-oo-san-ches, "all his life thrown into the front of battle and danger." He carries a white buffalo skin on his lance. Field sketch by George Catlin. Reproduced from Catlin, *Letters and Notes,* II, 55–57, 68

Sherburne had noted additional details that suggest the very typicality of that ranchería in the social and economic world of the southern Plains at that moment. Relatively small in size, with about forty adults and "numerous" children, the Kiowas held an extraordinary five hundred horses, which they offered to sell to the expedition for twenty dollars a head. The Americans, suspicious of the animals' provenance and quality, declined. Less scrupulous were the five "Mexicans who proved to be traders from Santa Fe" also resident in the camp. These comancheros expressed relief at the arrival of the Americans, for they had "about exhausted their stock of goods and feared robbery and perhaps murder from the Indians." A single encampment on an autumn day contained Kiowas, Mexicans made Kiowa by either volition or force, mixed Kiowa-Mexican children, New Mexican comancheros, and a huge horse herd of dubious origin all operating as agents and victims of the borderland economy.[13]

13. [Sherburne], *Through Indian Country,* ed. Gordon, 84, 87. Since Sherburne counted twenty adult men in the Kiowa camp, even a high estimate of fifteen horses per man would

FIGURE 12. *Kaiowa Indians Removing Camp.* c. 1851.
By Heinrich Balduin Möllhausen. Courtesy Yale Collection of Western Americana, Beinecke Rare Book and Manuscript Library

Nor did time or space neatly bound such moments. Taking advantage of the expedition's need for guidance west through the sand hills, the comancheros traveled alongside for several days, during which they were able to sell the Americans bison robes for their beds. Soon the two parties were joined by a third, a mixed band of about eight New Mexican and Pueblo Indian comancheros "just from Mexico" that Sherburne initially took for Comanches "clothed in buckskins." These claimed no luck in finding Indians with whom to trade their flour and bread for robes and horses, despite the signals they had sent by setting the prairie on fire. Yet, if they were indeed returning northward from Mexico, the pack mules they had conveniently left "some miles behind" were likely the reward for an illegal cross-border foray that Mexican authorities were finding increasingly common among their brethren to the north. Even before the American conquest in 1846 rewrote New Mexicans' nominal nationality, Mexicans had reported "mexicanos desnaturalizados" traveling with Indian bands and among those pillagers striking their settlements below the Río Grande. These included some whom, by the "perfection with which

yield a maximum utilitarian herd of three hundred animals, with two hundred available as surplus for exchange and sale.

they spoke castellano, and especially by their dress," authorities believed to be *bejareños* (from San Antonio) or *badeños* (from San Miguel and San José del Vado). Appearing as Comanches might not have been simply a matter of rustic style for the comancheros but a useful subterfuge. Firing the grasslands behind them also obliterated their tracks in case of pursuit. Soon the mixed band set out northward to find the Comanches, while the comancheros returned the two hundred miles to New Mexico, with what animals and effects they had gathered, to announce the imminent arrival of the Americans.[14]

In essence, the southern Plains Indian economy expanded territorially and in "capital on the hoof" at the same time as Kiowas, Comanches, and Apaches suffered demographic crises and a rapid depletion of bison herds occurred with aggressive growth in the American hide trade. As their labor needs crested, livestock raiding and captive assimilation reoriented their economies and repopulated their rancherías, allowing for their survival. The four decades after 1830 were the fullest florescence of the mixed-ethnic borderland communities. New Mexican and Indian llaneros developed extensive and reliable connections among themselves and to the market resources of Mexico and the United States. Although they grew dependent upon those resources, they continued to wield almost complete control over the terms of exchange within their shared region. Not content with the limitations of supply and demand, however, they proceeded with their customary command economy, plundering southward to acquire the livestock and captive labor crucial to the expansion of their societies.[15]

Although in general terms we can talk about expanding and vital border-

14. Ibid., 89–90; for "extraños" among the Indian invaders of the 1840s, see Vizcaya Canales, *La invasión de los indios bárbaros*, 55–60, quoting José Marcelo Hinojosa on June 17, 1841, and José Antonio Arredando on Nov. 15, 1849, 56. Vizcaya believes the badeños referred to in the latter's report might have been from the settlement of San Juan Bautista del Río Grande, where a ford had long been in use. But the ubiquity with which citizens of San Miguel and San José del Vado in New Mexico were referred to by contemporaries as badeños and those communities' deep involvement in the Plains (and contraband) trade suggest the affiliation attributed here.

15. For the rapid depletion of Great Plains bison herds by Indian hunters between 1830 and 1860, see Andrew C. Isenberg, *The Destruction of the Bison: An Environmental History, 1750–1920* (Cambridge, 2000), chap. 4, "The Ascendancy of the Market," 93–122; for specific treatment of Plains Apache–Mexican relations, see William B. Griffen, *Utmost Good Faith: Patterns of Apache-Mexican Hostilities in Northern Chihuahua Border Warfare, 1821–1848* (Albuquerque, N.Mex., 1988).

FIGURE 13. *A Kioway Indian on a Mule,—in His War-dress.* 1845. Watercolor by Lt. James W. Abert. Courtesy Yale Collection of Western Americana, Beinecke Rare Book and Manuscript Library

land economies during this period, in practice, the participants—whether New Mexican villagers, Plains Indians, pastoral Navajos, or their various mixed cultural communities of interest and affinity—experienced almost constant social and economic pressure as well. They maintained their vitality only through the creative elaboration of tactical responses that preserved their semiautonomous economies and ways of life. A closer look at the manner in which these communities met challenges emanating outside their regions of control reveals the bonds and weaknesses of communities of interest in the Southwest Borderlands.

They Identify Themselves with the Savage Tribes

In a remarkable echo of the uprising at San Miguel del Vado in 1805, late in the summer of 1837 New Mexico experienced a violent, chaotic, and short-lived rebellion against the Mexican government in Santa Fe. Erupting from a contested judicial decision and popular misconceptions of the direct-taxation elements of President Antonio López de Santa Anna's centralizing departmental plan of 1836, New Mexican borderlanders and more than a few Pueblo Indian coconspirators rose up. The rebels expressed their contempt for Mexican authority by piercing *á lanzadas* ("in the style of the ciboleros"), beheading, and mutilating the bodies of Governor Albino Pérez, his secretary of government Jesús María Alarid, and former governor Santiago Abreú. Perhaps as many as a dozen members of elite society died in this manner. Yet, from the revolution's outset, its positive goals were poorly defined and its adherents difficult to categorize by class or ethnicity. Some months later, the counterrevolutionary governor Manuel Armijo would claim,

> The aim of the factions . . . was to remain independent of the government of the Mexican nation; to put an end to every person who has an average education; to be governed by no established law, which was their excuse for sentencing all the archives to the flames; to destroy fortunes in a general sack; and to live without subjection to any precept or authority, identifying themselves with the savage tribes and putting themselves on the same level, making the same cause with their same interests.[16]

In Armijo's mind, at least, the rebellion seemed part of a larger cultural instability in New Mexico, and contemporary observers agreed. Josiah Gregg reported that, although Pueblo Indians bore the brunt of blame, "the insurgent party was composed of all the heterogeneous ingredients that a Mexican population teems with." Many New Mexicans shared similar uncertainties about the root causes of the revolt. Padre Antonio Martínez of Taos sought to lay the blame at the feet of American adventurers in Taos and beyond, with whom he

16. *Diario del gobierno de la republica Mexicana,* IX, no. 45, Nov. 30, 1837, 361–362; Lecompte, trans., *Rebellion in Río Arriba, 1837* (Albuquerque, N.Mex., 1985), 139.

long waged a struggle for political influence in Río Arriba. Donaciano Vigil, however, although a descendant of a prominent Río Abajo family and a solid Mexican nationalist, saw the problems lying with a lack of will toward modernization within the Mexican state and incompetent outside appointees like Pérez. Vigil, in fact, served as secretary to the short-lived revolutionary government, although he later claimed to have done so under duress.[17]

And the rebels themselves? The only document issued by the revolutionary Cantón is vague and perhaps intentionally misleading. Proclaiming that they would "sustain God and the nation and the faith of Jesus Christ" and "defend our country until the last drop of blood is shed to achieve the desired victory," the rebels claimed to stand opposed, first, to the departmental plan of 1836, which subordinated New Mexico and local village governance to the central authority of Mexico. Second, they were against any taxation and, third, the excesses of any authorities who sought to impose the preceding elements. The first complaint was broadly shared throughout Mexico's borderlands and provoked rebellions in Zacatecas, Sonora, Sinaloa, Tamaulipas, Coahuila, Texas, California, and the Yucatán. The opposition to taxation seems a misunderstanding by the rebels, for New Mexico had long been excused from that burden, and efforts were underway to make this clear in the departmental plan. The rebels' few rico allies, however, made much of this issue and purportedly spread rumors that taxation would extend to "compelling husbands to pay a tax for sleeping with their own wives." The final complaint probably focused more on dislike for Governor Pérez's personal style, which seemed ostentatious to an extreme.[18]

Yet a closer look at the background of the revolt reveals continuity with tensions by now familiar and probably considered common knowledge by the rebels. Unhappiness with Mexican administrators had been brewing since at least 1831, when Governor José Antonio Chávez prohibited unlicensed Indian trade and bison hunts. The commerce persisted, of course, but its illegality now allowed governors and their deputies to confiscate contraband and impose fines under the guise of maintaining stable government. No less unpopular

17. Josiah Gregg, *The Commerce of the Prairies,* ed. Milo Martin Quaife (Lincoln, Nebr., 1966), 126; Donaciano Vigil, "Arms, Indians, and the Mismanagement of New Mexico," in David J. Weber, trans. and ed., *Southwestern Studies Series,* no. 77 (El Paso, Tex., 1986), ix–50.

18. Lecompte, trans., *Rebellion,* 20; Weber, *The Mexican Frontier, 1821–1846: The American Southwest under Mexico* (Albuquerque, N.Mex., 1982), 31–35, 260–261; W. W. H. Davis, *El Gringo, or New Mexico and Her People* (Santa Fe, N.Mex., 1938), 87.

during the years 1832 to 1833 was Governor Santiago Abreú, whom the rebels of 1837 took real delight in slaying. Insurrection simmered in the summer of 1834 against the administration of Governor Francisco Sarracino, whose corruption ranged from fleecing traders and misapplying public funds to taking bribes from Spanish priests threatened with expulsion from Mexico after independence. Pérez's first acts as governor included his appointment of the detested Sarracino as *subcomisario* in charge of raising funds for the local government and its troops.[19]

But Pérez's imposition in July 1837 of several novel political provisions in keeping with the new constitution brought long-simmering resentments to a flash point. He ordered the *ayuntamiento* of Santa Cruz de la Cañada dissolved because most of its seven members were related by birth or marriage. He also imposed property qualifications for council members consistent with legislation passed in Mexico on March 20, 1837, that required an annual income of at least five hundred pesos. The assault on customary kin-based village political organization and elitist restrictions in citizenship rights outraged the residents of La Cañada, who refused to recognize the order. Concurrently, Antonio Abad Montoya, a relative of Alcalde Juan José Esquibel, bribed his *primo* (cousin) to release him from the local jail after he had failed to gain an appeal for some unexplained "grave crime." Pérez immediately issued orders for his reimprisonment and a fifty-peso fine against Esquibel. Again, the locals refused to obey the orders.

Still serving as alcalde, Esquibel next dismissed the complaint of Víctor Sánchez of Taos against two vecinos of La Cañada, who, Sánchez claimed, owed him money for the customs duties he had paid on their behalf in Chihuahua, where they had recently traveled to sell "their work of wool and leather." Pérez ordered the prefect of Río Arriba, don Ramón Abreú, to overrule the alcalde and place him in chains. In late July 1837, Esquibel's faction promptly freed him from jail by force of arms, and on August 1 the revolutionary Can-

19. Chávez to Vizcarra, Oct. 23, 1831, *Mexican Archives of New Mexico,* New Mexico State Records Center, Santa Fe, N.Mex. (hereafter cited as *MANM),* roll 13, frame 488. For Mexican law pursuant to contraband, in which the public treasury was to receive roughly half the value of the confiscated goods, with the remainder shared among denouncers, apprehenders, and administrators, see Susan Calafate Boyle, *Los Capitalistas: Hispano Merchants and the Santa Fe Trade* (Albuquerque, N.Mex., 1997), 51; for the "scandalous political movements" of 1834, which seem to reflect local tumult inspired in part by Santa Anna's assumption of the conservative mantle earlier that year, see two manifestos from Governor Sarracino, June 30, 1834, docs. 129, 130, Sender Collection, New Mexico State Records Center.

tón was born. A week later the governor and his two hundred presidiales and Pueblo auxiliaries were routed by a combined vecino and Pueblo force of fifteen hundred to two thousand men at La Mesilla, just north of La Cañada. All of Perez's Indian troops and ten presidiales deserted once the battle had joined. The governor and twenty-three remaining faithful fled for Santa Fe, but by dawn the next day Pérez's head was being kicked about the dusty streets of the villa.[20]

Although seemingly minor issues, the contested decisions at La Cañada point directly to struggles between local and national authority. One historian has called the events of 1837 a "failure of . . . hope for a democratic New Mexico," and in a certain sense this seems correct. But democracy meant different things to different people, and in La Cañada it meant the right of interrelated mestizo families to create their own village-based systems of government and conflict resolution. This is, not to argue the rightness or wrongness of Esquibel's actions, but to point out that the constitution of 1836 contained some decidedly antilocal elements, especially in creating a nation of citizens bound first to the state and only secondarily to customary relations of kith and kin. The dissolution of the ayuntamiento struck directly at the prerogatives of kinship. The attempt to override Esquibel's judgment, which may have relatively simple class undertones (a dispute between a man with cash and two men without), similarly offended customary autonomy.[21]

In the early days of the rebellion, a second set of complaints had emerged that also point to diverging interests between local New Mexicans and the Mexican state, or in this case the Catholic Church, which had discovered a new friend in the politically mercurial Santa Anna. Padre Fernando Ortiz of La Cañada found himself confronted with a list demanding that the church expect no contributions beyond the customary *primicias* (the early yield of fields and flocks) and that burials be permitted inside church walls. The rebels actually forced Ortiz and Padre Martínez in Taos to conduct such burials at gunpoint.[22]

20. Lecompte, trans., *Rebellion,* 19–20, 33–34, 97, 162 n. 29. Lecompte's note incorrectly dates the governor's announcement of the political provisions as July 14, 1833, rather than 1837. For legislation reorganizing ayuntamientos and new property qualifications, see Manuel Dublán and José María Lozano, *Legislación mexicana ó colección completa de las disposiciones legislativas espedidas desda le independencia de la república,* III (Mexico, 1876), 333. I thank Daniel H. Calhoun for noting the incorrect date above.

21. Ibid., 75.

22. Ibid., 21, 125.

Resistance to church levies makes sense when considered in the general antitaxation and antitithe atmosphere prevailing in New Mexico since at least 1805. The burial issue is more opaque. In 1833, Mexico City had suffered a massive cholera outbreak, and in response the Gómez Farías government instituted a set of sanitary regulations that included prohibitions of burials within any church building used for regular worship. The new campos santos, well away from public buildings, became more often internment grounds for people unable to pay burial fees sufficient to sway the local padre into a church burial and thus became the focus of both spiritual and economic resentments. After the expulsion of the Regular Orders of the Catholic Church in the late eighteenth century, New Mexican parishes gradually became self-supporting, and local padres like Ortiz and Martínez probably used sacramental, baptismal, and burial fees to support their own survival. The emergence of the lay brotherhood *Cofradía de nuestro padre Jesús Nazareno* (or the *Penitentes)* was one consequence, a lower-order attempt to meet the spiritual and economic needs of the local populace in the absence of church support.[23]

Beneath these issues of local authority and class conflict lay cultural tensions that fueled rebellion as well. The most radical faction among the insurgents came from Taos, headed by the former alcalde of Taos and lieutenant colonel of militia Pablo Montoya and by José Angel Gonzales, a genízaro from Ranchos de Taos nine miles south. Montoya's background is shadowy. Contemporaries would claim him a "brigand" with a history of troublemaking, who owned no home or property and was "engaged in no occupation." This is unlikely, given his position in the village government and his officer's status. His local support base, however, drew upon poor vecinos and Indians from the nearby pueblo, people "as abandoned and desperate as their rebellious chief." Mon-

23. C. A. Hutchinson, "The Asiatic Cholera Epidemic of 1833 in Mexico," *Bulletin of the History of Medicine,* XXXII (1958), 1–23. For the origins and functions of the Penitente Brotherhood, see Frances Leon Swadesh, *Los Prímeros Pobladores: Hispanic Americans of the Ute Frontier* (Notre Dame, Ind., 1974), 60–89; Fray Angélico Chávez, *But Time and Chance: The Story of Padre Martínez of Taos, 1793–1867* (Santa Fe, N.Mex., 1981); Marta Weigle, *Brothers of Light, Brothers of Blood: The Penitentes of the Southwest* (Albuquerque, N.Mex., 1976); José A. Hernandez, *Mutual Aid for Survival: The Case of the Mexican American* (Malabar, 1983), chap. 1; Paul Kutsche and Dennis Gallegos, "Community Functions of the Cofradía de Nuestro Jesús Nazareno," in Kutsche, ed., *The Survival of Spanish American Villages,* The Colorado College Studies, no. 15 (Spring 1979), 91–98; Albert L. Pulido, "Mexican American Catholicism in the Southwest: The Transformation of a Popular Religion," *Perspectives in Mexican American Studies,* IV (1993), 95–109.

toya's connections to Indian peoples certainly extended well onto the Plains, given the history of trade between Taos and Plains groups and the frequency with which Taoseños were reported among comanchero and cibolero caravans in the 1830s. Montoya likely would have led such viajes, now illegal. Judging from his actions ten years later, he held a particular antipathy for extranjero elites like Charles Bent and Antoine Robidoux as well as New Mexican ricos who prospered from the legal St. Louis trade.[24]

Of José Gonzales we know more. Baptized "José Angel, vecino" on April 14, 1799, Gonzales's parents were of mixed descent—his father José Antonio of coyote and genízara parentage and his mother an *india natural del pueblo de Taos.* In adulthood, Gonzales married three times, once into Taos Pueblo, again into Picurís Pueblo, and finally into the Bernals, a vecino family from Santa Cruz de la Cañada. Most of his adult years are obscure, but, on August 8, 1837, the Cantón at La Cañada elected Gonzales their revolutionary governor.[25]

Contemporary counterrevolutionaries like Albino Chacón claimed that Gonzales's "only talent was knowing how to kill buffalo." The rebel governor, therefore, was probably a mixed-descent cibolero who maintained kin ties with at least two Pueblo and two New Mexican communities. But Chacón and other writers also termed the 1837 uprising the Chimayó Rebellion and tagged the rebels as "treacherous deceivers . . . men of the braided hair . . . who have abandoned the looms to rebel against the country." The village of Chimayó, some eight miles upstream from Santa Cruz de la Cañada, had been fully settled by 1785. In 1822, its plaza held twenty-two households of some one hundred residents (including seven *acasiados,* or house servants of unknown ethnicity). Although located on the western side of the Sangre de Cristo range, the plaza often furnished men for the Plains Indian trade, men whose "braided hair" might not have been their only affiliation with the "savage tribes." Attempts to establish a textile industry for exports to Chihuahua dated from the middle 1790s and had received impetus from the Mexican government's prohibition of imports of ready-made clothes after 1821. Chimayó would eventually become the center of the Río Grande weaving tradition, but in the 1830s wages

24. See proclamation by provisional governor Donaciano Vigil, Jan. 22, 1847, in Michael McNierney, trans. and ed., *Taos 1847: The Revolt in Contemporary Accounts* (Boulder, Colo., 1980), 41–42. In 1832, Texans encountered two separate groups of Taoseño Indian traders and bison hunters on the Plains; see Kavanagh, *Comanche Political History,* 205.

25. Chávez, "José Gonzales, Genizaro Governor," *New Mexico Historical Review* (hereafter cited as *NMHR),* XXX (January 1955), 190–194.

were low and inconsistent, and the contraband trade beckoned. Chimayoses and the villagers of Río Arriba generally resisted easy assimilation into a pliant labor force of carders and weavers, preferring instead the uncertain rewards of their locally controlled exchange economy.[26]

The strategies Gonzales employed to organize defenses against the counterrevolution emerging in the Río Abajo also reveal his links to the eastern Plains. Conferring with the American trader Elisha Stanley, he supposedly offered an alliance that would have brought New Mexico under United States sovereignty. Whether this offer referred to formal political incorporation within the United States or to a more informal immediate alliance with the mixed cultural trading interests of the Arkansas and their St. Louis bankers remains unclear. Gregg noted during his visit to New Mexico shortly before the rebellion that, among the Pueblo Indians, at least, "prophecies" had circulated that "a new race from the east was about to appear to redeem them from the Spanish yoke." On its surface, Gregg's statement seems a self-serving flourish in the interests of Manifest Destiny, but the Pueblo prophecies might have referred as much to the growing cultural force of the Plains communities as to westering Americans.[27]

Pablo Montoya also maintained familial connections with vecino villagers of La Cañada, midway between Taos and Santa Fe. Two Montoyas from Santa Cruz, the brothers Antonio Abad and Desiderio, were signatories to the Cantón's *Pronunciamiento* and subsequently suffered decapitation in the counterrevolution. That Pablo survived the counterrevolutionary terror (only to lead the Taos revolt in 1847) suggests that his associations with Taos Pueblo, and by extension to other Pueblo Indians, made Mexican authorities more hesitant to

26. [Albino Chacón], "An Account of the Chimayó Rebellion, 1837," c. Sept. 21–Oct. 18, 1837, in Lecompte, trans., *Rebellion,* 101. For the Chimayó role in the rebellion, see the three *décimas* on the rebellion, in Lecompte, trans., *Rebellion,* 147–151. For the 1822 population, see Virginia Langham Olmsted, comp., *Spanish and Mexican Censuses of New Mexico, 1750–1830* (Albuquerque, N.Mex., 1981), 210–211. For Chimayó's settlement history and development as a weaving center, see Donald James Usner, "The Plaza del Cerro in Chimayo: Settlement and Function" (master's thesis, University of New Mexico, 1991), 55–61. For history of New Mexico's weaving economy, see Suzanne Baizerman, "Textiles, Traditions and Tourist Art: Hispanic Weaving in Northern New Mexico" (Ph.D. diss., University of Minnesota, St. Paul, 1987), esp. 76–79, 130–131.

27. Testimony of Tomás Zuloaga, Aug. 28, 1837, in Lecompte, trans., *Rebellion,* 116; Gregg, *Commerce of the Prairies,* ed. Quaife, 121.

mete out injudicious punishments to people who retained a power base within Indian communities than to those without such support.[28]

Such precautionary measures are reflected in the gentle handling of Pueblo rebels during the fall of 1837. Although Pueblo warriors from Santo Domingo were directly responsible for Pérez's assassination and for the mutilation and death of Santiago Abreú, Armijo's counterrevolutionary Plan de Tomé called only for the Pueblos to remain neutral and self-governing during his attempts to subdue the Río Arriba. The Pueblos, numbering some ten thousand of a total departmental population of sixty thousand, still were potential spoilers in this effort. Neutrality was the best Armijo could hope for, and he apparently got it, for the Pueblos would remain relatively quiescent for the next decade.[29]

Although its details remain sketchy, and little additional documentary evidence is likely to emerge to cast clarity on the exact causes and alliances it mobilized, the rebellion of 1837 reflects a wider constellation of tensions and forces at work late in the Mexican Period. Manuel Armijo's ostensibly polemical claim that the insurgents shared interests and causes with the "savage tribes" probably carries more weight than heretofore accorded it. The Río Abajo's interests seem allied with Chihuahua and the formal trade from St. Louis, so much so that, when Armijo and his rico allies promulgated the Plan de Tomé in September 1837, they received 410 pesos in loans from American trading interests to maintain their troops. On the other hand, the Río Arriba villagers depended more on the informal network of commerce radiating between the Arkansas valley, the eastern Plains, and their trading center at Taos. The departmental plan, with all of its explicit and implicit threats to local autonomy and intercultural commerce, proved the lightning rod of popular discontent. The next major event of community defense would also center on the high valley beneath Taos Mountain—with strong evidence for tactical links to the peoples of the Plains.[30]

28. Lecompte, trans., *Rebellion,* 20, 70–71.

29. Ibid., 34, 52.

30. The Bents' friend and partner Manuel Alvarez arranged these loans, drawing also upon funds from Jesse Sutton and the Robidoux brothers (ibid., 55). Philip Reno sees no evidence to support Mexican historian Carlos María Bustamante's assertion that Americans angered by customs duties fomented the rebellion. See Reno, "Rebellion in New Mexico—1837," *NMHR,* XL (July 1965), 197–213. For Bustamante's version, see Bustamante, *El Gabinete mexicano . . . ,* I (Mexico, 1842), 33–36.

Not One in a Hundred is Content

Manuel Armijo, hero of the counterrevolution of 1837 and twice governor since that triumph, fled New Mexico in August 1846 as Brigadier General Stephen Watts Kearney approached from the east. Kearney's "bloodless conquest" followed as many prominent New Mexicans hastened to make accommodation with their new rulers. But, within six months, blood would flow, not so much in retribution for Mexico's national humiliation as in another expression of local outrage over threats to local control. The Taos revolt of 1847 would show another, more expansive, aspect of New Mexico's borderland communities.

New Mexico's ambiguous position in the center of capital flows between St. Louis and Chihuahua grew throughout the 1840s. Texans had their own designs on the region, especially wishing to divert the Santa Fe trade through Texas, to explore New Mexico's purported mineral resources, and to develop the grasslands of the llano estacado as rich forage for an emergent Texan cattle culture to the north and west. Texans had claimed New Mexico—at least to the eastern bank of the Río Grande—since 1836 and sought once in 1841 and twice in 1843 to plunder and conquer that province. None of the expeditions proved successful, but the Texan *filibusteros* do seem to have awakened a growing sense of shared interests between Plains Indians and New Mexican llaneros, both of whom would have suffered under Texan suzerainty. These threats precipitated a political reaction late in 1845. When news of John Slidell's attempts to purchase New Mexico and California for the United States reached Santa Fe in December, citizens responded, not from an offended sense of Mexican nationalism, but as New Mexicans. Led by Armijo and endorsed by prominent leaders like Donaciano Vigil, they proposed instead to form an independent state, *La República Mexicana del Norte.* Vigil had earlier chided the Mexican Congress for imposing duties on the import of guns and munitions to the department from the United States, considering these crucial to his homeland's ability to resist both Indian depredations and American adventurism. After General Kearney's arrival in Santa Fe, Vigil continued to play the middle role. Accepting appointment as territorial secretary to the new governor, Charles Bent, on September 22, 1846, he also joined 104 New Mexican citizens in signing a lengthy letter to the Mexican president four days later that asserted their patriotic willingness to resist the American conquest, had they enjoyed proper leadership.[31]

More than self-serving instrumentalism (although it certainly was that), this kind of negotiation was characteristic of the New Mexican situation in general. Still uncertain of the outcome in the shooting war then raging to their south, and misled by press reports of Mexican victories, New Mexicans scrambled to find some middle position that would allow them flexibility in the long term. By October of 1846, however, both ricos and pobres, for their own reasons, began to fear that the American conquest would transform the customary divisions of power and resources with which they had grown familiar. Two rebellions began brewing, one in the Río Abajo and another in the traditional crucible of insurrection, the Río Arriba.

The Río Abajo movement seems a matter of disgruntled ricos, led by don Tomás Ortiz, Colonel Diego Archuleta, and Captain Dimasio Salazar, who took offense at their exclusion from the new government and hence from positions that would have allowed them to protect property holdings and social status. The Río Abajo rebels hoped, in the words of one historian, "to gain through rebellion what they had failed to acquire through cooperation or silence." In this respect the ricos' tactics mirrored their opportunism of 1837, when they proved more than willing to stand by as Governor Pérez met his end, only to step into the chaos as "stabilizers" once the killing had ended. American military strength was dispersed after Kearney's departure for Cali-

31. For the 1841 debacle, underwritten personally by Texan president Mirabeau B. Lamar, see George Wilkins Kendall, *Narrative of an Expedition across the Great Southwestern Prairies, from Texas to Santa Fé . . .* (New York, 1845); for the 1843 ventures, the first of which was a vengeance raid on the village of Mora in response to the imprisonment of the 1841 expedition, and the second a freebooting expedition on the St. Louis–Santa Fe trade endorsed by new president Sam Houston, see Rufus B. Sage, *Wild Scenes in Kansas and Nebraska, the Rocky Mountains, Oregon, California, New Mexico, Texas, and the Grand Prairies . . .* (Philadelphia, 1855); for relations between Texas and New Mexico after 1845, see Mark J. Stegmaier, *Texas, New Mexico, and the Compromise of 1850: Boundary Dispute and Sectional Crisis* (Kent, Oh., 1996); "Protest by Citizens of New Mexico, the Governor, Etc., Who Fear That the Mexican Government in Its Treaties Might Allow New Mexico to Become a Part of the United States for a Price, December 20, 1845," *MANM,* Miscellaneous, microfilm, frames 646–648; Vigil, "Arms, Indians, and the Mismanagement of New Mexico," in Weber, trans. and ed., *Southwestern Studies Series,* no. 77, ix–50; Max L. Moorhead, trans. and ed., "Report of the Citizens of New Mexico to the President of Mexico, Santa Fe, September 26, 1846," *NHMR,* XXVI (January 1951), 69–75.

fornia, and the moment seemed ripe. Colonel Sterling Price, commander of the troops who remained in Santa Fe, ordered artillery batteries fixed at the entrances to the plaza. Word came that San Miguel del Vado "was in a state of insurrection" and the paymaster's wagon train targeted for attack. On Christmas Day, three hundred warriors from Santo Domingo Pueblo joined the insurgency but dispersed after Price threatened to level their adobe town with his artillery. After U.S. scouts intercepted several requests for Mexican assistance, however, the ringleaders of the Río Abajo sedition were arrested and confined by December 28. Both Colonel Price and Governor Bent thought the danger past.[32]

But in Río Arriba conspiracy continued and displayed a face markedly different from events in the south. This resistance drew upon the intercultural connections developed by New Mexicans and Indians across the preceding generations and would be geographically wider and more internally complex than the Río Abajo movement. Fermenting in Taos, where occupying troops of the Missouri Volunteers had wreaked havoc after discovering the pleasures of Turley's "Taos Lightning," the rebellion also claimed adherents east of the Sangre de Cristos. Longtime trapper and trader Lawrence Waldo wrote his brother David early in January,

> It seems a general mistake has been made by all that were acquianted with the *gente* of this Territory in regard to their willingness to be subject to the rule of the United States . . . not one in ten is *a gusto,* and as I can judge I am well acquainted with the eastern side of the mountains, not one in one hundred is content.[33]

The extensive nature of seditious plotting was manifested in two central figures, Pablo Montoya and Manuel Cortés. Montoya, of course, had led the Taos faction during the 1837 rebellion. Cortés hailed from the village of Mora, where he seems to have had contacts with tribes including Cheyennes, Jicarilla

32. McNierney, trans. and ed., *Taos 1847,* 3–4. Captain Salazar first achieved notoriety as the leader of the civil militia that foiled the first Texas–Santa Fe expedition in 1841; see Kendall, *Narrative of an Expedition across the Great Southwestern Prairies,* 299; William A. Keleher, ed., *Report of Lieut. J. W. Abert, of His Examination of New Mexico in the Years 1846–'47* (1847; Albuquerque, N.Mex., 1962), 138–141.

33. Lawrence Waldo to David Waldo, Jan. 13, 1847, quoted in Ralph Emerson Twitchell, *The History of the Military Occupation of the Territory of New Mexico . . .* (Denver, Colo., 1909), 331.

Apaches, and the Comanches. Together, the men managed to field a multi-ethnic coalition numbering some two thousand fighters to disrupt the imposition of American control.[34]

The rising began on the evening of January 19, when a delegation from Taos Pueblo demanded the release of two prisoners held by Sheriff Stephen Lee in San Fernando de Taos. When refused, they killed Lee and the prefect Cornelio Vigil, then attacked Governor Bent in his home. Dying with Bent were his brother-in-law Pablo Jaramillo, Charles Beaubien's son Narcisio, and James Lee, circuit judge for the territorial government. Kit Carson's New Mexican wife, Josepha Jaramillo, her sister, Ignacia Jaramillo Bent, and Bent's daughter Teresina all escaped with the aid of a loyal criada, María Guadalupe Bent, who dug an exit through the adobe walls. Parading Bent's scalp on a pole, the Indians returned to their pueblo, joined by a growing crowd of Mexican insurgents.[35]

Within twenty-four hours, the revolt spread north and east. Several hundred New Mexicans and Pueblo Indians marched north to Arroyo Hondo, where Turley's Mill and Distillery stood as evidence of American entrepreneurial success. Besieged for almost two days, seven of the eight defenders, including Simeon Turley, died in the battle. Continuing north, the rebels attacked an American settlement on the Rito Colorado, killing Mark Head and William Harwood. By this time, January 23, the rebels got word of Colonel Price's departure from Santa Fe with a force of 350 army regulars and volunteers. Under the command of Montoya, Jesus Tafoya, and Pablo Chávez, some fifteen hundred to two thousand New Mexicans and Pueblo Indians marched south to meet them near La Cañada.[36]

Manuel Cortés appears to have left Taos for Mora on the evening of the nineteenth, for he was in the village when a party of eight American traders, including Lawrence Waldo, arrived on the twentieth. Waldo's premonition about the unruliness of the llaneros bore out, for the Americans quickly found them-

34. James W. Goodrich, "Revolt at Mora, 1847," *NMHR*, XLVII (January 1972), 49–60.

35. "Teresina Bent's Account of Her Father's Death," in McNierney, trans. and ed., *Taos 1847*, 14–15; see also Hubert Howe Bancroft, *The History of Arizona and New Mexico: 1530–1888* (Albuquerque, N.Mex., 1962), 428–437.

36. John Albert survived the mill fight to tell George Ruxton his tale, from which we get the details of the fray. See George F. Ruxton, *Adventures in Mexico and the Rocky Mountains* (Norman, Okla., 1982), 221–224. See also U.S. Government Circular, Feb. 15, 1847, in McNeirney, trans. and ed., *Taos 1847*, 43–45.

selves surrounded by armed villagers, and within minutes they lay dead in the dirt street. One villager loyal to the Americans rode south to Las Vegas, bearing news of the killings.[37]

On January 24, Captain Israel R. Hendley and eighty Missouri Volunteers set out from Las Vegas to punish the rebels at Mora. They found Cortés and some two hundred men defending the fortified plaza. Cortés skillfully defended the plaza and defeated the Americans, who retreated to Las Vegas with their dead leader tied to a mule.[38]

Affairs went better for the Americans under Price on their march up the Río Grande to Taos. At La Cañada, they engaged the rebel force on the evening of the twenty-fourth and by sundown had driven the New Mexicans from their positions on the surrounding ridges, killing thirty-six, including Jesus Tafoya. Breaking through a rebel defense at El Embudo, Price's troops arrived in Taos on February 3, where they found the rebels fortified in the pueblo church. When artillery failed to breach the walls, Price ordered an assault that finally scattered the defenders, who retreated into the pueblo itself. The American batteries proceeded to lob canisters of grapeshot into the village, and, by morning, the defenders sued for peace. Some 150 New Mexicans and Pueblo Indians had died in the attack, including Pablo Chávez. The Americans had lost seven dead and forty-five were wounded, many of whom subsequently died. Pablo Montoya was captured and hanged on the seventh of February after a perfunctory trial. In his report of the campaign, however, Price noted that Cortés was "still at large."[39]

Indeed, most of the Mora rebels escaped punishment at this time. Americans under Captain Jesse I. Morin had returned to the village on February 1 but found it largely deserted. Morin's Missouri Volunteers set out to destroy the town and its subsistence base, torching the village and burning thousands of pounds of stored grain. The action ultimately proved self-destructive, for the Americans were left without food and feed for their own forces during the harsh winter.[40]

Denied the support of their base at Mora, Manuel Cortés and his followers, numbering some two or three hundred men, retreated to the Plains and began

37. Goodrich, "Revolt at Mora," *NMHR*, XLVII (January 1972), 52.

38. Ibid., 54–55.

39. "Report by Colonel Sterling Price to the Adjutant General, February 15, 1847," in McNeirney, ed., *Taos 1847*, 45–53, esp. 53.

40. Goodrich, "Revolt at Mora," *NMHR*, XLVII (January 1972), 56–57.

a guerrilla campaign that lasted into March of 1848. During these fourteen months, the mixed-cultural nature of the borderlands confounded American troops charged with pacifying the llano. American officers consistently reported Cortés's force to include three or four hundred Indians, usually identified as "Shians [Cheyennes] and Apaches." Given that the southern Cheyennes were still allied with the Bent family through marriage and the market, and that American soldiers were seldom well versed in Indian ethnonyms, the first identification seems questionable. The much deeper association between New Mexicans and Comanches, Kiowas, and Kiowa Apaches suggests that the raiding force would have been of that customary composition. Indeed, Comanches participated in ten of twenty reported Indian attacks on caravans along the Santa Fe Trail during 1847. In two major actions in June and July, the victims identified the raiders as approximately 250 to 300 Comanches and "renegade Mexicans" almost certainly associated with Cortés. In a separate incident on June 14, Major D. B. Edmondson reported to Price in Santa Fe that a "marauding party" of "Indians and Mexicans" under "the outlaw Cortés" had, one month earlier, struck an army grazing party near Wagon Mound, killing one, wounding two, and making off with some 250 horses. A few days later, raiders hit an ox caravan at Santa Clara springs, and, although repulsed, they drove off the oxen and slaughtered them in order to strand the convoy. Edmondson's retaliatory foray stumbled into a rebel encampment and was forced to withdraw, leaving one man dead on the field. The major estimated the Indian and New Mexican force at four hundred to six hundred men.[41]

On June 27, raiders stole stock from Las Vegas, and the American scout detachment sent in pursuit suffered ambush at Las Vallas, losing four men. Major Edmondson's retaliatory raid netted forty townspeople who had supported the insurgents. Two weeks later, at the grazing camp of La Cienega east of Taos, Cortés's rebels killed six men and stole all the stock as well as "property of every description." Edmondson mounted a new campaign in July, destroyed the village of Las Pias, then moved up the Pecos through Anton Chico to La Cuesta, where Cortés and 350 insurgents barely escaped his attack, fleeing

41. The only Cheyennes likely to have felt real enmity toward Americans would have been young men cut out of the horse and marriage economy, but the Bents would probably have noticed and reported this development. For Comanche and renegade Mexican attacks on June 24–26 and again on July 4, 1847, see Kavanagh, *Comanche Political History*, table 6.2, 318; "Major D. B. Edmondson to Sterling Price, June 14, 1847," "Magoon's Report to Secretary of War—1900," in McNierney, trans. and ed., *Taos 1847*, 87, 91–94.

to the mountains. Fifty of his followers were made prisoner. That American military units destroyed villages and arrested civilians points to the depth of support the rebels held in the countryside.[42]

Edmondson's campaign failed to put an end to the Cortés rebellion. Santa Fe newspapers reported that he and his mixed band of insurgents plagued the region for nearly another year. These accounts also hint at efforts by Cortés to widen the arena of conflict, especially by enlisting Mexico's support for his guerrilla war. In December of 1847, the *Santa Fe Republican* declared that "Cortés has with him 2 or 3 hundred [New] Mexicans and a large party of Indians, making in all some 6 or 7 hundred well-armed and mounted." After requisitioning thirty-one sheep from a New Mexican grazing outfit near Las Vegas, Cortés was said to have delivered a "receipt, to be collected from the Mexican government, which he said would be good in a few days." Some days later, he entered a rancho and killed fifteen head of beef "for subsistence of his troops, which are mostly Indians."[43]

Later in January, the *Republican* noted with alarm that Cortés had been commissioned a captain by Governor Angel Trías of Chihuahua, with Juan Antonio Guerro of Taos as his lieutenant in a "company of the [Mexican] National Guard." In the decade before the Mexican-American War, Chihuahuan governors José Joaquín Calvo and Trías had made efficient use of mercenary fighters and scalp hunters like James "Santiago" Kirker, who brought in 487 Apache scalps for bounty payments between 1837 and 1846. Although nominally agents of the Mexican state, these freelancers chose their own objectives, and some evidence exists that a few of Kirker's Shawnee and Delaware compatriots joined in the Taos rebellion. The idea of a subsidized fighting force of the Mexican National Guard roaming the eastern Plains in search of white scalps brought Americans in Santa Fe close to panic.[44]

42. Unfortunately, neither of these place-names (Las Vallas and Las Pias) applies to known locations. They probably refer to sites in the Pecos valley and its tributaries downstream from Anton Chico (Sterling Price to the Adjutant General, Jul. 20, 1847, in McNierney, trans. and ed., *Taos 1847*, 95–96).

43. *Santa Fe Republican,* Dec. 25, 1847, Jan. 1, 1848, microfilm in New Mexico State Records Center.

44. Lewis H. Garrard reported that one of the bravest defenders in the American assault on the Taos Pueblo church was a Delaware Indian named Big Nigger, who had served with Kirker and a Shawnee chief named Spy-Buck from about 1836 on, often visiting at Bent's Fort. Kirker had received a trading license for the Apaches from Governor Albino Pérez

Much to their relief, in March came the "glorious news" that a Captain Armstrong and forty men had surprised Cortés and some sixty followers in their camp outside of Socorro, forcing them to flee without much of their equipment and "one cooked beef." Among the materials left behind were printed broadsides declaring the Taos rebels "true patriots of the Mexican nation." Cortés was thought to have been wounded in the attack, but the newspaper later reported that "this was but a slight wound in one of his legs." Finally, news reached Santa Fe that Cortés had disbanded his "banditti" and fled for the relative safety of Chihuahua.[45]

Still, depredations by mixed bands continued for the next several years. A band of Jicarilla Apaches, perhaps once allied with Cortés, destroyed an American trading caravan in June 1848 on Manco Burro Pass, taking captive two children whom they later sold to a Taos merchant for $160. New Mexicans would not mount another rebellion, but over the next several years they would solicit support from both Mexico and their Plains Indian neighbors to do so. James S. Calhoun accused New Mexican "wandering merchants" of being the agents of these seditious plots, arguing in 1849 that as long as New Mexican comancheros were "permitted a free and unrestrained access to the wild and roving Indians of this country, just so long are we to be harassed by them, and their allies."

---

in 1835, and from Governor Armijo after order was restored in 1837. See *Wah-to-yah and the Taos Trail . . .* (Norman, Okla., 1955), 186–187; see also a sketch of Kirker's career in the *Santa Fe Republican,* Nov. 20, 1847, microfilm in New Mexico State Records Center. Ralph A. Smith reports that Kirker's Delaware associates at Taos included Big Nigger, Jim Swanick, Kin Dickey, and Little Beaver and that all managed to escape the American suppression. See "The 'King of New Mexico' and the Doniphan Expedition," *NMHR,* XXXVIII (January 1963), 29–55, esp. 37–38. Smith has authored the definitive biography of Kirker in *Borderlander: The Life of James Kirker, 1793–1852* (Norman, Okla., 1999). For Mexican contracts with Kirker and other freelance bounty hunters, often fighters from emigrant tribes like the Delawares and Shawnees, see Smith, "Mexican and Anglo-Saxon Traffic in Scalps, Slaves, and Livestock, 1835–1841," *West Texas Historical Association Yearbook,* XXXVI (1960), 98–115; Smith, "Indians in American-Mexican Relations before the War of 1846," *Hispanic American Historical Review,* XLIII (February 1963), 34–64; Smith, "Scalp Hunting: A Mexican Experiment in Warfare," *Great Plains Journal,* XXIII (1984), 41–81; Smith, "Comanches' Foreign War: Fighting Head Hunters in the Tropics," *Great Plains Journal,* XXIV–XXV (1984–1985), 21–44.

45. *Santa Fe Republican,* Mar. 8, 1848, microfilm in New Mexico State Records Center.

> These traders go where they please without being subjected to the slightest risk, but one, not of their fraternity, dare not advance an inch abroad without risking life and property.[46]

The editors of the *Republican* agreed with Calhoun. Comanches, they claimed, continued to steal "thousands of head of cattle, horses, mules and sheep . . . and made women and children prisoners," whom they later sold to "wandering" New Mexican traders and traffickers. These middlemen in turn submitted claims for indemnification to stockowners or reluctant American administrators. However, the latter felt compelled to uphold article eleven of the Treaty of Guadelupe Hidalgo, which bound the United States to eliminate commerce in contraband, repatriate Mexican captives, or compensate Mexico for her losses. Despite his belief that New Mexican plainsmen were complicit in the traffic, Calhoun engaged the services of Encarnación García of Mora to seek out Mexicans held captive by Comanches and other Plains tribes. In March 1850, García delivered four Mexicans into Calhoun's hands.[47]

Comanches had seized twelve-year-old Refugio Picaros from the rancho de Papascal (Santiago Papasquiaro), Durango, in 1848, then sold him to Mescalero Apaches. García's compadre José Francisco Lucero purchased the boy for "four knives, one plug of tobacco, two fanegas of corn, and six yards of red Indian cloth." Powler Sandoval of Mora purchased Teodoro Martel of Saltillo, age ten or twelve, for a mare, a rifle, a shirt, a pair of drawers, thirty charges of powder, some bullets, and a buffalo robe. He had been two years in captivity. Sandoval also traded for Rosalie Taveris of Monclova, age twenty-five, in return for two stripped blankets, ten yards of blue cotton drilling, ten yards of calico, ten yards of cotton shirting, two handkerchiefs, four plugs of tobacco, one bag of corn, and one knife. The young woman had been taken only a few months earlier along with eight other captives whose fate she did not know. Her husband Santiago Costellan and her four-year-old daughter had been slain in the raid. At the time of her redemption she was being held at a place called Cerro del Queso (Cuesta?), a trading rendezvous on the llano, where Calhoun under-

46. Lecompte, "The Manco Burro Pass Massacre," *NMHR*, XLI (October 1966), 305–318; Calhoun to Medill, Oct. 15, 1849, in Abel, ed., *Official Correspondence of Calhoun*, 51.

47. "Indian Depredations," in *Santa Fe Republican*, Apr. 2, 1848, microfilm in New Mexico State Records Center; for Calhoun's frustration at having to deal with New Mexican comancheros like García, see Calhoun to Commissioner Orlando Brown, Oct. 9, 1850, in Abel, ed., *Official Correspondence of Calhoun*, 170–172.

stood that "parties of Apaches and Comanches are constantly going out and coming in with horses, mules, sheep, goats, cows, goods, money, and captives." Señora Taveris complained of hard work and rough treatment and had been "spared but one humiliation." One doubts that she would have made public a sexual assault in any case, given the stigma attached to cross-racial rape, but Comanche adoption might have prevented her violation. Given that all the goods exchanged for her were those valued by Comanche women, she might have found some security in fictive kinship with (or ownership by) a prominent Indian woman. Vicente Romero of Mora freed the last captive, twelve-year-old Caudalans (Candelario?) Galote, for the price of corn, tobacco, "one knife, one shirt, one mule, one small package of powder, and a few balls." The boy was four years in captivity. All were more than a thousand miles from their homes and would have to wait several months for formal repatriation procedures to be implemented. In June, Calhoun managed to deliver a total of thirteen Mexicans to Comandante José Prieto in El Paso del Norte. Few more would follow. Comanche reluctance to part with valuable social and labor resources, and American reluctance to compensate redeemers generously, made article eleven a sore point between the United States and Mexico for another generation.[48]

Some New Mexican comancheros did find a way around the poor recompense associated with repurchased captives: they dealt directly with those families able to reward the labors of rescue. This was not a covert commerce, for agents placed on behalf of grieving families advertisements in St. Louis and Santa Fe newspapers offering rewards for captive redemption. Responding to American reward notices posted in 1837, New Mexican plainsmen from San Miguel del Vado ransomed Sarah Ann Horn from Comanches for "a horse, four bridles, two blankets, two looking-glasses, two knives, some tobacco, and some powder and balls," which she estimated at a value of eighty dol-

48. Calhoun to Brown, Mar. 31, 1850, Jul. 15, 1850, enclosure from Prieto, June 27, 1850, all in Abel, ed., *Official Correspondence of Calhoun,* 181–183, 226–227; Kavanagh, *Comanche Political History,* 339–341. In fact, the only easy appropriation Calhoun ever received from Congress was a $1,500 bounty for the redemption, ultimately unsuccessful, of Mrs. White and her "fair daughter," taken in November 1849. Comanches resisted repatriation as well. When Calhoun bungled a diplomatic visit by the Comanche captain Eagle Feathers in May 1851 and inadvertently rescued his fifteen-year-old captive, Andrés Martínez, held seven years after his seizure from Rancho el Gallo in Durango, the Comanche left behind a trail of slaughtered cattle and empty horse corrals from Santa Fe to Anton Chico. He claimed he had "not forgotten or forgiven the loss of his captive." See Calhoun to Commissioner Luke Lea, Jul. 28, 1851, in Abel, ed., *Official Correspondence of Calhoun,* 390–391.

lars. Her subsequent "captivity" in the mercantile household of the American Benjamin Hill seemed to her more offensive than her seventeen months among the Comanches. In 1848, John Potts placed announcements that urged "young adventurers to make a dash for Comanche country" in search of eight-year-old Ramón López, held by the Comanche captain Antonio, himself a Mexican captive turned Comanche. In this case, someone might have reaped the reward money of two thousand dollars, for in 1856 López was attending school in Austin, Texas.[49]

Despite such alternative economic incentives, lower-order New Mexicans remained unhappy with the American conquest. With their Comanche allies they began to engage in larger diplomatic negotiations aimed at preserving their control of the southern Plains economy. Geopolitical tension between the United States and Mexico opened opportunities for play-off diplomacy like those employed during the era of empires. Panic again gripped Santa Fe in 1852, when U.S. Indian agent John Greiner received word that the Comanche captain Pahayuca had visited Mexico City with the intent of "forming a league among the wild tribes" to expel the Americans from New Mexico. At the same time, "several desperadoes conspicuous in the revolution of 1847" (unfortunately unnamed) turned up in Santa Fe to "foment discontent among the lower classes." Commanding officer Edwin V. Sumner garrisoned a new outpost at Albuquerque with infantry and artillery to block the advance of Mexican forces, which to their great relief did not materialize.[50]

Despite the failure of their grand alliance, New Mexican villagers continued to make military and trade alliances with their Plains Indian neighbors when opportunity seemed ripe. Although less dramatic than the revolt suppressed at Taos, Manuel Cortés's Plains campaign anticipated the strategy for the next thirty years. The consistent objectives in these guerrilla and brigandage campaigns were threefold. First, these equestrian raiders needed mounts, and they extended horse-stealing expeditions into Texas and Mexico. Second,

49. "Sarah Ann Horn's Narrative of Her Captivity among the Comanches . . . ," in Carl Coke Rister, *Comanche Bondage: Dr. John Charles Beales's Settlement of La Villa de Dolores on Las Moras Creek in Southern Texas of the 1830's* (Lincoln, Nebr., 1989), 165–176, esp. 171; *Santa Fe Republican,* Jan. 29, 1848, microfilm in New Mexico State Records Center; J. Ignacio Gallegos, *Compendio de historía de Durango, 1821–1910* (Mexico, 1955), 95, cited in Smith, "Comanches' Foreign War," *Great Plains Journal,* XXIV–XXV, no. 5 (1984–1985), 28.

50. For correspondence relating to the "grand union" of Indians and Mexicans, see John Griener to Luke Lea, Apr. 30, 1852, and related items, in Abel, ed., *Official Correspondence of Calhoun,* esp. 525.

they needed commodities with which to purchase arms and ammunition and knew that the market most rewarded horses, cattle, and captives. Finally, Plains groups needed to maintain their own populations and so continued their customary assimilation of Mexican and Texan captives as kinspeople and slaves. Similar needs organized relations between New Mexicans and Navajos in the western plateau country but found distinct expression in their pastoral borderlands.

Some Difficulty Exists between the Owners and the Captors

Even as the repercussions of the Taos revolt and its wider insurrections ebbed and flowed across the eastern Plains, James Calhoun became territorial governor by presidential appointment early in 1851. Governor Calhoun found relations between New Mexicans and Navajos west of the Río Grande no less vexing than those to the east. While revolutionary violence posed a threat in the east, Calhoun faced the continuing violence of the pastoral raiding economy that had plagued his Mexican and American predecessors since 1821. Navajo ladrones owned the frontier. As early as 1846, Brigadier General Stephen Watts Kearney had authorized Mexicans and Pueblos "to form War Parties, to march into the Country of their enemies, the Navajoes, to recover their Property, to make reprisals and obtain redress for the many insults received from them." But the rebellion of 1847–1848 brought an abrupt suspension of the American military's willingness to endorse these informal militias. Calhoun reported early in February 1851 that since the American conquest the Río Abajo counties of Santa Ana and Bernalillo had lost 150,231 sheep, 893 horses, 671 asses and mules, and 1,234 cattle to Indian raiders, primarily Navajos. During the same period, New Mexican militia raids had netted 8,500 Navajo sheep, 11 head of cattle, 467 horses, and at least 40 Navajo slaves. The imbalance was obvious. Desperate to stem the loss of capital on the hoof, on March 18, 1851, Governor Calhoun reversed the stance he had so adamantly defended in 1849 and authorized civilians "to form Volunteer Corps to protect their families, property, and homes. The property which may be captured from any hostile tribe of Indians, by any company raised under the foregoing provisions, shall be disposed of in accordance with the laws and customs heretofore existing in the territory." He might have known that he would be adding fuel to the fire rather than dampening the flames. But his choices were few.[51]

51. Frank McNitt, *Navajo Wars: Military Campaigns, Slave Raids, and Reprisals* (Albuquerque, N.Mex., 1972), 101. For livestock losses, see Calhoun to Lea, Feb. 2, 1851, in Abel,

Navajo livestock raiding soared during the first decade of American administration not simply because U.S. authorities had suspended "the pleasurable excitement of reprisal" or because the military presence in the territory was so thin. Internal dynamics continued to drive the reciprocal raiding economy. Navajo Indian agent Captain Henry Dodge reported in 1853 that the tribe numbered about eight thousand, "of whom near 2,000 are warriors." He praised their dedication to agriculture, which yielded in a single year sixty thousand bushels of corn as well as wheat, beans, pumpkins, and orchard fruit. Their sheep flocks he estimated at 250,000 animals, in addition to which they owned 20,000 horses and 150 "head of horned cattle." A prosperous people, but there was a catch. Dodge claimed that a mere "one hundred men in the tribe" owned 100,000 of those sheep and 15,000 of the horses, and some of those ricos held "40 or 50 peons to attend to their herds." At an average household size of five members, Dodge's report meant that perhaps 100 of 1,600 families (6 percent) held 40 percent of the nation's sheep-wealth and 75 percent of the horse-wealth, the key cultural commodities for affinal kinship and social prestige. Wealth distributions in Navajo society at the turn of the twentieth century seems to indicate that another cohort of one hundred moderately wealthy families, linked by clan or marriage to the ricos, held an additional 20 percent of the sheep-wealth and probably most of the remaining horses. Fully 65 percent of Navajo households held flocks of fewer than two hundred animals, and 15 percent of these might have held no sheep at all. Flocks of fewer than 190 animals fell below the minimum to maintain both animals and owners under bad weather or stock-loss conditions. At least one thousand Navajo households lived in the shadow of hunger, social marginality, and dependency. Little wonder then that Dodge concluded Navajos "rarely kill, but consider theft a great virtue."[52]

Federal Indian policy in the middle of the nineteenth century focused on a combined program of military pacification, reservation, and agricultural instruction for Indians of the western territories. In New Mexico, the settled and self-supporting Pueblos had provided a model for Governor Calhoun's vision: territorially bounded "tribes" who would "cultivate the soil, and raise

---

ed., *Official Correspondence of Calhoun;* for militia mobilization, see 300–302. For recaptures, see years 1847–1851, in Appendix B, below.

52. These figures come from a report by Navajo agent Henry Dodge in 1853, published as "The Arrival of Captain Dodge," in *Santa Fe Gazette,* Dec. 31, 1853, microfilm in New Mexico State Records Center; for wealth distributions, see Klara B. Kelley, "Navajo Political Economy before Fort Sumner," in Linda S. Cordell and Stephen Beckerman, eds., *The*

FIGURE 14. *Navajos.* c. 1851. One of these ladrones wears a first-phase Navajo "chief's blanket"; note also the Spanish saddles and stirrups. Courtesy Yale Collection of Western Americana, Beinecke Rare Book and Manuscript Library

flocks and herds for a subsistence." Although he thought Plains groups like the Comanches too "wild" for such a solution, he believed otherwise about the Navajos:

> [They are] rich in all the necessaries of life. They cultivate the soil very successfully, raise, and collect by stealing, numerous herds of sheep and goats, fine horses and mules, and make the finest blankets I have ever seen. . . . so far as the Navajoes are concerned, not one dollar would be necessary to subsist them.[53]

If only the stealing could be suspended. Predilections to thievery were ascribed to Navajos and New Mexicans alike by American observers, but few explicitly made the link to social inequalities in the Indians' respective societies. A rare exception to the notion of cultural degredation came from Samuel Yost, who became U.S. agent to the Navajos, Zuñis, and Hopis in the summer of 1858.

Versatility of Kinship (New York, 1980), 320–323; Lawrence David Weiss, *The Development of Capitalism in the Navajo Nation: A Political-Economic History* (Minneapolis, 1984), 31.

53. Calhoun to Brown, Feb. 12, 1850, in Abel ed., *Official Correspondence of Calhoun,* 141, 149–150.

In a letter to the editor of the *Santa Fe Weekly Gazette,* he explained that the Navajo

> rich men are opposed to war, for they have all to lose and nothing to gain; while the poor are anxious for any commotion or enterprise which may possibly better their condition and certainly not reduce them lower than they were before. The ricos have peons or slaves, just as they have in the South, except they are Indians.[54]

Perhaps better aware of Navajo social stratification through the loss of their own kinsmen, other Indians also made the connections. When Americans began to recruit Utes as allies in military actions against the Navajos, Capote Ute headman Delgarito offered Albert H. Pfeiffer, their U.S. Indian agent at Abiquiu, his understanding of the situation:

> The rich Navajoes, who are few, want peace, but all the poor who live in Chelle, Tchusca, and Tchacco want war and, as they say, they want to steal all the Animals from the [New] Mexicans as soon as they get in good condition.

In almost perfect accord with the distribution of wealth and poverty recalled by Navajo oral historians, the Ute leader knew that differentials in wealth, rather than ancient enmities or cultural predispositions, underlay the endemic violence among his neighbors to the south. Yet his eagerness to get "his people ready to invade the Navajoe Country" was doubtless based on his unspoken desire to partake of the latent profits vested amid those canyons and mesas.[55]

Substrata of economic contest were most evident in growing disputes over how New Mexican militias might reasonably profit by the risks they took in attempting to rescue flocks stolen from their rico patrones. Customary division of spoils had provoked friction between ricos and pobres as early as 1851, when Ramón Luna, prefect of Valencia County, reported to Calhoun, "Some difficulty exists between the owners of the recovered stock and the captors. The former claim the sheep as their property, and can prove it by their brand, while the latter maintain that [the sheep] are in the same position with other goods, and should be subject to the same condition." Luna referred to 5,000 sheep, 150 horses and mules, 11 oxen, and 48 captives that had been taken in a reprisal

54. Yost to editor, *Santa Fe Weekly Gazette,* Sept. 9, 1858, microfilm in New Mexico State Records Center.

55. Pfeiffer to Collins, May, 15, 1859, National Archives, Office of Indian Affairs, record group 75, New Mexico Superintendency, Letters Received, C 2087/1859, enclosure.

raid in November of the previous year, a considerable reward for the militiamen's risk. Men in the western border villages along the Río Puerco considered this tradition a customary privilege associated with frontier defense. For the sheep ricos of the Río Grande, however, these rescues differed little from the initial Navajo raids. Like Mexican officials before 1846, Americans came to see that using civil militias to recapture livestock simply enhanced opportunities for pobre-Indian collaboration and exacerbated class tensions within New Mexico. Colonel E. V. Sumner, military commander of the territory, managed to hobble the full effectiveness of civil militias by refusing to distribute arms and ammunition to local leaders. But the siphoning continued, and by 1857 sheep ricos pressured the territorial legislature into passing laws that limited militia compensation to 30 percent of the recapture. Since this accounting took place in the field, militia members still stood to profit substantially if they could avoid the official gaze.[56]

Anecdotal evidence suggests that roughly one-half of stock seized on a given raid would be recovered either in the initial pursuit or in later raids on Navajo rancherías (although these might have been entirely different animals). Using the statutory 30 percent compensation rate as a conservative baseline, local militias might have acquired through recapture and customary divisions some 48,000 of the 158,000 sheep taken from Navajos between 1800 and 1860. Given that sheep flocks reproduce themselves in a range of 10 to 30 percent annually, not surprisingly the nacajalleses of the Puerco found their own system preferable to that of the partido, since neither would the increase be diluted by the 20 percent lamb and wool "interest" nor would they ever need to repay the principle.[57]

Sheep were not the only booty seized in these raids. Between 1800 and 1870, when the borderland economy thrived in the west, more than 1,200 Navajo captives received baptism in New Mexican parishes. Concurrently, Navajos seized Paiutes, Utes, Hopis, and New Mexicans by the score, retaining them either as binaalté, adopted kinspeople, or potential bargaining chips in hos-

56. See enclosure of dispatch from Luna to Vigil, in Sarracino to Calhoun, Jan. 20, 1851, Secretary of War Conrad to Sumner, Apr. 1, 1851, Sumner to Jones, Nov. 20, 1851, all in Abel, ed., *Official Correspondence of Calhoun,* 283–286. As the politics of the territorial legislature turned from antislavery to proslavery, the Militia Act of 1851 was amended again in 1860 to exclude the governor as ultimate dispenser of captured people and property, leaving this prerogative to "any man of experience any good character who shall raise a force" (McNitt, *Navajo Wars,* 385–386 n. 2).

57. See Appendix B, below.

tage exchanges. But this went beyond a simple two-way traffic. The internal divisions noted above worked themselves out in the captive trade as well. New Mexican nacajalleses might take Navajo women and children in their reprisal raids, but they also acquired captives by purchasing them from the schismatic Diné Ana'aii. In March 1851, Cebolla Sandoval, that band's headman, delivered eighteen of his own "brethren" to Americans at Cebolleta. More would follow. As at least nominally converted Catholics, Diné Ana'aii now had two cultural categories into which captives could be incorporated, either the Navajo naalté status or the ceremonial kinship established through Catholic baptismal god-parenthood. These marginals now served as scouts for organized New Mexican campaigns or freebooted as raiders of sheep and captives. Their quarry could be Utes, Paiutes, Hopis, or their Navajo cousins.[58] Tiana Bighorse, in her biography of her father Gus Bighorse (born c. 1845), remembered his view on these enemies within:

> And it isn't only the other tribes we have to look out for. Even our own people work against us. That's the way it is with Ahidigishii. He is Navajo, the enemy of his own tribe, raiding upon us. With him travel several men and women. They are a tough gang. . . . [they] went raiding other tribes and made enemies against the Navajos. He made innocent people suffer and pay with their lives.[59]

Indian captives often entered New Mexican households to become servants and slaves through the agency of other Indian groups. Once bartered, the women and children were either resold to rico families in the Río Grande valley or retained in the households of their captors. Captives were commodities with real market value, weavers and laborers in the pastoral system, and prestige items in status competition.

Although Americans failed to comprehend fully how critical class divisions

58. David M. Brugge, *Navajos in the Catholic Church Records of New Mexico, 1694–1875* (Tsaile, Ariz., 1985), 22–23. Navajo baptisms for the period total 1,241 (McNitt, *Navajo Wars,* 26–51, 310, 364). See also Calhoun to Brown, Oct. 12, 1850, Calhoun to Lea, Mar. 31, 1851, in Abel, ed., *Official Correspondence of Calhoun,* 262–264, 307–308. For American accounts of Diné Ana'aii slaving against other Navajos, see Lansing Bloom, "The Reverend Hiram Walker Read, Baptist Missionary," *NMHR,* XVIII (April 1942), 113–147; for the Hopi view of these raids, see Katharine Bartlett, "Hopi History, No. 2: The Navajo Wars, 1823–1870," *Museum Notes,* VIII (January 1936), 35.

59. Tiana Bighorse, with Noël Bennett, ed., *Bighorse the Warrior* (Tucson, Ariz., 1990), 18–21.

and generational tensions were to the raiding economy, they did express growing awareness of just how the borderland phenomenon bore resemblance to the issue at the forefront of national consciousness east of the Mississippi: racial slavery. An anonymous letter to the *Gazette* in the summer of 1852 hints at the manner in which customary servitude in the borderlands would become embroiled in that national struggle. Responding to an effort in the territorial legislature to bring New Mexico into the Union as a Free Soil state, the author countered:

> There is in this country a state of things existing which is much more worthy the efforts of your philanthropists, your Abolitionists and your nigger-loving white, than the question of slavery; and that is the fact that there are thousands, I might say, of Indian women and children who have been stolen from their families and sold into slavery, worse than *Southern Slavery.*[60]

Yet, where the South featured an ideological, if not biological, commitment to the separation of the races and maintenance of white supremacy, New Mexico presented a more complicated racial landscape. U.S. territorial attorney William W. H. Davis detailed the dilemma when he observed in 1857,

> Of the pure Castilian . . . as light and fair as the sons and daughters of the Anglo-Saxon race . . . there are only a few families among the *ricos* who pride themselves in not having Indian blood in their veins. . . . The great mass of the population are very dark, and cannot claim to have more than one fourth or one eighth part Spanish. . . . The system of Indian slavery which exists in this country conduces to this state of things. The people obtain possession of their children by purchase or otherwise, whom they rear in their families as servants . . . when they grow up to a man's or woman's estate, many of them marry with the lower class of Mexicans, and thus a new stream of dark blood is added to the current.[61]

Although mestizaje as part of borderland slavery had long been a concern among caste-conscious Spaniards, Americans harbored even more intense anxieties about miscegenation born of their long experience with the enslavement and sexual exploitation of African women. Racial mixture of white with African or Indian blood destroyed stable social hierarchies and produced "mongrel" races incapable of self-government and hostile to American prin-

60. Unsigned letter to *Santa Fe Weekly Gazette,* Jul. 20, 1852, microfilm in New Mexico State Records Center.

61. Davis, *El Gringo,* 216.

ciples of discipline and democracy. These prejudices had prevented the annexation of yet more of Mexico after the victory of 1847 and were borne out also in the way many Americans understood events in New Mexico territory after its conquest.

Kirby Benedict, who arrived in New Mexico in 1853 and became chief justice of the territorial supreme court in 1857, estimated that the number of Indians, predominantly Navajo, held in bondage in New Mexico ranged somewhere between 1,500 and 3,000; "The more prevalent opinion seems to be they considerably exceed 2,000." Hence, Indian slaves constituted at least 3 percent of an aggregate 1850 population of 61,525 (excluding Pueblo Indians). In a rare case of habeas corpus brought before him as district judge of Valencia County in 1855, he ordered the twelve-year-old Navajo slave girl of Marcelina Otero y Chaves set free. Although the "courts were open to them," he felt few slaves sought legal remedy because they were "so influenced [by] the circumstances which surround them" that "their right to freedom" seemed a distant consideration. Situated in households where bondage and kinship often felt synonymous, few Indian slaves availed themselves of the Americans' legal avenues toward liberty. In 1857, as chief justice of the New Mexico Supreme Court, he heard the peonage case of *Mariana Jaramillo* v. *José de la Cruz Romero*, in which he freed the girl from her service since it was a debt owed by her father, not herself, that had initiated her indenture. Thus peonage, slavery, and the circumstances that confounded their interdiction grew largely from the way in which New Mexican slavery blended into relations of kinship, however exploitative. Benedict noted that the proportion of Indian–New Mexican mixed bloods was much higher than the simple representation of slaves in the territory, since when Indian slave girls grew "to womanhood, they sometimes become mothers from the natives of the land, with or without marriage." By the custom of the country, these children were "not regarded as property which may be bought and sold as had been their mothers. . . . They marry and blend with the general population." The vagueness of cultural distinctions between slave and kin would grow only more perplexing to Americans in the years to come.[62]

62. See Benedict's testimony, given on Jul. 4, 1865, as "The Testimony of Chief Justice Kirby Benedict before the Doolittle Committee, July 4, 1865," in "Condition of the Indian Tribes," in *Annual Report of the Commissioner of Indian Affairs, 1865* (Washington, D.C., 1866), 325–327. For census figures, see Francis A. Walker, *A Compendium of the Ninth Census (June 1, 1870)* . . . (Washington, D.C., 1872), 108, which lists figures for 1850, 1860, and 1870. For *Marcelino Otero y Chaves v José Castillo*, 1854–1855, see the records of the district court,

By the 1850s, social marginals on all sides used the extensive network of exchange that had developed in the pastoral borderlands to acquire the key items of wealth and prestige in Navajo and New Mexican society alike: sheep and slaves. In doing so, the marginals preyed directly or indirectly upon the wealth of their own societies. New Mexican villagers recaptured the sheep of their rico patrones, the Diné Ana'aii took captives from their wealthy cousins, and Navajo ladrones expanded the network to seize captives from Hopi, Pima, Mohave, Paiute, Havasupai, Zuñi, Ute, and Chiricahua and Mescalero Apache bands on the fringes of Navajo territories. From these nineteenth-century captures developed the captive or slave clans that stood in subordinate status to the fully enfranchised Navajo clans. Although damaged to some degree by this redistribution, wealthy Navajos and New Mexicans lacked both the capacity and the will to interdict the traffic—their best warriors and soldiers were its principal agents, and they too received benefits, either in the form of bride-wealth payments or in a steady supply of household servants. In the next decade a wider field of conflict revolving around slavery and servitude in North America would come to encompass the pastoral borderlands and begin to replace customary webs of dependency and inequality with new distinctions of freedom. But, in the northern mountainous headwaters of the Arkansas River, fissures in those mixed-ethnic communities prefigured some of the weaknesses that Americans would later exploit in subduing the Southwest Borderlands.

Shooting and Crying and Shouting

The Plains tribes and New Mexican villagers were not the only borderland groups to sense a growing threat to their autonomy in the early 1850s. In the mountain valleys of the Arkansas and Río Grande Rivers, various Ute bands also saw their control over terms of exchange slipping away and themselves declining into a risky dependency. Throughout the eighteenth century, Ute and New Mexican montañeses had developed a local exchange economy in

Valencia County, Habeas Corpus, Indian Peonage, New Mexico State Records Center; for *Mariana Jaramillo v José de la Cruz Romero,* see Aurora Hunt, *Kirby Benedict, Frontier Federal Judge: An Account of Legal and Judicial Development in the Southwest, 1853–1874 . . .* (Glendale, Calif., 1961), 107–111. The authority to which Benedict turned in these cases, and that remains the standard reference, was Gustavus Schmidt, *The Civil Law of Spain and Mexico* (New Orleans, 1851), 113–114.

peltries, Paiute captives, horses, and grains that met their respective needs for subsistence but kept them relatively isolated from the economic developments in the pastoral and plains borderlands. After 1821, the Utes allowed seasonal visits by American traders and, after 1834, small-scale settlements on the upper Arkansas, for these offered them some access to arms and ammunition they needed to protect themselves from Comanches, Cheyennes, and Navajos. But with few products of real commercial value to trade, they gradually fell behind their competitors in military potential.

Although they enjoyed generally good relations with ordinary New Mexicans between 1821 and 1844, the Muache, Capote, and Weeminuche bands fared less well with the agents of Mexican Indian policy. Their willingness to allow passage on the Old Spanish Trail and assist in Navajo campaigns put them at the bottom of the list for gift disbursements, which more often went to those Comanches and Kiowas who maintained threatening postures toward New Mexico. Mexican officials too often treated the Utes as easily dismissed.[63]

In 1843, for example, Governor Armijo had authorized a freelance slave raid against the Navajos by the Frenchman José Portelance and the Englishman Alexander Montgomerie, who instead struck a Ute camp, killing ten and taking three captives. Demanding justice, more than a hundred Utes arrived in Santa Fe, but the new Governor Mariano Martínez contemptuously murdered eleven of the leading men while they met in his quarters. The remaining Utes fled north, killing several New Mexicans en route, then ransacked Antoine Robidoux's trading fort on the Uncompahgre River in central Colorado. They killed seven of Robidoux's New Mexican workers and took their Indian wives into captivity but sent word through a surviving American that the trader's peltries were untouched, a clear indication that they sought revenge only, not the elimination of commercial ties. Official relations remained strained henceforth, and the Capotes and Weeminuches did not allow New Mexican shepherds to bring flocks to summer in the San Luis Valley without demanding that some duties on the hoof be paid for the privilege.[64]

63. Although the *Fondo de Aliados* (Fund for Allies, maintained to purchase gifts for Indian diplomacy) at the Santa Fe presidio seldom met the diplomatic gift requirements of any indios gentiles, the Utes always ranked lowest for what little disbursements were available. See Daniel Tyler, "Mexican Indian Policy in New Mexico," *NMHR*, LV (April 1980), 101–120.

64. "Manifesto que el gobernador del departmento de Nuevo-Mexico hace a sus habitantes, 8 de septiembre, 1844," *MANM*, reel 35, frames 1018–1022; "Documentos relati-

The American conquest altered little the administrative stance vis-à-vis these Ute bands. While the treaties with Plains groups in 1851 and 1853 delivered annuity payments that included arms and ammunition, the Utes received no such useful supplies, only a single feast of mutton and beef and several thousand dollars worth of flour and trinkets in November of 1852. The disparity in armaments put the Utes at a terrible disadvantage with Cheyennes and Arapahos, who often made forays into the San Luis Valley to raid Ute herds and take captives. The construction of Fort Massachusetts in the upper valley failed to discourage Plains raiders, who, although increasingly suspicious of American designs, had little choice but to maintain ties with William Bent and Charles Autobees, fostered by those men's marriages into each tribe.[65]

These two resentments—the absence of useful annuity payments and the Arkansas traders' affiliations with Cheyennes and Arapahos—lay at the heart of events that stunned New Mexico on December 24, 1854. Early that morning, a band of Muaches under "Tierra Blanca" stole 73 head of cattle, 13 horses, and 2 mules from Marcelino Baca's placita on the Hardscrabble but left the inhabitants, including Baca's Pawnee wife, untouched. The Utes proceeded down the Arkansas toward El Pueblo, and within thirty minutes the people at Baca's heard the sound of distant "shooting and crying and shouting." Then silence. Five hours later Baca, Felipe Cisneros, and José Barela ventured an inspection of El Pueblo, and found eighteen dead. Two boys—Felix and Juan Isidro Sandoval—and Chepita Miera, the Indian wife of Juan Blas Martín, were carried into captivity. Felix would be returned eight months later at Abiquiu, but the Utes sold Juan Isidro to a Navajo, who kept him for nearly six years before his mother could redeem him for about "$300 in silver and merchandise, including a Hawken Rifle."[66]

In the following days, events along the Arkansas illustrated just how complicated the network of alliances and tensions had grown since the 1830s. On December 25, some Arapahos surprised Tierra Blanca's Utes in their camp, killing several and stealing in turn some of Baca's horses. The enraged Utes

---

vos al alzamiento de la tribu Yuta," *La Verdad: Periodico del Nuevo-Mejico,* I, Sept. 12, 1844, *MANM,* reel 37, frames 537–545, New Mexico State Records Center; Weber, *The Taos Trappers: The Fur Trade in the Far Southwest, 1540–1846* (Norman, Okla., 1971), 215–217; Lecompte, *Pueblo, Hardscrabble, Greenhorn,* 137–138; Frances Leon Quintana, *Pobladores: Hispanic Americans of the Ute Frontier* (Aztec, N.Mex., 1991), 65–66.

65. Lecompte, *Pueblo, Hardscrabble, Greenhorn,* 237–245.

66. Ibid., 246–250, esp. 248, 250.

killed Chepita Miera in revenge. The Arapahos apparently acted out of solidarity with Charles Autobees, who had earlier been warned by the Utes to cease trading corn and wheat to his Arapaho relatives. Between December 27 and January 19, the Utes, augmented now by Jicarilla Apache allies, struck all the Arkansas settlements above William Bent's new fort at Big Timbers. They stole nearly two hundred head of livestock and killed seventeen men, including nine Cherokee teamsters who were helping the settlers retreat to safety at Bent's. By the fall of 1855, only Charles Autobees and William Bent remained on the Arkansas, protected solely by their Arapaho and Cheyenne connections.[67]

Operating out of Fort Massachusetts in the San Luis Valley, Lieutenant Colonel Ceran St. Vrain and five companies of New Mexico Volunteers set out to punish the Utes and Jicarillas in February 1855. In a series of engagements over several months, the troops destroyed camps, killed a dozen Apache and Ute fighters, took livestock, and returned to Fort Union with "fifty squaws and their little ones." In September, the Muaches and Jicarillas signed a treaty with the Americans at Abiquiu. Henceforth they would remain at peace with New Mexico, and would provide inestimable service to Kit Carson in his Navajo campaign early in 1864 and in his actions against the Kiowas and Comanches in the autumn of that year.[68]

By 1855, the Utes and Jicarillas found themselves settling into a dependent role as auxiliary fighters for American military campaigns, a tactical surrender of autonomy that in the long run would allow them to retain some abbreviated holdings in their traditional ranges. Likewise, New Mexicans from the Río Arriba country—twice risen in rebellion against the imposition of state authority—began a quiet retreat into their mountain villages and ventured new settlements in the San Luis Valley. By the end of the century Utes and New Mexicans would reach a surprising reconciliation. But on the Plains and across the pastoral plateaus a new generation of borderlanders was just beginning its final, twenty-year attempt to maintain negotiating space within a shrinking domain.

67. Ibid., 250–253.

68. "Memoirs of Major Rafael Chacón: Campaign against the Utes and Apaches in Southern Colorado, 1855," *Colorado Magazine,* XI (1934), 108–112, esp. 111; in this campaign, the first Adobe Walls fight, 72 Ute and Jicarilla scouts served with Carson's 260 regulars and volunteers in return for a "promise of all the plunder they might acquire"; see Captain George H. Pettis, "Kit Carson's Fight with the Comanche and Kiowa Indians," *Publications of the Historical Society of New Mexico,* no. 12 (1908), 1–35.

8

CLOSER AND CLOSER APART

Spring, 1874: Río Chama Valley

Ute headman Ignacio and his band of Weeminuches had allowed the passage of arrieros carting New Mexican produce to the San Juan silver fields since 1868. These seasonal journeys, much like the earlier sheep drives along the Old Spanish Trail, offered opportunities for small-scale bartering in furs and the occasional sale of a Paiute captive. Ute service as scouts in the Navajo wars had also nurtured generally good relations between Weeminuches, Capotes, and New Mexicans. Weeminuches visited their agency at Tierra Amarilla for annuity disbursements of grain, coffee, and sugar, as their Capote cousins did at Abiquiu. The Muache bands held out against settler encroachments at their Cimarron agency on the eastern slope of the Sangre de Cristos and traded a few buffalo robes to the western bands during multiband gatherings at Tierra Amarilla.[1]

But, in the spring of 1874, Ignacio heard more disturbing news: several New Mexican families were northbound up the Chama with, not trade, but settlement in mind. Gathering a group of warriors, he set out to intercept the pobladores. The amity of the preceding generation seemed on the verge of dissolution.

As the two groups drew within sight, Ignacio rode forward, ahead of his men. A man from among the New Mexican force spurred his horse into a gallop to engage Ignacio. Suddenly, the two men reined up within a few feet of each other and broke into smiles. Speaking Ute fluently, Francisco Manzanares greeted the headman, probably in the language of kinship. Manzanares had been born a Ute, captured by New Mexicans as a boy, and taken into the José

1. James Jefferson, Robert W. Delany, and Gregory Coyne Thompson, *The Southern Utes: A Tribal History* (Ignacio, Colo., 1972), 29–43.

Antonio Manzanares household as a criado, and now—with his New Mexican wife, two adult sons, and two grown daughters with their husbands—he wished to establish a settlement along the San Juan River at its confluence with the stream in Cañon Largo.

Riding forward to join Manzanares and Ignacio, José Salomé Jáquez also extended greetings in Ute. Utes had raised Jáquez in captivity, until his New Mexican family in Abiquiu found the means to ransom him. Manzanares's sons-in-law, Epifanio Valdez and Cruz Antonio Archuleta, also spoke Ute fluently and added themselves to the discussion. The men finally agreed to travel as a group to the Tierra Amarilla agency, where the agent explained that, under the Brunot Agreement of 1873, the Utes had indeed ceded land rights up to the Colorado line. Facing legal realities and mollified by the cultural familiarity of the pobladores, Ignacio acceded to the settlers' plans, and the first permanent New Mexican village on the San Juan River was soon christened "Largo." By 1880, the village included not only the Ute–New Mexican families but Juan Mateo Casías as well, a Navajo captive raised in the home of Miguel "El Grande" Casías of Los Pinos.[2]

The Largo settlement was only the first of dozens of such family-based migrations into Ute territory, and, soon, onto the reservation itself. Ironically, this new mixed society took hold in the old Dinetah, from which coalescing bands of Athapaskans had emerged as the "Indios Apaches del Navaju" some two centuries earlier. The canyons and mesas of the San Juan and its tributary rivers, little suited to extensive pastoralism and never the home of major bison herds, would continue to shelter experiments in multiethnic conflict and accommodation. The incident on the Chama in 1874 was one of the more sanguine local adjustments as the political economy of the borderlands gave way

2. Frances Leon Quintana, *Pobladores: Hispanic Americans of the Ute Frontier* (Aztec, N.Mex., 1991), 103–107. Manzanares must have been captured sometime in the 1820s or 1830s, for he shows up as an adult serviente in the José Antonio Manzanares household (*Seventh Census of the United States, 1850,* New Mexico Territory, Town of Abiquiu, 37–39, originals in New Mexico State Records Center, Santa Fe, N.Mex.). For ubiquitous kinship terminology between Southern Utes and New Mexicans, and the problems posed for later tribal membership criteria, see Louise Lamphere, "The Problem of Membership in the Southern Ute Tribes," *Tri-Ethnic Research Project Report,* no. 41 (1963), TS, Western History Collection, University of Colorado, Boulder. For an earlier (1849–1850) experiment in Ute–New Mexican amity in the San Luis Valley of Colorado, see Thomas G. Andrews, "Tata Atanasio Trujillo's Unlikely Tale of Utes, Nuevomexicos, and the Settling of Colorado's San Luis Valley," *NMHR,* LXXV (January 2000), 5–41.

to modernization with the capitalist incorporation of the Southwest. Across the pastoral and plains borderlands, however, violence surged in the years between 1850 and 1880, as the moral and military conflicts generated by the Civil War engulfed those regions.

I Demand That the Indians Pay for My Boy

Americans came only haltingly to see that Indian slavery in the Southwest Borderlands bore consideration, whether positive or condemnatory, in the same light as chattel slavery in the South. The region, of course, had attracted much argument and attention in the decade preceding the Compromise of 1850, since slaveholding Texas had long claimed sovereignty over Santa Fe County, which ranged from the Pecos River to the eastern bank of the Río Grande. The failed Texan invasion of 1841 and a foray in 1843—when Texan freebooters stole horses and slaughtered innocents in the village of Mora and attacked a New Mexican militia on the Santa Fe Trail—had both been conducted under the legal fiction of fulfilling that claim. Their ineffectiveness meant that the issue remained unresolved even after the Mexican-American War and would become a point in the debates leading up to the Compromise.

Submerged within the territorial dispute lay the question of slavery. President James K. Polk had declared in 1848 that the Missouri Compromise line of 36° 30′ should extend to the Pacific, by which both New Mexico Territory and the southern half of California would be slave states upon their admittance to the Union. Yet California was clearly pursuing statehood under the free-state banner. New Mexico, therefore, must under the Missouri Compromise be admitted as a slave state, despite the fact that it was under U.S. Army administration after the Taos revolt and most of its residents opposed the extension of chattel slavery within its borders. That opposition did not, however, imply a deep commitment to free labor but rather a continuing antipathy toward anything Texan. Statehood, favored by St. Louis–Santa Fe merchant classes both Anglo and New Mexican, presumed self-rule and a favorable boundary settlement in the Supreme Court. Territorial status, supported by the military, local judiciaries, and traditional New Mexicans, would set aside the political issues in favor of federal protection (and spending). As pro-statehood and pro-territorial political factions contended between 1848 and 1850, neither side felt it necessary to make public comment on the slavery controversy nor to meddle with customary systems of bondage in the region, which provided cheap labor that rendered the importation of black slaves impracticable and unnecessary. Although the statehood party found electoral victory in the summer of 1850 and sent a constitution to Washington the next month, the July death of President Zachary Taylor, who would have supported their stance, ended New Mexico's hopes for statehood. Millard Fillmore favored Henry Clay's compromise points, and by September the Texas–New Mexico boundary was settled: Texas gained 33,000 of the 70,000 acres it sought and a five-million-dollar payment by the federal government. New Mexico remained a territory with slavery an open question. Abolitionist groups like the American Missionary Society quickly sent agents there, but they found a cool welcome from its inhabitants, who were as much opposed to the missionaries' Protestant moralizing against Santa Fe's gambling halls and fandangos as to their stance on slavery, which few residents felt was worth engaging.[3]

But chattel slavery was not absent in the Southwest Borderlands, especially along their eastern frontiers. In their relocations to Indian Territory throughout the 1830s, slaveholding elites among Cherokees, Choctaws, Chickasaws, Creeks, and Seminoles had brought with them approximately five thousand black slaves (6 percent of the aggregate population), whose labor played a major role in the rapid ascendancy of slaveholders to prominence in the territory. Likewise, thousands of illegally imported black slaves comprised 25 percent of the non-Mexican population of Texas at the time of its independence in 1836. Black slaves in Indian Territory and Texas knew well that Mexico had abolished the institution in 1829 and that freedom awaited if they could find safe passage across several hundred miles of open plains.[4]

And some tried. The American captive James Hobbs—himself from a slaveholding family in Missouri—claimed that, in 1836 or 1837, while he was resident in the ranchería of Comanche captain Old Wolf, a scout party brought "six

3. For the Texas–New Mexico boundary dispute and internal debates over the extension of slavery, see Mark J. Stegmaier, *Texas, New Mexico, and the Compromise of 1850: Boundary Dispute and Sectional Crisis* (Kent, Oh., 1996), esp. 32, 34, 53, 67–68; Lawrence R. Murphy, *Antislavery in the Southwest: William G. Kephart's Mission to New Mexico, 1850–53*, Southwestern Studies, no. 54 (El Paso, Tex., 1978); Howard Roberts Lamar, *The Far Southwest, 1846–1912: A Territorial History* (New Haven, Conn., 1966), 61–70.

4. For numbers, see Michael F. Doran, "Negro Slaves of the Five Civilized Tribes," *Annals of the Association of American Geographers*, LXVIII (1978), 335–350, esp. 340, 346; for the institution among the Cherokees, see Theda Perdue, *Slavery and the Evolution of Cherokee Society* (Knoxville, Tenn., 1979); for Texas, see Paul D. Lack, "Slavery and the Texas Revolution," *Southwestern Historical Quarterly*, LXXXIX (1985), 181–202.

negroes" into camp as captives. They had escaped from their masters in the Cherokee Nation and were attempting to reach freedom in Mexican territory. Old Wolf and his band found the exhausted and frightened runaways a great curiosity. Instead of re-enslaving them, however, he played host for eight days, fed them back to strength, and finally gave them an escort to the "main road to Mexico," perhaps the Santa Fe Trail itself. In 1845, Charles Bent, Hobbs's onetime employer, warned Manuel Alvarez, the U.S. diplomatic representative in Santa Fe, that comancheros from Río Arriba had recently arrived in Taos with "five negroes . . . no doubt runaways from the United States," whose fugitive status threatened relations between the U.S. and Mexico. Claiming that treaty agreements between the two nations stipulated the reciprocal return of "prisoners taken by the allies of either nation," Bent said that Alvarez "should demand these negroes and send them to the U.S." He had done his part to preserve the relationship, he argued, since he had bought several New Mexican captives off the Pawnees (in U.S. territory) and returned them to their homes in San Miguel del Vado and Taos. Alvarez seems not to have acted on Bent's proposal. Two years later on the Upper Arkansas the English adventurer George Ruxton met an "American Negro," formerly a slave in the Cherokee Nation, who had lived some years with his Comanche captors before being sold to a Kiowa, who resold him to the American trader William Tharpe. The former slave was then the preferred fiddler at Fort Pueblo's fandangos, having passed through several versions of the institution.[5]

Other blacks found new identities or manumission in the borderlands. The African presence among the Delaware Indian hunters and trappers who worked at Bent's Fort on the Arkansas was sufficiently manifest that the Cheyennes called them Black Shawnees. One of these was Big Nigger, a Delaware Indian who married a woman of Taos Pueblo and who fought fiercely on the side of his affines and fellow insurgents in 1847, when American troops stormed the church at the pueblo. Opposing him in the American vanguard was Charles Bent's slave Dick Green, given the name Turtle Shell by the Bents' Cheyenne relatives, who sought to avenge the death of his master. Some Ameri-

5. James Hobbs, *Wild Life in the Far West: Personal Adventures of a Border Mountain Man* (Glorieta, N.Mex., 1969), 30–31; Charles Bent to Manuel Alvarez, Mar. 30, 1845, in Benjamin Read Collection, box 1, no. 71, New Mexico State Records Center (I have corrected Bent's singular approach to spelling in these quotations); George Frederick Augustus Ruxton, *Ruxton of the Rockies*, ed. Le Roy R. Hafen, coll. Clyde Porter and Mae Reed Porter (1950; Lincoln, Nebr., 1982), 268.

cans thought that Big Nigger died at Taos, but Ruxton encountered him two months later trapping with three other Delawares (Jim Dickey, Jim Swannick, and Little Beaver) on the upper Arkansas. Although there was a bounty on his head, his Indian companions had "taken the delinquent under the protection of their rifles," and Ruxton thought him safe from capture. Where this "Black Indian" found freedom among the "sturdy race of half-breeds" in the mountain borderlands, Dick Green attained his in the American way: he was manumitted by William Bent in reward for his loyalty and lived out his remaining days in St. Louis. Also fighting on the American side at Taos (at least to hear him tell it) was the free mulatto, trapper, and Crow Indian affine James Beckwourth, who would soon open a cantina in Santa Fe. Still empty of enslaved blacks, these fugitives, Black Indians, freed slaves, and free mulattoes might all have been among the twenty-two "free Negroes" enumerated in New Mexico's first territorial census in 1850.[6]

They would be among the last. New governor James Calhoun quickly called for the exclusion of free blacks from the territory, claiming, "The disgusting degradation to which society is subjected by their presence, is obvious to all, and demands a prohibatory [sic] act of the severest nature." Calhoun died in 1852, but others took up his cause. In 1857, the territorial legislature passed an Act Restricting the Movement of Free Negroes to the Territory, excepting those already in residence, who were cautioned that their freedom depended on "good behavior." In contrast to the reluctant acceptance that many Americans accorded sexual unions among enslaved Indians and New Mexicans, this act prohibited the marriage of a male Negro or mulatto, free or slave, to a white woman. Since the "colored serving woman" of a Mrs. White had disappeared into Indian captivity in 1849, the first black slaves to enter the territory securely were "Hannah" and "Benjamin," sold by then-lieutenant James H. Carleton to Governor William Carr Lane in 1851. By 1860, sixty-four black slaves re-

6. George Bent to George Hyde, Mar. 19, 1906, Oct. 3, 1911, Western Americana MS, 32, Beinecke Library, Yale University, New Haven, Conn. For Big Nigger, see Ruxton, *Ruxton of the Rockies,* ed. Hafen, coll. Porter and Porter, 266; Lewis H. Garrard, *Wah-to-Yah and the Taos Trail . . .* (Norman, Okla., 1955), 186–187. For the notoriously imaginative Beckwourth, who alternately contracted as a hunter with the Bents, lived among his Crow kinspeople, ran his Santa Fe cantina, and served as a scout in Colonel John Chivington's murderous assault on Black Kettle's Cheyennes at Sand Creek in 1864, see Beckwourth, *The Life and Adventures of James P. Beckwourth* (Lincoln, Nebr., 1972); for 1850 "free Negroes," see Francis A. Walker, *A Compendium of the Ninth Census (June 1, 1870) . . .* (Washington, D.C., 1872), 108.

sided therein, most of them personal servants for army officers stationed in Santa Fe.[7]

Borderland slavery and the American system converged in multiple tragedies in the summer of 1858. At Fort Defiance, established in September 1851 to interdict Navajo ladrones from Cañon de Chelly before they could reach the Río Grande, a visiting Navajo with a bow and arrow shot Jim, a black "servant boy" belonging to Brevet Major William Brooks. It took the teeenage boy four days to die. The Navajo, a member of the rico Cayetano's outfit, had been at the fort "trying to sell a couple of blankets . . . to a camp woman," Brooks reported to his superiors. When he saw Jim passing near the woman's quarters, he had leapt on his horse and shot downward, over the boy's shoulder blade and through his chest. He then "put whip to his horse and left over the hill." As he lay in agony, the boy insisted he had done nothing to incite the attack. Brooks immediately called in Zarcillos Largos (Long Earrings), a prominent Navajo rico and *hataali* (spiritual practitioner), and demanded that the murderer be turned over to authorities for prosecution. If not, the "great atrocity" would be countered by war on his people.[8]

The Navajo headman, called Naat'allee (Peace Chanter) by his people, tried to delay the vengeful American. The killer was no *pelado* like those who usually bartered and gambled at the fort but a member of a powerful headman's family, which Zarcillos Largos did not wish to confront. While Major Brooks prepared for war, Special Navajo Agent Samuel Yost arrived at the fort and conducted his own investigation. Yost lamented the death of the boy but also attempted to find some explanation for the violence. After interviewing several Navajos, he determined that the killer had "had a difficulty some days before with one of his women."

> He wished her to go to some place with him, she refused, and at a dance he tore from her all the clothing that covered her person. She still refused;

7. Calhoun quoted in Murphy, *Antislavery in the Southwest,* 90; for the exclusion act and its connection to an emerging proslavery faction, see Aurora Hunt, *Kirby Benedict, Frontier Federal Judge: An Account of Legal and Judicial Development in the Southwest, 1853–1874 . . .* (Glendale, Calif., 1961), 112–133; Loomis Morton Ganaway, "New Mexico and the Sectional Controversy, 1846–61," *NMHR,* XVIII (July 1943), 205–246.

8. Brooks to Assistant Adjutant General, July 15, 16, 1858, quoted in J. Lee Correll, comp. and ed., *Through White Men's Eyes: A Contribution to Navajo History: A Chronological Record of the Navajo People from Earliest Times to the Treaty of June 1, 1868* (Window Rock, Ariz., 1979), II, 133–134.

> whereupon, to appease his feelings, he started out (as is the custom of the Navajo Indians) to kill some one outside of his nation. This he succeeded in doing in the person of the negro boy. The Indian returned to the place where his woman was, and she proceeded with him to the place originally desired by the Indian.

Yost believed that the Navajo man had targeted Jim by simple happenstance, that the "commander of the post" might as easily have been slain had "an opportunity presented itself." Subsequent events suggested otherwise.[9]

Despite reassurances from Zarcillos Largos and even Sandoval, headman of the Diné Ana'aii, that peace-seeking Navajos were doing all they could to reach some resolution and surrender the murderer, the army moved to punish Navajos in general. Colonel Dixon Miles took command at Fort Defiance and announced that notice would soon be given to "the Mexicans and Pueblo Indians to strike in, capture, and slay." In August, an American detachment supported by New Mexican auxiliary militia struck a peaceful Navajo ranchería at Ojo del Oso, killing as many as ten and taking four captives. Other expeditions were planned, but, suddenly, on September 7, Sandoval arrived at the fort and announced that Jim's killer had been pursued by Navajos into the Chuska Mountains, where he had resisted their arrest and had suffered severe wounds as a consequence.

The next day, Sandoval returned to report that the man had died and to request a wagon with which to bring the body in. Yost offered a mule, and, as some three to five hundred Navajos watched anxiously from the nearby hills, several riders escorted the corpse into the fort's parade ground. Major Brooks immediately requested the post's surgeon to identify the man and perform an autopsy. The body turned out to be that of a "Mexican captive boy five feet two or three inches high, and not over eighteen years old." In fact, some recognized him as a frequent visitor to the garrison. The surgeon declared he had been shot "through the liver and lungs by a rifle ball, while he was in a reclining position—probably asleep. This not being fatal, he was then dispatched by a pistol held near his head." With real dismay Samuel Yost informed the gathered Navajos that his "functions as agent had ended with them for the present" and that the military men were now in command. In October, the Americans determined that the boy "was a slave to an Indian who could speak Spanish—probably Vicente Baca or Juan Lucero," both mixed-blood members of the

9. Yost to Collins, Aug. 31, 1858, ibid., 149.

Diné Ana'aii. By then Colonel Miles had carried an indiscriminate punitive campaign deep into the Navajo heartland, burning winter stores and confiscating thousands of sheep, goats, and horses. Jim's killer was never found. Juan Anañe, the New Mexican naalté held by Herrera, told Miles that the man had taken refuge among Utes north of the San Juan River.[10]

Two slaves had died brutally and without warning, with war the result. On the surface the incident seems a simple tragedy, the consequence of a homicidally enraged Navajo man striking at random the most vulnerable target within his reach. The delivery of the slain naalté can be seen, as it was by the Americans, as an attempt to bring the issue to a close through clumsy and dishonorable subterfuge. The outraged Major Brooks initially seemed to perceive the murder of the naalté as an inhumane act and the substitution as an offense to his honor. Yet the twin murders concealed deeper cultural logics that simultaneously mark cross-cultural confusion and a noteworthy convergence in the meaning of justice, slavery, and identity.

Yost's Navajo interviewees had pointed to conflict between the killer and one of his wives as the heart of the crisis. The man's behavior toward the woman was well outside the bounds of customary relations between Navajo men and women—Yost himself noted that a "striking singularity" among the Navajos was "the position and influence of their women. Some of these have as large property, and their opinions are as much respected, if not more, in grave matters affecting the weal of the nation, as the men." To strip her naked in public would have been a shocking affront to Navajo traditions of female modesty and conflict avoidance. The only explanation for such behavior that would make cultural sense to Yost's Navajo informants was that the man was either bewitched or somehow spiritually diseased through contact with ghosts or aliens. His behavior at Fort Defiance might have been an extension of his ruptured *hozho,* or harmony, a desperate attempt to reintegrate himself by initiating alone some elements of the balance-restoring Enemyway. An act of violence toward someone outside his nation would perhaps bring him back inside of his nation. He was not angry, he was mad, and culturally so.[11]

10. Yost to Collins, Sept. 9, 18, 1858, McKee to Yost, Sept. 9, 1858, Yost to editor, Sept. 9, 1858, Miles to Wilkins, Oct. 14, 1858, all ibid., 153, 154, 156; Frank McNitt, *Navajo Wars: Military Campaigns, Slave Raids, and Reprisals* (Albuquerque, N.Mex., 1972), 335–337, 341–362.

11. Yost to editor, Sept. 9, 1858, in Correll, comp. and ed., *Through White Men's Eyes,* II, 152; for customary Navajo understandings of dispute resolution, see Robert Yazzie, "*'Hozho Nahasdlii'*—We Are Now in Good Relations: Navajo Restorative Justice," *St. Thomas Law*

Targeting Jim also made sense in an atmosphere made tense by simmering conflict between Major Brooks and the young Navajo headman Manuelito, who had been feuding over ownership of grazing pastures used by the Americans for several months. In May, Brooks had slaughtered forty-eight of Manuelito's cattle and eight of his horses. If Jim's killer needed to feel as if his Navajo kinsmen would support his actions, he chose his target well. He would avenge Manuelito's loss of property by striking the property of his antagonist, and in that act kill someone outside both the Navajo's and the American's nation, thus avoiding, rather than triggering, a cycle of revenge. Under Navajo understandings of compensatory justice, the delivery of a dead slave, again of an alien nation, would be honorable and sufficient. The Navajos who delivered the naalté to Fort Defiance had taken compensation one step further, for they also returned "60 or 70 ponies and mules" recently stolen by ladrones in a raid on the Río Grande. Major Brooks's rejection of the effort by Zarcillos Largos and Sandoval to restore balance seemed to signal a notable difference in the cultural meaning of the reciprocal killings. His moralism was drained of its significance and cultural distinctiveness, however, when, at the conclusion of Colonel Miles's campaign, he raised the issue of compensation by questioning whether his superior would "make any demand upon the Indians for the payment of this boy." Brooks seemed satisfied when Miles suggested that, in lieu of the murderer's surrender, which had been explicitly exempted in the subsequent treaty negotiations, Brooks would be permitted to enter a claim against the Navajo livestock captured during the expedition. Despite the massive misunderstandings swirling around the tragedy at Fort Defiance, both Navajos and Americans agreed—in this case, at least—that slaves were set apart culturally from their owners and constituted property whose alienation, even in death, could be remedied with compensatory payments.[12]

Review, IX (Fall 1996), 117–129. For penetrating textual analysis of American perceptions of Navajo women and gender roles, see Carol Douglas Sparks, "The Land Incarnate: Navajo Women and the Dialogue of Colonialism, 1821–1870," in Nancy Shoemaker, ed., *Negotiators of Change: Historical Perspectives on Native American Women* (New York, 1995), 135–156. For witchcraft, see Clyde Kluckhohn, *Navaho Witchcraft* (Boston, 1989).

12. For the Brooks-Manuelito dispute, see McNitt, *Navajo Wars,* 316–317, 320–321; Miles to Asst. Adj. General, Sept. 17, 1858, in Correll, *Through White Men's Eyes,* II, 154. For Brooks's complaint, see McNitt, *Navajo Wars,* 359.

Not a Single Cent for His Services

Navajos and Americans in the pastoral borderlands shared some common notions about slavery yet could not mesh their respective systems into stable relations of intercultural commerce. More adept were New Mexican villagers, who continued their creative adjustments to participate in the rewards of the borderland economies. Bison hunting, Indian trading, contrabandismo, and participation in the slave network all presented opportunities for lower-order vecinos to prosper, even as American capitalist development began to supplant these options. The carefree days of bison chases and tax evasion were drawing to a close, and the New Mexican llaneros found themselves operating within new systems of commerce that would ultimately render them homebound.

In adopting the buffalo-hunting economy of their Plains Indian neighbors, ciboleros over the course of the nineteenth century developed social and cultural expressions that mirrored those of their neighbors yet expressed a distinctly New Mexican flavor. Like the Comanches' and the Cheyennes' collective hunts, a cibolero expedition often included men and women from more than one village. A single caravan could include as many as 150 members, 500 horses, pack mules, and 50 carretas drawn by teams of oxen. Converging at a customary rendezvous on the llano, the men elected from among themselves a comandante "whom they obeyed without question"; they acted in much the same role as Plains Indian "hunt police," like the Koi'tseñko society of the Kiowas. Julio Hurtado of San Miguel del Vado recalled that, when the band spotted a herd, the comandante would call the men together and order them to recite *un credo,* "the Apostles Creed." Fanning out in a broad arc, with the fastest "lance horses" and most skilled *cazadores* (hunters) on the flanks, the comandante gave the order to charge: *"Ave, María Purisima!"* Once the killing was over, meat and hide processing occurred. The comandante then took charge of allotting the meat to each family, although the "smaller pieces were anybody's property in any quantity desired." José Librado Aron Gurulé of Placitas detailed the many uses to which the hides were put upon return. "From them were made most of the clothing of the men, as were the *tewas* (moccasins) worn by everyone in the village." Ox harnesses were fashioned from long strips of hide, and complete hides furnished floor rugs. Women without combs for carding wool substituted by laying the wool upon the "clean, hard undersurface for the beating of the wool with sticks, which they gave it instead of combing." Even the holiday sport of "La Pelota" required a ball made from the "tough, durable hide of the buffalo." Gurulé felt that, since game like antelope and deer were still to be had in the Sandía Mountains, these hides were even more important than the meat gained in the cibolero hunts.[13]

However much ciboleros emulated Indians in hunting tactics and methods of processing the harvest, they suffered one sanction Indians did not: their viajes were usually illegal. From the 1830s forward Mexican directives prohibited bison hunting and Indian trading on the grounds that they diverted citizens' energies from respectable (and taxable) farming and manufacturing. Yet ciboleros ventured out despite threats of confiscation and fines. American governors like James Calhoun, William Carr Lane, and Abraham Rencher attempted repeatedly to arrest the commerce or at the very least regulate its practitioners. By the 1860s, governors required cibolero and comanchero expeditions to post bonds toward their good behavior of as much as one thousand dollars before they departed. This succeeded only in securing the resentment of the poorer of their subjects and redirecting the "legitimate" commerce to rico mercantilists who sponsored the viajes.[14]

Beyond their illicit material returns, bison-hunting expeditions inspired cultural forms. Oral traditions from the llano yield the poetry of tragedy and the possibility of romance as well as dramatize the risks involved and the discipline necessary for success. A young cibolero named Manuel Maes from Galis-

13. See Manuel Jésus Vasques (b. 1856), "History of a Buffalo Hunter," interview by Simeon Tejada, Mar. 31, 1939, Taos, N.Mex., in *Musuem of New Mexico Archives,* Santa Fe, N.Mex. (hereafter cited as *MNMA).* For a large expedition in 1853, see William Watts Hart Davis, *El Gringo, or New Mexico and Her People* (Santa Fe, N.Mex., 1938), 43–44; Julio Hurtado (b. 1846), "Buffalo Hunting," interview by Mary A. Fulgenzi, June 1, 1936, Works Progress Administration interviews (hereafter cited as WPA), 5-5-50, no. 20, TS in *MNMA;* Wesley R. Hurt, Jr., "Buffalo Hunters," *New Mexico Magazine,* XIX (November 1941), 9, 35–36. See also "Life in the Old Houses, Part VI," interviews by Lou Sage Batchen, Placitas, N.Mex., June 30, 1939, WPA interviews, 5-5-49, no. 18.

14. José Antonio Chávez to José Antiono Vizcara, Oct. 23, 1831, roll 13, frame 488, *MNMA;* Manuel Armijo to Minsterio de Guerra y Marina, Sept. 7, 1840, *Mexican Archives of New Mexico,* New Mexico State Records Center, roll 27, frame 1091; Calhoun to Medill, Oct. 15, 1849, in Annie Heloise Abel, ed., *The Official Correspondence of James S. Calhoun, while Indian Agent in Santa Fé and Superintendent of Indian Affairs in New Mexico . . .* (Washington, D.C., 1915), 51. For Lane, see Abel, ed., "Indian Affairs in New Mexico under the Administration of William Carr Lane, from the Journal of John Ward," in *NMHR,* XVI (April 1941), 206–232.

teo once ignored a dream in which he lay dying in his mother's arms and set out on his *caballo alazan* (sorrel horse) for a hunt. His story became enshrined in a local ballad, whose author is long forgotten. As Maes raced across the llano, disaster struck:

De los caballos llevamos	Of the horses we brought
Mi caballo es más ligero	Mine was the most swift
Y me cayó la desgracia	Yet this disgrace befell me
Se me cayó en un tusero	A prairie-dog hole threw him
Y se me solto la lanza	And I lost hold of my lance
Y me paso el cuerpo entero	And it pierced my body through

Young Manuel expired on the distant dusty plains, calling to his mind images of his beloved sister María Romana, his younger brother Dominguito, his parents, and the lovely *"cerro de Lauriano que de mi casa te ves"* (Lauriano peak that can be seen from my house). His only comfort lay in knowing that

Quando la noticia llegue	When this news travels
Al Nuevo Mexico entero	Across all of New Mexico
Como no la sentiran	Will they not feel
La muerte de un caballero?	The death of such a horseman?
Dia y noche llororan	Day and night will they weep,
De que veian mi sombrero	Even more when they see my hat.[15]

Hunting and trading forays intensified contact between Indians and New Mexicans, posing greater opportunities for both intimacy and danger. Beyond the tragedy that befell young Maes, the Plains held perils of the heart, born of borderland slavery. Vicente Romero of the plaza of Córdova recalled one visit to the Plains when he and his compañero Anaclete Mascarenas nearly "brought calamity on our little *escuadra* (squadron)." Having joined with a band of Comanches for trading purposes, he and Mascarenas met "a young girl of the tribe" who turned out to be a captive taken from San Antonio del Arbol in Texas. Although now the wife of one of her captors, she pleaded with the young men to rescue her, promising that her father would pay them "in gold

15. "Manuel Maes," collected from an unnamed informant, interview by Lorin W. Brown, Oct. 1, 1937 (author's translation), WPA Federal Writer's Project Files, no. 230, TS in New Mexico State Records Center.

and cattle, should we return her home." Although not swayed by the potential of reward, Romero did entertain "dreams of taking this really *'muy bonita'* captive as a bride, and enjoying the surprise she would cause when our folks saw her" as they returned to Córdova in triumph.

But their comandante vetoed their request. "No, it can't be done. Any effort to free her . . . might destroy our whole party." When Mascarenas persisted, he was "seized and bound until he gave up his plan and promised to obey of leader's orders in everything. . . . So the *pobrecita* stayed there with the Indians, perhaps for life. *Asi le tocó* [Thus it happened]."[16]

Vicente Romero might have failed to secure a wife from the Comanches, but he did go on to find rewards in cibolero and comanchero trading expeditions. The trade goods they carried were similar to those of the preceding generation—salt, Navajo serapes, strips of iron for arrowheads, dried apples and plums, and *trincas* (large woven sacks) of "*pan de comanche,* a very hard [unleavened] bread, which our wives baked especially for trading to the Indians." From Peñasco Valley villages, comanchero bands of thirty or more men traveled over the Sangre de Cristos and down onto the Plains to Mora, where they picked up more traders. Waiting until nightfall, they would slip quietly below Fort Union (est. 1851) since "the Americans did not want us to go into Comanche country because it might cause trouble." After they came across "the trail of a large group, in which there were signs of women and children," they would pitch camp and light signal fires to announce their presence. If all went well, by morning a band of Comanches or Kiowas would have established their own camp nearby and "after a sort of feast" would start in to trade.

These culturally mixed encampments brought participants into closer social contact as well as economic exchange. In order to relieve the tedium of bartering, the younger men engaged in wrestling matches, horse races, and "contests with the bow and arrow." Large bison kills were increasingly scarce and comancheros now desired either fine Comanche horses or stolen cattle. For each trinca of bread, Comanches were willing to part with one or two horses, suggesting both the size of their herds and perhaps the level of their growing hunger. After the comancheros had exhausted their supplies and the cambalache came to a close, the Comanches "escorted [them] for three days out of their country," on guard against Apache raiders and American scouts from Fort Union alike. Nearing the Peñasco Valley the men would fire their

16. See Vicente Romero (b. 1850s), "Los Comanches," interview by Lorin W. Brown, Apr. 6, [1937?], 5-5-9, WPA Federal Writer's Project Files, *MNMA.*

rifles in a *Salva á San Antonio,* alerting their relatives who stood "on the rooftops counting us as we rode down into the village, to see who was missing." These sorties skirted conflict both with American authorities and Comanche trading partners. Peaceful conclusions to the expeditions were cause for relief and celebration.[17]

Not all comanchero expeditions were as bucolic as these remembered by old villagers in the WPA interviews of the 1930s. What had once been opportunities for lower-order men of equal status to engage in subsistence and exchange economies beyond the reach of their social superiors had become by the 1860s enterprises suffused with class implications. The Peñasco Valley expeditions themselves suggested such changes. Some were sponsored by a village rico, don Juan Policarpio Romero, who held the peon Manuel Jesus Vasques and the Navajo slave Juan Jesús Romero among his household members. He provided the horses, mules, and some of the trade goods. Simeon Tejada, who recounted the oral history, declared that, whereas don Juan Policarpio paid some of his men (although no more then 50 cents per day), the peon Vasques never received "a single cent for his . . . services as a buffalo hunter or horse trader with the Indians." While a patrón lived, Vasques "never held one single penny in his hand." Instead, Policarpio "kept" Manuel and his family. After Policarpio's death, Manuel received four goats; the rico's sons insisted that he sign an affidavit declaring himself well satisfied with his inheritance.[18]

This shift in emphasis—from self-provisioning to the resale of Plains commodities and from self-organized village-based viajes to more formal, patron-sponsored expeditions—points to a transformation of the comanchero trade indicative of growing integration within larger relations of capital, finance, and state-regulated markets. The transition was gradual, inconsistent, and not without attempts to subvert its progress.

Some Became Big Chiefs among the Tribes

During the years that New Mexican ciboleros and comancheros were voyaging onto the Plains, Comanches and Kiowas sought to defend the borders of their regional economy from threats both eastern and western. In the East,

17. Romero, "Los Comanches," interview by Brown, WPA Federal Writer's Project Files, *MNMA.*

18. Manuel Jesus Vasques, "History of a Buffalo Hunter," as told to Simeon Tejada, coll. Lorin W. Brown, Apr. 17, 1939, WPA Federal Writer's Project Files, *MNMA.*

forces unleashed by the growing crisis around American slavery would begin to impinge on Plains autonomy. To the West, Plains groups and New Mexicans found themselves at odds over a shared resource that once had seemed limitless: the southern Plains buffalo herds. Beginning in 1852, New Mexican ciboleros and Plains Indian bison hunters met in conflict in what one historian has termed the Cibolero War. Market hunting, intrusive bovine diseases, and grazing competition from some 2.5 million horses had, by the 1850s, reduced the southern Plains bison herds below the reproductive threshold estimated at 6 million animals. American Indian agents reported seasonal starvation among the Arapahos, Cheyennes, and Comanches in 1852 and 1853. Not surprisingly, Comanches began to halt cibolero caravans and threaten them with loss of "all their animals and wagons" unless they returned to New Mexico empty-handed. The Comanches later relented but allowed ciboleros to hunt only if they brought no more than a few pack animals to carry their take.[19]

The Cheyennes proved more violent, probably spurred on by William Bent's willingness to purchase any goods they took from New Mexican parties. Cheyennes turned back a group of ciboleros from San Miguel del Vado in the autumn of 1853, capturing more than eighty oxen and destroying twenty carretas. In the spring of 1854, while New Mexican militias pursued the Utes and Jicarillas, Cheyennes went on an offensive in eastern New Mexico, killing fourteen New Mexicans in San Miguel County alone and taking captive eleven boys from Tecolote and Las Vegas. In November, Cheyennes attacked a party of twenty-five ciboleros from Taos Pueblo near the Raton Mountains, killing eleven men. American officials did little to interdict these forays, since William Bent informed them that "the [New] Mexicans were to blame" for the hostilities. Finally, in 1858 Kit Carson arranged a treaty among the Cheyennes, Arapahos, and the Taoseños that allowed at least those Pueblo Indians free passage on the Plains.[20]

19. Dan Flores, "Bison Ecology and Bison Diplomacy: The Southern Plains from 1800 to 1850," *Journal of American History*, LXXVIII (1991–1992), 480–485. For reference to Comanche starvation in 1852, see Rupert Norval Richardson, *The Comanche Barrier to South Plains Settlement: A Century and a Half of Savage Resistance to the Advancing White Frontier* (Glendale, Calif., 1933), 212–213; Colonel Philip St. George Crook to Major W. A. Nichols, Jan. 29, 1854, quoted in Charles L. Kenner, *The Comanchero Frontier: A History of New Mexican–Plains Indian Relations* (Norman, Okla., 1994), 108.

20. New Mexico governor David Meriwether reported to Commissioner of Indian Affairs George Mannypenny that the Cheyenne agent Thomas Fitzpatrick had approved the sale "of the property of Mexican hunters" to the Bents; see Mar. 15, 1845, N/246, New Mexico

While the Cheyennes limited intrusions on their resources from New Mexico, they and other Plains tribes perceived yet another threat brewing in the east. This involved the Indian policy of the Kansas–Nebraska Act then under debate in Washington. Even while Congress wrangled over the extension of slavery and popular sovereignty in the territories, the Indian Office had begun negotiating with the emigrant tribes for a reduction in their holdings in Kansas Territory, compensated in some cases by annuity payments and in others by new lands in the western Indian Territory. By June 5, 1854, nine treaties with fourteen tribes were in place that would clear the eastern areas for white settlement.[21]

Plains Indians understood that these negotiations constituted a new threat to the buffalo plains from the north and east. The emigrant tribes would now be within hunting range of the rapidly shrinking southern Plains bison herd. Accordingly, in mid-July 1854, Kiowas, Comanches, Kiowa Apaches, Cheyennes, Arapahos, Osages, and some Crows allied themselves "to wipe out all frontier Indians they could find on the plains." As evidence for the seriousness with which the Plains groups understood this effort, the campaign was one of only five occasions when the Cheyennes moved their sacred Medicine Arrows against an enemy. A combined force of fifteen hundred Plains warriors—probably the largest multitribal force assembled to that time—set out for the Smoky Hill River in western Kansas, where they engaged fewer than one hundred well-entrenched Sauk-Foxes armed with American rifles. These "frontier Indians" proceeded to kill sixteen and wound another hundred of the attackers in a fight lasting some three hours. Shocked and humiliated, the Plains allies turned their wrath on the hapless Pawnees, overwhelming a party of 113 who had risked a summer buffalo hunt.[22]

Superintendency, Office of Indian Affairs, Letters Received, record group 75, National Archives, Washington, D.C. (hereafter cited as NA); William Bent to Governor Meriwether, Feb. 15, 1854, quoted in Kenner, *Comanchero Frontier*, 109; for Carson's diplomacy, see Kenner, 111.

21. Francis Paul Prucha, *The Great Father: The United States Government and the American Indians* (Lincoln, Nebr., 1984), 118–119.

22. For the Plains alliance against the emigrant tribes, see letters of Agent James, Sept. 1, Agent Whitfield, Sept. 27, Superintendent Cummings, Sept. 30, 1854, all in *Annual Report of the Commissioner of Indian Affairs, 1854* (Washington, D.C., 1854), 285, 297, 312. For Cheyenne memories of this engagement, in which legendary headman Old Whirlwind "had putnear all the feathers shot out of his war-bonnet," see George Bent to George Hyde, Apr. 3, 1904, Jan. 7, 1905, Western Americana MS, 32, box 1, folder 2, Beinecke Library, Yale Univer-

With their honor restored, but still in dire strategic straits, the combined tribes regrouped around their one reliable American affine, William Bent, who continued to trade with them until 1860 from his small stone fort at Big Timber. Plains groups now shifted the focus of their actions to the south, where Texas and Mexico offered promising livestock substitutes for a dangerous dependency upon bison.[23]

New Mexican llaneros also refocused their strategies southward, since it seemed that the Americans would not protect them in ventures on the Arkansas River plains. Relations with the Comanches and Kiowas remained tense, but each group needed the other to make its economy work. Comanches and Kiowas needed buyers for captives, cattle, and horses, the only commodities they could produce through raiding and grazing. New Mexicans needed suppliers for the same commodities, since the demand for domestic servants in rico households remained strong; likewise, both New Mexicans and Americans presented a market for livestock. Hence, the multiethnic communities of interest survived. But, at a more general level, all of these various groups were functioning in some respects as a single, mixed cultural unit by the 1850s, attributable in large part to the ongoing exchanges and incorporations of the captive system.[24]

Thomas Fitzpatrick, an old Arkansas River trader turned Indian agent for the Plains tribes, reflected on the issue of captive seizure and cultural mixing when he described the difficulties he faced in coming to terms under treaties he helped to negotiate between the United States and southern Plains tribes in 1851 and 1853. Matters of territorial boundaries and annuity payments proved not nearly so vexing as his attempts to meet the conditions of article eleven

---

sity. For the Kiowa perspective, see James Mooney, "Calendar History of the Kiowa Indians," *Seventeenth Annual Report of the Bureau of American Ethnology*, part 2 (Washington, D.C., 1979), 297; Captain W. P. Clark, *The Indian Sign Language, with Brief Explanatory Notes of the Gestures Taught Deaf Mutes in Our Institutions for Their Instruction . . .* (Philadelphia, 1885), 283–288.

23. After 1860, Bent and his Cheyenne wife moved back to the junction of the Purgatoire and Arkansas Rivers, where they farmed and ranched until Bent's death in 1869. See David Lavender, *Bent's Fort* (Garden City, N.Y., 1954), 371–384.

24. Chief Justice Kirby Benedict, who arrived in New Mexico in 1853, reported, "The rich, and those who have some quantities of property" provided the greatest market for "Indian slaves" in the territory; see "The Testimony of Chief Justice Kirby Benedict before the Doolittle Committee, July 4, 1865," in "Condition of the Indian Tribes," in *Annual Report of the Commissioner of Indian Affairs, 1865* (Washington, D.C., 1866), 326.

of the Treaty of Guadalupe Hidalgo, whereby the United States agreed to suppress the trade in captives and seek the repatriation of Mexicans currently held by Indian groups. Fitzpatrick explained,

> For a long time these tribes have been in the habit of replenishing their *caballadas* of horses from the rich valleys and pasture lands that border upon the Rio Grande. . . . They seldom return without having acquired much plunder, as well as many captives. . . . The consequences of those expeditions are twofold, for while they serve to sharpen the appetite for pillage and rapine, they also tend to keep up the numbers of the tribe. The males thus taken are most commonly adopted into the tribe, and soon become the most expert war leaders and most accomplished of marauders. The females are chosen wives and share the duties and pleasures of the lodge. In fact, so intermingled amongst these tribes have most of the Mexican captives become that it is somewhat difficult to distinguish them. . . . Upon this account the chiefs of the nations refuse positively and distinctly to entertain any proposals or make any treaties having in view giving up those captives now dwelling amongst them.[25]

In fact, these raids fulfilled more than the replenishment of herds and reconstruction of tribal populations, since both livestock and captives served commodity functions as well. Captives retained their customary value in the informal marketplace of borderland exchanges. George Bent, the mixed-descent son of William Bent and Owl Woman, remembered the scale of the trade and its intersection with the needs of poor Mexicans in his letters to George Hyde early in the twentieth century. If an accurate reflection of practices on the ground, Bent's recollections suggest that, by the middle years of the nineteenth century, an impressive multiethnic Plains coalition had formed that combined customary forms of captive exchange with market capitalism in plundering the northern provinces of Mexico.

> Kiowas, Comanches and Apaches made raids into Old Mexico them days and drove from there herds of ponies. These ponies were glad to get away from their masters down there. One Indian would get two or three *peones* to help him with his herd of ponies. They did not take so many women, only young women they could use, but the males [came] in more useful.

25. Agent Fitzpatrick to the secretary of war, Apr. 30, 1853, in *Annual Report of the Commissioner of Indian Affairs* (Washington, D.C., 1854), 363.

FIGURE 15. *Comanches.* c. 1851. They appear to be wearing Mexican serapes. By Heinrich Balduin Möllhausen. Courtesy Yale Collection of Western Americana, Beinecke Rare Book and Manuscript Library

> Lots of these peones got to be Chiefs among these three tribes. Lots of the peones made big hauls from Old Mexico of horses, mules, and other plunder. They had [a] better chance to find out from Mexicans where to go for better plunder as lots of poorer Mexicans stood in with these raiders. . . . My father bought 2 [of] these *peones* as prisoners from the Kiowas. One of them is now living at Kiowa Agency, he is 82 years old [in 1906].[26]

Bent's father was not the only Anglo-American to take advantage of the regional trade in captive labor. According to George, Texas cattle baron John Chisolm bought Mexican captives from Comanches to work in his cattle outfits, and, hewing to regional custom, adopted them, at least in name:

> In 1867, John Chisolm traded with Wichitas, Caddoes, and Comanches. Chisolm told me that these Indians were rich in horses that they stole from Old Mexico and they had lots of Mexican prisoners. Chisolm used to trade for some of these prisoners and use them to break unbroken horses that he

26. George Bent to George Hyde, Mar. 19, 1906, Western Americana MS, 32, box 1, folder 2, Beinecke Library, Yale University.

bought off the Kiowas and Comanches. When I met him on the Arkansas in 1867 he had one of these Mexicans. He called him "Jack Chisolm."[27]

Mexicans seized in slave raids continued to face a range of possible fates from full cultural assimilation through subordinate labor status to resale among the expectant capitalists of American Texas. Long the source of victims in the captive trade, Mexican peons who "got to be Chiefs" among the tribes confirm the parallel and continuing pattern of informal local alliances and cultural fluidity within the transborder raiding peoples. Among those who "stood in" with Comanche, Kiowa, and Apache raiders were the Mexican citizens of San Carlos, Chihuahua, a farming village established in 1774 to support the short-lived Presidio San Carlos, just south of the Río Grande. The American boundary surveyor William Emory reported in 1851 that these villagers "maintained amicable relations" with both Lipan Apaches and Comanches (no small diplomatic feat) and allowed Comanche raiders to make "San Carlos a depôt of arms for their annual excursions into Mexico." San Carlos also harbored an "escaped Mexican peon" who went by the name Toro Mucho, no doubt a reference to his stock in trade. The American surveyors encountered thirty or forty Kiowa warriors, of whom Toro Mucho served as chief, near the "Comanche springs." The Kiowa raiding band and their Mexican chief had "quite one thousand animals" that they were driving northward to the informal markets of Texas and New Mexico. In an effort to assure William Emory of the prominence of his local connections, Toro Mucho displayed with pride an immense silver cross he wore around his neck, a gift, he claimed, from the bishop of Durango. The American wondered if he had not snatched it from the bishop's neck. Cynicism aside, this Mexican man does appear to have maintained successful relations of patronage with Kiowa warriors, peons on local haciendas, the residents of San Carlos, and legitimate regional authorities in ways that were typical for agents of the borderland economy.[28]

27. George Bent, letter of Aug. 22, 1913, ibid.

28. William Hemsley Emory, "Report on the United States and Mexican Boundary Survey . . . ," House ex. doc. no. 135, 34th Congress, 1st session (Washington, D.C., 1857–1859), 86–89; for Presidio San Carlos, which was abandoned in 1784, see James E. Ivey, *Presidios of the Big Bend Area* (Santa Fe, N.Mex., 1990). For the continuation of such relationships as late as 1881, when a raiding band of Indians, presumably Apaches, was said to have included some thirty men from San Carlos "disguised, armed and painted" like Indians, see Isidoro Vizcaya Canales, *La invasión de los indios bárbaros al noreste de México en los años de 1840 y 1841* (Monterrey, 1968), 96.

FIGURE 16. *Toro-Mucho, Chief of a Band of Kioways.* c. 1851. He is wearing a Mexican serape. By Heinrich Balduin Möllhausen. Courtesy Yale Collection of Western Americana, Beinecke Rare Book and Manuscript Library

San Carlos could not protect all of its seasonal visitors, however. In the autumn of 1853, the Mexican freelance Indian hunter Celedonio Villa apprehended the Comanche captain Antonio Salcido at the site of the former presidio and brought him to Victoria de Durango for trial and execution. Mexican authorities granted Villa the extraordinary bounty of 2,199 pesos in this case (50 to 200 pesos was the standard range), since Salcido stood accused of treason. He had been captured as a young man in the Comanche invasions of 1841, baptized under a Spanish name, catechized, and educated by his Mexican master. For twelve years he had resided in Victoria de Durango and had served as interpreter and scout for the city's public security cavalry. He had only rejoined his Comanche kinsmen in March of 1853 as they swept through the region in a foray that lasted much of the summer. Fifty-seven prominent citizens of Durango had contributed funds toward his capture.[29]

Denationalized and renationalized transborder raiders like Toro Mucho and Antonio Salcido probably did not shrink from including Mexican captives in their plunder caravans, since Comanches, Kiowas, and Texan cattlemen all seemed eager to find new social locations or labor roles for them across the northern border. By 1855, Mexicans claimed that the northern state of Durango alone had lost 1,446 women and children to Comanche and Kiowa slave raids in the preceding twenty-three years, an index of deracination and heartbreak that pales only when compared to the 11,704 vecinos and militiamen who died in the assaults. James Calhoun had created another potentially powerful market by offering to repurchase Mexican captives in order to meet the United States's treaty obligations to Mexico. Subsequent Indian agents recognized the diplomatic and moral imperatives that drove this new arrangement but expressed some misgivings at its cost and economic illogic. John W. Whitfield, who replaced Fitzpatrick as southern Plains Indian agent in 1854, cautioned New Mexico governor David Meriwether, "We cannot establish the precedent of buying Mexican prisoners, if we were . . . only to pay for what the [Cheyenne] Indians now have in my Agency it would Bankrupt your Treasury—I am certain the Comanches and Kiowas have [an additional] one thousand." Providing new markets would be counterproductive when attempting to end a system of slavery in which, unlike the slaveholding states of

29. Salcido's case is reported in *El registro oficial* (Victoria de Durango), Sept. 4, 9, Oct. 19, 1853, cited in Ralph A. Smith, "The Comanches' Foreign War: Fighting Head Hunters in the Tropics," *Great Plains Journal,* XXIV–XXV (1984–1985), 36, 43 n. 45.

the South, the procurement trade acted as the engine of the borderland social system.[30]

So Much Cheaper Than the Risk of Capital in Slaves

Throughout the 1850s, most of the practitioners of the captive trade came to see the American government as their wealthiest and most reliable buyer for victims of the commerce, whether drawn from the haciendas of northern Mexico or the Navajo rancherías west of the Río Grande. Driven by treaty obligations to redeem captives or by the opposite desire to become slaveholders in the west, both antislavery and proslavery Americans became implicated in underwriting the borderland economy, so extensive and customary had the local form of slavery become by the 1860s. In its farthest reaches, the system extended from Sonora and Chihuahua in northern Mexico to California in the west, to say nothing of its eastern extensions under the control of llaneros or its northern manifestations in Utah and Colorado by Ute and New Mexican montañeses. Violent, competitive, yet based in cultural transfers and intercommunity alliances, the political economy of captivity in the borderlands merged with larger economic systems but remained almost entirely under the control of the local people. As such, it posed a viable alternative and substantial barrier to free-labor capitalism in the Southwest.

Some Americans recognized their nation's implication in the regional slave system and understood that the United States would become responsible for its future. If slaves could not be rescued from their immediate captors by military interdiction or humanitarian redemption, perhaps the government should redeem them from their final owners. Governor Calhoun once complained to his superiors,

> Trading in captives has been so long tolerated in this Territory that it has ceased to be regarded as a wrong; and purchasers are not prepared willingly to release captives without an adequate ransom. . . . Unless the [New]

30. Report in *La ensaña republicana*, Jul. 17–Oct. 30, 1856, Pastor Rouaix, *Diccionario geográfico, histórico y biográphico del estado de Durango* (Mexico, 1946), 34, both cited in Smith, "The Comanches' Foreign War," *Great Plains Journal*, XXIV–XXV (1984–1985), 40–41; J. W. Whitfield to Governor Meriwether, Sept. 29, 1854, quoted in Kenner, *Comanchero Frontier*, 111.

> Mexicans are paid for such captives as they have purchased and have now in their possession, but very few of them will be released.[31]

The governor and his successors pleaded for "some congressional action" regarding the peculiar brand of slavery practiced in the borderlands, but Washington could hardly be bothered to address an institution so far away and presumably different from the one that had the nation on the edge of war. Although administrators like William Carr Lane and David Meriwether were Whigs with ambivalent attitudes toward slavery, by 1857 President Buchanan appointed as governor a solid North Carolina Democrat, Abraham Rencher.[32]

Although antislavery reformers decried the existing system, other Americans saw real possibilities in it. Writing in 1857, United States attorney William Watts Hart Davis sought to settle eastern concerns that the territory might elect to enter the Union as a slave state:

> A greater barrier than climate is the cheapness of peon labor, which is less expensive to the proprietor; and even in the southern parts, where more tropical productions could be raised, their labor would fully supply the place of the negro. A peon can perform as much work, and can be hired for about what it will cost to clothe and feed a negro, with the further advantage that the master having no capital invested in him, which he must lose at the death of the slave. The present labor of the country is so much cheaper than any that could be introduced, that a person would hardly be justifiable in risking his capital in slaves with so little prospect of profitable return.[33]

Yet politics in the east gave real impetus to those who wished to extend slavery across the west to the Pacific, however uncompetitive its economic return. By the late 1850s, when some American residents of the territory became wholesale supporters of chattel slavery's extension, they sought to combine their Democratic party's defense of chattel slavery in North America with an absorption of the local system. Allied with the New York–educated rico and avid politician Miguel Antonio Otero and Alexander Jackson, an old friend

31. Calhoun to Commissioner of Indian Affairs Orlando Brown, Mar. 31, 1850, in Abel, ed., *Official Correspondence of Calhoun,* 181–183; for the lack of progress in suppressing the captive trade, see Calhoun to Commissioner Luke Lea, Aug. 27, 1851, ibid., 405–406.

32. See *Territory v Harriet Brown* (1859), *Territory v John Winters* (1861), District Court, Santa Fe County Criminal Cases, New Mexico State Records Center.

33. Davis, *El Gringo,* 216, full quote at 108.

of Jefferson Davis, defenders of the southern institution set to work on the passage of a slave code for the territory. Jackson, at least, saw the political connections between the two institutions, claiming in a letter to Robert Downs in Santa Fe that he had informally "assured the [New] Mexicans that [the Slave Code] would protect their own system of peonage."[34]

On February 3, 1859, a territorial legislature composed of three Anglo-American Democrats and thirty-four New Mexican rico allies passed an Act for the Protection of Property in Slaves, taking explicit care to state that the act did not apply to existing peonage and that the word "slave" designated only a member of the "African race." To have termed Indians in bondage "slaves" would have exposed the fiction that Indians had always been free under Mexican rule, a status that the United States had confirmed in the Treaty of Guadalupe Hidalgo. Modeled on the codes of southern states like Mississippi, and almost ludicrously detailed given the presence of only sixty-four slaves in the territory, the document spoke to the aspirations of the proslavery faction. Its thirty-one sections included prohibitions against slave movement and travel, denied slaves the right to testify in courts, and, in a nod to local custom, restricted owners' rights to arm slaves except when necessary in defending against Indian raids.[35]

In Washington, congressional Republicans attempted to disapprove the legislation in House Resolution no. 64, which passed the House ninety-seven to ninety on May 10, 1860, but later died in committee in the Senate. Hoping to expand their political base and take advantage of the scores of Navajo captives spiraling into the system with renewed warfare and militia forays, in the autumn of 1860 the proslavery advocates in the territorial legislature recklessly enlarged the scope of the earlier law to include "male or female Indians that should be acquired from the barbarous nations." Governor Rencher vetoed that amendment, however, in an annual address that managed to finesse the constitutionality of the Otero Slave Code, confirm the illegality of Indian slavery, and retain the latter institution for its practitioners. Arguing that the territorial legislature could "neither create nor abolish slavery" but only regulate it where it already existed, he put his stamp of approval on the Otero Slave

34. Alexander Jackson to Robert Downs, Santa Fe, Aug. 16, 1858, cited in Ganaway, "New Mexico and the Sectional Controversy," *NMHR,* XVIII (July 1943), 205–246, esp. 236.

35. For text of the Otero Slave Code, see "Slavery in the Territory of New Mexico," *Records of the 36th Congress,* 1st session, report no. 508, House of Representatives (Washington, D.C., 1860), 1–39.

Code by suggesting that African slavery existed anywhere in United States territory where it was not prohibited. Rencher went on to confirm that the "native condition of our Indian tribes is that of freedom" and that they could not be made slaves "either by conquest or purchase." In the spirit of providing social uplift to barbarous peoples, citizens could, however, "hold them as captives or peons," by which Rencher positioned Indian slavery safely outside the national debate and back in the realm of local custom.[36]

In that ill-defined legal space, local courts did occasionally uphold rights in Indian slave property. In 1862, Sydney Hubbell, associate justice of the New Mexico Supreme Court, ruled in favor of Francisco Montoya and against Mariano Yrrisarri in a dispute over "a certain Indian girl named Juana" valued at five hundred dollars. Montoya had acted as agent for Yrrisarri in the girl's purchase but had not been fully compensated, and Hubbell ordered Juana delivered to Montoya to fulfill the contract. He did not comment on the legality of the girl's servile status. In other cases, usually where "Indian servant girls" became the focus of divorce or abandonment proceedings, local judges quietly affirmed their customary status as property.[37]

Abraham Lincoln's election resulted in Governor Rencher's replacement by Henry F. Connelly, a pro-Union Democrat who soon delegated all but nominal power to the military government of General James H. Carleton, the man who had sold the first black slaves in the territory. In his titular role, Connelly issued a proclamation on May 4, 1864, that prohibited "the traffic in captive Indians." By then, the war against slavery in the east was well under way and had begun to be felt in the borderlands as well.[38]

36. Fourth annual message of Governor Rencher, N.Mex., Dec. 6, 1860, quoted in Hunt, *Kirby Benedict*, 117–118.

37. *Mariano Yrrisarri v Francisco Montoya*, Bernalillo County, case no. 262 (1862); see also *Apodaca v Chavez*, Valencia County, case no. 329 (1861), in which "an Indian girl" figures in an adultery and divorce case, and Yrrisarri's later abandonment case of *Mariano Yrrisarri v Vicenta Arranda*, Bernalillo County, case no. 302 (1864), in which Vicenta, his estranged wife, claimed to have brought "two Indian Servant girls" into the marriage as a portion of her dowery, all indexed under "Indian Slavery" in New Mexico State Records Center. See also Ganaway, "New Mexico and the Sectional Controversy," *NMHR*, XVIII (July 1943), 205–246, 325–348; Murphy, *Frontier Crusader: William F. M. Arny* (Tucson, Ariz., 1972), 115–134.

38. For Connelly's proclamation, see "Condition of the Indian Tribes," in *Report of the Joint Special Committee Appointed under Joint Resolution of March 3, 1865* (Washington, D.C., 1867), 333.

They Cannot Prey upon Them as Formerly

Local attempts to codify Indian slavery within the Territorial Slave Code in 1860 were suspended by President Lincoln's election. During the Civil War, however, Union commanders in New Mexico realized that the regional slave trade disrupted any movement toward pacification of the Indians and therefore sought in the 1860s to extend the eastern war against slavery into the Southwest Borderlands. If the Civil War was a racially charged economic conflict in which free-labor capitalism triumphed over slave-labor capitalism, the extension of this conflict to the Southwest meant the triumph of state-sponsored capitalist development over the exchange economies of the borderland peoples. This campaign involved eliminating the use of livestock and captives as exchangeable resources in the system, placing Indians on reservations to disrupt their exchange economy, and replacing kin-based subjectivity with state-sponsored individual autonomy—all to clear the way for a capitalist system. Although more successful in the former than the latter, this strategy began to sever the links that had long bound the borderland communities together.

The changing role of New Mexican civil militias proved crucial to this transformation. With the advent of the Civil War in April 1861 and an invasion of Confederate forces from Texas in July of that year, Colonel Edward R. Canby authorized the formation of two volunteer infantry regiments, one under the leadership of Kit Carson of Taos, the other under Miguel E. Pino of Albuquerque. Driven by a long-term antipathy toward American Texans, who had twice attempted to invade New Mexico, and drawn by the promise of wages, bounties in hard cash, and forgiveness of peonage debts, more than 2,800 New Mexican men joined these and local militia units by February 1862. Although they played only minor roles in the defeat of General Henry H. Sibley's forces at Glorieta Pass in late March, these militia units stood ready one year later, when General Carleton, after first subduing the Apaches of the Sacramento and Guadalupe Mountains, began his war of relocation against the Navajos.[39]

Carson's First New Mexico Volunteers figured prominently in this scorched-earth campaign. Here, local enthusiasm waxed warm, for the action against the Navajos conformed closely to customary practices. As he carried his cam-

39. Darlis A. Miller, "Hispanos and the Civil War in New Mexico, a Reconsideration," *NMHR,* LIV (April 1979), 105–123.

paign deep into the Navajo heartland, Carson pleaded with Carleton for continued rewards in Navajo captives for local militias and Ute scouts. Military census materials from 1865 bear out his successful avoidance of Carleton's prohibition. When Ute Indian agent Lafayette Head counted 148 Indian captives held in households in Costilla and Conejos counties, Colorado Territory, 112 were Navajos, 48 of whom had been acquired during the 1863–1864 campaign. Their masters had acquired them from Ute warriors and New Mexican militiamen in nearly equal numbers. In all, 788 Navajo war captives were baptized in New Mexican parishes between 1860 and June 1868. Likewise, the Carson campaigns confiscated at least 100,000 sheep from Navajo rancherías. Unable to provide for safe shepherding, the army destroyed many of these in the field and set thousands aside for military provisioning. But tens of thousands were also distributed as rewards to members of the New Mexico militia.[40]

The most telling if incomplete achievement of the Carson campaign, however, was its ideological redefinition of Navajos from captors and captives in the borderland economy to involuntary dependents of the United States. Carson's Navajo campaign was largely complete by March 1864. In July, 6,000 Navajos were held at Bosque Redondo, and by Christmas 1864 they numbered 7,800. Finally, nearly 9,000 Navajos came abjectly under the dominion of the federal government, where their traditional talents as farmers and herders were to be wed to the formal market economy and Christian instruction. The prisoners agreed, according to James L. Collins, "to abandon their nomadic, marauding way of life, to settle on a reservation away from their cherished mountain homes, and to devote themselves to the pursuit of industry as their means of support." Yet bad weather, corrupt administration, poor provisioning, and Navajo resistance undercut Carleton's experiment almost from the start. As early as October 1864, Carleton himself suggested that his impoverished charges raid the Comanches to rebuild their horse and cattle herds. Navajos recalled that expedition as a near disaster, since the Comanches chased

40. For Carson's request that Ute scouts be allowed to retain and resell captured Navajo women and children to New Mexicans, see Carson to Carleton, Jul. 24, 1863, and Carleton's response of Aug. 18, in Lawrence C. Kelly, ed., *Navajo Roundup: Selected Correspondence of Kit Carson's Expedition against the Navajo, 1863–1865* (Boulder, Colo., 1970), 29–32. For the Costilla and Conejos censuses, see app. D, "The Traffic in Slaves," in McNitt, *Navajo Wars,* 441–446; for Navajo baptisms from 1860–1868, see David M. Brugge, *Navajos in the Catholic Church Records of New Mexico, 1694–1875* (Tsaile, Ariz., 1985), 37, table 6; for sheep figures, see Appendix B, below.

them so hard on their return to Fort Sumner that "only a few of the strongest horses were left." Some young Navajo men slipped past military sentries to raid local New Mexican settlements and American military herds for livestock. These so threatened the security of their imprisoned kinspeople that the headman Manuelito, who joined his interned relatives in 1866, had executed forty of them as witches by 1868.[41]

Most of the first Navajo internees at Bosque Redondo were pelados who had lived east of the mouth of Cañon de Chelly. The four hundred or so members of the Diné Ana'aii, now led by their headman Delgadito, were horrified to find themselves transported to the Bosque as well, where they suffered resentment and violence from the peoples upon whom they had once preyed. Like Manuelito, some ricos who escaped the initial roundup eventually tired of continuous hiding and harassment from Ute and New Mexican raiders and gave themselves up. Ganado Mucho did so in the spring of 1866, and the arrival of his large herds and flocks at the Bosque brought some relief to his fellow Navajos. Barboncito likewise returned to the reservation in November of the same year. Most ricos, however, managed to avoid the worst of the formal and informal military pillaging, unlike their less wealthy people. Hashkeneinii, Daghaa Sik'aad, K'aayelii, and Spane Shank were among those still free when superintendent of Indian affairs for New Mexico Michael Steck claimed late in 1864 "that less than one-half the tribe have surrendered; that the prisoners embrace the poor, while the strength and wealth of the tribe remain in the western part of their country." Gus Bighorse recalled at least thirty headmen who escaped incarceration at the Bosque. Many of their names, when translated into English, suggest their socioeconomic status: Ram Sheep, Big Man, Many Horses, Many Goats, White Goats, Much Horses, Silversmith. These ricos apparently took shelter near the Grand Canyon or with Paiutes north of the San Juan River, from whom they had variously seized captives, purchased children as pawns, or taken wives. With these holdouts would survive the institution of Navajo slavery—Louisa Wetherill would inherit Hashkeneinii's thirty-two Ute slave women in 1909.[42]

41. For numbers, see Gerald Thompson, *The Army and the Navajo* (Tucson, Ariz., 1976), 66–68; Katherine Marie Birmingham Osburn, "The Navajo at the Bosque Redondo: Cooperation, Resistance, and Initiative, 1864–1868," *NMHR*, LX (October 1985), 399–413, esp. 400; for Manuelito's witchcraft prosecutions, see Kluckhohn, *Navajo Witchcraft*, 63–64.

42. William Haas Moore, *Chiefs, Agents, and Soldiers: Conflict on the Navajo Frontier, 1868–1882* (Albuquerque, N.Mex., 1994), 7–9, 35; Steck quoted in Robert S. McPherson, *The*

Significantly, the success of the campaign came to strike many New Mexicans as dubious. In Carson's deposition to Congress at the conclusion of his victory, he noted, "Some New Mexicans now object to the settlement of Navajos at the Bosque, because they cannot prey upon them as formerly." Over the next four years, two political factions argued in New Mexico's newspapers about the merits of internment. Sensing that the future of wealth in the liberal order lay with control over land, New Mexican sheep ricos generally praised the policy, perhaps in part because they could now safely graze their immense flocks on former Navajo territories. Opposing them, an odd combination of borderlanders, old Democrats, Indian traders, and philanthropists complained about the collapse of the local economy now that the Indian commerce had vanished and the immense drain that internment placed on public finance.[43]

Indeed, borderland villagers suffered both cultural crisis and economic subordination in the aftermath of the pacification of New Mexico. Military service under Carson, while bringing much-desired hard currency, also involved the acceptance of military discipline, an issue that grated on the borderlander's sense of honor. According to former militia veterans from the village of Las Huertas, submission to military discipline expressed itself in Carson's orders that they must shear their "long and braided hair. Those braids proclaimed [a man] a good and honorable citizen . . . short hair was a brand, a silent declaration of dishonor." Although the men "wept and begged," Carson remained adamant, and so the day of enlistment "marked the disappearance of braids from the heads of men, except for the old men. They refused to part with their braids." Mustering out of military service in the 1870s, few found stable employment and in many cases returned to the relations of peonage of which they had once thought themselves free.[44]

Northern Navajo Frontier, 1860–1900: Expansion through Adversity (Albuquerque, N.Mex., 1988), 9–10; for relations with Paiutes, see 11–14. See also Tiana Bighorse, *Bighorse the Warrior,* ed. Noël Bennett (Tucson, Ariz., 1990), 40–41.

43. Testimony of Colonel Christopher Carson, in "Condition of the Indian Tribes," in *Annual Report, 1865,* 96–97; see the running editorial debate between the *Sante Fe Weekly Gazette* (supporting internment) and the *New Mexican* (opposing it) in issues between 1864 and 1868, in New Mexico State Records Center.

44. "*El Pelón:* An Old Native Custom," June 19, 1940, interview by Lou Sage Batchen. Interviewees include José Librado Aron Gurulé, age eighty-nine, and José Garcia y Trujillo, age ninety-four, both of whom served under Carson. Originals in New Mexico State Records Center.

Yet other villagers, especially those east of the Sangre de Cristos, managed to keep their old ways alive during and after the war years. Carleton's decision to impound the defeated Navajos and Apaches at Fort Sumner brought cruelties beyond uprooting these peoples from their traditional territories. Inadequate troop strength and poor command left the Bosque Redondo reservation practically defenseless against raids by Plains Indians. In addition to the many hundreds who died from malnutrition, disease, and heartbreak, uncounted scores of Navajo women and children were lost to Plains raiders and slave-snatching comancheros, whose very name was becoming "synonymous with evil" to Americans and New Mexicans alike.[45]

The tiny parish of Nuestra Señora de Guadalupe in Sapello, at the junction of the Mora and Sapello Rivers, provides evidence for this aspect of the Plains captive trade. Totaling only 123 people in the census of 1860, the baptismal registers from the parish church tell a story of continuing misery. Between 1861 and 1871, forty-nine indios or indios Navajoses received baptismal names, twenty-nine in the period of Navajo internment between 1864 and 1868. Thirty-one of these were children under the age of ten; thirty-four were female. Their padrinos at baptism—almost certainly their purchasers—represent thirteen different village families, but that of Nazario Gallegos sponsored fourteen such baptisms alone. New Mexican natives dominated as padrinos, but the Americans Louis Rudolph and Benjamin Minsk also participated, Rudolph sponsoring the boy Juan de Dios, age seven, and Minsk standing up for eighteen-year-old Maria Romona Minsk. In five cases, the mothers of the "infant" baptismal subjects were noted as an anonymous india and the father as *padre no conocido* (father unknown), strong testimony to the continuing practice of concubinage.[46]

All the parishes on the eastern side of the Sangre de Cristos held similar entries. At least four hundred Indians were brought into New Mexican households in that area between 1860 and 1875. All baptismal entries exhibit a dramatic spike, approximately double the annual average, between 1864 and 1868 when Navajos lay vulnerable at Bosque Redondo. Although these four hun-

45. For hardships at Bosque Redondo, and the negotiations that finally brought Navajos back to a portion of their homeland, see John L. Kessell, "General Sherman and the Navajo Treaty of 1868: A Basic and Expedient Misunderstanding," *Western Historical Quarterly,* XXII (July 1981), 251–272; Kenner, *Comanchero Frontier,* 155.

46. *Archdiocesan Archives of Santa Fe* (hereafter cited as *AASF),* Sapello Baptisms, books 34, 35, Jan. 20, 1861–Mar. 5, 1871, microfilm in New Mexico State Records Center.

dred represent fewer than 10 percent of the population in eastern villages during the period, they attest to the continuation of borderland slavery even after chattel slavery had been eliminated in the East. Where informal markets remained strong and the U.S. military presence relatively weak, the custom of the country overruled the law of the nation.[47]

The Wild Tribes Could Go to War against the North

Whether they tried to ransom captives under treaty obligations between 1847 and 1856, to legalize their private purchase between 1857 and 1860, to sanction covertly war captures between 1862 and 1868, or to pursue redemption for humanitarian reasons after 1868, American actions in New Mexico worked to support the institution of slavery. Concurrent with American involvement in sustaining the trade in border captives came additional complications that bolstered the very economy in which slavery was embedded. A cattle industry blending Anglo and Mexican traditions was developing in the southern Plains and the Río Grande border region, and by 1860 some 3.6 million Iberian longhorn cattle grazed the open range in Texas alone. Although New Mexicans had always maintained some cattle among their mixed herds, sheep grazing predominated until the late 1850s, when the demand from quartermasters in American forts suddenly provided a cash incentive for cattle ranching. The expansion of the cattle industry fed the two components that sustained the captive exchange economy, a supply of livestock and a demand for dependent laborers. After a military outpost was established at Alexander Hatch's ranch thirty-three miles below Las Vegas on the Gallinas River in 1856, several Americans sought to extend cattle operations even further onto the Plains, with initially disastrous results.[48]

47. Baptismal registers for the parishes of Pecos, San Miguel del Vado, San José del Vado, Anton Chico, La Cuesta, Tecolote, San Gerónimo, Las Vegas, Montón de Alamos, and Mora list 384 Indian captives receiving baptism during the period 1860–1875; 229 (some 60 percent) did so between 1864 and 1868. This survey does not include parishes immediately west of Bosque Redondo (Punta del Agua, Manzano, Torreón, and Tajique), so these numbers remain incomplete. See baptismal registers in *AASF,* microfilm in New Mexico State Records Center. The decade of 1860–1870 featured the largest number of Navajo baptisms in New Mexico (790); see Brugge, *Navajos in the Catholic Church Records,* 22–23.

48. Terry G. Jordan, *North American Cattle-Ranching Frontiers: Origins, Diffusion, and Differentiation* (Albuquerque, N.Mex., 1993), 208–240. For the role of the United States

Samuel Watrous was the first American to venture an enterprise on the llano, and his foreman, a Mr. Bushman, paid the price. Bushman established a ranch on the Canadian River in 1857, on approximately the same site that Pablo Montoya had worked in the 1830s. Shortly thereafter, Bushman hired three Mexican vaqueros, who had long lived among the Comanches as captive herders but who now offered those skills for wages. Within a few days, four Comanche warriors rode up to the ranch, and, reassured by his ranch hands, Bushman met them unarmed. The Comanches quickly dispatched the foreman, torched the ranch buildings, and ran off Watrous's livestock. They also sent their former captives to New Mexico with word that the Americans "should not settle there, for the Comanches would kill any who attempted it." The following year, Comanches took hostage members of an American expedition surveying the Canadian River and only released them at the behest of the expedition's New Mexican employees, "whose own safety was never in jeopardy." Neither Comanches nor their New Mexican partners were ready just yet to relinquish their Plains to Anglo ranchers.[49]

Although Comanches, Kiowas, and New Mexican contrabandistas would not give over control of their regional economy, they were forced to make adjustments that would make them both agents and victims of capitalist expansion on the southern Plains. The key transition years were those of the Civil War, when Union military goals included the pacification of "wild Indians" and the rationalization of local exchange economies. The Plains proved somewhat difficult in this regard, for throughout the 1860s certain powerful American interests benefited considerably from their covert relations with the peoples of the Plains.

These complications stemmed from two factors. First, Comanches, Kiowas, and other Indian groups shared more interests with the Confederate secessionists than with the Unionists who held Colorado and New Mexico. Second, from 1864 well into the 1870s, Anglo cattle barons in New Mexico found that the most efficient route to stocking their rangelands lay in purchasing stolen Texan and Mexican cattle from the mixed-culture raiders and traders of the llano estacado.

Plains Indians and New Mexicans shared certain cultural values with those

---

military in New Mexican economic development, see Miller, *Soldiers and Settlers: Military Supply in the Southwest, 1861–1885* (Albuquerque, N.Mex., 1989). Fort Biddle was founded by Captain W. L. Elliott in November 1856; see Kenner, *Comanchero Frontier,* 122–123.

49. Kenner, *Comanchero Frontier,* 124–127, esp. 126.

southerners who waged war in defense of their own economic system in 1861. Both were societies whose extended kinship networks organized much in the way of exchanges of people and property, although in the southern case this did not apply overtly to kin linkages with their slave population. Both were societies that held the highest expression of manhood to be the equestrian fighter, guided by a shared code of honor among men to defend the virtue of their dependent women and children. Proslavery southerners and llaneros both perceived, in distinctive ways, that liberal capitalist development in the form of wage-based manufacturing and family farming would destroy their customary way of life. Despite the antipathy that Plains Indians and New Mexicans had held for Texans since at least the 1840s—a hatred exacerbated by Texan attempts to clear Comanches and Kiowas from the western cattle ranges—the Civil War's effects on the West would drive the llaneros into a short-lived, but analogously suggestive, alliance with the Confederacy by 1865. The broader terms of settlement imposed by the North's victory over the South, by which traditional economic forms and customary social relations were suppressed and capitalism instated, would not reach the Plains for another decade.

Whatever the shared ideologies, Plains Indians finally sought accommodation with Confederate agent Albert Pike in 1865, not because of affinity, but because of offenses committed by Union troops late in 1864. Even though the Confederate invasion of New Mexico early in 1862 had been soundly whipped at Glorieta Pass, Union commanders in New Mexico continued to fear another expedition from across the Plains. General Carleton had seldom trusted New Mexican comancheros and early in 1864 began to restrict their trade with their Plains Indian neighbors. When Kiowa and Comanche warriors attacked Union supply trains and killed Americans but allowed New Mexican members to proceed unharmed, Carleton surmised that a dangerous combination was brewing. He summoned Kit Carson, fresh from his victories over the Navajos, to lead a punitive expedition.[50]

New Mexico Superintendent of Indian Affairs Michael Steck opposed Carleton's plan, as did most ordinary New Mexicans. But the general pushed

50. In the summer of 1861, Pike succeeded in bringing factions of the Five Civilized Tribes into military alliance with the Confederacy and had even signed nonaggression pacts with leaders of the eastern Comanche bands. But the 1865 negotiations were aimed at a military alliance between a reeling Confederacy and desperate Plains tribes. For Pike's early negotiations, see Alvin M. Josephy, Jr., *The Civil War in the American West* (New York, 1991), 322–330; Kenner, *Comanchero Frontier*, 143–147.

ahead, finally cobbling together a force of 335 volunteer cavalry and 75 Ute and Jicarilla scouts. Wittingly or not, Steck subverted Carleton by granting trading permits to two parties of comancheros, who appear to have warned the Kiowas and Comanches and resupplied them with arms and ammunition. When Carson reached the Bents' abandoned trading outpost at Adobe Walls on the Canadian, he ransacked a Kiowa village of 150 lodges but suddenly found his force surrounded by a combined Comanche-Kiowa cavalry of one thousand fighters. Skillful use of two mountain howitzers prevented annihilation of Carson's men, who managed a night retreat with losses totaling three dead and twenty-five wounded.[51]

During the fight at Adobe Walls, Captain George Pettis noted several details that gave evidence of persistent alliance between Plains Indians and New Mexicans. The pickets who warned the Indians of Carson's advance yelled in Spanish, "bene-acá, bene-acá *[sic]*" ("come here, come here") to their comrades. During the daylong fight, each bugle call ordered by Carson was countermanded by a call emanating from the Indian ranks: "When our bugles sounded the 'advance,' he would blow 'retreat'; and when ours sounded the 'retreat' he would follow with 'advance.' " Carson insisted later that a "white man" gave these countermanding signals. Finally, upon his return to Fort Bascom, Carson discovered that two comancheros, Jesús Amalla and José Castillo, had been apprehended returning from the Kiowas and Comanches with a large herd of recently bartered cattle—no doubt compensation for the arms and ammunition used in the fight. Carson complained that Steck had allowed the men to betray his campaign, "knowing perfectly well that we were at war with the Indians, and that the Mexicans would take what they could sell best, which was powder, lead, and caps."[52]

Just four days after Carson's self-proclaimed victory at Adobe Walls, Colonel John M. Chivington—the hero of Glorieta Pass—and his Third Colorado Cavalry destroyed a peaceful encampment of Cheyennes and Arapahos at Sand Creek. After the slaughter, some two hundred Indians, two-thirds of them women and children, lay dead and mutilated "Indian-fashion." It was little

51. Kenner, *Comanchero Frontier,* 148–149.

52. Captain George H. Pettis, "Kit Carson's Fight with the Comanche and Kiowa Indians," *Publications of the Historical Society of New Mexico,* no. 12 (Albuquerque, N.Mex., 1908), 14, 23; Carson to Carleton, Dec. 16, 1864, in *War of the Rebellion: A Compilation of the Official Records of the Union and Confederate Armies* (Washington, D.C., 1880–1989), 1st Ser., XLI, part 1, 943.

wonder that, in May 1865, fourteen Indian nations met at Camp Napoleon, Indian Territory, to conclude a military alliance with the Confederate agent Pike under orders from General E. Kirby Smith. Smith had it on good authority that the "Comanches and other wild tribes of the Plains . . . were enraged against the United States . . . desiring to bring their wives and children to a place of safety near our lines where they could leave them secure while they could go to war against the North." In return for food and weaponry, the Indians promised their assistance in a Confederate expedition against Union forts in New Mexico. Of course, the alliance proved useless to the Indians with the Confederate surrender in April. General Stand Watie, the slaveholding Cherokee Confederate guerrilla leader, could manage only symbolic resistance on the part of his people and laid down his arms in June of 1865, the last Southerner to do so.[53]

Lee's surrender might have brought an end to chattel slavery in the South, but not on the Plains. In fact, Carleton and Carson's internment of Navajos and Apaches at Bosque Redondo actually reinvigorated the customary trade, revulsion against which finally brought the full force of American emancipatory and regulatory programs to the West. Concurrently, llaneros both Indian and New Mexican made a stepwise adjustment in their pastoral economy and commenced the "great comanchero cattle-trade." The two developments were the concluding flare of the multiethnic Plains economy, combining centuries-old customary exchanges with almost complete subsumption in the expansion of capitalist commercial relations.[54]

53. For an Indian view of the Sand Creek Massacre, see George E. Hyde, *Life of George Bent Written from His Letters,* ed. Savoie Lottinville (Norman, Okla., 1968), 151. George Bent was William Bent's mixed-blood son by his Cheyenne wife and survived the attack; for an overview, see Josephy, *Civil War in the West,* 305–316. The Indian nations present at Camp Napoleon were the Kiowas, Comanches, Cherokees, Choctaws, Creeks, Chickasaws, Seminoles, Caddos, Osages, Cheyennes, Arapahos, Lipan Apaches, Northern Caddos, and Anadarkos. See Smith to Adair, Apr. 8, 1865, in *War of the Rebellion,* 1st Ser., LXVIII, part 2, 1266–1269; Josephy, *Civil War in the West,* 385.

54. Kenner, *Comanchero Frontier,* 155.

Their Theft Was an Important Advance in Our Industry

American agents became less willing to pay cash redemption for captives after the Civil War, yet many Americans proved more than willing to render cash payments to Indian raiders for stolen Mexican and Texan cattle. Captain E. H. Bergmann, commander at Fort Bascom in 1864, supplied comanchero middlemen with trade goods for Plains Indians in return for hundreds of cattle delivered to the fort. After his retirement in 1868, he established a ranch on the Canadian and stocked it largely with stolen cattle. A ring of army officers led by Patrick Healy nearly monopolized the comanchero trade between 1866 and 1867 before being denounced by more reputable men. Civilians also enjoyed the trade—one year before his appointment to the territorial supreme court, John Watts received a license to trade with the Comanches through comanchero intermediaries.[55]

At least 400,000 Texan cattle entered New Mexico through the illicit trade between 1860 and 1875. Mexican livestock losses numbered even more. Of the four million head of cattle in Texas in 1860, three million were considered "feral," or without recognized Anglo-Texan owners. So numerous were these herds that, in the 1870s, when hide prices soared on international markets, Texan and Mexican adventurers organized skinning raids and counter-raids on both sides of the Río Grande. Chihuahuan and Coahuilan *hacendados* (ranchers) suffered most during these "skinning wars," for a Mexican investigation commission of 1873 found that fully 90 percent of the cattle hides transshipped through Brownsville and Corpus Christi, some 100,000 per year, featured Mexican brands. The commissioners noted that Mexican ranchers south of the Río Grande no longer attempted to market their cattle or horses across the border, so depressed were prices by illegal competition. Although to the west of Eagle Pass, Texas, Kiowas and Comanches were accused of most of this pillage, the investigators found that, even in the more "civilized" areas of the lower Río Grande, local sheriffs and justices of the peace were not above organizing midnight forays across the all-too-shallow river. They estimated Mexico's financial losses between 1848 and 1868 at twenty-eight million dollars, a severe blow to the "stability of the nation." Since the going rate in New

55. Kenner, *Comanchero Frontier,* 156–161, 173.

Mexico for stolen cattle was about two dollars per head, a conservative rendering of cattle and horses thieved by Indian and comanchero raiders would equal one million animals. Their legitimate market value was nearly twice that figure, and the American buyers grew rich, for a while, at the expense of their brother cattlemen beyond and below the llano estacado.[56]

The mixed New Mexican–Indian nature of the great cattle trade was apparent to all observers. "Comanche" raiding parties often spoke perfect Spanish, and New Mexicans driving stolen cattle were occasionally arrested dressed "in Indian disguise." These raiding parties sometimes combined their forces—Herman Lehmann, an Anglo-Comanche captive, recalled one in which 60 New Mexican comancheros joined 140 Comanches in raiding a cattle herd west of Fort Griffin, Texas. In combining customary raid and trade with cash sales to "respectable" American buyers, llaneros both New Mexican and Indian came to act as agents for the creation of a full-blown commercial cattle industry.[57] The fact was not lost on American analysts. In 1880, Clarence Gordon of the tenth census commented on the trade in stolen cattle:

56. Charles Goodnight claimed that 300,000 head of Texas cattle and an additional 100,000 horses were lost to the comanchero trade between 1860 and 1867. See "Goodnight Deposition," in Indian Claims Case no. 8532 (1898), 15–16, cited in J. Evetts Haley, "The Comanchero Trade," *Southwestern Historical Quarterly,* XXXVIII, no. 3 (1935), 155–176, esp. 169. For feral cattle in the Texan economy, see Terry G. Jordan, *North American Cattle-Ranching Frontiers: Origins, Diffusion, and Differentiation* (Albuquerque, N.Mex., 1993), 208–227. For "skinning wars," see David Montejano, *Anglos and Mexicans in the Making of Texas, 1836–1986* (Austin, Tex., 1987), 53; for Mexican analysis, see *Informe de las comisión pesquisadora de la frontera al ejecutivo de la union sobre depredaciones de los indios y otros males que sufre la frontera mexicana* (Mexico, 1874), 81–83, 108, 112, 160. In 1871, the *Daily New Mexican* reported 30,000 Texas cattle brought in during a three-month season (Kenner, *Comanchero Frontier,* 174); between 1848 and 1870, nine villages in Coahuila suffered 608 attacks by Comanche and Apache raiders, in which were lost 2,289 horses and 2,474 head of cattle. They also suffered 276 dead, 92 wounded, and 52 carried into captivity. See also Joseph A. Stout, Jr., " 'Filibusteros' and Indians on the Northern Frontier, 1848–1912: Mexican Sources and Interpretations," in Virginia Gueda and Jaime E. Rodríguez O., eds., *Five Centuries of Mexican History: Papers of the VIII Conference of Mexican and North American Historians, San Diego, California, October 18–20, 1990,* II (Irvine, Calif., 1992), 426–433; *Daily New Mexican,* Jul. 14, 1866, 3, microfilm in New Mexico State Records Center.

57. Herman Lehmann's story can be found in Lehmann, *Nine Years among the Indians, 1870–1879,* ed. J. Marvin Hunter (Albuquerque, N.Mex., 1993), 92–97; Kenner, *Comanchero Frontier,* 167.

> Stockmen from New Mexico fitted out expeditions into the dangerous country and purchased the herds. Many thousand cattle were thus secured for New Mexico, especially for the northeastern section. This constituted an *important advance* in the New Mexican stock occupation.[58]

By the late 1860s, however, American military and developmental planners came to see that the illicit cattle trade stood in the way of regularizing social and economic relations in the Southwest; they began a concerted effort, like that of refusing to ransom captives, to bring an end to cattle stealing and trading. General Philip Sheridan recognized that any efforts to subjugate Indian tribes by destroying their buffalo herds would have little effect should they maintain themselves through a new form of borderland pastoralism.

In the summer of 1869, Sheridan issued orders stating flatly that any New Mexicans found with supplies or cattle on the llano estacado would find that "their goods will be burned and their stock killed." General William Tecumseh Sherman's return of the Navajos to their western homelands the previous year had already removed one major source of victims for the captive trade, and the demand for cattle declined with stronger military surveillance. Still, the trade continued on a smaller scale, with comancheros making use of secret trails to reach their trading points at Cañon del Rescate, Quitaque, and Valle de las Lágrimas (Valley of Tears). Increasing numbers of New Mexican and Pueblo comancheros were intercepted by patrols and brought to court in the territory, but local juries found little reason to convict their neighbors for cattle trading. The fifty-one cases presented in 1871 led to no convictions. Finally, in 1872 the U.S. Army switched to a strategy of cooptation, hiring seasoned comancheros like Jesus Tafoya and his compadres to guide punitive expeditions against Kiowa and Comanche raiders and occasionally against their New Mexican kinsmen. Once the cavalry could cross the llano confident of finding water holes and hidden trading canyons, the days of the Plains communities were numbered.[59]

Efforts to suppress the cattle trade and a concerted campaign to eliminate

58. Clarence Gordon, "Report on Cattle, Sheep, and Swine Supplementary to Inumeration of Live Stock, on Farms in 1880," in *Tenth Census of the United States, 1880* (Washington, D.C., 1883–1886), III, 989, cited in Kenner, *Comanchero Frontier,* 174.

59. Proclamation printed in *Republican Review,* Jul. 30, 1869, cited in Kenner, *Comanchero Frontier,* 183; Chief Justice of New Mexico to President Grant, Feb. 20, 1871, Chronological Files, New Mexico, no. 53, Department of Justice, record group 60, NA, cited in Kenner, *Comanchero Frontier,* 176–200, esp. 189.

bison from the southern Plains triggered the last futile resistance by Comanches, Kiowas, and comancheros. By 1872, Americans had largely suppressed the comanchero trade, and two years later the last glimmer of military power among Plains Indians would be snuffed at Adobe Walls. Attacking a group of Anglo buffalo hunters in the summer of 1874 at the outpost first established by William Bent in 1845, Quanah Parker and his Quahada band kinsmen suffered a tactical defeat that concluded with the U.S. Army's brutal Red River campaigns of 1874–1875. By the end of the year, 1,400 Comanches delivered themselves to their agency headquarters at Fort Sill. Although they continued to hunt buffalo on reservation lands, their take dwindled precipitously. In 1876, Comanches and Kiowas sold robes worth $70,400 to their agency buyers; by 1879, they could deliver only $5,068 worth.[60]

Nor could New Mexican ciboleros cope with transformations in the region's economy. Those who tried to compete with Anglo buffalo hunters sometimes became prey themselves—Anglo hunters killed six ciboleros on the Pecos in August of 1874 and another dozen late in the 1870s on the Pease River in west Texas. "Forty or fifty" ciboleros from Taos Pueblo conducted their last bison hunt in 1884, killing fifty-four whom they found "grazing peacefully" among a cattle herd. By then, José María Rendón, an old cibolero and comanchero from the village of Las Vegas, would discourage his son Gabino from even learning to ride a horse. Looking back on his life, he would say to his wife, "It is the horses that make men wild. With a horse under me, I myself am no better than a Comanche. Gabino must get no taste for them." Gabino did not. As a grown man he went on to become a field missionary for the Board of National Missions of the United Presbyterian Church. Both the Pueblos and their New Mexican neighbors had begun a retreat to their adobe villages, where they settled into subsistence farming, small livestock raising, and seasonal wage labor. Their extraordinary years of cultural innovation and aggressive economic experimentation would be obliterated by a later generation of American ethnographers who hailed their retrenched post-borderland societies as timeless models for antimodern utopian movements.[61]

60. Robert M. Utley, *The Indian Frontier of the American West, 1846–1890* (Albuquerque, N.Mex., 1984), 174–178; Kenner, *Comanchero Frontier*, 209. In the Red River campaigns, the army hounded fleeing Comanche families throughout the winter and spring.

61. Kenner, *Comanchero Frontier*, 208–209; Gabino Rendón, as told to Edith Agnew, *Hand on My Shoulder*, rev. ed. (New York, 1963), 12. By the 1890s, a new borderland "industry" of tourism was dawning, and the survival economy of these peoples became reinscribed

He Assumed a Debt That This Woman Had Contracted

Like bison hunting and the illicit trade in cattle, Indian slavery in New Mexico took decades to die. A story that begins in the summer of 1865 serves as a parable for the complex campaigns and negotiations that brought an end to slavery in the region. The case of an anonymous Hopi woman in the New Mexican village of Cubero illustrates the continuing vulnerability of women and children in the borderland economy. An executive order from President Andrew Johnson places her experience in national context. The response of the New Mexican Indian superintendent demonstrates just how difficult the suppression of Indian slavery in the territory would prove, given the customary practices against which emancipation would compete. The Hopi woman's ultimate fate, if it can be recovered at all, raises the question of how peonage, slavery, and kinship could remain inextricably intertwined well into the 1870s.

On August 12, 1865, a Hopi woman staggered into the office of Lieutenant Colonel Julius C. Shaw, commanding officer of Fort Wingate, some thirty miles west of Cubero. Her hair clotted with blood from a head wound, she declared to Shaw that, while she and her nine-year-old daughter were walking the wagon road between the village of Cubero and Fort Wingate, two men from the village overtook them, hammered her with their rifle butts, and left her stunned beside the trail. When she recovered consciousness some hours later, her daughter was missing. Retracing her steps to Cubero—where she had "lately been residing"—she discovered that the men had kidnapped her daughter, and they refused her requests to see the child. She walked to Fort Wingate to plead for Shaw's intercession in the kidnapping. Shaw reported to Major Benjamin Cutler, his superior in Santa Fe, that he would dispatch

---

as a model of moral virtue for a generation of ethnographers and makers of United States Indian policy. See Leah Dilworth, *Imagining Indians in the Southwest: Persistent Visions of a Primitive Past* (Washington, D.C., 1996). For the reciprocal influence of Pueblo Indian women on American feminists during the progressive era and beyond, see Margaret D. Jacobs, *Engendered Encounters: Feminism and Pueblo Indian Cultures, 1879–1934* (Lincoln, Nebr., 1999). For similar relationships between ethnographers and New Mexican villagers, see Suzanne Forrest, *The Preservation of the Village: New Mexico's Hispanics and the New Deal* (Albuquerque, N.Mex., 1989).

First Lieutenant George McDermott to Cubero to investigate the "particulars concerning the affair."[62]

A presidential directive and local reply provide larger historical and cultural context for the meaning within the Hopi woman's dilemma. Although particular in certain of its details, the sufferings of this anonymous woman prove symptomatic of the experience of women and children caught up in the region's violence, exchange, and state regulation. Hopi captives in villages like Cubero and Cebolleta became so numerous that a surname, "Moquino" (from "Moqui," another term for the Hopi), appeared in documentary records by the early nineteenth century, as did a village of the same name in the 1860s.

Two months before the incident at Fort Wingate, President Andrew Johnson had issued a directive to the secretaries of the interior and war departments regarding the question of Indian slavery in the territory of New Mexico. Declaring the practice in violation of "the rights of Indians" and territorial "organic law," he ordered his subordinates to engage in "an effective suppression of the practice."[63]

The president's letter elicited a quick response from New Mexico, one thoroughly in keeping with customary defenses of Indian slavery. Within a month, New Mexico's Superintendent of Indian Affairs Felipe Delgado wrote to Commissioner of Indian Affairs William Dole in an attempt to clarify the local practice. "Allow me to say," he replied, "that the representations made to the government upon this subject have been greatly exaggerated." He claimed,

> It is true that there are among the citizens of this country a large number of Indian captives belonging to various tribes, that have been acquired through purchase from the Utahs, Navajos and some other tribes, but the object in purchasing them has not been to reduce them to slavery, but rather from a Christian piety on the part of the whites to obtain them in order to instruct and educate them in Civilization, and at the same time to leave them at full liberty whenever the Indian desires it, or—in some cases—to remain until they were twenty one years of age.

Pleading more context, Delgado continued:

62. Lieutenant Colonel Shaw to Major Benjamin Cutler, Aug. 12, 1865, NA, New Mexico Superintendency (hereafter cited as NMS), microcopy T-21, roll 6, film in Center for the Study of the Southwest, Fort Lewis College, Durango, Colo.

63. Copy, President Andrew Johnson to the Executive Departments, June 9, 1865, NA, NMS, 1863–1865, T-21, roll 6.

> This has been the practice in this country for the last century and a half and the result arising from it has been to the captives, favorable, humane, and satisfactory. When these Indians wish to marry, their guardians do not object, but rather, treat them as their adopted children, and give them pecuniary aid at the time of marriage. When the guardian dies, they usually leave something to the captives, as their adopted children.[64]

Emphasizing the captive trade as a multilateral affair among Indian groups and customary slavery as a Spanish civilizing mission, Delgado's reply underscores the depth of historical and cultural processes that underlay the phenomenon. The case of the Hopi woman provides further evidence of the extent to which the system permeated local society.

Lieutenant McDermott delivered his report to Lieutenant Colonel Shaw within twenty-four hours. Having arrived in the village of Cubero, McDermott interviewed several residents about the case of the Hopi woman and discovered that one of her attackers was a local vecino, Filomeno Sánchez, commonly known as Chato. This man indeed held the woman's daughter against her will but defended his action by claiming that "he had assumed a debt which this woman contracted" and had taken both the mother and daughter as security against that debt. Soon after doing so, he asserted, the mother and child attempted to escape, so he and a compadre pursued the fugitives and "beat the woman on the head with his rifle until senseless, then carried the child away."[65]

Under pressure from McDermott, Chato fetched the child and returned her to her mother in the presence of the alcalde ordinario, Manuel Garcia. When asked to point out her assailant, she indicated Chato, which McDermott noted as occurring in the presence of several other witnesses. But with martial law recently suspended in the West with the end of the Civil War, McDermott could do little more, and he harbored doubts that the civil authorities would take "any steps to punish this fellow." To support this judgment, he added a postscript, noting that Alcalde Garcia himself had in his possession "two small Moqui [Hopi] Indians" that "he held as his property."[66]

When Chato Sánchez claimed that he held the women and child as security against a debt, he probably spoke the truth as he saw it. Although pur-

64. Felipe Delgado, superintendent of Indian affairs in the territory of New Mexico, to Commissioner of Indian Affairs William T. Dole, Jul. 16, 1865, NA, NMS, T-21, roll 6.

65. Lieutenant George McDermott to Lieutenant Colonel Shaw, Aug. 13, 1865, NA, NMS, T-21, roll 6.

66. Ibid.

portedly made distinct in the territory's master and servant laws after 1851, peonage and slavery became densely interwoven, and, despite numerous attempts by some American reformers to eliminate debt bondage, provisions for enforcement were so ignored that involuntary servitude remained common practice. By 1865, the price of "a likely girl, not more than eight years old, healthy and intelligent" could reach "four hundred dollars or more"; therefore, the "debt" for which the Hopi woman was responsible (which probably included her daughter) totaled at least eight hundred dollars. Her bondage might well be considered perpetual.[67]

The merger of peonage and slavery provides the likely explanation of how the Hopi woman had come to reside in Cubero in the household of Chato Sánchez. Analysis of baptismal records indicates that thirty-seven Hopis received baptism in New Mexico in the later nineteenth century, all of them "definitely servants acquired by purchase or capture." Navajo raiders had struck the Hopi mesas several times in the 1860s, taking corn and captives. This might be when the woman became a commodity in the system.[68]

Although we cannot be certain, the Hopi woman appears never to have found freedom, despite her own and Lieutenant McDermott's best efforts. In the 1860 census Chato Sánchez appeared as a common laborer in the household of Decidero Trujillo; in 1870, five years after the event at Fort Wingate, he headed a household in Cubero that included a woman named Serafina and her unnamed daughter. The woman carries no matronym, suggesting obscure origins. She was designated as "keeping house" and her daughter "at home." Sánchez seems to have made the remnants of the borderland slave system work quite well. In addition to acquiring a wife and child through capture, by 1870 he

67. For the Law Regulating Contracts between Masters and Servants of 1851, see folder titled "Laws and Resolutions Passed by the Legislature of the Territory of New Mexico, 1851," in United States Senate Territorial Documents, 32d Congress, record group 46, NA; section 17 of that act, pertaining to indenture of minors, left Indian slavery in question, since it allowed minors between the ages of fourteen and twenty "not under parental jurisdiction" to "celebrate the contract specified therein"; see Murphy, "Reconstruction in New Mexico," *NHMR*, XLIII (April 1968), 99–115, esp. 100; "Testimony of Benedict before the Doolittle Committee," in "Condition of the Indian Tribes," in *Annual Report, 1865*, 225–226.

68. Brugge, *Navajos in the Catholic Church Records*, 22–29, esp. 28. Navajos seem to have struck both the Hopi and Zuñi pueblos at intervals of two or three years during the 1850s and 1860s, especially around harvest time, in order to steal corn and take captives. See Correll, *Through White Men's Eyes*, II, 311, 379; for alternating patterns of trade and warfare, see Ruth Underhill, *The Navajos* (Norman, Okla., 1956), 64–66.

claimed two hundred dollars in real property and one hundred dollars in personal property. His experience may be extrapolated for many of the ambitious poor in the region.[69]

The case of the Hopi woman is just one example of the general ineffectiveness of efforts to end Indian slavery in New Mexico. Local resistance to emancipation and Carleton's belief that "enslavement was an effective method for punishing Indians for their depredations" contributed to the de facto persistence of slavery and peonage for another decade and a half. Stronger moral and military sanctions did subdue the continuing traffic in captives after Sherman took control of Indian affairs in 1868. His position reflected the consensus formed by the victorious modernizers at the end of the Civil War, a policy of pacification and liberal economic development that had long been debated but not implemented due to the disruptions of the conflict. Policy makers on the national level concurred, and they believed that gradual market dependency through connections with rail-linked commercial centers would produce salutary effects: more regular, efficient animal husbandry practices and wage employment in industry and mining for "surplus," dangerous young men.[70]

Who Will Take Care of Me if Not My Slaves?

The decades following the Long Walk era (1864–1868) proved to be times of social and economic crisis for the Navajos, yet as a people they surmounted these with considerable success. Stripped of their herds, removed from their canyon-sheltered cornfields, and hundreds of miles from their raiding zones along the Río Grande, they had initially little choice but to turn to paltry federal aid for subsistence. When Sherman negotiated a return to their old

69. See household no. 1949, "Free Inhabitants in the Village of Cubero in the County of Valencia, Territory of New Mexico," MS enumeration, Sept. 16, 1860, in *Federal Census of 1860,* 218, household no. 105, "Inhabitants in Precinct No. 9, Cubero, in the County of Valencia, Territory of New Mexico," MS enumeration, Sept. 15, 1870, in *Federal Census of 1870,* 9, both in New Mexico State Records Center.

70. The territorial legislature abolished peonage in New Mexico on March 2, 1867, but the practice was still common in the late 1870s. See Murphy, "Reconstruction in New Mexico," *NMHR,* XLIII (April 1968), 99–115. For a treatment of Grant's peace policy (1869–1882) and its roots in postbellum liberal reformers, see Robert H. Keller, Jr., *American Protestantism and United States Indian Policy, 1869–82* (Lincoln, Nebr., 1983); Prucha, *Great Father,* 122–127.

homelands in 1868, he both promised and threatened an end to local slavery and urged them to abandon pastoralism to become "self-supporting farmers." Securing the allegiance of "progressive" ricos like Henry "Chee" Dodge—the mixed-descent son (b. 1860?) of Captain Henry Dodge and a Navajo woman—by making them dispensers of annuities, Indian agents brought pressure to bear on the more troublesome elements. By 1872, many of the young men who had once profited from ladronismo found themselves drafted into the Navajo Cavalry, a police unit that punished renegades and assisted the U.S. Army in campaigns against the Chiricahua Apaches. In 1883, they were put to the task of protecting the new railroad right-of-way through the Río Puerco valley over the protests of Tohyelte, a member of the Cañoncito Navajos, once known as the Diné Ana'aii. This two-pronged strategy of economic patronage to secure the loyalties of ricos and military mobilization to co-opt marginal young men had proved useful in earlier Indian wars and in the aftermath of the Civil War. Hence, the solution to the Navajo problem had its place in the larger liberal capitalist restructuring of North America.[71]

The new reservation shifted the Navajo homelands westward, away from their New Mexican neighbors, and seldom again would they share "the pleasurable excitement of reprisal" with their distant cousins. With customary patterns of redistribution thus foreclosed, problems of inequality intensified, as a few Navajo bands controlled most of the bottomlands, sheep flocks, and government annuities. In 1915, Peter Paquette, superintendent of the agency at Fort Defiance, conducted a detailed census of the Chinle, Ganado, Agency, and St. Michael's Districts within his jurisdiction. The returns revealed that the wealthiest 10 percent of Navajos held more than 50 percent of the livestock wealth, the top 20 percent over 70 percent. Fenced and cultivated lands showed similar disparity among a people whom ethnologists were celebrating as egalitarian cultural models. The Diné Ana'aii, once central in the borderland economy, suffered vilification and separated themselves on a tiny reservation of their own at Cañoncito, west of Albuquerque.[72]

Slavery also persisted among the Navajos. In 1882, Navajo agent Dennis Riordan attempted to repatriate some three hundred binaalté held by Navajo

71. Moore, *Chiefs, Agents, and Soldiers,* 20–30, esp. 23, 100; Frank D. Reeve, "The Government and the Navaho, 1883–88," *NMHR,* XVIII (January 1943), 17–51, esp. 23–25.

72. McPherson, "Ricos and Pobres: Wealth Distribution on the Navajo Reservation in 1915," *NMHR,* LX (October 1985), 415–434; Myra Ellen Jenkins, "A History of the Cañoncito Navajos," MS in Center for the Study of the Southwest, Fort Lewis College, Durango, Colo.

ricos. Riordan reported that "one old villain" objected and asked "who was to take care of him if his slaves were taken away from him." The agent responded firmly that "I would take care of him and the whole band if they were *not* set free." The old rico finally freed his six Paiute binaalté, but they returned to their master the next day. In other cases Riordan's victory was short-lived as well, for he reported one year later, "Most beat a hasty path back to the hogans of their masters." Juanita, thought by Americans to be the captive New Mexican wife of the legendary Manuelito, likewise refused liberation with others of his New Mexican binaalté after the headman told them they were free to go. The following year, John Bowman, Riordan's successor, argued that the only way to "free" these slaves "would be to take them away entirely, confine them, and subsist them at public expense." In 1909, when Louisa Wetherill inherited Hashkeneini's thirty-two Ute slaves, worried Navajos came to her and reported that "the Ute slave women are giving away their sheep. They are already in need. They are your slaves and you must give them work to do." When she protested her ownership, they confirmed her responsibility: "They are your slaves. Are you not the granddaughter of Hoskinini?" Wetherill reluctantly accepted her new role and built them hogans near her own house, "fed them when they were hungry, and gave them work to do when they asked for it." They came and went only with her permission and always "returned as to one who had the right to decide on their coming and going."[73]

In New Mexico, too, the legacy of the captive trade lingered. While the military and legal arms of the American state succeeded in suppressing the traffic, emancipation itself was hindered by the persistence of customary kin and culture bonds. In early 1868, Special Commissioner for Indian Affairs William W. Griffin, a confirmed radical Republican, prepared 363 cases against residents of Taos, Santa Fe, and Río Arriba counties, who still held peons and Indian slaves, for presentation to a local grand jury. His cases provide a clear view of how such social inequality was distributed in the northern region. Peonage accounted for nearly 20 percent (70) of the cases, Indian slavery 80 percent (295). Both peonage and Indian slavery were widely dispersed; 87 percent of house-

73. Riordan quoted in Reeve, "The Government and the Navajo," *NMHR*, XVIII (January 1943), 22, and in Brugge, *Navajos in the Catholic Church Records,* 142–143. See also Bowman to commissioner of Indian affairs, Sept. 3, 1884, *Annual Report of the Commissioner of Indian Affairs for the Year 1884* (Washington, D.C., 1884), 401; Moore, *Chiefs, Agents, and Soldiers,* 267–268; Frances Gillmor and Louisa Wade Wetherill, *Traders to the Navajos: The Wetherills of Kayenta* (Albuquerque, N.Mex., 1953), 179–180.

holds with peons contained only one, and 85 percent of those holding Indian slaves contained only one or two. Some ricos, however, had amassed substantial numbers. Jesus María Pacheco held five peons; Pablo Trujillo owned eight slaves, Vicente Mares nine, and Juan Benito Valdez ten. After taking testimony, only fragments of which exist, Griffin freed sixty of the seventy peons and all but one of the Indian slaves. He dismissed those accused of holding peons in violation of the Civil Rights Act of 1866, citing local custom and misunderstandings of the new law. But he bound over 171 slaveholders to appear before a grand jury of the New Mexico District Court. That jury, however, composed of prominent citizens, found few of his charges compelling and ruled that, unless the victims would swear to their "forcible restraint or ill-treatment," indictments would not be issued. U.S. attorney S. B. Elkins summarized the dismissals as being a matter of "the accused not intentionally or maliciously violat[ing] the law," since holding Indian slaves "had become a part and parcel of the social system of the country."[74]

Griffin had released Indian slaves from bondage, whereas the grand jury excused slaveholders from legal punishment. But, in spite of legal strictures, the bonds were not so easily broken. When Manuel Vizcarra, president of the grand jury, interviewed Juan Santistevan about the four Indian slaves that he and his mother, Rosalia Medina, held in their home, Santistevan's testimony illustrated just how intertwined slavery and kinship had become in New Mexico. Santistevan confirmed the presence of the slaves and explained that "for as long as he could remember" Indian captives had been "brought back and sold into slavery by parties making a campaign." "In the years past Pahutahs [Paiutes] before the American conquest used to sell and trade their children to the citizens of New Mexico as slaves" as well, but in all cases the Indians were "there of their own free will." As evidence, he added that the Indians in question had remained with him and his mother even after Griffin liberated them. That decision had probably rested in part on his unremarked statement that one of the women was a mother of two young children, "an infant and the other about four years old." All of those slaves had been purchased within the last "3 or 4 years," so at least one child had been born in captivity. The father never received mention; perhaps Santistevan held a deeper involvement

74. See Appendix C, "Taos County Cases," below; Elkins's endorsement to summary of Grand Jury President Manuel Vizcarra, July 1868, *Territorial Papers of the U.S. Senate* (hereafter cited as *TP USS)*, record group 46, NA; Murphy, "Reconstruction in New Mexico," *NMHR*, XLIII (April 1968), 106–107.

FIGURE 17. *Lawrie Tatum, First Kiowa Agent.* 1872. Tatum is shown with a group of "redeemed" Mexican captive boys. Photograph by William Stinson Soule (?). Courtesy National Anthropological Archives, Smithsonian Institution

than he wished to expose publicly. More than a few Indian slaves made the decision to maintain their servitude rather than sever kin relations, however coercive those relations might have been. In 1872, General Oliver O. Howard of the recently defunct Freedmen's Bureau arrived in New Mexico to facilitate the repatriation of several hundred Navajo slaves who continued to be held in New Mexican households. Some, especially women with children, refused the offer. For women with children and little means of support, perhaps seized too young to recall their Navajo kinspeople, the expectation of food and shelter might not lightly be traded for "freedom."[75]

During the same period, Plains Indians continued to take New Mexican children into captivity, although at only a fraction of the rate that Indian

75. Manuel Vizcarra, "Extract and Synopsis of Evidence before the U.S. Grand Jury, July 1868," fragment in "W. W. Griffin, Summary of Actions Regarding Peons and Slaves Held in Taos, Santa Fe, and Rio Arriba Counties, March 16 to November 28, 1868," *TP USS,* record group 46, NA. For O. O. Howard's cases, see Moore, *Chiefs, Agents, and Soldiers,* 100, esp. 267–268, for later refusals of repatriation.

groups suffered losses. Those whom they did take served increasingly as hostages in deals with their reservation agents. From 1860 forward, we see a corresponding increase in Americans entering Plains Indian captivity, some of whom did pen captivity narratives. Comprehensive and detailed counts of such captives do not exist, but the war department considered eight Texas counties most vulnerable, and one of them, Jack County, lost more than two hundred settlers to captivity between 1859 and 1871. Montague County lost forty-three and reclaimed twenty-nine in 1866 alone. Kiowa agent Lawrie Tatum redeemed fourteen American and twelve Mexican captives for a total price of $1,500 in 1870. It is not unreasonable to estimate American captives taken between 1860 and 1875 at roughly one thousand. Mexican losses are even more difficult to estimate, especially between 1857 and 1867, when the Mexican nation experienced the wars of the Reforma and the French Invasion. The upheavals of 1857 through 1867 allowed even less military protection than the earlier era, when Durango lost more than fourteen hundred citizens. Even a conservative estimate based on a continuing loss rate of fifty-seven Mexicans annually would bring another 1,026 captives into the Plains, for a total of 2,467 Mexicans between 1832 and 1875.[76]

Like American authorities in New Mexico before them, reservation agents like Lawrie Tatum and Commissioner of Indian Affairs William L. Cady anguished over their own nation's implication in the captive trade. Finally, in late 1870, Cady instructed his superintendents that "the practice of ransoming captives must be stopped, as it is only an inducement for the Indians to commit depredations and capture white women and children." Reservation annuity goods would be suspended if captives were not surrendered. Although it took time to become effective, the new policy, combined with military defeat and the Indians' increasing dependency on rations, gradually reduced the commerce. Fewer than fifty captives existed among Comanche bands enumerated in censuses between 1879 and 1901. In all likelihood, Mexican captives among the Comanches and Kiowas had been slipping (or cast) away from bondage since at least 1868, when reservation life, poverty, and military oversight began to eliminate the benefits of their servitude. Based on known cases of the end

76. Carl Coke Rister, *Border Captives: The Traffic in Prisoners by the Southern Plains Indians, 1835–1875* (Norman, Okla., 1940), 141–143; Lee Cutler, "Lawrie Tatum and the Kiowa Agency, 1869–1873," *Arizona and the West,* XIII (Autumn 1971), 221–244, citing Governor E. J. Davis to President Ulysses S. Grant, Mar. 22, 1871, Letters Received, Office of Indian Affairs, roll 377, NA.

FIGURE 18. *Vittoriano, a Mexican-Kiowa Captive.* 1872. Photograph by William Stinson Soule (?). Courtesy National Anthropological Archives, Smithsonian Institution

of slavery in other pastoral societies, emancipation often meant no more than walking away from it—the bonds of kinship and coercion that had once tied slaves to their masters were sufficiently strong to bind during the heights of its success, and sufficiently brittle when things fell apart, that bondage and freedom were in some part contingent on the relative security one felt in either condition.[77]

77. Cady to Hoag, Sept. 9, 1870, cited in Rister, *Border Captives,* 175; Thomas Kavanagh, "Playing a Numbers Game: Counting the Comanches in History and Anthropology" (1998), paper in possession of the author. Smith argues that the many Spanish surnames among long-resident families in western Oklahoma derive, not from late-nineteenth-century migrations, but from former captives who became country cousins to their reservated captors and kinspeople after 1875 ("Indians in American Mexican-Relations before the War of 1846,"

For He Had Learned to Love Them

Mescalero Apaches seized ten-year-old José Andrés Martínez and his younger nephew Pedro from the pastures above San Gerónimo in October 1866, trading Andrés shortly thereafter to the Kiowa headman Setdayaite (Many Bears). Renamed Andali, he grew to manhood among Kiowas and played a role similar to the Ute Francisco Manzanares in the closing years of the borderland communities. He left the Kiowa-Comanche reservation and returned to his family in 1884. His aged mother received him warmly, but after four years in New Mexico he went back to Anadarko, feeling "his interests were all identified with the Kiowa, and he had learned to love them."[78]

But he also felt the tides of history turning and converted to Methodism in 1890. Under the tutelage of the Reverend J. J. Methvin, he acted as a lay minister to his people and began teaching industrial arts in the mission school. In 1893, he married (his fourth) the Methodist matron Emma McWhorter. Unable to have children of their own, Andrés and Emma adopted two orphan girls, one a Cherokee and the other a Mexican-Kiowa mixed-blood. In 1894, Andrés began a new role as interpreter and spokesman for his people, traveling to Washington, D.C., with a Kiowa, Apache, and Comanche delegation to oppose allotment of reservation lands under the Dawes Severalty Act of 1887. He lived until 1930, mediating between two worlds and participating in the emergence of the syncretistic Native American (Peyote) Church among his friends and relatives. In a single life, Andrés combined nearly all the customs and innovations that this study has addressed.[79]

Hispanic American Historical Review, XLIII [February 1963], 41). For comparative cases, see Stephen Baier and Paul E. Lovejoy, "The Tuareg of the Central Sudan: Gradations in Servility at the Desert Edge (Niger and Nigeria)," in Suzanne Miers and Igor Kopytoff, *Slavery in Africa: Historical and Anthropological Perspectives* (Madison, Wisc., 1977), 391–411; Suzanne Miers and Richard Roberts, eds., *The End of Slavery in Africa* (Madison, Wisc., 1988).

78. Andrés's capture is reported in the Oct. 20, 1866, edition of the *Daily New Mexican,* 2, microfilm in New Mexico State Records Center. He later told his story to the Reverend J. J. Methvin, missionary to the Kiowa agency at Anadarko, Indian Territory. See Methvin, *Andele, the Mexican-Kiowa Captive: A Story of Real Life among the Indians* (Albuquerque, N.Mex., 1996), esp. 80.

79. Methvin, *Andele,* 80. The Dawes Act of 1887 proposed to extinguish tribally held lands in favor of private ownership.

FIGURE 19. *Andrés Martínez (Andali)*. 1894. Photograph by John K. Hillers. Courtesy National Anthropological Archives, Smithsonian Institution

Francisco Manzanares, the Ute captive-turned–New Mexican poblador, succeeded in bringing the first New Mexican families to the San Juan River in 1874. Within a few years, the Utes began selectively inviting New Mexicans to join them on their southern Colorado reservation. Persuading their agent to issue grazing permits to the New Mexicans, the Utes initiated an accommodation that would help build a stable and enduring multiethnic community on their reservation lands. When William Stollsteimer, a German-born Civil War veteran who had married a French–New Mexican daughter of the trader Antoine Robidoux, established a small farm at Francés on the Piedra, the Utes managed to get him appointed their Indian agent.

Under Stollsteimer's agency (1885–1887), a local policy developed of soliciting New Mexican villagers to settle on the reservation, clear land, build farms, and operate them on shares for their Ute landlords. Dozens of New Mexican families from the Chama River region moved north under this agreement. This extraordinary system of tenant farming, emerging at the same time that sharecropping developed as the labor solution in the postslavery South, met the needs of both parties but drew sharp criticism from Anglo farmers who wished to condemn Ute lands under the Dawes Act.[80]

The connection to the South was more than simply structural. In the 1880s, John Taylor, son of a slave and a former Buffalo Soldier in the all-black Ninth Cavalry, arrived on the Ute reservation. There he courted Kitty Cloud in the custom of the country. In a photograph taken on their "wedding" day in 1894, John Taylor lies on a blanket surrounded by gun-toting Ute warriors both afoot and on horseback. One man holds a buffalo lance to Taylor's breast, but Taylor smiles serenely. The metaphor combining captivity, adoption, and marriage is inescapable.[81]

In 1899, John and Kitty had a daughter, Euterpe Taylor, who lived outside Ignacio and reigned as the matriarch of the multigenerational, multiracial Black Ute Clan until her death in 1995. Euterpe spoke fluent Spanish, English, and Ute—in fact, she taught Ute in the reservation schools. In conversation, she switched her self-identification from "African" to "Indian" without hesitation and took great pride in both her African heritage and her Ute history—she believed the African element allowed her descendants to resist

80. Quintana, *Pobladores,* 103–144. Ute relations with their U.S. Indian affairs agents and Catholic missionaries were not so easy. See Katherine M. B. Osburn, *Southern Ute Women: Autonomy and Assimilation on the Reservation, 1887–1934* (Albuquerque, N.Mex., 1998).

81. William Loren Katz, *Black Indians: A Hidden Heritage* (New York, 1986), 182.

FIGURE 20. *Ute Indians at Play.* 1894. John Taylor's "Wedding." Photograph by H. S. Poley. Courtesy Denver Public Library, Western Collection

the ravages of alcoholism on the reservation. Relatively wealthy by the standards of the Southern Ute tribe, her surviving relatives suffered racial prejudice from resentful full-blood Utes and Anglos alike, even into the late twentieth century.[82]

While Utes, New Mexicans, and Africans were creating a multiethnic accommodation in southern Colorado, American control of the Plains east of the Sangre de Cristos did not go uncontested by New Mexican villagers after 1880. But the resistance henceforth would largely utilize tactics consistent with struggles against incorporation into a strong state. In the late 1880s and early 1890s, night riding *Las Gorras Blancas* (White Caps) from San Miguel County engaged in seventy-eight actions of fence cutting, hay burning, and livestock rustling. But the real power base for these night riders lay with a coterie of upwardly aspiring professionals and politicians of New Mexican descent. The Herrera brothers of Las Vegas supported their bandito cousins through the popular press and political parties like El Partido del Pueblo Unido, seeking,

82. Author's field notes, interview with Euterpe Taylor, Jul. 6, 1993, Ignacio, Colo. See also James F. Brooks, "Confounding the Color Line: Indian-Black Relations in Historical and Anthropological Perspective," *American Indian Quarterly,* XXII, nos. 1, 2 (1998), 125–133, for more treatment. The Denver Public Library Western Collection lists Taylor's first name as "Jim."

not autonomy in the sense of an earlier era, but reform within the existing structures of state power. Although the thunder of hooves on a moonlit night might evoke memories of the Plains defense, the orderly concentration of Hispano votes for county sheriff proved to be the future path of community preservation.[83]

83. Robert J. Rosenbaum and Robert W. Larson, "Mexicano Resistance to the Expropriation of Grant Lands in New Mexico," in Charles L. Briggs and John R. Van Ness, eds., *Land, Water, and Culture: New Perspectives on Hispanic Land Grants* (Albuquerque, N.Mex., 1987), 269–310. For other studies of local conflict and resistance movements within the context of a strengthening American state, see Altina Waller, *Feud: Hatfields, McCoys, and Social Change in Appalachia* (Chapel Hill, N.C., 1988); Christopher Waldrep, *Night Riders: Defending Community in the Black Patch, 1890–1915* (Durham, N.C., 1993); John Walton, *Western Times and Water Wars: State, Culture, and Rebellion in California* (Berkeley, Calif., 1992).

EPILOGUE

REFUGIO GURRIOLA MARTÍNEZ

Not everyone turned out for the winter celebration of "Los Comanches" in New Mexican villages at the close of the nineteenth century. In San Fernando de Taos, Refugio Gurriola Martínez stayed at home, her hand-stitched *cortinas* drawn against the music and tumult.

Born in the village of Magdalena, Sonora, Refugio was captured by Yaqui Indians in 1858 at age fifteen. About one year later, her Yaqui captors sold her to Chiricahua Apaches, with whom she lived another five years, serving her Apache owner, Great Deer, along with six other captive Mexican girls. But among the men in Great Deer's ranchería was another Mexican captive, a boy named Tomás. They formed a secret friendship and awaited the opportunity to escape. Their chance came in 1864.

Traveling at night across the recently pacified (and largely depopulated) Navajo borderlands, Refugio and Tomás made it to Tierra Amarilla, site of the Weeminuche Ute agency. Under the protection of the U.S. military, Refugio eventually ended up at Fort Union, east of the Sangre de Cristo Mountains. There she met Teófilo Martínez, a rank-and-file soldier who wooed her and sent her to live with his family in Taos until he mustered out. Their marriage brought happiness to Teófilo's family, for their youngest son had little property and was "tímido con las mujeres" (timid with women). Refugio became "una verdadera Taoseña" (a genuine member of the village) and gained local renown as a seamstress and dressmaker. But, when Los Comanches came to town, she trembled with fear until the dancers became Taoseños again.[1]

1. Jacobo M. Bernal, "La Cautiva," TS, Nov. 26, 1971, 19, 24, and Myrtle R. Bernal, "La Cautiva: A True Story," TS, n.d., both in the archives of the Kit Carson Foundation, Taos, N.Mex. Refugio and Teófilo were great aunt and uncle to Jacobo, who delivered their story to a meeting of the Taos County Historical Society. For Yaqui relations with the Mexican state, and for the liberal reforms instituted by Sonoran governor Pesqueira after 1854 that heightened tensions between the Yaquis and Mexican vecinos, see Evelyn Hu-Dehart, *Yaqui*

Refugio's story encompasses several themes prominent throughout this work. A young woman in a borderland village, she was particularly likely to become a victim of the commerce in slaves. Seized in Sonora and sold to Apaches, only to find redemption in northern New Mexico, Refugio's "middle passage" describes the extraordinary geographic and cultural breadth of the slave system of the borderlands. Of the six other Mexican women in her ranchería, María had been a captive since age seven and "seemed quite satisfied with her life." Twenty-one-year-old Josefa, however, saw her husband and two children die in the Apache attack that took her into bondage, and Refugio worried for her safety, since she "was quite open in her resentment." Refugio's ability to make a successful escape with Tomás across hundreds of miles of high desert attests to their personal courage and resourcefulness, a theme we have seen repeatedly in these pages. Present around Great Deer's hearth was the full spectrum of women's experience in borderland slavery.[2]

Refugio's life also reflects some of the broad historical changes witnessed herein and underscores how thoroughly one woman's experience could depend on forces well beyond her influence. The defeat and internment of the Navajos at Bosque Redondo probably made it possible for the two refugees to reach Tierra Amarilla; otherwise, they might well have become binaalté in a Navajo outfit or criados in a Cebolleta household. The emancipatory focus of American moral and military might throughout North America in 1864 brought Refugio into the protective embrace of the U.S. Army at Fort Union. There, her future husband Teófilo—who might earlier have been a captive-taking nacajallese or comanchero himself—had found wage employment within the military apparatus of the expanding American state.

Refugio's ultimate fate depended on local factors as well. Teófilo's shyness with women might have derived from his position as the youngest son of a family of limited means. His two older brothers, Inocencio and Nestor, had already married, and what little land the Martínezes farmed was no doubt already allocated to feeding the growing extended family. Teófilo had few re-

---

Resistance and Survival: The Struggle for Land and Autonomy (Madison, Wisc., 1984); Hu-Dehart, "Peasant Rebellion in the Northwest: The Yaqui Indians of Sonora, 1740–1976," in Friedrich Katz, ed., *Riot, Rebellion, and Revolution: Rural Social Conflict in Mexico* (Princeton, N.J., 1988), 141–175, esp. 154–162. For a wider view of Sonora in the colonial and early national periods, see Cynthia Radding, *Wandering Peoples: Colonialism, Ethnic Spaces, and Ecological Frontiers in Northwestern Mexico, 1700–1850* (Durham, N.C., 1997).

2. Jacobo Bernal, "La Cautiva," TS, 9–10.

sources with which to attract a bride; thus his family's delight at his good fortune. Torn from her Sonoran family's support, Refugio herself had no dowry with which to solicit a husband. Although their marriage proved a happy one, it was a union of two people balanced at the very margins of security, where the winds of fortune might easily have blown tragedy instead of romance. And, despite her long life, Refugio's security vanished each Christmas Eve, when the strange combination of hand drums and violins awakened terrible memories of her passage into adulthood.[3]

Refugio Gurriola Martínez was just one of thousands of women and children swept into the intercultural exchange network treated here as a borderland political cultural economy. This analytical framework emerges from overwhelming evidence that native Americans and New Mexicans, despite their cultural differences, shared an understanding of the production and distribution of wealth as conditioned by social relations of power. At the same time that captives entered the borderland economy, many hundreds of thousands of sheep, goats, horses, mules, and cattle were moving between native American, New Mexican, and Mexican societies. If these livestock served as capital on the hoof, captives represented a type of cultural capital. Captured women and children served as objects of men's contestations for power while simultaneously they enriched the cultures in which they found themselves lodged through their own social and biological reproductive potential.[4]

Captives' numerical representation may seem insignificant when compared to the commerce in stolen livestock, but this story suggests that the slave system of the Southwest Borderlands provided the ideological and cultural fuel that fed the larger economy. Historians of the South have argued that, although the majority of whites did not own slaves, most believed that their own economic prospects and racial dominance depended upon the perpetuation of that region's political economy. Slave ownership in native American and New

3. Life stories like that of Refugio Gurriola also abound in Africa. For cases that reveal the "interplay of institutional or structural elements with situational, idiosyncratic actions," see Marcia Wright, *Strategies of Slaves and Women: Life Stories from East / Central Africa* (New York, 1993), 1.

4. Pierre Bourdieu notes that, in oral-historical social formations without the literary apparatus for objectifying symbolic and cultural capital, household power relations define and conserve the value of rights in persons. See *Outline of a Theory of Practice* (Cambridge, 1977), 88–95.

Mexican societies was smaller in scale and equally restricted by wealth, but the traffic in captives offered lower-status raiders real opportunity to accumulate power and prestige. And, although slavery in the borderlands never exhibited a hardening of racial distinctions as in the South, hierarchies of status did exist in both native American and New Mexican societies. These exhibited cultural variation, however, given the particular circumstances confronting Navajos, Comanches, Kiowas, and Apaches. Navajos, whose population actually grew during the eighteenth and nineteenth centuries, unlike other Indian groups, seem to have begun to use their binaalté as symbolic boundary markers to help stabilize and purify the essence of being Navajo. Comanches and Kiowas confronted population crises from the 1780s forward and therefore allowed relations of inequality to be more fluid between themselves and their captives, although in specific cases the experience of the slave could be grim indeed.[5]

Although many borderland Indian and New Mexican men, like many southern whites, found comfort and economic potential in their regional systems of human bondage, the Southwestern case also is in contrast with the southern institution. Its foundation in indigenous and Iberian customs of capture and kinship—by which slaves gradually shed their status as war captives and became full, if subordinate, household members—provoked comparison to African cases throughout this work. The dynamic role of kinship cannot be underplayed in either Africa or the Southwest Borderlands, for in both cases the incorporation of captives as kinspeople moderated some of the worst abuses latent in slave systems and prevented full momentum toward racial dichotomization. Whereas racial mixing was ubiquitous throughout the South, acknowledgment of kinship, with its attendant rights and obligations, was fundamentally absent there.[6]

Native Americans' and New Mexicans' adoption, marriage, and recognition of the captives' offspring as culture-group members mirror most African cases. This aspect foregrounds one of the painful contradictions found in kin-based slave systems. Although most scholars differ in their views on the dividing line

5. James Oakes, *The Ruling Race: A History of American Slaveholders* (New York, 1982).

6. Ironically, this suggests that Eugene D. Genovese's deeply criticized conceptualization of the South as a precapitalist political economy organized around kinlike paternalism might have found more support if applied to indigenous or Hispanic America. See *The Political Economy of Slavery: Studies in the Economy and Society of the Slave South* (New York, 1961).

between kinship and slavery in Africa, they agree that kin incorporation provided some opportunities for intercultural accord yet simultaneously stimulated demand for more slaves to replace those absorbed into kinship statuses. Where accommodation did occur, this meant that slaving wars had to expand into new territories, thereby perpetuating violence and exploitation.[7]

Slavery in the Southwest Borderlands, and probably wherever capture and kinship occurred in the Americas, presents a similar paradox. Based in the biological necessity for intermarriage between small communities, marital exchanges often involved mutualistic or competitive patriarchal exchanges of women. Parallel institutions of reciprocal adoption fostered trade between Indian groups but also often involved the violent seizure, sacrifice, or assimilation of war captives. Patricia Albers's trenchant observation that intercultural human exchanges always contained "the grounds for conflict" and "embodied (quite literally) the terms of reconciliation" encapsulates this paradox succinctly. Long before mestizaje became the rallying cry of Mexican nationalism or the preoccupation of modern scholars, native American groups went about the pragmatic and often violent business of mingling families and producing hybrid cultures. In colonial New Mexico, the Iberian customs of migrants from New Spain meshed all too well with the autochthonous tradition, and, as borderland societies matured, so too did the range and volume of local slave raiding.[8]

This book addresses several areas of contemporary debate in native American, Spanish Borderland, and North American history. It highlights patriarchal competition for women and children and the accumulation of indigenous units of social wealth as crucial factors in triggering violence within and between native American societies. As such, it casts shadows across a tenaciously sunny romanticism that sees indigenous peoples on the fringes of Euramerican expansion operating within subsistence-and-exchange economies that produced little intergroup conflict. As one scholar cautioned, the challenge of the "new Indian history" is to "stop treating Indians like sacred, one-dimensional

7. Claude Meillassoux, *The Anthropology of Slavery: The Womb of Iron and Gold* (Chicago, 1991); Suzanne Miers and Igor Kopytoff, eds., *Slavery in Africa: Historical and Anthropological Perspectives* (Madison, Wisc., 1977).

8. Patricia C. Albers, "Symbiosis, Merger, and War: Contrasting Forms of Intertribal Relationship among Historic Plains Indians," in John H. Moore, ed., *The Political Economy of North American Indians* (Lincoln, Nebr., 1993), 128.

European myths and begin the hard, terribly difficult and unpredictable quest of regarding them as human beings."[9]

The study at hand suggests that, when natural resources were scarce or unevenly distributed among Indian groups, customs of exogamous marriage and reciprocal adoption that usually fostered intergroup exchange could shift to a violent and competitive commerce that reaped sorrow. Although modern scholarship has worked to integrate ecological and cultural theories for indigenous American warfare and accommodation, the role of gender, kinship, and status imperatives deserves deeper investigation. A focus on the tensions and resolutions within a universally adoptive indigenous culture raises the possibility that native North America before the advent of political "tribes" might have been more than a patchwork landscape of families and bands. Rather, the adoptive impulse wove a vast web of interethnic tensions and alliances that constituted a social formation equal in territorial scale and social complexity to that of Europe.[10]

The Southwest Borderlands offer a complicated and dynamic history where power and identities were in perpetual turmoil, negotiation, and regeneration. Looking at these myriad forces within the framework of a regional political economy, one can see that social inequalities, largely born of asymmetrical gender relations within all the participant societies, contributed significantly to patterns of conflict and movements toward intergroup alliances. Social inequality in Navajo and New Mexican societies helped to create the ladrones and nacajalleses who stole from the rich to give to those men who controlled access to wives and cultural enfranchisement. Sometimes the men thus gifted were the same as those who had been earlier robbed. The New Mexican institution of rescate, a thinly disguised slave market, encouraged Comanches to sell their war captives rather than adopt them. Yet, when Comanches were threatened by disease or American expansion, they raided New Mexico and Mexico for captives who could quickly "become Comanche." When Utes found them-

9. Michael Dorris, "Indians on the Shelf," in Calvin Martin, ed., *The American Indian and the Problem of History* (Oxford, 1987), 98–105, esp. 105.

10. Albers, "Symbiosis, Merger, and War," in Moore, ed., *Political Economy of North American Indians*, is the best example of integrated analysis and helped to highlight the focus here on kin dynamics and captive taking. For an earlier effort, see Thomas Biolsi, "Ecological and Cultural Factors in Plains Indian Warfare," in R. Brian Ferguson, ed., *Warfare, Culture, and Environment* (Orlando, Fla., 1984), 141–168.

selves falling behind the Comanches in military power, they became allies with New Mexicans and raided both Navajos and Comanches for slaves. But, as customary retribution and redistribution moved resources within and between contending groups, the articulation of their borderland economy with the expanding Atlantic economy fostered new inequalities and accommodations.[11]

In the South, no matter how earnestly defenders of southern slavery mobilized metaphors of paternalism to explain their commitment to the institution, they could not conceal their dependence upon slave traders and markets to create and maintain their wealth, which in turn exposed the cynicism of the family metaphor. In the Southwest Borderlands, the quest for captives and their incorporation into Euramerican or Indian households never achieved the determining power of chattel slavery in the South, but, as commercialization of the system expanded during the nineteenth century, market forces eroded its institutions of kinship. In an ironic twist, the willingness of U.S. Indian agents to redeem captives with cash created yet another market for slaves after 1850. As in the cases of the postwar South and colonial Africa, integration with a capitalist economy did not bring free-wage labor to the borderlands. New forms of peonage, such as sharecropping, and dependency on conquest governments appeared during the late nineteenth century in all these regions. Hence, the military and economic solutions to the "Indian Problem" between 1860 and 1880 in the West had strategic connections to the Civil War and Reconstruction eras. It would become clear with time that liberal capitalism only lent its support to those autonomous individuals already possessed of the means of independence in both regions.[12]

All this suggests that the volatile matrix created by the borderland economies actually brought some significant sectors of the colonial population into the indigenous social formation proposed above. Thus, North America featured nascent social alternatives to nativistic resistance or European expan-

11. Some important predecessors in raising questions of gender, sexuality, and the creativity of Indian identity include Ramon A. Gutiérrez, *When Jesus Came, the Corn Mothers Went away: Sexuality, Love, and Conquest in New Mexico, 1500–1846* (Stanford, Calif., 1991); Gary Clayton Anderson, *The Indian Southwest, 1580–1830: Ethnogenesis and Reinvention* (Norman, Okla., 1999).

12. Michael Tadman, *Speculators and Slaves: Masters, Traders, and Slaves in the Old South* (Madison, Wisc., 1989); Steven Deyle, "The Domestic Slave Trade in America" (Ph.D. diss., Columbia University, 1995).

sionism. Profoundly important studies of the Great Lakes region, the cis-Mississippi frontier, and the deep colonial South have announced similar phenomena.[13]

Extending the history of early America in the Southwest Borderlands into the late nineteenth century allows some insights into how the borderland societies both confronted and participated in American westward expansion—and how Mexican state-building influenced their formation and disintegration. Without a weak Mexico as a source of cattle and captives, the border societies might well have withered by the 1820s. Without the military and economic consolidation of Mexico and the United States after 1877, they might still be raiding today. The imposition of state order in the pastoral borderlands of New Mexico produced contradictory effects. Severing customary links of violence and exchange, it brought a measure of security to many women and children, the most vulnerable members of both societies, and a measure of independence to freed slaves. Economic dependency on Federal annuities and poorly paid wage labor followed, with especially damaging results in the early years of the twentieth century. In subduing the pastoral borderlands, the American and Mexican states sundered long-term connections of kinship and community and superimposed new, "state-sponsored" ethnic identities upon a complex mélange. Without the pain and terror that beset borderland travelers like Refugio Gurriola Martínez, the cultural exchanges and transformations wrought by her and those like her might have offered some alternative to the alienation and poverty that flowed in the wake of American freedom.

13. Richard White, *The Middle Ground: Indians, Empires, and Republics in the Great Lakes Region, 1650–1815* (Cambridge, Mass., 1991); Daniel H. Usner, Jr., *Indians, Settlers, and Slaves in a Frontier Exchange Economy: The Lower Mississippi Valley before 1783* (Chapel Hill, N.C., 1992); Andrew R. L. Cayton and Fredrika J. Teute, eds., *Contact Points: American Frontiers from the Mohawk Valley to the Mississippi, 1750–1830* (Chapel Hill, N.C., 1998); Claudio Saunt, *A New Order of Things: Property, Power, and the Transformation of the Creek Indians, 1733–1816* (Cambridge, 1999).

CHRONOLOGY

DATE	SOUTHWEST BORDERLANDS	NORTH AMERICA
1265	*Las Siete Partidas* set Spanish laws of slavery	
1500s	Athapaskan Migrations	
1520	Cortéz's conquest of Mexico	
1540–1542	Coronado's *entrada*	
1587		Roanoke Colony est.
1598	First Spanish settlement est. in New Mexico at San Gabriel del Yunque	
1607		Jamestown Colony est.
1610	Santa Fe est.	
1620		Plymouth Colony est.
1670s	Spanish Inquisition in New Mexico	
1675–1676		King Philip's War
1676		Bacon's Rebellion
1680	Great Southwestern Revolt	
1681	*Recopilación de las Indias* reiterates ban on Indian slavery in New World	
1692–1696	Spanish *reconquista* of New Mexico	
1700s	Comanche migration to southern Plains	
1701–1714		Queen Anne's War
1720	Villasur Massacre	
1740s–1750s	Navajo migrations out of Dinetah	
1754		Seven Years' War commences
1763		Treaty of Paris
1765	Bourbon reforms instituted in New Spain	
1769	Presidios San Diego and Monterey est. in California	

1775		American Revolution commences
1776	*Provincias Internas* organized	
1776–1777	Domínguez-Escalante expedition	
1777–1779	Drought in Southwest	
1779	Defeat of Cuerno Verde	
1779–1781	Smallpox epidemic	
1780	Analceño resistance	
1781		Spain declares war on Great Britain
1783	Great Britain recognizes U.S. independence	
1786	Spanish-Comanche Peace Spanish-Navajo Treaty Comanche-Ute Peace	
1786–1787	San Carlos de los Jupes est.	
1805	Comanche-Kiowa alliance San Miguel insurgency Narbona's campaign into the Cañon de Chelly	
1807	Zebulon Pike arrested in New Mexico	
1810	Mexican war for independence commences	
1819		Adams-Onís Treaty
1820–1821	Missouri Compromise	
1821	Spain recognizes Mexico's independence St. Louis–Chihuahua Trail est. via Santa Fe	
1824	First Mexican constitution ratified	
1828–1829	Ruíz-Berlandier expeditions	
1829	Old Spanish Trail links New Mexico and California Mexico abolishes chattel slavery	
1834	Bent's Fort est.	
1836	Lone Star Republic (Texas) est.	

1837	Río Arriba rebellion	
1845	Texas annexed to U.S.	
1846	Mexican-American War commences	
1848	Treaty of Guadalupe Hidalgo	
1847–1848	Taos revolt	
1850		Compromise of 1850
1859	New Mexican legislature attempts to codify Indian slavery	
1861–1865		Civil War
1862	Confederate invasion of New Mexico	
1864	Sand Creek massacre	
1864–1868	Navajo internment at Bosque Redondo	
1865		Thirteenth Amendment abolishes slavery in U.S.
1865–1885	Santa Fe ring gains control of Mexican land grants	
1868		Fourteenth Amendment establishes citizenship for ex-slaves
1868–1872	Griffin inquests on Indian slavery	
1874	Plains Indians attack American bison hunters at Adobe Walls	
1875	U.S. Army's campaigns into Red River area	
1887		Dawes Severalty Act

GLOSSARY OF SPANISH AND NATIVE AMERICAN TERMS

acequia (irrigation ditch)
aguacil mayor (sheriff)
alcalde mayor (executive officer of district or town)
alcalde ordinario (member of municipal government, local magistrate)
ana'i (Navajo: lit., alien, enemy)
arriero (mule packer, driver)
ayuntamiento (municipal council)
bando (official document announcing law, act, event)
binaalté (see *naalté)*
b'yisná (captives)
cambalache (barter)
capitalistas (merchant capitalists)
carga (unit of measure, approx. 200 lbs.; load)
casta (descendants of mixed unions between Indian, mestizo, black, and Spanish parents)
castellanos (Castilians)
castizo (of pure blood, descent)
cautivo (captive)
cibolero (bison hunter)
cofradía (Catholic lay brotherhood)
collotes, coyotes (of mixed Indian-mestizo descent)
comanchería (region under Comanche control)
comanchero (Indian trader)
comerciante (merchant trader)
compadrazgo (Catholic godparenthood)
compadre (fictive coparent)
convivencia (coexistence)
cordón (trading caravan)
corrales (livestock corrals)
criadas / criados (lit., "those raised up"; servants; adopted within system of Catholic godparenthood)
crianza (adoptive servitude)
criollo (creole, Spaniards born in Americas)
Cupirittaka (Pawnee: Evening Star)
diligencia (inquiry, investigation)
diligencias criminales (inquiries into criminal activities)
diligencias matrimoniales (premarriage inquiries)
Diné Ana'aii (Navajo: Enemy [alien] Navajo)
Dinetah (Navajo homelands along the San Juan River)
efectos del país (items of domestic manufacture or provenance)
empresario (holder of entrepreneurial land grant)
encomendero (holder of *encomienda)*
encomienda (royal grant of Indian labor and tribute rights to Spaniard in return for commitment to religious instruction and physical safety)
entrada (entrance, gateway)
estancia (large farm or ranch, livestock operation)
estanciero (livestock rancher)

expediente (administrative directive)
extranjeros (foreigners)
fanega (grain measure, approx. 2 bushels, 100 lbs.)
feria (trade fair involving nomadic Indians, Pueblo Indians, and Spanish colonists)
frazada (heavy blanket of cotton or wool)
genízaro (lit., Janissary; in New Mexico, detribalized nomadic Indians reduced to slavery, converted, resettled in Spanish homes or villages and deployed as military auxiliaries)
gente de razón (people of reason; Christianized Spanish subjects)
guía (commercial passport)
hermano mayor (head of *cofradía)*
huérfano (orphan)
indios bárbaros ("barbarous Indians"; not under Spanish dominion)
indios gentiles ("heathen Indians")
jacal (small structure of interwoven posts and saplings, covered with adobe plaster)
jefe principale (Indian divisional chief)
jinetes (equestrian raiders)
Kwuhúpu (Comanche: assimilated captive)
labradores (farmers)
ladrones (lit., thieves; Navajo livestock raiders)
limosnas (alms)
llaneros (plainsmen)
maestro de los obreros (master of workers; foreman)
Ma'ideshgizni (Navajo: "Coyote Pass," or Jémez Clan)
majordomo (head of association, foreman)
manojo (handful)
merced (grant of land)
mestizaje (racial and ethnic mixing)
mestizo / mestiza (person of mixed Spanish-Indian descent)
milicias activas (volunteer civil militias, serving forty-five-day terms)
montañeses (people of the mountains)
naalté (Navajo: slave; plural, *binaalté)*
nacajalleses (Navajo: New Mexican livestock and slave raiders)
Nakaídiné (Navajo: Mexican Clan)
na'nil (Navajo: servant, dependent laborer)
na'taani (Navajo: band headman)
Notádiné (Navajo: Ute Clan)
numunahkahni (Comanche: local residence band)
obraje (textile workshop)
padrinos (baptismal godparents)
paraibo (Comanche: band captain, chief)
paraje (resting and provisioning place on road or trail)
partidario (obligee under *partido* sheep lending and raising system)
partido (livestock lending and raising system; contract for same)
pastores (sheepherders)
pelado (lit., "peeled"; poor person)
pesos fuertes (lit., strong pesos, silver pesos)
pieza (slave, esp. captured child)

placita (small village)
población (small frontier settlement)
poblador (settler)
pobre (poor, or a poor person)
presidiales (frontier soldiers)
Protector de Indios (legal representative for Christian Indians)
Provincias Internas (Internal Provinces; administrative unit established in 1776 to include the Californias, Sonora, New Mexico, Coahuila, Nueva Vizcaya, and Texas)
pueblo (town, village)
puesto (outpost)
punche (native tobacco)
quintal (unit of measure, 46 kg, 130 lbs.)
ranchería (usually, nomadic Indian encampment; residential agricultural compounds among Spanish and Navajos)
ranchero (rancher)
real (monetary unit and coin, one-eighth of a peso)
reconquista (lit., "reconquest," of Iberian Peninsula in late medieval and Early Modern periods and New Mexico after 1692, when don Diego de Vargas resettled the colony)
reducción (Christian settlements of nomadic or dispersed Indians)
repartimiento (allotment of Indian labor to Spaniards)
rescate (lit., ransom; commercial events at which Indian slaves were purchased by Spanish subjects)
rico (rich, or a rich person)
serapes, sarapes (blankets of wool, worn by men)
Las Siete Partidas (Alfonso X's [1252-1284] legal code)
tai'vo (Comanche: "slave"; later, *na'raivo,* "black man")
teniente (lieutenant, assistant magistrate)
teniente general (lieutenant general; when applied to Indians, "sub-chief")
testamento (testament; written will)
torreón (defensive tower of adobe or stone)
traficante (trader, usually illicit)
Upirikutsu (Pawnee: Morning Star)
vara (Spanish yard, approx. 33 inches)
vecino / vecina (citizen)
velorio (wake, death vigil)
vergüenza (lit., shame, or sense of honor)
viaje (journey, trip)
villa (formal settlement, smaller than a city *[ciudad]* but larger than a *pueblo* or *población)*
yisná' (Navajo: war captive)

APPENDIX A

Navajo Livestock and Captive Raids, 1780–1864

These figures represent approximate data on Navajo raids on New Mexican, Pueblo, and, in some cases, Apache settlements wherein livestock and/or captives were taken.[1]

Date	Location	Sheep & Goats	Cattle	Horses & Mules	People Killed/ Captured
5/1780	Río Abajo	>30		30	
1/1783	Keres			9	
3/1783	Abiquiu	[<100]			
6/1783	Río Grande			11	
9/1783	Jémez/Zía	55			
3/1785	Albuquerque			27	2/
3/1786	Abiquiu			23	
1/1788	Gila			49	
5/1791	Gila				/71
3/1795	Albuquerque	[<100]			/1
4/1800	Cebolleta	[<500]	55	12	12/2
4/1804	Jémez/Zía	>1,000			
4/1804	Jémez/Zía	>1,000			
4/1804	Cebolleta	>1,000	58	24	
4/1804	Río Arriba			7	
3/1805	Río Grande	>1,000	100	40	
5/1805	La Cañada		10	2	
5/1805	Jémez			39	
11/1807	Mescalero				15/4
9/1815	Mogollon				1/6
3/1818	Jémez		[<200]	[<100]	
6/1818	San Mateo	[<500]			1/
7/1818	Abiquiu	400		2	
7/1818	Abiquiu			17	
9/1818	Cebolleta	[<500]			
9/1818	Taos			30	
10/1818	Mora			[<50]	1/
2/1822	Río Abajo	[>500]	[>200]	[>100]	

Date	Location	Sheep & Goats	Cattle	Horses & Mules	People Killed/ Captured
2/1824	Cebolleta			[<100]	
4/1824	Abiquiu		5		
10/1824	Laguna			[<50]	
12/1824	Santa Ana	6	7	5	
3/1825	Belén	>1,000			
5/1827	San Juan			40	
6/1827	La Cañada	[<500]			
8/1827	Belén	29			
3/1829	Jémez	130			
8/1829	Abiquiu	30			
8/1829	Santa Ana			4	
9/1829	Jémez			8	
1/1830	Cebolleta	11			
7/1832	San Juan			10	
2/1834	Zía			1	/2
7/1834	Jémez			4	
1/1835	Jémez	50		14	
3/1835	Albuquerque		[>200]		
6/1835	Socorro	>2,000	[>200]	[<50]	/1
9/1839	Cebolleta	[<500]			1/
8/1839	El Sabinal			90	
12/1840	Jémez			11	
6/1843	Belén	500			
6/1843	Jémez		25	2	
11/1843	Río Arriba	[>500]			/6
3/1844	Abiquiu		14	3	
7/1844	Rincon		13		
10/1844	Río Abajo			[<50]	
11/1844	Río Abajo	16,000			
9/1846	Río Abajo	[<500]	[<200]		
10/1846	Polvadera		[<200]	[<50]	
10/1846	Cubero			40	
10/1846	Albuquerque	5,000			/6
11/1846	Valverde	800			
12/1846	Río Arriba	250			

Date	Location	Sheep & Goats	Cattle	Horses & Mules	People Killed/ Captured
1846–1860	New Mexico	60,000			/50
2/1849	Puerco	6,000–8,000			
9/1849	Sandía	[<500]			5/
10/1849	San Mateo	[<500]			2/1
10/1849	La Cañada			115	
10/1849	San Ysidro			[<50]	
11/1849	Santa Ana	[<500]	[<200]	[<50]	
11/1849	Cebolleta		16	5	
1/1850	Zuñi			[<50]	/2
5/1850	Puerco	4,400			
6/1850	Abiquiu	[<500]		[<50]	/2
6/1850	Jémez	[<500]		20–30	1/
6/1850	Puerco	15,000			
6/1850	Chama			30	
7/1850	Corrales	2,000			1/
8/1850	Zuñi	[<500]			3/
10/1850	Cebolleta	3,869			
11/1850	Valverde	2,000			
12/1850	Cebolleta	5,822			
1846–1850[2]	New Mexico	150,231	1,234	1,654	
1/1851	Corrales	[<500]			1/1
2/1851	Albuquerque		30		
1848–1850[3]	New Mexico	47,300	788	181	83/13
3/1851	Río Abajo	[<500]	100	30	
3/1851	Pajarito		68	11	
3/1851	Manzano	3,000			
6/1851	Isleta	[<500]			
7/1851	Mora	>1,000	[<200]	[>100]	3/3
8/1851	Pajarito	>1,000			1/
5/1853	Abiquiu				1/3
5/1853	Socorro	5,600			
6/1853	Abiquiu	3,000			

Date	Location	Sheep & Goats	Cattle	Horses & Mules	People Killed/ Captured
1/1856	Puerco			14	
3/1856	Puerco	11,000			3/
5/1856	Peña Blanca	300			2/
9/1856	Puerco			30	
12/1856	Puerco	2,000			
1/1857	Puerco	1,235			
1846–1854[4]	New Mexico	80,263	1,364	884	
3/1857	Puerco	3,100			
6/1857	Río Abajo		100	15	
2/1858	Zuñi			150	
3/1858	Abiquiu	2,000			
9/1858	San Ildefonso	>1,000			
10/1858	Cebolleta		100		8/
11/1858	Isleta	2,300			
4/1859	Laguna			61	
4/1859	Jémez	3,200			
5/1859	Abiquiu		30	8	
5/1859	Zuñi			47	
5/1859	Chama			[<100]	
5/1859	Río Abajo	3,000			
5/1859	Cebolleta	1,000			4/
6/1859	Puerco	300			
1858–1859[5]	New Mexico	5,565	89	93	
9/1859	Corrales			75–100	
11/1859	Puerco			22	
11/1859	Pajarito	1,200		3	/3
11/1859	El Sabinal	900	20		1/
1/1860	Fort Craig	6,000–7,000			/4
1/1860	Belén		30		
1/1860	Los Lunas	12,000			/4
2/1860	Paraje	5,000	70		
1861[6]	New Mexico	50,000			
1862[7]	New Mexico	30,000			

Where documents say simply *algunos* (some), *muchos* (many), *rebaño* (flock [of sheep]), *manada* (herd [of cattle]), *caballada* (herd [of horses]), estimates are placed in brackets as follows: *algunos* (sheep) [<100]; (cattle) [<50]; (horses) [<20]; *muchos* (sheep) [<500]; (cattle) [<200]; (horses) [<100]; *rebaño* [<1,000]; *manada* [>100]; *caballada* [<100].

1. Unless otherwise noted, figures are drawn from entries in J. Lee Correll, comp. and ed., *Through White Men's Eyes: A Contribution to Navajo History: A Chronological Record of the Navajo People from Earliest Times to the Treaty of June 1, 1868* (Window Rock, Ariz., 1979), I, II. Individual entries may be found in text by date and location.

2. James S. Calhoun's estimation of stock losses by Navajos and other Indians for years since U.S. conquest (ibid., I, 284).

3. Tabulation for eighteen months' losses between March 1848 and September 1850 by General George A. McCall, ibid., I, 279–280.

4. Claims submitted by Commissioner of Indian Affairs George Mannypenny to Secretary of Interior McClelland, Mar. 2, 1857, summarizing stock losses attributed to Navajo raids (ibid., II, 75–84).

5. New Mexico Indian Superintendent Collins to Navajo Agent Baker, summarizing New Mexican stock losses to Navajo raids between Aug. 15, 1858, and Dec. 25, 1859 (ibid., II, 270–272).

6. Estimates from L. R. Bailey, *If You Take My Sheep: The Evolution and Conflicts of Navajo Pastoralism, 1630–1868* (Pasadena, Calif., 1980), 217.

7. Gerald Thompson, *The Army and the Navajo* (Tucson, Ariz., 1976), 10.

APPENDIX B

New Mexican Livestock and Captive Raids, 1780–1864

These figures represent approximate data on New Mexican militia actions, both official and unsanctioned, against Navajos wherein livestock and/or captives were taken.[1]

Date	Location	Sheep & Goats	Cattle	Horses & Mules	People Killed/ Captured
6/1785	Gila				40/
7/1804	Navajo			22	4/10
8/1804	Navajo		33	16	57/5
12/1804	Navajo			8	1/3
1/1805	Navajo	350		30	118/34
12/1818	Navajo	2,300		73	7/2
3/1819	Navajo	470		24	36/20
9/1821	Navajo	2,112		400	21/7
10/1821	Navajo			5	7/1
6/1823	Navajo	722	87	91	50/36
4/1825	Navajo				14/22
4/1829	Navajo				17/24
10/1834	Navajo	3,000		15	16/3
8/1836	de Chelly	6,604	109	14	35/4
9/1836	Navajo/Zuñi	1,537		108	20/1
12/1836	Río Salado	3,500			
12/1836	Chuska Mts.	7,300		98	28/19
9/1838	Tunicha Mts.	2,060		226	78/56
12/1838	Tunicha Mts.			20	3/6
10/1839	Navajo	9,253		>222	34/7
10/1840	Navajo			39	33/14
9/1843	Navajo	14,000	300	[>100]	15/22
2/1844	Ojo Caliente	1,600	200		19/18
11/1845	Tierra Amarilla				4/3
10/1847	Navajo	1,500		75	10/40
8/1849	de Chelly			242	
7/1850	Corrales	2,000			

Date	Location	Sheep & Goats	Cattle	Horses & Mules	People Killed/ Captured
11/1850	Valverde	5,000	11	150	/52
3/1851	Cebolleta				/18
5/1856	Valle Grande	300			2/
2/1857	Puerco	1,120		80	
3/1857	Puerco	1,000			
3/1858	Abiquiu				5/3
4/1858	Navajo	117			
9/1858	de Chelly			24	10/4
9/1858	de Chelly	6,000		5	6/6
10/1858	Chuska	6,500		80	10/
10/1858	Cebolleta				9/
10/1858	de Chelly		5	100	1/
10/1858	Navajo	20		10	/20
10/1858[2]	New Mexico	13,000		275	/25
11/1858	Navajo	1,500			
11/1858	de Chelly	300		35	4/
1859[3]	New Mexico	15,000			
1/1860	Fort Craig	6,500			
2/1860	Navajo	6,000			
2/1860	de Chelly	12,000			
2/1860	Chuska	6,420	97	13	13/
3/1860	Río Abajo	17,000	100		28/
9/1860[4]	Navajo	2,440			/115
1861[5]	Navajo	8,000			34/
1862–1864[6]	Navajo	2,533		134	56/269

Where documents say simply *algunos* (some), *muchos* (many), *rebaño* (flock [of sheep]), *manada* (herd [of cattle]), *caballada* (herd [of horses]), estimates are placed in brackets as follows: *algunos* (sheep) [<100]; (cattle) [<50]; (horses) [<20]; *muchos* (sheep) [<500]; (cattle) [<200]; (horses) [<100]; *rebaño* [<1,000]; *manada* [>100]; *caballada* [<100].

1. Unless otherwise noted, figures are drawn from entries in J. Lee Correll, comp. and ed., *Through White Men's Eyes: A Contribution to Navajo History: A Chronological Record of the Navajo People from Earliest Times to the Treaty of June 1, 1868* (Window Rock, Ariz., 1979), I, II. Individual entries may be found by date and location.

2. General Nelson Miles, summary of 1858 campaigns, ibid., II, 188–189.

3. Major Ruff to Wilkins, summary of sheep taken during campaigns of 1859, Nov. 4, 1859, ibid., II, 317.

4. Four campaigns by New Mexico militia, May–September, 1860, in L. R. Bailey, *If You Take My Sheep: The Evolution and Conflicts of Navajo Pastoralism, 1630–1868* (Pasadena, Calif., 1980), 212–213.

5. Bailey, *If You Take My Sheep,* 210.

6. Figures from Carson's Navajo campaign. The actual number of livestock and captives are, of course, many thousands higher. The Navajos arrived at Bosque Redondo with only 6,962 sheep, 2,757 goats, 3,038 horses, and 143 mules, in the possession of 1,782 families totalling 8,354 persons. Even with the depletions of the preceding years, flocks left behind, either to perish from neglect or among those outfits that escaped internment, must have numbered in the hundreds of thousands. For Carson's reports, see Lawrence C. Kelly, *Navajo Roundup: Selected Correspondence of Kit Carson's Expedition against the Navajo, 1863–1865* (Boulder, Colo., 1970), 38–39, 54–55, 75–77, 98–100, 161–163. For Bosque Redondo totals, see Bailey, *If You Take My Sheep,* 249.

APPENDIX C

New Mexican Peonage and Slavery Hearings, 1868

W. W. Griffin, "Summary of Actions regarding Peons and Indian Slaves Held in Taos, Santa Fe, and Río Arriba Counties, New Mexico Territory, March 16 to November 28, 1868," in Papers Relating to the Cases of W. W. Griffin, Indian Commissioner of Territory of New Mexico, Indian Peonage, United States Senate Territorial Documents, New Mexico, record group 46, National Archives.

TAOS COUNTY CASES

Case No.	Defendant	Form of Bondage	Proceedings
1	Jacobo Vigil	peonage	peon freed, defendant discharged
2	Florentino Suaz	peonage	peon freed, defendant discharged
3	Bartolo Valdez	peonage	insufficient evidence, defendant discharged
4	Francisco Santistevan	peonage	peon freed, defendant discharged
5	Juan Domingo Mestas	peonage	peon freed, defendant discharged
6	Antonio Torres	peonage	insufficient evidence, defendant discharged
7	Antonio Torres	peonage	insufficient evidence, defendant discharged
8	José Dolores Duran	peonage	peon freed, defendant discharged
9	José Dolores Duran	peonage	peon freed, defendant discharged
10	Francisco Cordova	peonage	peon freed, defendant discharged
11	Jesusito Medina	peonage	peon freed, defendant discharged
12	Juan Bautista Sanchez	Indian slavery	slave freed, defendant arraigned
13	Tomás Vigil	peonage	peon freed, defendant discharged
14	Juan Antonio	peonage	peon freed, defendant discharged
15	Tomás Vigil	peonage	peon freed, defendant discharged
16	Fernando Lopez	peonage	peon freed, defendant discharged
17	Juan de Jesus Trujillo	peonage	peon freed, defendant discharged
18	Jesus María Pacheco	peonage	peon freed, defendant discharged
19	Jesus María Pacheco	peonage	peon freed, defendant discharged
20	Jesus María Pacheco	peonage	peon freed, defendant discharged
21	Jesus María Pacheco	peonage	peon freed, defendant discharged
22	Jesus María Pacheco	peonage	peon freed, defendant discharged
23	Julian Vigil	Indian slavery	slave freed, defendant at large
24	Ramón Medina	Indian slavery	slave freed, defendant arraigned
25	Ramón Medina	Indian slavery	slave freed, defendant arraigned

TAOS COUNTY CASES

Case No.	Defendant	Form of Bondage	Proceedings
26	Rafael Chacón	peonage	peon freed, defendant discharged
27	José Dolores Medina	peonage	peon freed, defendant discharged
28	Jesus Ortega	peonage	peon freed, defendant discharged
29	S. Durán	Indian slavery	slave freed, defendant arraigned
30	Pedro Seiba	peonage	peon freed, defendant discharged
31	Nicolas Montoya	peonage	peon freed, defendant discharged
32	Antonio Maez	Indian slavery	slave freed, defendant arraigned
33	José Albino Vigil	Indian slavery	slave freed, defendant arraigned
34	Felipe Cisneros	Indian slavery	slave freed, defendant arraigned
35	Julian Durán	peonage	peon freed, defendant discharged
36	Dionicio Dominguez	peonage	peon freed, defendant discharged
37	Dionicio Dominguez	peonage	peon freed, defendant discharged
38	Antonio Guadalupe Cordova	peonage	peon freed, defendant discharged
39	Antonio Guadalupe Cordova	peonage	peon freed, defendant discharged
40	Antonio Guadalupe Cordova	peonage	peon freed, defendant discharged
41	Francisco Trujillo	peonage	peon freed, defendant discharged
42	José Cordova	peonage	peon freed, defendant discharged
43	Jesus Rodriguez	Indian slavery	slave freed, defendant arraigned
44	Jesus Rodriguez	peonage	peon freed, defendant discharged
45	María Josefa Barela	Indian slavery	slave freed, defendant arraigned
46	Eugenio Baca	peonage	peon freed, defendant discharged
47	José Gabriel Gallegos	Indian slavery	slave freed, defendant arraigned
48	Augustine Lecome	Indian slavery	slave freed, defendant arraigned
49	Jesús María Lucero	Indian slavery	slave freed, defendant arraigned
50	José Romulo Martinez	Indian slavery	slave freed, defendant arraigned
51	Mariano Lucero	Indian slavery	slave freed, defendant arraigned

TAOS COUNTY CASES

Case No.	Defendant	Form of Bondage	Proceedings
52	Mariano Lucero	Indian slavery	slave freed, defendant arraigned
53	Mariano Lucero	Indian slavery	slave freed, defendant arraigned
54	Mariano Lucero	Indian slavery	slave freed, defendant arraigned
55	Tomás Garcia	Indian slavery	slave freed, defendant arraigned
56	Juan Garcia	Indian slavery	slave freed, defendant arraigned
57	Ramón Archuleta	Indian slavery	slave freed, defendant at large
58	Davíd Armijo	Indian slavery	slave freed, defendant arraigned
59	José Manuel Quintana	Indian slavery	slave freed, defendant arraigned
60	Meleton Trujillo	Indian slavery	slave freed, defendant arraigned
61	Juan Antonio Baca	Indian slavery	slave freed, defendant arraigned
62	Juan Geronimo Garcia	Indian slavery	slave freed, defendant arraigned
63	José María Cortez	Indian slavery	insufficient evidence, defendant discharged
64	Juan Trujillo	Indian slavery	slave freed, defendant arraigned
65	Ygnacio Trujillo	Indian slavery	slave freed, defendant at large
66	Meleton Trujillo	Indian slavery	slave freed, defendant arraigned
67	Meleton Trujillo	Indian slavery	slave freed, defendant arraigned
68	Simon Trujillo	Indian slavery	slave freed, defendant arraigned
69	Pascual Martinez	Indian slavery	slave freed, defendant arraigned
70	Pascual Martinez	Indian slavery	slave freed, defendant arraigned
71	Pascual Martinez	Indian slavery	slave freed, defendant arraigned

TAOS COUNTY CASES

Case No.	Defendant	Form of Bondage	Proceedings
72	José Francisco Martinez	Indian slavery	slave freed, defendant arraigned
73	Jesús Martinez	Indian slavery	slave freed, defendant arraigned
74	Julian Jaramillo	Indian slavery	slave freed, defendant arraigned
75	Manuel Gomez	Indian slavery	slave freed, defendant at large
76	Julian Espinosa	Indian slavery	slave freed, defendant arraigned
77	Rafael Cordova	Indian slavery	slave freed, defendant sick
78	Antonio Rivera	peonage	peon freed, defendant discharged
79	Juan Ysidro Romero	peonage	peon freed, defendant discharged
80	Juan Ysidro Romero	peonage	peon freed, defendant discharged
81	Antonio Rivera	peonage	peon freed, defendant discharged
82	Juan Ysidro Romero	peonage	peon freed, defendant discharged
83	Juan Ysidro Romero	peonage	peon freed, defendant discharged
84	Antonio Vargas	peonage	peon freed, defendant discharged
85	Antonio Vargas	peonage	peon freed, defendant discharged
86	Santiago Valdez	peonage	peon freed, defendant discharged
87	Santiago Valdez	peonage	peon freed, defendant discharged
88	José Rafael Vigil	peonage	peon freed, defendant discharged
89	Charles Holmes	Indian slavery	slave freed, defendant arraigned
90	Rafael Cordova	peonage	peon freed, defendant discharged
91	Julian Mondragon	peonage	peon freed, defendant discharged
92	Antonio Sandoval	Indian slavery	slave freed, defendant arraigned
93	Antonio Sandoval	Indian slavery	slave freed, defendant arraigned
94	José Dolores Vigil	Indian slavery	slave freed, defendant arraigned
95	Ramón Medina	Indian slavery	slave freed, defendant arraigned
96	José Dolores Medina	Indian slavery	slave freed, defendant arraigned
97	José Dolores Medina	Indian slavery	slave freed, defendant arraigned
98	Juan Antonio Duran	Indian slavery	slave freed, defendant arraigned

TAOS COUNTY CASES

Case No.	Defendant	Form of Bondage	Proceedings
99	Juan Antonio Duran	Indian slavery	slave freed, defendant arraigned
100	Ronaldo Sanchez	Indian slavery	slave freed, defendant arraigned
101	Nicolas Martinez	Indian slavery	slave freed, defendant at large
102	Pablo Cordova	Indian slavery	slave freed, defendant arraigned
103	Juan Sanchez	Indian slavery	slave freed, defendant arraigned
104	Juan Romero	Indian slavery	slave freed, defendant at large
105	Pedro Roibal	peonage	peon freed, defendant discharged
106	Faustín García	peonage	peon freed, defendant discharged
107	Juan Antonio Sanchez	Indian slavery	slave freed, defendant arraigned
108	Florentino Suaz	peonage	peon freed, defendant discharged
109	Pedro Maez	Indian slavery	slave freed, defendant arraigned
110	Albino Ortega	Indian slavery	slave freed, defendant arraigned
111	Prudencio Martinez	Indian slavery	slave freed, defendant arraigned
112	Antonio Sandoval	Indian slavery	slave freed, defendant arraigned
113	José Mateo Cordova	Indian slavery	slave freed, defendant arraigned
114	Antonio Maez	peonage	peon freed, defendant discharged
115	Juan Sanchez	Indian slavery	slave freed, defendant arraigned
116	Juan Duran	peonage	peon freed, defendant discharged
117	Vicente Cordova	peonage	peon freed, defendant discharged
118	Antonio José Medina	peonage	peon freed, defendant discharged
119	Matias Medina	Indian slavery	slave freed, defendant arraigned
120	Juan Martinez	Indian slavery	slave freed, defendant arraigned
121	Prudencio Martinez	Indian slavery	slave freed, defendant arraigned
122	José Albino Vigil	Indian slavery	slave freed, defendant arraigned

TAOS COUNTY CASES

Case No.	Defendant	Form of Bondage	Proceedings
123	José Armijo Duran	Indian slavery	slave freed, defendant arraigned
124	Pedro Vasquez	peonage	peon freed, defendant discharged
125	Esquinipulo Martinez	peonage	peon freed, defendant discharged
126	Esquinipulo Martinez	Indian slavery	slave freed, defendant arraigned
127	Juan Lovato	peonage	peon freed, defendant discharged
128	Ant. Guadalupe Cordova	Indian slavery	slave freed, defendant arraigned
129	Ant. Guadalupe Cordova	Indian slavery	slave freed, defendant arraigned
130	Ant. Guadalupe Cordova	Indian slavery	slave freed, defendant arraigned
131	Ant. Guadalupe Cordova	Indian slavery	slave freed, defendant arraigned
132	José Dolores Martinez	Indian slavery	slave freed, defendant arraigned
133	José Dolores Martinez	peonage	peon freed, defendant discharged
134	Blas Guillen	Indian slavery	slave freed, defendant arraigned
135	Juan Antonio Duran	Indian slavery	slave freed, defendant arraigned
136	Vicente F. Mares	Indian slavery	slave freed, defendant arraigned
137	Vicente F. Mares	Indian slavery	slave freed, defendant arraigned
138	Vicente F. Mares	Indian slavery	slave freed, defendant arraigned
139	Vicente F. Mares	Indian slavery	slave freed, defendant arraigned
140	Vicente F. Mares	Indian slavery	slave freed, defendant arraigned
141	María A. Means	Indian slavery	slave freed, defendant arraigned
142	María A. Means	Indian slavery	slave freed, defendant arraigned
143	María A. Means	Indian slavery	slave freed, defendant arraigned
144	María A. Means	Indian slavery	slave freed, defendant arraigned

TAOS COUNTY CASES

Case No.	Defendant	Form of Bondage	Proceedings
145	María A. Means	Indian slavery	slave freed, defendant arraigned
146	Juan Santistevan	Indian slavery	slave freed, defendant arraigned
147	Juan Santistevan	Indian slavery	slave freed, defendant arraigned
148	Gabriel Nissel (?)	Indian slavery	slave freed, defendant arraigned
149	Benigna Lee	Indian slavery	slave freed, defendant arraigned
150	Benigna Lee	Indian slavery	slave freed, defendant arraigned
151	Benigna Lee	Indian slavery	slave freed, defendant arraigned
152	Benigna Lee	peonage	peon freed, defendant discharged
153	Pablo Beaubien	Indian slavery	slave freed, defendant arraigned
154	Aloys Scheurich	Indian slavery	slave freed, defendant arraigned
155	Aloys Scheurich	Indian slavery	slave freed, defendant arraigned
156	María Francisca Trujillo	peonage	peon freed, defendant discharged
157	Luz Tafoya	Indian slavery	slave freed, defendant arraigned
158	Luz Tafoya	Indian slavery	slave freed, defendant arraigned
159	Gabriel Vigil	Indian slavery	slave freed, defendant arraigned
160	Vicente Romero	Indian slavery	slave freed, defendant arraigned
161	Vicente Romero	Indian slavery	slave freed, defendant arraigned
162	Elfegio Branch	Indian slavery	slave freed, defendant arraigned
163	Manuel Martinez	peonage	peon freed, defendant discharged
164	Antonio José Valdez	Indian slavery	slave freed, defendant arraigned
165	Antonio José Valdez	Indian slavery	slave freed, defendant arraigned

TAOS COUNTY CASES

Case No.	Defendant	Form of Bondage	Proceedings
166	Antonio José Valdez	Indian slavery	slave freed, defendant arraigned
167	Vicente F. Mares	Indian slavery	slave freed, defendant arraigned
168	Vicente F. Mares	Indian slavery	slave freed, defendant arraigned
169	Vicente F. Mares	Indian slavery	slave freed, defendant arraigned
170	Vicente F. Mares	Indian slavery	slave freed, defendant arraigned
171	José Rafael Vigil	Indian slavery	slave freed, defendant arraigned
172	José Rafael Vigil	Indian slavery	slave freed, defendant arraigned
173	José Rafael Vigil	Indian slavery	slave freed, defendant arraigned
174	José Rafael Vigil	Indian slavery	slave freed, defendant arraigned
175	María Pabla Lovato	Indian slavery	slave freed, defendant arraigned
176	María Pabla Lovato	Indian slavery	slave freed, defendant arraigned
177	María Pabla Lovato	Indian slavery	slave freed, defendant arraigned
178	Meleton Trujillo	Indian slavery	slave freed, defendant arraigned
179	Meleton Trujillo	Indian slavery	slave freed, defendant arraigned
180	Julian Espinosa	Indian slavery	slave freed, defendant arraigned
181	Julian Espinosa	Indian slavery	slave freed, defendant arraigned
182	Pascual Martinez	Indian slavery	slave freed, defendant arraigned
183	Nestor Rivera	Indian slavery	slave freed, defendant arraigned
184	Albino Suazo	Indian slavery	slave freed, defendant arraigned
185	Tranquilino Gallegos	Indian slavery	slave freed, defendant arraigned

TAOS COUNTY CASES

Case No.	Defendant	Form of Bondage	Proceedings
186	Tranquilino Gallegos	Indian slavery	slave freed, defendant arraigned
187	Tranquilino Gallegos	Indian slavery	slave freed, defendant arraigned
188	José Francisco Martinez	Indian slavery	slave freed, defendant arraigned
189	Juan Trujillo	Indian slavery	slave freed, defendant arraigned
190	Juan Trujillo	Indian slavery	slave freed, defendant arraigned
191	Juan Trujillo	Indian slavery	slave freed, defendant arraigned
192	Juan Trujillo	Indian slavery	slave freed, defendant arraigned
193	Juan Trujillo	Indian slavery	slave freed, defendant arraigned
194	Juan Trujillo	Indian slavery	slave freed, defendant arraigned
195	José Gregorío Valdez	Indian slavery	slave freed, defendant arraigned
196	José Gregorío Valdez	Indian slavery	slave freed, defendant arraigned
197	Ignacio Jaramillo	Indian slavery	slave freed, defendant arraigned
198	Pedro Vigil	Indian slavery	slave freed, defendant arraigned
199	Pedro Vigil	Indian slavery	slave freed, defendant arraigned
200	Benito Cortez	Indian slavery	slave freed, defendant arraigned
201	Benito Cortez	Indian slavery	slave freed, defendant arraigned
202	Benito Cortez	Indian slavery	slave freed, defendant arraigned
203	Gabriel Lucero	Indian slavery	slave freed, defendant arraigned
204	Gabriel Lucero	Indian slavery	slave freed, defendant arraigned
205	Nieves Lujan	Indian slavery	slave freed, defendant arraigned

TAOS COUNTY CASES

Case No.	Defendant	Form of Bondage	Proceedings
206	Nieves Lujan	Indian slavery	slave freed, defendant arraigned
207	Miguel Rivera	Indian slavery	slave freed, defendant arraigned
208	Miguel Rivera	Indian slavery	slave freed, defendant arraigned
209	Juan Antonio Baca	Indian slavery	slave freed, defendant arraigned
210	Juan Antonio Baca	Indian slavery	slave freed, defendant arraigned
211	Juan Antonio Baca	Indian slavery	slave freed, defendant arraigned
212	Luisa Branch	Indian slavery	slave freed, defendant arraigned
213	José Antonio Valdez	Indian slavery	slave freed, defendant arraigned
214	José Antonio Valdez	Indian slavery	slave freed, defendant arraigned
215	José Antonio Valdez	Indian slavery	slave freed, defendant arraigned
216	José Antonio Valdez	Indian slavery	slave freed, defendant arraigned
217	Pablo Romero	Indian slavery	slave freed, defendant arraigned
218	Gabriel Jeantet (?)	Indian slavery	slave freed, defendant arraigned
219	Gabriel Vigil	Indian slavery	slave freed, defendant arraigned
220	Gabriel Vigil	Indian slavery	slave freed, defendant arraigned
221	José Benito Martinez	Indian slavery	slave freed, defendant arraigned
222	José Benito Martinez	Indian slavery	slave freed, defendant arraigned
223	José Benito Martinez	Indian slavery	slave freed, defendant arraigned
224	José Benito Martinez	Indian slavery	slave freed, defendant arraigned
225	José Benito Martinez	Indian slavery	slave freed, defendant arraigned

TAOS COUNTY CASES

Case No.	Defendant	Form of Bondage	Proceedings
226	José Benito Martinez	Indian slavery	slave freed, defendant arraigned
227	Juan Ysidro Valdez	Indian slavery	slave freed, defendant arraigned
228	Juan Ysidro Valdez	Indian slavery	slave freed, defendant arraigned
229	Juan Ysidro Valdez	Indian slavery	slave freed, defendant arraigned
230	Juan Ysidro Valdez	Indian slavery	slave freed, defendant arraigned
231	George Romero	Indian slavery	slave freed, defendant arraigned
232	Santiago Martín	Indian slavery	slave freed, defendant arraigned
233	Juan Santistevan	Indian slavery	slave freed, defendant arraigned
234	Juan Santistevan	Indian slavery	slave freed, defendant arraigned
235	Juan Santistevan	Indian slavery	slave freed, defendant arraigned
236	Joseph Clonthies (?)	Indian slavery	slave freed, defendant arraigned
237	Joseph Clonthies (?)	Indian slavery	slave freed, defendant arraigned
238	Manuel Gomez	Indian slavery	slave freed, defendant arraigned
239	Ygnacio Trujillo	Indian slavery	slave freed, defendant arraigned
240	Luís Duran	obst. justice	insufficient evidence, defendant discharged
241	Juan Benito Valdez	Indian slavery	slave freed, defendant arraigned
242	Juan Benito Valdez	Indian slavery	slave freed, defendant arraigned
243	Juan Benito Valdez	Indian slavery	slave freed, defendant arraigned
244	Juan Benito Valdez	Indian slavery	slave freed, defendant arraigned
245	Juan Benito Valdez	Indian slavery	slave freed, defendant arraigned

TAOS COUNTY CASES

Case No.	Defendant	Form of Bondage	Proceedings
246	Juan Benito Valdez	Indian slavery	slave freed, defendant arraigned
247	Juan Benito Valdez	Indian slavery	slave freed, defendant arraigned
248	Juan Benito Valdez	Indian slavery	slave freed, defendant arraigned
249	Juan Benito Valdez	Indian slavery	slave freed, defendant arraigned
250	Juan Benito Valdez	Indian slavery	slave freed, defendant arraigned
251	Charles Holmes	Indian slavery	slave freed, defendant arraigned
252	Charles Holmes	Indian slavery	slave freed, defendant arraigned
253	José Antonio Archuleta	Indian slavery	slave freed, defendant arraigned
254	José Antonio Archuleta	Indian slavery	slave freed, defendant arraigned
255	José Antonio Archuleta	Indian slavery	slave freed, defendant arraigned
256	Jesus María Lucero	Indian slavery	slave freed, defendant arraigned
257	Davíd Armijo	Indian slavery	slave freed, defendant arraigned
258	Augustin Lucero	Indian slavery	slave freed, defendant arraigned
259	Augustin Lucero	Indian slavery	slave freed, defendant arraigned
260	José Gabriel Gallegos	Indian slavery	slave freed, defendant arraigned
261	José Gabriel Gallegos	Indian slavery	slave freed, defendant arraigned
262	Francisco Salazar	Indian slavery	slave freed, defendant arraigned
263	Juan Geronimo Martinez	Indian slavery	slave freed, defendant arraigned
264	Juan Geronimo Martinez	Indian slavery	slave freed, defendant arraigned
265	Joaquin Garcia	Indian slavery	slave freed, defendant arraigned

TAOS COUNTY CASES

Case No.	Defendant	Form of Bondage	Proceedings
266	Joaquin Garcia	Indian slavery	slave freed, defendant arraigned
267	Joaquin Garcia	Indian slavery	slave freed, defendant arraigned
268	Joaquin Garcia	Indian slavery	slave freed, defendant arraigned
269	Mariano Lucero	Indian slavery	slave freed, defendant arraigned
270	Abad Romero	Indian slavery	slave freed, defendant arraigned
271	Abad Romero	Indian slavery	slave freed, defendant arraigned
272	Juan Manuel Lucero	Indian slavery	slave freed, defendant arraigned
273	Juan Manuel Lucero	Indian slavery	slave freed, defendant arraigned
274	José Romulo Martinez	Indian slavery	slave freed, defendant arraigned
275	José Romulo Martinez	Indian slavery	slave freed, defendant arraigned
276	José Francisco Martín	Indian slavery	slave freed, defendant arraigned
277	José Francisco Martín	Indian slavery	slave freed, defendant arraigned
278	José Francisco Martín	Indian slavery	slave freed, defendant arraigned
279	José Francisco Martín	Indian slavery	slave freed, defendant arraigned
280	Lorenzo Romero	Indian slavery	slave freed, defendant arraigned
281	Lorenzo Romero	Indian slavery	slave freed, defendant arraigned
282	Antonio María Chavez	Indian slavery	slave freed, defendant arraigned
283	Raymundo Cordova	Indian slavery	slave freed, defendant arraigned
284	Antonio Martinez	Indian slavery	slave freed, defendant arraigned
285	Antonio Martinez	Indian slavery	slave freed, defendant arraigned

TAOS COUNTY CASES

Case No.	Defendant	Form of Bondage	Proceedings
286	Antonio Martinez	Indian slavery	slave freed, defendant arraigned
287	Antonio Martinez	Indian slavery	slave freed, defendant arraigned
288	Antonio María Sanchez	Indian slavery	slave freed, defendant arraigned

SANTA FE AND RÍO ARRIBA COUNTY CASES

Case No.	Defendant	Form of Bondage	Proceedings
289	Marta Romero	peonage	insufficient evidence, discharged
290	Vicente de Herrera	peonage	insufficient evidence, discharged
291	Vicente Aragon	Indian slavery	slave freed, defendant arraigned
292	Cruz Borrego	Indian slavery	slave freed, defendant arraigned
293	Antonio José Salazar	Indian slavery	slave freed, defendant arraigned
294	Antonio José Salazar	Indian slavery	slave freed, defendant arraigned
295	Juan Y. Salazar	Indian slavery	slave freed, defendant arraigned
296	Rafaelito Aguilar	Indian slavery	slave freed, defendant arraigned
297	Guadalupe Alvares	Indian slavery	slave freed, defendant arraigned
298	María Antonia Lucero	Indian slavery	slave freed, defendant arraigned
299	Pablo Trujillo	Indian slavery	slave freed, defendant arraigned
300	Pablo Trujillo	Indian slavery	slave freed, defendant arraigned
301	Pablo Trujillo	Indian slavery	slave freed, defendant arraigned
302	Pablo Trujillo	Indian slavery	slave freed, defendant arraigned
303	Pablo Trujillo	Indian slavery	slave freed, defendant arraigned
304	Pablo Trujillo	Indian slavery	slave freed, defendant arraigned

SANTA FE AND RÍO ARRIBA COUNTY CASES

Case No.	Defendant	Form of Bondage	Proceedings
305	Pablo Trujillo	Indian slavery	slave freed, defendant arraigned
306	Pablo Trujillo	Indian slavery	slave freed, defendant arraigned
307	Matias Chacón	Indian slavery	slave freed, defendant arraigned
308	Juan B. Lopez	Indian slavery	slave freed, defendant arraigned
309	Antonio Casados	Indian slavery	slave freed, defendant arraigned
310	Juan Desedirío Valdez	Indian slavery	slave freed, defendant arraigned
311	Candelarío Archuleta	Indian slavery	slave freed, defendant arraigned
312	Gabriel Valdez	Indian slavery	slave freed, defendant arraigned
313	Vicente Aragon	Indian slavery	slave freed, defendant arraigned
314	Vicente Aragon	Indian slavery	slave freed, defendant arraigned
315	Vicente Aragon	Indian slavery	slave freed, defendant arraigned
316	Vicente Aragon	Indian slavery	slave freed, defendant arraigned
317	Vicente Aragon	Indian slavery	slave freed, defendant arraigned
318	José María Bustos	Indian slavery	slave freed, defendant arraigned
319	José Antonio Lopez	Indian slavery	slave freed, defendant arraigned
320	Francisco A. Mestas	Indian slavery	slave freed, defendant arraigned
321	Matias Velarde	Indian slavery	slave freed, defendant arraigned
322	Matias Velarde	Indian slavery	slave freed, defendant arraigned
323	José de la Luz Lujan	peonage	insufficient evidence, discharged
324	José A. Velarde	Indian slavery	slave freed, defendant arraigned
325	Justo Montoya	Indian slavery	slave freed, defendant arraigned

SANTA FE AND RÍO ARRIBA COUNTY CASES

Case No.	Defendant	Form of Bondage	Proceedings
326	Juan Domingo Valdez	Indian slavery	slave freed, defendant arraigned
327	Teodoro Valdez	Indian slavery	slave freed, defendant arraigned
328	Julian Gutiérrez	Indian slavery	slave freed, defendant arraigned
329	Manuel Valdez	Indian slavery	slave freed, defendant arraigned
330	Manuel Valdez	Indian slavery	slave freed, defendant arraigned
331	Manuel Valdez	Indian slavery	slave freed, defendant arraigned
332	Manuel Valdez	peonage	insufficient evidence, discharged
333	Manuel Valdez	peonage	insufficient evidence, discharged
334	Manuel Valdez	peonage	insufficient evidence, discharged
335	Benito Sarragite	Indian slavery	slave freed, defendant arraigned
336	José Antonio Vigil	Indian slavery	slave freed, defendant arraigned
337	José Antonio Vigil	Indian slavery	slave freed, defendant arraigned
338	Louis Clark	peonage	insufficient evidence, discharged
339	Guadalupe Alvarez	Indian slavery	slave freed, defendant arraigned
340	María Antonia Lucero	Indian slavery	slave freed, defendant arraigned
341	Ramón Garcia	Indian slavery	slave freed, defendant arraigned
342	Ramón Garcia	Indian slavery	slave freed, defendant arraigned
343	Pedro Mestas	Indian slavery	slave freed, defendant arraigned
344	Pedro Mestas	Indian slavery	slave freed, defendant arraigned
345	Vivian Lopez	Indian slavery	slave freed, defendant arraigned
346	Alejandro Manzanares	Indian slavery	slave freed, defendant arraigned
347	Antonio M. Vigil	Indian slavery	slave freed, defendant arraigned

SANTA FE AND RÍO ARRIBA COUNTY CASES

Case No.	Defendant	Form of Bondage	Proceedings
348	José Vicente Cordova	Indian slavery	slave freed, defendant arraigned
349	Luis Ortiz	Indian slavery	slave freed, defendant arraigned
350	María Y. Montoya	Indian slavery	slave freed, defendant arraigned
351	Rafael Martín	Indian slavery	slave freed, defendant arraigned
352	Nicolas Vigil II	Indian slavery	slave freed, defendant arraigned
353	Juan Antonio Naranjo	Indian slavery	slave freed, defendant arraigned
354	Polonio Vigil	Indian slavery	slave freed, defendant arraigned
355	Ramón Vigil	Indian slavery	slave freed, defendant arraigned
356	Ramón Vigil	Indian slavery	slave freed, defendant arraigned
357	Francisco E. Vigil	Indian slavery	slave freed, defendant arraigned
358	Francisco E. Vigil	Indian slavery	slave freed, defendant arraigned
359	Francisco E. Vigil	Indian slavery	slave freed, defendant arraigned
360	Ramón Salazar	Indian slavery	slave freed, defendant arraigned
361	Jesus M. Vigil	Indian slavery	slave freed, defendant arraigned
362	Jesus M. Vigil	Indian slavery	slave freed, defendant arraigned
363	José A. Vigil y Salazar	Indian slavery	slave freed, defendant arraigned

PEONAGE

Total individuals in peonage: 70
Peons set free: 60
Peons not set free: 10
Total peon holders: 53
Female peon holders: 3

NUMBERS OF PEONS HELD PER HOUSEHOLD

Peons	Households	Proportion of Total Number of Peons
1	41	77 percent
2	9	19 percent
3	2	
4	0	
5	1	

INDIAN SLAVERY

Total Indians in slavery: 292
Slaves set free: 291
Slaves not set free: 1
Total number slaveholders: 171
Female slaveholders: 9

NUMBERS OF SLAVES HELD PER HOUSEHOLD

Slaves	Households	Proportion of Total Number of Slaves
1	111	65 percent
2	34	20 percent
3	10	6 percent
4	8	5 percent
5	3	
6	2	
7	0	
8	1	
9	1	
10	1	

DISTRIBUTION BY TYPE OF BONDAGE

Peonage	19.3 percent
Slavery	80.7 percent

REPRESENTATION OF PEONAGE AND SLAVERY BY COUNTY

County	Total Households	Households with Peons	Households with Slaves
Taos	2,820	48	128
Santa Fe and Río Arriba	4,438	5	43

Total household estimates based on Francis A. Walker, *A Compendium of the Ninth Census (June 1, 1870)* . . . (Washington, D.C., 1872), table XLVI, "Areas, Families, and Dwellings," 540–541.

ACKNOWLEDGMENTS

This project began over coffee in Ray and Sadie Cordova's kitchen in Weston, Colorado, in 1988. While conducting research on Hispano miners in the southern Colorado coal fields, I had spent a summer collecting oral histories among the older residents of villages along the "Picketwire" (Purgatoire) River valley. Ray Cordova—knees shot from working seams only three feet high and voice reedy from miner's lung—had just finished reciting a family genealogy that cast back in time from Colorado coal camps to the mountain village of Las Trampas, New Mexico, to Early Modern Spain itself. It mattered to Ray that I understand he descended from peninsulares and conquistadores. When he left the kitchen for a moment, however, Sadie whispered conspiratorially, "His grandmother was Apache, you know."

When I later recounted the conversation to a fellow student at the University of Colorado, he nodded knowingly and reflected, "When Pawnees back home want to discredit my family, they say we're not 'real Indians, just Mexicans.'" I wanted to get to the bottom of those contradictory histories. I began to listen more carefully. That in these instances I feel obliged to cloak identities with pseudonyms or anonymity points to just how difficult those conversations continue to be, more than a century after the historical dynamics that underlay them drew to a close.

Yet this book owes its existence to the collective memory of many people, Indian and Hispano alike, who kept alive and were willing to speak the often discomforting truths that bind their histories together in the Southwest Borderlands. I hope the details herein provide some useful substantiation to the many family stories shared with me over the years and might make it possible for hitherto private memories to be spoken publicly.

I brought the questions provoked by these conversations to the University of California, Davis. Guided by the gentle heart and ruthless pen of Vicki L. Ruiz and the inspirational presence of Jack D. Forbes, they grew into a master's thesis. But so too did the questions grow. In the subsequent Ph.D. dissertation, John Walton reminded me that questions are but "cases" in disguise and pushed me to search for clarity as well as complexity. Clarence E. Walker, never one to mince words, drilled home another point—any historical explanation must include "the dross of history: namely, facts." It remained, however, for my Chair, Daniel H. Calhoun, to bring his limitless intellect and equally unlimited patience to the task of guiding my efforts at real understanding. He continues to serve as my most constant scholarly companion.

Other faculty and graduate students at U.C. Davis deserve my thanks as well. Members of the Cross-Cultural Women's History Program read chapters along the way and refined my thinking on issues of gender and power. Likewise, members of the Hemispheric Initiative on the Americas—Patricia Erikson, Charles Hale, Jr., Carol Smith, Circe Sturm, Stefano Varese, Andrew Wood, to name but a few—criticized drafts and pressed, always, for "more theory!" Martha J. Macri of the Native American Studies Department offered boundless good humor and two solid years of employment with the Maya Hieroglyphic Database Project. In the History Department, Cynthia Brantley, Catherine Cocks, Austin Jersild, John Logan, Jennifer Selwyn, Carl Sjovold, Alan Taylor, and Lisa Trivedi all knew the dissertation better than they might have wished. Tom Adams brought comradeship (and freshly baked bread) to my time in Davis.

At the University of Maryland I found an exciting if contentious community of scholars who deepened my appreciation for the study of slavery and its implications in the history of the Southwest. Ira Berlin provided a steady hand as I embarked on my career and, as James Henretta and David Grimsted did, read many chapter revisions. Bill Bravman offered an enduring friendship and helpful discussions on African parallels. Michael David-Fox, Gary Gerstle, James Gilbert, James F. Harris, John Lampe, Hayim Lapin, Clare Lyons, Robyn Muncy, Stephan Palmié, Leslie Rowland, David Sicilia, Richard Wetzell, Daryle Williams, and Madeline Zilfi each found ways to support me through early parenthood and to enrich my work. The office staff of Christy Davila, Darlene King, and Catalina Toala offered remarkable goodwill to we who often deserved much less.

A year at the School of Social Science at the Institute for Advanced Study in Princeton as National Endowment for the Humanities Fellow brought welcome reimmersion among anthropologists and social theorists. Steve Caton taught me not to fear the poetry that lies within history; Joan W. Scott casually provided, in a one-sentence comment, resolution to a long perplexing problem of conceptual framing; and Clifford Geertz reminded me that, although books may end, the past does not. Adam Ashforth, Cathryn Carson, Mauro Guillen, Debra Keates, and Deborah Koehler each brought distinctive insights to this and other projects.

The School of American Research in Santa Fe provided a delightfully rewarding way station in our cross-continental return to California. Lee Goodwin, Ellie Gossen, Gary Gossen, Nancy Owen Lewis, Mary Eunice Romero, Martha A. Sandweiss, Doug Schwartz, Ruth Van Dyke, and Kathy Whitaker all helped to keep alive Edgar Lee Hewitt's vision of a vastly interdisciplinary "science of man." That year in New Mexico reinforced my belief that the Greater Southwest is its own community of interest, where nonacademics take their history seriously and academics must listen carefully to the voices around them. Any morning coffee break at the Archives and Historical Services division of the New Mexico State Records Center will make this clear. I would have been lost without the generosity of Director Sandra Jaramillo or the patience of staff members Arelene Padilla, Al Regensberg, and Robert Torrez. Beyond those walls roams a band of similarly learned and welcoming archaeologists, cultural specialists, and historians: David M. Brugge, Kathy Bustamante, Tom Chávez, Helen Silva Dunn, Francisco Gonzales, Jake Ivey, Elizabeth Jameson, Janet Lecompte, Hartman Lomawaima, Natalie Alexis Lopez, Dedra McDonald, Devon Mihesuah, Josh Mihesuah, Miguel Montoya, Rain Parrish, Frances Quintana, Miguel Quintana, Soge Track, Carlos A. Valdez, and Angelina Veyna all contributed to my education. David H. Snow, David J. Weber, and Peter H. Wood in particular were extraordinarily giving of time, knowledge, and manuscript critiques.

More generally but no less crucially, archivists at the American Philosophical Society, the Bancroft Library at the University of California, Berkeley, the Eugene C. Barker Texas History Collection at the University of Texas, Austin, the Beinecke Rare Book and Manuscript Library at Yale University, the Library of Congress, the National Archives, and the Smithsonian Institution in Washington, D.C., earned my thanks many times over. Funding from the American Philosophical Society, the National Endowment for the Humanities, the University of Maryland, and the University of California, Santa Barbara, made it possible to spend extended time in these locations and to write up the research. My new colleagues at UCSB, especially W. Elliot Brownlee, Sarah Cline, Patricia Cline Cohen, Mario Garcia, Harold Marcuse, Ann Marie Plane, Jack Talbott, and Dean David Marshall demonstrated their confidence in this work by bringing my family and me west again, to our great happiness. Additionally, I would like to express my gratitude at having the opportunity to try out some of the ideas in this monograph, in different form, in *American Quarterly, American Indian Quarterly, Feminist Studies,* and the collections *Power and Place in the North American West,* edited by Richard White and John M. Findlay, and *The Many Legalities of Early America,* edited by Christopher L. Tomlins and Bruce H. Mann.

Making a book of those words, however, fell to Editor of Publications Fredrika J. Teute and Manuscript Editor M. Kathryn Burdette at the Omohundro Institute of Early American History and Culture. However much we might have tried each other's patience, never have sharper eyes nor clearer heads addressed a manuscript. Jennifer Baker at UCSB saved me many embarrassments with her proofreading skills. Their efforts, and those of the teachers, friends, and colleagues mentioned above, make any remaining errors, oversights, and failures of interpretation within these pages all the more my own.

Finally, I wish to thank my parents, Margaret and Robert Brooks, for raising me in the Rocky Mountain Southwest "amid the dust of many horses" and in nurturing my interest in the past. Jeremy Hinton "Forrest" Brooks and Lila Anne Brooks, who arrived midstream and grew along with this book, awakened a visceral sense of kinship that had too long been a cerebral abstraction. Rebecca Anne Allahyari—ever willing to remind me, "It is more complicated than that"—continues to grace my life with her profoundly simple passion to understand and live in the unity of ideas and emotions.

INDEX